Progress in IS

More information about this series at http://www.springer.com/series/10440

Volker Nissen

Editor

Digital Transformation of the Consulting Industry

Extending the Traditional Delivery Model

 Springer

Editor
Volker Nissen
Department of Economic Science and Media
Ilmenau University of Technology
Ilmenau
Germany

ISSN 2196-8705   ISSN 2196-8713   (electronic)
Progress in IS
ISBN 978-3-319-70490-6   ISBN 978-3-319-70491-3   (eBook)
https://doi.org/10.1007/978-3-319-70491-3

Library of Congress Control Number: 2017957206

Printed on acid-free paper

This Springer imprint is published by Springer Nature
The registered company is Springer International Publishing AG
The registered company address is: Gewerbestrasse 11, 6330 Cham, Switzerland

I dedicate this book to my children with love.

Für Leon und Hanno.

Volker Nissen

Preface

When I was a small child, the watchmaking industry was reigned by watches from European or American companies. Then, around 1970, the first electronic quartz watches became available to a broad market. During the next 15 years, the watchmaking industry changed completely. Former leading companies were often marginalized or became extinct. The mass business shifted from traditional mechanical watches to electronic watches, where producers were often located in Asia. Moreover, the price level for an average wristwatch dropped dramatically. However, in the long run, also the attitude toward watches changed. The wristwatch has increasingly mutated from a simple chronometer into an actual piece of fashion. Moreover, smartwatches appeared and revolutionized what a watch can be. Thus, new markets opened up and producers experience new chances for profitable growth.

Consulting firms can learn a lot from these developments that changed the appearance of the watchmaking industry forever. Within the next years, the business and delivery models of consulting have to be redesigned and partly reinvented. Technology-based consulting solutions will gain ground. The importance of IT and associated qualifications rise, and the war-for-talents in consulting will get even tougher than today. Consulting services will be unbundled and become more modularized with considerable consequences for sales. Moreover, the pressure on prices for standard services also puts your margins at risk. Digitalization and decreasing customer loyalty intensify competition in consulting. Clients require solutions that integrate aspects of strategy-, process-, and IT-consulting with design challenges. Concurrently, new billing models need to be introduced.

However, you can turn threats into opportunities for new business. Prepare for the new and promote the change. New models, like crowdsourcing-supported or self-service consulting, new tools for data- and process mining, and the maturing of AI all offer possibilities to complement and optimize the existing service portfolios of consulting providers. Incumbents and technology-driven newcomers in the consulting market can work fruitfully together. Automated low-cost consulting solutions can open up whole new segments of clients that would otherwise never approach a consulting firm. In this book, you will find inspiration and help to accomplish the digital transformation in business consulting.

A book like this is the result of hard work of different parties. I would like to thank all people who contributed to this book! This not only includes the various authors, but also my doctoral students, in particular Mr. Henry Seifert, and staff at my chair at the University of Technology Ilmenau, especially Mrs. Anne Füßl, as well as the editorial office at Springer, in particular Mr. Christian Rauscher as the executive editor. It was a pleasure to work with you all!—I would also like to express my gratitude to colleagues and seniors during my more than 12 inspiring years in the consulting business. Finally, I wish to thank my wife Iska for her support and understanding during the long formation phase of this book.

It would certainly make me happy if this volume provided not only some scientific contribution in the field of Consulting Research, but also concrete practical help to consulting companies in their own digital transformation initiatives. If you have comments on the book, or need further support and advice, please contact me at volker.nissen@tu-ilmenau.de.

Enjoy the book!

Ilmenau, Germany   Volker Nissen
August 2017

Contents

Editor and Authors

About the Editor

Volker Nissen holds the Chair of Information Systems Engineering in Services at Technische Universität Ilmenau, Germany, since 2005. Prior to this, he pursued a consulting career, including positions as manager at IDS Scheer AG, director at DHC GmbH, and CEO of NISSCON Ltd., Germany. In 1994 he received a Ph.D. degree in Economic Sciences with distinction from the University of Goettingen, Germany. His current research interests include the digital transformation of the consulting industry, the management of IT-agility, metaheuristic optimization, and process acceptance research. He is author and editor of 19 books and some 200 other publications, including papers in Business & Information Systems Engineering, Information Systems Frontiers, IEEE Transactions on EC, IEEE Transactions on NN, and Annals of OR.

About the Authors

Mats-Niklas Ackert is a consultant at Sopra Steria Consulting, a technology and management consultancy with focus on digital transformation. He completed his Master degree in industrial engineering and management with specialisation in automation and strategic management at Technische Universität Ilmenau, Germany and wrote his Master thesis about the virtualization of consulting at the Institute for Business Information Systems Engineering.

Friedrich Augenstein is a Professor for Consulting and Corporate Management at the Baden-Württemberg University of Cooperative Education Stuttgart and head of department for Business Management–Services Management. He is also the owner of CONMETHOS GmbH corporation for consulting methods. He studied Business Engineering at the University of Karlsruhe, was researcher and doctorate at the Institute of Computer Science at the University of Freiburg and has more than 20 years of professional experience as a consultant (Senior Manager at KPMG,

Principal at Capgemini). Since 2005, Friedrich is a full-time Professor at the Baden-Württemberg University of Cooperative Education.

Marco Blumenstein has studied Business Information Systems Engineering at Technische Universität Ilmenau, Germany. There he was also involved in a research project on the virtualization of consulting services and specifically examined the expectations of consulting clients and developed a method to support the selection of a particular virtualization technology. He graduated as a Master of Science in 2017. Since 2013, he has been working as a working student at X-CASE GmbH, in the area of SAP ERP consulting. Since 2017, he is a SAP Consultant focused on logistics and e-commerce processes within the SAP ERP.

Matthias Book is Professor for Software Engineering at the University of Iceland. His research focus is on facilitating communication between distributed business and technical stakeholders in large software projects, and on pragmatic approaches to requirements engineering and modeling of complex software systems.

Ricardo Buettner is a Professor of Data Science at Aalen University. He studied Computer Science (Dipl.-Inf.), Industrial Engineering and Management (Dipl.-Wirtsch.-Ing.), and Business Administration (Dipl.-Kfm.) and received his Ph.D. in Information Systems from Hohenheim University. After nine years working with the BMW Group, with experience in the fields of finance/controlling, marketing, strategy, R&D and HR, Ricardo joined the FOM University of Applied Sciences in 2009 before he moved to Aalen University in 2017.

Oliver Christ is a lecturer and senior researcher at the Institute for Quality Management and Business Administration (IQB) at the FHS University of Applied Sciences St. Gallen, Switzerland (FHS). After studying business administration, Oliver Christ worked as research assistant at the University of St. Gallen and finished his Ph.D. in 2001. For 10 years, he was employed by SAP, first as assistant to the CEO and commencing 2006 as Research Director SA0P Switzerland, where he established the local research organization and managed the distributed organization with 3 locations including a team of +40 international researchers. Over the last 18 years, Oliver Christ worked as lecturer and researcher with different Swiss Universities and teaches courses on bachelor and master level on Enterprise Systems, Business Intelligence, Business Process Management, Emerging Technologies and Organizational Theories.

Michael Czarniecki is a lecturer and project manager at the Institute for Quality Management and Business Administration (IQB) at the FHS University of Applied Sciences St. Gallen, Switzerland (FHS). He worked on projects in Switzerland and abroad for private and public institutions. The projects involved maturity development, market introduction and market research projects. Michael Czarniecki is co-founder and member of the Management Board of Solid Chemicals GmbH since

2001 and was Managing Director from 2007 to 2011. Michael Czarniecki is also the co-founder of BeeUp GmbH. Michael Czarniecki holds both a M.A. in economics and teaching degree at the University of St. Gallen as well as a CAS in management in the life sciences of the EPFL in Lausanne.

Thomas Deelmann Thomas Deelmann is Professor for Public Management at the University of Applied Sciences for Public Administration and Management of North Rhine-Westphalia (FHöV) in Cologne, Germany. Until 2016, he was Professor for Corporate Consulting and Management at BiTS Iserlohn as well as the head of the strategy development department for a leading global ICT service provider. His professional experiences as a consultant at one of the largest international consultancies, as an inhouse consultant, as a strategic sourcer for consulting services and as a client of consulting services form the basis for his teaching and research. Currently, he serves as the editor for a consulting handbook and as a jury member of the WirtschaftsWoche's "Best of Consulting" award.

Jim Eidmann is an apprenticeship specialist in application development at the Dr. Kuhl Unternehmensberatung. His main focus is the development of software prototypes.

Matthew Flynn is a postdoctoral research fellow at the Queensland University of Technology and PwC Chair in digital economy. Matthew's keen interest in the future of work has led to a growing research portfolio that includes digital disruption of industries, jobs and tasks, disruptive innovation, employability, educational and industry partnerships, and innovative educational approaches to address future of work challenges. Matthew also possesses extensive real world experience as a consultant and trainer to large organizations and SMEs on innovative learning and development projects, evaluations, and industry research projects.

Moritz Fröhlich is a Master student of Applied Computer Science at HTW Berlin. Additionally to his studies, he is a software developer for Java and C#. He develops web applications in different branches like healthcare, e-commerce and public sector. In agile projects, he executes the role of a developer and the role of the Scrum Master and supports his team colleagues with qualified knowledge. His expertise are the usage of graph databases like Neo4J and the hosting of web applications in the cloud.

Anne Füßl is a doctoral candidate at the Chair of Information Systems Engineering in Services at Technische Universität Ilmenau, Germany. Her research interests focus on the development of a learning and decision-making knowledge model (iKnow) to support consulting services in the context of digital transformation. In 2015, Anne has already contributed to the research and development of the knowledge model iKnow in two publications. She holds a Master's degree in

Business Information Systems Engineering, was a student assistant and worked as product manager at Magnitude Internet GmbH for an online portal.

Franz Felix Füßl is a consultant in Software Engineering and holds a Dr.-Ing. (2016) in Computer Engineering from Technische Universität Ilmenau, Germany. He gained his expertise mainly in the field of software engineering, especially in the area of web development and software architecture. During his doctorate, he dealt with learning systems and computer-assisteddecision-making. Today, he is working on web-based software systems to increase the efficiency of processes in industrial production, production automation and key figure analysis.

Simon Grapenthin is Co-CEO of Interaction Room GmbH and doctoral candidate at paluno – The Ruhr Institute for Software Technology at the University of Duisburg-Essen. As an Interaction Room Coach, he has led over 50 Interaction Room workshops at organizations in the financial service, trade and healthcare domains. His research areas are agile software development practices and pragmatic modeling techniques.

Tobias Greff is a professional researcher at the AWS-Institute for digitized products and processes. He holds a Master's degree in Business Information Systems from the Saarland University. His main research topics focus on consulting research, especially future trends in software development tools for the consulting domain and on digital business development in start-up environments.

Volker Gruhn holds the Chair for Software Engineering at the University of Duisburg-Essen. His research focus is on methods for industrial software engineering, as well as the effects of digital transformation on enterprises. He is Co-Founder and Chairman of the supervisory board of adesso AG, one of Germany's largest independent IT service providers with more than 2200 employees in 18 locations in Europe.

Christoph Hardt born 1980 in Gießen is one of the two founders of COMATCH. He is an expert in B2B marketing and sales and previously worked at McKinsey & Company, Inc. as a project manager for large international companies, particularly in the chemical, energy and logistics industry for more than seven years. He studied Business Administration with the degrees in Business Studies and Dr. rer. pol. at the University of Bayreuth and the EDHEC in Nice. He holds several teaching assignments in B2B marketing and sales.

Erik Hebisch is Co-CEO of Interaction Room GmbH and doctoral candidate at paluno—The Ruhr Institute for Software Technology at the University of Duisburg-Essen. As an Interaction Room Coach, he has led over 15 Interaction Room workshops at organizations in the insurance and financial service domains and is responsible for the training of new coaches. His research focus is on the impact of quality and non-functional requirements on software architecture.

Peter Hufnagl studied Mathematics and Statistics at the Academy of Mining Freiberg. He focused firstly on medical image analysis and developed frameworks for tumor characterization and drug research. In the late nineties, he started do built telemedical solutions for doc-to-doc communication and emergency care for ships and aircrafts. As head of Digital Pathology at the Institute of Pathology at Charité Berlin, he is engaged in the application of virtual microscopy systems and machine learning in histology. In 2016, he founded the Center for Biomedical Image and Information Processing (CBMI) at the HTW University of Applied Sciences Berlin.

Markus Kleffmann is a doctoral candidate at paluno—The Ruhr Institute for Software Technology at the University of Duisburg-Essen and the lead developer of the Augmented Interaction Room software. His research focus is on human factors in software engineering, visualization and interaction techniques involving large interactive screens, and traceability between software model elements and artifacts.

Thorsten Knape is a researcher at the CBMI and has more than 15 years of experience as a senior manager and consultant in the medical devices industries and research institutions. He holds a Diploma in the field of Business Administration and Engineering, and a Master's degree in Computer Sciences from the Beuth University of Applied Sciences Berlin. His current research interests focus on the design and implementation of future digital consulting services, business model innovations of medical apps and data-driven services.

Marek Kowalkiewicz is an academic and industry leader with extensive experience in conducting academically sound research, co-innovating with industry and university partners, and delivering innovative products to the market. Currently, as Professor and PwC Chair in Digital Economy, as well as leader of the embracing digital age research theme, he leads Queensland University of Technology's research agenda to inform and influence a robust digital economy in Australia. Marek manages a contemporary research portfolio and converts industry driven opportunities into research outcomes of global relevance. He is an invited government expert, university lecturer and project lead, as well as an inventor and author.

Hendrik Kräft studied Social Sciences (Diplom Soz.-Wirt) with a focus on media and communication in Göttingen. He is a consultant and project manager at the Dr. Kuhl Unternehmensberatung and manages the business field of project management. His focus is the methodical development of project management and the consulting of midmarket customers in the digitization of business processes.

Jochen Kuhl studied economics with a focus on business informatics in Braunschweig and Göttingen. He obtained his Ph.D. in Business Informatics at the University of Göttingen. Jochen is Managing Director of Dr. Kuhl Unternehmensberatung and specialized in the optimization and digitization of management and business processes in midmarket companies. Furthermore, he is Managing Director of MeyerundKuhl Spezialwäschen GmbH, which is specialized in innovative washing and impregnation processes.

Jakob Reiter is a Master student of Business Information Systems Engineering at Technische Universität Ilmenau, Germany. He holds a Bachelor of Science and is currently finishing his Master studies with research on digitalized consulting products at the chair of Prof. Volker Nissen. Besides his study, he works as a freelance web developer.

Lukas Andreas Scherer is the managing director of the Institute for Quality Management and Business Administration (IQB) and professor at the FHS University of Applied Sciences St. Gallen, Switzerland (FHS). As lecturer, researcher and consultant he focusses on strategic management and entrepreneurship in SME and multinationals. After studies of Business Administration at the University of St. Gallen and at the Stockholm School of Economics (University Stockholm) and the Ph.D. at the University of St. Gallen he was business consultant for private and public organisations. In 1998 he joined the first private university in Switzerland as Dean and CEO. Besides these business activities he is engaged in several non-profit organisations.

Henry Seifert is a graduate engineer for media technology and since 2011 working as a management consultant. His main focus is on the automotive industry and artificial intelligence, analytics, process optimization and requirements management. He works in projects in the area of sales and after sales processes as well as professional learning. As doctoral candidate at the Group for Information Systems Engineering in Services at Technische Universität Ilmenau, he examines the digital transformation in the consulting industry. The goal of his dissertation is to demonstrate the opportunities and limitations of virtualization, as well as the design of artifacts that enable the realization of virtual consulting services.

Detlef Streitferdt is currently senior researcher at Technische Universität Ilmenau heading the research group Software Architectures and Product Lines since 2010. The research fields are the efficient development of software architectures and product lines, their analysis and their assessment as well as software development processes and model-driven development. Before returning to the University he was Principal Scientist at the ABB AG Corporate Research Center in Ladenburg, Germany. He was working in the field of software development for embedded systems. He received his doctoral degree from Technische Universität Ilmenau in the field of requirements engineering for product line software development in 2004.

Ingo J. Timm received a Diploma degree (1997), Ph.D. (2004), and Venia Legendi (2006) in Computer Science from University of Bremen. Ingo has been a Ph.D. student, research assistant, visiting and senior researcher at University of Bremen, Technische Universität Ilmenau, and Indiana University Purdue University, Indianapolis (IUPUI). In 2006, he was appointed full Professor for Information Systems and Simulation at Goethe-University Frankfurt. Since the fall of 2010, he has held the Chair for Business Informatics at Trier University. In 2016, he founded and is now heading the Center for Informatics Research and Technology (CIRT) and its Research Lab on Simulation (TriLabS).

Dirk Werth is leading the AWS-Institute for digitized products and processes, a private independent non-profit research center focusing its research on digitization of businesses and society. Before he worked at the German Research Center for Artificial Intelligence (DFKI) for more than a decade, where he served in different management positions. He has been responsible for numerous international and national research and consulting projects in the area of innovation by ICT. He holds Diplomas in Business Administration and in Computer Sciences as well as a Ph.D. in Economics.

Digital Transformation of the Consulting Industry—Introduction and Overview

Volker Nissen

Abstract Even though the total turnover in the consulting industry is increasing year after year, the competitive playing field for consultancies is changing rapidly. This is due to recent developments in potentially disruptive technologies used by successful digital newcomers, but also substantial changes and evolving requirements on the client side. In the face of new challenges and changing framework conditions, consultants should continually assess their service portfolio and critically review the traditional personnel-intensive 'face-to-face' delivery model of consulting. Like many of their clients, consulting firms are facing a digital transformation process that will lead to partially or completely virtualized processes, adapted organization structures and digital business models. Virtualization promises innovative possibilities for optimized performance and service delivery, thereby strengthening the competitive position. A serious analysis with regard to the potentials of virtualization within the different phases of consulting projects, within the consulting organization and in cooperation with customers and partners is necessary. To this end, knowledge should be accumulated at an early stage and a comprehensive vision should be developed that combines traditional and digitalized consulting approaches in a value-adding way. This introductory article reviews and structures the recent technology and market developments, provides examples of virtual consulting services, and outlines how a digital transformation initiative in consulting can be set up.

V. Nissen (✉)
Chair of Information Systems Engineering in Services,
Technische Universität Ilmenau, Ilmenau, Germany
e-mail: volker.nissen@tu-ilmenau.de

© Springer International Publishing AG 2018
V. Nissen (ed.), *Digital Transformation of the Consulting Industry*,
Progress in IS, https://doi.org/10.1007/978-3-319-70491-3_1

1 Motivation and Background

1.1 *All Is Well, Isn't It?*

There can hardly be doubts that business consulting is flourishing, and has been so for quite a while. Figure 1 shows exemplary the rise in total turnover in the German consulting market between 2010 and 2016. And the positive development continues. For 2017, the Association of German Business Consultants (BDU e.V.) expects another increase of 8.3%, reaching a total German consulting market volume of an estimated €31.4 billion (BDU, personal communication). On an international level the turnover increased from \$205 billion (including financial advisory) in 2011 to around \$250 billion in 2016. Thus, the global consulting sector is one of the largest and most mature markets within the professional services industry, according to Consultancy.uk (2017).

The figures seem to suggest that all is well in the consulting sector and steady growth for most companies can be anticipated for the next years, too. However, continued success can make you lazy and inattentive for potentially disruptive competitors. Or, as Christensen et al. (2013) put it, "there may be nothing as vulnerable as entrenched success". Much of the growth we see in consulting today may be attributed to some form of co-management or 'body leasing', where clients essentially remove management layers and replace permanent staff by support services from consultancies (see also the contribution of Deelmann 2017 in this volume).

Two difficulties of modern strategic planning, already identified by Igor Ansoff in 1975, may contribute to the danger of misinterpreting the overall situation with regard to future developments. First, strategic information about impending threats and opportunities is often perceived too late to permit timely and effective response. Second, the corporate planning cycle is too long to react in time to fast-developing

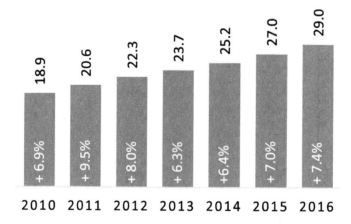

Fig. 1 Total turnover in the German consulting market 2010–2016 (BDU 2017)

events. Thus, Ansoff (1975) suggested that companies should look for 'weak signals' in strategic foresight as early indications of effective changes or trends in the company environment. Those companies may gain a competitive advantage that are able to recognize weak signals at an early stage, interpret them properly and act accordingly.

Some trends that may be interpreted as 'weak signals' in the context of a potential digital disruption of the consulting industry are:

- there is a 'digitalization of society', most people use digital ways of interaction,
- digital natives more and more get into decision maker positions,
- soaring online trade creates a well-established digital ecosystem,
- artificial intelligence has 'grown up' and become a key issue with growing relevance,
- the importance of data-based services is generally rising,
- complementary technical developments, such as data analytics/big data, mobile and cloud gain broad attention,
- ever shortening technology and product cycles render the follower strategy problematic,
- businesses engage in digital products and services that formerly were allocated solely to technology-focused companies,
- for standard consulting services the framing conditions have become increasingly competitive, the margin erodes, thus cost-effective measures are required,
- in fields closely related to business consulting, such as legal advice, wealth management, and auditing, technology-based approaches are gaining ground for some time.

With the consulting market conditions changing, as described in more detail below, and technologies like machine learning and analytics advancing, it can be expected that much of future growth in consulting goes to those who successfully create technology-based business opportunities and delivery models that better meet client requirements at lower cost. A closer look at the current trends in consulting will help to assess the situation more completely.

1.2 Markets Are Changing—Current Trends in Consulting

1.2.1 Trends in Technologies

Some of the most important current megatrends that also have an effect on consulting providers refer to complementary technological developments. Technologies like mobile devices and virtual personal assistants (VPAs) add to the channels to reach customers, while also changing the habits how people want to consume services. Moreover, these technologies enable instant responses and access to vast amounts of information that could be used on the client as well as on

...

the consultant side. According to Gartner (2014), by 2018, more than 50% of users will go to a tablet or smartphone first for all online activities.

Cloud computing radically changes the cost structure of technology-intensive service offers, cutting down fix costs that so far may have provided a barrier to market entry for technology-based competitors. Moreover, large business software providers like SAP with S/4 Hana Cloud intensified their efforts to provide their customers with Software-as-a-Service offerings that are largely pre-configured in the sense of standardized processes (Denecken 2017; Schmitz and Bischoff 2017). For IT-oriented consultants this means that their classical implementation business in the context of large on premise installations of business software with intensive need for individual tailoring will go down. It is increasingly replaced by smaller projects, focusing on the best possible use of such software on the client side, and associated change management. This is confirmed by a recent report from Forrester Research (2016) who assert that cloud applications and packaged deployments will require significantly less technical expertise to deploy and maintain than previous generations of systems.

Big data and analytical applications, in particular when combined with artificial intelligence/machine learning, provide capabilities that raise consultants' productivity and quality of results. The potential is immense, as according to McKinsey Global Institute (2016) most companies are capturing only a fraction of the potential value from data and analytics. Next to analytical capabilities, the focus should be on the integration of massive amounts of data of various formats and from different sources to enable discovery, gain new insights, and support innovation. Consulting companies will become increasingly 'data-driven'. On the one hand, they can integrate data and analytical competencies more closely into their services, thus improving their added value for the clients. On the other hand, the business model of consulting providers can be significantly modified if data are used to digitalize the service provision and enable automated consulting approaches that clients use autonomously.

The latter concept is further supported by current developments in natural language processing and chatbots, which provide an automated conversation interface that can be used to replace human communication partners. Gartner (2017) considers chatbots and AI/machine learning as two of the top ten technologies to support digital business. A recent survey amongst 150 service providers (USU 2017) concludes that as people feel more and more comfortable with digital communication and self-service channels, chatbots will gain a substantial share in customer interaction, providing information on standard topics automatically. McKinsey Global Institute (2016) estimates that 45% of work activities (cross industries) could potentially be automated by current technologies, with machine learning as a major enabler. Breakthroughs in natural language processing could expand that impact even further.

While data is abundant, it is the ability to integrate, analyze and use it intelligently that will make the difference. Consulting companies should strive to harness these capabilities in order to differentiate themselves from competitors and create value for their clients. For consulting HR departments this implies a strong demand to search for talented staff with the right qualification, intensifying the war for talents with entrepreneurial thinking, broad architectural skills, change management abilities, and deep knowledge in analytics, AI and other key technologies.

It is worth mentioning that big software companies make large investments in integrating analytical applications, machine learning, block chain, Internet-of-Things and related technologies, as exemplified by SAP Leonardo (SAP 2017) to provide their customers with what is marketed as a 'digital innovation system'. Again, this could in the long run, reduce the necessity for consulting support, as the business software increasingly provides "intelligent" functionality to support the client. On the other hand, challenging technological concepts inside products like SAP S/4 Hana Cloud and SAP Leonardo require a whole new and non-trivial set of technical skills from consultants. Moreover, Forrester (2016) ascertains that the work of many technology consultants by 2020 will have shifted from technical implementation toward areas of business model and customer experience design as well as highly specialized areas in analytics, security, mobility, and artificial intelligence.

Finally, digitalization and integration are megatrends in practically all industries. In the digital age, what can be digitalized, will be digitalized—if not by us, then by our competitors! Taken together with the ever shortening technology and product life cycles, this serves as a clue to understand that waiting what the others will do, i.e. adapting the classical follower strategy, will not work in most cases. From a management perspective, it is necessary to take risks, test alternative options of digitalization, drop the ones that do not seem to work within due time, and turn the other ones into economic success and competitive advantage. This must be supported by a more frequent (re-)assessment and potential change of resource allocation in budgeting processes.

It must be stressed that digitalization is not primarily about process optimization, but about new business models and innovations at the customer interface. Digital solutions should solve customer problems better than classical approaches. Different digitization approaches with differing focus are required in the various fields of action, such as marketing and distribution (focus: channels, customer journeys), products and services (focus: digital products and add-ons), ecosystems (focus: digital networks, collaboration), and processes (focus: automation).

Networking with other employees, partners and customers, but also interconnecting products is important. Platform thinking is required—IT-platforms grant access to market demand, communities and information exchange. The implicit trust problem that comes along with using such a solution must be solved, though. It basically reads: who is hosting the platform, gets the data, i.e. is in the strongest position among market players. Essentially platform economy may be characterized by a struggle between trust and convenience.

1.2.2   Developments on the Provider Side of the Market

The consulting and IT services industries meanwhile face a truly global competition while traditional boundaries between market segments are disappearing. As a result, vendors' offerings are converging and clients find it increasingly difficult to perceive differences between service providers in each segment (Parakala 2015). This reduces the pricing power of consulting firms as they become more exchangeable. Furthermore, concerning standard services ('commodity consulting'), the market is characterized by massive pressure on margins from freelancers and providers from low-wage countries (Nissen 2013). Aggressive competition in the area of commoditized services is seriously impacting the profitability of many consulting companies (Parakala 2015).

The situation is further aggravated by the clients growing tendency to unbundle consulting engagements and buy modular pieces from different providers, aiming for best-of-breed solutions in all aspects. Consequently, consulting providers should respond by applying flexible delivery models that are adaptable to clients' rapidly evolving needs. Facets of such flexibility include pricing, proving ROI, way of collaboration with clients, co-design and co-management, methodologies, standards and tools used, as well as delivery through onsite teams, competence centers, software tools and virtual workgroups. This is certainly a challenging requirement for many consulting companies, as was already pointed out in a Source Information Services Report in 2013 (p. 8): "Of all the characteristics of the successful consulting firm of the future, flexibility is arguably the most significant because it challenges the very foundations on which many firms are built".

A particular reaction to this best-of-breed attitude of clients is the business model of consulting providers like Eden McCallum (EMC). They analyze every project and compile a team of experienced freelance consultants to tackle it. For clients, that means tailored expertise at highly competitive rates, while consultants remain free from internal demands of traditional consulting companies and can opt to work on those projects they are really interested in, which puts this approach in the neighbourhood of professional employer organizations (Klaas et al. 2005). Companies like EMC can compete at lower rates than traditional consulting providers because they do not carry the fixed costs of unstaffed time, expensive buildings, recruiting, and training. While initially only serving small customers from its London base, EMC is meanwhile internationally established and supports leading companies (Christensen et al. 2013).

This setting also helps new competitors with innovative business models and technology-driven consulting concepts to enter the market, challenging incumbent firms in the long run (Christensen et al. 2013). Many of them do not aim to be providers of overarching 'one-stop-shopping' consulting services, but rather supply innovative solutions for a particular step in the consulting process, such as automated data analysis and interpretation (e.g. Narrative Science, Inspirient), process mining and modeling (e.g. Celonis), or creating innovative solutions with the help of an international community of experts (e.g. 10EQS, Wikistrat, Kaggle). The functional spectrum of services reaches from quickly connecting a client to an expert to provide on demand business advice (e.g. Clarity) to processing an entire consulting project in a fully digital manner. Many of these new consulting providers rely on web-based IT-platforms as a medium of communication and data exchange.

As a result, a certain modularization can be witnessed on the supply side of the consulting market. This reduces the primacy of integrated solution shops, which are designed to execute all aspects of the client engagement within the same consulting company. This shift is frequently triggered when customers feel they are paying too much for features they do not value and they want greater speed, responsiveness, and control (Christensen et al. 2013).

A result of modularization in consulting is a shrinking volume of individual engagements, which leads to rising sales and marketing efforts. New sales concepts and distribution models for 'small consulting services' are to be developed, such as consulting web-shops, consulting product configurators, pay-per-use and subscription-based payment models. The classical pay-per-diem concept does not fit many of the new consulting concepts that are currently introduced by potentially disruptive market entrants.

A group of new competitors in the consulting market provides asset-based consulting solutions. Christensen et al. (2013) describe asset-based consulting as involving "the packaging of ideas, processes, frameworks, analytics, and other intellectual property for optimal delivery through software or other technology". One could also say that this consulting approach heavily relies on software solutions, tools, models, algorithms and data-based assets. Consequently, the amount of human intervention is generally less than what traditional consulting requires. As a result, these services can be multiplied and scale much better than traditional consulting. Asset-based consulting is generally provided at a lower price than traditional people-based consulting, because of a substantial increase in efficiency, speed and productivity. Basically, more projects can be successfully conducted with the same consulting workforce, eventually improving operating margins at consultancies. Forrester (2016) expects project size to shrink, because asset-based consulting, cloud applications, and agile methodologies are creating environments that can support smaller, more iterative projects. Simultaneously, project teams tend to be more cross-disciplinary with higher seniority and specialization due to the complex demands of transformational client projects.

Asset and platform-based consulting concepts render geographic borders and distances irrelevant, thus extending the reach of providers. Expert knowledge becomes instantly and globally available. Additionally, in particular asset-based consulting contributes to consistent and repeatable project output, potentially adding to consulting quality. For clients, the ROI of consulting engagements becomes easier to grasp when consulting relies primarily on tools and software, reducing the opacity that is often criticized with regard to consulting.

Forrester Research (2016) estimates that by 2020 asset-based consulting will have substantially changed revenue and delivery models of consulting. When such tools are embedded by clients, they provide ongoing engagement outside the traditional project-based consulting model. Moreover, intelligent tools can be used to monitor business activities and processes at clients, communicating conspicuous features or operational problems to consultants and clients alike. Thus, new opportunities for consulting business might be automatically revealed through this monitoring. The Internet-of-Things will further add to such automated surveillance options.

Some established consulting firms, such as McKinsey, have early adopted the trend to asset-based consulting and added corresponding solutions (McKinsey Analytics) to complement their service portfolio. More recently, other major providers have followed this example, including Deloitte and BearingPoint. It is reported (Bakalova 2015) that asset-based consulting, as a strategic focus area, accounted for approximately 15% of BearingPoint's 2014 revenue, and will continue to expand its share to over 20% in 2020. Interestingly, also business software vendors such as Salesforce (having acquired the enterprise analytics provider BeyondCore in 2016) follow a similar path, adding new competition to traditional consulting companies.

Next to these technology-based approaches, other innovative concepts and methodologies have been introduced in consulting and IT services that aim for an improved coverage of changing client demands, more pragmatic solutions, and greater speed in delivery. These include Lean Start-up Approaches (Ries 2011), Design Thinking (Brown 2009), Innovation Labs & Think Tanks, and Professional Employer Organizations (Klaas et al. 2005), to name just a few.

As many incumbents lack the required technological and design capabilities to provide high-quality digital transformation consulting to their clients or use digital channels for active marketing in a masterly manner (not to mention digitalizing their own service portfolio), there has been intensive consolidation with M&A activity in the consulting sector over the last years (Parakala 2015). Examples how large firms in the consulting sector augmented their digital capabilities include the acquisition of BGT, a digital creative consultancy by PwC in 2013, while Accenture bought the design firm Fjord. In 2014, McKinsey acquired Agiliti, BCG picked up Strategic & Creative, and in 2016 IBM acquired exc.io (Desai 2016). Through this, large international consulting companies position themselves as 'one-stop-shopping providers', integrating competencies from strategy, operations, design and technology. This is an attempt to offer services in all areas required to solve their clients' challenges. However, a recent survey (Cardea 2016) revealed that more than two thirds of the clients currently perceive the multi-specialists to be lacking breadth and depth of specialized expertise. Consequently, these clients rather turn to specialist consultants when looking for certain expertise.

Small and medium-sized consulting companies face particular challenges in reacting to the current market trends. They have fewer resources, making it difficult to acquire digital capabilities, create asset-based consulting products, or buildup new competencies quickly. Thus, they are in danger of falling-back in terms of competition. In this situation, cooperation and focusing are two options smaller consulting companies should build upon. Cooperation with other consulting providers can extend the individual portfolio of competencies and services while focusing on specialized service offerings aims, as a complementary strategy, at deploying the available resources in the best possible way. By thoughtfully digitalizing their specialized services, smaller consulting companies are able to compete in their particular niche on an international level. Specialists with deep technological knowledge, industry know how, and innovation capabilities are in strong demand by clients.

With the high complexity of client projects in transformation consulting, the focus in hiring consultants is more and more on a consultant's ability to develop innovative and viable solutions at a reasonable price-performance ratio in complex market conditions (Cardea 2016). While this should make recruiting and staffing of projects more difficult, a recent survey by Cardea & NEWCOVENTURE (2016) reveals that consulting companies do see the challenge here but do currently not view these issues as primary barriers to making business.

1.2.3 Developments on the Client Side of the Market

The buyer side of the consulting market has also changed. An increasing professionality and an enhanced price consciousness of the clients regarding consulting services can be observed (Mohe 2003). In the realm of consulting purchase there is a stronger centralization, formalization and standardization of the processes. The client organizations' increasing sophistication about consulting services is often attributed to the vast number of former consultants now working inside client organizations (see e.g. Christensen et al. 2013), and adding to the professionalism and methodological knowledge of consulting customers.

Individualization is also a strong trend among clients. According to Scheer (2017), there is an increasing desire for more choice between in-house effort and external procurement, fueling the demand for highly qualified freelancers.

The megatrend digitalization further changed the buying behavior of consulting customers significantly. Following a general trend in B2C trade, clients increasingly use digital channels to search information on eligible consulting providers for their projects. Here, digital marketplaces and online communities already exceed the importance of the known search engines and portals (e.g., LinkedIn, XING) according to a survey by Cardea & NEWCOVENTURE (2016). Consequently, there is a stronger need for active (digital) marketing in consulting to increase the marketplace visibility and improve brand recognition and reputation.

When assessing the demand for consulting services in more detail, it is helpful to apply a differentiation of client projects with respect to overall complexity. Here, Maister (2003) suggested the three categories outlined in Table 1.

Brain projects are characterized by a client problem at the forefront of professional or technical knowledge and extreme complexity. It requires a high professional craft of its staff, since creativity and innovation are essential, while few procedures in these projects are routinizable. This project type requires mainly senior consulting staff and, hence, allows for only a low leverage.

Grey hair projects require a lesser degree of innovation and creativity in the actual performance than *Brain* projects would. While the output must still be highly

Table 1 Categorization of client projects with respect to complexity (based on Maister 2003)

	Brain	Grey hair	Procedure
Client problem	New or rather unique, very complex	Not unfamiliar, similar to others	Familiar and frequently solved
Required consultant skills	Creativity, innovation, pioneering of new approaches, concepts and techniques	Usable prior knowledge, judgment and transfer capabilities	Procedural knowledge, efficiency, tools
Leverage (ratio junior to senior level)	Low	Middle	High
'Hire us because…'	We are smart!	We have been through this before!	We know how to do this efficiently!

customized in meeting the client's needs, the problem to be solved is not unfamiliar, and the activities to be performed may be similar to those of other projects, though some judgment and transfer capabilities are essential. Consequently, the fraction of junior consulting staff and, thus, the leverage in these projects can be higher than in *Brain* projects.

Procedure projects address client problems that are very familiar. While there is still a need to customize to some degree, the required steps to solve the problem are somewhat programmatic. Clients often have the ability to perform the work themselves, but turn to consultants, because internal resources are needed elsewhere, or consultants can provide more efficient solutions. The use of procedure models, templates and tools allows for a high fraction of junior staff, leading to a high leverage in this class of projects.

Interestingly, the indication of leverage in the project class *Brain* could change in complex digital transformation projects of clients. While senior staff is certainly necessary to structure and steer such projects, the up-to-date technological knowledge of young professionals (digital natives) might be more useful and required in consulting today than ever before.

According to a recent industry survey (Parakala 2015), clients are becoming much more selective and modular about what they are buying, often seeking services in smaller well-defined scopes of work. Where large service providers are unable to meet expectations, clients are willing to explore partnerships with smaller, more agile and innovative consulting companies. Clients demand leveraging digital technologies to streamline operational processes and bring about fundamental changes in the business model. This requires consulting and IT service providers to increasingly co-create solutions in close cooperation with clients that face a globalized and volatile business environment.

In this situation, the clients have become more demanding and professional, and they are more closely examining whether they really need consulting services and which consulting company they want to use (Cardea 2016). Moreover, new and potentially disruptive consulting delivery models become more acceptable with clients, when they better account for their needs and provide a clearer ROI.

It can be observed, that for commodity consulting (*procedure projects*) business consulting has been changing towards a buyers' market. Here the price, speed, and value for money are foremost, as competition amongst providers is intense and clients hire consultants mainly because they are more efficient or helpful in pushing decisions. Moreover, self-service solutions will be offered and consumed more extensively, according to Forrester (2016), where clients need an ongoing capability, and the consulting activities can be automated. According to Deelmann (2009) as well as Brynjolfsson and McAfee (2016) tasks with a routine character are at the most risk of being replaced by digitalized solutions.

On the other hand, as complex and uncertain market conditions present new challenges, consulting customers face difficult problems that call for complex analyses, and innovative solutions (*brain projects*). The versatile business context demands fast and complex transformations of clients' business models, value chains and product offerings (Cardea 2016). Digital transformation projects require globally consistent systems, organizational structures and processes, which increases the scope, risk, and impact of such projects. Clients also expect that consultants understand the clients' customers. Consultants thus need more detailed knowledge and supporting data on how customers research, buy, and use their clients' products and services (Forrester 2016), adding further complexity to consulting. Here the challenge will be to stay ahead of the clients in order to be able to add actual value.

A closer look at the future consulting market was taken in the recent study by Cardea & Newcoventure (2016) and Cardea (2017). Consulting providers as well as clients predict an increasing segmentation of the consulting market in three major segments:

- high-value strategy consulting (covered by international top consultancies),
- large-scale 'low-cost' consulting projects solving well recognized problems,
- spot-consulting/high-value specialist consulting.

While procedure and brain projects clearly persist, it appears that there might be some form of 'erosion of the middle' (*grey hair projects*) in terms of project complexity.

A recent study conducted by Cardea (2016) revealed that almost two third of the surveyed clients stated that it is difficult or very difficult for them to find the right consultants for their businesses. At the same time, the majority of clients in this study said that digital media and channels are gaining importance for seeking the right consulting service providers. As a consequence, a further increase in market share for digital matching platforms (such as consultingsearcher, Comatch, and Klaiton) can be expected that aim to provide transparency over the consulting market and intermediate between companies searching for consultants, and consultants (including independent freelancers) seeking project engagements. This in turn has substantial influence on the required marketing and sales activities of consulting providers.

In the third market segment, high-value specialist consulting, new entrants with radically different consulting approaches, such as crowd labor markets (e.g. OnFrontiers), crowd contests (e.g. kaggle) or technology-driven functional tools enter the market. The newcomers in this segment build on the clients' trend to unbundle consulting engagements, and buy consulting from different providers in a modular way to achieve best-of-breed solutions. With their innovative consulting approaches, they use delivery models that provide high-quality results for specific aspects in the consulting process at greater speed and lower costs compared to established firms, making it very attractive for clients to choose them.

1.3   Lessons from Related Branches of Industry

Today digital attackers can be found in most industries, but particularly in services. How fast and fundamentally knowledge-intensive professional services can be digitally transformed can be seen by a quick look at investment counseling, legal advice, and auditing.

Regarding money investments, a turn of the era is in progress—in future assets will be largely managed by means of sophisticated software (Weimer 2016; Anonymous 2016a). This is demonstrated by companies like Easyfolio, which offer automated fund management to their investors. The investment tool, also called Robo-Advisor, automatically invests the client's money in different funds depending on the customers' willingness to take risks.

Similar developments can be observed in legal advice. Companies with web-based offers like LegalZoom, Otris, Agreement24 and RocketLawyer directly invade the business branch of lawyers and solicitors. As an example, Swedish online provider Agreement24 provides software for the automatic design of legal documents, such as contracts and testimonials, for private and business customers. Moreover, the companies' webpage attracts users with detailed information on different legal areas. The juristic start-up Legalist aims to identify promising law-suits by means of historical trial data. Intelligent algorithms are supposed to determine the chances of success and the estimated duration of a lawsuit (Anonymous 2016b).

Meanwhile analysis tools are also available for auditing, so that relevant business processes, in the course of the annual audit, can be automatically reconstructed and audited for financial reporting (Werner 2012). Companies like Zapliance build on the digitization of business processes and internal control systems that opens up new opportunities for audit automation and audit digitization. Similar procedures apply to internal audits in a company (Jans et al. 2011). Companies like PwC expect an almost complete change in the professional job profile of public accountants since auditing will be (almost) fully automated in the future. As a result, PwC intensified its cooperation with Google and moves in the direction of a more technology-oriented company that strives for digital business models and offers digital products to complement its service portfolio (PwC 2017).

1.4 There Is a Need for Action in the Consulting Industry

"Businesses intensively need to deal with questions of how their core business will run in the future. It is therefore necessary to develop an efficient digital strategy. Classical approaches no longer apply here. Industries need to redefine themselves to prevail against innovative competitors and challenges." This statement given by Marcel Nickels, chairman of the executive board of BearingPoint GmbH, Germany, in an interview for the Lünendonk—Handbook Consulting 2016, also applicably describes the situation of consulting service providers today.

As was outlined above, the consulting sector is constantly confronted by new challenges and changing market conditions. Consulting providers should therefore repeatedly review their service portfolio in a critical way. Even though they strengthen the competitiveness of their clients by innovative solutions and substantially take part in the development of new concepts for digitalization, consulting services are often only done by the traditional face-to-face approach.

According to Parakala (2015) the same disruptive forces that have changed the way many industries operate have now started to seriously impact the consulting and IT services sector. This is also clearly expressed in the following statement of Hans-Werner Wurzel and Kai Haake, respectively the president and manager of the Association of German Business Consultants (BDU e.V.): "When it comes to the mega trend digitalization, consultants should not only find answers to clients' questions. They should become master minds on their own account, because digital transformation will also turn the classical business models of the 'People Business' consulting upside down" (Wurzel and Haake 2016, translated).

A recent study amongst the members of the BDU reveals that 84% expect the consulting portfolio, business models and processes of consulting companies to change significantly in the course of the coming years. 79% can also imagine that new solutions are being developed in close cooperation with established software vendors in the fields of data analysis, business intelligence and cloud. And 75% (large providers 92%) see the fight for digital talents in full swing (BDU 2016).

Consulting meta-researcher Fiona Czerniawska (2017) estimates that 72% of the consulting market could be taken over by "a new breed of intelligent machines". Expressed differently, almost three quarters of the traditional consulting industry could disappear over the next ten years, particularly in the area of commodity consulting. According to her, 98% of senior US clients think that digital technology will change the way consulting is done. Data gathering and work done by junior consultants will fall victim to automation first.

The demographic change and the intensifying War-for-Talents provide further arguments to look at options of digitalization. Today's younger employee generation (often referred to as the 'Generation Y') are accustomed to digital media and tools from early childhood on ('digital natives'), so they have no fear or skepticism towards using innovative technologies (Dahlmanns 2013). They are further characterized by strong individualism (Parment 2013). These young people are aware of the shortage of qualified applicants on the consulting job market, while loyalty to employers has declined considerably (Buck et al. 2002). This provides young professionals with a position to make demands on their employers. Members of 'Generation Y' value the opportunity to travel less and work flexible hours, as this adds to their Work-Life-Balance (WLB).

In our survey on the status of WLB in German IT-consulting (Nissen and Termer 2014) 95% of the IT consultants asked said that they actively strive for a balance between professional and private life. But 59% state that their profession does rather not or not at all enable them to realize a WLB. Improvements concerning the flexibility of place of work and the organization of working time are most important to raise WLB from the viewpoint of more than 80% of the surveyed consultants. A change of corporate culture was judged as a decisive factor in consulting to generally upgrade the importance of WLB measures. This is supported by a recent result from the Lünendonk consulting market survey (2016) that also concludes employees want to work more flexibly. It is precisely these issues that the digital transformation of consulting delivery models could enable and support, as they reduce the need for face-to-face interaction on-site with clients. Clearly, raising the extent of WLB would be a powerful argument in the recruitment of highly qualified staff for consulting and enforce their bonding to the company. Thus, also for recruiting reasons the topic digitalization should be prioritized more by the consulting management.

While some of the large and established consulting firms have realized the signs of the times, and started digital transformation initiatives (McKinsey Solutions and Bearing Point Asset-based Consulting are examples), most companies are still in the early stages regarding the digitalization of their own business, as the results of our survey show (Nissen and Seifert 2016, see also the contribution of Nissen and Seifert 2017a in this volume). Incumbent firms demonstrate a lack of business model innovations and high-degree virtualizations of consulting services (up to full automation), building on disruptive technologies. Instead, the focus in the majority of consulting companies is on low levels of virtualization, where technology is merely used to increase personal productivity of consultants, improve the quality of existing services, and reduce travel times.

Traditional consulting companies have typical problems when it comes to the digitalization of their services and business models. First, they have not changed their business models for a long time. This laziness can be explained by the generally positive market development in the past. As a result, internal structures and corporate culture are not supportive to change. Second, traditional consulting providers established highly selective and standardized operations to ensure a high level of quality in their services. As a consequence, they easily fall victim to what Christensen (1997) calls the 'innovator's dilemma'. According to this logic, established organizations, focused on excellence, at first do not take possible disruption seriously. For too long these firms ignore potentially disruptive new market entrants. The reason is that new competitors initially have innovative but immature products and gain only small fractions of the market in niches unattractive for incumbents. Over time, the new competitors develop further, improve their products and rapidly broaden their customer base. But then it is too late for the established organizations to come up with a response in due time that is suitable to defend their market position. A further problem here is that incumbents, focused on excellence, have problems to internally integrate innovative but immature solutions, even though they may be available to them. Third, traditional consulting is an opaque business (Christensen et al. 2013), with consulting services considered complex and expensive. But the consulting solutions offered by technology-driven new market entrants are often cheaper with a clearer ROI, easier to understand and use, and instantly available at an international level, which makes them attractive also for the clients of established consulting providers.

There are sufficient examples what happens when disruptive competitors are under-estimated or key technologies are adopted too late or unsuccessfully, both at the level of individual companies as well as the level of whole industries. The following two short cases will serve to demonstrate this.

The German trading firm Quelle was founded in 1927 in Fürth, Bavaria. In the 1980s it was one of the top five trading companies in Germany, internationally represented, with a maximum of about 8000 employees. The mail order business model focused on sales through printed catalogues and mailings. The company substantially underestimated the importance of e-commerce and emerging online competitors like Amazon (founded in 1994). The management tried too late and in an unprofessional way to change to an omni-channel sales concept. The result was the liquidation of the enterprise in 2009. Quelle collapsed because it ignored too long emerging digital competitors and failed at its own digital transformation.

In the watchmaking industry, most European and American market leaders were too late in adopting the new electronic quartz watches that became available to a broad market around 1970. As a result, former leaders were marginalized, resulting in a massive loss of jobs. The volume business shifted from traditional mechanical watches to cheaper electronic watches, where producers were often located in Asia. The dramatic local impact of this development can be seen in the employment figures of the watch industry of Baden-Württemberg, one of the German states and a former stronghold of mechanical watch production in Germany. While this industry employed more than 31,000 people in 1969, this figure went down to below 9000 in 1989 and merely 1369 in 2009,[1] documenting the decline of a former flourishing business.

---

[1]For more details see http://www.sozialgeschichte-uhrenindustrie.de/2014/06/22/vom-niedergang-der-uhrenindustrie-strukturwandel-in-der-region-schwarzwald-baar-heuberg/.

2   Virtual Consulting Services

2.1   What Is a Virtual Consulting Service?

In order to remain strong in the market, established consultancies need to critically evaluate their business models as well as the way they provide their services to clients. Incumbents can gain a sustainable competitive advantage if they use new and disruptive technology to innovate their consulting processes. Technology-fueled tools and digital products can distinguish a provider from its competitors by optimizing and sustainably extending the service-portfolio. Asset-based consulting services can offer new starting points to lower ones' own costs and recover marginal scope. Through rethinking the delivery-process of consulting itself consultancies can reshape the interaction with the client and open up segments of new customers. A promising approach to achieve these goals is virtualization.

Consulting traditionally is expected to be a 'people business'. Normally consultants will be sent to clients in order to interactively solve business problems. A virtual process is in comparison a process during which the physical interaction vanishes. The transition of a physical process towards a virtual process is termed 'process virtualization' (Overby 2008). Central virtualization mechanisms are digitalization and networking. Virtualization is omnipotent nowadays. Online banking and social media are only two examples, which show that virtualization has meanwhile taken an ever more important role in everyday life.

Virtualization is a trend which should also be applied by consulting companies to their own business processes. In view of the described market challenges, virtualization of consulting services can be an innovative strategy to secure lasting business success. The aim of virtualization is to reasonably reduce the amount of face-to-face interaction between consultant and client by the suitable use of information and communication technologies (ICT) (Christensen et al. 2013; Greff and Werth 2015; Nissen et al. 2015). It can thus be referred to as the strategy for digital transformation of the consulting business.

Virtual services can supplement classical offers of business consulting in an attempt to optimize ones' performance, and complement the existing service portfolio as well as delivery modes. Virtualization can introduce new digital business models of consulting which increase the efficiency, flexibility and effectiveness of consulting services. In combination with a standardization of the consulting service, the door to fully automated consulting solutions is opened in some fields. In practice, the strongly virtualized forms of business consulting, e.g. self-service consulting, have only been used occasionally so far. As a matter of fact, it was observed that some consultants have adverse tendencies, specifically towards an automatization of consulting services (Deelmann 2015). The potential of such a digital transformation of consulting is, however, gradually being recognized (Nowak 2015; Werth et al. 2016a).

Virtualization opens up new markets that would otherwise be out of geographical reach, or simply not suitable for traditional forms of consulting—see, for instance, bestprax.de as an example of virtual strategy consulting for dentists. Virtualization can be the cornerstone of new forms of collaboration and integration with the clients. Thus, the way in which consultants and clients work together changes fundamentally, introducing both chances and risks (Nissen et al. 2015; Nissen and Seifert 2015).

Consultancies, which do not or only superficially deal with virtualization, run the risk to fall behind in the competitive field and weaken their position in the consulting market. In the following section, the wide spectrum of the virtualization of consulting services will be explained.

2.2 Spectrum of Virtual Consulting Services

In consulting, virtualization is understood as a spectrum of possible services, where the extreme points of these services are determined, on the one hand by a mere supportive use and on the other hand by an exclusive use of information and communication technology (Fig. 2). The latter is termed full virtualization where the personal consulting service is completely substituted by technology based solutions. Here the client uses consulting products autonomously. If required he can, however, obtain supplementary personal consulting. Between these extremes there are numerous variants of virtual consulting services.

The lower the degrees of virtualization, the more often direct face-to-face interaction between the participants of the consulting process is performed. This means that workshops, meetings or dialogues take place directly and personally. Occasionally tools are used to communicate with each other independently from the location. Standardization and automation are specifically used in the form of procedure models and templates. The delivery of services is not automated.

With an increasing degree of virtualization, the direct, personal contact between the consultant and his client, but also between a consultant and another consultant, is minimized. When the service has a very high degree of virtualization, there will only be direct contact between the participants, especially between the consultant and the client, in the case of critical activities and problems. The more the consulting process is virtualized, the more often collaboration tools like instant messenger, video applications, shared file repositories or virtual workspaces are used (Schuster 2005).

A crucial added value can be achieved when automation is used with an increasing degree of virtualization. This way the service delivery can be detached from a single consultant and is extensively, up to fully substituted by software products. This allows for an optimal multiplication of knowledge and scaling of consulting services. Moreover, they may be applied even in remote regions (Nowak 2015). On the other hand, the deployment of such consulting products brings new forms of pricing along. Automated consulting applications may e.g. be sold at a fixed price or distributed via licenses.

Degree of Virtualization of Consulting Services

little virtualized

fully virtualized

▪ mainly direct interaction	▪ mainly direct interaction	▪ mainly indirect interaction	▪ mainly automated interaction
▪ sporadic usage of web conferences, chat applications, and similar tools	▪ frequent usage of web conferences, chat applications, and similar tools	▪ predominant usage of web conferences, chat applications, and similar tools	▪ predominantly automated solutions for consulting tasks
	▪ sporadic usage of online collaboration	▪ frequent deployment of tools for automated solving of individual consulting tasks	
Example Scenario: Software implementation with developers at the client on-site. Sporadic usage of desktop sharing tools and video conferences.	**Example Scenario:** Additional programming with nearshore-teams. Regular video conferences and online workshops. Requirements workshops usually take place at the client.	**Example Scenario:** Process mining for business process optimization with workshops at the client on-site. Analytical tasks, however, are performed remotely as much as possible via corresponding digital services.	**Example Scenario:** Clients are supplied with a digital consulting application, which analyzes the client's data, interprets tendencies, and automatically suggests measures to be taken.

Fig. 2 The virtualization of consulting services as a continuum (Nissen et al. (2015) in source: Deelmann T, Ockel DM, in collaboration with BDU e.V. (eds) Handbuch der Unternehmensberatung, loose-leaf book, state 2017, KZ. 7311, courtesy of Erich Schmidt Verlag GmbH & Co. KG, Berlin 2017, more about the loose-leaf book at http://www.esv.info/978-3-503-07846-2)

A different categorization of virtual consulting services, suggested by Werth et al. (2016a) is shown in Fig. 3. It is based on the degree of integration with either the client or the consultant side. Virtual consulting can be found in any of the four quadrants of Fig. 3, which again points to the diversity of services and application scenarios conceivable.

Specific features of service research can be used to characterize virtual consulting services in an even more differentiated way (Fig. 4). *Interactivity* of a virtual consulting service describes the amount of interaction between the consultant and the client. The *degree of digitalization* illustrates to what extent information and communication technologies are used to deliver virtual consulting services. The *degree of standardization* illustrates how many components, procedures and results of a virtual consulting service are predetermined. *Integrativity* describes to what extent the resources of clients and consultants are brought into the consulting process. *Modularity* characterizes how a consulting service can be differentiated into complete, by clear interfaces separated, subservices.

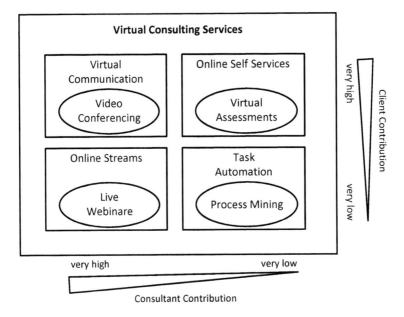

Fig. 3 Classification of virtual consulting services in terms of respective consultant and client contribution in the service co-creation (after Werth et al. 2016a)

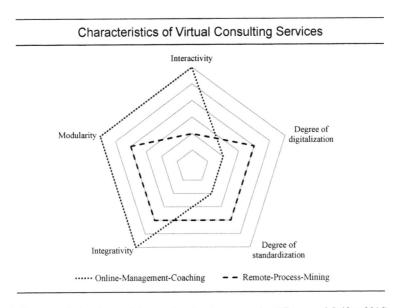

Fig. 4 Features of virtual consulting services for two examples (Nissen and Seifert 2016)

For instance, an online management coaching that is being offered as HR-consulting presents other characteristic attribute values than a remote process mining which is being used for IT-consulting. By taking the example of interactivity, the difference can be explained. During online coaching, the consultant and the assisted person work interactively with each other. Ideas, opinions and experiences are lively exchanged. In the case of remote process mining, however, there is hardly any interaction with the client. Here the focus is on the proper implementation of mining tools by the consultant and the correct analysis of the generated process models.

Further examples of virtual consulting services, which each have different characteristic attribute values, are the following:

- Video conferences between consultants are very interactive, but not really standardized.
- A podcast for the client about an actual topic, which is not interactive, but on the other hand, is completely digitalized.
- A data mining tool for analysis purposes used by the consultant, which is marked by a high modularity and degree of integration.
- A web-based assessment to determine the client's maturity level of project management, which is little interactive, but is standardized and modularized.
- A tablet consulting app about project management with a high level of digitalization.
- An interactive, virtual assistant for clients which can advise the client in a digital and standardized way.

Virtual consulting services can thus take different shapes. By the combination of virtual service modules, new virtual consulting products can be created. It also becomes clear that virtualization is not a completely new phenomenon. In present daily routine of consulting, various technologies, especially in the context of lowly virtualized services, are already used. For instance, video conferences or project platforms are already components of many projects today.

The ambitious vision of a digital transformation of the consulting industry requires suitable artefacts. These include technology-driven software solutions, such as web-based consulting platforms, mobile consulting applications, data mining and cooperation tools. Likewise, concepts are required to assess the virtualizability of consulting tasks and develop solutions, which can link conventional and virtualized consulting in a unified service portfolio to better address clients' needs. Methods and techniques for virtualization have to be created. Here is still a substantial need for research (Seifert and Nissen 2016).

2.3 Examples of Virtual Consulting Services

2.3.1 Foundation—An Idealized Consulting Process

Before discussing examples of virtual consulting, the basic structure of an idealized consulting process will be briefly outlined (Fig. 5). This process then serves as the basic structure to present the examples afterwards. The process starts with considerable activities of marketing and sales during the project acquisition phase. When the deal is won and the contract is agreed with the client, the project is initiated, which includes staffing and planning activities, creating a project organization, setting up an infrastructure for the project, determining tools and standards for project management, and finally, the kick-off meeting of consultants and clients. Project management, of course, remains a permanent task for the rest of the project. In the next phase, data is gathered and analyzed to deepen the understanding of the client's problems. Based on a diagnosis of the client situation, planning is further detailed and work packages for the next phases are assigned. Then, one or more solutions are developed to solve the client's issues, based on results of the problem analysis. The solutions are presented to the client management, who decide which solution is to be implemented in the next project phase. During project closure, various activities take place on the consultant and client side. Consultants should evaluate the project internally and record lessons learned. Clients usually approve the project results and should also check project success w.r.t. the goals set and their expectations of the project. Then, from the perspective of the consulting provider, the after sales phase starts that aims for further business with this client.

2.3.2 Project Acquisition, Planning and Setup

Content-marketing is an established form of virtualization in the marketing of consulting. Particularly large, international companies frequently use published studies, articles and blogs to demonstrate their competencies and attract customers. Practically all consultancies further provide written project references and success stories on their web pages. However, a wide range of marketing instruments (such as search engine optimization) and channels (such as online business networks, e.g. LinkedIn) are available to raise brand reputation and gain client attention.

A recent study by Cardea (2017) concludes that while personal client relationships are still the most important success factor for the future growth of consulting firms, the second most important factor is brand, closely followed by visibility and ease of being found. The same study, though, also states that consulting companies

Fig. 5 Idealized consulting process plus integration with sales & marketing

do not yet appear to find the right approach for their digital marketing strategies. As a consequence, they are leaving important opportunities to increase their visibility and brand reputation in the web unexploited.

An interesting application for project planning (but also other project tasks) with a moderate degree of virtualization is the *Augmented Interaction Room* developed by Hebisch et al. (2017). The setting used by the authors to highlight their approach is software development, where the method is, for instance, applicable in sprint planning within agile software projects, or in distributed project scoping and controlling. But the virtualization described is basically useful in all complex projects with heterogeneous (and potentially distributed) teams. Core objectives of the method include improved communication and fostering of information as well as a better mutual understanding within the project team.

To facilitate communication and cooperation in interdisciplinary teams, Book et al. (2012) previously introduced the *Interaction Room*, a consulting method that uses large whiteboards to help team members identify the key risk, value and effort drivers of their projects early. In the *Augmented Interaction Room*, the classical whiteboards are replaced by software that runs on several connected large interactive displays, mimicking the look and feel of traditional whiteboards, but offering additional features that provide higher usability and versatility. At its core, the *Augmented Interaction Room* enables the sketching of models on the interactive screens with a pen whose movements are translated into digital ink strokes in real time. The digital ink strokes can be grouped, rearranged and resized on the interactive display with simple touch gestures. Model elements can be annotated by dragging and dropping icons from an annotation palette, while additional background information (notes, web links etc.) can be associated with each annotation icon. As a result, models, plans and sketches created during workshops are immediately visible and editable by all stakeholders regardless of their location. Moreover, relations in the content between the different digital whiteboards used are recognized and digitally linked, dependencies and conflicts between models become automatically visible. Furthermore, workshop results can be easily stored and distributed for platform-independent viewing. Summarizing, the goal of digitization in the *Augmented Interaction Room* method is to improve the quality of workshop discussions and project planning, to increase the long-term influence of workshop results, and to include remote stakeholders.

Recent developments at the sales front-end of consulting include online shops for consulting solutions. An example is the *Scheer Marketplace*, outlined in the contribution of Greff and Werth (2017) in this volume. It allows consultancies to offer modular consulting services via a webstore. Clients can select, compare, customize, configure and buy consulting services online, while the consulting service itself is still delivered traditionally on-site.

Already very popular are consulting procurement marketplaces. They act as a digital intermediary between companies (clients or consultancies) in need of external support with projects and requirements on the one side and consultants (mostly individual freelancers, but sometimes also consulting companies) with their capabilities and available capacities on the other side. At the moment, the majority of digital marketplaces are focusing on the placement of independent consultants respectively, on freelancers in compiled teams. Frequently, admittance to the marketplace is granted to consultants on the basis of a quality assessment that might include a CV check, a required threshold of industry experience, and/or interviews with representatives of the marketplace.

COMATCH, as an example, matches independent consultants and companies in need of external support for projects. The matching is based on a combination of technology and personal experience, which nicely demonstrates the limits of full automation in sensitive business areas. With a network of already more than 2000 experienced consultants, the service is offered worldwide but focusing on the German speaking countries (DACH), the Nordic, Benelux, France and the Middle East. Next to the matchmaking functionality, the marketplace offers administrative services, such as contracting, time-tracking and billing as well as feedback tools. Feedback includes a regular evaluation of the consultant by the hiring company, concerning work quality, interaction and professional behaviour. The consultant also gives feedback to the client in return and both parties evaluate how satisfied they are with the COMATCH service. This helps to keep consulting quality at a high level and reduces the risk associated with procuring previously unknown personnel for a project via a digital marketplace. More details concerning COMATCH are given in the contribution by Hardt (2017) in this volume.

2.3.3 Problem Analysis

For consulting companies it will be increasingly important to improve the productivity of the individual consultant in order to stay competitive. This can be achieved by employing innovative software tools that speed up data-intensive routine tasks during problem analysis and solution development. As an example, many projects require the modeling and analysis of as-is business processes, which traditionally is a more or less manual task with the help of 'drawing tools' such as MS Visio, possibly augmented by a database and some supporting functionality.

A science- and technology-driven newcomer in this field who provides a disruptive new solution is *Celonis* (2017). Building on the results of researchers like the Dutch professor van der Aalst (2016), *Celonis* has developed the process mining software *Pi* that automatically analyzes available log-data of business software (like ERP systems). It then not only comes up with a visualization of the way processes are really operated in the client company (standard process and any number of deviations), but can also provide suggestions for improvements, based on process analysis and machine learning techniques. This is classical consultant work and would normally consume a significant amount of time and budget. Moreover, working manually, it would be virtually impossible to give an account of all process variants actually present at a company. Thus, *Celonis Pi* can provide more results faster and at potentially lower cost, while some data collecting and preprocessing is required beforehand as data quality is crucial for good results. It should be noted that process mining tools can only be used if data is available. Moreover, social aspects of processes and 'soft factors' that are not mirrored in the data, are difficult to include in automatic analytic approaches. Consequently, consultants are not replaced by such tools, but it shifts their focus on the more creative and social aspects. In the end, process mining tools speed up the analysis phase of projects, raising productivity and agility of the consultants and potentially also the attained quality of results.

This also holds for more general analytical applications, which operate based on classical statistics as well as modern computational intelligence techniques (such as artificial neural networks and metaheuristic approaches). An example here is the product provided by consulting newcomer *Inspirient* (Wittenburg 2017a, b). Basically, *Inspirient* treats data analysis as a search for insights in large amounts of data, which is also labeled data mining. Here, the analytical routine work of (junior) strategy consultants is automated. Just a few years ago this would not have been deemed possible. Business data records, for example in the form of an MS Excel file, are analyzed within a very short time using methods from statistics and artificial intelligence. As a result, the user is presented with a prioritized selection of relevant analysis results in the form of ready-to-use presentation slides, including natural-language descriptions of the analysis results.

The tool-based solution is brought to the market above all by deals with large classical consulting companies, where data analysis is part of the day-to-day business. However, it could as well be used by clients directly, and is particularly attractive for small and medium-sized companies that would usually not afford expensive strategy consulting. A logical next step in the advancement of analytical applications such as *Inspirient's* solution is a combination of the algorithms with industry expertise, e.g. for credit assessment, patent analysis, and fraud detection.

A completely different approach is used by crowd-contest based companies, where *kaggle* is a good example. The business model of *kaggle* (2017) is to connect people with a problem and the associated data to experts all around the world who can create predictive models fitting the data. The connection is 1:n so that a multitude of different models based on a variety of techniques is developed for a given problem in the form of a crowd contest. Only the best model is later sold to the client of *kaggle*. This way, data science and analytics are converted to an open and transparent competition, with public rankings and international team forming. Thus, a form of gamification takes place that builds largely on the motivation of people to provide better results than others. Moreover, the *kaggle* platform provides many community and feedback functions, free data sets, job adverts and related functions that make joining the *kaggle* crowd even more attractive.

Our final example is an automated digital assessment. In the case of *bestprax.de* (Stummeyer 2017, 2018) the customers in focus are dentists. Owners of dental practices may be good in their profession, but often lack comprehensive business knowledge. Thus, they would frequently need advice from a professional strategy consultant on how to improve their business. However, given the revenue size of a common dental practice, fees for a professional management consulting project are simply not in financial reach for most dentists. This issue is solved with the self-service consulting solution offered by *bestprax.de*. By conducting a benchmarking study of their dental practice using an online platform for interaction and a large database of comparable practices in the background, the dentist gains access to a proven consulting method and receives an objective perspective on strengths and weaknesses of his practice. *Bestprax.de* offers its' service in the form of a digital expertise, and at a very low price compared to standard rates in strategy consulting. This self-service opens up a whole new group of clients who would normally not approach a business consultant for help.

2.3.4 Solution Development and Implementation

Crowdsourcing provides interesting opportunities to solve certain tasks cost-effectively, rapidly and creatively in the consulting project phases solution development and implementation. Crowds are largely intrinsically motivated, for example by the desire to learn or compete with others. This increases when people themselves can choose which problems they are working on. According to Boudreau and Lakhani (2013) four different forms of problem solving through the crowd can be differentiated with the following purposes:

- *Crowd contests* can be used to generate high-value solutions to complex or novel problems through large-scale and diverse independent experimentation.
- *Crowd collaborative communities* aggregate a large number of diverse contributions into a value-creating whole.
- *Crowd complementors* enable a market for goods and services to be built on some core product or technology, effectively transforming that product into a platform that generates complementary innovations.
- *Crowd labour markets* are essentially about efficiently and flexibly matching talent to discrete tasks.

Crowd contests are a relatively straightforward way to engage a crowd. A sponsor, in our case a consulting company, creates a contest and describes the specific problem. Moreover, it agrees to pay the winner a certain amount of price money and defines a deadline. Afterwards the contest is started and the crowd will try to generate good solutions. Finally, the sponsor selects a winner and hands over the price. Thereby the consulting company acquires the corresponding rights, e.g. authorship of the solutions. *Kaggle* is an example of a crowd-contest based company in the field of data science, as was already outlined above.

A digital provider that basically operates as a collaborative community is *Wikistrat* (2017). It is an international platform that aims to model the forces of globalization and forecast the outcomes of geostrategic issues. For consulting clients the crowd-sourced platform is of particular interest due to the opportunity to receive support in strategic planning by identifying and discussing 'strategic surprises', and to provide help for decision-makers to identify solutions of complex strategic challenges. *Wikistrat* is based on an expert pool of currently 2200 subject matter experts (historians, physicists, former diplomats etc.) instead of highly paid business consultants. If a customer places an order with the crowd consultancy on a certain topic, Wikistrat selects between 50 and 100 analysts from their fundus, who then work to create appropriate scenarios. The online platform supports working collaboratively to increase speed and quality of results. *Wikistrat* promises the generation of diverse and interdisciplinary insights unavailable through traditional analysis, with transparent methodology and client interactivity. The payment for crowdworkers results from a fixed amount per analysis as well as a bonus system that rewards the quantity, but also the quality of the contributions measured by other experts on the platform. It is reported that Ernst & Young and Deloitte have already commissioned *Wikistrat* (Röper 2016).

Criticism and challenges in crowd-based consulting include confidentiality aspects, as it must be avoided that client-internal sensitive data diffuses to competitors. Moreover, results created through an external crowd may experience company-internal resistance in implementation ('not invented here' syndrome). In this situation, Christ et al. (2017) argue that an iterative approach is necessary in order to enhance the maturity of the crowdsourced solution and overcome the organization's resistance to change. They term this approach 'K-crowdsourcing' by analogy to biology. This form of crowdsourcing can create new processes, business models and strategies.

The implementation of this approach yielded a K-crowdsourcing-based innovation method named *BeeUp*, developed at the University of St. Gallen and the University of Applied Sciences in St. Gallen. It mixes activities of consultants with activities of crowds (teams) registered on the *BeeUp* crowdsourcing platform. Based on the analysis of the client's situation, a consultant develops an anonymised case study which describes the company's current problems. The case study is published on *BeeUp's* online platform (www.beeup.com) where it can be studied by the crowds. Crowds are motivated by the learning incentives offered by the platform and the participating educational institutions. The *BeeUp* teams start working independently on the published case in a form of crowd contest. What follows, is iteration between crowds and consultants, where the crowd teams propose a solution and receive feedback and more detailed and sensitive information on the case from the consultants. The better the team's proposal, the more time the consultants put into the team's training and development by means of repeated rounds of coaching and feedback. Once the solution is matured and has reached a high level of quality it is presented to the company (Christ et al. 2017). With this stepwise approach that aims for mature solutions to business development problems, the two problems of crowdsourcing mentioned before can be tackled, namely avoiding the rejection of immature solutions by the client organization, and the uncontrolled dissemination of sensitive information in the crowd.

Crowd labor markets aim at matching the requirements of the requested tasks with the skills of people in the crowd. They can be implemented particularly meaningful in the implementation phase of a project when it is clear what the solution should look like and which skills are necessary to get the work done. A provider operating on the crowd-labour market model is *upwork* (2017), a large freelancer marketplace, where companies can post their tasks. Clients can browse freelancer profile pages to compare skills and previous customer ratings. Freelancers in turn can bid on the jobs posted on the platform. Just like COMATCH, *upwork* offers administrative support, such as payment services and timesheet collection. Payment can be by the hour or a fixed price for the entire task. Chat and filesharing functions on the *upwork* platform support the cooperative work process in the project.

Some digital marketplaces offer focused remote assistance by qualified experts from potentially all around the world. The support can be very short, a telephone call or skype session with a subject matter expert, which will be charged by the minute, something referred to as 'nano consulting' here. An example and pioneer of this kind of service is *Clarity* (2017). By means of requested focus areas, the platform can indicate to the client which experts are suitable, and it also reveals their competence profiles with additional ratings and reviews by previous clients. Moreover, the cost rates of the different experts are transparent, which can differ substantially based on knowledge and region. At a price of up to US$50 per minute (with very good client ratings), it can be expected that the consulting is top quality.

2.3.5 Project Closure and After Sales

Business consulting is a knowledge-intensive service. The professional management of the strategic resource knowledge should therefore have a central role in consulting firms (Nissen 2012). On the one hand, it is a permanent task within consulting companies, as should be reflected by the role of a knowledge manager in the organization with associated duties and responsibilities. On the other hand, transferring the lessons learned of a project in a digital format that can be re-used in later situations anywhere in the organization is one of the last and most important tasks of project management. Numerous IT-systems are available to assist in knowledge management, such as document management systems, file sharing systems, yellow pages in the intranet, or mindmaps.

Interesting software is offered under the brand name '*TheBrain*' (Brain 2017). Basically, it offers an advancement of classical mind map visualization, with a stronger focus on connecting information that may not be hierarchically structured. In principal any number of 'thoughts' (knowledge items, ideas, tasks) can be visualized, digitally arranged, connected to each other, and linked with external information (such as text documents, spread sheets, web pages, and business process models). The user literally creates a digital memory and navigates this network of knowledge, where connections help to locate and discover information that would later otherwise be overlooked. With dynamic animated views, search functions, and a database in the background, *TheBrain* offers useful digital features to support the knowledge management tasks within the context of project management.

After sales activities include releasing success stories of important projects, and publishing professional articles and interviews to demonstrate ones competencies. Today, this should frequently be done in an online format. Large scale digital expert platforms are available to spread such information, improve the consultancies image, and attract potential clients as well as young professionals. A typical example is *Consultancy.uk*, an online platform for the advisory and consulting industry. This website claims to attract more than one million visitors per year, ranging from professionals active in consultancy roles (external/internal), students, job seekers and potential clients of consultancies. *Consultancy.uk* presents news and trends in the sector, follows the developments and publications of consulting firms across 60+ industries and functional areas and provides an overview of career opportunities for professionals interested in working in consultancy (Consultancy. uk 2017). By collaborating with more than 100 consulting firms active in the UK plus selected partner companies, by distributing a weekly industry newsletter, posting banner advertisements, and through the use of social media channels such as LinkedIn and Facebook, the online platform offers extensive possibilities for digital marketing and after sales activities of consulting providers.

3 Exemplary Related Research[2]

3.1 Research on the Digitalization of Consulting

There are many terms used in the literature synonymously for the virtualization of consulting services, such as e-consulting, electronic consulting, internet consulting, online consulting or distance consulting (Allegra et al. 2000; Wurdack 2001; Türk 2004; Deelmann 2009). The amount of publications on this topic is up to now fairly manageable, but a notable increase in the last few years can be witnessed, fueled by the widely known contribution of Christensen et al. (2013) who argue the consulting industry is facing essentially the same forces of disruption that have already reshaped other industries. Only a part of these contributions is design-oriented, aiming to support consulting providers with the creation of artefacts. Examples include the publications of research groups around Scheer and Werth (Greff and Werth 2015; Johann et al. 2016; Werth et al. 2016a, b) as well as Nissen and Seifert (2015, 2017b, c; Nissen et al. 2017a, b). In short, it can be observed that so far there is still a shortage of scientific concepts and pilot solutions, which companies can use to support the design and implementation of virtualized consulting solutions. Several contributions in this volume address this issue.

In the context of an early empirical study, Türk (2004) e.g. investigates which forms of virtualized consulting services are used by the client, respectively offered by the consulting companies. During her investigation she found that there is a fundamental interest in virtual consulting services as seen from the perspective of the client. Furthermore she emphasizes that the complementary use of virtualized consulting services has priority and, moreover, that there is a tendency, which aims towards the substitution of human consulting services.

---

[2]For a more complete review see the contribution of Seifert and Nissen (2017) in this volume.

Deelmann (2009) analyzes whether full automation of consulting services is possible and whether the use of technology will fundamentally change the nature of consulting. With this contribution he gives important stimuli for the discussion about the virtualization of consulting services. He comes to the conclusion that under certain conditions consulting services can be fundamentally automated. This automation is, however, significantly determined by the respective consulting approach (advisory consulting, expert consulting, organizational development, systemic consulting). Advisory (or fact-based) consulting offers most potential for a straightforward full automation, which presents a form of content-oriented consulting, where a consultant, based on specific knowledge, suggests a solution to a client problem in the form of a report (Bamberger and Wrona 2012). Deelmann points out that the client's approval of fully automated consulting services needs to be further investigated, as it is critical for the success for such consulting services. Nissen et al. (2015) provide answers to precisely this question, elaborating on the benefits and risks of virtual consulting, as well as the change in quality criteria when the level of virtualization rises in consulting services.

Nissen and Seifert (2016) survey the status quo of digital transformation in the German consulting market (see also their contribution on the status quo in this volume). They conclude that the significance of virtualization as an innovation driver, that paves the way for new business models and consulting services, will increase in the consulting industry. However, in most companies the current state of practice is not very advanced when it comes to digital initiatives w.r.t. own consulting processes. Fully virtualized and automatic consulting services have a subordinated significance to the consulting business according to the participants of this survey. The integration of clients into the design and development process of virtual consulting services will be crucial for success, while at the same time the current lack of demand and low acceptance for virtualized consulting services are seen as the main barriers to such digital initiatives.

The scientific discussion on virtual consulting and digital transformation in the consulting industry has a certain proximity to the topic of service modularization (Carlborg and Kindström 2014; Dörbecker and Böhmann 2013; Rahikka et al. 2011). Service modularity in general appears to be a promising concept to cope with the dilemma of increasing diversification of customer demands on the one hand and the need for standardization and efficiency for service providers on the other (Lubarski and Pöppelbuß 2016). Through standardization and modularization, the virtualization of individual tasks and sub-processes in consulting can be prepared. Distinct modules can, where necessary, be combined newly in order to meet the demands and thus form the basis of innovative consulting services. Research on service modularization emphasizes that it is essential for the provider to understand the client's wishes and to already include them during the service development (Rahikka et al. 2011).

3.2 Process Virtualization Theory

The transition of a physical process to a virtual process is referred to as 'process virtualization'. Overby developed the generic 'Process Virtualization Theory (PVT)' and introduced the term 'process virtualizability' (Overby 2008, 2012). He views the usage/acceptance and quality of the process results as the basis to measure the virtualizability of a process (as dependent variable) ex post. Furthermore, he names a succession of variables, which have an influence on the possible virtualization of a process.

According to PVT, especially the following features have a negative influence on the virtualizability of a process: high sensory requirements (as physical interaction is no longer in focus), high requirements concerning the personal level of the relationship of the participants and thereon following constructs, such as trust, high requirements concerning the synchronicity of activities during the process and high identification and control requirements in the process (as the actual interacting can be readily concealed during virtualization).

In contrast, the following features of the IT-based virtualization mechanism temper the mentioned process characteristics and thus have an influence on the virtualizability of a process: The capability of IT to present process relevant information (representation), the capability of IT to allow a time- and location-independent process participation (reach), as well as the possibility to generate an authentication of the process participants and to monitor the process (monitoring capability).

Balci and Rosenkranz (2014) note that so far it has hardly been empirically investigated how measurable the virtualizability of processes actually is. In their own research, they found empirical confirmation for the PVT, though at the same time there were indications of its incompleteness. In particular factors concerning characteristics of the process participants (e.g. IT-knowledge) also play a role.

The contribution of Nissen and Seifert (2017c) on evaluating the virtualization potential of consulting services in this volume further elaborates on PVT and suggests a three-step procedure to assess the virtualizability of processes in consulting.

3.3 Consulting Research

Scientific contributions on virtual consulting can be subsumed under the larger field of Consulting Research (Nissen 2007), which encompasses the scientific investigation of consulting services, consulting firms and the consulting market with its various participants on the supplier and the buyer side. Consulting Research has two concerns: Firstly, the scientific penetration of the topic of consulting, with the focus on the scientific knowledge being abstracted from individual consulting projects. Secondly, the transfer of scientific theories, knowledge and methods to consulting practice with the overall goal of solving consulting tasks better.

In this context, the author uses the following formal definition: Consulting can be defined as a professional service, which is carried out by one or more person(s), generally professionally qualified, and hierarchically independent from the advised client. This service is time-limited and usually paid for. The objective is to define, structure and analyze economic problems of the commissioned company interactively with the client, to develop or enable solutions for the problems and, if wanted, to plan their implementation and realize them, together with representatives of the client, in the company (Nissen 2007).

On an abstract level, four types (modes) of corporate consultancy can be differentiated: advisory consulting, expert consulting, organizational development/coaching and systemic consulting (Walger 1995; Nissen 2007; Deelmann 2012). They differ mainly in the way the client organization is viewed and, consequently, the role of the consultant in the transformation process.

Very briefly, in advisory consulting, the consultant, based on specific knowledge, suggests a solution to a client problem in the form of a report (Bamberger and Wrona 2012). He is usually not involved during the (optional) implementation of these proposals. Expert consulting is the dominant type of consulting today. It assumes a doctor-patient relationship between consultant and client. Here the expert solves complex problems due to superior knowledge, and together with the client's executives, he actively realizes a change in the client company. In organizational development client employees essentially solve the business problems by themselves, but consultants help them through external reflection and active guidance. The consultant is seen as a coordinator in this development, and an initiator of the clients' learning processes. In the view of systemic consulting, which is based on systems theory, organizations are regarded as social autopoietic systems. Such systems are recursively closed and self-regulative. They cannot be specifically changed from the outside. Consultants in this approach take on the role of an observer who tries to find out the client organizations' characteristic behavior and communication patterns that reproduce the problem. He then attempts to 'irritate' constitutive perceptual and explanatory models of the client's system, also pointing to complex interrelationships in the effect of potential actions. As a result processes are disturbed that generate the problem. Of central importance in systemic consulting is also the self-reflection of clients on their modes of observation, communicative and behavioral patterns.

4 Managing the Digital Transformation in Consulting

In the face of digital transformation, companies must develop digital business models and services, create an agile organization, develop new skills, change existing mind-sets, digitalize processes and redesign them with a strong customer-focus. The risk is high as reported failure rates of large-scale change programs hover around 70%. Consequently, a digital transformation takes up a large share of a leadership's and an organization's time and attention. It requires bold decisions from the CEO and enormous energy to realize the necessary degree of change (Bucy et al. 2016). Even with a successful start, there is always the danger that the legacy organization will exert a gravitational pull that drives a reversion to established practices. Without a transformation of core aspects of the company, such as value proposition, people, processes, and technologies, digital initiatives are likely to fail in the long run (Dahlström et al. 2017). In the following, some focus points for transformational success will be highlighted.

4.1 Create a Digital Transformation Strategy

Digitalization is not a value in itself but must create added value within the respective processes and in particular for the consulting clients. The first thing, therefore, is to identify the goals of a digital transformation initiative. These should be measurable and corresponding metrics are required to measure success later. At this stage, a lot of vision and creativity is necessary, as new business models that leverage technologies such as big data, analytics, cloud, machine learning, and AI will often strongly deviate from existing forms of making business. Talking to digital start-ups and analyzing their way of business can deliver first insights. According to Islam et al. (2017) the cooperation of incumbents with start-ups is frequently a good idea, since strength and weaknesses on both sides tend to be complementary. Moreover, it is certainly useful to also talk to key clients, understand their experience with our company, as well as their evolving requirements and how digitalization and new technologies could better account for them.

Dahlström et al. (2017), based on their practical experience, recommend thinking through the possibilities of using connectivity and data to transform the customer experience or to reshape services by allowing customers to interact with them in new ways. The basic line of thought should be to identify where value is migrating in the future and set the ambition of the business accordingly.

In order not to set the targets too low, but instead to identify a company's full potential, Bucy et al. (2016) recommend that top management assumes the mind-set, independence, and tool kit of an activist investor or private-equity acquirer. To do so, they must step outside the self-imposed constraints and define what is truly achievable. 'Think great' would be the message, aiming rather for a bold creative leap than incremental development.

There are certainly different approaches to achieve a successful transformation, just as the digitalization of business models can take on different intensities. However, an important element to successfully integrate the entire coordination, prioritization, and implementation of digital transformations within a firm is the formulation of a digital transformation strategy. A digital transformation strategy is a blueprint that supports companies in governing the transformations that arise owing to the integration of digital technologies. It should also support operations after a digital transformation. Digital transformation strategies go beyond the process paradigm, and include changes to and implications for products, services, and business models as a whole. Moreover, it is critical to align the digital transformation strategy with the IT strategy and other organizational and functional strategies (Matt et al. 2015).

Independent of the industry or firm, digital transformation strategies have certain elements in common, according to Matt et al. (2015). These elements can be structured in four dimensions: *use of technologies, changes in value creation, structural changes, and financial aspects.*

The use of technologies addresses a company's attitudes towards new technologies as well as its ability to exploit these technologies. Is the firm aiming for market leadership in technology use, or will it resort to already established standards as a means to enable business operations?

Concerning changes in value creation the top management must decide how far future digital activities deviate from traditional business and, thus, how strongly the firm's value chain will be impacted by the digital transformation initiative. Matt et al. (2015) point out that while further deviations offer opportunities to expand and enrich the current services portfolio, they are often accompanied by a stronger need for new competencies and higher risks owing to less experience in the new field.

Digitalization initiatives must set up supporting structures and management practices to govern these complex transformations. Structural changes especially concern the placement of the new digital activities within the corporate structures. If the extent of expected changes is large, it might be reasonable to create a separate subsidiary.

The financial aspects of a digital transformation strategy refer, on the one hand, to a firm's urgency to act because of deteriorating core business, and on the other hand, its ability to finance a digital transformation initiative. Low financial pressure on the core business may reduce the perceived urgency to act. High financial pressure can result in problems to externally finance a large-scale transformation project. An early and unprejudiced assessment of the need and options to conduct a digital transformation are therefore recommended.

It clearly is essential to closely align the four dimensions. Finally, since digital technologies are subject to constant change and the underlying assumptions of digital transformations are associated with high uncertainty, a digital transformation strategy must be regularly reviewed, and its assumptions as well as the progress made should be critically assessed (Matt et al. 2015).

4.2 Create Digital Business Models

Potential benefits of digitization are manifold and, among others, include increases in sales or productivity, innovations in value creation, as well as novel forms of interactions with customers. As a result, entire business models can be reshaped or replaced (Downes and Nunes 2013). Rethinking ones business models and creating new digital business models is, therefore, a crucial step in succeeding with a digital transformation. With a business model, a model is meant that describes essential functions of an enterprise and the means by which it generates profits and value, taking into account the company's individual situation, as well as current environmental factors and trends (Osterwalder and Pigneur 2011). The success of a business model requires an appropriate accompanying transformation of the business organization.

Of particular interest in consulting is the ability of digital business models to scale well. By contrast, traditional consulting scales badly, as value for clients is delivered through personal expertise. It is a 'people business', meaning staff is the dominant resource required to execute projects. Hence, if a traditional consultancy wants to double the number of projects in a given time then approximately twice the people is needed. By contrast, the technology-fueled business models of newcomers scale far better. Thus, the question arises what traditional consultancies can do to improve the scalability of their own business. The contribution by Werth and Greff (2017) in this volume addresses this issue, and basically comes up with four options:

- separate and digitalize information-based parts of the consulting process,
- engage in sharing economy, use external resources instead of internal via an IT-platform,
- enable clients and partners, integrating them into the service processes in various ways,
- apply fully automated services and algorithmic processing.

Business models describe companies as activity systems of three related submodels: the performance model, the value-added and the yield model. The competitiveness of these systems results from unique, one on top of the other tuned configurations of these partial models (Clauß 2016).

A consulting company's performance model includes the respective portfolio of consulting services, and the markets and customers addressed. As an example, how digitalization may introduce changes in this model, digital sales channels could be implemented in the course of an online shop where clients can buy individually customized services in straightforward digital applications according to their own preferences.

The value-added model encompasses the resources, processes, and partnerships that enterprises use to deliver services. Many companies that succeeded in digital transformation have chosen to establish a kind of 'digital ecosystem' around them (Klimmer and Selonke 2016). Often, digital processes can be organized decentralized and outsourced to cost-effective specialists around the world. Digitization also enables new forms of communicating and collaborating with partners and clients, using digital platforms.

The yield model includes the income channels and profit formulae that companies use. In the digital world, there are approaches to achieving revenue through cross-subsidies, even if the actual service is sold below cost or with a low margin.

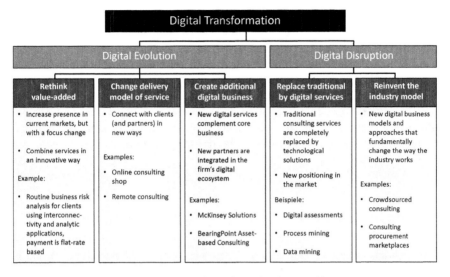

Fig. 6 Five types of digital business model transformation in consulting

In an attempt to structure digital business model transformations in consulting, building on some fundamentals of Westerman et al. (2014), Bonnet et al. (2015) and Stummeyer (2017), the differentiation shown in Fig. 6 is suggested.

The change induced in business models through digital transformation and innovative new technologies can vary between more evolutionary and more disruptive. Nevertheless, as pointed out by Clauß (2016), one should keep in mind the following success factors in shaping digital business models:

- The logic of current business models should be questioned in the course of a digitization initiative. This clearly is a strategic task of the top management.
- Business models should be considered as a whole. The mentioned examples of innovations in the dimensions of the business model are not to be viewed separately from each other. If a change is implemented by means of digitization in one area, the configuration of the entire business model should be questioned. Only when the performance model, the value-added model and the yield model are coordinated can the full potential be exploited.
- Digital transformation is not a one-time process but a continuous process. Companies must therefore continue to be agile and changeable in the future.

There is currently an open debate, whether it is better to approach digital transformation in full scope or to begin with smaller, more manageable initial steps and then broaden the initiative. Clauß (2016) advocates to 'think big but start small'. Business models are often complex. While an attempt should be made to strategically realign the company digitally, in order to make risks and financial constraints manageable, he recommends an iterative process of change for many companies. On the other hand, Klimmer and Selonke (2016) report on an empirical basis that of their interview partners many have chosen a 'turbo entry' into the topic. They have launched large-scale projects that build as much as possible on the knowledge and ideas of the workforce.

Anyway, for incumbent consulting firms in practice it is sensible to use multiple business models in parallel. Virtualization promises innovative possibilities for optimizing a company's performance and for differentiation from the competition. However, virtual consulting services will not replace conventional on-site consulting in general. Instead, they should be seen and analyzed as mostly complementing the current portfolio of services, replacing traditional services here and there.

4.3 Manage Operational Aspects of Digital Transformation

A digital transformation is foremost a change in corporate culture and organization. Ultimately people (internal and external) and processes matter most, not technology. This does not mean that IT is not important, quite the contrary, but it is more of an enabler in this scenario that requires adequate deployment and decisions w.r.t. the 'back end' of a companies' enterprise architecture. In the following, some key aspects are discussed that support a sustained success in digital transformation.

4.3.1 Successful Leadership and a 'Digital' Corporate Culture

A recent survey (Maor et al. 2017) suggests that for their transformations to succeed, organizations need employee buy-in at all levels, consistent communication, and better people strategies. In successful companies, CEOs and senior leaders are in general more visibly engaged and committed to the transformation. Moreover, two-thirds of respondents said they provide regular access to information on the transformation's progress, compared with 28% of those with failed transformations.

A major problem is that in average companies, the combination of skills, mind-sets, and ongoing commitment required to succeed in large-scale transformation is rarely available. According to Bucy et al. (2016) many companies perform under their full potential through a combination of poor leadership, a deficient culture and capabilities, and misaligned incentives that favour local units over the success of the business as a whole. The top management is used to running business in a fairly stable environment rather than in rapidly changing ones. Thus, executives may struggle to come to terms with the demands of a digital transformation, and can be reluctant to lead rather than delegate when they are faced with disruptive competition. But even if leaders and employees take a great initial effort and corporate results improve, it frequently happens that those involved declare victory prematurely. Then, slowly the company slips back into its old ways. As a result, transformations degrade rather than visibly fail (Bucy et al. 2016).

To avoid these traps, overcome organizational inertia, and achieve a sustainable digital transformation process, companies need to achieve alignment and lasting commitment via successful top management leadership. Bucy et al. (2016) point out that a CEO is required who recognizes that only a new approach will dramatically improve the company's performance. Top management support is essential along the whole transformation process since there may be resistance in different areas of the company. To deal with such resistance, transformation leadership skills are essential and require the active involvement of the different stakeholders affected by the transformations (Matt et al. 2015).

For driving the day-to-day effort in the transformation a group of senior leaders is needed. Thus a key decision for the CEO is selecting the right members of this team and empowering them to help drive the digital transformation. One criterion for inclusion has to be skill in and knowledge of digital business models and technologies. For this reason, the position of a chief digital officer (CDO) or Chief Transformation Officer (CTO) was created in the course of many digital transformation projects. But as a digital transformation affects almost every aspect of the business and requires a high level of coordination across the entire organization, any leadership group has to include executives from multiple functions. In the team, there should be a well-balanced mix of skills, including digital vision, change management experience, and a deep understanding of the company's business models and processes. Moreover, team members should represent the key values of a digital culture, i.e. customer-orientation, tolerance for risks, and a collaborative mind-set (Dahlström et al. 2017).

To achieve alignment and commitment amongst the employees, it is necessary to create incentives, remove barriers, and provide a clear, consistent and audience-tailored line of regular communication about the vision, goals and progress of the transformation initiative. Dahlström et al. (2017) recommend that the CEO should focus first on winning over influencers both inside and outside the company, then on propagating the change to their networks. For employees there should be no more than three objectives in a transformation, with an outsized payout for outsized performance. According to Klimmer and Selonke (2016) the turbulences of large-scale transformation projects that build on the ideas and knowledge of the workforce generate a bearing wave of companywide alignment. Additionally, diversity in the core teams appears to be important—in terms of study, gender and hierarchy, as well as age groups.

Corporate culture is an important factor in the transformation process. Maybe one of the most complex issues in the course of a digital transformation is adapting the corporate culture to represent the required key values of digitalization. Here, technology-driven start-ups frequently have an advantage, apart from superior skills and knowledge in core technologies. Innovative newcomers in consulting are often characterized by a collaborative and open mind-set, technology affinity, a common set of values with digital as value creation, a commitment to permanent innovation and change, flat hierarchies, a tolerance for failure and risks, and a fresh customer-centred look at consulting that is prepared to do things completely different from traditional firms. Crowdsourcing-based providers are just one example.

While changing a corporate culture may be difficult for incumbents, it is not impossible. Klimmer and Selonke (2016) report that their entire top management interview partners found ways to establish formats for the breakthrough of current hierarchies in digital transformation projects. These were often focus group formats, targeted individual discussions with stakeholders in the organization, special projects on individual questions and joint workshops with suppliers. This was frequently associated with a reduction of hierarchical elements. Certainly, the culture change should also be reflected in the incentive system of the company.

To sustain and further improve the achieved level of performance, even when the transformation project as such is over, Bucy et al. (2016) advise that top management must anchor a repeatable process to deliver better and better results in the organization. This can be achieved by taking over patterns of the transformation management (e.g. meetings' cadence, financial reviews, focus on execution) in the basic business routines.

4.3.2 Critical Roles and Responsibilities in Transformation

The wide scope, complexity and high risk of large-scale transformations require ensuring adequate and clear responsibilities for the definition and implementation of a digital transformation strategy. As a result of an extensive online survey in June 2016 with 1487 participants representing the full range of regions, industries, company sizes, functional specialties, and tenures, Maor et al. (2017) suggest the following critical roles in the course of a digital transformation:

- The *CEO* should be the face of the change in large-scale transformations. He should act as a visionary leader who shows the organization the way by communicating a compelling change story and being a visible advocate for the changes taking place. Moreover, he puts the critical teams in place to lead the day-to-day effort in major work streams of the transformation.
- *Senior leaders* should act as mobilizers of both the message and the people in their organizations. Senior leaders must support companywide coordination by sharing aligned messages and providing transparent communication across the organization—on both the changes that will take place and the desired outcomes. They lead work stream teams and ensure that team members are committed to the changes.
- According to Maor et al. (2017), few survey respondents recognize *heads of human resources* as a critical player in their transformations' outcomes. However, in companies with the most successful transformations, HR leaders are best at connecting the high-level transformation objectives with employees' day-to-day work and communicating about this link to employees.
- *Leaders of program-management offices (PMOs) or transformation offices* act as problem solvers, identify barriers to change in the organization, serve as thought partners to senior managers, and help to disseminate transformation-related knowledge and best practices across the organization.

- *The leaders of individual transformation initiatives* have clear ownership of their initiatives in the most successful transformations. They work well with their peers leading other initiatives, and understand the significance of their contribution within the broader transformation effort.
- *Line managers* have an important role as motivator for front line employees, whose involvement and buy-in is very important to a transformation's success. They must make the transformation efforts tangible and digestible to the frontline employees and motivate their teams to adopt the changes in their daily work routines.
- *Change agents* work as facilitators or agents of the transformation, and support other employees in developing new capabilities and mind-sets essential for success. They are most valuable to a transformation as role models for others throughout the organization, demonstrating the shifts in mindsets and behaviors that the transformation requires.

Bucy et al. (2016), following their experience in transformation projects, further elaborate on the 'transformation office' (TO) as an important institution in digital transformation. The TO oversees the transformation, constantly pushes for decisions, and thus drives the change at a faster speed than daily routine business. According to them, this faster clock speed is one of the most defining characteristics of successful transformations. Collaborating with senior leaders across the entire business, the TO must have the grit, discipline, energy, and focus to drive forward five to eight major work streams. All of them are further divided into perhaps hundreds of separate initiatives, each with a specific owner and a detailed, fully costed bottom-up plan.

Moreover, the position of a Chief Transformation Officer should be created, an authority to push the organization to its full potential: "The chief transformation officer's job is to question, push, praise, prod, cajole, and otherwise irritate an organization that needs to think and act differently. (…)The CTO must be dynamic, respected, unafraid of confrontation, and willing to challenge corporate orthodoxies" (Bucy et al. 2016, p. 6).

4.3.3 Achieve Process Acceptance

Business processes are designed as a blueprint for delivering products and services. The virtualization of consulting tasks and processes constitutes a change that can potentially lead to rejection by process stakeholders. In business practice, it can frequently be observed that while some business processes are well accepted and executed in a compliant manner, other processes are refused, and employees create unofficial processes and shadow organizations, which carry with them substantial risks from a company perspective.

In designing and optimizing processes in companies and other organizations often the topics effectiveness and efficiency are in focus. Insufficient attention is given to the people who ultimately take part in these processes. Process acceptance

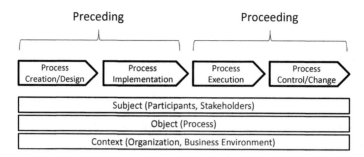

Fig. 7 Overall structure of process acceptance (Müllerleile et al. 2015; Nissen et al. 2016)

research addresses this issue by taking into account social aspects of process execution and investigates what the acceptance of business processes generally depends upon. As a result the foundations of a process acceptance theory have been developed on an empirical basis (Müllerleile and Nissen 2014; Müllerleile et al. 2015, 2016; Nissen et al. 2016; Nissen and Müllerleile 2017) yielding a structure of the process acceptance phenomenon. This structure enables sorting the success factors into an overall logical framework (Fig. 7).

Reasons for missing process acceptance could be classified into four different categories. These categories can be further merged in two groups preceding and proceeding the process usage. The first two categories include process creation/design and process implementation. The next two categories include process execution and process control and, if necessary, process change. The factors in each category are arranged according to their respective acceptance dimension into subject (process stakeholder), object (the process) and context (organization, business environment). These are relevant in projects that aim for a virtualization of existing consulting processes and tasks.

The results reveal that process acceptance is driven by different forces and that their influence varies along the process lifecycle. Table 2 summarizes the results. In the beginning of the process lifecycle, process acceptance is mainly driven by the subjects and the process itself (object). Interestingly, context variables become more important during the process execution and maintenance phase. In general, the process implementation and the execution phase incorporate the most factors.

Some findings, like the inclusion of process stakeholders in almost all process lifecycle phases, seem self-evident. These factors may appear obvious, but, as our empirical data shows, are infrequently applied. This is especially the case for all communication pertaining to the process. Stakeholders are keen to be informed, but this communication should take place via the official channels. Unfortunately, managers often avoid direct communication with their employees, especially if unpleasant information is to be disseminated.

During the implementation and execution phase process properties play an important role, and bad process design is revealed. Questionable process design

Table 2 Key factors for process acceptance (Müllerleile et al. 2015; Nissen et al. 2016)

Phase	Subject (Participants)	Object (Process)	Context (Environment)
Creation/ Design	Stakeholder Inclusion, Communication on Involvement		
Implementation	Explain Reasons, Pre-Implementation Training, Peer Group Involvement, Process Guidance	Transparency, Structure	Implementation Strategy, Implementation Context, Information Strategy
Execution	Interdependence, Hierarchy, No. of Organizational Units Involved, Responsibility, Communication	Process Feedback, Failure Tolerance, Task Heterogeneity, Perceived Process Length, Standardization	Cross Process Consistency, Organizational Overhead, Time and Resource Constraints, Bureaucracy
Control/ Change	Stakeholder Inclusion	Process Stability/ Process Age	Management Ignorance/Override, Process Maintenance

decisions can be prevented by incorporating stakeholders in the whole process lifecycle. This may also help to tap into potential for future process improvements.

The empirical data also demonstrated that stakeholders value processes as a normative structure for their daily work routine. To a certain extent, process acceptance requires that these processes can function as a normative structure. If this is threatened by a chaotic and inconsistent context, process acceptance will suffer. Establishing a process friendly organizational structure is therefore important.

Process acceptance can be improved by influencing three basic factors (Ritter et al. 2016). These factors are the behaviour and attitude of the subjects involved, the process properties, and the context properties. The first option offers potential for short term benefits, e.g. using incentives. The second option, changing process properties, requires redesigning processes, and thus offers potential for medium term benefits. Improving process acceptance could, for instance, be achieved by incorporating process feedback, reducing the number of participants and interdependencies, or making a process fail-safe. The third option, changing the organizational culture, is a strategic effort, and may only yield benefits in the long run.

4.3.4 Listen to Clients, Cooperate with Start-Ups, and Create a Digital Ecosystem

In their empirical study on digital leadership Klimmer and Selonke (2016) identified informal 'reverse coaching' as a useful recipe for CEOs in the course of successful digital transformation. They let digital natives within their companies conduct pilot projects in digitalization, accepting the risks associated with it. The CEOs learn in and through the project, in the discussion with the team members.

Another very typical example is the detailed analysis of start-up business models. Unfortunately, incumbent firms are burdened with high fixed costs, rigid structures, and regressive cultures that tend to hinder business model innovation (Richter and Niewiem 2004). But incumbent firms and start-ups complement each other and have the potential to collaborate with each other in an appropriate form. The technological and organizational enabling factors in incumbent firms are similar to the inhibiting factors in start-ups, and the corresponding inhibiting factors in incumbent firms are similar to the enabling factors in start-ups, according to an analysis by Islam et al. (2017).

In consideration of how inhibitors can develop into enablers, incumbent firms as well as start-ups can approach each other to overcome their respective inhibiting factors. Traditional consulting providers can form new partnerships with digital newcomers. Newcomers have agile business models and are trained in deploying latest technology. As a consequence, previously unsolvable problems may become more transparent and accessible for the established consulting firm. Incumbent firms can use start-ups to create an entrepreneurial organization and stimulate the expansion of competence across all departments (Islam et al. 2017). Moreover, new business areas can be pursued by collaborating with start-ups. On the other hand, start-ups gain access to a broad customer base by joining forces with incumbent firms, whose consultants bring along a trustful partnership with many clients.

According to a recent survey by Klimmer and Selonke (2016), successful top managers often establish a kind of 'digital ecosystem' around them in the course of digital transformation. The basic idea is to leverage the benefits of digitalization through an ecosystem of specialized partners, which focus on specific tasks. Using current technologies, they perform more efficient and effective, while cooperation and exchange can be conveniently arranged on digital platforms. Where to position the firm within such a digital ecosystem is a crucial decision.

CEOs need to figure out which capabilities, skills, and technologies available in the ecosystem complement and support their company's strategic ambitions. Moreover, they should think of how to secure the company's most valuable assets. For consulting this clearly is the trustful relationship with clients, and the bonding of excellent consultants to the company. Consequently, how much to rely on relationships in the digital ecosystem and how to structure them are also crucial decisions (Dahlström et al. 2017).

New models of interaction with partners and consulting clients can be implemented in digital ecosystems, including for instance open innovation and co-design, consulting self-services and configurable products, crowdsourced consulting approaches, and digitalized consulting procurement. Different IT-platforms may be linked together to extend the portfolio of available functions and services.

Many interview partners of Klimmer and Selonke (2016) had an institutionalized approach of listening to customers on a regular basis. But the issue of digitalization is often the reason for additional large-scale visitor programs to ensure the requirements of customers are understood and enter the digital agenda.

The consultant-client relationship as well as the quality of services rendered are of crucial importance in consulting. Previous models of collaboration with clients are being revolutionized in parts by virtualization since new forms of communication and cooperation with less personal contact are established. Moreover, the currently low demand for these services is the greatest obstacle on the way to a deep penetration of virtualization in consulting practice (Nissen and Seifert 2016). Against this background, the knowledge of the quality requirements as well as the expectations and fears of clients is of central importance for the success of a digitalization project in consulting.

Ultimately, virtualized consulting products and services must also be marketed so that customer acceptance and trust will increase. The aim is to build up references and to communicate to customers that conceptual thought-out virtual consulting services can add value to classic consulting approaches in certain areas. The early integration of core clients and complementary technology providers into the development and implementation of virtual consulting services is thus a key to success.

4.3.5 Rethink Enterprise Architecture and the Use of IT

With a focus on technology-enabled solutions it is clear that IT and the technology stack of a company as a whole are crucial enablers of digital transformation in consulting. The traditional focus of IT is on implementing the requirements of the business units as effectively and efficiently as possible into high-quality IT services. Industry frameworks such as ITIL support this role. In digital transformation, IT is increasingly challenged to actively shape the company as a whole and proactively identify technological innovations. A company's ability to change increasingly depends on the ability to change its IT, something referred to as 'IT agility' here (Nissen 2008). High IT agility can contribute to increased business agility and thus create a competitive advantage. IT-agility is attributed a strong value proposition to corporate success, however, the required level of IT-agility is seldom achieved in companies (Nissen and von Rennenkampff 2013, 2017). Moreover, business-IT alignment is particularly important to enable IT a more proactive role in digital transformation.

With their current set-up, many IT departments cannot meet these new requirements because as rather reactive service providers they do not have the necessary structures, processes and abilities to systematically develop business innovations. Additionally, they are often perceived as bureaucratic, static, and not on a par with the business departments. Consequently IT functions have to change to meet the challenges of digital transformation. Concepts like bimodal (or two-speed) IT, co-location with business units, cross-functional digital teams, active IT innovation management and enterprise architecture management can be understood as precursors of the additional role of IT as an advisor and innovator for business. Moreover, developments like cloud computing simplify the outsourcing of elements of the IT value chain (Urbach et al. 2017).

Table 3 Digital transformation requires a different model for managing enterprise architecture, according to Bossert and Laartz (2017)

Elements of enterprise architecture	Traditional model	Perpetual evolution model (Digital transformation)
Business operations	Focus on product- or service centered processes	Focus on customer-centric journeys
Business capabilities	Reliance on one operating model	Use of multiple operating models (working at 2 speeds)
Business applications	Emphasis on interdependency	Emphasis on decoupling applications
IT integration platform	Use of heavyweight bus	Use of lightweight connections
Infrastructure services Information and communication technology	Software development managed centrally Managed as precious asset	Software developers and IT operations jointly build new products and features (DevOps) Managed as commodity

Bossert and Laartz (2017) observe that the enterprise architecture in traditional firms typically reflects a bygone era, when it was unnecessary for companies to shift their business strategies, release new products and services, and incorporate new business processes at great speed. Companies did not have an acute need to continually infuse new IT-enabled business capabilities into their operations. With disruptive digital competitors, traditional companies need to adopt a different approach to designing and managing their processes, operating models and technology stack. Bossert and Laartz (2017) suggest a model they call 'perpetual evolution' that supports the changing out or adding of elements of enterprise architecture quickly, incorporating latest technology. It is strongly built on modular design and decoupling of business capabilities as well as technologies supporting them (Table 3).

An enterprise architecture built for perpetual evolution differs from a traditional one in six ways (Bossert and Laartz 2017). When considering business operations, the emphasis is on end-to-end customer journeys rather than discrete product- or service-oriented processes. As a critical element of the approach, companies use two operating models rather than one. Processes and systems are grouped into two categories: digital business capabilities that are differentiating for the customer experience and those that support transactional capabilities with a focus on efficiency. Companies must be able to continually improve business capabilities without fear of disrupting entire systems.

When considering the application landscape, the focus is on applications and systems to be modular and work independently rather than being tightly coupled via a single heavyweight enterprise service bus. As the number of connections increases exponentially in a digital environment, the enterprise architecture features a central integration platform that boasts lightweight connections to avoid the connection layer become a bottleneck. In this way, the IT can upgrade core applications module by module and application migration can happen quicker and at lower risk.

While traditionally IT-infrastructures are often centrally managed with development and operations split in separated teams, under the perpetual evolution model the IT organization deploys an application-development model based on DevOps, so that development and IT operations work closely together to test and launch new software features quickly. This way, new digital business capabilities can be designed and brought to the market rapidly.

Finally, advances in connectivity, cloud computing, and other technologies have created a situation where prior investments are no longer necessarily a big competitive advantage or barrier to market entry. As a result, information and communications technology is viewed as a commodity rather than a strategic factor under this enterprise architecture model.

4.3.6 Refocus and Digitalize Back Office Functions

Digital transformation can affect both external and internal processes of a consulting firm. Consequently, consultancies should think about digitalization opportunities not only in terms of customer-faced processes but also processes that occur in back offices and without any client interaction. In many companies there are shared-service organizations that deliver technical and administrative support in areas common to all business units, such as human resources and finance. However, digital capabilities (with the obvious exception of the IT function) tend to be underdeveloped in shared-services organizations. Often they have been candidates for outsourcing to 'service factories' in remote locations as the management focus is predominantly on costs with these services.

According to Chandok et al. (2016) companies that digitalize their back office activities have an opportunity to realize significant savings in time and money—e.g. up to 50% increases in efficiency in some activities. Given their expertise in efficient delivery of services, coupled with the value of back-end data, these organizations have a key role to play in the digital environment. In the course of digital transformation, Chandok et al. (2016) suggest the focus of shared services organizations' performance objectives to shift. For instance, large-scale automation and total cost to serve should be in focus on the operational level, while analytics-based decision making and new service lines would be objectives for business outcome. Shared services should think of themselves as centers of expertise with more time spent devising and launching innovative and efficient service options. A redefining of the skills is required to serve an increasingly digital business. Process automation and networking are increasingly important, using technology platforms that can deliver higher-order benefits to the entire company. In this digital environment, shared services can partner with the business units to determine how best to realize digital strategies, improve front-end customer interactions, digitally transform end-to-end processes, and increase internal productivity.

4.3.7 Adapt Budgeting and Create Governance Structures

Even the best design of a digital transformation initiative cannot prevent unexpected events and new developments that have to be taken into account. In this situation, it is useful to establish a governance, rules and procedures in advance that provide a framework for the required decisions and allow for course corrections to keep the transformation on track. Associated controlling measures must be in place that allow the CEO to monitor the progress on key initiatives within the program. Dahlström et al. (2017) point out that yardsticks that focus on short term success, like ROI, can be misleading, as a digital transformation is a long-term effort. They advocate using nontraditional measures that evaluate digital adoption, such as new registrations on digital channels or digital-engagement levels.

The pace within a digital transformation is higher than in normal day-to-day business. This should be reflected in the way resources are allocated in the project. Funding should follow the mind-set of a venture capitalist. The impact and success probability of sub-projects within the transformation initiative must be constantly monitored and challenged. Considering the high uncertainty and risks associated with any large-scale transformation it can be expected that while some ideas and initiatives are successful, others are not. The CEO must decide when to stop funding sub-projects that lack behind expectations, and free resources to invest in other, more successful areas of the transformation.

In this context, Dahlström et al. (2017) recommend shifting budgeting from annual to quarterly or even monthly cycles. Succeeding with a digital transformation often requires cutting budgets for legacy operations. Moreover, to maximize the chances of success and raise the motivation of employees, CEOs should decide how to sequence the transformation for quick wins and cumulative effects, "so the business builds towards a cohesive digital whole rather than a jumble of loosely affiliated programs" (p. 7).

5 Possible Future Consulting Directions

Although virtual consulting will not replace traditional consulting with its reliance on personal interaction and talent completely, the proportion of the consulting market which could be taken over by a new breed of intelligent machines could be significant (Czerniawska 2017). Thus, there is a considerable pressure on traditional consulting firms to adjust their competitive positioning and define differentiating factors w.r.t. other providers in the market. Else they will suffer from increasing pressure on margins despite the so far general positive development of turnover in the consulting industry as a whole. In the end, there is a need to devise better ways to support their clients' business in an agile and value-adding way.

If one thinks about innovative digitalized consulting services, the analogy to another important field within the service sector can be helpful: logistics. The digitalization of logistics is far more advanced than in consulting. Virtual processes, working in networks and the intensive exchange of digital data between logistic service providers, customers and partners are reality today and, in fact, have been for quite a while.

Several concepts that are in use in logistics today can, in the authors view, be transferred 'in spirit' to virtual consulting services. Of course logistics mainly deals with physical goods, while consulting is highly immaterial. However, on a higher level of abstraction, concepts of close digital integration between service provider and customer make sense in both fields. Virtualization will enable new forms of client integration, with a common data base providing the basis for innovative consulting services. Similarly, the idea of outsourcing certain tasks that require highly specialized knowledge can be taken from logistics to consulting. These ideas will be elaborated a bit more in the following sub-sections.

5.1 Consultants Watching Over Clients

Many innovative models of partnership have been devised in logistics, on a strategic as well as operative level. One particular popular concept is Vendor Managed Inventory (VMI). For those not so familiar with logistics, the basic idea of VMI in now briefly outlined. Let us assume the interaction of a manufacturer (supplier) and a retailer (his customer). Traditionally, the management of inventory levels at the retailer (with associated risks, such as out-of-stock situations or high inventory costs) would be solely the retailer's issue. So, when he runs low in stock, the merchant would order goods supply from the manufacturer, who then in turn delivers these goods and issues a corresponding invoice. However, logistics is not a core competency of many retailers. So, in an act of logistics outsourcing, the retailer might come to a VMI-agreement with his manufacturer.

In VMI, it is the manufacturer who controls the goods supply for VMI-articles of the retailer. The manufacturer thus generates the orders of the merchant concerning these goods. He manages the stock of the retailer regarding own products to stay within a contractually agreed volume corridor. For this to be possible, the retailer periodically provides the manufacturer with internal logistics data, especially the current inventory level, the amount of sales and the quantity of stock outs per VMI-article.

This has a number of advantages on both sides, e.g. lower stock levels in the supply chain, higher service levels in retail, reduced process costs through auto-mated communication, simpler planning and the ability to focus more strongly on strategical issues for the retailer, a strengthening of the strategic position and optimized capacity utilization for the manufacturer, and generally an increased customer-supplier linkage. Disadvantages include substantial initial setup costs and the required disclosure of sensitive data by the retailer which makes him potentially more vulnerable within the competitive field, if this data is misused.

Let us now transfer the basic idea of VMI to consulting. In this scenario, the client represents the customer (retailer) while the consulting firm is the supplier (manufacturer).

With the advent of new media and analytical technologies, such as big data, intelligent analytics, process mining etc., there will be an increasing number of clients (in particular of small and medium size) who are not in a position to apply these technologies adequately, due to a lack of resources and skills. Moreover, the advancing digitalization at the client, further fueled by the Internet-of-things, will create abundant data that could potentially be analyzed and used to improve products, processes and business models of the client on an ongoing basis (rather than only in the course of a limited consulting project).

In this situation, a client may outsource analytic tasks and the monitoring of internal or market data to a consulting provider, who specializes in analytics. The consultancy gains remote access to critical data streams of the client. With its specialists it then applies modern analytical instruments on a regular basis to identify early 'weak signals' of future critical issues (market shifts, process deficiencies, IT problems etc.) at the client or develop ideas for business improvements (in a form of open innovation). Thereby, the consultants watch over the client. They alert the client early on issues that suggest management action to prevent substantial problems or take advantage of a market situation. As this service is provided on an ongoing basis, new payment models are reasonable, such as a monthly flat fee. Part of the analytical capabilities might even be provided automatically in the form of software tools that collect and analyze data from within the client company. As a result of such an automatic or external monitoring, also new traditional consulting business may be created when the analysis generates input for business optimization projects at the client.

Seen from a more abstract perspective, digitalization and networking enable new forms of client integration, with a common data base providing the grounds for innovative virtual consulting services. As in logistics, the necessary disclosure of sensitive client data is a critical issue that must be accounted for.

5.2 Digital Consulting Platforms

Internet-based platforms, such as social networks and trading platforms are becoming increasingly important. Uber, Airbnb, and Facebook are prominent examples. Uber, the largest company in passenger transportation worldwide, owns no taxis. Airbnb, the world's largest provider of sleepover opportunities, owns no real estates. Facebook is the biggest international media provider, but produces no original content. And even more noticeable: none of these companies existed 15 years ago! They have all grown exponentially through the use of digital platforms that actively manage and monetize ecosystems of providers and consumers. Frequently, this is supported by collecting and analyzing large amounts of data generated through user interactions on or with the platform.

As Uber etc. have demonstrated the development of platforms has the potential to change markets and market structures very quickly. The network effects of digital platforms are creating a winner-take-most dynamic in some markets (McKinsey Global Institute 2016). The infrastructure independence of digital platforms and their potential usability from any internet connection are the main reasons for the possibility of exploiting direct and indirect network effects. Positive direct network effects arise through the direct networking of a large number of consumers, i.e. the size of the network. The benefit increases directly with the number of other participants (example Facebook). Positive indirect network effects arise when two or more groups (often buyers and sellers) interact on a platform. Thus the attractiveness of a platform for the one side increases as more users are on the other side (example ebay).

Consulting experts, such as the German Professor Scheer (2017), CEO of Scheer GmbH, also expect the consulting market to change very strongly in the direction of virtual and digitalized platform companies. The author is of the same opinion. Again, an analogy with logistics might be helpful to better understand the potential of digital platforms in consulting. This time we take a look at Fourth Party Logistics (4PL).

4PL is a form of logistics outsourcing. A 4PL provider, as a supply chain integrator, assumes the leading role for the management of complex supply chains. All definitions are consistent with the fact that the use of new technologies is one of the key competencies of a 4PL, as well as the ability to manage complex cross-company business processes while complementing its own capabilities through complementary service providers (Nissen and Bothe 2002). Essentially, the 4PL is the bridge head into a potentially large network of service partners with specialized skills, required to put together an overall solution that covers all requirements of the 4PL's customers. Cost-effective networking is of central importance within the service integrator function of the 4PL provider. For this purpose, the 4PL uses a digital platform, which connects to customers and logistics service providers and includes the software functions for the implementation of the 4PL tasks.

If one transfers this idea from logistics to consulting, the result could look somewhat similar to Fig. 8. The supported cross-company processes and platform functionality are sketched in Fig. 9. The author's vision is that consultants and sales representatives, independent of the question whether they are working from remote or on-site at the client company, start their work by accessing a digital platform that provides them with content, connectivity and tools to support their daily work. Tools would include communication and cooperation functionality like web-conferences and desktop sharing, for instance, but also modeling, knowledge management, process mining and analytical tools to speed up difficult routine tasks in the analysis and problem solving phase of consulting projects. A full integration with the main IT-systems (ERP, CRM, APS etc.) of clients would ease these tasks

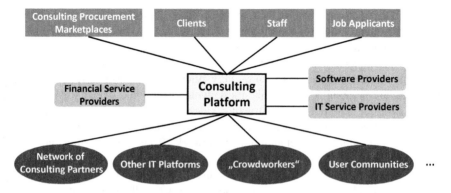

Fig. 8 Digital consulting platform as enabler and integrator of a digital ecosystem

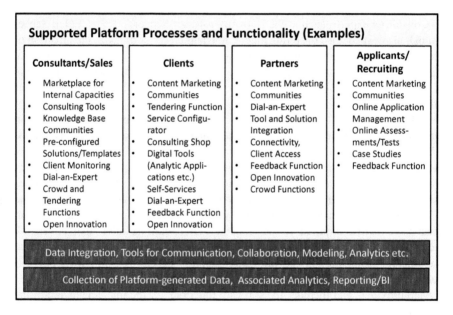

Fig. 9 Supported processes and functionality on a digital consulting platform

and provide the basis for monitoring and alert options as outlined in 5.1. Basically, the whole lifecycle of consulting and sales should be supported by corresponding tools, available via the digital platform. Content could be made available for supporting consulting projects through access to knowledge and data bases, project histories, customized industry solutions, templates and guidelines, to name only a few options. Another stream of functionality on this IT platform would support HR in dealing with job applications online and provide content that attracts applicants in the war for talents.

Some of the value-adding tools should be made available to clients, too, who also log on the platform to consume content marketing, post calls for proposals, configure complex consulting services interactively in pre-sales, or use self-service consulting solutions, such as digital assessments and knowledge bases. Clients could be offered pre-defined and validated analytical services that enable them to explore their data either autonomously or guided by an expert of the consulting firm. Moreover, a dial-an-expert function creates the opportunity for clients (and consultants) to quickly clarify pressing issues with a functional expert from within the ecosystem of partners, who are also linked to the digital platform. Chat rooms, blogs, forums and such like, are available to enable user communities that could be managed or monitored by consultants of the platform provider. Valuable pre-sales information would be generated this way. Moreover, new groups of clients can be reached using these online possibilities that would not be in a financial position to use traditional consulting options. This increases sales with very little marketing effort.

A network of specialized partners is also accessible through the digital platform—maybe even a managed crowd of freelance subject matter experts on a worldwide scale. This enables the consulting firm to scale business at very low cost. The digital platform provides clients and partners with a broader range of services. Furthermore, the ecosystem grants access to specialized skills and a large knowledge base of people. This raises the quality and operational efficiency within consulting projects, and improves the agility in providing solutions to customers.

Platforms and associated digital ecosystems are shifting competitive advantages from corporate to network level. Thus, the crucial challenge for platform providers is to constantly sustain and foster an innovative ecosystem around their platform, keeping up with evolving requirements of clients and the pace of modern technologies. Platforms of different providers may be linked to further increase the capacities, knowledge and capabilities reachable. Excess capacities of the consulting firm could be made available to consulting procurement marketplaces or advertised via the digital platform.

Certainly, more is possible, but even implementing the functionality and processes mentioned here would be a big step forward in using digitalization in consulting to its full extent. Established consulting companies are trusted partners of clients. They are, therefore, in a unique position to extend their customer reach and improve their competitive position through digital platforms that integrate internal solutions with external services (including technology-based newcomers) and manage an ecosystem that is attractive and value-adding for clients. New payment models are required, though, to account for these varied forms of customer services, as the classical per-diem payment usually is not applicable here. These new models could, for instance, be based on flat rates, pay per use, transactional volume, or fixed prices for packaged services.

The management of a digital ecosystem is not an easy task. It involves finding the right business models, designing business processes and ecosystem, solving issues of IT architecture and platform technology, as well as planning and monitoring regular operation. Moreover, it must be ensured that digital platforms can be continuously updated. Adhering to established technological standards is a key issue here.

6 Conclusions

Although consultancy firms strengthen the competitiveness of their clients through innovative solutions and are decisively involved in the development of new concepts and the use of digitalization, traditional face-to-face approaches are mostly applied in the consulting process. This must be critically reviewed. Like many of their clients, consulting firms are facing a digital transformation process that will lead to partially or completely virtualized processes, adapted organization structures and digital business models.

With new technology-driven competitors and changing framework conditions, consultants should continually assess their service portfolio. Virtualization is a promising approach to optimize consulting processes and supplement the service portfolio, thereby creating a sustainable competitive advantage. Using state-of-the-art ICT enables consulting firms to deliver customized solutions anytime and anywhere while the individual work load of every consultant can be optimized. The downside of virtualization is a reduced direct interaction of clients and consultants and thus the risk of weaker client-consultant-relationships—a critical resource of consulting companies. Virtualized consulting services will not generally replace conventional on-site consulting. It is a value-adding combination of traditional and digital approaches that consulting providers should aim for. Whether virtualization is the right approach for a specific client or project has to be clarified within a sound decision process based on appropriate assessment criteria.

Digital can cannibalize classic business—but a company should rather do this on its own than leave it to others. The complexity of modern technologies, and digital transformation as a whole, suggest getting involved early and building up experience and knowledge without expecting immediate breakthroughs. The biggest issue here is digital leadership, i.e. active management of the transformation. In many branches of industry, the topic is today driven by lower management or customers, while a digital strategy is missing. But as already Christensen (1997) explains when discussing the 'Innovator's Dilemma': "(…) we cannot expect our customers to lead us toward innovations that they do not now need". Technology-based products may be ahead of current client needs, but maybe ideal to serve these clients tomorrow. This implies taking first steps in this direction today, adopting a more experimental approach instead of long-term planning, and also accepting the risk of failure in certain digital initiatives.

Digital transformation in the consultancy sector is a complex undertaking, creating barriers to competitors. Those who accumulate relevant knowledge early and execute successful pilot projects can in the long term be expected to generate and defend competitive advantage. This requires a high degree of creativity and strategic thinking that reaches far beyond the pure 1:1 transfer of conventional consulting processes into the virtual world.

References

Allegra M, Fulantelli G, Chiazzese G, Stanford-Smith B, Kidd PT (2000) Distance consulting for small and medium-sized enterprises. In: E-business: key issues, applications and technologies. IOS Press, Amsterdam, pp 953–959

Anonymous (2016a) Angriff der Robo-Advisor. Online-Vermögensverwaltung auf dem Vormarsch. http://boerse.ard.de/anlagestrategie/geldanlage/angriff-der-robo-advisors100.html. Accessed 29 Aug 2016

Anonymous (2016b) Algorithmus rechnet Chancen aus. http://www.n-tv.de/wirtschaft/wirtschaft_startupnews/Peter-Thiel-investiert-in-Klage-Start-up-article18508141.html. Accessed 29 Aug 2016

Ansoff HI (1975) Managing strategic surprise by response to weak signals. Calif Manag Rev 18:21–33

Bakalova E (2015) BearingPoint satisfies client needs by coupling tools with consulting. https://www.linkedin.com/pulse/bearingpoint-satisfies-client-needs-coupling-tools-elitsa-bakalova Accessed 18 Aug 2017

Balci B, Rosenkranz C (2014) Virtual or material, what do you prefer? A study of process virtualization theory. Proc ECIS 2014, Tel Aviv

Bamberger I, Wrona T (2012) Konzeptionen der strategischen Unternehmensberatung. In: Wrona T (ed) Strategische Unternehmensberatung, 6th edn. Gabler, Wiesbaden, pp 1–44

BDU (2016) Facts & Figures zum deutschen Beratungsmarkt 2015/16. BDU e.V., Bonn

BDU (2017) 1960 – Unternehmensstrategie, Vertrieb und Marketing rücken in den Fokus. http://www.zeitstrahl.bdu.de/. Accessed 27 Feb 2017

Bonnet D, Buvat J, Subrahmanyam KVJ, Digital Transformation Research Institute (2015) Rebooting the business model for the digital age. White Paper. CapGemini Consulting

Book M, Grapenthin S, Gruhn V (2012) Seeing the forest and the trees: focusing team interaction on value and effort drivers. In: 20th international symposium on the foundations of software engineering (ACM SIGSOFT 2012/FSE-20) New Ideas Track. ACM, New York, NY, art. no. 30

Bossert O, Laartz J (2017) Perpetual evolution—the management approach required for digital transformation. Digital McKinsey Article (Jun 2017)

Boudreau KJ, Lakhani KR (2013) Using the crowd as an innovation partner. Harvard Bus Rev 91(4):60–69

Brain (2017) Analysis of publically available material on the webpage http://www.thebrain.com/. Accessed 3 Sept 2017

Brown T (2009) Change by design: how design thinking transforms organizations and inspires innovation. Harper Business, New York

Brynjolfsson E, McAfee A (2016) The second machine age: work, progress, and prosperity in a time of brilliant technologies, Paperback edn. W.W. Norton & Company, New York

Buck H, Kistler E, Mendius HG (2002) Demografischer Wandel in der Arbeitswelt. Chancen für eine innovative Arbeitsgestaltung, Fraunhofer IAO, Stuttgart

Bucy M, Hall S, Yakola D (2016) Transformation with a Capital T. McKinsey Q (Nov 2016)

Cardea (2016) Trends in the consulting market 2016. Cardea AG. https://www.consultingsearcher.com/eng/Cardea-competence-centre/The-consulting-market/Executive-Survey-Consulting-Market-Trends. Accessed 12 Aug 2017

Cardea & NEWCOVENTURE (2016) Consulting 4.0 – die marktorientierte Digitalisierung. Research Report. Cardea AG & NEWCOVENTURE GmbH, Zurich & Neckarhausen

Cardea (2017) Digitization of consulting 2017. Cardea AG. https://www.consultingsearcher.com/eng/Cardea-competence-centre/The-consulting-market/Survey-Digitization-of-Consulting-20163. Accessed 12 Aug 2017

Carlborg P, Kindström D (2014) Service process modularization and modular strategies. J Bus Ind Mark 29(4):313–323

Celonis (2017) Web page analysis of Celonis. https://www.celonis.com/. Accessed 1 Sept 2017

Chandok P, Chheda H, Edlich A (2016) How shared-services organizations can prepare for a digital future. McKinsey Article (Feb 2016)

Christ O, Czarniecki M, Scherer L (2017) Improving business development through crowdsourcing supported consulting—a methodical approach. In this volume

Christensen CM (1997) The innovator's dilemma. When new technologies cause great firms to fail. Harvard Business School Press, Boston, MA

Christensen CM, Wang D, van Bever D (2013) Consulting on the cusp of disruption. Harvard Bus Rev 91(10):106–114

Clarity (2017) Analysis of publically available material on the webpage https://clarity.fm/. Accessed 2 Sept 2017

Clauß T (2016) Digitale Geschäftsmodelle gestalten. Wirtschaft Nordhessen 3:16–17

Consultancy.uk (2017) Global Consulting Market Development and other publically available information on the website http://www.consultancy.uk/consulting-industry/global. Accessed 18 July 2017

Czerniawska F (2017) Five big numbers for 2017 (#3). Blog contribution. http://www.sourceglobalresearch.com/blog/2017/03/07/3-five-big-numbers-for-2017. Accessed 18 July 2017

Dahlmanns A (2013) Generation Y and personnel management. Practice-oriented personnel- and organization research. Rainer Hampp, Mering

Dahlström P, Desmet D, Singer M (2017) The seven decisions that matter in a digital transformation: a CEO's guide to reinvention. Digital McKinsey article (Feb 2017)

Deelmann T (2009) Internetberatung - Einige Überlegungen zu Möglichkeiten einer sinnhaften Vollautomation von Beratungsleistungen. In: Fischer S (ed) Informatik 2009. Im Focus das Leben - Beiträge der 39. Jahrestagung der Gesellschaft für Informatik e.V. (GI), Bonn, pp 3745–3759

Deelmann T (2012) Organisations- und Prozessberatung. In: Nissen V, Klauk B (eds) Studienführer consulting. Gabler, Wiesbaden

Deelmann T (2015) Organisation der Managementberatung im Wandel. Organisationsentwicklung (ZOE) 34(1):69–71

Deelmann T (2017) Does digitization matter? Reflections on a possible transformation of the consulting business. In this volume

Denecken S (2017) SAP S/4HANA cloud: revolutionizing the next generation of cloud ERP (Blog posted 13 Feb 2017). https://blogs.saphana.com/2017/02/13/sap-s4hana-cloud-revolutionizing-the-next-generation-of-cloud-erp/. Accessed 16 Aug 2017

Desai F (2016) The rise of digital consultancies. Blog contribution. https://www.forbes.com/sites/falgunidesai/2016/03/23/the-rise-of-digital-consultancies/#27fe62f16a79. Accessed 17 Aug 2017

Dörbecker R, Böhmann T (2013) The concept and effects of service modularity—a literature review. In: Proceedings of the 46th Hawaii international conference on system sciences 2013, IEEE, Piscataway/NJ, pp 1357–1366

Downes L, Nunes PF (2013) Big-bang disruption. Harvard Bus Rev 91(3):44–56

Forrester (2016) The future of consulting through 2020. research report, 11 Feb 2016

Gartner (2014) Gartner news on the user of mobile devices. http://www.gartner.com/newsroom/id/. Accessed 17 Aug 2017

Gartner (2017) Top 10 personal technologies to support digital business. http://www.gartner.com/smarterwithgartner/top-10-personal-technologies-to-support-digital-business/ Accessed 17 Aug 2017

Greff T, Werth D (2015) Auf dem Weg zur digitalen Unternehmensberatung. IM + io - Magazin für Innovation, Organisation und Management. IMC, Saarbücken, pp 30–34

Greff T, Werth D (2017) Scalability in consulting: insights into the scaling capabilities of business models by digital technologies in consulting industry. In this volume

Hardt C (2017) The best of two worlds: digitization of matchmaking between consultancies and independent consultants. In this volume

Hebisch E, Grapenthin S, Book M, Klaffmann M, Gruhn V (2017) Experiences with the digitization of the interaction room method for IT strategy development and software project scoping. In this volume

Islam N, Buxmann P, Eling N (2017) Why should incumbent firms jump on the start-up bandwagon in the digital era?—A qualitative study. In: Proceedings of Wirtschaftsinformatik 2017 (St. Gallen, Feb 2017)

Jans M, Alles M, Vasarhelyi M (2011) Process mining of event logs in internal auditing: a case study. In: Proceedings of the 2nd international symposium on accounting information systems

Johann D, Greff T, Werth D (2016) On the effect of digital frontstores on transforming business models. In: Shishkov B (ed) Proceedings of the 6th international symposium on business modeling and software design. Rhodes, pp 64–72

Kaggle (2017) Your home for data science. Analysis of publically available material on the webpage https://www.kaggle.com/ and company films on Youtube. Accessed 1 Sept 2017

Klaas BS, Gainey TW, McClendon JA, Yang H (2005) Professional employer organizations and their impact on client satisfaction with human resource outcomes: a field study of human resource outsourcing in small and medium enterprises. J Manag 31(2):234–254

Klimmer M, Selonke J (2016) Digital leadership. Springer, Berlin

Lubarski A, Pöppelbuß J (2016) Methods for service modularization—a systematization framework. In: Proceedings of the Pacific Asia conference on information systems (PACIS), Chiayi, Taiwan

Lünendonk (2016) Consulting 4.0—Mit Analytics ins digitale Beraterzeitalter. Mindelheim

Maister DH (2003) Managing the professional service firm. Simon & Schuster

Maor D, Reich A, Yocarini L (2017) The people power of transformation. McKinsey Res Study

Matt C, Hess T, Benlian A (2015) Digital transformation strategies. Bus Inf Syst Eng (BISE) 57(5):339–343

McKinsey Global Institute (2016) The age of analytics: competing in a data-driven world. McKinsey Res Rep (Dec 2016)

Mohe M (2003) Klientenprofessionalisierung. Strategien und Perspektiven eines professionellen Umgangs mit Unternehmensberatung. Metropolis, Marburg

Müllerleile T, Nissen V (2014) When processes alienate customers: towards a theory of process acceptance. In: Nonopoulos A, Schmidt W (eds) Proceedings of S-BPM One (LNBIP). Springer, Berlin, pp 171–180

Müllerleile T, Martinovic D, Joenssen D, Orner M, Grimm M, Nissen V, Reuss H (2016): Fully charged: process acceptance of different EV charging processes (4 Sept 2016). Available at SSRN: http://ssrn.com/abstract=2834600

Müllerleile T, Ritter S, Englisch L, Nissen V, Joenssen D (2015) The influence of process acceptance on BPM: an empirical investigation. In: Proceedings of the 2015 IEEE 17th conference on business informatics (CBI 2015). IEEE, Piscataway/NJ, pp 125–132

Nissen V (ed) (2007) Consulting research. Unternehmensberatung aus wissenschaftlicher Perspektive. DUV, Wiesbaden

Nissen V (2008) Einige Grundlagen zum Management von IT-Agilität, Technical Report 2008-03, TU Ilmenau

Nissen V (2012) Wissensmanagement. In: Niedereichholz C, Niedereichholz J (eds) Das Beratungsunternehmen - Gründung, Aufbau und Strategie, Führung, Nachfolge. Oldenbourg, München, pp 203–226

Nissen V (2013) Stand und Perspektiven der informationsverarbeitungsbezogenen Beratung. HMD Praxis der Wirtschaftsinformatik 50(4):23–32

Nissen V, Bothe M (2002) Fourth Party Logistics – ein Überblick. Logist Manag 4(1):16–26

Nissen V, Kuhl J, Kraeft H, Seifert H, Reiter J, Eidmann J (2017a) ProMAT—a project management assessment tool for virtual consulting. In this volume

Nissen V, Müllerleile T (2017) Prozessakzeptanzforschung. Warum manche Prozesse gelebt und andere umgangen werden. In: Corsten H, Roth T (eds) Handbuch Dienstleistungsmanagement. Vahlen, München, pp 1049–1073

Nissen V, Müllerleile T, Kazakowa E, Lezina T (2016) Analyzing process acceptance with IT-enabled experimental research. Vestn Econ 3:109–129

Nissen V, Seifert H (2015) Virtualization of consulting—benefits, risks and a suggested decision process. In: Pavlou P, Saunders C (eds) Proceedings of AMCIS 2015, vol. 2, Puerto Rico, pp 1380–1391

Nissen V, Seifert H (2016) Virtualisierung in der Unternehmensberatung. Eine Studie im deutschen Beratungsmarkt. BDU, Bonn

Nissen V, Seifert H (2017a) Digital transformation in business consulting—status quo in Germany. In this volume

Nissen V, Seifert H (2017b) Ermittlung des Virtualisierungspotenzials von Beratungsleistungen im Consulting. In: Leimeister JM, Brenner W (eds) Proceedings of Wirtschaftsinformatik 2017, St. Gallen

Nissen V, Seifert H (2017c) Evaluating the virtualization potential of consulting services. In this volume

Nissen V, Seifert H, Ackert MN (2017b) A process model for the virtualization of consulting services. In this volume

Nissen V, Seifert H, Blumenstein M (2015) Virtualisierung von Beratungsleistungen: Qualitätsanforderungen, Chancen und Risiken der digitalen Transformation in der Unternehmensberatung aus der Klientenperspektive. In: Deelmann T, Ockel DM (eds) Handbuch der Unternehmensberatung, 25th edn. Erich Schmidt Verlag, Berlin

Nissen V, Termer F (2014) Women and their work-life balance in German IT-consulting. In: Rode JA, Wulf V (eds) Proceedings of gender IT 14—gender and IT appropriation, Siegen. European Society for socially embedded technologies. ACM Digital Library, pp 1–9

Nissen V, von Rennenkampff A (2013) IT-Agilität als strategische Ressource im Wettbewerb. In: Lang M (ed) CIO-Handbuch, vol 2. Symposon Publishing, Düsseldorf, pp 57–90

Nissen V, von Rennenkampff A (2017) Measuring the agility of the IT application systems landscape. In: Leimeister J M, Brenner W (eds) Proceedings of Wirtschaftsinformatik 2017, St. Gallen (AISeLibrary)

Nowak S (2015) Karibik ohne Strand und Sonne – Wie digitale Beratung Projekte in außergewöhnlichen Regionen ermöglicht. IM + io - Magazin für Innovation, Organisation und Management. IMC, Saarbücken, pp 74–79

Osterwalder A, Pigneur Y (2011) Business model generation: Ein Handbuch für Visionäre, Spielveränderer und Herausforderer. Campus, Frankfurt am Main

Overby E (2008) Process virtualization theory and the impact of information technology. Organ Sci 19(2):277–291

Overby E (2012) Migrating processes from physical to virtual environments: Process virtualization theory. In: Dwivedi YK, Wade MR, Schneberger SL (eds) Information systems theory. Explaining and predicting our digital society. Springer, New York, pp 107–124

Parakala K (2015) Global consulting and IT service providers trends, an industry perspective. Technova

Parment A (2013) Die Generation Y. Mitarbeiter der Zukunft motivieren, integrieren, führen. 2nd edn. SpringerGabler, Wiesbaden

PwC (2017) Personal communication with PWC representatives

Rahikka E, Ulkuniemi P, Pekkarinen S (2011) Developing the value perception of the business customer through service modularity. J Bus Ind Mark 26(5):357–367

Richter A, Niewiem S (2004) The changing balance of power in the consulting market. Bus Strategy Rev 15(1):8–13

Ries E (2011) The lean startup, how today's entrepreneurs use continuos innovation to create radically successful businesses. Crown Business, New York

Ritter S, Müllerleile T, Nissen V (2016) Akzeptanz – Der Schlüssel für gelebte Prozesse. Qualität und Zuverlässigkeit 61(6):38–41

Röper N (2016) Unternehmensberatung nach Feierabend. FAZ Online 21 Nov 2016. http://www.faz.net/aktuell/wirtschaft/netzwirtschaft/wikistrat-beraet-mit-der-crowd-14518185.html. Accessed 28 Aug 2017

SAP (2017) SAP Leonardo—the digital innovation system for rapid, scalable transformation (Product Brochure). SAP SE

Scheer AW (2017) Interview with Prof. Dr. A W Scheer on market developments in consulting. IM + io 2017 (1):10–14

Schmitz A, Bischoff J (2017) 11 Fragen zu SAP S/4HANA Cloud (SAP News). http://news.sap. com/germany/11-fragen-zu-sap-s4hana-cloud/. Accessed 16 Aug 2017

Schuster K (2005) E-Consulting; Chancen und Risiken. Dissertation, University of Mannheim

Seifert H, Nissen V (2016) Virtualisierung von Beratungsleistungen: Stand der Forschung zur digitalen Transformation in der Unternehmensberatung und weiterer Forschungsbedarf. In: Nissen V, Stelzer D, Straßburger S, Fischer D (eds) Proceedings of MKWI2016. Ilmedia, Ilmenau, pp 1031–1040

Seifert H, Nissen V (2017) Virtualization of consulting services: state of research on digital transformation in consulting and future research demand. In this volume

Source for Consulting (2013) The consulting firm of the future. Source Information Services Ltd., London

Stummeyer C (2017) Personal communication

Stummeyer C (2018) Case study: digital consulting for dental practices by benchmarking. In: Nissen V (ed) Advances in consulting research. Springer, Berlin (to appear)

Türk B (2004) E-Consulting: Der Einsatz webbasierter Technologien in der Unternehmensberatung - eine empirische Untersuchung aus Sicht von Klienten- und Beratungsunternehmen. Dissertation, University of Leipzig

Upwork (2017) Analysis of publically available material on the webpage https://www.upwork. com/ and company films on Youtube. Accessed 2 Sept 2017

Urbach N, Drews P, Ross J (2017) Digital business transformation and the changing role of the IT Function. Editors' comments on the special issue. MIS Q Exec 16(2):II–IV

USU (2017) Chatbots - (R)Evolution im Service? (Survey by USU AG) https://www.kcenterusu. com/file/113909/chatbot-studie-2017. Accessed 17 Aug 2017

van der Aalst W (2016) Process mining. Data science in action. 2nd edn. Springer, Berlin

Walger G (1995) Idealtypen der Unternehmensberatung. In: Walger G (ed) Formen der Unternehmensberatung: Systemische Unternehmensberatung, Organisationsentwicklung, Expertenberatung und gutachterliche Beratungstätigkeit in Theorie und Praxis. Otto Schmidt, Cologne, pp 1–18

Weimer M (2016) Frankfurter Bank kauft Fintech-Startup Easyfolio. http://www.gruenderszene. de/allgemein/robo-advisor-privatbank-easyfolio-hauck-aufhauser. Accessed 29 Aug 2016

Werner M (2012) Einsatzmöglichkeiten von Process Mining für die Analyse von Geschäftsprozessen im Rahmen der Jahresabschlussprüfung. In: Plate G (ed) Forschung für die Wirtschaft. Cuvillier, Göttingen, pp 199–214

Werth D, Greff T (2017) Scalability in consulting: insights into the scaling capabilities of business models by digital technologies in consulting industry. In this volume

Werth D, Greff T, Scheer AW (2016a) Consulting 4.0 - Die Digitalisierung der Unternehmensberatung. HMD Praxis der Wirtschaftsinformatik 53(1):55–70

Werth D, Zimmermann P, Greff T (2016b) Self-service consulting: conceiving customer-operated digital IT consulting services. Conference paper. In: Proceedings of AMCIS 2016, San Diego

Westerman G, Bonnet D, McAfee A (2014) Leading digital. Turning technology into business transformation. Harvard Business Publishing, Boston

Wikistrat (2017) Wikistrat—Crowdsourced Consulting. Analysis of publically available material on the webpage http://www.wikistrat.com/ and company films on Youtube. Accessed 2 Sept 2017

Wittenburg G (2017a) Interview with G. Wittenburg (Co-founder) on the business model and solution of Inspirient. IM + io 2017 (1):22–27

Wittenburg G (2017b) Company information brochures of Inspirient, and personal communication

Wurdack A (2001) E-Consulting - Entwicklung eines Rahmenkonzeptes: Aufbau und Darstellung einer E-Consulting-Lösung im Beratungsunternehmen der Zukunft. Dissertation, University Mannheim

Wurzel HW, Haake K (2016) Vorwort. In: Seifert H (ed) Nissen V. Virtualisierung in der Unternehmensberatung. Eine Studie im deutschen Beratungsmarkt. BDU, Bonn

Author Biography

Volker Nissen holds the Chair of Information Systems Engineering in Services at Technische Universität Ilmenau, Germany, since 2005. Prior to this, he pursued a consulting career, including positions as manager at IDS Scheer AG, director at DHC GmbH, and CEO of NISSCON Ltd., Germany. In 1994 he received a PhD degree in Economic Sciences with distinction from the University of Goettingen, Germany. His current research interests include the digital transformation of the consulting industry, the management of IT-agility, metaheuristic optimization, and process acceptance research. He is author and editor of 19 books and some 200 other publications, including papers in Business & Information Systems Engineering, Information Systems Frontiers, IEEE Transactions on EC, IEEE Transactions on NN, and Annals of OR.

Part I
Scientific Contributions

Virtualization of Consulting Services: State of Research on Digital Transformation in Consulting and Future Research Demand

Henry Seifert and Volker Nissen

Abstract The theme of virtual consulting services still is in its early stages considering practice but also scientific research. For this reason, we conducted a structured literature review to reveal what the main topics of research in this field currently are, which "blind spots" are noticeable and, thus, where fruitful avenues for continued research can be found. Some of the major issues have already been addressed in this volume.

1 Introduction

Despite a positive development and also positive growth forecasts (BDU 2017), consulting providers are confronted by numerous challenges. One of these challenges is the potential of technology-based consulting services and internal processes, and thus the virtualization of consulting (Christensen et al. 2013; Greff and Werth 2015; Nissen and Seifert 2015; Nissen 2017). Really innovative forms of consulting with a high degree of virtualization are, so far, only used occasionally (Nissen and Seifert 2016, 2017a). A negative trend has actually been noticed among consultants, specifically towards an automation of consulting services (Deelmann 2015). The potential of a digital transformation of consulting, rethinking the traditional business and delivery models, seems to be gradually perceived by some providers. However, virtualization is, so far, rather an option for specialists, than a generally accepted approach in consulting services. Thus, there seem to be obstacles, which impede a broad virtualization initiative in consulting.

Against this background, the current contribution focuses on presenting the status quo of research on the theme of virtualization in consulting. For this purpose, we initially describe our methodical procedure and then summarize the acquired

H. Seifert (✉) · V. Nissen
Technische Universität Ilmenau, Ilmenau, Germany
e-mail: henry.seifert@infosysconsulting.com

V. Nissen
e-mail: volker.nissen@tu-ilmenau.de

© Springer International Publishing AG 2018   61
V. Nissen (ed.), *Digital Transformation of the Consulting Industry*,
Progress in IS, https://doi.org/10.1007/978-3-319-70491-3_2

results. In conclusion, we will point to some, in our opinion, fruitful avenues for further research.

2 Objective and Research Questions

The main objective of our overall research stream on the virtualization of consulting is the construction of scientifically sound and practically relevant artefacts (process model, decision guidance, methods etc.). Thereby, the consulting providers shall be supported to meaningfully alter and extend their current service portfolios. In order to achieve this, it is essential to analyze the state of research first and then start constructing the missing artefacts.

Firstly, we want to present an overview of relevant scientific concepts and approaches to the virtualization of consulting services. Secondly, this serves as a basis to identify blind spots in research and interesting future research questions. Thereby, we hope to foster further research projects and to stimulate continuing research efforts on the virtualization of consulting.

Thirdly, this contribution should help to prevent the duplication of work, and identify important previous results that can be used as inputs of current research (Fettke 2006). In particular, the following three questions, inspired by Overby et al. (2010), will guide our efforts and form the scope for our research on the virtualization of consulting processes:

(1) How should a virtual consulting process be designed?
(2) How and why do clients and consultants use virtual processes as compared to traditional face-to-face consulting processes?
(3) What are the consequences of migrating traditional consulting processes into a virtual environment?

The literature review, considering these three central questions, will form the basis to construct artefacts (Hevner et al. 2004) for the virtualization of consulting services, such as a process model, checklists, and methods to support individual steps in the design and implementation of virtual consulting services. The review can be understood as a method of explorative research in the context of the problem identification and research motivation of a design science process model (Peffers et al. 2007; Briggs and Schwabe 2011).

Balci (2014) conducted a comprehensive literature review on the Process Virtualization Theory (PVT) of Overby (2008, 2012). According to him, the following areas constitute the majority of application areas of PVT: information systems in a general sense, e-learning, e-commerce, communication and/or relationship, business processes, health care, and mobile technology. Professional services, such as business consulting, are not explicitly mentioned in his review.

Balci (2014) remarks that the virtualizability of processes is, so far, the element of PVT, which has been investigated least of all. The current contribution links to

Balci's work and investigates, to what extent virtualization, in the context of consulting services, is covered by the present research literature. In the following section, the methodology used to analyze the status of research is described before the individual results will be discussed.

3   Methodology and Data

To achieve the above mentioned objectives, a review was conducted according to the methodical guidelines, which were suggested by Webster and Watson (2002). This procedure was completed by the analysis steps according to vom Brocke et al. (2009). At the beginning of the investigation keywords, based on our objectives were defined. These keywords are suitable for the investigation of relevant contributions (see Table 1). To be able to find suitable key words, it was first analyzed which denominations for the virtualization of consulting services are being used in the present literature. This input was then used to create corresponding search strings.

The search for relevant literature was only done from the year 1990 onwards, as from a technological perspective earlier contributions would not be expected. The selection of scientific databases, which were used for this investigation, is based on the MIS Journal Ranking of the Association for Information Systems (AIS). Thus, those databases were used for this investigation, which included at least one of the top ten scientific journals according to this ranking (see Table 2).

Subsequently a backward search following Webster and Watson (2002) was conducted. The relevance of each contribution was first evaluated by means of a title analysis, and then a keywords and abstract analysis. Relevant contributions were added to the list of found contributions. In the following step of the investigation a forward search was conducted for the contributions so far found. Thus, it was analyzed which papers cited the contributions identified so far (Webster and Watson 2002). Moreover, each of the contributions found, was analyzed to find relevant references of other contributions and every new contribution was again

Table 1 Key words and search strings (English and German search) in our review

#	Search string (English)	#	Search string (German)
1	"E-consulting" OR "Electronic Consulting" OR "Internet Consulting" OR "Automatic Consulting" OR "Web based Consulting" OR "Virtual Consulting" OR "IT-enabled Consulting" OR "Distance Consulting"	4	"Internet Beratung" OR "Online Beratung" OR "Computergestützte Beratung" OR "Virtuelle Beratung"
2	"Virtualization" AND "Consulting"	5	"Virtualisierung" AND "Beratung"
3	"Digitization" AND "Consulting"	6	"Digitalisierung" AND "Beratung"

Table 2 Searched databases and hits per search string

Database	Search string 1	Search string 2	Search string 3	Search string 4	Search string 5	Search string 6
IEEE Xplore	21	3	3	0	0	0
Wiley Online	292	347	1058	10	1	37
JSTOR	14	1	21	0	0	0
Science Direct	708	507	1171	5	0	33
ACM Digital	19	505	240	0	1	0
HBR Library	0	2	1	0	0	0
Informs	2	4	60	0	0	0
Google Scholar	3600	3	1	62	0	0
EBSCOhost	146	81	90	1	0	0

tested for its relevance. For this purpose, again the title, keywords and abstracts were interpreted.

In this review, contributions were assessed as relevant, which explicitly dealt with virtualization of consulting services. Contributions, which dealt with the virtualization of other services or processes, were not considered in the scope of this review. Regardless of this limitation, the authors are aware of the fact, that in particular the research fields of Service Engineering and Management, Collaboration Engineering as well as Computer Supported Cooperative Work have relevance in the broader design process, and especially for the construction and evaluation of new artefacts for the virtualization of consulting services.

Finally, it should be noted that only contributions in English and German were considered and that our review may therefore exclude relevant research results in other languages. Furthermore, other contributions could have been published after we had completed our investigation. Altogether 41 contributions on virtual consulting services were identified.

4 Literature Analysis and Synthesis

Webster and Watson (2002) recommend doing the literature analysis—and synthesis in the form of a concept matrix. In this concept matrix, the contributions are consolidated and analyzed according to relevant criteria (see Fig. 1). In order to define the applied criteria for our analysis, we orientate ourselves towards the elements of Process Virtualization Theory, the artefacts of Design Science (DS) research approaches, and the concepts of the consulting research field.

#	Contribution (chronological)	Requirements of the consulting process	Features of virtualization mechanism	Virtualizability of the consulting process	Strategy consulting	IT consulting	Human Resources-Consulting	Organizational and process consulting	Expert Consulting	Advisory Consulting	Systemic Consulting	Organizational development/ Coaching	Development of virtual consulting services	Usage of virtual consulting services	Consulting provider	Client	Virtualization concept	Methods of Virtualization	Reference model	Consulting tool
	Legend: − = not addressed ○ = addressed, without reference to PVT ● = addressed, with reference to PVT																			
1	Nissen & Seifert (2017b)	●	●	●	●	●	●	●	●	●	●	●	●	-	●	-	-	●	●	-
2	Johann et al. (2016)	○	○	○	-	○	-	-	○	○	-	-	○	○	○	○	○	-	○	○
3	Werth & Greff (2016)	○	○	○	○	○	○	○	○	○	○	○	-	-	○	○	-	-	-	-
4	Werth et al. (2016b)	○	○	○	○	○	○	○	-	○	○	-	○	○	○	○	○	-	-	○
5	Nissen & Seifert (2016)	●	●	●	●	●	●	●	●	●	●	●	●	●	●	●	-	●	●	●	-
6	Werth et al. (2016a)	○	-	-	○	○	○	○	○	○	○	○	○	○	○	○	○	-	-	○
7	Nissen & Seifert (2015)	●	●	●	○	●	●	●	●	●	●	●	●	●	●	●	●	●	●	●	-
8	Nissen et al. (2015)	●	●	●	○	●	●	●	●	●	●	●	●	-	●	●	-	●	●	-	-
9	Greff & Werth (2015)	○	-	-	○	○	○	○	○	○	○	○	○	-	○	○	-	-	-	-
10	Nowak (2015)	○	-	-	-	○	-	-	○	-	-	-	-	-	○	○	-	-	-	-
11	Burin (2014)	○	○	○	○	○	○	○	○	-	-	-	○	-	○	○	-	○	-	-
12	Martensen (2014)	-	○	○	○	○	○	○	○	-	-	-	-	○	○	-	○	-	○	-
13	Christensen et al. (2013)	-	○	-	○	○	○	○	○	○	○	○	-	○	○	○	-	-	-	-
14	Robinson (2013)	-	○	-	○	○	○	○	○	-	-	-	-	○	○	○	○	-	-	-
15	Hoven et al. (2012)	○	○	-	○	○	○	○	-	○	-	-	○	○	○	-	○	○	-	○
16	Schumann et al. (2012)	○	○	○	○	○	○	○	○	○	○	○	-	○	○	○	○	-	-	-
17	Korytko (2011)	○	-	-	○	○	○	○	○	-	-	-	-	○	○	-	○	-	○	-
18	Strehlau & Sieper (2009)	-	○	-	○	-	-	-	○	-	-	-	-	○	○	-	○	-	○	-
19	Deelmann (2009)	○	○	○	○	○	○	○	○	○	○	○	○	-	○	-	○	-	-	-
20	Richter et al. (2009)	-	-	-	○	○	○	○	○	-	-	-	-	○	○	-	○	-	-	-
21	König (2009)	-	○	-	-	○	-	-	○	-	-	-	○	-	○	-	○	○	○	○
22	Steir (2007)	-	○	-	○	○	○	○	○	○	○	○	-	○	○	○	○	-	-	-
23	Schulze et al. (2006)	○	○	○	○	○	-	○	○	○	-	-	○	-	○	○	○	○	-	-
24	Schuster (2005)	-	○	-	○	○	○	○	○	-	-	-	-	○	○	○	○	○	-	-
25	Czerniawska (2005)	○	○	○	○	○	○	○	○	-	-	-	○	○	○	○	○	-	-	-
26	Türk (2004)	○	○	○	○	○	○	○	○	○	○	○	-	○	○	-	○	-	-	-
27	Lindhorst et al. (2004)	○	○	-	○	○	○	○	○	○	-	-	○	-	○	-	○	-	○	○
28	Davison et al. (2003)	○	○	-	-	○	-	-	○	-	-	-	-	○	○	-	○	-	-	-
29	Fulantelli & Allegra (2003)	-	○	-	○	○	○	○	○	-	-	-	-	○	○	○	○	-	-	○
30	Zeißler et al. (2003)	○	○	-	○	○	○	-	○	-	-	-	-	○	○	-	○	-	-	-
31	Fink (2002)	-	○	-	○	○	○	○	○	○	○	○	○	-	○	-	○	-	○	-
32	Evans & Volery (2001)	○	○	○	○	○	○	○	○	○	-	-	○	-	○	-	○	-	-	-
33	Fulantelli et al. (2001)	○	○	-	○	○	○	○	○	-	-	-	-	○	○	-	○	-	-	○
34	Wurdack (2001)	○	○	○	○	○	○	○	○	○	○	○	○	○	○	○	○	○	○	-
35	Bätz (2001)	○	○	○	○	○	-	○	○	○	○	○	-	○	○	○	○	○	○	○
36	Najda (2001)	○	○	○	○	○	○	○	○	-	-	○	○	○	○	○	○	○	○	○
37	Allegra et al. (2000)	-	○	-	○	○	○	○	○	-	-	-	-	○	○	-	○	-	-	-
38	Baum (2000)	-	○	-	○	○	○	○	○	○	○	○	-	○	○	-	○	-	-	○
39	Katz (1998)	○	○	-	○	○	○	○	○	-	-	-	-	○	○	-	○	○	-	-
40	Kordes (1992)	○	○	○	○	○	○	○	○	-	-	-	○	-	○	-	○	-	-	-
41	Neuert (1990)	○	○	○	○	○	○	○	○	○	○	○	○	-	○	-	○	○	○	-

Fig. 1 Concept matrix on the state of research on the virtualization of consulting services

The PVT describes the factors, which influence the virtualizability of a physical process (Overby 2008; Overby et al. 2010). These are differentiated into sensory, relational-related, synchronicity-related, as well as identification- and control-related factors. The virtualizability of a physical process is furthermore influenced by features of the virtualization mechanism (e.g. digitalization using ICT). Relevant features are the representation, reach and monitoring capabilities. In our review, we investigated, whether the contributions dealt with the virtualizability of consulting processes, the features of the virtualization mechanism or the requirements of the physical consulting process.

Artefacts in the sense of Design Science can be, for example information systems, concepts, methods or models (Hevner et al. 2004; Gregor and Jones 2007; Frank 2007; Peffers et al. 2007; Sinz 2010). During the analysis of the contributions, the following aspects were tested: whether artefacts in the form of a reference model (process model in the sense of an action and design oriented design-theory), methods (e.g. to assess the degree of virtualizability of a consulting task), applications and information systems (consulting tools) or concepts (for consulting, sales, integration) were described in the contributions. Besides this artefact oriented analysis, it was evaluated, whether the different consulting fields (strategy-, organizational/process, IT- as well as HR-consulting) and consulting approaches (expert consulting, advisory consulting, organizational development/coaching, systemic consulting) and thus varying perspectives of consulting research were covered. Other criteria inspired by consulting research, which we included in the concept matrix, were the focus of the contribution (consulting firm versus client) and the question whether the contribution dealt with the development and/or the usage of virtual consulting services.

5 State of Research

5.1 Design of Virtual Consulting Processes

The question regarding the way how virtual consulting processes should be designed, includes the question how the virtualizability of consulting tasks can be evaluated, likewise which technologies and tools are suitable, as well as the roles and responsibilities for the realization of virtualization (Overby et al. 2010). Our literature review reveals that only Nissen and Seifert (2016, 2017b) developed a method to assess the virtualizability of tasks in consulting in the context of PVT. Other authors, however, implicitly deal with this issue through the investigation of relevant service attributes, such as standardization, interactivity, integrativity, as well as the consideration of automation potential. Key studies on these determining factors of virtualization were supplied by Neuert (1990), Wurdack (2001) and Deelmann (2009). The issue regarding suitable technologies and tools is dealt with by Neuert (1990), Najda (2001) and Schuster (2005) in the form of typologies and checklists for the selection of suitable virtualization technologies. The authors, though, do not refer to PVT and its elements. These authors provide a technological reference framework, which could be expanded by actual technologies and tools as well as by useful, new dimensions such as a consulting field, or consulting approach. The issue regarding the responsibility for the realization of virtualization is dealt with by Wurdack (2001), Christensen et al. (2013) and Nissen and Seifert (2015). They refer to the management of the consulting provider. A useful expansion of this concept would be the assignment of roles and responsibilities to distinctive business processes of a consulting company, as was exemplary done by Nissen et al. (2015).

5.2 Usage of Virtual Consulting

The review shows, that so far, there are only two empirical studies addressing the usage of virtual consulting processes. One (Nissen and Seifert 2016) is described in a contribution of this volume (Nissen and Seifert 2017a). Before this study, solely Türk (2004) investigated why clients and consulting firms use virtual consulting services, which technologies they deploy and which chances and obstacles they observe. Türk limits her investigation on virtual consulting services as "project related subservices" to e-coaching services and e-intermediation (Türk 2004). Full virtualization and automated consulting services have not been part of her investigation, neither the analysis of various levels of virtualizations during the consulting. Both is addressed in Nissen and Seifert (2016) on a high level that aims for determining the status quo in the German market w.r.t. the digital transformation of consulting.

An explicit investigation on the factors, which influence the elements of the success chain (design, acceptance, usage, satisfaction—see Bruhn 2002) of virtual consulting services, has not been conducted yet. This seems to be essential, though, in order to construct effective artefacts for virtualization, and finally apply virtualization successfully. Further contributions, which also deal with the usage of virtual consulting services, are qualitatively designed. They focus on the description of the implementation of exemplary virtual consulting solutions and derive from these recommendations for action. Allegra et al. (2000), Baum (2000), Bätz (2001), Fulantelli et al. (2001), Fulantelli and Allegra (2003), Strehlau and Sieper (2009) and Werth et al. (2016b) show how a virtual consulting service can be used.

5.3 Consequences of Migrating Classical Consulting to the Virtual Space

So far, there are no empirical studies about the consequences of consulting virtualization. Contributions, which deal with this topic so far had a conceptual character. Wurdack (2001), Deelmann (2009), Christensen et al. (2013), Greff and Werth (2015) and Werth et al. (2016a) all describe which consequences can be expected regarding business strategy, organization and processes of a consulting provider in the case of virtualization. Likewise it was not, so far, empirically investigated whether the expected impact on the interaction and relation with the client really takes place. In the key contributions of Wurdack (2001), Deelmann

(2009) as well as Nissen and Seifert (2015), these aspects were conceptually described.

The review revealed that on the theme of virtual consulting services there is a considerable need for continued research. This demand will be made more specific in the next section.

6   Future Research Avenues

6.1   *Process Model for the Virtualization of Consulting Services*

After it was determined which phases and finally which activities of a consulting service can be virtualized and whether virtualization provides an advantage to conventional consulting, consulting companies should actually develop these virtual consulting services. To reduce the complexity of this digital transformation, a process model should be constructed, which considers the features of virtualization of consulting services and the results of preliminary research, for example the client's quality requirements (Nissen et al. 2015). The conception of the process model should especially include the critical analysis of existing reference models of Service and Software Engineering and evaluate these in a consulting context. This research question is addressed in the contribution of Nissen et al. in this volume (2017b). Moreover, individual steps in the process of designing and implementing a virtual consulting service require supporting methods and tools. The paper by Nissen, Seifert and Blumenstein (2017c) in this volume takes up this issue for the selection of adequate technologies in order to virtualize a given consulting task. However, other steps of the process model of virtualization thereafter remain unsupported up to now.

6.2   *Virtual Consulting Services in Practice*

So far, research is insufficient when it comes to questions of practical usage of virtual consulting. It remains unclear which kind of virtual service could usefully be implemented in which consulting field, consulting type, consulting companies and client industries. At this point, it is therefore necessary to investigate to which extent virtualization has already penetrated the consulting practice. This would be generally helpful in terms of transparency for research and practice. Moreover, a state-of-practice overview could also provide valuable insights concerning the virtualizability of consulting services.

It would also be interesting to characterize the different forms of virtual consulting services and tools already used in practice. Which technologies and tools are used to support which phase of a consulting process (or internal process)? What is their practical impact? How do incumbent consulting providers react when technology-driven competitors invade their markets? And finally, there is, of course, a practical as well as scientific interest in designing purposeful virtual consulting products that can be applied in practice. At this point, a fruitful cooperation between consulting researchers and practitioners is called for. The contribution by Nissen et al. (2017a) as well as the paper by Füßl et al. (2017) in this volume are examples of such design efforts.

6.3   Influence of Virtualization on the Client's Behavior and the Consultant-Client-Relationship

After virtual consulting services have been implemented, future investigations should more closely investigate their consequences in practice. Especially the influence of virtualization on the client's behavior, as well as the consultant-client-relationship should be researched, as these aspects are decisive for the success of consulting services (Nissen and Seifert 2015). Here an explorative empirical research approach seems adequate, where primarily the application and impact of IT and technology-based services is investigated (Österle et al. 2010). The research results should subsequently be evaluated, to optimize existing artefacts, such as the process model of virtualization.

6.4   Influence of Virtualization on the Business Processes, Business Model and the Organization of Consulting Providers

The consequences of virtual consulting services on other processes of consulting companies should likewise be part of future research efforts. Such research could be based on the consulting reference model proposed by Nissen and Seifert (2008). Of particular interest is the influence on sales, knowledge management, partner management, recruiting, and staff development. Following the conceptual work on changing business models in consulting, e.g. by Christensen et al. (2013), it is now the time for empirical investigations to practically understand the actual influence of digital transformation on the organization and business model of consulting. Johann et al. (2016) as well as Werth and Greff (2016) indicate that there could occur fundamental changes to the business models—depending on the technologies and virtual services that will be created.

References

Allegra M, Fulantelli G, Chiazzese G, Stanford-Smith B, Kidd PT (2000) distance consulting for small and medium-sized enterprises. E-business: key issues, applications and technologies. IOS Press, Amsterdam, pp 953–959

Balci B (2014) The state of the art on process virtualization: a literature review. In: Proceedings of the 20th Americas conference on information systems (AMCIS 2014), Savannah

Bätz V (2001) Internetbasierte Abwicklung von Consulting-Projekten und-Analysen im Umfeld betriebswirtschaftlicher Softwarebibliotheken. Dissertation, University of Würzburg

Baum BJ (2000) Ernie—four years of online consulting. Consult Manage 11(1):25–29

BDU (2017) Facts & Figures zum Beratermarkt 2016/2017. BDU e.V., Bonn

Briggs RO, Schwabe G (2011) On expanding the scope of design science in IS research. In: Jain H, Sinha AP, Vitharana P (eds) Service-oriented perspectives in design science research (DESRIST 2011). Proceedings., Milwaukee, 5–6 May 2011. Springer, Berlin, pp 92-106

Bruhn M (2002) E-services - eine Einführung in die theoretischen und praktischen Probleme. In: Bruhn M, Stauss B (eds) Electronic Services. Gabler Verlag, Wiesbaden, pp 3–41

Burin C (2014) Competing in knowledge intensive service: the dichotomy between talent and technology. Dissertation, University of Pretoria

Christensen CM, Wang D, van Bever D (2013) Consulting on the cusp of disruption. Harvard Bus Rev 91(10):106–114

Czerniawska F (2005) Will consulting go online. In: Greiner LE, Bennigson LA, Poulfelt F (eds) The contemporary consultant: handbook of management consulting: insights from world experts. Thomson South-Western, pp 329–343

Davison R, Fuller M, Hardin A (2003) E-consulting in virtual negotiations. Group Decis Negot 12:517–535

Deelmann T (2009) Internetberatung - Einige Überlegungen zu Möglichkeiten einer sinnhaften Vollautomation von Beratungsleistungen. In: Fischer S (ed) Informatik 2009. Im Focus das Leben-Beiträge der 39. Jahrestagung der Gesellschaft für Informatik e.V. (GI), Bonn, pp 3745–3759

Deelmann T (2015) Organisation der Managementberatung im Wandel. Organisationsentwicklung (ZOE) 34(1):69–71

Evans D, Volery T (2001) Online business development services for entrepreneurs: an exploratory study. Entrepreneurship Reg Dev 13:333–350

Fettke P (2006) State-of-the-art des State-of-the-art. Wirtschaftsinformatik 48(4):257–266

Fink D (2002) Building the Professional Services E-practice. In: Burgess S (ed) Managing information technology in small business: challenges and solutions, pp 246–260

Frank U (2007) Ein Vorschlag zur Konfiguration von Forschungsmethoden in der Wirtschaftsinformatik. In: Lehner F (ed) Wissenschaftstheoretische Fundierung und wissenschaftliche Orientierung der Wirtschaftsinformatik. GITO mbH Verlag, pp 155–184

Fulantelli G, Allegra M (2003) Small company attitude towards ICT based solutions: some key-elements to improve it. J Educ Technol Soc 6:45–49

Fulantelli G, Chiazzese G, Allegra M (2001) Distance training as part of a distance consulting solution. In: Proceedings of ED-MEDIA 2001 world conference on educational multimedia, hypermedia & telecommunications. Tampere, Finland, 25–30 June 2001, pp 527-532

Füßl A, Füßl FF, Nissen V, Streitferdt D (2017) A reasoning based knowledge model for business process analysis. In this volume

Greff T, Werth D (2015) Auf dem Weg zur digitalen Unternehmensberatung. IM+ io - Magazin für Innovation, Organisation und Management. IMC, Saarbücken, pp 30–34

Gregor S, Jones D (2007) The anatomy of a design theory. J Assoc Inf Syst 8:312–335

Hevner AR, March ST, Park J, Ram S (2004) Design science in information systems research. MIS Q 28(1):75–105

Hoven G, Steffens A, Deelmann T (2012) Prototypischer Versuch einer automatisierten Beratung. In: Deelmann T, Petmecky A (eds) Schriften zur Unternehmensberatung, Siegburg, Dusseldorf, pp 1–22
Johann D, Greff T, Werth D (2016) On the effect of digital frontstores on transforming business models. In: Shishkov B (ed) Proceedings of the 6th international symposium on business modeling and software design. Rhodes, pp 64–72
Katz JA (1998) Distance consulting: potentials and pitfalls in using the internet to deliver business development services to SMEs. Report to the Donor Committee on Small Enterprise Development, Saint Louis University
König S (2009) Ein Wiki-basiertes Vorgehensmodell für Business Intelligence Projekte. In: Baars H, Rieger B (eds) Perspektiven der betrieblichen Management-und Entscheidungs-unterstützung, pp 34–51
Kordes T (1992) Expertensystemgestützte Beratung von Organisationen. In: Wagner H, Reineke R (eds) Beratung von Organisationen. Gabler Verlag, Wiesbaden, pp 157–191
Korytko MO (2011) Whether management consulting can be successfully conducted online? Dissertation, University of East Anglia
Lindhorst A, Suhl L, Nastansky L (2004) Konzept und prototypische Implementierung für die webbasierte, kundenindividuelle Konfiguration von Beratungsprojekten. Paderborn University, Diploma
Martensen M (2014) Einsatz von Social Software durch Unternehmensberater: Akzeptanz, Präferenzen, Nutzungsarten. Springer, Wiesbaden
Najda L (2001) Informations- und Kommunikationstechnologie in der Unternehmensberatung: Möglichkeiten, Wirkungen und Gestaltung des Einsatzes. Dissertation, University of Hohenheim
Neuert UW (1990) Computergestützte Unternehmensberatung; Möglichkeiten und Grenzen der Computerunterstützung unter besonderer Berücksichtigung der Strategieberatung. Dissertation, Universität Marburg
Nissen V (2017) Digital transformation of the consulting industry—introduction and overview. In this volume
Nissen V, Kuhl J, Kraeft H, Seifert H, Reiter J, Eidmann J (2017a) ProMAT – A Project Management Assessment Tool for Virtual Consulting. In this volume
Nissen V, Seifert M (2008) Das Consulting C – Grundzüge eines Prozessreferenzmodells für IV-Beratungsunternehmen. In: Bichler M, Hess T, Krcmar H Lechner U, Matthes F, Picot A, Speitkamp B, Wolf P (eds) Multikonferenz Wirtschaftsinformatik, Proceedings of REFMOD 2008. GITO, Berlin, pp 1661–1674
Nissen V, Seifert H (2015) Virtualization of consulting—benefits, risks and a suggested decision process. In: Pavlou P, Saunders C (eds) Proceedings of AMCIS 2015, Puerto Rico, vol 2, pp 1380–1391
Nissen V, Seifert H (2016) Virtualisierung in der Unternehmensberatung. Eine Studie im deutschen Beratungsmarkt. BDU, Bonn
Nissen V, Seifert H (2017a) Digital transformation in business consulting—status quo in Germany. In this volume
Nissen V, Seifert H (2017b) Ermittlung des Virtualisierungspotenzials von Beratungsleistungen im Consulting. In: Leimeister JM, Brenner W (eds) Proceedings of 13rd International Conference on Wirtschaftsinformatik, WI2017, St. Gallen, pp 1348–1362
Nissen V, Seifert H, Ackert MN (2017b) A process model for the virtualization of consulting services. In this volume
Nissen V, Seifert H, Blumenstein M (2015) Virtualisierung von Beratungsleistungen: Qualitätsanforderungen, Chancen und Risiken der digitalen Transformation in der Unternehmensberatung aus der Klientenperspektive. In: Deelmann T, Ockel DM (eds) Handbuch der Unternehmensberatung, 25th edn. Erich Schmidt Verlag, Berlin
Nissen V, Seifert H, Blumenstein M (2017c) A method to support the selection of technologies for the virtualization of consulting services. In this volume

Nowak S (2015) Karibik ohne Strand und Sonne – Wie digitale Beratung Projekte in außergewöhnlichen Regionen ermöglicht. IM+ io - Magazin für Innovation, Organisation und Management. IMC, Saarbücken, pp 74–79

Österle H, Winter R, Brenner W (eds) (2010) Gestaltungsorientierte Wirtschaftsinformatik; Ein Plädoyer für Rigor und Relevanz. Infowerk, Nuremberg

Overby E (2008) Process virtualization theory and the impact of information technology. Organ Sci 19(2):277–291

Overby E (2012) Migrating processes from physical to virtual environments: process virtualization theory. In: Dwivedi YK, Wade MR, Schneberger SL (eds) Information systems theory. Explaining and predicting our digital society. Springer, New York, pp 107–124

Overby E, Slaughter SA, Konsynski B (2010) Research commentary—the design, use, and consequences of virtual processes. Inf Syst Res 21:700–710

Peffers K, Tuunanen T, Rothenberger MA, Chatterjee S (2007) A design science research methodology for information systems research. J Manage Inf Syst 24(3):45–77

Richter A, Kneifel D, Ott F (2009) Fallstudie: Social Networking bei Accenture. Wirtschaftsinformatik & Management 1:78–81

Robinson M (ed) (2013) Consulting firm of the future. Source Information Services Ltd.

Schulze H, Papirny P, Spiller A, Zühlsdorf A, Mellin M, Staack T (2006) Verbindung von agrarökonomischer Forschung und Beratung durch neue Formen des E-consulting: Aufbau eines internetgestützten Benchmarkingsystems für landwirtschaftliche Direktvermarkter. GIL Jahrestagung, pp 265–268

Schumann JH, Wünderlich NV, Wangenheim F (2012) Technology mediation in service delivery: a new typology and an agenda for managers and academics. Technovation 32:133–143

Schuster K (2005) E-consulting; Chancen und Risiken. Dissertation, University of Mannheim

Sinz EJ (2010) Konstruktionsforschung in der Wirtschaftsinformatik: Was sind die Erkenntnisziele gestaltungsorientierter Wirtschaftsinformatik-Forschung? In: Österle H, Winter R, Brenner W (eds) Gestaltungsorientierte Wirtschaftsinformatik. Ein Plädoyer für Rigor und Relevanz. Infowerk, Nuremberg, pp 27–33

Steir R (2007) The on-demand virtual advisory team: a new consulting paradigm? Glob Bus Organ Excellence 26:37–46

Strehlau R, Sieper M (2009) E-consulting 2.0: der Einsatz von Web 2.0 im Beratungsgeschäft. Zeitschrift der Unternehmensberatung 4(2):57–61

Türk B (2004) E-consulting: Der Einsatz webbasierter Technologien in der Unternehmensberatung - eine empirische Untersuchung aus Sicht von Klienten- und Beratungsunternehmen. Dissertation, University of Leipzig

vom Brocke J, Simons A, Niehaves B, Riemer K, Plattfaut R, Cleven A (2009) Reconstructing the giant: on the importance of rigour in documenting the literature search process. In: Proceedings of European Conference on Information Systems, ECIS 2009, Verona, pp 2206–2217

Webster J, Watson R (2002) Analyzing the Past to prepare for the future: writing a literature review. MIS Q 26(2):13–23

Werth D, Greff T (2016) Digitale Beratung, ein Modell für den Mittelstand. IM+ io - Magazin für Innovation, Organisation und Management. IMC, Saarbücken, pp 82–87

Werth D, Greff T, Scheer AW (2016a) Consulting 4.0 - Die Digitalisierung der Unternehmensberatung. HMD Praxis der Wirtschaftsinformatik 53(1):55–70

Werth D, Zimmermann P, Greff T (2016b) Self-service consulting: conceiving customer-operated digital IT consulting services. In: Proceedings of AMCIS 2016 conference paper, San Diego

Wurdack A (2001) E-consulting - Entwicklung eines Rahmenkonzeptes: Aufbau und Darstellung einer E-consulting-Lösung im Beratungsunternehmen der Zukunft. Dissertation, University Mannheim

Zeißler G, Remus U, Thome R (2003) Internetbasierte E-Business-Strategieberatung. FORWIN-Bericht, Bayerischer Forschungsverband Wirtschaftsinformatik

Author Biographies

Henry Seifert is a graduate engineer for media technology and since 2011 working as a management consultant. His main focus is on the automotive industry and artificial intelligence, analytics, process optimization and requirements management. He works in projects in the area of sales and after sales processes as well as professional learning. As doctoral candidate at the Group for Information Systems Engineering in Services at Technische Universität Ilmenau, he examines the digital transformation in the consulting industry. The goal of his dissertation is to demonstrate the opportunities and limitations of virtualization, as well as the design of artifacts that enable the realization of virtual consulting services.

Volker Nissen Volker Nissen holds the Chair of Information Systems Engineering in Services at Technische Universität Ilmenau, Germany, since 2005. Prior to this, he pursued a consulting career, including positions as manager at IDS Scheer AG, director at DHC GmbH, and CEO of NISSCON Ltd., Germany. In 1994 he received a Ph.D. degree in Economic Sciences with distinction from the University of Goettingen, Germany. His current research interests include the digital transformation of the consulting industry, the management of IT-agility, metaheuristic optimization, and process acceptance research. He is author and editor of 19 books and some 200 other publications, including papers in Business & Information Systems Engineering, Information Systems Frontiers, IEEE Transactions on EC, IEEE Transactions on NN, and Annals of OR.

Does Digitization Matter?
Reflections on a Possible Transformation
of the Consulting Business

Thomas Deelmann

Abstract Consulting firms have the ambition to help their clients in the area of digitization. Digitization might affect the consulting industry, too. This paper reviews different long-term views and evaluates current developments of the industry in order to work towards an answer to the question: Does digitization matter and will it transform the consulting business? The paper comes to the conclusion that consulting firms will at least be impacted with respect to their client engagements and internal measures for efficiency increase. Especially for those consulting firms, which offer large-scale professional services, there will be an impact on their core business, too. Many of them have the size to be attractive for embedded automation efforts.

1 Introduction

1.1 Motivation

Consulting is an economic and social success model as three observations may show: (i) Consultants[1] are preferred employers for students, young and experienced professionals alike. (ii) Considering the relatively small total workforce, its media presence and influence seems quite large. (iii) Over the last decades the overall market has grown in both economically good and bad times. Especially the last aspect refers to the industry's flexibility to adapt to new situations emerging in the business area and the public sector, e.g. internationalization, marketing, strategic planning, change management, enterprise resource planning (Krizanits 2015).

---

[1]This paper uses the terms "consultant" and "consulting firm" synonymously. They both shall refer to an entity, which offers consulting services. This can be a freelance consultant or a multi-national company with several thousand employees. However, if the paper focuses on an individual, this person will be the addressed accordingly e.g. as an "individual consultant".

T. Deelmann (✉)
FHöV NRW, Cologne, Germany
e-mail: thomas.deelmann@fhoev.nrw.de

© Springer International Publishing AG 2018
V. Nissen (ed.), *Digital Transformation of the Consulting Industry*,
Progress in IS, https://doi.org/10.1007/978-3-319-70491-3_3

A current trend topic for (but not limited to) the consulting industry is digitization (e.g. Brynjolfsson and McAfee 2012, 2014).

Consultants use the insecurity of client companies on how to deal with the omnipresent *digitization*, which comes under the labels of Industrial Internet, Industry 4.0, Internet of Things, New Work, Digital Natives etc., to generate new business and a steady revenue flow. For example, in the timespan of one morning only, the author received several newsletters with success stories from consultants (e.g. Boston Consulting Group, McKinsey, Experton, Detecon) on how they had helped clients to digitize.

Additionally, consultants are using latest digital technology to streamline their internal operations and become more efficient. High resolution video conferencing, fast knowledge databases working with semantic technology and business intelligence technology are only three areas of application.

As stated above, consultants are excellent advisors to their clients on how to cope with digitization in order not to become out-dated and be forced to exit their market. Internally, they are much more reluctant. In a recent Delphi study conducted by the author, consultants refuse the statement that in a couple of years a significant amount of their business activities will be automated (Deelmann 2015). In contrast to this introspection, there are several studies stating that basically all business areas will undergo a process of digitization and automation, e.g. research results by the German Federal Employment Agency (Bundesagentur für Arbeit, BA) and the Institute for Employment Research (Institut für Arbeitsmarkt- und Berufsforschung, IAB), prominently featured by the German broadcasting network ARD (Dengler and Matthes 2015; ARD 2017).

1.2 Intention of This Paper and Research Question

Taking the given description into account, the goal of this paper is to examine what kind of impact digitization has to the consulting business. It aims to give an outlook on the overall industry development and recommendations for both consulting companies and individual consultants.

1.3 Outline

After this introductory first section, the paper is organized in three main sections. In the second section, several long-term developments on the industry will be briefly sketched out. This seems helpful to put the current digitization debate in place within an overall development path of the industry. Three aspects seem promising to characterize the consulting industry from a macro perspective:

- Firstly, the framing conditions of the consultant's clients. During the last decades, the economic environment of client companies was full of challenges and opportunities—whereas the spirit in the consulting industry seems to be constantly excellent.
- Secondly, the overall market development. The growth rate of the consulting market can be viewed stand-alone (BDU 2016) or in relation to the overall economic growth rate of an economy. Interestingly enough, the perception of consultants and consulting services was not always positive. Since their first appearance on the professional services market, reports about consultants and their services are full of so called low lights (e.g. N.N. 1956, 1962). Since the 1960s, the perception oscillated constantly between good and bad. Today the overall reputation of consultants can be described best as dichotomous. However, these changes do not seem to have a significant impact on the market.
- And thirdly, the type of consulting services. Consulting services are being offered in a more classical or in a broader, pragmatic sense and should therefore be distinguished sufficiently for making statements about the industry.

Section three focuses on current topics of the industry that might have the power to challenge the existence of single firms and the actual predominant people-oriented business model. Again, three developments are singled out to characterize the actual state of the consulting industry:

- The first major issue is the (perceived) consolidation of the industry. Especially the *Big Four* professional services firms with their traditional portfolio of auditing, tax and financial advisory strengthen their management consulting as well as IT consulting capabilities and are acquiring several *Hidden Champions*. For many consulting firms, they became an increasingly stronger competitor: In 2011 they were not considered as a strong competitor; this changed during the years to 2015—now they are seen as a serious competition (Lünendonk 2015). The field of digital consulting services is especially attractive for the *Big Four*.
- A kind of role reversal between consultants and clients is the second development. On the one hand, client employees become more and more familiar with typical consulting techniques and methods: Either they have spent some time working as a consultant or the techniques are taught at universities and business schools and are common knowledge. Clients are now able to perform tasks which were a core competency of consultants just a couple of years ago. On the other hand, clients followed their consultant's advice and downsized their administrative workforce. However, they have often not followed the recommendation to implement sufficient digitization initiatives to compensate the shorter workforce. Now they are keeping numbers of consultants busy with tasks which were performed by own employees before the downsizing (Deelmann 2015).
- The third topic, digitization in the consulting industry seems to be the prevailing issue today. As outlined above, digitization is (i) the trending topic in the client-consultant-relationship, (ii) a driver for consulting firms themselves to become more efficient, and (iii) a real threat for individual business models of

consulting firms in case of not only digitization but automation of consulting business processes (Nissen and Seifert 2016a, b; Chui et al. 2016; Christensen et al. 2013).

The fourth section of the paper uses a combination of the sections two and three in order to make predictions on how the consulting business will develop and transform over the next years: How will the size of the market change, how will the consulting workforce increase or decrease, how should consulting firms act in order to cope with e.g. digitization, and how can an individual consultant cope with the anticipated developments.

A summary, a conclusion and an outlook on future research questions close the paper. The developments and predictions are meant to have a certain global applicability. However, for the sake of a consistent argument, the data and used examples are taken from the area of German speaking countries.

1.4 Consulting Characteristics

Several definitions of the term consulting give a very general and a quite heterogeneous interpretation of the institutional and functional perspective of consulting (e.g. Sangüesa Sanchez 2003; FEACO 2004; Smith and Smith 2003; Kieser 2002). To be sufficiently flexible towards various roles of consultants in the foretime as well as those in the future, the following definition of organizational consulting is suggested:[2]

Organizational consulting is a (1) professional, (2) contractually appointed (3) service and transformation process of an (4) intervening attendance by a (5) consulting firm system for the (6) analysis, description, and solution of a (7) problem of the client system—under the tenor of a (8) work on decision premises—with the goal of (9) transformation.

This definition builds on nine elements. For the purpose of this paper, two of them should be explained in more detail:

(4) *Intervening attendance*: This is an open genus with respect to the several types of consulting, containing different kinds of intervention: expertise-oriented consulting, expert-oriented consulting, process-oriented consulting, and systemic consulting. The term "attendance" distinguishes from other forms of cooperation (e.g. co-management) or replacing work (e.g. interim management).

(8) *Work on decision premises*: The client is the only one who can decide for the client organization within a consultant-client-relationship. The act of consulting only supports the realization, evaluation, and (if necessary) change of decision premises, decided on in the past. This situation points out the relevant difference between consulting firms and the client: The decision is exclusively made by the client. This is also true if the consultant influences the client in a more or less strong way.

---

[2]This section is a shortened version of (Deelmann et al. 2006).

2 Review of Long-Term Developments

2.1 Selected Framing Conditions

Looking back several decades and taking a more diagnostic approach towards the consulting industry, one can identify a change in the leading paradigm and in the dominating topics for the business environment every couple of years (this section bases on: Krizanits 2015). These changes impacted the consulting industry and created mostly growth opportunities. Therefore, the review in this section will be matched with market data (cf. Sect. 2.2) and will be later on used for creating long-term scenarios and predictions (cf. Sect. 4).

- Until the *mid of the 1960s* the major issue for most businesses was about the *organization of the core production and sales functions*. Mass production and mass consumption were the outcomes. In the German speaking countries, business consultants were mainly unknown until this time. Specific consulting demand was met e.g. by the RKW (founded in the 1920s as "Reichskuratorium für Wirtschaftlichkeit in Industrie und Handwerk"). Since the end of the 1950s resp. in the 1960s, the first American consulting firms opened European branches and offices.
- The framing conditions changed at the *end of the 1960s and in the 1970s*. The Club of Rome's powerful report *The Limits of Growth* articulated criticism towards the consumer society. The markets became saturated and sellers markets changed to buyers markets. The crisis around the Limits of Growth became a good entry point for consultants. They could help their clients with new tools and concepts to defeat this crisis. With e.g. strategy consulting, corporate planning and marketing, the consultants became accepted in Europe.
- During the next phase, roughly the *1980s*, many companies faced a situation where (international) competition significantly increased. The prevailing paradigm became the *internal optimization*. For the consulting industry, this became a boom period with respect to their capabilities to sell new concepts and to publish new management literature. The client's requests covered both more classical topics and approaches (e.g. introducing cost accounting) and new services (e.g. development of information systems, benchmarking).
- The *1990s* saw the end of the Cold War and the break-up of the two dominating political blocs. This gave way for approaching new geographical rooms and new markets. Companies used this situation, the continued rise of the information technology and the deregulated communications markets for new growth, e.g. in the new economy and via the globalization trend. In this decade, especially IT consulting boomed thanks to the chances and options by the roll-out of enterprise resource planning software (e.g. SAP, Oracle), the so called dot.com boom and the Year-2000-Problem.
- During the *first years of the 21st century* companies had to cope with the effects of globalization and were *shaping globalization* at the same time. The BRIC countries were the carriers of hope for a new round of *economic growth* and jobs

Major narratives of the (Western German) economy ...
... and selected consulting topics and examples:

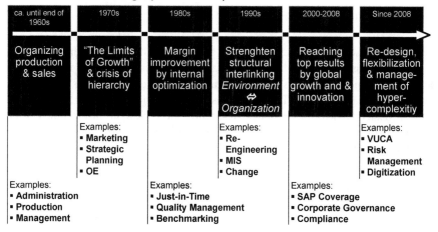

Fig. 1 Major narratives for clients and selected consulting topics

were transferred to low cost countries. On the one hand, consulting firms profited from a boom of new organizational concepts. On the other hand, they faced challenges like new inhouse consulting expertise and a loss in reputation (e.g. after the cases of Enron and SwissAir) which led to a shake-up of the consulting industry.

- *Since* the beginning of the financial and economic crisis in *2008* companies are in need to *re-dimension and re-design* themselves. The core premise of many (Western) countries, the assumption of ever increasing growth seems to be no more valid. For consulting firms, the crisis initially meant again a setback. However, especially the digitization of everything, the Internet of Things and the defense of subsequently anticipated cyber-attacks are new growth topics.

Figure 1 gives an overview of the discussed paradigms and responses by consulting firms.

2.2 Overall Market Development

After the more qualitative description of the industry's framing conditions, an additional view and assessment on the overall market development will be given in the following section. This might be helpful to fully understand the development of the last decades and to lay a foundation for an outlook.

For the German consulting market, the Association of German Business Consultants (BDU e.V.—a German consulting industry group) publishes regularly

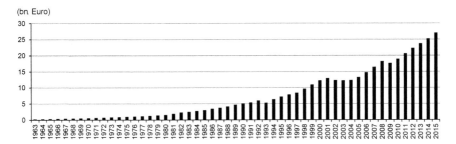

Fig. 2 Consulting market volume in Germany, 1963–2015 (Deelmann 2016a and literature cited there; BDU 1993, 2017; additional approximations and calculations by the author)

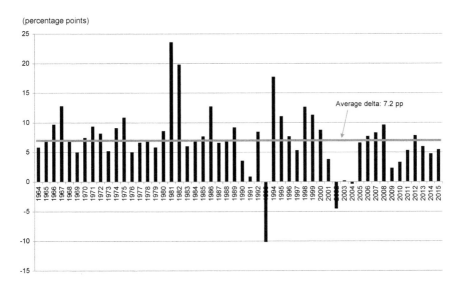

Fig. 3 Delta between the change of the German consulting market volume (vs PY, in %) versus the change of the German GDP (vs PY, in %) in percentage points, 1964–2015 (Deelmann 2016a and literature cited there; BDU 1993, 2017; additional approximations and calculations by the author)

market data, e.g. its volume (e.g. BDU 2016). With some approximations and calculations for single missing years it is possible to calculate the market volume back until 1963 (see Fig. 2).

The increase of the market volume seems impressive. However, this period covers the "Wirtschaftswunder" as well as the German Unity—which both certainly had *special effects* on the consulting industry. Therefore, it seems more appropriate to calculate relative changes in the market (actual volume versus the previous year's volume); step (1). The results can be compared with the overall economic development in Germany, measured by the change of the Gross Domestic Product

(GDP); step (2). Fig. 3 shows the delta between the relative change of the consulting market and the relative change of the GDP for the years 1964–2015. For example: In 2015 the German consulting market saw an increase of 7.14% versus 2014; the GDP increased by 1.66% versus 2014; the delta between the development of the consulting market and the development of the GDP is 5.48% points.

In most years, the development of the consulting market outperformed the development of the GDP. For the last 52 years, the average delta was 7.2% points. This underlines not only the absolute growth as shown above, but points out the relative strength of the consulting industry in Germany, too.

Due to the steady outperformance regardless of the existing (positive as well as negative) circumstances, it seems fair to presume a future growth of the consulting market—also in times of an increased digitization of the industry (cf. Sect. 4 for an outlook).

2.3 Emergence of Two Kinds of Consulting Services

Based on this rapid development of the consulting industry (in Germany alone there are more than 110,000 consultants in 2015—up from 21,000 in 1985 and 68,000 in 2005) and in order to gain an understanding about the possibilities and limitations of a digitization and automation of this *people business* one has to evaluate, what kind of consulting services are being offered.

There are several ways to divide the market into segments. One popular method is to split along the fields of consulting like strategy, HR or IT (e.g. BDU 2016; FEACO 2004). Another common split goes along the forms of consulting like expertise-driven consulting, expert-oriented consulting, process-oriented consulting, and systemic consulting (Walger 1995). In this paper, an additional way is suggested: *Consulting in a narrower sense* versus *Consulting in a broader sense*.

Practical experience shows that in most cases under the label of *Consulting* all kinds of support services are summarized, which are delivered by consultants to their clients. This is a pragmatic and oversimplifying view.

Following the self-presentations of several consultants, these support services consist in giving advice, in helping to solve a problem, in supporting a transformation journey etc. Popular as well as research oriented literature comes up with definitions, focusing on these aspects (cf. for example Sect. 1.4). These activities can be interpreted as the classical kind of consulting. They can be referred to by *Consulting in a narrower sense*.

However, experience shows that not all services being offered and requested under the label of *Consulting* can cope with the self-set resp. self-defined ambitions. Or to make a point: often one cannot be sure that the contents match the label.

Mostly the consultants are pragmatically working on their client's problems— but very often not with the above mentioned intention to work only on decision premises and in form of an intervening attendance. On the contrary, often there are other forms of co-operation like co-management, interim management or the

Kind of consulting service ("Label")	Consulting in a narrower sense	Consulting in a broader sense
Examples ("Content")	• Giving advice • Helping to solve a problem • Supporting a transformation journey	• Making decisions for the client organization • Acting as the responsible project manager • Bridging resource gaps for the client
Selected characteristics	• Work on decision premises • Work in form of intervening attendance	• Support services which are delivered by the consultant to the client • Does not match the characteristics of "Consulting in a narrower sense"

Fig. 4 Two kinds of consulting services

so-called body leasing. With body leasing, consultants take over tasks of the client's line functions. Following the above introduced differentiation of *Consulting in a narrower sense*, consulting services shall be called *Consulting in a broader sense* in cases that they are helpful for the clients but do not fit into the type of *Consulting in a narrower sense*. Figure 4 contrasts the two described kinds of consulting services.

While the overall consulting market is quite well defined and measured (cf. above) an empirical separation of *Consulting in a narrower sense* and *Consulting in a broader sense* seems to be difficult. This can root in at least two causes.

Firstly, a consultant typically will not admit that he sells consulting-like activities under the label of *Consulting in a narrower sense*. This damages the reputation. Also the remuneration typically differs: Real consulting services are priced higher than other professional services like body leasing.

Secondly, customers typically will not confess that they are buying consultants for relatively high fees when they could save money via purchasing body leasing services for lower fees.

Both sides of the market have little intentions to speak openly over a differentiation of the two types of consulting. However, a dilution of the core consulting market can be assumed: Strategy consultants are said to have spent 30 years ago approximately 60–70% of their time with *Strategy Consulting* and 30–40% with other consulting services. Over time, the share of *Strategy Consulting* went down to approximately 20% (statement by Tom Rodenhauser (of the consulting research and advisory firm Kennedy Research; since 2015 part of ALM) cited in Christensen et al. 2013). This shift can be seen as symptomatically for the total market.

For the time being it should be assumed that *Consulting in a broader sense* is not just an insignificant appearance but covers a significant share of the market.

The differentiation between two kinds of consulting services will be helpful to predict some effects of digitization on the consulting business itself (see Sect. 4).

3 Selected Recent Developments and Their Relation to the Current Digitization Debate in Consulting

3.1 Industry Consolidation

Sometimes the consulting industry is described as mature. Often heard statements— either as support for the maturity thesis or standalone—concern the increasing industry consolidation and the huge number of acquisitions in the industry (e.g. Christensen 2017; BDU 2014; Cardea 2016; Bartsch 2014). However, looking at the numbers, the subjective impression seems to be stronger pronounced than a measurable approach.

In 2002, the ten largest management consulting firms in Germany had a market share of 34.2% (i.e. fields of strategy consulting plus organization & process consulting). Their share declined steadily to 23.8% in 2012 (the last year for which adequate data is available) as Table 1 shows.

A declining market share of the industry's largest players does not seem to support claims of industry consolidation.

Table 1 Market share for the top 10 consulting firms in Germany 2002–2012 (for the market share cf. Deelmann 2016a; based on data provided by Lünendonk 2003–2013; BDU 2002–2013)

	Market volume (in bn Euro)			Top 10 consulting firms	
Year	Strategy	Organization & processes	Sum	Revenue (in bn Euro)	Market share (%)
2002	2.93	4.33	7.26	2.48	34.2
2003	2.93	4.31	7.24	2.45	33.8
2004	3.02	4.38	7.40	2.42	32.7
2005	4.00	4.50	8.50	2.43	28.6
2006	4.48	4.95	9.43	2.69	28.5
2007	3.99	7.22	11.21	2.94	26.2
2008	4.31	8.08	12.39	3.11	25.1
2009	4.17	7.57	11.74	2.88	24.5
2010	4.52	8.16	12.68	2.94	23.2
2011	4.94	8.56	13.50	3.28	24.3
2012	5.46	9.77	15.23	3.62	23.8

Number of deals

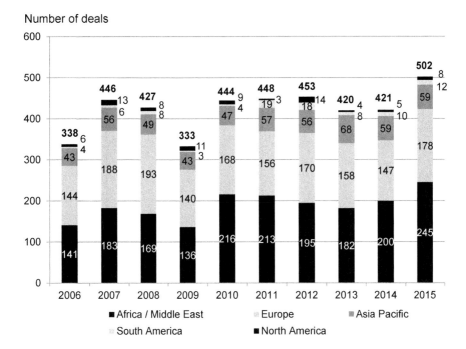

Fig. 5 Number of management consulting M&A deals worldwide, 2006–2015 (Equiteq 2016)

On a global scale, the number of mergers & acquisitions in the management consulting sector reached a high in 2015 with 502 deals. This significantly tops the pre-crisis number of 446 in 2007. The increase is mainly driven by deals in North America while Europe is catching up but still lies below the pre-crisis level (see Fig. 5).

Looking to selected sub-sectors of Management Consulting (Table 2), one can identify a peak for strategy consulting in 2015 and a strong increase for transformation & change management consulting as well as for compliance, regulation, governance consulting. This might be driven by a boom in these areas after the crisis.

Press coverage is often with large mergers & acquisitions. However, the largest number of the deals is small in size: 35.8% of all deals have a transaction volume <5 million US-Dollar and 70.7% are below 70 million US-Dollars. In Europe, most of the deals in 2015 took place in the UK (43%) and France (14%) with Germany coming third (8%); (Equiteq 2016. Please note: the latter figures are for all kinds of mergers & acquisitions in the consulting sector, not only management consulting.).

To summarize this, the number of mergers & acquisitions reached (on a worldwide level) again the pre-crisis level, when most of them took place in North America. However, they tend to be small in size and often take place in consulting niches.

Table 2 Number of M&A deals in selected sub-sectors of management consulting (Equiteq 2016; own calculations)

Sub-sectors	Years						
	2010	2011	2012	2013	2014	2015	Total
Strategy consulting	40	49	39	42	47	58	275
Operations consulting	39	57	55	57	54	52	314
Transformation & change management	29	39	32	38	55	60	253
Financial advisory	106	97	119	90	101	109	622
Compliance, regulation, governance	30	29	34	33	40	42	208
Others	200	177	174	160	124	181	1016
Total	444	448	453	420	421	502	2688

With respect to the overall development, the "market remains steady—with an overall balance of consolidation and fragmentation" (Equiteq 2016) and does not show significant signs of consolidation.

3.2 Role Reversal

Role reversal in short means that consultants do classical client's work and clients possess and apply the classical consultant's competencies.

Clients Possess and Apply the Classical Consulting Competencies: The basis for the role reversal can be found by the consulting firms themselves. Based on the "up or out" principle and with the respect to the personal plans of the individual consultants many former individual consultants are actually employees in client companies. They are now applying their consulting knowledge and competencies in their day-to-day business. These knowledge ranges from knowledge about industries and competitors over the usage of analytical methods and procedures to the point of creating optically faultless presentations, e.g. with PowerPoint charts.

The so called asymmetry of knowledge between service provider and customer is diminishing—and the traditional consulting sales pitch vanishes for wide parts of consulting engagements. However, consultants have often a knowledge advance with new and very specialized topics like digitization.

Consultants Do Classical Client's Work: In parallel it can be observed that over the last years in many client organizations personnel reductions took place. This would be not worth mentioning if together with the personnel reduction a streamlining of tasks and processes had taken place, too. Unfortunately this was often not the case. Client companies therefore face the situation that they do not have enough staff to fill all the line positions needed to execute the required regularly tasks. In order to fill this gap, support from third parties is needed—and these third parties are often consultants.

The thesis of a role reversal is based on these two observations. It got in principle high approval rates in a Delphi study with consultants, clients and market observers (Deelmann 2015).

Especially the second part of the role reversal can be seen as one attempt to explain the enormous increase in consulting market volume and manpower (cf. Sect. 2.2).

3.3 Digitization

Perhaps the most attention-grabbing current development is digitization. Often, digitization is seen uniformly. However, at least three different views should be taken into account: Digitization as a consulting topic, digitization for an increase in internal efficiency, digitization as a first step towards an automation of consulting services. The consulting topic and the measure for efficiency improvements can be handled rather short; the idea of automation the *people business* requires some more coverage.

Firstly, Digitization as a Consulting Topic: Market observers, clients and consultants see the field of digitization on top of the agenda. For example: The business paper Wirtschaftswoche in 2016 dedicated a special price section for digitization within its *Best of Consulting* award for the first time (Wirtschaftswoche 2016), the research company Lünendonk covers Consulting 4.0 and the consultant's use of data in a special report (Lünendonk 2016), the market researcher ALM featured in the "State of the industry 2017 Webinar" digitization (ALM 2017), and the Association of German Business Consultants (BDU) identifies digitization as the driver of the overall market growth (BDU 2016).

Clients jump on the bandwagon trying to digitize and transform their businesses and look towards the consultants for help and guidance. The consultants respond to this happily, as a few examples might show: Accenture has actually grouped the market facing operations in five units; one is called *AccentureDigital* (Accenture 2017). McKinsey sees digital disruption as one of seven global themes and has set-up *Digital/McKinsey* (McKinsey 2017) and even for the IT consulting start-up Mindeight is digital transformation in the midst of their offering portfolio (Mindeight 2017).

Secondly, Digitization to Increase Internal Efficiency: Web-conferences, knowledge management systems and techniques for data analytics are widely established tools for improving efficiency. Additionally, consultants have the option to digitize selected functions like the sales process, the gathering of intelligence and analytical insight, and the sourcing and combination of resources. With the front-line processes help is offered e.g. through the *eConsulting Store* (AWSi 2017) or digital market places *ConsultingSearcher* (Cardea 2017) and *Fiverr* (2017). With respect to the gathering of analytical insight *Wikistrat* seems to be a fresh example on how to collaborate in new ways (Wikistrat 2017). A novel way of setting up consulting projects and combining team members can be seen for example at *Comatch* (2017) or *Eden McCallum* (2017).

Thirdly, Digitization as a First Step Towards a Possible Automation of Consulting Services: It has to be investigated if and how consulting activities could be digitized (i.e. electronically performed and delivered with the help of Internet technologies; Nissen and Seifert 2017) and automated (i.e. the transfer of tasks previously performed by humans onto artificial systems). Such automation would inevitably lead towards a significant transformation of the traditional consulting business model—which is often called a *people business*. In order to realize this, digitization has to exceed the above mentioned support for more efficient processes. It has to substitute classical core processes with automated solutions.

Three lines of thought could help to assess the overall prospects of automation as well as where to begin and how to find a good starting point.

- The above conducted differentiation between *Consulting in a narrower sense* and *Consulting in a broader sense* (cf. Sect. 2.3) can be used to make estimations on the automation potential of these two service types. *Consulting in a broader sense* offers just a more or less valuable and pragmatic support service and should have a relatively huge digitization and automation potential. This assumption is supported by two considerations.

  - There are structural aspects to keep in mind. This type of consulting services is people-intensive and goal of the consulting firm will classically be to increase the so called leverage. Leverage means the relation between partners and *normal* consultants. If the leverage increases, the delegated tasks get easier to manage (with respect to giving instructions, monitoring and controlling). However, the easier the tasks get, the higher should be their digitization and finally their automation potential.
  - Additionally, one can compare *Consulting in a broader sense* with other related professions. Consultants, lawyers, auditors etc. are collectively seen as professional services (firms). Lawyers and auditors have very strict access mechanism to their profession and a very good reputation. In both groups tasks, which were typically performed by junior staff in the past, become more and more automated. For example the extensive research of documents for key words can be performed by IT much faster. As a result, less junior staff will be needed. In parallel, professional services firms have to adapt their fee system if they do not want to lose the revenues previously generated by the juniors.

  With this background it is hard to understand why large parts of *Consulting in a broader sense* could not also be automated. *Consulting in a narrower sense* could simply be a business model with too little starting points or repeated tasks (cf. below) for automation.

- It has already been argued before that there are situations and *aspects which can more easily be automated than others* (Deelmann 2016b; see for an alternative approach and study results Nissen and Seifert 2016a, b). Five perspectives were taken into account:

- With respect to the forms of consulting, the assessment-based consulting seems to have more automation potential than expert-based consulting, organizational development and systemic consulting.
- Looking to the fields of consulting, IT and financial consulting seem to have the most and strategy consulting the least automation potential. HR as well as organizational and process-focused consulting are in the middle.
- Over the three typical phases of a consulting engagement, the analysis phase has the most automation potential, followed by the problem solving and then the implementation phase.
- During consulting engagements different kinds of expertise are often necessary. Fact-based consulting has the highest automation potential, interpretation-based and experience-based consulting have less.
- And last but not least, one can consider the degree of transparency on the consulting issue or demand. An explicitly articulated demand has much better chances for automation than a non-explicitly articulated demand resp. a hidden agenda.

Figure 6 summarizes these thoughts.

- The *concept of embedded automation* (Sawhney 2017) builds on the combination of products and services. Product companies are used to offer value adding services together with their products in order to gain a competitive advantage. However, with service companies the complementary idea is relatively new. Consulting firms have to systematically analyze their services and look for

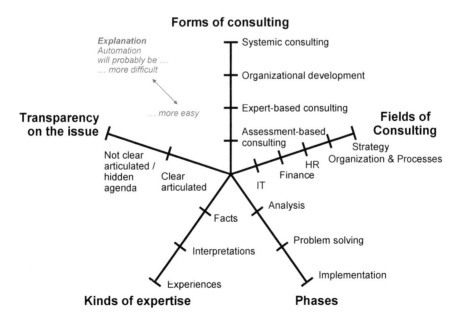

Fig. 6 Perspectives and facets of the automation of consulting services

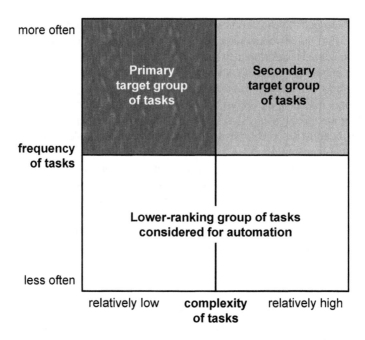

Fig. 7 Frequency and complexity of tasks as guidelines for embedded automation potential

patterns. These patterns often point towards data transformations which could have automation and value added potential. The value added potential makes the service itself more valuable for the client and the embedded automation makes the service provisioning more efficient for the consulting firm.

For example, a consulting firm might realize that it performs increasingly often data analytic tasks during their client engagements. These analytical tasks could be automated as well as the creation of a well looking results report. The good looking and automatically generated report adds value for the client during the overall consulting engagement.

Figure 7 shows the ranking of tasks that could be considered for embedded products resp. embedded automation. Ideal are tasks that have a high frequency and a relatively low complexity: the less complex, the easier the automation. The secondary target group consists of tasks that have a higher complexity than the first group but are quite frequent, too. Embedded automation seems to be feasible due to learning effects and economies of scale. Only if a task is performed frequently, there is a chance that automation makes economically sense. Therefore are the less often performed tasks parts of a lower-ranking group with respect to a consideration for automation—regardless of their complexity.

Wohlgemuth estimates for the Swiss market that in 1980 the share of industrialized consulting services was at approximately 30% and grew to 78% in 2007 (Wohlgemuth 2008; with additional calculations by the author). *Industrialized* means consulting services which are e.g. standardized, have a specified quality level and can performed with a division of labor. Even if this description remains relatively vaguely and *industrialized* is far from *already automated*, this statement can be interpreted as a proxy for a large automation potential.

4 Predictions and Recommendation

4.1 Overview

Before looking at the industry, company and individual level, a very short summary of the reviewed long-term elements plus the selected recent developments and their respective key messages may be helpful. They are the foundations for the predictions and recommendations in this section:

- *Selected Framing Conditions*: The clients went through several paradigm changes and got support by their consultants. Change and uncertainty is the natural habitat of the consulting industry and hence one should not be afraid of digitization.
- *Overall Market Development*: The long-term market development is impressive and shows considerably higher growth rates than the GDP.
- *Emergence of Two Kinds of Consulting*: The combination of *Consulting in a narrower sense* and *Consulting in a broader sense* under one roof (i.e. brand or consulting firm) could become critical due to the significant differences in their respective business model.
- *Consolidation of the Industry*: There are mergers and acquisitions, but they are actually on a *business as usual* level.
- *Role Reversal*: The fact that a consultant performs more often the client's activities and less often the usual consulting tasks might become critical for the classical consulting business model.
- *Digitization*: Digitization will play a role as an engagement topic and for increasing internal efficiency. Especially for *Consulting in a broader sense* there might be a significant potential for embedded automation in its core business. *Consulting in a narrower sense* might just have not the size to start automation activities economically in the near future.

4.2 Industry Level

On a macro level, it seems impressive that the industry was able to grow and outperform the GDP development significantly—regardless of the social and economic circumstances (cf. Sect. 2). Therefore this sub-section abstracts from

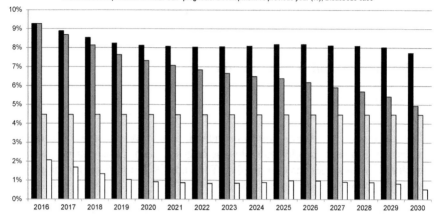

Fig. 8 Four scenarios with yearly growth rates regarding the development of the German consulting market

individual developments (e.g. technology, client's needs) and offers four scenarios for a long-term market development until 2030. They all start with the current consulting market volume and have different basic assumptions and growth models (see Fig. 8 on the following page).

The first and least positive case is built on the assumption that the consulting market will see no real growth and will develop in-line with an economist's GDP prognosis for Germany (Oxford economics 2016). For that the major part of the consulting industry is focused on growth, this development will have significant effects on business models, utilization, reputation, recruiting, promotions etc. and is therefore called *disastrous case*. This development of the yearly growth rates is shown with the white columns in Fig. 8.

The second scenario works with a constant growth rate of 4.5%. This is the compound annual growth rate (CAGR) for the consulting market of the decade from 2000 to 2010 where two crises hit the market significantly. A *pessimistic* observer might come to the conclusion that this decade was not an exception but will become normal and that the industry should prepare for more crises and shorter recovery times to come so that the long-term average growth rate will roughly equal the rate from 2000 to 2010. Therefore the light grey columns reflect this assumption and remain on the same height.

The *base case* builds on the fact that the market development in the past laid 7.2% points above the development of the GDP (cf. Sect. 2.2). Additionally it takes into account that there is a good chance that the outperformance continues but the delta between market growth and GDP development shrinks. The base case calculates with a reduction of the outperformance by 0.2% points per anno

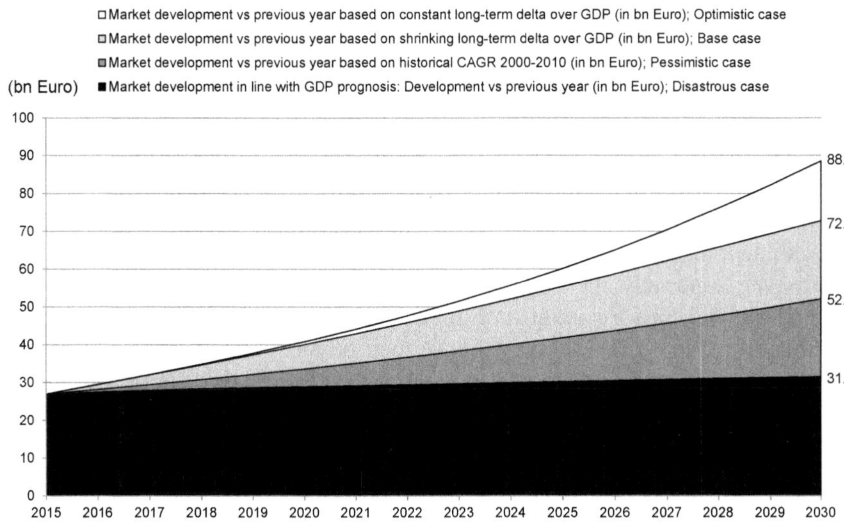

□ Market development vs previous year based on constant long-term delta over GDP (in bn Euro); Optimistic case
□ Market development vs previous year based on shrinking long-term delta over GDP (in bn Euro); Base case
▣ Market development vs previous year based on historical CAGR 2000-2010 (in bn Euro); Pessimistic case
■ Market development in line with GDP prognosis: Development vs previous year (in bn Euro); Disastrous case

(bn Euro)

Fig. 9 Scenarios for the absolute development of the German consulting market

(i.e. 1st year: GDP growth rate in % plus 7.2% points; 2nd year: GDP growth rate in % plus 7.0% points; 3rd year: GDP growth rate in % plus 6.8% points etc.).

The *optimistic case* builds on the assumption that the market development in the last several decades laid 7.2% points higher than the development of the GDP. The prognosis is that this outperformance will last for the next years, too. In Fig. 7 the black columns come close to the 8% line (while the GDP growth rate is expected to be just below 1%) and remain there for the next years—unlike the dark grey columns (base case).

Based on these growth rates it is now possible to model the overall market volume for the years until 2030 (Fig. 9). All four scenarios for the German consulting market start at a volume of 27 bn Euro. The *disastrous case* only moves slightly upward with a CAGR of 0.96% and ends up in 2030 with a market volume of 31.5 bn Euro.

For the *pessimistic case* growth is visible in the chart. A CAGR of 4.47% leads to a market volume of 52.0 bn Euro. And just for playing with the numbers: If the per capita revenue from 2015 is transferred to this market volume (i.e. the positive and negative financial effects resulting from fee developments, utilization rate changes, effects from digitization etc. are balancing themselves), the number of consultants will nearly double from 110,000 to approximately 210,000.

A CAGR of 6.66% is leading the *base case* to a market volume of 72.8 bn Euro in 2030—and a workforce of nearly 300,000 consultants at constant per capita revenues.

The *optimistic case* finally would reach a market volume of 88.6 bn Euro. This reflects a CAGR of 8.17%. If the revenue per consultant does not change, the market will consist of roughly 360,000 consultants in 2030.

4.3   Company Level

For the individual consulting company at least three of the four scenarios seem to be preferable. However, there are some dangerous developments in the market that might bring several consulting firms into trouble.

Digitization and automation are inevitable and will change the industry. At least, the ways of doing work will adjust. For many consulting firms the engagement topic of client digitization will be a source for future revenue streams.

However, especially the companies which perform *Consulting in a broader sense* will be attacked by automation initiatives and providers with a streamlined cost structure. These providers might have their origins in the classical consulting business or are newcomer from related professional services fields or the outside. If not consulting firms trigger changes, the outsiders will identify the sweet spots and enter the market with innovative offerings.

Additionally, the role reversal should get a closer look. Over the last years, recruiting candidates got used to the stories of helping the client's top-management, comfortable travelling and ever-changing projects. If they join a consulting firm based on these stories, these *new hires* might become disappointed very quickly after their start—and this disappointment will spread fast under existing colleagues, potential recruiting candidates and the clients.

Companies should evaluate if they want to offer *Consulting in a broader sense* and act like the large professional service firms with their franchise structure or if they want to stay with the classical advisory role and offer *Consulting in a narrower sense*. This decision heavily impacts the business model. Following both business models simultaneously might work under certain circumstances. However, this combination will probably cause internal frictions due to different earning structures, utilization targets, self and third party perceptions etc.

The larger the market gets and the higher the growth rates are, the more necessary it seems to be for many consulting firms to stretch and broaden the classical consulting business models and to diversify—like e.g. McKinsey and Accenture did successfully over the last years. McKinsey launched e.g. McKinsey Solutions (web-based applications as part of or additional to a consulting engagement) and started Lumics Consulting (a shared company between McKinsey and Lufthansa). Accenture diversified in other, consulting-related professional services fields (cf. e.g. the acquisition of SinnerSchrader, a German digital agency) and balances its outsourcing and consulting businesses.

To summarize: while a large part of the consulting process is getting digitalized and automated, consulting firms will have to evaluate carefully their business model and eventually adjust it.

4.4 Individual Level

As for the company level most of the individual consultants will face a relatively attractive (digitized) future, too.

On the positive side, clients will articulate a strong demand for both types of consulting, the classical consulting services and the pragmatic professional services. The expected growth of the industry will offer attractive career paths.

On the other hand, the number of consulting firms who operate in the *classical* way, i.e. *Consulting in a narrower sense*, could be smaller than expected. Balancing this, many more individual consultants than expected could end up working in the project business, in professional service franchise corporations, in out-tasking companies, as a member of a freelancer network etc. – this is the area of *Consulting in a broader sense.*

Within this field of work the probability of getting one's work digitized and automated should be higher than in the field of *Consulting in a narrower sense.*

To summarize: the consulting industry remains highly attractive—if one can adapt to the new circumstances and find an individual role.

Figure 10 gives an overview of the predictions and recommendations for the company and individual level.

5 Conclusion

Since the 1960s, the perception of *consulting* oscillated constantly between favorable and negatively. Since their first appearance on the professional services market, reports about consultants and their services are full of so-called low lights.

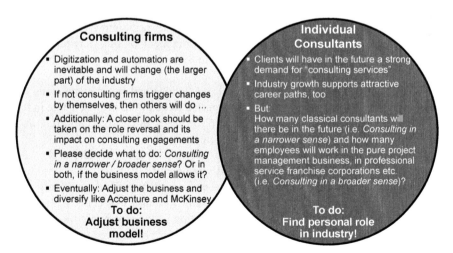

Fig. 10 Predictions and recommendations for the company and individual level

Today, the overall reputation of consultants can be described best as dichotomous. In this environment, consulting firms cope with the ambition to help their clients in the area of digitization. It is not decided yet if consultants are the better advisors or other professional groups like digital design agencies, technology service provider or even university staff.

With this background, the paper aimed to examine different perspective of the industry and to work on the question: Does digitization matter and will it transform the consulting business?

The paper came to the conclusion that there will be an impact on the core business especially for these companies, which offer *Consulting in a broader sense*. Many of them have the size to be economically attractive for *embedded automation* initiatives. They should evaluate how to digitize and to automate their business— before third parties enter the industry with disruptive ideas. Here, a change of the business model might be required. Beside this kind of professional services firms, which often operate in a kind of a franchise system, there are companies which offer *Consulting in a narrower sense*, e.g. the classical advisory role. It can be questioned if the latter part of the consulting industry is large enough in order to justify automation efforts from an economical perspective primarily or at a later stage in time.

Within the overall consulting sector there are some perspectives (e.g. forms and fields of consulting, phases of an engagement, kinds of expertise and transparency of the issue) and some facets where automation is easier implemented than in others.

For both groups of consulting firms digitization has two impact categories which might change the way business is done—but not essentially the business model itself. Digitization can be used to make the internal organization more efficient and digitization will be for the next couple of years a trending consulting topic and a source of revenue flows.

This paper has argued that the consulting business was successful in helping its clients in various economic situations and under various paradigms. This gave way to the modeling of four scenarios for the development of the German market volume until 2030 with a range from circa 32 to 89 bn Euro, starting by 27 bn Euro in 2015.

Finally and alongside the industry level, predictions and recommendations for the company as well as individual level suggested to be aware of the change in the industry structure and to find an individual place either as part of *Consulting in a broader sense* or *Consulting in a narrower sense*.

The paper wanted to put the question of *digitization* on a broader scale with respect to (a) the historical and (b) actual developments.

This, of course, leads toward a high degree of uncertainty. This is not only—as the saying goes—because predictions are difficult to make, especially if they are related to the future. Additionally, the interpretation of the past is not much easier and often topic of heated disputes. Future research might help to reduce uncertainty and vulnerability in both directions, past and future.

A further limitation lies on the strong focus on the German consulting market. Here, again, future research might help to broaden the focus, identify national or regional differences as well as similarities. A first hypothesis might be that the results are basically transferable to other industrialized western countries.

And, finally, if the answer to the paper title's question "Does digitization matter?" is that "The market will grow and it will continue to be attractive to become a consultant!", then there is today little clue if this development is because or despite the digitization of consulting. Hopefully these reflections may help to stipulate discussions and research.

References

Accenture (2017) About accenture. https://www.accenture.com/us-en/company. Accessed 28 Feb 2017

ALM (2017) State of the industry 2017. Documentation of the webinar, 2 Feb 2017

ARD (2017) Job-futuromat. https://job-futuromat.ard.de/. Accessed 4 Jan 2017

AWSi (2017) eConsulting Store—Prototyp des AWS-Instituts. https://www.aws-institut.de/digitale-beratung/econsulting-store/. Accessed 28 Feb 2017

Bartsch B (2014) Ende eines Mythos. https://www.brandeins.de/wissen/brand-eins-thema-unternehmensberater/unternehmensberater-vom-besserwisser-zum-bessermacher/unternehmensberaung-strukturwandel-ende-eines-mythos. Accessed 25 Feb 2017

BDU (1993) Jahresstatistik 1993. http://bdutime.live.kmf01.kmf-port.de/wp-content/uploads/2014/09/BDU-Jahresstatistik-80er-300x214.jpg. Accessed 27 Feb 2017

BDU (2002–2004, 2006–2016) Facts & Figures zum Beratermarkt [2002–2004, 2005/2006–2015/2016]. BDU e.V., Bonn

BDU (2005) Geschäft der Unternehmensberater in Deutschland zieht langsam wieder an. BDU e.V., press release Feb 2005

BDU (2017) 1960—Unternehmensstrategie, Vertrieb und Marketing rücken in den Fokus. http://www.zeitstrahl.bdu.de/. Accessed 27 Feb 2017

Brynjolfsson E, McAfee A (2012) Race against the machine. Research brief. MIT Sloan School of Management, Cambridge

Brynjolfsson E, McAfee A (2014) The second machine age—work, progress, and prosperity in time of brilliant technologies. WW Northon & Company, New York

Cardea (2016) Beratungsmarkt Trendstudie 2016. Zurich

Cardea (2017) Geprüfte Berater & Consulting Unternehmen - consultingsearcher. https://www.consultingsearcher.com/. Accessed 28 Feb 2017

Christensen CM (2017) Die Kunden haben heute für viele Probleme interne Experten. Interview Harvard Bus Manag 39(3):30–31

Christensen CM, Wang D, van Bever D (2013) Consulting on the cusp of disruption. Harvard Bus Rev 91(10):106–114

Chui M, Manyika J, Miremadi M (2016) Where machines could replace humans—and where they can't (yet). McKinsey Q 53(3):58–69

Comatch (2017) COMATCH—the consulting marketplace. https://www.comatch.com/en/home. Accessed 28 Feb 2017

Deelmann T (2015) Managementberatung in Deutschland—Grundlagen, Trends, Prognosen. Springer, Wiesbaden

Deelmann T (2016a) Consulting in Zahlen. 2nd edn. Berlin

Deelmann T (2016b) Keine Tabuzone—Möglichkeiten der Automatisierung von Beratungsleistungen. In: Lünendonk J, Canibol H-P (eds) Handbuch consulting 2016. Fakten & Köpfe, Kelsterbach, pp 80–85

Deelmann T, Huchler A, Jansen SA, Petmecky A (2006) An empirical analysis of internal corporate consultancies. In: Deelmann T, Mohe M (eds) Selection and evaluation of consultants. Rainer Hampp, München & Mering, pp 197–210

Dengler K, Matthes B (2015) Folgen der Digitalisierung für die Arbeitswelt. IAB-Forschungsbericht 11/2015, Nuremberg

Eden McCallum (2017) Eden McCallum—Consulting redefined. http://edenmccallum.com/. Accessed 28 Feb 2017

Equiteq (2016) The global consulting mergers & acquisitions report 2016. New York

FEACO (2004) Survey of the European management consultancy market 2003. Brussels

Fiverr (2017) Fiverr/search results for 'business consultant'. https://www.fiverr.com/search/gigs?utf8=%E2%9C%93&source=guest-homepage&locale=en&search_in=everywhere&query=business+consultant&page=1&filter=auto. Accessed 1 Mar 2017

Kieser A (2002) Wissenschaft und Beratung. Winter, Heidelberg

Krizanits J (2015) Entwicklungen in Gesellschaft, Organisationen und Unternehmensberatung. In: Deelmann T, Ockel DM (eds) Handbuch der Unternehmensberatung. Erich Schmidt, Berlin

Lünendonk (2003–2013) TOP 25 der Managementberatungs-Unternehmen in Deutschland [2002–2012]. Bad Wörrishofen

Lünendonk (2015) 3xD—Trends und Entwicklungen in der Beratung—Vor dem Hintergrund von Digitalisierung, Diskontinuität und Disruption. Mindelheim

Lünendonk (2016) Consulting 4.0—Mit Analytics ins digitale Beraterzeitalter. Mindelheim

McKinsey (2017) How we help clients—Digital McKinsey. http://www.mckinsey.com/business-functions/digital-mckinsey/how-we-help-clients. Accessed 28 Feb 2017

Mindeight (2017) Startseite. http://www.mindeight.de. Accessed 28 Feb 2017

Nissen V, Seifert H (2016a) Digitale transformation in der Unternehmensberatung: status quo in Deutschland. In: Deelmann T, Ockel DM (eds) Handbuch der Unternehmensberatung. Erich Schmidt Verlag, Berlin, pp 7312–7319

Nissen V, Seifert H (2016b) Virtualisierung in der Unternehmensberatung. Eine Studie im deutschen Beratungsmarkt, BDU, Bonn

Nissen V, Seifert H (2017) Ermittlung des Virtualisierungspotenzials von Beratungsleistungen im Consulting. In: Leimeister JM, Brenner W (eds) Proc. 13rd Intl. Conference on Wirtschaftsinformatik, WI2017, St. Gallen, pp 1348–1362

N.N. (1956) Betriebsberatung—Anruf beim Vatikan. Der Spiegel 10(49):22–24

N.N. (1962) Firmenberatung—Verkaufe Bratenduft. Der Spiegel 16(41):58–65

Oxford economics (2016) Global Macro Monitor—Germany. Oxford

Sangüesa Sánchez M (2003) Modell zur Evaluierung von Beratungsprojekten. Dissertation, Berlin

Sawhney M (2017) Wie Produkte Mehrwert schaffen. Harvard Bus Manag 39(3):42–49

Smith B, Smith D (2003) The global consulting marketplace 2003: key data, forecasts & trends. In: Kennedy Information, Inc. (ed) Market intelligence. Peterborough

Walger G (ed) (1995) Idealtypen der Unternehmensberatung. In: Formen der Unternehmensberatung: Systemische Unternehmensberatung, Organisationsabwicklung, Expertenberatung und gutachterliche Beratungstätigkeit in Theorie und Praxis. Otto Schmidt, Cologne, pp 1–18

Wikistrat (2017) Wikistrat—Crowdsourced Consulting. Analysis of publically available material on the webpage http://www.wikistrat.com/andcompanyfilmsonYoutube. Accessed 2 Sept 2017

Wirtschaftswoche (2016) Best of consulting—Preisverleihung. http://award.wiwo.de/boc/preisverleihung/. Accessed 28 Feb 2017

Wohlgemuth AC (2008) Konstanz und Wandel in der klassischen Unternehmensberatung. In: Wohlgemuth AC, Gfrörer R (eds) Management Consulting. NZZ Libro, Zurich, pp 17–46

Author Biography

Thomas Deelmann Thomas Deelmann is Professor for Public Management at the University of Applied Sciences for Public Administration and Management of North Rhine-Westphalia (FHöV) in Cologne, Germany. Until 2016, he was Professor for Corporate Consulting and Management at BiTS Iserlohn as well as the head of the strategy development department for a leading global ICT service provider. His professional experiences as a consultant at one of the largest international consultancies, as an inhouse consultant, as a strategic sourcer for consulting services and as a client of consulting services form the basis for his teaching and research. Currently, he serves as the editor for a consulting handbook and as a jury member of the WirtschaftsWoche's "Best of Consulting" award.

Opportunities and Risks of Digital Business Model Innovation for Behemoths in Consulting

Matthew Flynn and Marek Kowalkiewicz

Abstract This chapter focuses on the opportunities and risks of digital business model innovation for large incumbents in the consulting industry. It summarises a study analysing major themes observed by large organisations currently leading in the industry and analysis potential future scenarios, specifically focusing on opportunities and risks of new business approaches in this industry.

1 Introduction

Consulting firms typically solve complex problems for their clients in tax, accounting, IT, and management. In recent times, the large incumbent consultants (behemoths) have experienced disruption to parts of their business from newcomers via "new business models through facilitated platforms that uproot traditional markets, break down industry categories, and maximise the use of scarce resources" (Allen and Berg 2014). We are seeing a growing number of consulting firms like 10EQS employ platform technologies and data analytics, and offer comprehensive consulting solutions (10EQS 2017). These newcomers tend to be nimbler and more cost-effective compared with incumbents. At the same time, new technologies are an opportunity for incumbents to innovate their traditional business models and become the best integrator of services in their ecosystem.

M. Flynn (✉) · M. Kowalkiewicz
Business School of Management, Queensland University
of Technology, Queensland, Australia
e-mail: m6.flynn@qut.edu.au

M. Kowalkiewicz
e-mail: marek.kowalkiewicz@qut.edu.au

© Springer International Publishing AG 2018
V. Nissen (ed.), *Digital Transformation of the Consulting Industry*,
Progress in IS, https://doi.org/10.1007/978-3-319-70491-3_4

2 Review of Technologies and Business Models Disrupting in Consulting

2.1 Disruption to Incumbents, Making Room for Newcomers

Big changes are happening in the business world. Consulting firms are not immune to these changes, particularly technological breakthroughs that redefine business models and change client expectations (see Table 1 on the following page). There are opportunities and risks for consultants and their clients. Entry barriers for start-up consulting firms are minimised through digital technology, while the large incumbents tend to be slower to adopt new technology. The theory of disruptive innovation explains these phenomena as "a process whereby a smaller company with fewer resources is able to successfully challenge established incumbent businesses" (Christensen et al. 2015). Therefore, some incumbents are fearful about their resilience and relevance, given the digital capability of newcomers. In our review of the literature and company websites and reports, we identified three interconnected areas of digital transformation that are potential opportunities and risks for consulting firms: (i) analytics and algorithms, (ii) technology platforms, and (iii) disintermediation.

2.2 Analytics and Algorithms

The survival of consulting firms in the digital economy depends on their ability to support their clients to make strategic decisions. And yet more broadly, incumbents continue to make critical decisions about their own businesses, and their clients without access to optimal information (Bazerman and Chugh 2006). As consulting firms increase their reliance on analytics for decision-making for themselves and their clients, jobs for data analysts will grow (Chartered Accountants Australia and New Zealand 2015). The major advantage is scalability. Machines scale better than

Table 1 Megatrends and digital technologies disrupting incumbent consulting firms

Global megatrends	Digital megatrends	Disruption of consulting
Climate change & resource scarcity	People & the internet	Analytics for decision making
Shift in global economic power	Computing, communications & storage everywhere	Automation of routine tasks
Technology breakthrough	The internet of things	Platforms
Demographic & social change	Artificial intelligence & big data	Disintermediation
Rapid urbanization	Sharing economy & distributed trust	

humans and can detect patterns in big data better than humans. Moreover, machines are not prone to irrational biases although they are increasingly prone to fraud and cyber-attacks. It is critical that incumbents invest in analytics infrastructure and become expert at using it for decision-making.

If incumbents do not recognise and react to the potential application of software analytics and algorithms, there is a risk that routinized tasks will be disrupted and replaced by firms with this capability. There is an opportunity for all consulting firms (incumbents and newcomers) to automate existing activities to enable high growth scale and dramatically lower costs. Predictions for the future of knowledge workers, including those in consulting are grim. Manyika et al. (2013) estimated that "knowledge work automation tools and systems could take on tasks that would be equal to the output of 110–140 million full-time equivalents". As a result, routinized jobs in consulting will rapidly decline, particularly those in the accounting profession including general accountants, management accountants, and external and internal auditors (Frey and Osborne 2013). Routine tasks will be performed by machines, while non-routine tasks have until recently not been understood by computers.

2.3 Technology Platforms

Technology platforms connect producers and consumers in exchanges of value (Parker et al. 2016). The most obvious examples outside of the consulting industry are Alibaba, Airbnb and Uber. If incumbents do not seize the potential opportunities technology platforms offer, they will face disruption and replacement in traditional markets. There is also a significant opportunity for consultants to leverage the exponential power of platforms networks. Much of the success of newcomers in consulting can be attributed to the positive network effects of their platform business models. As more people use a consultant's platform, the more value there is to members of the network (Parker et al. 2016). For instance, Wikistrat's online platform enables over 2000 subject-matter experts to collaborate and solve complex problems (Wikistrat 2017). Some newcomers, like Wikistrat, control the key resources that "create value for the majority of users"—the platform itself (Parker et al. 2016). At the same time, other newcomers target niche markets by complementing larger incumbents within existing networks. In this way, Gigwalk extends the capacity of Deloitte with their cloud-based workforce management platform (Gigwalk 2016). Complementary firms are potentially disruptive to incumbents, particularly if they operate across multiple networks and build their positive network effects. Assuming there is demand for both, there will be positive network effects for newcomer and incumbents (Gawyer 2014).

2.4 Disintermediation

At the heart of some of the most successful 20th century business models were intermediaries in finance, manufacturing, real estate, music, education, law, and the large consulting firms. From a consumer perspective, the intermediary is a barrier to entry, and prevents access to certain markets, products and services (Lin 2016). Perhaps the most currently discussed digital disintermediation example relevant to the consulting industry is blockchain. Blockchain is defined as a distributed database of records: "a public ledger of all (Bitcoin) transactions that have ever been executed. It is constantly growing as completed blocks are added to previous blocks forming a chain" (Nakamoto 2008). At the very least, blockchain may signal the removal of intermediaries (even large consultants) in supply chains. Fanning and Centers (2016) envisage blockchain impacting the financial services industry. It offers the potential to remove time consuming processes for recording syndicated loan transactions that normally involve extensive negotiation through lawyers, and can take up to 20 days to complete a transaction. For this reason, blockchain is potentially a source for innovation in the consulting industry. Deloitte announced their partnership with ConsenSys in May 2016, with the purpose of creating new value for customers by "consulting on how blockchain technologies can improve their traditional financial products and services" (Allison 2016).

2.5 New Business Models

What has been surprising is "that many of the business models used by many of the traditional consulting firms have not changed in decades, leaving them, just like many of their clients, exposed to becoming victims of digital disruption (Llewellyn 2016). Perhaps the success of some incumbents in the 20th century has hindered them from innovating their business models. Clayton Christensen described how some experienced consultants "scoffed at the suggestion of disruption in their industry, noting that (life and change being what they are) clients will always face new challenges" (Christensen et al. 2013). 20th century consulting business models were steeped in supply-side thinking, however from a modern client's perspective these models are expensive, complicated, and for people with high levels of expertise (Christensen et al. 2013). Generally, new business models have given rise to products and services that are more affordable, globally accessible, and simpler to use.

Newcomers in consulting are demonstrating an adaptive capacity to reconfigure the four elements of the business model: (i) value proposition, (ii) resources, (iii) processes, and (iv) profit formula. Unfortunately, the incumbents are anchored by high fixed costs, rigid structures, and regressive cultures that tend to hinder business model innovation (Richter and Niewiem 2004). Newcomers are solving client problems in more efficient ways than incumbents by creating digital products and services for tasks that clients are already attempting to do manually: that is a genuine value proposition for clients (Christensen and Johnson 2009). In terms of acquiring the resources to solve complex client problems, newcomers are adopting fatter structures, growing global platform networks of crowd-sourced subject-matter experts, and investing in predictive technologies and data analytics (Lin 2015; Parker et al. 2016). Kaggle is one example, running competitions among data scientists to solve problems for some of the world's largest firms (Kaggle 2017). Whereas, incumbents in consulting are somewhat confused about what resources are required for the modern world, while at the same time holding fast to existing structures.

Incumbents have traditionally delivered value for clients through personal expertise, closed local networks, reputation and trust. Processes for newcomers are almost entirely explicit, easily scalable and repeatable through digital platforms, involve open global transparent networks, and are sometimes connected to social enterprise. Finally, major changes in other industries are influencing how profit is derived in consulting. Take for example the zero cost assumption customers have for navigation systems (Google maps), recruitment services (LinkedIn) and education (MOOCs). Hence, the revenues for incumbents are at risk because client assumptions about value for money have completely changed in the 21st century. Products and services supplied by newcomers are significantly cheaper for clients and have lower fixed costs for providers, particularly in terms of the inherent resources needed to deliver value. Incumbent models are hindered by unsustainable top-heavy partner structures and other inflexible fixed costs (Richter and Niewiem 2004).

There are a growing number of newcomers who have their own digitally enabled business model, but with different approaches to large incumbents. For instance, IDEO adopts design thinking which is a "human-centred approach to innovation that draws from the designer's toolkit to integrate the needs of people, the possibilities of technology, and the requirements for business success" (IDEO president and CEO, Tim Brown). The firm started in 1991 and now employs 600 people, solving complex problems in most industries. Another example is Axiom, who is disrupting traditional legal services through technology, having amassed $200 million and 150+ employees across three continents. Axiom clients' have access to analytics that translate static legal documents into structured data that can be searched and analysed to verify contractual obligations with customers and supply chains. Examples of some of the newcomers to the consulting industry that we reviewed are listed in Table 2.

2.6 Research Question

Having discussed the relevant literature on digital technology trends, types of business models disrupting consultants, we asked the following question to guide our research.

Table 2 Newcomers in the consulting industry

Newcomer	Description
OnFrontiers	Online platform where professionals connect to get insights and share knowledge about emerging markets
10EQS	A comprehensive platform solution for consulting firms, investors, and global enterprises
Wikistrat	A global network of subject-matter experts working collaboratively via an online crowd-sourced platform to help decision-makers identify solutions to complex strategic challenges
Kaggle	A platform for predictive modelling and analytics on which companies and researchers post their data and statisticians and data miners from all over the world compete to produce the best models
HeroX	Enables everyone, anywhere in the world, to create a challenge that addresses any problem or opportunity, build a community around the challenge and activate the circumstances that can lead to a breakthrough
Expert360	An online platform structured like a standard freelance marketplace as it provides the tools to potential employers to post and manage jobs of interest to independent consultants in the upper employment market
IDEO	An international design and consulting firm. They use design-thinking methodology to design products, services, environments and digital experiences. The company has become increasingly involved in management consulting and organisational design
Narrative science	A technology company that uses artificial intelligence and a platform to generate advanced natural language to create perfectly written reports with meaningful narratives for any intended audience

What are the risks and opportunities of digital transformation for large incumbents in the consulting industry?

3 Methodology

Phase one of this research involved a structured review of literature, which is presented in section two of this chapter (Webster and Watson 2002). We began by developing a concept matrix of relevant concepts: analytics, algorithms, platforms, disintermediation, and business models. A single unit of analysis, 'disruptive innovation', then augmented our concepts and enabled us to review the literature as it related to disruption in the consulting industry. Major contributions were from journal articles, but it was also important to review company websites and reports. We elicited a significant volume of secondary data that was publicly available on 50 firms.

Phase two followed a qualitative case study method to answer the research question (Yin 2009). Semi-structured interviews were conducted. A purposeful

Table 3 Research themes

Theme	Description
1	Incumbents demonstrate an adaptive capacity when experiencing disruption from smaller and newer consulting firms
2	Incumbents tend to partner with smaller firms that possess digital technology capability (particularly platforms and analytics) and agile business models
3	Incumbents acknowledge that their business models are not appropriate for all ecosystems
4	Incumbents see themselves as the best integrator of services in their ecosystems, because they provide value for customers and can ensure trust and independence
5	Advances in technology provide opportunities for incumbents to deliver efficiencies and to augment new capability, but are also a risk with opportunities for newcomers to disrupt incumbents at scale

sampling technique was applied where we intentionally selected individuals from four different large (Behemoths) consulting firms to help us understand the risks and opportunities for incumbents. All participants interviewed hold senior national and/or international roles within their firms, and are responsible for innovation and digital technology strategies. We reduced the volume of data by assigning codes and sorting into categories related to the research question, different business models and the theory of disruptive innovation. The coding was an iterative process, and it involved back and forth discussion within a team of three, plus others external to the immediate process to validate the code development. Thematic analysis of patterns in the data from the interviews and documents were aggregated together to form major themes and are presented in the findings section of this chapter.

4 Findings

Five themes emerged from the dataset, which are presented in Table 3.

4.1 Risks and Opportunities of Adapting to Disruption from Newcomers

The first theme found from across the dataset was that: *incumbents demonstrate an adaptive capability when experiencing disruption from smaller consulting firms.* The disruption was only evident in some parts of incumbent firms. For instance, we found that new firms with specific digital capability can disrupt parts of incumbent's activities, as described in the extract below:

Newer and smaller consulting firms pick off certain things that (incumbent firms) do and try to commoditise it, disrupt it. If I think about what would really disrupt incumbents it is not pulling off one piece at a time. If you pull off one piece at a time we will (incumbent) just add other pieces. New types of firms are challenging incumbents, like Kaggle, engineering firms, and the tech players like Accenture. They (newcomers) have the potential to disrupt rather than reality, because they struggle regarding reputation and implementation (A1).

Interview data demonstrated that incumbents are able to adapt their consulting services despite disruption from newcomers. The interview extract below shows this:

We are seeing AI and Robotic Process Automation augmenting people. Tasks that use to take our teams days of work can now be automated and replicated much more quickly and repeatedly. I see consulting as one the most heavily disrupted industries in the market. We are just really good and quick at adapting because our livelihood as partners depends on our ability to adapt (B1).

The above extract also shows that incumbents are willing to implement digital technologies that augment the abilities of employees. These technologies are a risk if incumbents do not implement them because their clients may contract smaller and cheaper firms with these capabilities. However, the participant believes that their firm's partnership model helps protect them from the risk of disruption. It should be noted that the interviewee in this extract was a partner within their firm.

Interview data showed that it is much harder to adapt tax and audit services, although if disrupted would do significant damage to incumbents because these services contribute a large percentage of revenue. The extract below explains this scenario:

A genuinely disruptive newcomer would be one that can implement an innovative approach to independence and trust. Independence and trust in audit and tax services are essential to the competitive advantage of incumbents (A1).

Despite the potential risk of disruption from newcomers, one participant believes that newcomers are not trusted by companies in the same way that incumbents are:

The problem I have seen is that industry based companies [newcomers] think they are going to be the leader and that all of the companies in the industry are going to give them their data, no one is going to trust them. You need an independent firm like [large incumbent] to be trusted to manage all of that. This is where [large incumbent] can benefit from its DNA in audit and tax and risk assurance (C1).

All participants in this research commented on how they believed that their firms were good at adapting when there is a risk of disruption from newcomers. The representative extract below verifies this theme:

We are good at looking at new capability, horizon 1, 2, 3. Internally we have an innovative culture. Real disruptors would disrupt the ability to connect across multiple services. I do not think I have seen that yet (D1).

4.2 Opportunities to Partner and Form Alliances with Newcomers

The second theme found was that most *incumbents tend to partner with smaller firms that possess digital technology capability (particularly platforms and analytics) and agile business models.*

The extract below provides a representative example of how one large incumbent partners with a smaller firm to extend their own capability:

> We partner with 10EQS as a platform based business. I have had a number of engagements with them, very effective way of delivering expertise. 10EQS is exceptionally good at answering a specific question about something that is quite detailed. For example, if you want to know what the benchmark operational performance of a mine in Mongolia should be, it is very difficult to find that information. But through 10EQS you can find an individual, or a series of individuals across organisations very quickly and find information you can use to then base a project off or build a business case (A1).

We were also able to find a significant amount of publically available documentary data in company reports and websites to verify various partnership/alliance arrangements between all the large incumbents and smaller organisations. For example, we found that large incumbent participants were partnering with Xprize and Singularity University to offer membership-based consulting programs to educate business leaders on the domains of technological change that is disrupting Fortune 500 companies.

4.3 Business Model Risks and Opportunities

The third theme we found was that *incumbents acknowledge that their business models are not appropriate for all ecosystems.* The time and materials business model that endures in parts of large incumbents is not competitive in digital ecosystems, where newcomers are offering clients more flexible payment options.

> We have to adjust to product centric type business models that are not necessarily tied to hours, but value for clients. So, we're moving away from hour based business models to value based business models, which is a real shift for some parts of the business, but reasonably familiar for other parts of the business (A1).

> What I saw of some other firms, not [large consultants], but when I was at [international bank] for example, were effectively a slide pack or strategy and an invoice for their time. But they in some cases might create tens of millions of dollars of value for the client but they're only charging the 50 or 100 K for their time. We know we can create significant value for our clients, because of the IP, and the skills and experience we bring. We should we be looking for a share of the profit value rather than a share of the time (B1).

The extract above demonstrates that large incumbents believe they can extract more value from their services if they adapt their business models away from charging for time and materials.

> Where we share the risk, it is working as a strategy. Because the clients often do not want to
> take the risk (B1).

However, with the opportunity to extract more value from clients is increased risk. In some cases, large incumbents are contributing capital toward client ventures for a share in the profit.

Interestingly, some large incumbents were found to have adopted new business models that are similar to successful newcomers (e.g. Fintech solutions), however the participant in the extract below acknowledged that they are unable to offer solutions at the same rates as newcomers.

> The fee for service subscription model, like Xero is more and more common nowadays.
> Microsoft have shifted from "give us $1000 for Office" to "subscribe for $100 a month"
> because they cannot continue with that old model. So, this is one of the increasing pressures
> and opportunities coming into the consulting industry. The example of Xero is an example
> of a solution we have embedded [incumbent digital initiative]. We do not necessarily see
> ourselves competing against those, in becoming those in the future, we would be misguided
> if we thought we could do it with our high cost model (D1).

We also found that incumbents believe their value proposition is more compelling for clients than what the newcomers offer. A consistent theme across the dataset was the value of assurance offered by incumbents, despite their costs being higher. The extract below shows a representative extract:

> If I look at some of our largest clients, the reason they use us [or one of the other large
> incumbents] is because they want assurance of the outcome. The reason you would use a
> taxi and not get in some random car is because of the assurance. So, Uber came along and
> gave people the assurance through a validation or check they have done, so I think the
> disruption that would come to consulting is if clients could get that assurance in some other
> means to meet their needs and confidence. And I am not sure if any of these new firms
> (newcomers) do that yet. If that a body could come along and do that for whatever these
> services were then that would be a real disruption I feel.

4.4 Opportunities for Incumbents to Lead Their Ecosystem

The fourth theme we found was that *incumbents see themselves as the best integrator of services in their ecosystems because they provide value for customers and can ensure trust and independence.*

> We want to be the best integrator of services, whether those services are internal or external.
> I do not think it matters as long as we are seen as the integrator of those capabilities. We
> provide value through that (A1).

Secondary data consistently verified that newcomers to consulting recognise the importance of being able to integrate multiple services. This is why almost all the firms that we reviewed use platforms as the means to integrate services. Interview data also showed that incumbents recognise how platforms can enable them to integrate services:

We have to adjust to product centric type models, we need to own IP and holistic solutions and platforms, which we use and distribute services from (B1).

Sometime incumbents may elect to acquire smaller firms as a means of integrating and demonstrating their capacity to lead their ecosystem, which is shown in the extract below:

It could be a strategy to acquire a firm like 10EQS, but sometimes firms like that can be better on the outside be more agile and innovative in the way they do things (A1).

One large firm were found to be very proactive in leading their ecosystem having partnerships and alliances with many newcomers to the consulting industry.

We have relationships with 10EQS, Kaggle, MIT Singularity and Xprize, Gigwalk, Salesforce are all strategic partners of ours (A1).

4.5 Technology Risks and Opportunities

The fifth and final theme was that *advances in technology provide opportunities for incumbents to deliver efficiencies and to augment new capability, but are also a risk with opportunities for newcomers to disrupt incumbents at scale.*

One participant spoke at length about the risks to their consulting clients from software solutions that can quickly become out-dated with rapid advances in technology. The extract below explains this risk issue for consulting clients:

Is that solution going to grow with me and is the provider going to continue to innovate? Does it remain on the front of the curve, or does it start to fall away? Xero versus MYOB is a great example. So, as a firm and as company and I've done this over my whole career you carry the short and long term risks, and it's not unusual for companies to take a 3 or 5-year horizon or less than that on a lot of these solutions. We know that there will be new technology in 3–5 years and we do not know what that is. We're very much running down a managed service path where we share the risk with a client and that might be us and two others, we might partner with a software provider and a software integrator, take some of that risk, but also with the client potentially share some of the upside (profit) (B1).

All the participants interviewed described the Blockchain, Artificial Intelligence and other technologies as potentially disruptive, while at the same time recognising the opportunity to improve their own internal efficiencies and to provide consulting services to their clients. However, they also recognise the potential risk if newcomers can provide similar types of technology-consulting services to clients at cheaper rates. The extract below describes the risk for incumbents:

Anything that challenges the time-and-materials business model and delivers outcomes for our traditional customers faster, cheaper and with the same level of confidence is absolutely disruptive. Blockchain shows promise in some areas but not yet, artificial intelligence shows promise in a lot of areas to automate the work we do and disrupt knowledge workers (D1).

Below is an extract from one participant who described in depth how they are looking to leverage technology as an opportunity to provide new services to their clients.

> This one might be 1:100 scenario where if we for example build a global industry database from an industry point of view. If you are a marketing manager sitting at flight centre and we knew everything that would affect flight centre's business over a year. And so, we knew everything about their customers and their competitors, we knew everything about travel, about disruptive things happening in the world. Could we then create a database and create products and services off that into all different parts of the industry, into travel, into flight centre, airlines, freight, if we knew demand and we help people match demand into a market (C1).

5   Discussion

To analyse what the possible future may be for the consulting services' industry, we employed scenario thinking (Wright and Cairns 2011). It is a research technique exploring possible and plausible futures to assist strategy development and prepare for possible outcomes of future events. Scenario thinking helps determine potential level of impact and uncertainty of various trends.

When developing scenarios, we used two independent factors as key variables: level of progress (particularly in the *Disruption of Consulting* megatrend, as explored earlier in the chapter) and consumer sentiment/uptake of new trends (both technologies and business models). We selected level of progress, as we expect that technology and business progress will have a high impact on the industry, and there is a high level of certainty that major new technologies and business models will emerge over the next 5–10 years. Consumer sentiment and uptake of new trends was selected as ultimately it will be customers who will decide whether to adopt a new trend in technology and business. Given high reliance on human-intensive services, it is possible that customers will prefer traditional models to newly developed ones (although, as described above, this would be one of potential outcomes). Below, we provide a summary description of each of four scenarios.

Each scenario could be placed in a two-dimensional matrix (progress vs. demand) in one of the four corners of the matrix (see Fig. 1 on the next page). We refer to each of them following a glass is empty/full metaphor. *Glass is empty* is a scenario where there is low progress in technology and business, and low demand for new technologies or business models (progress is low, demand is low). *Glass is half empty* describes a scenario where progress is high—with new technologies and business models available, and customer demand—need for new ways of doing business—is low (progress is high, demand low). *Glass is half full* is where customers demand new ways of doing business, but the progress is low, below expectations (progress low, demand high). Finally, *Glass is full* describes a scenario where there is high progress and respectively high demand for new technologies and business models (progress high, demand high).

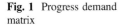

Fig. 1 Progress demand matrix

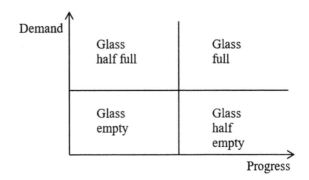

In describing the scenarios, we focused on the five themes identified during our chapter. In *Glass is empty* future, it is business as usual for incumbents. There are no major newcomers disrupting the market and as such there is no need to partner with newcomers. Customers do not expect new business models to be developed, and so incumbents stay in their existing positions, occasionally competing with other incumbents. As there are no major new technologies developed, no risks or opportunities arise in this space.

Glass is half empty is a future where despite major focus of organisations on deploying new business models, newcomers entering the markets, new opportunities to create partnership networks, the customers remain very conservative. As they avoid any unusual ways of doing business models, efforts of incumbents to adapt to disruption, create partnerships, lead with new technologies, do not cause major changes to their position in the market. Many incumbents conclude that their efforts on innovation are simply a waste of time and resources.

In *Glass is half full* future, customers take the lead. Despite challenges incumbents and newcomers face, customers expect technologies and new business models to be top-notch, surprise and delight them, being superior to previous ways of doing business. In this future, customers, unhappy with lack of progress from their traditional service providers, seek new providers, or experiment with novel approaches, only to be disappointed later. It is a challenging future, where service providers need to work very closely with customers to help them understand that many of their needs and requirements simply cannot be fulfilled yet.

The *Glass is full* future is where incumbents need to fully focus on exploration of new ways of doing business, as customer demand is high, and newcomers are readily disrupting the industry. Incumbents need to continuously adapt to disruption, form alliances with newcomers, develop new business models and finally look for options to lead the entire ecosystem, before some of the newcomers rise to the role of the leader.

Whether any of the scenarios summarised above materialises, remains to be seen. We expect that the future may be a mix of the scenarios we proposed. The distinct scenarios make it easy to review them and plan strategic responses. Our finding from the scenario thinking task showed that (1) economic, social and political factors will accelerate and slow trends, (2) there is high uncertainty for some of the trends discussed, (3) lack of information about new business models and newcomers, as well as progress in technologies and business models, makes it much harder for organisations to respond, (4) incumbents are in a position to influence many of the trends, as well as customer demand.

6   Conclusion

Our work identifies the five themes of potential disruption in consulting. The findings provide policy makers and practitioners with specific knowledge about the opportunities and risks of digital business model innovations in consulting. Researchers will gain insights and options to pursue new areas of research. Further work may be required to understand the perception of industry newcomers, adding a valuable perspective of non-traditional participants of the industry. Similarly, a good understanding of customers' expectations will allow for a better understanding of which of the futures described in previous sections are more likely to materialise.

References

Allen D, Berg C (2014) The sharing economy: how over-regulation could destroy an economic revolution. Institute of Public Affairs, Australia. https://ipaorg.au/portal/uploads/Sharing_Economy_December_2014.pdf. Accessed 7 Nov 2015

Allison I (2016) Deloitte to build ethereum-based 'Digital Bank' with New York City's ConsenSys. Intl. Bus Times. Available at http://www.ibtimes.co.uk/deloitte-build-ethereum-based-digital-bank-new-york-citys-consensys-1557864

Bazerman H, Chugh D (2006) Decisions without blinders. Harvard Bus Rev. Available at https://hbr.org/2006/01/decisions-without-blinders. Accessed 12 June 2017

Chartered Accountants Australia & New Zealand (2015) Disruptive technologies: risks, opportunities—can New Zealand make the most of them? http://www.charteredaccountants.com.au/futureinc/Publications. Accessed 12 June 2017

Christensen CM, Johnson MW (2009) What are business models, and how are they built? Harvard Business School

Christensen CM, Wang D, van Bever D (2013) Consulting on the Cusp of Disruption. Harvard Bus Rev 91(10):106–114

Christensen CM, Raynor M, McDonald R (2015) Disruptive innovation—what is disruptive innovation? Harvard Business Review Press

EQS (2017) Open innovation challenges, staff augmentation, advanced digital manufacturing, oil and gas capital investment, civil aviation vendor analysis, cost structure analysis, mobile fashion apps, steel scrap recycling market. https://www.10eqs.com/. Accessed 1 Apr 2017

Fanning K, Centers DP (2016) Blockchain and its coming impact on financial services. J Corp Account Finance 27(5):53–57

Frey CB, Osbourne MA (2013) The future of employment: how susceptible are jobs to computerisation.http://www.oxfordmartin.ox.ac.uk/downloads/academic/The_Future_of_Employment.pdf. Accessed 12 June 2017

Gawyer A (2014) Bridging differing perspectives on technological platforms: toward an integrative framework. Elsevier, 43(7). doi:10.1016/j.respol.2014.03.006

Gigwalk (2016) Gigwalk. http://www.gigwalk.com/. Accessed 12 June 2017

Kaggle (2017) Your home for data science. Analysis of publically available material on the webpage https://www.kaggle.com/andcompanyfilmsonYoutube. Accessed 1 Sept 2017

Lin N (2015) Applied business analytics: integrating business process, big data, and advanced analytics. Pearson Education LTD, Upper Saddle River, New Jersey

Lin TCW (2016) Infinite financial intermediation. Wake forest law Review 50(643), Temple University Legal Studies Research Paper No. 2016–06. Available via https://ssrn.com/abstract=2711379

Llewellyn R (2016) How digital democratised consulting. In: Stewart B, Anshuman K, Schatz R (eds) Phantom ex machina: digital disruption's role in business model transformation. Springer, Cham

Manyika J, Chui M, Bughin J, Dobbs R, Bisson P, Marrs A (2013) Disruptive technologies: Advances that will transform life, business, and the global economy 180. McKinsey Global Institute, San Francisco, CA

Nakamoto S (2008) Bitcoin: a peer-to-peer electronic cash system. https://bitcoin.org/bitcoin.pdf. Accessed 12 June 2017

Parker G, Van Alstyne W, Choudary SP (2016) Platform revolution: how networked markets are transforming the economy and how to make them work for you. W.W. Norton & Company Inc, New York

Richter A, Niewiem S (2004) The changing balance of power in the consulting market. Bus Strategy Rev 15(1):8–13

Webster J, Watson R (2002) Analyzing the past to prepare for the future: writing a literature review. MIS Q 26(2):13–23

Wikistrat (2017) Wikistrat—Crowdsourced Consulting. Analysis of publically available material on the webpage http://www.wikistrat.com/andcompanyfilmsonYoutube. Accessed 2 Sept 2017

Wright G, Cairns G (2011) Scenario thinking: practical approaches to the future. Palgrave Macmillan UK. doi:10.1057/9780230306899

Yin RK (2009) Case study research: design and methods, 4th edn. SAGE, Thousand Oaks, California

Author Biographies

Matthew Flynn is a postdoctoral research fellow at the Queensland University of Technology and PwC Chair in digital economy. Matthew's keen interest in the future of work has led to a growing research portfolio that includes digital disruption of industries, jobs and tasks, disruptive innovation, employability, educational and industry partnerships, and innovative educational approaches to address future of work challenges. Matthew also possesses extensive real world experience as a consultant and trainer to large organizations and SMEs on innovative learning and development projects, evaluations, and industry research projects.

Marek Kowalkiewicz is an academic and industry leader with extensive experience in conducting academically sound research, co-innovating with industry and university partners, and delivering innovative products to the market. Currently, as Professor and PwC Chair in Digital

Economy, as well as leader of the embracing digital age research theme, he leads Queensland University of Technology's research agenda to inform and influence a robust digital economy in Australia. Marek manages a contemporary research portfolio and converts industry driven opportunities into research outcomes of global relevance. He is an invited government expert, university lecturer and project lead, as well as an inventor and author.

Scalability in Consulting: Insights into the Scaling Capabilities of Business Models by Digital Technologies in Consulting Industry

Dirk Werth and Tobias Greff

Abstract Scalability is the major success factor for digital business models. Facing an upcoming trend to also digitize consulting industry, the leading question is how to transform conventional business models of consulting firms into successful digital ones. This paper addresses scalability in knowledge intensive services like consulting services. The authors analyze instruments that contributed to a scalability in business models of other domains and transfer those into the consulting domain. Besides of this theoretical work, they also present individual use cases, where those instruments have already been realized by consulting firms. In summary, the paper can help consulting executives to realign their business models, to select appropriate digital technologies and to build up new digital services incorporating scalability in the consulting domain.

1 Introduction

Digitization is eating the world. In the current age, this major trend is heavily affecting the way businesses are operating. It requires companies to transform their business models and processes for which they often need external support. This is one of the reasons, why the global market for consulting companies is continuously growing. In 2016, global consulting companies reached about 251 billion USD of revenue in total, compared to 205 billion USD in 2011 (Consultancy.uk 2016, see Fig. 1 on the following page). Even though revenues are growing, the consulting branch itself faces radical changes in their own business models: Digitization influences the way consulting will look like in the near future, their business models will get digitized, too. More and more consulting firms establish digital labs, digital think tanks or own business units focusing on the development of new, digitized

D. Werth (✉) · T. Greff
AWS-Institute for Digitized Products and Processes, Saarbrücken, Germany
e-mail: dirk.werth@aws-institut.de

T. Greff
e-mail: tobias.greff@aws-institut.de

© Springer International Publishing AG 2018
V. Nissen (ed.), *Digital Transformation of the Consulting Industry*,
Progress in IS, https://doi.org/10.1007/978-3-319-70491-3_5

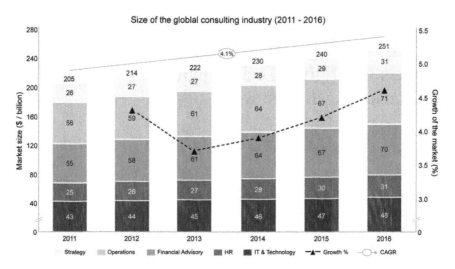

Fig. 1 Growth of the global consulting market 2016 (Consultancy.uk 2016)

business models (Odgers Berndtson 2015). They aim on using the Internet for sales and distribution, on improving the quality of their consulting service or on raising the efficiency of their internal processes. The paper at hand addresses this issue by focusing on the major success factor for digital business models, namely scalability. We analyze how scalability is realized in digital businesses and transfer this findings into the consulting business. Revealing four core variants of implementing this scalability, we finally depict dedicated use cases and underlying digital technologies that realize this concept for specific consulting scenarios.

2   Digital Enterprises and Digital Business Models

The first question to address when talking about business model transformation is to clarify the meaning of the term "business model", since several definitions and understandings of models exist (El Sawy and Pereira 2013; DaSilva and Trkman 2014). In this work, we restrict ourselves to the definition that a business model "describes—mainly textual on a highly aggregated level—the business logic of an underlying company by a combination of interdependent offering, market, internal as well as economical business model components in a static and dynamic way beyond the company's borders. Furthermore, it is not limited to a certain type of business or industry and is thus generally applicable and intended for internal as well as external addressees." (Burkhart et al. 2011). The advantage of this definition is that it explicitly incorporates the generic applicability of business model concepts as well as the consideration of external addressees. As we see later, these aspects are crucial to set up proper digital business models, especially when we consider a transformation of business models with the approach that "the business model concept shifts focus from the resources firms have to how they use them" (McGrath 2010).

In the digital age, research on business models concentrates on the field of digital business models. There are numerous definitions of electronic or digital business models (DBM). They vary largely, and even reviews of IS literature draw different conclusions of what are the key values of digital business models (Timmers 1998; Al-Debei et al. 2008; Veit et al. 2014). Different terms have been introduced and accordingly, the actual search terms may critically influence the outcome of a literature review, though the content that was intentionally searched for would be the same. As an example keep in mind that the terms *virtual*, *electronical* and *digital* are often used synonymously without an explicit remark. To summarize these terms in a broader sense, we will use the term digital business models basically for all those business models that are enabled by the efficient and effective use of information and communications technology (ICT) concepts (Johann et al. 2016). This sets a focus on business models based on IT-driven business processes and digital eco systems (El Sawy and Pereira 2013). But there are even more criteria to consider. Therefore this broader understanding has to be elaborated.

Defining digital enterprises as such companies that incorporate digital business models in their main business fields, the last years have shown an increased number of digital enterprises that have been becoming large in a very short time. On the other hand, there are plenty of startups that are digital enterprises as well, even if they did not grew up to a significant size yet. Thus, it is favourable to specify the definition of a digital enterprise by depicting the characteristics that constitutes them (Werth 2016) and by the way digital business models are established in opposite to traditional ones.

Typically, a redesign of business models is driven by development of technologies and—in particular—new products and solutions. In contrast to that, successful companies of the digital era like Apple or Google rather drive the innovation of business models first (Zott and Amit 2010). Hence, a digital business model is not built around the actual product portfolio, but focuses on new ideas and technologies first. The business model canvas (Osterwalder and Pigneur 2013) has developed into a well-designed product, suited by software solutions that allow to easily get an overview of a current business model. Yet, it is unbiased in the sense that it is not focused on digital transformation. However, the question remains what to put in the center of a digital business model? Several previous works on digital business models state that IT should be put into the core of the business model (Slywotzky 1996; Slywotzky et al. 2001; Zeng and Li 2008). Studies that evaluated how the usage of IT influences the firm performance showed a positive correlation (Rai et al. 2006; Swafford et al. 2008; Liu et al. 2013; Luo and Bu 2016). Consequently, a guideline for adapting business models must consider how IT can be properly focused by business and research units.

Digital Business Model

To sum up our understanding, *a digital business model (DBM)* is a continuously evolving business model, where all essential value-generating and business-operating factors are enhanced or automated using digital technologies and which is steadily adjusted to changes in the economic and technical environment by concerning concepts to gain competitive advantages by deploying those technologies.

An example for such a DBM is the online business platform around the Amazon Marketplace. It presents an optimal way for offering services and products to a large audience and is able to easily increase the number of reached customers. The DBM is continuously evolving around the customer needs with the goal to grow by competitive advantages based on technology. For example they steadily adjust their product portfolio by adding digital services like Amazon Prime, Amazon Instant Video or by offering platform-enlarging products like the Kindle, the Amazon Fire Stick, Amazon Echo or the Amazon Dash Button.

Such a business platform like the Amazon Marketplace puts requirements on the way products are presented, offered and delivered—this holds for physical products that are offered via web stores as well as for digitized services, as we will discuss in detail below when we apply our guideline to the consulting industry. Platforms usually are external business partners collaborating even with direct competitors. For example, Amazon Marketplace offers similar products from different vendors. Yet, individual companies can benefit from the platform by the large number of potential customers. Other than that, a company may think about implementing a new platform for the own product or service portfolio. Even here, it might be advantageous to allow seemingly direct competitors to offer their products side-by-side, since more customers can be attracted.

Since outsourcing is necessary to provide flexibility with respect to digital innovation (Ismail 2014), the business network of a company gains importance. A network is able to provide collaboration, either by co developing products and services or by reselling products. New competitors can either be incorporated into the current network or serve as indicators to new technologies, triggering a new iteration of business model digitization. And lastly, a company's partners also have their own partner network that should be used as much as possible to extend the own network. And when looking for new business partners in the digital era, it is of large interest not to look at pure skills or business numbers, but also at the strength of a potential partner's network.

3   Scalability as a Requisite for Digital Business Models

Digital business models incorporate specific characteristics. Empirically it is undoubtful that those models are economically successful nowadays (Weill and Woerner 2013; Veit et al. 2014). However, it remains the question, why? Looking especially on those digital business models that often exponentially increase, the main requirement for a high impact and economic success is that the business model scales (Ismail 2014). In this respect scalability describes the growth potential of a digital business model and its underlying function (Stampfl et al. 2013).

Consequently, there are two facets of scalability to be considered: One facet is the ability to grow with increasing profits: Only if the revenues can be increased highly faster than the costs, a digital business will take profit of scalability. Additional services, concerning quality as well as quantity, should lead to proportionally smaller, additional costs. For digital technologies, this factor is mainly based on a very low margin cost setting.

Second facet is the ability to grow per se: investigating successful digital businesses, it can be revealed that they usually grow exponentially. This means that the increase of volume (may it be users, content or revenues) is significantly high, often more than 100% per year. Such growth rates are hardly realizable in conventional businesses.

To reach scalability, digital business models need to have a clear strategic growth perspective. But how to create scalability within a digital business model? Based on the characteristics of those models, we can derive four instruments that affect the scaling effect and thus will lead to this effect to be incorporated into the DBM. Those instruments, which promise success for future digital enterprises have proven success in the past by established successful and exponentially growing digital enterprises (Stampfl et al. 2013).

3.1   Separating Information-Based Parts

ICT allow the digitization of many services. This in particular holds for information-based services. As information flows are per se digitizable, every service based on communication, could be delivered through information technology. For example, this has been shown in the educational sector, in which e-learning has reached a new level by the introduction of MOOC's. MOOC's are massive open online courses, which are created and optimized for a large scale of students consuming lectures via an e-learning platform (Fini 2009). The advantages arise from the fact that such a lecture has to be built and prepared only once. Afterwards, no human resource is required anymore to hold that lecture, which has a large impact on costs. The main challenge remains to create the right incentives for learners to participate consistently in those courses as it does a lecturer. Another aspect, which should not be neglected, is that parts of manual service offerings and provisioning can be digitized as well. Therefore, using well designed web interfaces is the main key, which allows to digitize support processes of the manual services as appointments, upstream activities, ratings or bookings.

However, the same principle is also applicable to all services, even those that are not information-based. Every service can be separated into a physical and an informational part. While the physical part usually cannot be digitized today (replacing every physical part by connected robots may be a future scenario), the information part can be, using the mechanisms described above. The given information can be utilized by information technology, leading to an effect of scalability. Additionally, by digitizing the information-based parts of a service, a configuration by the customer becomes possible. For example services can be individually offered in more detail or initial services, which could be free services for a first customer contact to identify or discuss identified problems, can be offered, too.

In the consequence, scalability is achieved by a more efficient use of the physical resources. Additionally, concerned products and services become more flexible, individual in concerned information-based parts and cheaper in total.

3.2 Leveraging Assets and Sharing Economy

The sharing economy is one of the leading principles in digitization. Resources are not used exclusively, but shared with others. Vice versa, the consuming party is not building up resources by their own, but using external ones. It arises an externalization of resources and assets. This can be seen as the central activity for digitizing a business model. Although at first sight this might look like a raise in purchasing costs in opposite to build-up in-house services, it may pay off in the long run, since externalization offers two central advantages: First, the external partners typically are highly specialized companies that focus on a specific task. They are in general more efficient and more effective in performing this task, they can easily use the most modern techniques and—since they offer their capabilities to several companies—their investments pay off faster than for a company needing these investments for internal use only. This gives rise to cost efficiency, a fact typically considered when talking about outsourcing (Holcomb and Hitt 2007). Parts of the automotive industry have for example profited largely from externalizing the construction of car parts, which shows that the concept is not exclusively a topic of digitization, but is again in focus due to the high requirements in development speed (Milovanović et al. 2016). Even more, external capabilities additionally allow a highly flexible adaption of business models and strategies. If you identify new technologies that may suit your business models, there are usually already companies with at least some expertise in the field. Using their knowledge advantage can help to be the first company in the own business sector offering a specific product and fulfilling customer needs while others may still prepare their in-house resources. This is also not a new concept, but is again largely improved by the possibilities of distributed working of knowmads. Thereby, we contradict previous claims that outsourcing in general negatively affects innovativeness (Stanko and Olleros 2013) and long-term development of companies (Hoecht and Trott 2006), given that information sharing between partners is optimized (Yozgat et al. 2013). Note that a company may use partners redundantly to ensure reliability in critical areas. A positive side-effect of partnering with other companies is eventual co-development, if the business model of partners and the own company align with each other (Chesbrough and Schwartz 2007). Note that externalization of previously internal resources requires a good supply chain management, ideal communication and data exchange with partners. That is why digitization of business models necessarily needs to internally empower IT of core functionalities.

In respect to scalability, using external resources creates a leverage effect: Less capital is on short time necessary to build up an offering, compared to a full purchase and internal operations. Thus, with the same capital at stake, the offering can be wider and/or deeper. Also in terms of speed, there is a gain, since using existing, external resources takes far less time than building them up by themselves. In practice, companies incorporating this principle often operate a sharing platform, but they do not own any resources distributed through the platform. By charging the process of connected suppliers and customers, the company offers its own paid service. This aspect of outsourcing processes to users reduces the amount of services directly offered by the company, leading to scalability of the remaining services.

3.3 Enabling Customers and Partners

Customer engagement and excitement is obviously a driver that mainly affects the connection between a company and its customers. Apple as a brand has reached customers all around the world extremely successful, which can be derived from the crowds queuing in front of Apple stores days before the release of new products. And if customers are successfully excited and engaged in marketing activity, the effect of campaigns can scale almost arbitrarily, since the digital transformation opened up new communication channels to customers. For example, viral marketing techniques based on social media platforms can easily reach large groups of people, the number of potentially addressed buyers is growing almost exponentially with every shared post, comment or image. And on the same time, costs for marketing campaigns can be reduced dramatically (Scott 2015). When engaging customers, one must keep in mind that digitization enables automation, customization and individualization. Individualized products are more attractive to the customer but mostly expensive. And automatized productive processes allow to reduce costs at typically increasing quality—although quality and price being two tightly entangled aspects when offering products and services (Olbrich et al. 2016).

Consequently, this principle focuses on integrating customers into the service processes. There are multiple types of customer engagement. If processes are mainly done by the customer for his own, it is called self-services

(Meuter et al. 2000). If customers are involved to inspire the company, it is called crowd-innovation or for example if customers develop parts of software, it is part of open source approaches. By outsourcing several parts of a process to customers, companies are, on the one hand, able to reduce their own expenses and on the other hand they can directly include the customers into formerly internal processes and thereby interact with them via the used platform. This can, for example, lead to more market-based results (e.g. product development). It can also lead to more individualized services for customers.

By enabling customers and partners, scalability is realized in additional services, which do not directly lead to an increased need for resources. Additionally, by outsourcing processes, companies reduce their expenses and the amount of time invested in the services and products. The main activity remaining is to support the customers and supervise the processes.

3.4 Automation and Algorithmic Processing

This final principle is indeed the first coming in mind when talking about digitization. Machinery takes over tasks from the human. And if this machinery is digital technology, then the scaling effect of this automation is obviously enormous. And some specific services can be completely automated. Especially in the financial sector, this trend is very common. By using huge amounts of data and mining methods, trends and especially anomalies can be detected. This algorithmic services can give insights into every kind of business data and identify organizational weaknesses. Additionally they can support decision-makers by providing case relevant data. As a further example insight engines based on machine learning algorithms are able to analyze the whole email traffic of customer-service companies and built up knowledge clusters to optimally solve customer problems with integrated software support and partially generate automated answers (mindbreeze.com).

In this case, scalability is realized by fully automated services, which do not directly lead to an increased need for human resources. Employees then primarily supervise the services.

4 Conceptual Model for Consulting Industry

Consulting companies are mostly not a good example for scalability: Projects typically depend on the consultants, who are usually bound to a small number of projects for a longer time. It is their knowledge, experiences and abilities that enable them to work in those project—and vice versa those projects depend on them. Consulting is considered a highly human-centric domain. In the consequence, there is a clear correlation between people and project activities. In other words, for a consulting firm in order to perform more projects, it requires more consultants. More precisely, doubling the projects requires (ceteris paribus) doubling the number of consultants. Thus, there is a linear correlation between projects (i.e. project effort) and headcount, i.e. consulting scales linearly.

In this respect, consulting firms are typical representatives for knowledge-intensive services. They are based on highly-creative and people intensive products and services. A typical consulting project is intellectually challenging, often there are problems never solved in exactly that setting. In many cases there is a need for an intensive solution transfer or innovative restructuring. It all leads to the insight that with each new project a raised head count is needed.

However, considering this linear relation as a kind of natural law is neglecting the effects of digitization that has been already demonstrated in other domains. Also in accommodation, it was assumed that there is such a linear correlation. However, Airbnb has successfully shown that they can build up an exponentially scaling digital business model. So, in order to conceive the possibilities to incorporate scalability into the consulting domain, we investigate the ways how scalability has been achieved in other domains.

In the previous section, we already described the base properties of digital business models that enable scalability. In order to systematically assess the options for the consulting domain, we therefore focus on each of those instruments shown above and analyze how they could be transferred for consulting services respectively for business models of consulting firms. By doing so, we create a conceptual model for applying digital business models to the consulting domain (see Fig. 2 on the following page).

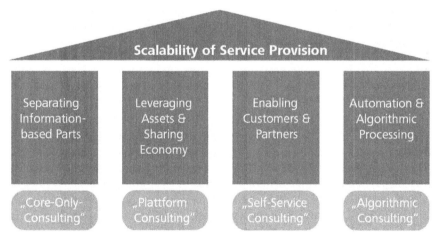

Fig. 2 Scalability for consulting services

4.1 Core-Only Consulting

This approach bases on the *separating information-based parts* instrument. We have shown that if the provider keeps the information-based segments of services disjunctive from the physical segments, then the provider receives the possibility to realize those information-based parts by information technology. In the same way as hairdressers create a digitally supported business model (mylocalsalon.com.au), consulting firms can adopt those techniques.

In respect to the consulting domain, these information-based parts exist too and are already partially realized by ICT today. They consist of process activities like choosing the right consultant, finding an appointment or invoicing. All activities of those characteristics can be efficiently realized by information technology in a more holistic way by focusing on IT-based processes and customer needs. Moreover, the customers that are now interacting with those IT systems, obtain the possibility to configure the consulting services by themselves or potentially to purchase additional digital goods (such as web-based-trainings or digital content). Another large potential by separating information based parts evolves from the virtualization of consulting services, which largely increases spatial and temporal flexibility of consultants (Nissen and Seifert 2015).

In consequence, the activities of consultants are reduced to their knowledge-based tasks. Consultants have the ability to focus on their primary competences; we call this *Core-Only Consulting*. Consulting services can be provided more flexible, more individualized and more cost efficient. In terms of scalability, core-only consulting means that not the full consulting service is scaling, but only the information-based segments. However those segments greatly scale, mainly without marginal costs. This results in an overall scaling ability that is higher than linear, if the company is able to realize an appropriate flexible and efficient scaling of the remaining physical resources.

4.2 Platform Consulting

Scalability in a digital business model can also be achieved by using external resources instead of the own ones. We have seen that this instrument leads to a leverage effect on capital and growth. A common way to incorporate this instrument into a digital business setting is through a software platform. This *platform thinking* (Rochet and Tirole 2003) leads to the question, which resources must be provided by the company and which resources can be handled just as well by external partners. As an example consider Amazon, which does both. It provides their own offerings as well as those from other suppliers resp. partners. Often it is even the case that both offer the same product, in a competitive situation. And this is per se not limited to physical products, but can also be applied to services. Even more, companies may externalize essential internal resources, such as human resources.

This is the way, consulting firms can realize a digital business model that uses the potentials of *Leveraging Assets and Sharing Economy*.

Transferring this instrument into the consulting market, we conclude that this market can be aligned by a two-sided market platform as well. Such a software platform is shaping a digital business model for the consulting domain that we call *Platform Consulting*. The consulting firm implementing this business model profits primarily of the successful intermediation. It is paid by both user roles—customers and providers of consulting services. Basically, there are two different possibilities for the business orientation of a consulting platform. On the one hand there are platforms for the *people-oriented mediation* of consultants and freelancers on the other hand there are platforms for the *product-oriented mediation* of consulting services. Both options profit from the intensive usage of external capabilities and consultants and thereby their ecosystem scales.

4.3 Self-service Consulting

Enabling customers has been proven as another effective principle to create scalability. This *Ikea*-effect has been applied to many domains, but not into consulting industry. Here it would mean that work, which is originally carried out by consultants, is now performed by the customer instead, i.e. by employees of the customer's company. It is obvious that this requires a support by digital technologies, because otherwise the customer would not require the consulting service at all. This technological support needs to focus on the knowledge aspects of the activity to be carried out and enables the customer's personnel to take the role of an assisted consultant. The result is a *Self-Service Consulting*.

In the area of assessments, such services already exist. They are often freely/cheaply offered software services, which are dialogue-based and automatically provided. They empower the customer to solve company specific problems by him/herself. Nowadays, self-service consulting offers are mainly designed for standardized and generally small cases. They often are a structured guidance for the customers to collect their knowledge and input. Based on this input, self-assessment products can evaluate present circumstances of the customer in an automatically generated report and explain possible, following steps. While customers are doing their self-assessments, they are supported by consultants. By enabling customers and partners, consulting companies reduce their expenses and the amount of time invested by consultants in the services.

This approach creates scalability by providing consulting firm just with a minor own effort. In comparison, it is the customer who puts in the majority of the personnel effort which does not necessarily produces extra efforts, if the resources bound by specification and co-working hours in consulting projects are concerned. This way, the respective business model highly scales in regards to the company's offering of self-service consulting.

4.4 Algorithmic Consulting

Automation is often considered as the primary paradigm of digitization. Even through this is not the case, automation is indeed an effective way to realize scalability. However in the knowledge-driven consulting domain, this is not as simple to incorporate as e.g. in the manufacturing industry (Deelmann 2015). On the other side, it is undoubtful that machinery is advancing in areas that have been dedicated domains for humans some years ago. Autonomic driving is just one of the few examples. Another is within the financial industry where automated financial advising services (so called *robo advisors*) succeed to realize similar or even better investment results than human investment managers.

In respect to the consulting domain, this is not fully transferable. Consulting processes are not primarily number-driven and results are not always easy to measure. The mainstream opinion is that consulting processes cannot be automated—or at least not with the digital technologies currently available. However, this is not fully right: Picking up specific consulting processes and decomposing them reveals process parts that can indeed be automated, especially those dealing with data analysis parts. Here, an algorithm can substitute and even improve the work of human consultants. We call this scenario where algorithmic computations are used within consulting processes *Algorithmic Consulting*.

For example, computers and algorithms can be used to automatically analyze process data in transactional systems to discover existing anomalies. In that case, the needed interventions will automatically be triggered. Besides, such algorithmic consulting systems can generate automated reports and decision support. The consultants' role in the process changes into supervising and decision supporting.

5 Use Cases in Consulting Firms

Having presented the four instruments above that enable scalability, it has been an analytical procedure to come up with those insights. It remains the practical question if those instruments are just of theoretical nature or if they can be deployed into practice. In order to answer this question, we have investigated the consulting market and queried for use cases that demonstrate the practical application of each of the four instruments. This work is presented below.

5.1 Use Case 1: Scheer Marketplace
(Core-Only Consulting)

The Scheer Marketplace is a suitable pilot example for the separation of physical and immaterial parts of the consulting process. It allows consulting firms to offer

Fig. 3 Scheer marketplace—customization and service purchase (Scheer 2017)

modular consulting services via a webstore solution. The customer can book services or request discounts and offers (Baldi et al. 2017). It includes sales, dispo-
sition and delivery processing of consulting services (Werth et al. 2016a).
Customers thereby are able to select, compare, customize, configure and buy
consulting services. The consulting service itself is still delivered traditionally
on-site (Fig. 3).

The process of purchase starts by assisting the customer in service selection,
where s/he looks for services matching her/his problem requirements. Afterwards, a
consulting service is chosen and the service is conceptualized. In this process, all
steps except the actual provisioning of the service, are digitally and automatically
covered by the store.

The store profits from the long tail (Oestreicher-Singer and Sundararajan 2012),
since the company can easily offer highly specialized products to a much larger
group of potential customers by the Internet. The largest impact on the business
model results from the raise in efficiency of the procedures before and after the
actual consulting service. Customers can look for their services themselves at any
time without direct contact to consultants. They may fix appointments and customize their service by modularly add or remove configurable parts. Besides that
they are able to invite offerings, add further conditions and negotiate prices.
Furthermore billing is also automatized in the concept of the Marketplace.

Scalability is reached by raising the efficiency of each consultant's main activities by liberating him/her from repetitive operational tasks.

5.2   Use Case 2: Clarity.fm (Platform Consulting)

Clarity.fm is a mentoring platform for start-ups and at the same time a suitable example for digital consulting platforms. It realizes the platform aspect by mediating between start-up mentors (mostly consultants) and start-up founders (customers). Clarity.fm offers a web-dashboard to search for the right consultant in different areas of start-up founding. Anytime it is possible to book an online live consulting session with the currently available consultants. The live consulting sessions are paid by use. It is possible to get minute-wise consulting or to get practical advises for several hours. The billing is automatically processed on a minutely rate. An essential part of the mediation platform is the rating of mentors and consultants offering their services on the platform. Thereby, the customer is able to publicly rank the quality of the consulting services. For the customers this ensures service quality and for consultants this allows to increase their charge per-minute with raising experience. To build trust and grant the correctness of references, the profiles have to be evaluated by the platform provider.

Traditionally, consulting firms offer large blocks of services on a daily rate. The digital business model of Clarity.fm allows to eliminate travel costs and time. Thus, it is possible to offer services on an hourly or even minutely rate. The consulting service thereby scales in two dimensions. First, the individual consultant gets more efficient by the reduced travel expenditures. But more interesting is the second way to scalability. It is achieved by the platform character of Clarity.fm. Every consultant in the addressed domain is able to offer his/her services on the platform. With each mediation the percentual profit of the platform raises with marginal costs close to zero (Fig. 4).

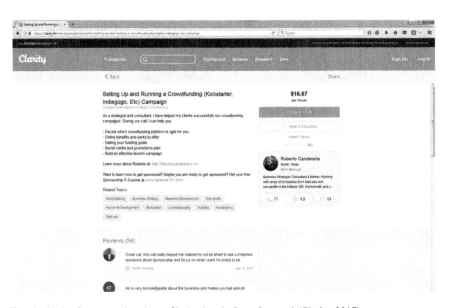

Fig. 4   Clarity.fm—consultant's profile in the platform frontend (Clarity 2017)

5.3   Use Case 3: IMP3rove Self-assessments (Self-service Consulting)

IMP3rove is a company offering different kind of consulting services in the domain of innovation management (www.improve-innovation.eu). One service category they offer consists of the *Innovation Management Assessments*. Traditionally assessments are on-site workshops leaded by consultants in which company's key drivers are identified and the performance of a business field or a whole company is evaluated. The business field evaluated by IMP3rove's Self-Service Assessments is the innovation management. To scale that consulting business, they digitized the classical on-site assessment. Therefore, the consultant is replaced by a digital self-service. By a form-based online assistance software the customer is enabled to do the assessment by him/herself online. The customer provides the information formerly collected on-site in a guided online questionnaire. After having completed an IMP3rove Assessment, companies can generate and download a customized, automatically-generated benchmarking report that compares their own innovation management capabilities and performance against the average results of a self-selected set of direct or indirect competitors. The IMP3rove Database encompasses more than 5000 datasets and is unparalleled in covering industries, size classes, and geographies (Fig. 5).

This online assessments aim to fully automated consulting services that are entirely managed by a software system, without an involvement of a consultant (Werth et al. 2016b). However, this only applies to the execution. In respect to designing and configuring such a service, it is still the consultant with his/her domain knowledge that is in the lead.

Deriving the self-service consulting process from assessment-like consulting is done by separating customer's and consultant's tasks and adjusting tasks according to the new self-service environment. The operational work and contribution of the consultant is, except of creating the questionnaire and defining report parameters,

Fig. 5 Sample of the automated evaluation report of an IMP3rove self-assessment (Imp3rove 2017)

completely replaced by the digital service. More precise, it is the software in collaboration with the customer, who is now in charge of the work: Now the customer, i.e. the different persons working in the customer company, are managing and performing all those tasks. This obviously requires a strong support and guidance that is provided by the digital self-service and thereby allows the service to scale with each customer independently of human resources.

5.4   Use Case 4: Inspirient (Algorithmic Consulting)

Inspirient is an artificial intelligence based consulting software. It enables companies to get relevant insights from its structured business data. The software is able to immediately create easy to understand reports for decision-makers and business leaders. The Inspirient software automatically analyses business data, prioritizes results, and visualizes them as management slides—just like popular presentation software. It is able to discover unexpected outliers, trends, hotspots and potentially critical processes. The software is basically domain independent and thus is able to analyze any kind of data, such as sales, production or financial data. Inspirient's artificial intelligence automatically harmonizes dates, country codes, number formats and currencies without data preparation. The discovered insights can be interpreted by customers or specialized consultants to derive further data-driven actions such as business recommendations or suitable countermeasures. Findings could be collaboratively discussed and shared with persons in charge. Inspirient fully automatizes the analytical parts of consulting tasks. Formerly, the consultant talked initially to the customer, got the data of the customer and afterwards had to go back to the office to analyze the data him/herself. With algorithmic consulting tools data can be analyzed live in front of the customer. This allows to improve the consulting process. With algorithmic consulting tools the consultant and the customer are able to discuss analytical results instantly and graphically on a user- and therefore customer-friendly interface. By reducing the requirement level of data analytics the software is able to scale with nearly zero need in consulting firm's headcount by empowering the customer to use the tools without assistance or to replace expensive analytical consultants by tool assistants (Fig. 6).

6   Conclusions

Using the model described in this paper, the concept of scalability can be introduced into the consulting domain. This is a mandatory requisite for the enablement of economically successful digital business models. In summary, scalability of consulting firm can be reached (i) by transferring all information-based activities to ICT leading to a more efficient use of the consultant's time, (ii) by the use of external consulting resources, (iii) by a strong involvement of the customers and by

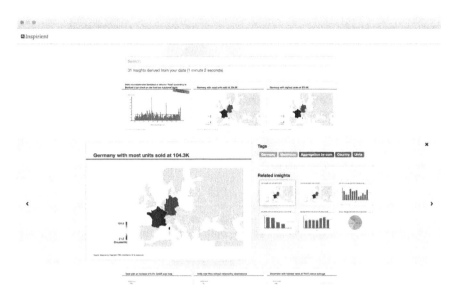

Fig. 6 Inspirient Webinterface: detailed view of identified hotspots and related insights (Inspirient 2017)

outsourcing processes to them, and (iv) by automating core consulting firm processes, which are only supervised by the consultants. In further research the goal would be to evaluate customer acceptance of the mentioned DBMs. All the use cases from the consulting domain are software pilot projects, smaller enterprises or start-ups. Their possibilities for success will be evaluated and analyzed in detail with the aim to collect state-of-the-art research information and to improve these DBMs.

References

Al-Debei MM, El-Haddadeh R, Avison D (2008) Defining the business model in the new world of digital business. In: Proceedings of the fourteenth Americas conference on information systems, Toronto ON, Canada, 14–17 Aug 2008

Baldi M, Lerch M, Schoenecker A (2017) Scheer Marketplace – ein Praxisbericht: Kundenorientierte digitale Beratungslösungen erfolgreich entwickeln. IM + io - Magazin für Innovation, Organisation und Management. IMC, Saarbücken, pp 42–47

Burkhart T, Krumeich J, Werth D, Loos P (2011) Analyzing the business model concept—a comprehensive classification of literature. In: Thirty second international conference on information systems, Shanghai

Chesbrough H, Schwartz K (2007) Innovation business models with co-development partnerships. Res Technol Manage 50(1):55–59

Clarity (2017) Clarity.fm – consultant's profile in the platform frontend. https://clarity.fm/robertocandelaria/expertise/setting-up-and-running-a-crowdfunding-kickstarter-indiegogo-etc-campaign. Accessed 1 Mar 2017

Consultancy.uk (2016) Global IT-consulting market. http://www.consultancy.uk/consulting-industry/it-consulting. Accessed 1 Mar 2017

DaSilva CM, Trkman P (2014) Business model: what it is and what it is not. Long Range Plan 47 (6):379–389

Deelmann T (2015) Managementberatung in Deutschland - Grundlagen, Trends, Prognosen. Springer, Wiesbaden

El Sawy OA, Pereira F (2013) Digital business models: review and synthesis. In: Business modelling in the dynamical digital space—an ecosystem approach. Springer, Heidelberg, pp 13–20

Fini A (2009) The technological dimension of a massive open online course: the case of the CCK08 course tools. Int Rev Res Open Distrib Learn 10(5)

Hoecht A, Trott P (2006) Innovation risks of strategic outsourcing. Technovation 26(5–6): 672–681

Holcomb TR, Hitt MA (2007) Toward a model of strategic outsourcing. J Oper Manage 25 (2):464–481

Imp3rove (2017) Sample of the automated evaluation report of IMP3rove self-assessment. https://www.improve-innovation.eu/our-services/assessments/improve-assessment/. Accessed 1 Mar 2017

Inspirient (2017) Inspirient Webinterface. https://www.inspirient.com. Accessed 1 Mar 2017

Ismail S (2014) Exponential organizations: why new organizations are ten times better, faster, and cheaper than yours (and what to do about it). Diversion Books

Johann D, Greff T, Werth D (2016) On the effect of digital frontstores on transforming business models. In: Shishkov B (ed) Proceedings of the 6th international symposium on business modeling and software design, Rhodes, pp 64–72

Liu H, Ke W, Wei KK, Hua Z (2013) The impact of IT capabilities on firm performance: the mediating roles of absorptive capacity and supply chain agility. Decis Support Syst 54 (3):1452–1462

Luo Y, Bu J (2016) How valuable is information and communication technology? A study of emerging economy enterprises. J World Bus 51(2):200–211

McGrath RG (2010) Business models: a discovery driven approach. Long Range Plan 43(2–3):247–261

Meuter ML, Ostrom AL, Roundtree RI, Bitner MJ (2000) Self-services technologies: understanding customer satisfaction with technology-based service encounters. J Mark 64 (3):50–64

Milovanović G, Milovanović S, Spasić T (2016) The role of contemporary web technologies in supply chain management. Ekonomika 62:43–58

Nissen V, Seifert H (2015) Virtualization of consulting—benefits, risks and a suggested decision process. In: Pavlou P, Saunders C (eds) Proceedings of AMCIS 2015, vol 2, Puerto Rico, pp 1380–1391

Odgers Berndtson (2015) Consulting-monitor 2015. http://www.odgersberndtson.com/media/2355/odgers_berndtson_consulting-monitor_2015.pdf. Accessed 2 Feb 2017

Oestreicher-Singer G, Sundararajan A (2012) Recommendation networks and the long tail of electronic commerce. MIS Q 36:65–83

Olbrich R, Jansen HC, Hundt M (2016) Effects of pricing strategies and product quality on private label and national brand performance. J Retail Consum Serv 34:294–301

Osterwalder A, Pigneur Y (2013) Business model generation: a handbook for visionaries, game changers, and challengers. Wiley, New York

Rai A, Patnayakuni R, Seth N (2006) Firm performance impacts of digitally enabled supply chain integration capabilities. MIS Q 30:225–246

Rochet J-C, Tirole J (2003) Platform competition in two-sided markets. J Eur Econ Assoc 1 (4):990–1029

Scheer (2017) Scheer marketplace—customization and service purchase. https://shop.scheer-group.com. Accessed 1 Mar 2017

Scott DM (2015) The new rules of marketing and PR: how to use social media, online video, mobile applications, blogs, news releases, and viral marketing to reach buyers directly. Wiley, New York

Slywotzky AJ (1996) Value migration: how to think several moves ahead of the competition. Harvard Business School Press

Slywotzky AJ, Morrison D, Weber K (2001) How digital is your business?. Crown Business, New York

Stampfl G, Prügl R, Osterloh V (2013) An explorative model of business model scalability. Int J Prod Dev 18(3–4):226–248

Stanko MA, Olleros X (2013) Industry growth and the knowledge spillover regime: does outsourcing harm innovativeness but help profit? J Bus Res 66(1):2007–2016

Swafford PM, Ghosh S, Murthy N (2008) Achieving supply chain agility through IT integration and flexibility. Int J Prod Econ 116(2):288–297

Timmers P (1998) Business models for electronic markets. Electron Markets 8(2):3–8

Veit D, Clemons E, Benlian A et al (2014) Business models. Bus Inf Syst Eng 6(1):45–53

Weill P, Woerner SL (2013) Optimizing your digital business model. MIT Sloan Manage Rev 54 (3):71–78

Werth D (2016) Educating digital leadership: Zur Frage der Weiterbildung von digitalen Führungskräften. In: Scheer A-W, Wachter C (eds) Digitale Bildungslandschaften, 1st edn. IMC AG, Saarbruecken, pp 186–201

Werth D, Greff T, Scheer AW (2016a) Consulting 4.0 - Die Digitalisierung der Unternehmensberatung. HMD Praxis der Wirtschaftsinformatik 53(1):55–70

Werth D, Zimmermann P, Greff T (2016b) Self-service consulting: conceiving customer-operated digital IT consulting services. In: Conference paper proceedings of AMCIS 2016, San Diego

Yozgat U, Demirbağ O, Şahin S (2013) The impact of knowledge sharing and partnership quality on outsourcing success. Int Proc Econ Dev Res 63:50. doi:10.7763/IPEDR

Zeng Q, Li X (2008) Evolution of e-business transformation strategy: a four dimension model. In: International conference on service systems and service management, IEEE, pp 1–5

Zott C, Amit R (2010) Business model design: an activity system perspective. Long Range Plan 43:216–226

Author Biographies

Dirk Werth is leading the AWS-Institute for digitized products and processes, a private independent non-profit research center focusing its research on digitization of businesses and society. Before he worked at the German Research Center for Artificial Intelligence (DFKI) for more than a decade, where he served in different management positions. He has been responsible for numerous international and national research and consulting projects in the area of innovation by ICT. He holds Diplomas in Business Administration and in Computer Sciences as well as a Ph.D. in Economics.

Tobias Greff is a professional researcher at the AWS-Institute for digitized products and processes. He holds a Master's degree in Business Information Systems from the Saarland University. His main research topics focus on consulting research, especially future trends in software development tools for the consulting domain and on digital business development in start-up environments.

Chances, Risks and Quality Criteria of Virtual Consulting

Volker Nissen, Henry Seifert and Marco Blumenstein

Abstract A consulting firm can only be successful in the long term if the quality of the consulting services meets or exceeds the expectations of the clients. Therefore, it is of central importance for the consulting firm to know the quality requirements as well as the expectations and fears of clients with respect to virtualized consulting services. Within this contribution, we analyze the expectations of clients through a literature-based Delphi study. Additionally, we investigate which quality criteria clients consider important and how these relate to the degree of virtualization in consulting services. Finally, we also highlight chances and risks of virtual consulting from the perspective of the consultants, based on a second Delphi study. On this basis, we derive implications for the consulting industry.

1 Introduction

Virtualized consulting processes go with reduced (or even without) direct face-to-face interaction between the advisor and the client in specific phases of the consulting project. Instead, information and communication technology (ICT) is specifically used (Overby 2008) to support, assist, control or even replace the consultant. For a more comprehensive introduction to the subject see Nissen (2017).

Whether or not a consulting service can be successfully virtualized is primarily dependent on the client's acceptance and expectations. Only when the clients accept the changed forms and procedures of consulting will they be prepared to make use of these services. To ensure a maximal acceptance regarding the virtual consulting services, it is necessary to clarify which opportunities and risks the clients anticipate

V. Nissen (✉) · H. Seifert · M. Blumenstein
Technische Universität Ilmenau, Ilmenau, Germany
e-mail: volker.nissen@tu-ilmenau.de

H. Seifert
e-mail: henry.seifert@infosysconsulting.com

M. Blumenstein
e-mail: marco.blumenstein@x-case.de

© Springer International Publishing AG 2018   137
V. Nissen (ed.), *Digital Transformation of the Consulting Industry*,
Progress in IS, https://doi.org/10.1007/978-3-319-70491-3_6

in virtual consulting. When the client accepts, and uses the virtual consulting service, he will be able to judge how satisfied he is with this service in the following step.

Consulting firms provide services in areas that are often of great relevance to clients, but also may involve substantial risks for the client. A consulting firm can only be successful in the long term when the quality of the performed consulting services satisfies the clients' expectations. For this reason, quality management (QM) becomes a central management task for consulting businesses (Nissen 2007). Therefore, it is necessary to assess which expectations the clients have regarding the quality of virtual consulting services.

2 Methods and Data

Exploring the expectations of clients forms the basis of the development of procedure models, decision guidance and methods to successfully virtualize consulting services. Eventually, artefacts should be created, according to Hevner et al. (2004), which support consulting businesses innovating their business models in the direction of digital transformation.

The first step in this research endeavour was a systematic multi-step literature review, following the procedure suggested by Webster and Watson (2002). The literature review was performed twice to determine established quality criteria for both traditional consulting services as well as electronic services (Nissen et al. 2015). The result was a catalogue with a preliminary set of quality criteria for virtualized consulting. Subsequently an expert panel evaluated this preliminary criteria catalogue from the client`s perspective. In this process four questions were prominent:

1. Is the catalogue of quality criteria for virtualized consulting services complete?
2. What relevance does the single criterion have?
3. What influence does the degree of virtualization have on the relevance of the criterion?
4. What chances and risks are anticipated by clients in the case of virtual consulting?

To find answers for these research questions a Delphi study, according to Häder and Häder (2000), Häder (2014) was conducted.

The participants of this client survey (Table 1) came from various business branches and they were experienced in working with consultants. It was made sure that the participants chosen had various expertise and that they also had different functions in the business. Experts from the IT and business departments were chosen for this study; representatives of the business dominated. Likewise, considerably more representatives of medium and big companies participated. Therefore, the results should be interpreted carefully against the background of small businesses.

Table 1 Features of the client panel of the Delphi study (first round)

How often do you have direct contact with consulting services?		
Sporadic	1×	The participants fundamentally corresponded to the target
Often	6×	group and have a good or very good knowledge of consulting
Daily	6×	
How many employees do you have in your company?		
51–250	1×	Participants mainly came from medium to big companies
251–1000	1×	
1001–2000	4×	
>2000	7×	
In which branch of industry is your company active?		
Automotive	5×	Mainly participants from the chemical and automotive
Industry (without further details)	1×	industry
Chemical	5×	
Energy	1×	
Financial services	1×	
In which department are you employed?		
Business department	11×	Mainly participants from business departments
IT department	2×	

The Delphi study had two questioning rounds. Results of the literature analysis formed the starting point for quality criteria of virtual consulting services. Furthermore, the experts had the opportunity to add their own quality criteria into free-text fields. Regarding the added value and risks of virtual consulting, the experts were asked in open questions to formulate their opinion. The second questioning wave was started two weeks after the first one. Hereby the results from the first survey were consolidated. The second survey was finished by ten clients (13 clients answered the questionnaire during the first round).

The question should also be clarified which opportunities and risks are observed by the consultants when virtualizing their services. For this goal a second Delphi survey was conducted (Nissen and Seifert 2015). In doing so, a panel of consulting experts was questioned in two rounds again (Table 2). Here the experts could also formulate their assessments freely in the first questioning round. The second round was used to consolidate the results and was finished by twelve consultants (20 participants finished the first questionnaire). In both Delphi surveys, the required minimum number of participants, according to Häder and Häder (2000), was thus achieved. Both surveys were conducted on-line with the aid of the software Questback. This was done in autumn 2014. For further details of the method see Nissen et al. (2015), as well as Nissen and Seifert (2015).

Table 2 Features of the consultant panel of the Delphi study (second round)

Expert No.	Professional experience (years)	Position/Department	Size of the company (employees)
1	14	Innovation Center, Sales	120
2	5	Managing Consultant/Advisory	100,000
3	5	VP Strategy Development/Strategy Development	50,000
4	20	Management Consultant/Security Service	400,000
5	30	Associated Partner/Management Technology	1000
6	9	Manager/Advisory/Sales	140,000
7	14	CEO/Consultant	30
8	20	Sales & Business Development/Sales	20,000
9	5	Technical Architect/Custom Solution Development/Sales	130,000
10	18	CEO/Sales	45
11	8	Senior Manager/Technology Architecture	280,000
12	19	Director Marketing & Sales	110
13	14	CEO/Innovation	100
14	22	CEO/Sales	80
15	9,5	Senior Project Consultant/Education/ Certification	50,000
16	20,5	Principal Enterprise Architect/ Business Technology	127,000
17	18	Senior Manager/IT-Consulting	180,000
18	15	Manager IT Consulting/Advisory	180,000
19	16	Senior Manager/Risk and IT-Service	180,000
20	18	CEO/Sales	200

3 Results and Discussion

3.1 Chances and Risks of Virtual Consulting from the Consultants' Perspective

Besides financial reasons, like sinking costs (e.g. due to reduced travel times), the improved flexibility of consulting services (spatio-temporal and regarding the involved knowledge carriers) plays an important role to the consultants. Virtual consulting services are not seen as premium services, but rather provide potential in the field of commodity services. Additionally, it is expected that virtualization brings advantages in the availability to the client (from increased use of ICT), as well as generally accelerating the consulting project. One also assumes that it will be easier for the employees to achieve a good work-life-balance due to the

Table 3 Chances and risks of virtualization from the perspective of the consultants (Nissen and Seifert 2015)

Chances	Risks
Greater temporal flexibility	Weaker client-consultant-relationships
More spatial flexibility	
Working across time zones	IT-security and data safety problems
Shorter reaction times	
Time savings	Increasing coordination and alignment efforts
Cost savings	
Better use of colleagues knowledge	Communication, coordination and cooperation difficulties
Better availability of resources	
Optimization of work-life-balance	Insufficient individualization
Better availability for the client	
Higher working rate	Uncontrollable project complexity
Better pricing options for services	

improved spatio-temporal flexibility of service deliveries as well as shorter travel times. Against the background of a generally high workload in business consulting, this could make the respective company a particularly attractive employer in the war-for-talents (Termer and Nissen 2011, 2012).

From a strategic point of view, the apprehended weakening of the consultant-client relationship should be emphasized among the risks. This can have a negative effect on the trust of the parties involved, while trust is a central asset in consulting (Glückler and Armbrüster 2003). In this aspect, standardization could lead to lesser individualization, which, in turn, may have a negative impact on the service delivery. From an operational point of view, in addition to security issues, uncontrollable project complexity is particularly feared. Associated problems in the fields of communication, coordination and cooperation are also apprehended. Table 3 summarizes the chances and risks of virtualization.

3.2 Chances and Risks of Virtual Consulting from the Clients' Perspective

It is surprising that the clients have similar expectations as the questioned consultants (see Table 4). In general, the clients expect a range of advantages from digital consulting services compared to conventional consulting forms. Clients assume that the reduction or even absence of consultant presence on-site and direct interaction results in lower prices. Another expected benefit on the client side is the higher reaction speed and work rate. The characteristics of the virtualization mechanism, especially the greater (spatial and temporal) reach of virtual services, promise faster working. Urgent client-problems could be solved faster as travelling

Table 4 Chances and risks of virtualization from the perspective of the clients (Nissen and Seifert 2015)

Chances	Risks
Higher reaction and working speed	Communication, coordination and cooperation difficulties
Lower prices of consulting services	Weaker client-consultant-relationships
Better flexibility in selecting consultants	Lower performance and quality of service
Easier international work	Higher chance of data abuse
Use of innovative consulting solutions	Lower level of trust
Better knowledge access and sharing	Lower level of loyalty
Better reuse of results and project documents	Insufficient individualization
Better flexibility in tasks management	High technological dependency
Better availability of consulting services	Higher chance of loss of control

time is not necessary. Additionally, standardized solutions that need only minimum effort for customization would be available instantly. The reach of the virtualization mechanism offers the possibility to select the right person from a greater pool of consultants. Even consultants that usually do not work in a specific region could be assigned to projects virtually. The surveyed clients expect increased flexibility in terms of where and when to cooperate with consultants because of use of ICT for distributed work.

Once the virtual consulting service started and the project is running clients expect benefits that relate to the continuous logging and monitoring capabilities of the virtualization mechanism. All the information that was exchanged within the consulting process and every tool or result could be monitored and stored more easily. This information could later be used for upcoming projects or in other projects that somehow relate to the current one. Clients expect that efforts for project documentation are lower as many processes and results are already digitally documented within a virtual consulting process. Additionally clients expect that sharing information becomes easier. On the other hand, virtualization implies a high technology dependency and may lead to data abuse and a loss of control over the project.

When virtualization is combined with standardization and automation the level of consulting quality is feared to be at risk by the clients. On the other hand, the uncertainty that comes along with engaging in consulting services would possibly be reduced via standardization (Dichtl 1998). Clients expect it would be easier to select a specific (virtual) consulting product among similar products, as their properties would be easier to compare. Clients do think that virtualization goes along with the opportunity to introduce and regularly use innovative consulting tools that will help them optimize their business autonomously. Partly or fully automated consulting services would help clients to gain flexibility within their daily business while always having the option to get in contact with experts when they are needed (Christensen et al. 2013).

3.3 Quality Criteria of Virtual Consulting Services from the Clients' Perspective

The conducted evaluation, amendment and prioritization by the experts resulted in an integrated catalogue of quality criteria for virtual consulting. In this catalogue the criteria of traditional consulting services and electronic services were combined and sorted as to the clients' quality preferences (Fig. 1). In the following the quality criteria are briefly explained. Thereafter the correlation between the degree of virtualization and the importance of the individual criteria will be dealt with.

System availability describes the correct and technically perfect functionality of a virtual consulting service. This includes the actuality of the data and information as well as a stable and retrievable consulting process in the Internet. This aspect seemed to be particularly important to the participants.

Fulfillment, also a high-ranking criterion, aims at the technical delivery of the consulting service. The assurances made when the virtual consulting service was offered will be compared with the actual solution and should agree with this. Contents and information, which are available within a corresponding consulting application, should not have any mistakes and should match the reality. This in particular has to do with the features of the used technology and tools. In that respect, this criterion differs from the criterion *Achieving objectives* of consulting quality, which aims at the actual solution of the business problem.

Quality Criteria of Virtual Consulting Services

Criteria of electronic services:

1. System availability
2. Fulfilment
3. Efficiency
4. Reaction capability
5. Privacy
6. Contact
7. Aesthetics
8. Compensation

Criteria of traditional consulting:

1. Professional consulting competencies
2. Achieving objectives
3. Social consulting competencies
4. Consulting process quality
5. Clients' integration
6. Quality of the relationship
7. Reputation of consulting provider

(Ranking in respective sections)

Fig. 1 Quality criteria of virtual consulting services—ranking in the respective sections. Nissen et al. (2015) in source: Deelmann T, Ockel DM, in collaboration with BDU e.V. (eds) Handbuch der Unternehmensberatung, loose-leaf book, state 2017, KZ. 7311, courtesy of Erich Schmidt Verlag GmbH & Co. KG, Berlin 2017, more about the loose-leaf book at http://www.esv.info/978-3-503-07846-2

Efficiency aims at features, which lead to high performance. Here it is necessary to deliver the consulting service as efficient as possible, specifically using ICT. This could include, among others, a user-friendly interface and navigation, good structuring of the online service, search functions and the pace at which the individual consulting results are provided. The efficiency is significantly responsible for the quality of a virtual consulting service and presents an added value in comparison with conventional consulting (Leimeister 2012).

Reaction capability describes the support in the case of (technical) problems and mistakes. The client evaluates the pace at which a solution for the problem can be initiated. The option to ask for help and to get a quick reaction can objectively be measured at the same time. A purely electronically conducted assistance can though lead to obscurities on the client's side so that consulting should critically evaluate this option. To improve the reaction capability and quality of problem solving in a virtual consulting process, different contact channels should be offered. This refers to both technical as well as professional problems, which can arise during usage.

Privacy aims for relevant data security and an adequate data protection according to the client's expectation. The protection of personal data as well as business data, and the secure dealing with these data needs to be guaranteed (Schuster 2005). Here the client evaluates the felt security of this data and the security mechanisms of the virtual consulting service offered for that reason.

Contact is a criterion describing the option to approach a consulting firm directly when questions and problems arise. Precast contact options, e.g. the often-used FAQs or contact forms, frequently are not satisfactory, so that the option should be offered to the client to have real-time contact with an expert (Wurdack 2001). Contact can be made by telephone, chat applications or similar functions. The quality of this criterion, therefore, on the one side is measured via the option of making this contact, but on the other side also via the interaction quality and regarding the client's wishes for feedback.

Aesthetics refers to the image and visualization of the consulting solution, respectively the website that was generated for the consulting service. A virtual consulting service of this criterion needs to be really good to outperform traditional consulting offers. Then it will be easier for the client to make use of the virtual solution.

Compensation describes to what extent a reimbursement will be offered to a client when there are problems during the (virtual) consulting process. When this criterion is largely fulfilled, then this will contribute to a high quality of the virtual consulting. This mainly involves fully virtualized and automated consulting services, where the client autonomously uses a consulting application. If there are any deficiencies when using the software based consulting product, corresponding compensation offers have to be available. Additionally, the client will then expect to have the option of personal consultation.

Professional consulting competencies is an exceptionally important aspect. With this criterion a mutual trust can be developed and the client's confidence can be enhanced. Criteria like knowledge of the industry and company-specific aspects, knowledge of methods and an easy access to high class information sources represent a substantial part of professional consulting competencies. When the professional expertise of the consultants is assessed, the client's opinion is always relevant. Competencies are thus only subjectively evaluated. Therefore, the assessment amongst different clients can vary a lot.

Achieving objectives aims at the economical and project specific requirements, which should be fulfilled on the client's side. In addition to accomplishing the consulting goals, factors like time (meeting the deadline), costs (adhering to the budget) and quality are used to determine the degree to which objectives were achieved. Partly it is a matter of quantifiable criteria which can be assessed, e.g. with the aid of a cost-benefit analysis, a should-is-comparison, or other methods which are used to measure the profitability. However, by using the example of acceptance of the consulting results, it is noticeable that several of these aspects can only be qualitatively assessed by the client.

Social consulting competencies are necessary to establish and develop a relationship with the client (Aldhizer et al. 2002). Due to the increasing competition in the consulting branch, this criterion has become more and more important for assessing the quality of a consulting service. The appearance and behavior of the consultant are possible criteria to assess these social consulting competencies and should not be neglected alongside the professional competencies. Soft skills like empathy and cooperativeness are also important aspects. Once more, only the client's opinion is relevant for assessing this criterion.

Consulting process quality refers to the quality of service delivery in a procedural respect. Client orientated working, as well as professional and flexible solutions are some aspects, which can be used to assess the quality of traditional and virtual consulting processes. A transparent and clearly structured project organization is the corner-stone for the successful handling of consulting service delivery. The pace of the service delivery, as well as the reaction capability to solve problems are further aspects having an influence on the quality of consulting processes. They carry weight during the generation of a satisfactory assessment.

Clients' integration relates to communication and working together with the client during the consulting project. The perceived level of how active the clients' side was involved in the consulting process serves as a qualitative measurement parameter. This criterion deserves special attention in the case of virtualized consulting services because face-to-face communication is reduced.

Quality of the relationship aims particularly at the personal relationship between the customer and the consultant. The compliance of the consultant's behavior and the client's expectation is one of the basic criteria to assess the quality of their relationship. Virtualization of consulting services results in a changed consulting process, which reduces direct contact between the consultant and the client. This consequently may put the quality of the relationship between the consultant and the client at risk. Particularly, it may reduce the client's trust in the consultant. From the client's perspective, trust and confidence in the consultant are of great importance. In particular, there exists a service-specific quality risk, respective information insecurity for the clients for both traditional as well as virtual consulting services. When the service is used for the first time, the client needs to be able to trust the promises made by the consultant. Commitment is a further component of the relationship quality. Commitment can be understood as "a feeling of inner commitment and can also be an expression of a psychological need for social recognition and belonging, as well as the wish to predict the behavior of business partners" (Jeschke 2007). The third factor assessing the relational quality is the clients' overall satisfaction with the consulting service.

Reputation of the consulting provider is the reputation of a consulting company, respectively of an individual consultant. Reputation is of major importance when clients decide whether or not to hire a consulting firm to solve their business problems. It is also a critical resource for the consulting provider (Ringlstetter et al. 2007). It is rather difficult to measure reputation. In general, modern equipment, a neat, professional appearance and convincing references will improve the reputation.

3.4   Influence of the Degree of Virtualization on the Quality Criteria

The Delphi study confirmed that the importance of the previously described quality criteria for the clients' total satisfaction varies depending on the degree of virtualization (Fig. 2). The quality of a highly virtualized consulting service is measured more strongly according to the criteria used for the quality of electronic services. A service with a lower virtualization degree is rather evaluated by the quality criteria of traditional consulting services. During the client's quality assessment, the professional and social competencies of the consultant, as well as the quality of the relationship between client and consultant become less important when the virtualization degree increases. Here factors like reaction capability, system availability, privacy and compensation rise in importance.

The survey also illustrated that all criteria should be included when assessing the quality of virtual consulting services. There is no single quality criterion that could be totally neglected from the client's point of view.

4   Some Implications for Consulting Providers

4.1   Implications for Design and Deployment of Virtual Consulting Services

In order to minimize the risks identified above, it is important from an organizational point of view to establish a good preparation and a feeling of cohesion between consultants and clients beyond the limitations of virtualization. Many participants in our study suggested that is desirable to always have access to a

Change in Importance with Rising Degree of Virtualization

Professional competencies of consultants	◑
Social competencies of consultants	◑
Quality of the relationship	◑
Clients' integration	◑
Reputation of consulting provider	➡
Achieving objectives	➡
Consulting process quality	➡
Reaction capability	◕
Efficiency	◕
System availability	◕
Fulfilment	◕
Privacy	◕
Compensation	◕
Contact	◕
Aesthetics	◕

◑ Importance goes down   ➡ Importance stays constant   ◕ Importance goes up

Fig. 2 Importance shift of the quality criteria with rising degree of virtualization. Nissen et al. (2015) in source: Deelmann T, Ockel DM, in collaboration with BDU e.V. (eds) Handbuch der Unternehmensberatung, loose-leaf book, state 2017, KZ. 7311, courtesy of Erich Schmidt Verlag GmbH & Co. KG, Berlin 2017, more about the loose-leaf book at http://www.esv.info/978-3-503-07846-2

consultant through personal contact if needed. Starting with the contract negotiations, followed by the conception of a fast and individual virtual solution, up to the acceptance of the consulting result, it is important in the opinion of the clients to have the continuous support of a direct contact person. The majority of the study participants therefore want a mix of virtualized consulting services and classical, personal consulting. This result is somewhat contradictory to the decreasing importance of the relational quality as the degree of virtualization of the consulting offer increases. This is probably reflected in the uncertainty of the interviewees, as highly virtual consulting services are still the exception today and their own experience among the customers is correspondingly low.

4.2 Implications for Quality Management

The quality management of a consulting firm can be divided into the following phases: quality planning, quality control, quality assurance and quality disclosure.

The first phase focuses on the planning and further development of the quality requirements for consulting services. The quality criteria of virtualized consulting services identified above should therefore be critically evaluated by the affected consulting firm in this phase. It should be noted that the importance of the criteria from the customer perspective is shifted depending on the degree of virtualization. In addition to these quality criteria, the opportunities and risks of virtualization, which have already been described, must also be considered during the quality planning phase. Through the increased use of ICT in the implementation of virtualization, the basic task of quality management is retained. In this phase, however, consulting firms have to expand their viewpoints by adding technology-specific aspects.

In the next phase, quality control, specific activities are carried out in order to meet the expectations of the clients. For this purpose, employee-related, organization-related, culture-related and technology-related instruments for quality assurance must be implemented. In particular, the last group of instruments should receive increased attention in the context of virtual consulting services, since in the case of customer-oriented planning and implementation additional value can be achieved compared to conventional consulting. For example, additional contact functions could be offered within a virtual consulting service in order to ensure, at any time, the support of an optimally qualified consultant for the respective task.

The quality assurance, third phase in quality management, evaluates the extent to which the quality requirements are met by the offered consulting service. Particularly against the background of lesser personal interaction between consultants and clients, the quality of virtualized consulting services should be continuously monitored through appropriate measuring methods and instruments. The increased use of ICT in the context of virtualization also provides service providers with new possibilities to receive, at any time and largely unbiased, feedback of their clients by digital functions such as e.g. mood barometer and electronic complaints. As indicated above, virtual consulting services require the measurement of quality characteristics of classical business consulting and quality features of electronic services.

The conclusion of a quality management cycle requires the disclosure of the company's own performance both with regard to the quality of the services offered as well as with regard to the internal processes and structures of the company. Audits are used to determine whether own requirements or requirements of established quality management standards are met or not. The documentation and disclosure of quality management and all aspects included in it can be carried out externally, for example, in the form of a certification, and internally in the form of a quality manual. If the consulting provider offers virtual services, then the virtualization-related features, such as specific quality criteria, have to be integrated into these forms of quality management. Quality management should be a holistic process that enables the monitoring of traditional and virtual consulting services. Consulting companies must therefore ensure that their existing quality management is able to meet the extended requirements of such an integrated consulting portfolio. Moreover, quality management aspects should already be taken into account during the design and implementation of virtual consulting services.

5 Conclusions

Summing up the identified benefits, it can be established that clients and consultants expect similar benefits. Higher flexibility and lower costs are the core benefits that have been mentioned from both panels. It is surprising that, considering the different characteristics of the two panels, almost identical benefits were stated. Based on our previous literature analysis, we expected consulting firms to mention some additional benefits: the potential to increase the service quality, the chance to create a better reputation, to create more transparency, to innovate their own business model or the extended potential for knowledge management (Christensen et al. 2013; Dichtl 1998; Polster 2012; Türk 2004; Wurdack 2001)—however, they were not stated in our surveys.

Clients and consultants share similar concerns in respect to risks of virtualization. Although the results generated from the client panel are more differentiated, the core of the concerns refers to communication difficulties, insufficient individualization and weak business relationships. We had expected more differentiated risks coming from the consulting panel. This may have been prevented by the high professional positions of the interviewed consulting experts. Consultants that have more project-oriented responsibilities might have delivered more detailed risks related to daily operative work.

Virtualization is a promising approach for consulting firms to optimize their consulting processes and thereby an innovative option to gain a sustainable competitive advantage. Using state-of-the-art ICT enables consulting firms to deliver customized solutions anytime and anywhere while the individual workload of every consultant can be optimized. The downside of the virtualization is the reduced direct interaction of clients and consultants and thus the risk of weaker client-consultant-relationships—a critical resource of consulting firms.

The results demonstrated in this paper are limited by the number of clients and consultants that were interviewed. Additional limitations must be made as high degrees of virtualization in consulting, including automation, are still relatively new and therefore broad experiences, both on client- and consultants-side, are generally missing. Furthermore, we focused on expert consulting as a basic consulting approach. Other forms of consulting, such as coaching or systemic consulting, may yield other results. Finally, research aiming at ensuring the quality of virtual consulting services will be crucial for a continued strong client-consultant-relationship.

References

Aldhizer GR III, Turner LD, Shank MD (2002) Determinants of consulting service quality for accounting and nonaccounting service providers. J Inf Syst 16(1):61–74

Christensen CM, Wang D, van Bever D (2013) Consulting on the cusp of disruption. Harvard Bus Rev 91(10):106–114

Dichtl M (1998) Standardisierung von Beratungsleistungen. DUV, Wiesbaden

Glückler J, Armbrüster T (2003) Bridging uncertainty in management consulting: the mechanisms of trust and networked reputation. Organ Stud 24(2):269–297

Häder M (2014) Delphi-Befragungen - Ein Arbeitsbuch, 3rd edn. VS Verlag, Wiesbaden

Häder M, Häder S (2000) Die Delphi-Technik in den Sozialwissenschaften - Methodische Forschungen und innovative Anwendungen. VS Verlag, Wiesbaden

Hevner AR, March ST, Park J, Ram S (2004) Design science in information systems research. MIS Q 28(1):75–105

Jeschke K (2007) Die Rolle des Beziehungsmarketings für Beratungsunternehmen. In: Nissen V (ed) Consulting research. Unternehmensberatung aus wissenschaftlicher Perspektive. DUV, Wiesbaden, pp 197–215

Leimeister JM (2012) Dienstleistungsengineering und -management, 2nd edn. Springer, Berlin

Nissen V (ed) (2007) Consulting Research—Eine Einführung. In: Consulting research. Unternehmensberatung aus wissenschaftlicher Perspektive. DUV, Wiesbaden, pp 3–38

Nissen V (2017) Digital transformation of the consulting industry—introduction and overview. In this volume

Nissen V, Seifert H (2015) Virtualization of consulting—benefits, risks and a suggested decision process. In: Pavlou P, Saunders C (eds) Proceedings of AMCIS 2015, vol 2, Puerto Rico, pp 1380–1391

Nissen V, Seifert H, Blumenstein M (2015) Virtualisierung von Beratungsleistungen: Qualitätsanforderungen, Chancen und Risiken der digitalen Transformation in der Unternehmensberatung aus der Klientenperspektive. In: Deelmann T, Ockel DM (eds) Handbuch der Unternehmensberatung, 25th edn. Erich Schmidt Verlag, Berlin

Overby E (2008) Process virtualization theory and the impact of information technology. Organ Sci 19(2):277–291

Polster T (2012) Innovation in Beratungsunternehmen. Gabler Verlag, Wiesbaden

Ringlstetter M, Kaiser S, Kampe T (2007) Strategische Entwicklung von Unternehmensberatungen - Ein Beitrag aus Sicht der Professional Services Firms Forschung. In: Nissen V (ed) Consulting research. Unternehmensberatung aus wissenschaftlicher Perspektive. DUV, Wiesbaden, pp 179–195

Schuster K (2005) E-consulting; Chancen und Risiken. Dissertation, University of Mannheim

Termer F, Nissen V (2011) Frauen und ihre Work-Life-Balance in der IT-Unternehmensberatung. In: Proceedings of Informatik 2011, LNI vol P-192 (CD, 12 pp)

Termer F, Nissen V (2012) Work-Life-Balance – Strategische Waffe des HR-Managements in der IT-Unternehmensberatung? In: Mattfeld D, Robra-Bissantz S (eds) Proceedings der MKWI 2012. GITO, Berlin, pp 369–380

Türk B (2004) E-Consulting: Der Einsatz webbasierter Technologien in der Unternehmensberatung - eine empirische Untersuchung aus Sicht von Klienten- und Beratungsunternehmen. Dissertation, University of Leipzig

Webster J, Watson R (2002) Analyzing the past to prepare for the future: writing a literature review. MIS Q 26(2):13–23

Wurdack A (2001) E-Consulting - Entwicklung eines Rahmenkonzeptes: Aufbau und Darstellung einer E-Consulting-Lösung im Beratungsunternehmen der Zukunft. Dissertation, University Mannheim

Author Biographies

Volker Nissen holds the Chair of Information Systems Engineering in Services at Technische Universität Ilmenau, Germany, since 2005. Prior to this, he pursued a consulting career, including positions as manager at IDS Scheer AG, director at DHC GmbH, and CEO of NISSCON Ltd., Germany. In 1994 he received a Ph.D. degree in Economic Sciences with distinction from the University of Goettingen, Germany. His current research interests include the digital transformation of the consulting industry, the management of IT-agility, metaheuristic optimization, and process acceptance research. He is author and editor of 19 books and some 200 other publications, including papers in Business & Information Systems Engineering, Information Systems Frontiers, IEEE Transactions on EC, IEEE Transactions on NN, and Annals of OR.

Henry Seifert is a graduate engineer for media technology and since 2011 working as a management consultant. His main focus is on the automotive industry and artificial intelligence, analytics, process optimization and requirements management. He works in projects in the area of sales and after sales processes as well as professional learning. As doctoral candidate at the Chair of Information Systems Engineering in Services at Technische Universität Ilmenau, he examines the digital transformation in the consulting industry. The goal of his dissertation is to demonstrate the opportunities and limitations of virtualization, as well as the design of artifacts that enable the realization of virtual consulting services.

Marco Blumenstein has studied Business Information Systems Engineering at Technische Universität Ilmenau, Germany. There he was also involved in a research project on the virtualization of consulting services and specifically examined the expectations of consulting clients and developed a method to support the selection of a particular virtualization technology. He graduated as a Master of Science in 2017. Since 2013, he has been working as a working student at X-CASE GmbH, in the area of SAP ERP consulting. Since 2017, he is a SAP Consultant focused on logistics and e-commerce processes within the SAP ERP.

Digital Transformation in Business Consulting—Status Quo in Germany

Volker Nissen and Henry Seifert

Abstract Within this contribution, we present the core findings of an empirical study on the virtualization of consulting services, which was conducted with the support of the Association of German Business Consultants at the end of 2015. More than 500 consultants participated in this study. The results document on the one hand, where the industry currently stands in the digital transformation process. On the other hand, we are also looking for answers to the questions of how the further development could look like in this area, what technologies are influencing and how the business models of classical business consulting are affected by the digital transformation.

1 Study Design and Data

In order to assess the status quo of the digital transformation in the German consulting market, consulting firms of all magnitudes and from all fields of business consulting (Strategy-, Organization-, Information Technology (IT)- and Human Resources (HR)-Consulting) were questioned. In the scope of the study described here, new data (primary data) were collected online. An online survey has numerous advantages over other forms of data collection, such as low costs, the elimination of manual data input and the fast availability of the data (Atteslander 2010). However, there are also some disadvantages (Pötschke and Simonson 2001). Due to the anonymity on the Internet, there is an increased risk, that the participant can take part more than once. There is also the risk, that inexperienced Internet users have problems with answering the questionnaire. These aspects were thus minimized as the Association of German Business Consultants (BDU e.V.) sent out specific invitations to their contacts for participation. Furthermore, the

V. Nissen (✉) · H. Seifert
Technische Universität Ilmenau, Ilmenau, Germany
e-mail: volker.nissen@tu-ilmenau.de

H. Seifert
e-mail: henry.seifert@infosysconsulting.com

© Springer International Publishing AG 2018
V. Nissen (ed.), *Digital Transformation of the Consulting Industry*,
Progress in IS, https://doi.org/10.1007/978-3-319-70491-3_7

153

Table 1 Structure of the online-questionnaire

#	Section	Content
1	Categorization of the participants	Enterprise size, consulting field, client branch and consulting experience
2	Importance of virtualization	General assessment, current and future
3	Use of virtualization	Depending on the level of virtualization and the project phase
4	Progress of virtualization	Progress of digital transformation in each of the questioned companies
5	Barriers to virtualization	Evaluation of barriers and obstacles to virtualization within the consulting business
6	Technologies of virtualization	Evaluation of the importance of each technology for the virtualization of consulting firm services
7	Determinants of virtualization	Evaluation of the determinants of virtualizability in consulting services
8	Applications of virtualization	Open question on the use and application possibilities of virtualization in consulting

Nissen and Seifert (2016a) in source: Deelmann T, Ockel DM, in collaboration with BDU e.V. (eds) Handbuch der Unternehmensberatung, loose-leaf book, state 2017, KZ. 7312, courtesy of Erich Schmidt Verlag GmbH & Co. KG, Berlin 2017, more about the loose-leaf book at http://www.esv.info/978-3-503-07846-2

comprehensibility of the questionnaire was given particular attention. This will be further discussed below.

The online-survey was carried out using the survey software 'Unipark Questback'. The questionnaire, with 18 questions, was divided into the topics illustrated in Table 1.

The questions were developed according to the principles of simplicity (avoiding complex sentences and technical terms), neutrality (avoiding suggestive formulations) and clearness (avoiding double questions) (Homburg 2015).

Subsequently a pre-test was done and the final completion of the questionnaire followed. The pre-test was carried out with both members of the research project at the University of Technology Ilmenau, Germany, as well as with experts of the BDU. By means of this test phase information on the following aspects could be collected: How comprehensible is the questionnaire, to what extent do the questioned persons have adequate information available, to what extent the answer categories are adequately illustrated and how much time is really necessary to answer the entire questionnaire (Diamantopoulos et al. 1994).

The survey was carried out from the 23rd November to the 18th December 2015. During the following editing and coding of the data, a data cleansing was done. Thus, those questionnaires, which were not completed by the participants were separated. Likewise, very incompletely processed questionnaires were excluded. Altogether 552 questionnaires could be considered for the statistical analysis.

Based on the structure of the German consulting market regarding the market share, businesses with a turnover of less than ten million Euro are somewhat

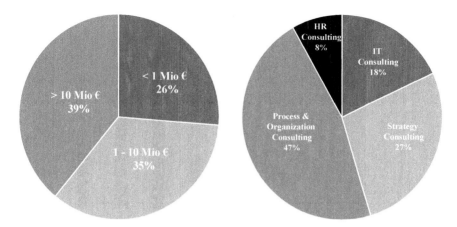

Fig. 1 Composition of the random sample in terms of the yearly turnover of the consulting business (left, n = 520) as well as the consulting field (right, n = 552). Nissen and Seifert (2016a) in source: Deelmann T, Ockel DM, in collaboration with BDU e.V. (eds) Handbuch der Unternehmensberatung, loose-leaf book, state 2017, KZ. 7312, courtesy of Erich Schmidt Verlag GmbH & Co. KG, Berlin 2017, more about the loose-leaf book at http://www.esv.info/978-3-503-07846-2

over-presented in the random sample (Fig. 1). Overall, the German consulting market is however well represented. Consultants from different consulting fields participated in this survey. Strategy consulting in Germany has a share of 24.8% of the total turnover, according to the Facts & Figures—study of the BDU (BDU 2015). Furthermore, organization- and process consulting has a share of 43.3%, HR-consulting 10.4% and IT-consulting 21.4%.

Even though the turnover was not considered in the random participant sample, it seems that the German consulting market is also adequately represented in this aspect. The sample was rather put together by choosing participants from various consulting fields. It should also be taken into consideration that a distinct assignment of consulting fields is often difficult, as consulting businesses offer services from different consulting fields and combine them with each other.

It was also important to investigate the involvement of both young, as well as very experienced consultants to attain valid assessments of the significance and future of virtualization. Moreover, it turned out that the opinion of consultants with different experience levels could be captured (Fig. 2). Furthermore, the participants were asked to estimate their present experience with virtual consulting services. Half of the questioned participants so far had acquired no experience, or were rather short on experience with virtualization of consulting services. A third of the participants stated that they already have acquired some experience, and almost a fifth of the consultants said that they have much, resp. very much experience in this area. These experience values point to the fact that virtualization is still at an early stage, and in particular experience with complex, virtual consulting services is still scarce.

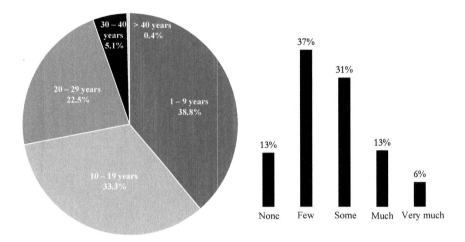

Fig. 2 Composition of the random sample in terms of work experience in consulting (left column: n = 552), as well as the participants' experience with virtual consulting services (right column n = 531). Nissen and Seifert (2016a) in source: Deelmann T, Ockel DM, in collaboration with BDU e.V. (eds) Handbuch der Unternehmensberatung, loose-leaf book, state 2017, KZ. 7312, courtesy of Erich Schmidt Verlag GmbH & Co. KG, Berlin 2017, more about the loose-leaf book at http://www.esv.info/978-3-503-07846-2

Moreover, later questions in the questionnaire revealed that the participants in our sample tended to overestimate their experience with virtual consulting.

In summary, it can be said that the data of this survey underlies a random sample, which can be looked upon as representative of the German consulting market. The number of participants of over 500 consultants enables us to derive trends and theses, which are well founded for the German consulting market. In the following, selected results of this survey will be described in more detail.

2   Principal Findings

2.1   Basic Attitude to Digital Transformation in Consulting

The classical way of business consulting is a personnel-intensive service. Virtualization involves a paradigm shift and aims at business models, which in specific sections replace human consulting services by technology. Thus, opposition and anxieties concerning virtualization can develop. A majority of the survey participants (Fig. 3) though rate virtualization as a chance to make use of the possibilities and potential of technologies during consulting.

Only one percent of the questioned consultants felt that virtualization was a threat. This distinct minority fears that technology-based consulting services can threaten their own business model and their own market position. The perspective

Fig. 3 Basic attitude concerning the virtualization of consulting services (n = 520). Nissen and Seifert (2016a) in source: Deelmann T, Ockel DM, in collaboration with BDU e.V. (eds) Handbuch der Unternehmensberatung, loose-leaf book, state 2017, KZ. 7312, courtesy of Erich Schmidt Verlag GmbH & Co. KG, Berlin 2017, more about the loose-leaf book at http://www.esv.info/978-3-503-07846-2

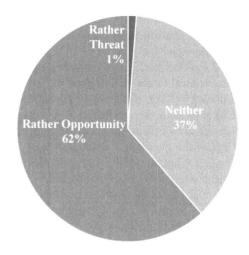

to expand existing services in a meaningful way, gives way to the fear of this group, that technology-based consulting services would make classical consulting irrelevant. This group is in danger to become a victim of the "innovator's dilemma" (Christensen 1997).

We want to advise the businesses, which especially see virtualization as a threat, to deal with the wide spectrum of virtual consulting services in a profound, open and unbiased way. This should include a differentiated analysis of their own service portfolio, the competitive context, clients and projects in terms of the possibilities, chances and risks of virtualization. This will then serve as a sound basis for a profound evaluation of the possible applications of the many variants of virtualization.

37% of the participants do not see virtualization as a clear threat nor as a chance. More than a third of the questioned consultants were thus not aware of the fact that virtualization can offer an added benefit when competing against other businesses. The question, how risks, which go along with virtualization, can be dealt with, also still seems to be unresolved. A crucial factor here is the acceptance and use of virtual consulting services by the clients. The active cooperation with clients and the mutual involvement with concepts of virtualization should be gently enforced.

Furthermore, businesses that are currently still neutral regarding the significance of virtualization, should deal in detail with the challenges, chances and consequences of virtual consulting services. It should also be considered that virtualization breaks with some habits of consulting. It is, for example, dubious whether the current accounting model, which is commonly based on the accounting of time units, will keep its supremacy (Deelmann 2009). The concurrency of the service creation and execution can also be changed by using technology (Deelmann 2009). Based on rather little experience, which participants so far have made with virtualization, additional educational work is necessary to explain the features, chances and risks thereof. Moreover, it is important to demonstrate prototypes and their successful application to show that complex variants of virtualization can also be used beneficially.

62% of the participants see virtualization as a chance. These participants realize that technical progress, specifically in the field of information and communication technology (ICT), will have significant effects on the future performance of consulting services. Meanwhile the current technology has sustainably changed the commercial world in all phases during the product- and service lifecycle. Two thirds of the questioned consultants are of the opinion, that the already high penetration of digitalization in many branches will eventually also influence the added value processes of consulting providers.

Virtual consulting services can be assigned to a wide spectrum, which reaches from video conferences via online business coaching to self-service applications. Already existing technology (e.g. conference tools or mobile apps) enables consulting businesses to optimize their internal and external processes. Virtualization technologies offer new potentials and chances to design consulting processes in a more rapid, efficient and client oriented way. These opportunities were recognized by a majority of the participants.

When looking at the assessment of virtualization, differences among the size groups of the questioned companies can be determined. Rather big consulting businesses with an annual turnover of over ten million Euros consider virtualization as a clear chance. Big providers often have complex service systems, where service portfolios are characterized by a broad spectrum of consulting services. Virtualization then has the potential to further differentiate their own value creation processes. The chances to better connect consultants with each other and to be able to exchange knowledge more rapidly supports the efficiency and quality of service delivery, which is particularly promising for large-scale consulting firms.

In summary, it seems that virtualization is rather noticed as a chance by the participants. Nevertheless, a third of the participants are unsure whether the chances of virtualization outweigh the risks. Therefore, it will be necessary to devise methods and tools, which will help to assess virtualization potentials correctly, to secure the positive effects of utilization and at the same time limit the risks of virtualization.

2.2 The Importance of Virtualization for the Consulting Business Model

Only 7% of the questioned consultants stated that virtualization is unimportant for the business model of their own company (Fig. 4). These consulting providers solely put emphasis on the personal and direct contact between client and consultant. As it can be assumed that these consultants use common means of communication like e-mail etc., virtualization can, however, be rudimentarily present.

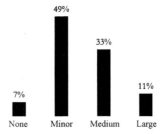

Fig. 4 Significance of virtualization for the *current* business model. Nissen and Seifert (2016a) in source: Deelmann T, Ockel DM, in collaboration with BDU e.V. (eds) Handbuch der Unternehmensberatung, loose-leaf book, state 2017, KZ. 7312, courtesy of Erich Schmidt Verlag GmbH & Co. KG, Berlin 2017, more about the loose-leaf book at http://www.esv.info/978-3-503-07846-2

A reason why virtualization is not very important may be found in the service portfolios of these consulting firms. It can be assumed that their service spectrum involves complex and interaction-intensive consulting services, which cannot be readily virtualized.

About half of the participants (49%) stated that virtualization as a business model is currently hardly of any importance for their own company. Virtualization is presently used here in a supportive way. Technology is deployed by these consultants to ensure the efficiency as well as location-independent communication and cooperation. Innovative virtual consulting services are barely offered by these companies.

Virtualization has a medium-sized relevance for 33% of the questioned consulting businesses. Initial concrete approaches and business ideas of virtualization are used to meaningfully extend the traditional delivery-model of the specific company. Eleven percent of the participants stated that virtualization plays an important role in their consulting. In this case, it can be assumed that relatively extensive offers of virtual consulting services are already available.

The actual significance of virtualization in their own business model is the largest for consulting providers with an annual turnover of more than ten million Euros. Here, virtualization is also most advanced in the implementation. Thus, the starting situation is especially advantageous to exploit the whole spectrum of virtualization. The great significance assigned by these consulting firms can also be attributed to an in-depth analysis of the topic virtualization that has already taken place in these companies.

The statistical evaluation shows that the assessment of the current significance of virtualization on behalf of IT- and HR-consulting is similar, and by tendency higher than the evaluation of strategy and organizational/process consulting. The fact that the consultants of IT-consulting rate the significance of virtualization higher, was to be expected, as IT-consulting is already strongly driven by technology and is subjected to an extremely high competitive pressure. Virtualization is here an essential means to ensure competitiveness. Moreover, the service portfolio of

IT-consulting shows a high virtualization potential. A virtual consulting service, which is already offered by these businesses, is for example a remote application management, thus the care and support of IT-applications via so-called helpdesks. Additionally, diverse virtual consulting services are already used for the selection and implementation of software in projects. Thus "customizing", which means the individualization of standard software, the testing of new software solutions and user trainings, are already performed in a virtual and technology-based way. The distinct technology orientation of IT-consulting service systems facilitates extensive virtualization.

Participants working in HR-consulting also give a high assessment to the significance of virtualization. One can conclude here, that particularly in the field of talent management, virtualization plays a big role. Virtualization makes it possible to evaluate a large pool of talents, independent of the location and time of each candidate. A virtual service, which is also provided by HR-consulting, is online-coaching. This makes a continuous support service for managers possible in the field of management diagnostics and development.

Consultants from strategy consulting state, by tendency, that virtualization is less significant for their business model. Consulting services for the development of e.g. marketing or sales strategies or in the field of business development and innovation are described as too complex and individual for virtualization to apply. According to these consultants, the creative processes necessary to solve a problem are not suited for virtualization, but rather require personal contact.

This resembles the significance of virtualization for consulting services of organizational and process consulting. Here participants assume that consulting services from the area of change management as well as reorganization and post-merger integration need the experience and the personal attendance of individual consultants. Using virtual consulting services for highly individual and partly sensible problems is regarded as unsuitable. Even though, this consulting field does offer significant potential for virtualization. Virtualization could bring forth new approaches to process optimization and performance management, which use the existing data from the clients' information systems to automatically model processes and generate performance data. Projects in the fields of customer relationship management and sales issues could result, via data- and technology based solutions, in the creation of new clients' accesses and integration opportunities.

In summary, it can be said, that virtualization nowadays is rather important to large IT-consulting firms as well as to large HR-consulting firms. Consulting companies, which have projects particularly in the areas of organizational and process consulting as well as strategy consulting, regard virtualization as less significant. The assessment of consulting firms with a turnover of less than ten million Euros are similarly moderate.

A look at the future (Fig. 5)—only 6% of the participants were of the opinion that the significance of virtualization for consulting services will not increase. This small number of participants gives traditional consulting approaches a higher ranking, even for the future. These participants might also have exhausted their

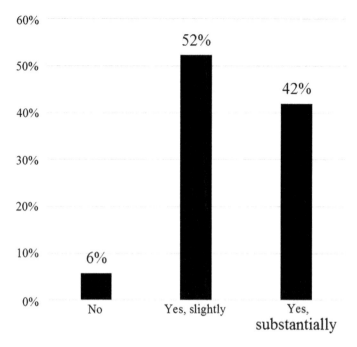

Fig. 5 Assessment of the *future* increase in significance for virtual consulting

capabilities of virtualization. On the other hand, 94% of the participants believe that the significance will increase, at least slightly (52%), whereas 42% believe that it will increase substantially. This result is also due to the extensive penetration of digitalization in all living- and business areas. Digitalization and consequently virtualization is omnipresent, and it changes products and services sustainably. The changes do not fail to leave their mark on consulting businesses. The general increasing acceptance of digitalization presents chances, which will redesign the service systems of consulting businesses and their own value chains in an innovative way. Consultants who are expecting an increase in the significance of virtualization have realized that this is not only an important impulse for their clients, but also for their consulting business.

The lowest increase in significance was predicted amongst businesses with a turnover of between one and ten million Euros. Consulting firms with a turnover of less than one million Euros and more than ten million Euros cannot really be significantly distinguished by their assessment. Thus, small and large consulting businesses expect a stronger increase of virtualization. Virtualization is currently of a rather minor significance for small consulting firms. In the future, it can offer the chance to exploit new client segments by innovative technology-based consulting services. These consulting businesses could operate in niches, which are currently still unexplored. The digital transformation of client-specific business processes leads to new problems, which need innovative consulting solutions. Here lies the potential to develop new consulting products, which will differentiate the business from the competition.

Employees of large consulting firms see an increase in the significance of virtualization, because the complexity of their own organizations, as well as that of the clients' organizations does increase. To keep up with the clients, and to be able to still work efficiently, it is useful to extend virtual service concepts in a meaningful way.

There is an insignificant difference amongst the various consulting fields regarding the expected significance increase of virtualization. This was a surprise, as it seemed plausible to believe that virtualization was more important to IT-consulting, than for the firms in other consulting fields. The reason therefore is that IT-consulting operates in an especially technology-oriented field and the daily rates for standard services decrease continuously. Virtualization and thus consulting concepts putting emphasis on automatization could offer valuable potential to lower the costs against this background. Hence, the margin for standard services would increase again. Respectively, lower prices could exploit new groups of buyers.

HR-consulting does not estimate the future significance increase of virtualization any higher than the other consulting fields. It is though important to note that HR- as well as IT-consulting do already use virtualization more often today than the other consulting fields. Organization- and process consulting, as well as strategy consulting have likewise realized that virtualization will become more important to them in future.

2.3   Virtualization of Different Project Phases

It is not feasible to equally virtualize every phase during the consulting process. The following factors have an influence on the acceptance of digital consulting services, and thus of the virtualization potential (Nissen and Seifert 2016b):

- High complexity has a negative influence.
- High interactivity has a negative influence.
- Great urgency affects the virtualization potential positively.
- Great trust of clients in the consultants has a positive effect.
- A high maturity level concerning virtualization has a positive effect.
- Availability of suitable consultants has a positive effect.

It can be assumed that the phases, which are particularly suited for virtualization are, by tendency first digitally transformed. To verify this assumption, the participants were asked to estimate to which degree each of their consulting phases are being virtualized. As mentioned before, virtual consulting can be assigned to a spectrum, which reaches from simple, supportive usage on the one side, to full

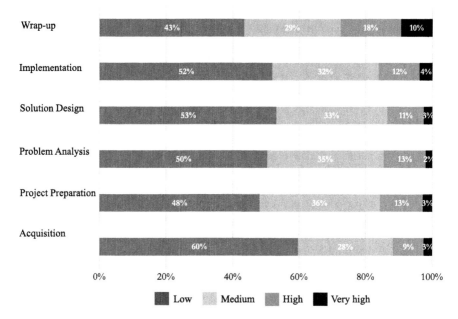

Fig. 6 Degree of virtualization of the individual project phases (n = 472). Nissen and Seifert (2016a) in source: Deelmann T, Ockel DM, in collaboration with BDU e.V. (eds) Handbuch der Unternehmensberatung, loose-leaf book, state 2017, KZ. 7312, courtesy of Erich Schmidt Verlag GmbH & Co. KG, Berlin 2017, more about the loose-leaf book at http://www.esv.info/978-3-503-07846-2

automatization on the other side. Using this spectrum, the participants were now able to indicate to which degree each individual project phase is being virtualized in their own consulting business. Concerning this question 472 responses could be evaluated (Fig. 6).

The customer acquisition, by tendency, shows the lowest degree of virtualization. However, concepts and approaches already exist to sell consulting services online in a type of consulting shop (Werth et al. 2016). There are also corresponding digital options for marketing purposes in the consulting business. Additional activities, which can directly be assigned to the acquisition phase, such as a demand analysis or the presentation of an offer are still conducted by personal contact with the client. Thus, the participants indicated that the individual starting situation and the individual consulting demand could only be adequately determined in a personal conversation on site. There are only isolated approaches to allow clients to configure their own consulting service in some form of a product configurator. The consulting fields do not differ significantly in this phase.

The project preparation phase is overall a bit more virtualized than most other phases are. This phase includes activities such as preparing a detailed project plan, setting up the project organization structure, determining standards, the establishment of a mutual communication level for the project members, the distribution of work packages for consultants and client employees and the project-kick-off. Virtualization is used here in the form of project platforms, audio- and video-conferences as well as knowledge management systems. Approaches for the simulation of project progress are still the exception. As the availability of data and new technologies to analyze these data increases steadily, many extensive opportunities will appear in the future to arrange the preparation in a more efficient and qualitative better way. In this phase, the consulting fields do not show significant differences. Problem analysis includes activities such as the diagnosis of present problems as well as accomplishing a deeper understanding of these problems, to be able to form a basis for the development of solution alternatives. During this phase, slightly less virtualization is currently used than during project preparation. In problem analysis, creative and analytical processes do already take place, which often require direct contact between the consultant and the client. Personal commitment of the consultants as analysts is here still customary. However, there are concepts to automate the analysis of very large quantities of data, such as data mining, analytics applications, and process mining. Virtualization concepts are particularly suited for standardized surveys and analyses. Questionnaires can be put on the Internet to conduct online-assessments for choosing a software product or to determine the maturity of an organization. Furthermore, the analysis phase provides potential to gather avatar-based and fully automated the current situation of the clients. In the scope of a self-service, the clients can be led through an individualized assessment, whilst e.g. technologies of artificial intelligence are being used to analyze individual responses of the clients, regarding the actual situation in the project. Similar virtualization during this phase is shown by all consulting fields in our survey.

The solution design phase, during which problems are solved, includes activities such as the preparation of one or more alternative solutions and presenting them to the decision makers, as well as the selection of the solution to be implemented. This phase has, by tendency, only a moderate virtualization level, and according to the participants, it has a low virtualization potential. The consultants stated that the preparation of a specific solution for the client is often only possible via personal exchange with the customer on site. Using full virtualization was regarded as unrealistic. Personal contact and creative consulting services are inevitable for having success. In this phase of solving problems, the virtualization level for IT-consulting is the highest. This is followed by HR-consulting. IT- and strategy consulting differ significantly. Strategy consulting is distinctly less virtualized than IT-consulting in this phase that may be attributed to the on average higher complexity of strategy consulting tasks.

Implementation includes the implementation of recommendations in the individual analysis areas. This phase is currently just as moderately virtualized as the two former phases. There are significant differences between IT- and strategy consulting during the implementation phase. Whereas IT-consulting already virtualizes its implementation, the activities of strategy consulting are mainly conducted in a traditional way.

The wrap-up work of a project includes activities such as the processing of rendered results for the purpose of re-use and knowledge storage. During this phase the evaluation of project members' individual performance and compiling references are also carried out. The virtualization level of this phase is comparatively high. This means that many activities are already carried out virtually. In most cases, a full virtualization is impossible, because the selection of information and documentation of knowledge needs to be done by a human consultant. In IT-consulting this phase is, in comparison to the other consulting fields, significantly higher virtualized. The other consulting fields do not differ much amongst each other.

Viewing the virtualization level of each phase, it can be determined, that similar to the assessment of the virtualization progress, larger consulting companies have developed their virtualization much further.

2.4 The Use of Different Virtualization Levels

Virtualization makes the formation of a broad spectrum of heterogeneous, innovative consulting services possible. The level of virtualization serves the differentiation of typical forms of virtual consulting offers within this spectrum. A consulting service with a particular low level of virtualization is featured by a low technology input and mainly by direct contact of the actors. The technologies used here, typically are e-mails, and also conference- and chat applications. A consulting service with a particularly high level of virtualization is not feasible without technology and contains concepts such as self-service consulting. These virtual consulting applications are complex individual software developments, which amongst others may contain the newest data analytics procedures.

The analysis of the participants' feedback shows that the frequency of usage decreases, whilst the level of virtualization increases (Fig. 7). Most frequently very low level forms of virtualization are employed. This encompasses the use of e-mails and conference tools for regionally separated and timely synchronized or asynchronized consulting.

Approaches to which a low level of virtualization can be assigned are still used regularly, but definitely less frequently. An example for this type of virtualization is regular virtual collaboration on collaboration platforms, also called "project places". Consulting with a medium level of virtualization is, by tendency, rarely used or not at all. These include approaches such as online coaching on professional topics, or concepts where the actors hardly have direct or personal contact with each other. Some approaches of automatization can also be found here. Of the participants, 63% state that they do not use a high level of virtualization at all. This level includes, for example, a remote-diagnostic-tool, which could be linked to the central ERP-system of the client.

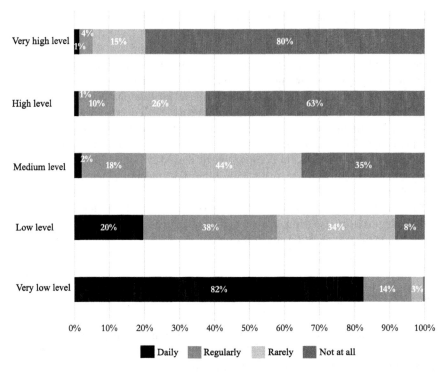

Fig. 7 The use of various levels of virtualization (n = 473). Nissen and Seifert (2016a) in source: Deelmann T, Ockel DM, in collaboration with BDU e.V. (eds) Handbuch der Unternehmensberatung, loose-leaf book, state 2017, KZ. 7312, courtesy of Erich Schmidt Verlag GmbH & Co. KG, Berlin 2017, more about the loose-leaf book at http://www.esv.info/978-3-503-07846-2

Consulting services and approaches with a very high level of virtualization, which are largely automated are not used at all, as stated by 80% of the participants. Only one percent of the consultants replied that they use this type of virtualization daily. This includes e.g. self-service consulting, such as a rule-based fully automatic online-assessment, which based on the data entered by the client creates an expert report.

The impression that virtualization in business consulting is still at the beginning, for the majority of the consulting providers, is strengthened by the analysis of the results received on consulting services with various levels of virtualization. The participants, who were questioned, use approaches with a middle to very high level of virtualization only very rarely. Here a lot of unused potential is concealed (because it is not fully understood). More in depth examination of the tasks, contents and procedures within a consulting phase could lead to valid starting points for a stronger virtualization. This also entails the examination of the data, technologies and actors, which may be needed to fulfil the tasks.

Full virtualization describes the extremum of virtualization where the human performance and the personal contact disappears almost completely. Avatars take over from business consultants and offer a comprehensive spectrum of automated solutions. Results are produced promptly, automated and personalized without requiring any contribution of an employee of the consulting business. Full virtualization basically offers the opportunity to be able to conduct routine consulting tasks most efficiently. Automated consulting services make a simple scaling possible and thus the short-term covering of similar customer requests. Another advantage of automatization is a quality standard, which guarantees a uniform service delivery and can thus be marketed accordingly. However, an automated consulting service has limits regarding the required individuality. Thus, full virtualization only enables the solution for a specific class of problems.

Clients with a very individual consulting requirement and a complex starting situation would hardly be advised to use automated approaches. Another aspect, which can be considered as a hindrance for full virtualization, is the client's skill to use this kind of self-service correctly. To be able to analyze what significance full virtualization will have in the future, the participants were asked to estimate the significance of automated consulting services for the next five years. There were 506 responses, which could be evaluated (Fig. 8).

16% of the participants stated that full virtualization will be irrelevant also in the future. The prior described disadvantages and particularly the apprehension that the provided service might not satisfy the clients' quality demands, contributes to this tendency. Just more than half of the participants (51%) refer to a minor significance of full virtualization in the future. The tendency can also be noted here, that human contribution to knowledge intensive services, like consulting, can hardly be replaced by virtualization. Full virtualization is seen as a niche solution by these participants. A group of 24% of the participants, however, allocate a medium

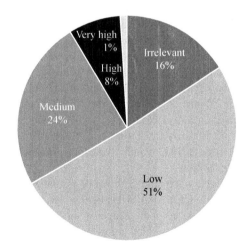

Fig. 8 Future significance of full virtualization in consulting (n = 506). Nissen and Seifert (2016a) in source: Deelmann T, Ockel DM, in collaboration with BDU e.V. (eds) Handbuch der Unternehmensberatung, loose-leaf book, state 2017, KZ. 7312, courtesy of Erich Schmidt Verlag GmbH & Co. KG, Berlin 2017, more about the loose-leaf book at http://www.esv.info/978-3-503-07846-2

significance to full virtualization and note that there will be a potential for the use of "self-service" and automated consulting solutions.

For the remaining 9% of the participants total virtualization has a high to very high significance. The consulting businesses of these participants have service portfolios and clients available, who enable them to render automated services at any time and in any place. Complex technical solutions will form the basis of these services. As the circumstances require, clients have to be supported and/or qualified while using these services, so that afterwards they will be able to use them effectively. Business consultants, who see a chance to use full virtualization, should incorporate potential clients in the conception of the new services at an early stage. The role of the clients during the development of virtual consulting services will be discussed again later. Basically, the point is to draw up present, possibly only low virtualized project references and to integrate virtual products into the right places so that their strength can be highlighted.

Small and large consulting firms assess the significance of full virtualization significantly higher than medium-sized consulting firms. Here the general tendency continues in the outcome of our survey, that small and large consulting firms see more potential in virtualization. Medium-sized consulting firms are, by tendency, still indifferent concerning the chances and risks of technology-based solutions. HR- and IT-consulting firms evaluate the future significance of total virtualization as the highest. In the case of HR-consulting full virtualization could help to conduct assessments faster, or to identify suitable candidates for an open vacancy in an automated way, analysing, for instance, social media data.

2.5 Possible Applications of Virtualization in Consulting

In the scope of this survey, the participants were asked to specify three possible applications of virtualization in their consulting business from their individual perspective (Table 2). Here the participants particularly often mentioned the application during geographically distributed cooperation. The motivation to use virtualization thus originates primarily from the need to work together independently from where the project members are. Thereby the participants explain the importance of one of the most fundamental surplus values of virtualization—temporal and local flexibility. Virtualization can also contribute to the improvement of work-life-balance during consulting (Termer and Nissen 2011, 2012; Nissen and Termer 2014), which makes the consulting businesses, as an employer, more appealing.

Even when simple forms of virtualization are used such as video conferences, it can provide a significant benefit for the client as well as for the consultant. The analysis done on the usage of various virtualization levels, furthermore, shows that this form of virtualization and virtual cooperation is already used extensively. Hence daily consulting cannot be imagined without virtualization.

Table 2 The 10 most frequently mentioned application priorities of virtualization in consulting, according to the consultants questioned

1. Online collaboration	6. Data mining and big data
2. Remote analysis	7. Virtual project management
3. Online coaching	8. Virtual assessment
4. Information distribution via internet	9. Online knowledge management
5. E-learning	10. Test of IT solutions

Nissen and Seifert (2016a) in source: Deelmann T, Ockel DM, in collaboration with BDU e.V. (eds) Handbuch der Unternehmensberatung, loose-leaf book, state 2017, KZ. 7312, courtesy of Erich Schmidt Verlag GmbH & Co. KG, Berlin 2017, more about the loose-leaf book at http://www.esv.info/978-3-503-07846-2

Another frequently mentioned application refers to the analysis of information and the opportunity to do this independently from a specific place, such as the client's office. Here is a particularly large potential in the problem analysis phase of the consulting process. In doing so, it has to be differentiated whether the virtualized analysis should be done manually, which means remote by a consultant, or technically based, which means extensively automated by an IT-tool. In both cases, there is no need to analyze the information at the client on-site. The process of gathering information can also be partly virtualized, whilst for example the required documents are automatically loaded onto a consulting portal or an analysis tool. The more steps of this analysis are technically based and automated, the higher would be the level of virtualization. According to these findings, there is still considerable potential to virtualize sub-tasks and to optimize the problem analysis as compared to the status quo.

The opportunity to conduct a professional coaching anytime and independently from the client's site was also mentioned as a good application area for virtualization. Such an online coaching, moreover, offers the opportunity to look after various participants at the same time, or to save conducted sessions so that they can be used again. Online coaching is currently often a component of blended learning —or e-learning programs. Moreover, nowadays online coaching is already offered on the Internet when specific demand exists. In the context of business consulting online coaching could specifically be used to support clients to solve their business problems, as well as supporting them with the usage of complex virtual consulting products.

The opportunity to prepare information and to pass it on to clients and partners were repeatedly mentioned by the participants as a possible application of virtualization. Information, which is digitally available can be managed, secured, distributed and specifically used in a better way. These are processes with a rather low to medium level of virtualization. During the analysis of the progress of virtualization and discussing the level of virtualization, it was already determined that virtualization should both take place internally (internal processes), as well as externally (sales and consulting processes). In the case of both variants, consulting companies are still at the beginning of the development. The distribution of information via the Internet rather refers to external communication by the use of webinars or podcasts. Testimony of competencies and client references can be distributed rapidly and efficiently via blogs and forums. During the acquisition, implementation and also the follow-up phases of a project, webinars can be used to distribute information to the clients.

The success of a consulting business is determined largely by the qualification of their own employees. Today virtualization, in the form of e-learning, already contributes to the advanced training of consultants. Thereby the local dispersion of consultants is considered. E-learning offers can be used for every phase in a consulting project, in order to provide the consultant with project-relevant knowledge.

A basis for the successful and profound usage of virtualization will be the ability to gather, structure and analyze large amounts of data rapidly and possibly automated. Data produced by the consulting business, data generated by the client and data generated by the partners or public institutions have to be consolidated and analyzed. In this way, new insights can be gathered very quickly and consulting results of a high standard are produced. This assumes that the exchange and the storage of data, as well as their application is legally protected. From the point of view of the survey participants, the topic of data protection does not really present an impediment. It should though be considered in a conclusive master plan. Furthermore, the participants stated that the necessary technologies do exist and can be obtained, if needed. For successfully virtualized consulting concepts, on the basis of big data and analytics (e.g. data mining solutions), a close cooperation with key clients is recommended. A sound analysis of realistic applications against the background of different virtualization potentials for individual tasks is recommended as well.

Nowadays the completion of projects is already supported by project platforms. These are mainly tools, which record the work progress and organize the cooperation. However, the actual consulting service is personally rendered by the consultants. It is conceivable that the larger part of communication among the project actors is processed via such platforms and also certain consulting services are available through this channel. As early as the times of virtual platforms like "second life", there were concepts to offer and conduct consulting services in a fully virtualized space.

The option, to conduct surveys, studies and assessments online, to investigate a variety of clients and companies in a standardized form and independently from time and location, presents a further, often mentioned approach for the usage of virtualization.

The opportunity to use and expand online knowledge management was also often mentioned by the study participants. Know-how is a critical resource of consulting businesses. Therefore, it has to be used effectively and efficiently during the service delivery, which means that it needs to be managed actively. At the same time virtualization offers new chances to continue developing the knowledge management of a consulting organization. On the one hand, elaborate knowledge management presents the basis for the design of virtual consulting services, since knowledge has to be analyzed and explicated in order to apply it in the form of innovative virtual consulting products. On the other hand, virtual consulting services and the correlated digitalization of information offer the basis for an efficient knowledge backup and distribution. Furthermore, knowledge management, which is closely integrated with operative consulting processes, is simplified where knowledge management systems are smoothly linked to digital consulting products. In this way, the results of a virtualized consulting project can simply be adapted and re-used in other consulting services. An example here could be a process mining-tool, which automatically designs processes based on the analysis of actual ERP-data of the client. These models are then abstracted from the specific situation of the client and are saved in a process database for later re-use in other contexts.

Another opportunity for virtual consulting, already known from experience, is the remote-testing of software. Without being directly on-site with the customer, the consultant can test the implemented software and document the results.

A trend of the participants was to use only a low to medium level of virtualization for the mentioned possible applications. High to fully virtualized consulting services were only mentioned in the field of online assessments. This result agrees with the other results of the study, where an actual focus on low to medium levels of virtualization was noticed. The presented examples refer to all phases of the consulting process. So far there are, however, only a few concrete ideas, of what highly virtualized consulting services could look like.

2.6 Relevant Technologies of Virtualization

The participants were asked to assess the relevance of possible technologies for the virtualization of consulting services (Fig. 9).

Digitalization in the business world and society is substantially characterized by the use of mobile technologies. Today mobile devices already have an important role in consulting and may gain further significance in the future. Mobile communication by means of tablets, smartphones or smartwatches allows the speedy and location-independent interaction with clients, partners and consultants in the context of virtualization. Internal business applications and client-specific apps could support consulting services or even serve as stand-alone consulting products. By constantly being available on corresponding devices, expert systems used for the fully automated, and location-independent analysis of bulk data, could be considerably useful to assess the client's situation, or to support decision making. However, even in the case of mobile technologies the initial situation of the client's company as well as the skills of individual clients need to be considered. The use of mobile technologies will be a clue for extensive virtualization in consulting. But these technologies demand the qualification and support of the internal employees as well as of the clients, which requires additional resources, in particular at the beginning of the product life-cycle.

In this study the significance of cloud technologies is, by tendency, rated at a high level. Cloud computing is a model, which allows accessing readily, at any time

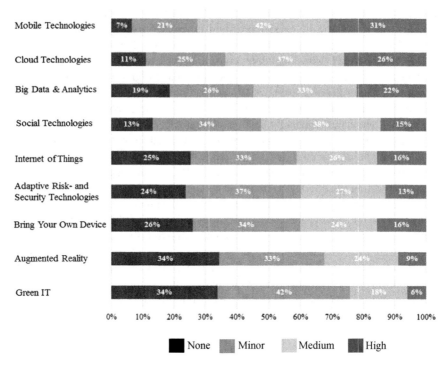

Fig. 9 The importance of technologies for the virtualization of consulting services (n = 419)

and everywhere a network of shared and configurable computer resources (e.g. networks, server, storage systems, application and services). In this way, virtualized consulting services can be readily developed, offered and flexibly scaled with minimum effort. Cloud-based software tools can be the basis for more efficient consulting processes and the modular combination of various tools opens up new possibilities. Cloud-based service networks, which integrate service portfolios of various consulting providers with different professional focus in a highly flexible and scalable manner, could sustainably change the added value of the consulting branch.

A similar high significance was assigned to technologies in the context of Big Data and Analytics. Big Data does not only provide concepts, but also concrete methods, technologies, IT-architectures, as well as analysis tools for the virtualization of consulting services. These are necessary in order to convert the exponentially increasing volumes, and continuously changing information into better consolidated and prompt decisions. The rate and quality of consulting services are supposed to be improved by analytics solutions. This was assessed as medium to highly significant by the participants.

Social technologies, such as forums, blogs, microblogs, social networking and instant messages can be platforms for the communication, cooperation and coordination of the actors during a consulting process. In the scope of virtualization, they serve the problem oriented exchange of ideas, questions and opinions among client, partners and consultants. The participants of this study assessed the significance of these technologies on average as medium important.

A similar rating was given for the Internet of Things (IoT). The IoT describes the communication of objects via corresponding networks, to gather and exchange data. In the case of business consulting, the IoT can make the development of consulting services possible, which, for example, are based on real-time information of linked-up production resources. By doing so, production processes of the client could be continuously monitored and analyzed, which again makes it possible to offer customized solutions for the optimization of processes. If e.g. logistic processes need to be optimized, then diagnostic- and modelling tools could give insights into the running logistic procedures in real-time on the basis of data mining approaches. The participants assessed such technologies on average as medium important. In particular consulting businesses, which do industrial projects, should in detail consider the chances, which virtual consulting services can offer. The *Smart Factory*, *Smart Product* or *Smart Services concepts* offer digital links to deploy accurately fitting virtual consulting services. On a more general level, the IoT offers great potential for client integration.

According to the assessment of the participants, adaptive risk and security technologies have a similar significance for virtualization. Therewith technologies are meant, which ensure a minimum of data security within virtual consulting services. Safety measures which autonomously recognize and evaluate risks, may be vital for the approval of the clients. Such concepts could, for example, be based on techniques of data and text mining as well as semantic technologies.

Not only social media can blur the line between private and professional lives, but technologies employed in virtual consulting services may also partly come from the private sphere. Consultants can use their own smartphones and laptops. This technology trend, which is referred to as "Bring Your Own Device" was assessed by the participants as medium relevant. It is assumed that security demands, which are posed for user devices, would prevent the use of private hardware.

The evaluation of the responses shows that augmented reality technology is considered only barely significant for virtualization. It includes, for example, the use of products such as data glasses, which can display additional information on processes, systems or products. There are concepts in other industries, such as engineering, where data glasses are used for the maintenance and analysis of machinery. Virtual data could be linked to real information like the optical condition of a machine. Even in the case of knowledge-intensive service industries, such as business consulting, technologies of the augmented reality could make new consulting approaches feasible. That way data about the client's company, the client market, benchmarks, and much more, could be accurately called at the right moment. New quality standards for decision making and working results seem to be attainable is this way. In order that these technologies are leveraged, the consultants should be qualified and supported by technology experts. The connection between the business and technological know-how is the key for realizing the technical surplus values of new technologies.

The technology trend Green IT seems not very relevant to the participants. Therewith ambitions are described to design information- and communication technology, so that they are environmentally- and resource-friendly during their whole life cycle. This would involve the process from designing the virtual consulting solution to the implementation and use.

Virtualization can only be successful when various technologies are meaningfully combined with each other. This requires the analysis of own processes as well as the client's procedures. Consultants need to learn how to use the technologies themselves, before implementing them for their clients. Consulting firms, which rather offer services without much technology, should look for partners to acquire this know-how. On the methodological side it is, however, essential to employ a method, which supports the process of determining whether consulting services can be virtualized meaningfully at all.

2.7   Barriers to Digital Transformation in Consulting

The participants were also asked to evaluate pre-defined barriers to virtualization, which will impede investments in virtualization in their consulting businesses. Moreover, they were given the chance to comment every barrier, and to mention additional barriers (Table 3) if desired.

The analysis shows that the client's lack of demand is the primary barrier (62% of the participants answered this way). One participant responded that, as no demand had been established so far, no knowledge had been accumulated. At this point, the German consulting branch seems to be in a standby situation. Virtual consulting services are thus only developed when the client directly asks for them. The question can though be asked, how clients are supposed to request innovative consulting services, when the consulting businesses cannot show any innovative product portfolios. The questioned consulting businesses state that financial means can be made available, if a demand is noticeable. They are, however, hesitating to invest in consulting products, which may only later arouse a certain demand.

Without a concrete demand from the client, and without a possible prospect of an order, an investment in virtualization will only be difficult to realize. The client, his acceptance and demand, as well as the resulting business case are the greatest barriers that need to be overcome. When these basic questions are positively resolved, the consulting business can attend to the acquisition of resources and the establishing of know-how that is initially needed. Technological and data protection-based aspects, which are associated with virtualization, were not assessed as a real barrier by most participants.

If consulting businesses want to attain (or keep up) a leading position on the consulting market, they should evaluate the creation of complex virtual products in depth. Only those consulting companies, which establish competencies in this field and which can demonstrate innovative virtual services, will be able to arouse a corresponding demand from the client. Whoever can show innovative reference

Table 3 Barriers to virtualization of consulting services (n = 493)

Barrier	Share of consultants, whom consider this factor a barrier (%)
Missing demand for virtual consulting services by our clients	62
Missing acceptance of virtual consulting services by our clients	43
Vague business value	38
The lack of a strategic fit to existing consulting services	34
Missing experts for the virtualization of our consulting services	32
Missing capacities of our consultants for the implementation of virtualization	31
Missing know-how of methods and tools used for virtualization	28
Missing know-how of which consulting services are suitable for virtualization	27
Missing know-how of technologies for virtualization	25
A low maturity level of the required technologies	25
Unresolved questions on the data security	24
Limited funding	23
Missing know-how on the application of methods and tools	20
Missing standards and norms	20
Problems associated with the general legal framework	16
Inadequate infrastructure (e.g. broadband communication)	14
Inadequate stability of the infrastructure	9
No interest from our management	9
Problems associated with the political framework	6

Nissen and Seifert (2016a) in source: Deelmann T, Ockel DM, in collaboration with BDU e.V. (eds) Handbuch der Unternehmensberatung, loose-leaf book, state 2017, KZ. 7312, courtesy of Erich Schmidt Verlag GmbH & Co. KG, Berlin 2017, more about the loose-leaf book at http://www.esv.info/978-3-503-07846-2

projects at an early stage has got good chances of a lasting competitive advantage. It is important not to wait too long with own initiatives. Otherwise there is substantial risk to become a victim of the "innovators dilemma", described by Christensen (1997) that might ultimately drive even big service providers out of the market when faced with disruptive innovations.

The missing acceptance of virtual consulting services by the clients is seen as another major barrier for the implementation of virtualization (43% of the participants). The acceptance for technology-based products or services are being influenced by factors such as the expected usage effort of the client, the expected performance of the service, the social influences on the client, the supportive framework conditions (e.g. availability of the infra-structure) or the client's age (Venkatesh et al. 2003). To attain maximum acceptance, the heterogeneous expectations of the clients and the relevant factors describing the initial situation, need to be considered. Thus, one participant states: "The opposite party does not have the know-how" and another participant reckons "The client is not prepared for this".

To receive as much acceptance as possible, it is required, from an organizational perspective, to establish a feeling of solidarity between the clients and consultants across the barriers of virtualization. If required, clients should still be able to make use of a personal contact to a consultant despite virtualization. Beginning with the negotiations for the contract, via the design of a speedy, individual solution to approval of the consulting results, it is important to have continuous support by the personal consulting counterpart (Nissen et al. 2015). The acceptance will increase when a client-oriented mixture of virtual and classical consulting services is offered. It can be presumed that a certain insecurity on the part of the client prevails, as virtual consulting is nowadays still the exception. This means that clients hardly have any experience with it.

More than a third of the participants (38%) find that a vague business value hinders the implementation of virtualization. One participant responded: "If we saw a surplus value for our clients or for ourselves, we would use it". On the other side, 62% of the questioned participants did not express any barrier caused by the business case. However, the added value for clients in the context of existing consulting services (strategy and organization) is not yet unambiguous. The low distribution of virtual, and, in particular, complex virtual consulting products indicates that the vague business value constitutes in fact a bigger barrier than stated by the participants.

Economic advantages of virtualization include scalability of virtual consulting products, the reduction of costs by reduced travelling activities and automatization, as well as the opening-up of new client segments that would rather not place an order for (expensive) classical consulting. Contrary to that are the investment and maintenance costs as well as the non-chargeable time used for the development of virtual services. The business case of a virtual consulting product should therefore integrate initial and ongoing efforts, quick wins and particularly long-term income potential, so that an investment in virtualization should be seen as an investment in the future of the consulting business.

Thirty-four percent of the participants are of the opinion that the strategic fit of consulting services is not suitable for their service portfolio, so that virtualization cannot be successfully implemented. Therefore, knowledgeable analysis is necessary to find out which services and products can be admitted into the service portfolio. Starting with the company strategy, consulting firms should be able to derive a strategy for virtualization (Wurdack 2001). Based on this general approach, a consulting portfolio can be defined, which combines traditional and virtual consulting services. To evaluate the strategic fit, the previous portfolio is confronted by strategic goals. The role of virtualization for achieving these goals is then elaborated. In this process, information about the actual and the expected development status of the markets, as well as information on industrial clients, are very important. Subsequently it has to be tested whether virtualization is suitable to sustainably cover future demands and the expected development of markets.

Only 32% see the shortage of experts as a barrier for virtualization. The majority of the participants disagrees with this. The participants indicate that the questioning on suitable resources should be treated as of secondary importance, and the questioning on the demand of the clients as a matter of priority. The application of virtualization in a customer project will be successful when consultants are capable of analyzing their own processes on a meta-level. Besides the professional know-how, which a consultant needs to apply to a client's project, he also needs methods and tools for the analysis of knowledge-intensive processes, and for the development of technology-based virtual services. Depending on the consulting field, specific qualification, particularly on the side of the consultant, is needed to implement virtualization successfully.

Less than a third of the participants (31%) state that inadequate capacities of their own consultants are the reason why virtualization cannot be implemented. The majority though states that resources are made available, when required and a directive of impact has been set. The participants also state that not enough try out time to experiment is a barrier on the way to more virtualization. One participant noted that the required training needed for the conversion of classical delivery-models of consulting, during the course of virtualization, is very time-consuming and therefore, a capacity related impediment.

Of the participants, 28% assessed that insufficient know-how of methods and tools is a barrier of virtualization. The virtualization of knowledge-intensive services demands a profound know-how on e.g. the areas: service engineering and management, software engineering, knowledge management, virtual organization, computer supported cooperative work, as well as business management. In order to be able to implement virtualization successfully, a consultant has to apply this knowledge in his own consulting processes. The analysis of own processes, tasks, information, actors and results requires corresponding methods for modelling and analyzing knowledge intensive services. After assessing the status quo, it should be possible to show the virtualization potentials. Subsequently client-oriented service concepts can be designed, which consist of sub-services with various levels of virtualization. For this purpose, engineering tools and methods are required. The following decision between the purchase of standard tools, and of the development of an individual solution, requires profound know-how of software engineering. If these concepts have been implemented in corresponding virtual products, they should be marketed. For this, know-how of service management is required. Overall, an engagement with the required knowledge to develop complex virtual consulting products on the one side, and the critical evaluation and advancement of own skills on the other side, are decisive for the success of the consultant.

Twenty-seven percent of the participants stated that they did not know which consulting services can be virtualized. Here the participants also pointed out that without any concrete customer demand and without a corresponding strategic goal, virtualization know-how is not required. At this point the consulting businesses under-estimate how complex the evaluation of virtualization can be. Various factors determine whether consulting processes or tasks can be virtualized. These factors should be accurately analyzed before virtual consulting products are developed.

A quarter of the participants feel that insufficient knowledge of technologies is a barrier. In this case, it would be necessary to examine precisely whether all possibilities of current technologies had already been researched, analyzed and evaluated sufficiently accurately. Non-technology consultants are here confronted by particular challenges concerning the virtualization of consulting services.

The maturity of the relevant technologies is considered as a barrier by 25% of the participants questioned. ICT is the vital virtualization mechanism. As has already been shown, various technologies have a different rating for digital transformation in consulting. Consulting providers have to succeed in assessing the application capabilities of various technology trends, and to choose the suitable technology for a consulting service.

Just less than a quarter of the participants (24%) consider that unresolved issues regarding data security are a barrier for virtualization. The responsible dealing with data is a fundamental basis for the success of digitalization, and consequently for the success of virtual consulting services. Consulting businesses need to deal firmly with the legal data security perspective of virtualization, to develop solutions which are legally valid on the one hand, and allow the client's trust on the other hand. At the end, it is all about consulting services, which are not only interesting and effective, but also secure. The client's trust is just as important during traditional consulting as during virtual consulting. Thus, it should be the goal of a consulting business to design digital consulting products, which establish trust and strengthen the relationship to the clients. Consequently, a high significance should be attributed to relevant security technologies and concepts.

Only 23% of the participants see the lack of financial means as a barrier for the implementation of virtualization, whereas 77% do not see it like that. They point out that financial means are provided, and investments taken as soon as the strategic usage and demand of virtual consulting services become clear. One participant responded: "Means are provided when it makes sense". The business case for the development and the implementation of a virtual consulting service should be given and the return-on-investment calculable. A missing business case is often the reason why complex (and by tendency expensive) forms of virtualization are not pursued.

Twenty percent of the participants see inadequate know-how on the applications of virtualization as a barrier. The parties state that they do not have the necessary "vision and imagination". Furthermore, they also respond that "no concrete approaches or business ideas exist", and "there is a lack of ideas for suitable digital implementation of consulting services", which delays the progress of virtualization. The maturity level of virtualization in the German consulting branch shows that virtual consulting services and in particular complex virtual products take up only a niche role at present. So far only a few consulting providers were successfully able to use the existing technologies to design innovative service systems.

A further 20% of the participants see the limited availability of standards and norms as a barrier. International as well as national standards and norms are crucial for virtualization, as corresponding standardized and normalized consulting products facilitate their distribution, and reduce their complexity. The standardization of technique-based consulting products forms a fundamental basis for the wide-ranging integration of various digital and traditional consulting processes and providers. When a consulting business considers valid standards and norms of virtualization, consulting services can be developed, which are more compatible with existing services, and can therefore be used more readily.

A group of 16% of the participants felt that legal conditions could be a hindrance to the implementation of virtualization. Regulatory requirements can promote or restrict virtualization. Compliance with legislation on the regulation of employee assignment is, for example, definitely necessary for both the client and the consulting business, as in the case of non-compliance substantial penalties may be imposed. This legal structure forces in particular clients to separate the consultant and the client's employees clearly from each other, to avoid the accusation of concealed employee assignment. Here e.g. standardized communication and organization of projects via a project platform can contribute to the establishing of consulting processes according to legal requirements.

Legislation can set bounds for the virtualization of consulting services, in particular in the case of data security. Especially complex virtual consulting products are based on large amounts of data from various resources. That way a specific consulting firm, on behalf of the client, could extract information about consumers (e.g. the buyers of a specific product) from market data, and process this information in the course of analytical applications. For virtualization to be successful, a legal approval has to be obtained for this data processing.

Only 14% of the participants find that the non-availability of suitable infrastructure hinders the implementation of virtualization. Increasing virtualization of technical resources by cloud-services favours virtualization, because new virtual consulting products can be made available sooner, and with a greater operating reach. Cloud architectures and software-as-a-service products provide the technical basis for flexible and scalable virtual consulting products. In order that the infrastructure does not present a barrier, consulting businesses ought to strive for a high extent of technical flexibility and compatibility. They should also be informed which infrastructure related requirements the clients have.

Not more than 9% of the participants feel that the stability of the infrastructure is inadequate and obstructive in the given context. It now applies that the existing technical base should be successfully utilized, and by implementing suitable virtual consulting products the available technologies should be beneficially installed.

Nine percent of the participants have the opinion that virtualization is hindered by absent interest of the consulting management. The commitment of the management is needed to define a vision and to derive strategies, processes and an organization in the context of virtualization. Even though the necessary attention of the management does predominantly exist, the consequent implementation of virtual consulting products does not take place among the consulting businesses questioned. It is inhibited by the distinctive factors—lack of client demand and low client acceptance. In this context, a key role is assigned to the management, namely to launch virtualization even if there is initially no obvious demand. The management has the responsibility to develop, and put onto the market a consulting service portfolio, in such a way, that it attracts clients.

Merely 6% of the participants questioned find that political circumstances cause a barrier. Currently a high significance, which also applies to the political side, is attributed to the digitalization of economy and society, as well as the concomitant challenges. Consulting businesses can make use of this trend by means of targeted cooperation with research institutes, clients and other actors from industry and science, to develop new, innovative consulting offers.

2.8 Organization of the Digital Transformation

In the context of virtualization of consulting services, the question arises, how the transformation of a traditional consulting service is typically organized. Here simple and complex virtual consulting services should be differentiated. The development of simple virtual consulting services requires comparatively little effort. For example, a virtual workshop about process mapping can be carried out without the development of special tools, merely by using a standard software.

Complex virtual consulting services, such as a consulting-app for the self-service of clients, first need to be designed and developed. Such a development project can be carried out in various ways. The participants were asked to name the typical organization form used for their transformation processes. The analysis of the data shows that, in most cases, virtualization is carried out during the preparation or execution of a client project (Fig. 10). In less than a third of all cases, virtualization takes place as an internal project without direct contact to a particular customer. Least often virtualization is implemented in the course of the wrap-up of a client project.

These results were to be expected in view of the revealed obstacles of virtualization, because these had shown that virtualization can barely be carried out without a concrete demand from clients. About two-thirds of the participants stated that virtualization is carried out before or during a client's project. In these cases, there is thus a customer and a concrete demand. If consulting businesses want to address new clients or client segments, and they want to use virtual consulting services to do this, then the design and development without a specific customer project might be necessary.

No significant correlation between the size of the consulting provider and the question, how the digital transformation is organized could be discovered in our study. Likewise, the organization of the transformation process seems to be independent from the consulting field. Should consulting firms intend to use

Fig. 10 Project context of virtualization (n = 397). Nissen and Seifert (2016a) in source: Deelmann T, Ockel DM, in collaboration with BDU e.V. (eds) Handbuch der Unternehmensberatung, loose-leaf book, state 2017, KZ. 7312, courtesy of Erich Schmidt Verlag GmbH & Co. KG, Berlin 2017, more about the loose-leaf book at http://www.esv.info/978-3-503-07846-2

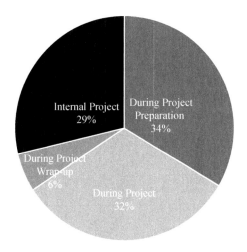

virtualization outside the context of a customer project, they can try to involve innovative clients to determine, at an early stage, whether their own ideas relate to the client's demand. This way, acceptance and chances of success of virtual consulting services can be improved, right from the beginning.

The development of virtual consulting services detached from a particular consulting project and unencumbered from daily business makes it easier to continuously and purposefully deploy resources. Should, however, virtualization concepts be developed alongside a proceeding client's project, the danger increases that the conceptual work done for the digital transformation comes short due to daily business.

The virtualization of consulting services can, therefore, be organized in different ways. The implementation certainly also depends on which application should be developed.

3 Maturity Model of Digital Transformation in Consulting

3.1 Four Maturity Levels

The virtualization of consulting services depicts a transformation process, where, in the simplest case, individual consulting services, and at the highest level of maturity, the complete business model of a consulting business are digitally transformed.

Digitalization as the decisive mechanism for virtualization makes the extensive networking among the actors of consulting processes possible. Hence the consultants, clients and partners are part of a transformation process. To be able to characterize this conversion, and for orientation in this challenging transformation process, we defined four maturity levels for consulting providers (see Fig. 11).

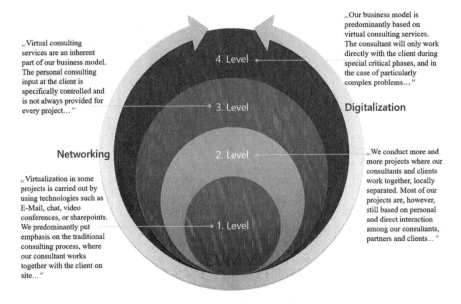

"Virtual consulting services are an inherent part of our business model. The personal consulting input at the client is specifically controlled and is not always provided for every project..."

"Our business model is predominantly based on virtual consulting services. The consultant will only work directly with the client during special critical phases, and in the case of particularly complex problems..."

Digitalization

Networking

"Virtualization in some projects is carried out by using technologies such as E-Mail, chat, video conferences, or sharepoints. We predominantly put emphasis on the traditional consulting process, where our consultant works together with the client on site..."

"We conduct more and more projects where our consultants and clients work together, locally separated. Most of our projects are, however, still based on personal and direct interaction among our consultants, partners and clients..."

Fig. 11 Consulting virtualization maturity model (Nissen and Seifert 2016b)

These four maturity levels are briefly characterized in the following. Later the classification of the participants from our empirical study in this maturity model will also be presented.

First Level—Basic The first level of the model describes a state in which virtualization is used by consulting companies in some projects through the use of technologies such as e-mail, chat, video conferences or sharepoints. The consulting provider predominantly puts emphasis on the traditional consulting process where the consultant personally works together with the client on-site. The consulting organization and the internal processes as well as the added value processes are based on the direct contact among consultants, internal employees, clients and partners. The issue of virtualization could possibly be further taken into account in the future, but at the moment it is only of minor importance.

Second Level—Upward Climber In the second level of virtualization, we assume that more and more projects are conducted where the consultant and client work together, although they are geographically separated. Most of the projects are, however, still based on personal and direct interaction among consultants, partners and clients.

The development of new consulting services with a stronger emphasis on technology is one of the strategic targets of a consulting business at this level. The company is already actively involved in the process of virtualizing internal processes and improves the network among employees of individual business areas through the targeted use of technology. The topic virtualization could possibly be considered more in future, and is currently, however, only of secondary significance.

Third Level—Established Virtual consulting services are an inherent part of the business model of consulting businesses on the third level. Personal consulting input at the client is specifically controlled and is not always provided for every project. The clients, internal employees, partners and consultants of a consulting business are already digitally well connected. Occasionally consulting services are offered, which can be performed fully automated. Virtualization is one of the strategic pillars, and will be inwardly (internal processes) and externally (added value) pushed ahead in the future.

Fourth Level—Master The business model of a consulting business on level four is predominantly based on virtual consulting services. The consultant will only work directly with the client during special critical phases and in the case of particularly complex problems. Many of the offered consulting services are carried out automatically and possibly with remote support by specialists. The consulting company is so well networked with its partners, clients and employees that future problems can be recognized at an early stage and appropriate consulting services can be developed and offered promptly and precisely. The subject of virtualization is of very high importance and is characteristic of this service provider.

As with every maturity model, it should to be noted, that one would be able to differentiate more levels and characteristics, than the four levels mentioned by us. Virtualization, as a digital transformation process, is fundamentally a continuum of changes. However, in order to be able to compare the current state of virtualization in the consulting market and to compare the situation of the different consulting firms, the four levels described above were helpful.

3.2 Maturity of the Consulting Providers in the German Market

We wanted to find out which of the four introduced virtualization maturity levels most likely reflects the situation in the businesses of our participants. Altogether 470 responses could be evaluated (Fig. 12).

Forty-five percent of the participants stated that the progress of virtualization in their company corresponds with level one, whereas 47% identified themselves most closely with level two of our model. Only 7% classified themselves at level three of the transformation process, and merely 1% of the participants stated that they had reached the top level of our model. Consulting businesses with a turnover of more than ten million Euros do, by tendency, have a higher maturity level of virtualization, than businesses with a lower turnover. Large consulting businesses do not only assign a higher significance to virtualization, their transformation process is also further advanced.

By tendency IT-consulting providers show the largest maturity, followed by HR-companies. The consulting providers, who assign a high significance to virtualization, are also more advanced in the transformation of their service systems

Fig. 12 Virtualization
maturity level of the
consulting providers
questioned (n = 470)

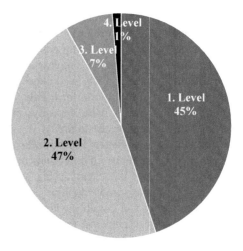

and business models. The actual progress of virtualization is though still inferior to the stated significance. Consulting businesses do not only have to define a strategy for virtualization, they consequently also have to implement this strategy. Other fields of consulting, namely strategy, organization and process consulting, still stand at the beginning of their respective transformation processes.

4   Summary and Outlook

Subsequently the central results of the survey will be summarized in the form of ten theses on virtualization in the consulting business.

> I. The significance of virtualization as an innovation driver that paves the way for new business models and consulting services, will increase in the consulting industry.

The study has shown that virtualization in consulting will become more important. Like other industries, the consulting industry also needs to follow the trend of digitalization and networking, and consequently the virtualization of their consulting services and internal processes. To stay competitive, the virtualization potential of one's own business needs to be investigated accurately, so that, at suitable parts of the service spectrum, process steps and even entire services can be virtualized. Moreover, completely new, digitalized services are to be developed and business models critically reflected and altered. The digital transformation calls for a self-critical and creative strategic perspective on one's own business model.

A service portfolio with complementary classical and virtual consulting products is aimed for. Virtualization can be varyingly useful, depending on the consulting issue and the phase of the project. This needs to be evaluated in a sophisticated manner.

In the simplest case, virtualization can be understood as a measure for securing efficiency and flexibility. At the highest evolution level, virtualization offers the opportunity to completely change the delivery model of the company. The consequence would be that the complete service system of the consulting business is changed, and the value chain is optimized. A majority of the consultants questioned in our study recognized this opportunity, and assigned a corresponding high significance to virtualization in the future.

II. Virtualization is particularly advanced in large consulting businesses.

Looking at the status quo of virtualization, it can be determined that simple variants of virtualization are already applied by most of the consulting providers. However, virtualization is more advanced in large businesses, even if the virtualization concepts are at first rather simple.

The starting situation for big consulting companies is good, and an important basis for the future development of more complex virtual services. In the case of small and medium consulting firms, virtualization will first be an important measure to secure efficiency. Moreover, virtual consulting services could exploit new client segments, to whom classical consulting is too expensive. For medium consulting businesses, virtualization may provide further chances for growth. A necessary basis is that digital transformation is solidly rooted in the business strategy, which requires a profound analysis as well as associated knowledge of the topic. Here partnerships with technology vendors or universities can be advantageous.

III. IT- and HR-consulting firms are more advanced in the digital transformation of their own services than is the case in strategy consulting as well as in organizational and process consulting.

Providers of IT- and HR-consulting services assess themselves as comparatively advanced in their digital transformation. It is not surprising that IT-consulting is leading here as it represents the most technology oriented consulting field. IT-consulting has direct access to the technologies, which could also change the service systems of the consulting businesses. HR-consulting services, in the fields of personnel recruitment, selection, and employee development are nowadays already simplified by virtualization. For example, recruiting measures in social media are implemented, or training programs are almost completely deployed online. The challenge for HR-consulting would rather be to successfully virtualize strategic consulting activities next to the operational ones.

IV. Fully virtualized and automatic consulting services have a subordinated significance to the consulting business according to the participants.

Full virtualization stands for the complete substitution of human work performance by suitable technologies. The majority of the participants in our study assessed the significance of full virtualization as slight, even in the future. Both the application and also the benefits of high- to fully virtualized-consulting services are more dependent on the willingness and skill of the client to use these, as is the case with lesser virtualized consulting offers. Through the automation of service delivery, parts of the human consulting service are substituted and other parts are shifted from the consultant's side to the client. Full virtualization, therefore, requires a substantial contribution from the client, who uses the consulting service independently. Here it is necessary that the client is equipped with the corresponding infrastructure, that he is prepared and has the ability to operate such a consulting application correctly, and that he is able to understand the results of the consulting, and wants to apply them. Full virtualization is, therefore, not suitable for every consulting task and is only implemented by those with know-how to bring key technologies, like big data, and suitable client segments together. At the same time, high requirements on the conception of such consulting products arise.

Our own opinion is that the participants though, underestimate the long-term potential of full virtualization for (selected) consulting services.

V. In the course of a typical consulting process, the preparation phase, problem analysis phase and the wrap-up phase of a project are more rapidly, and by tendency, stronger virtualized than other phases such as the acquisition and solution design.

The virtualization of consulting services necessitates the analysis of the phases of a typical consulting project and the differentiation of these phases according to the degree, to which they can be virtualized. The following typical phases, which are ideal during the consulting process, could be differentiated: the acquisition, project preparation, problem analysis, solution design, implementation and wrap-up work. When considering virtualization, it is necessary to analyze these individual phases, the assigned tasks and the actors in a differentiated way. Depending on the outcome, virtualization will be more or less advantageous. Currently, in particular the phases project preparation and wrap-up are stronger virtualized, as they are marked by a less complex interaction pattern. Fundamentally, technology for virtualization is nowadays potentially used in every project phase. The level of virtualization decreases, though, in the phases design and implementation of a solution. Here it is possible, that especially in the case of highly standardized services, changes will come in the future. These offer great potential for virtualization, up to automated self-service applications for the client, in the extreme case. The future significance of extensive automated, analytical applications, in the scope of the analysis phase, should also not be underestimated.

The development of web-based consulting portals, which may in the future be used for the virtual marketing, sales, initiation as well as the handling of consulting projects, should take place under the stipulation, that classical and virtual consulting services (with different levels of virtualization) should be depicted in a client-oriented way within a single "consulting environment". In this way, a platform for the continuous interaction between the client and the consultant is offered, which will intensify the consultant-client relation.

VI. Currently mainly supporting technologies for slightly virtualized consulting services are implemented. Automation, Virtual Reality and Artificial Intelligence are still in the early stages.

If one looks at the actual distribution of consulting services or internal processes with varying levels of virtualization, it becomes clear that only the slightly virtualized services are daily or regularly used. The higher the level of virtualization, the more rarely it is nowadays used in consulting practice. In order for stronger virtualized consulting processes to find their way into the company, and to make use of higher virtualization in internal processes, visions and substantial innovative power are needed. Here it is necessary to integrate the strategic, procedural and technological aspects meaningfully. This imposes high technical requirements on the consulting businesses, not only during the design and implementation of virtualized consulting concepts, but also in terms of the internal change management as well as the sales-related interface toward the clients. When, for example, technology oriented consultants think about meaningfully using their technological potential for virtualization, the competencies of other consulting fields, for example process consulting, are also in demand.

VII. The integration of clients into the design and development process of virtual consulting services will be crucial to their success.

Within this survey, we could show that the clients' attitude, their acceptance and trust is crucial to the success of virtual consulting services. To be able to develop and offer long-term, successful consulting services, close cooperation and coordination with key clients are needed, which does not necessarily have to be within a concrete client's project. From the first idea of an innovative consulting service, to its design, implementation and usage, the focus should be on the integration of particularly innovative, technology-affine key clients.

VIII. The so far low demand for (highly) virtualized consulting services is the largest obstacle on the way to the in-depth penetration of virtualization in the consulting practice.

The question, why consulting businesses do not invest in the development of innovative virtual consulting services, is predominantly answered by the low demand of the clients. Barriers, such as the lack of know-how, the availability of resources, financial obstacles or technologies are considered less critical. Our results show that the demand and acceptance of the clients, as well as a missing strategic fit within the consulting service portfolio, were the three determining impediments. According to the participants, know-how, technology and resources are either there, or they are acquired as soon as a business case is given. This attitude is reflected in the actual progress of virtualization in the consulting branch, and in the distribution of related tools and services. The client's demand for innovative and highly virtualized consulting services are absent in most of the consulting businesses. Consulting providers should, therefore, ask the question how the demand for virtual consulting services can be increased. Here the cooperation with key clients, and the active marketing of these pilot projects will be of vital significance. Concerning the topic of digitalization of their own processes and services, consulting businesses should not repeat the mistake other industries have already made, namely to adopt a strong waiting attitude. That way a chance would be wasted. The contrary is true. At an early stage, with a strategic foresight and creativity, consulting firms should occupy themselves with the chances and risks of virtualization, in view of their own service portfolio. They should also accumulate competitive know-how. Here it is also meaningful to experiment. We are convinced that parts of consulting businesses will in future proceed quite differently than it is the case today. Those who are conceptually involved at an early stage, have a long-term chance of a sustainable competitive advantage.

IX. Virtualization will enable new forms of clients' integration, where a common data base forms the foundation for innovative consulting services.

Previous models for the cooperation within consulting are partly revolutionized by virtualization, as new modes of cooperation, as well as communication- and cooperation-platforms develop. The adolescent generation is used to interact virtually and to exchange information online. In future this next workforce generation will have completely different expectations concerning the work and forms of cooperation with each other. This will increase the acceptance for virtual cooperation, and eventually also of virtual consulting services.

X. Consulting providers with no technology background should seek for cooperations with technology providers and universities, to secure their future competitive capability.

The starting situation of technology oriented consulting firms is better than that of other companies. The others should form strategic alliances with companies offering technologies relevant to virtualization in order to compensate their weaknesses, and nonetheless, have the chance of using virtualization.

For the consulting industry, virtualization promises innovative opportunities to optimize their own performance and to differentiate in competitiveness. A detailed analysis of their own service portfolio, in terms of the potential, which virtualization offers within the phases of consulting projects, within the internal consulting organization, and in cooperation with clients and partners, is necessary. For this purpose, knowledge should be accumulated at an early stage, and a consistent strategic vision should be developed, which meaningfully combines virtualization and the traditional consulting approach. The early involvement of technology-affine clients in the complete process, from the development to the implementation of virtual consulting products, will be the key to success.

References

Atteslander P (2010) Methoden der empirischen Sozialforschung, 13th edn. Erich Schmidt Verlag, Berlin

BDU (2015) Facts & Figures zum Beratermarkt 2014/2015. BDU e.V., Bonn

Christensen CM (1997) The innovator's dilemma. When new technologies cause great firms to fail. Harvard Business School Press, Boston

Deelmann T (2009) Internetberatung - Einige Überlegungen zu Möglichkeiten einer sinnhaften Vollautomation von Beratungsleistungen. In: Fischer S (ed) Informatik 2009. Im Focus das Leben - Beiträge der 39. Jahrestagung der Gesellschaft für Informatik e.V. (GI), Bonn, pp 3745–3759

Diamantopoulos A, Reynolds N, Schlegelmilch B (1994) Pretesting in questionnaire design—the impact of respondent characteristics on error detection. J Res Market Res Soc 36(4):295–314

Homburg C (2015) Marketingmanagement - strategie - instrumente - umsetzung - unternehmensführung, 5th edn. Springer Gabler, Wiesbaden

Nissen V, Termer F (2014) Women and their Work-Life Balance in German IT-consulting. In: Rode JA, Wulf V (eds) Proceedings of gender IT 14 – gender and IT appropriation, Siegen. European Society for Socially Embedded Technologies. ACM Digital Library, pp 1–9

Nissen V, Seifert H (2016a) Digitale Transformation in der Unternehmensberatung: Status Quo in Deutschland. In: Deelmann T, Ockel DM (eds) Handbuch der Unternehmensberatung. Erich Schmidt Verlag, Berlin, pp 7312–7319

Nissen V, Seifert H (2016b) Virtualisierung in der Unternehmensberatung. Eine Studie im deutschen Beratungsmarkt. BDU, Bonn

Nissen V, Seifert H, Blumenstein M (2015) Virtualisierung von Beratungsleistungen: Qualitätsanforderungen, Chancen und Risiken der digitalen Transformation in der Unternehmensberatung aus der Klientenperspektive. In: Deelmann T, Ockel DM (eds) Handbuch der Unternehmensberatung, 25th edn. Erich Schmidt Verlag, Berlin

Pötschke M, Simonson J (2001) Online-Erhebungen in der empirischen Sozialforschung – Erfahrungen mit einer Umfrage unter Sozial-, Markt- und Meinungsforschern. ZA-Inf 49:6–28

Termer F, Nissen V (2011) Frauen und ihre Work-Life-Balance in der IT-Unternehmensberatung. In: Proceedings of Informatik 2011, LNI vol P-192 (CD, 12 pp)

Termer F, Nissen V (2012) Work-Life-Balance – Strategische Waffe des HR-Managements in der IT-Unternehmensberatung? In: Mattfeld D, Robra-Bissantz S (eds) Proceedings der MKWI 2012. GITO, Berlin, pp 369–380

Venkatesh V, Morris MG, Davis GB, Davis FD (2003) User acceptance of information technology—toward a unified view. MIS Q 27(3):425–478

Werth D, Greff T, Scheer AW (2016) Consulting 4.0-Die Digitalisierung der Unternehmensberatung. HMD Praxis der Wirtschaftsinformatik 53(1):55–70

Wurdack A (2001) E-Consulting - Entwicklung eines Rahmenkonzeptes: Aufbau und Darstellung einer E-Consulting-Lösung im Beratungsunternehmen der Zukunft. Dissertation, University

Author Biographies

Volker Nissen holds the Chair of Information Systems Engineering in Services at Technische Universität Ilmenau, Germany, since 2005. Prior to this, he pursued a consulting career, including positions as manager at IDS Scheer AG, director at DHC GmbH, and CEO of NISSCON Ltd., Germany. In 1994 he received a Ph.D. degree in Economic Sciences with distinction from the University of Goettingen, Germany. His current research interests include the digital transformation of the consulting industry, the management of IT-agility, metaheuristic optimization, and process acceptance research. He is author and editor of 19 books and some 200 other publications, including papers in Business & Information Systems Engineering, Information Systems Frontiers, IEEE Transactions on EC, IEEE Transactions on NN, and Annals of OR.

Henry Seifert is a graduate engineer for media technology and since 2011 working as a management consultant. His main focus is on the automotive industry and artificial intelligence, analytics, process optimization and requirements management. He works in projects in the area of sales and after sales processes as well as professional learning. As doctoral candidate at the Group for Information Systems Engineering in Services at Technische Universität Ilmenau, he examines the digital transformation in the consulting industry. The goal of his dissertation is to demonstrate the opportunities and limitations of virtualization, as well as the design of artifacts that enable the realization of virtual consulting services.

Evaluating the Virtualization Potential of Consulting Services

Volker Nissen and Henry Seifert

Abstract Even though consulting firms strengthen the competitiveness of their clients by innovative solutions and substantially take part in the development of new concepts for digitalization, consulting services are often only performed by the traditional face-to-face approach. Virtualization is a megatrend, which consulting providers have to acknowledge in their own business processes. In this contribution, we derive a possible procedure to allow the ex ante assessment of the virtualization potential of consulting processes (or their sub-steps). This will be done theory driven and on the basis of supplementary empirical research.

1 Fundamentals and Motivation[1]

Despite a positive development of the turnover, the consulting sector is confronted by new challenges. On the one side, the competition with providers from low-wage countries and freelancers in the field of standard services increases. Furthermore, new competitors with innovative business models and technology-driven consulting approaches come in the market. On the side of the client an increasing professionality regarding the purchase and dealing with consulting, can be observed. The price sensitivity of clients has also increased and a trend to buy modularized consulting services from different providers can be observed (Nissen 2017).

Regarding the described challenges, virtualization of consulting services can be an innovative strategy to secure the lasting success of a company and to complement the classical offers of consulting. The aim of virtualization is to reduce the amount of face-to-face interaction between consultant and client by the suitable

---

[1]This contribution builds on Nissen and Seifert (2017).

V. Nissen (✉) · H. Seifert
Technische Universität Ilmenau, Ilmenau, Germany
e-mail: volker.nissen@tu-ilmenau.de

H. Seifert
e-mail: henry.seifert@infosysconsulting.com

© Springer International Publishing AG 2018
V. Nissen (ed.), *Digital Transformation of the Consulting Industry*,
Progress in IS, https://doi.org/10.1007/978-3-319-70491-3_8

implementation of information and communication technologies (ICT) (Greff and Werth 2015; Nissen et al. 2015). It can thus be referred to as the strategy for digital transformation of the consulting business.

For the realization of this ambitious vision, suitable artefacts are necessary, such as web-based consulting platforms, mobile consulting applications, semantic technologies, data mining and cooperation tools. Likewise, concepts are required to assess the virtualizability of consulting processes and to develop solutions, which can link the conventional and virtualized consulting as a whole. Methods and techniques for virtualization have to be created (Seifert and Nissen 2016).

While spatiotemporal flexibility of virtualization increases, the reduced personal interaction of consultant and clients can impair their relationship. Whether virtualization is the right approach to change a consulting process and how this can happen in the best way should be tested diligently. However, there is currently a shortage of resilient criteria and virtualization concepts. This leads to the following research question for the present contribution: *How can the potential for virtualization of a consulting service (or a sub-step) be assessed ex ante by means of resilient criteria?*

2 Methods and Data

2.1 Overview

In the first step to answer the research question, we go back to the theoretical foundation of the process virtualization theory by Overby (2008, 2012) and apply it to the domain of consulting. A supplementary empirical study in the German consulting market was done to investigate numerous factors influencing the virtualization potential and to obtain further clues for a useful evaluation process. In the third step a strategic perspective is taken, which additionally includes chances and risks of virtualization on the basis of a literature-supported Delphi-study with consultants and clients. This leads to a three-step evaluation process, which will be described in more detail in this contribution. The methodical basis will be briefly presented in the following.

2.2 Process Virtualization—Theoretic Foundation

A virtual process is a process in which the physical interaction disappears. The transition of a physical process to a virtual process is referred to as 'process virtualization' (Overby 2008, 2012). Overby developed the generic 'Process Virtualization Theory (PVT)' and introduced the term 'process virtualizability' (Overby 2008, 2012). Overby views the usage/acceptance and quality of the process results as the basis to be able to measure the virtualizability of a process (as dependent variable) *ex post*. Furthermore, he names a succession of variables, which have an influence on the virtualizability of a process and thus seem to be suitable for the here intended *ex ante* assessment of the virtualization potential of consulting processes. The PVT is a suitable theoretical anchor for this investigation as, compared with the Theory of Task-Technology-Fit, it does not evaluate the suitability of a technology for a specific task, but instead explains how well a task (as part of a process) is basically suitable for the implementation of technology. It is also preferable to the Technology-Acceptance-Model (TAM), as consulting services are primarily viewed as a co-creation between the consultant and the client, from a process perspective [and not in the sense of pure technology acceptance (Overby 2012)]. The TAM was also strongly criticized for its lack of relevance and its insufficient usefulness to design future systems in a better way (Bagozzi 2007).

According to PVT, especially the following process features have a negative influence on the virtualizability of a process: high sensory requirements (as physical interaction is no longer in focus), high requirements concerning the personal level of the relationship of the participants and thereon following constructs, such as trust, high requirements concerning the synchronicity of activities during the process and high identification and control requirements in the process (as the actual interacting can be readily concealed during virtualization).

In contrast, the following features of the IT-based virtualization mechanism temper the mentioned process characteristics and thus have an influence on the virtualizability of a process: The capability of IT to present process relevant information (representation), the capability of IT to allow a time- and location-independent process participation (reach), as well as the possibility to generate an authentication of the process participants and to monitor the process (monitoring capability).

Balci and Rosenkranz (2014) note, that the measurability of the virtualizability of processes has so far hardly been empirically investigated. In their own research, they find empirical confirmation for the PVT, though at the same time there are indications of its incompleteness. In particular factors, concerning characteristics of the process participants (e.g. IT-knowledge) also play a role.

2.3   Criteria of Process Virtualizability—Empirical Study

The fact that PVT is possibly incomplete is taken up for the given application area, consulting. This is done by a supplementary large survey on the criteria for virtualizability of consulting services. In cooperation with the Federal Association of German Business Consultants, BDU e.V., companies of all sizes in the entire German consulting industry were surveyed.

In the scope of this study, data were collected online by means of a survey software. An online-survey has numerous advantages, such as the low data collecting costs, the elimination of manual data input for the researcher, or the instant availability of the data (Atteslander 2010). As opposed to the advantages of an online-survey, there are, however, also disadvantages (Döring and Bortz 2015). Based on the anonymity in the Internet, there is a higher risk of multiple participation. This aspect was minimized insomuch that the BDU only sent invitations to their contacts among members. As the members of the BDU represent a good cross section of the German consulting landscape, biases of the results are hardly likely. Furthermore, a lot of value was placed on the comprehensibility of the questionnaire and it was verified by pre-tests.

The survey was done in the period from 23rd of November till 18th of December 2015. Altogether 765 participants clicked onto the link that led to the starting page of the online-survey, which was sent by e-mail. Of these participants, 654 began with the actual online survey. In the following editing and coding of the data, a data cleansing took place. In this process, 102 responses were excluded, as the answers of these questionnaires were rather incomplete. In total 552 questionnaires could be considered for further statistical analysis. Overall the German consulting market is well presented according to its turnover and consulting fields, so that extensive, representative results were obtained.

Regarding the age and work experience of the participants, it was shown that the opinions of consultants with various experience levels were gathered. The representative status of the sample is restricted inasmuch that the method to collect data is not without problems even though it has many benefits. Thus, this method expects that the participants are capable to use the online questionnaire appropriately. Participants, who are sparsely Internet-affine, could be excluded here (Döring and Bortz 2015). However, this will hardly have been the case as the target group contains business consultants.

The overall objective of this survey was to clarify the status quo and the perspectives of digital transformation in consulting in Germany. In this paper, only criteria will be considered, which are used to determine the virtualization potential of consulting services. For this purpose, a structured literature analysis, according to Webster and Watson (2002) was conducted in advance, to identify possible candidates for such criteria. Besides the original literature on the virtualization of consulting, other subject areas, such as teleworking, tele-cooperation, computer supported work, task analysis, e-government and e-services were also researched to identify potentially transferable results for consulting services. Furthermore, contributions quoted by Overby, or which quote Overby, were considered. Altogether 41 contributions could be identified for the investigation. Using the following literature synthesis, and drawing up a concept matrix, a list of criteria on the virtualizability of consulting services was compiled. These criteria can be clustered into three groups—client, consulting provider, and consulting task. The particular relevance of these three groups for the investigation of the virtualization of consulting services was highlighted in the literature by authors like Wurdack (2001). Furthermore, this grouping was already used in the context of standardization of consulting services (Dichtl 1998) and was also mentioned as key aspect in the area of modularization of services (Carlborg and Kindström 2014).

The group 'client' contains all the criteria relating to the integration of clients. This includes both the trust of the client in the consulting company and the acceptance of the client of virtual consulting services. Moreover, the technical requirements of the client, as well as the experience of the client with virtual consulting services, can be mentioned.

The second group 'consulting provider' contains all criteria relating to the consulting organization, thus the consulting company itself. To these belong the experience of the consulting firm with virtual consulting services and the maturity of the knowledge management. Furthermore, the workload of the consultants and their seniority are determining the virtualizability of consulting services.

The third group, consulting task, covers the criteria, which allow the evaluation of the virtualization potential on the level of the consulting task. This includes the criticality, hence the risk and conflict potential of the task, as well as the complexity and thus the changeability, number and variety of the task. Furthermore, it is important to determine the urgency, therefore the deadline pressure of the task as well as the importance, which means the individual significance of the task. Other criteria belonging to the third group are the confidentiality of the information and task, and the interactivity, hence the frequency, duration, type and intensity of the consultant-client interaction. An essential and final criterion of the group consulting task is the individuality and thus the entitlement of the client to receive an individual solution.

After the literature supported derivation of this initial criteria catalogue, the criteria had to be evaluated in the scope of a large survey of business consultants. To be able to evaluate the virtualization potential practically, it was also necessary to reduce the number of 15 criteria to a number, which is manageable in the future evaluation process.

The results of the review formed the foundation of a corresponding question in the online-survey, where the participant had to evaluate the relevance of the criterion by means of a six-step Likert-scale. The opportunity was also there to mention additional criteria in a free-text-field. In our study, the responses of 374 participants could be evaluated.

To characterize the criteria for the virtualizability of consulting services, the Exploratory Factor Analysis (EFA) suggests itself as a dimension reducing procedure. Herewith latent influencing factors can be identified (Cleff 2015). In this context, Cronbach's Alpha was calculated for the initial 15 criterion candidates. Cronbach's Alpha basically has a value between 0 and 1. The higher the value of Cronbach's Alpha, the higher is the correlation between the indicators and hence is the internal consistency-reliability (Churchill 1979). Thus, a Cronbach's Alpha value ≥ 0.7 should be achieved. In our study, the value was 0.83.

To conduct EFA the data set was initially cleansed by means of a complete-case analysis and then tested for its fundamental suitability for an analysis. Central criteria, which give information whether a data set is basically suitable for an EFA, are the KMO criterion and the Bartlett-test (1951). Here a KMO-value of over 0.5 points at the fact that the data show a specific correlation can thus be used for an EFA. In the present case, the KMO-value is 0.81. In the case where the null hypothesis is rejected, the Bartlett-test also points at the fundamental suitability of the data for an EFA. For the existing data, the result is significantly ($p < 0.001$) different from zero. The null hypothesis, that the correlation matrix is just accidentally different from the unit matrix, can be rejected, which means that the Bartlett-test also confirms the suitability of the data for an EFA.

Table 1 shows that the items can be selectively matched to the individual factors, as every item, with two exceptions, at a cutoff-value of 0.5 merely loads on one factor. At the same time, most of the items have a factor loading of over 0.7. As a result, the 15 criterion candidates can be reduced to seven factors. We gave them convincing names for their respective focuses. These now form the most important foundation to evaluate the virtualization potential of consulting services ex ante.

2.4 Chances and Risks of Virtualization—Literature- and Delphi-Study

The client related chances and risks of virtual consulting services were investigated by Nissen et al. (2015). This was done by a combination of a standard literature investigation and a Delphi-study with participants of various industries. The following relevant results were obtained on the strategical analysis level.

Clients connect virtualized consulting offers with the chance of greater flexibility and availability of consulting services, higher work and reaction speed in the project, as well as the hope that consulting services can be obtained at lower prices. Furthermore, the clients expect that by the more intensive usage of digitalization, it will become easier to acquire and re-use results. Standardized digital solutions that need only minimum effort for customization would be available instantly. There is also the chance of utilizing particularly innovative and partly automated consulting solutions.

Contrary to the above, there are also concerns and risks on the client's side. On the one side, these refer to possible communication, coordination and cooperation problems. Moreover, there is a stronger dependence on technical aspects during collaboration and the thereby associated dangers of data abuse and loss of control. On the other side, it is feared that the quality of the results could suffer as the relation between the consultant and the client deteriorates, trust and loyalty decreases and the individualization of the services diminishes.

The gained insights now flow into a multistage proposal for the evaluation of the virtualization potential of consulting services. In compliance with Overby (2008, 2012) and Bruhn (2002), the acceptance of the client is viewed as a result of the successful implementation of the virtualization potential, and is thus an objective and not an indicator.

Table 1 Factor analysis of the criteria for the evaluation of virtualization potential

Rotated component matrix	Complexity	Availability of suitable consultants	Acceptance of clients	Digital maturity level of the consulting provider	Urgency of the consulting service	Trust between actors	Interactivity
Criticality	0.888						
Complexity	0.856						
Confidentiality	0.770						
Individuality	0.693						
Seniority of consultants		0.859					
Workload of consultants		0.833					
Experience of client with virtualized consulting			0.843				
Requirements of client towards virtualization technology			0.701				
Acceptance/approval of client for virtualized consulting			0.574			(0.566)	
Experience of consulting provider with virtualized consulting				0.859			
Maturity of knowledge management				0.790			
Urgency					0.888		
Importance	(0.546)				0.627		
Trust of client in consulting provider						0.896	
Interactivity							0.757

Extraction method: Principal component analysis. Rotation method: Varimax with Kaiser-normalization. The rotation converged in six iterations. Coefficients with a value <0.5 are suppressed

3 Evaluating the Virtualization Potential of Consulting Services

3.1 Overview

The success chain (Bruhn 2002) of virtual consulting services describes the steps, which need to be completed to successfully implement virtualization in consulting (Fig. 1). The offer and design of a virtual consulting product ideally lead to high acceptance on the side of the client. Depending on alternative consulting possibilities, felt risks and advantages, the usage of the consulting product follows. The client assesses the quality, while using the service. When the quality meets his expectations, satisfaction occurs. Satisfaction of the client is a necessary prerequisite of the success of the provided virtualized consulting service.

The design of the virtualized consulting service is very important, because it will contribute to a high acceptance of the client and it will increase his intention to use it. Therefore, it is initially necessary to thoroughly investigate the virtualization potential, since not every consulting service is equally suitable.

Previous findings indicate that it makes sense to carry out the evaluation of the virtualization potential in the consulting sector in three separate steps, which now will be described in detail (Fig. 1). The first step, evaluation of the process-related virtualization potential, is based on the PVT by Overby, and investigates how features of the consulting process influence the virtualization potential. The second step, the organizational analysis, investigates key factors within the consulting company and how they influence the virtualization potential. In the third and strategical step the chances and risks of virtualization are investigated from both the perspectives of the client and the consulting provider in the scope of a business case. For the later project-based implementation, the client's quality expectations are decisive for success.

The evaluation process starts in step 1 with the PVT-oriented factors. The following evaluation steps apply the remaining criteria and complement them with results on the chances and risks of an actual virtualization decision. Consequently, the evaluation process becomes more and more specific and leads to a business case of the respective consulting company.

3.2 Analysis of the Process-Related Virtualization Potential

Influence of the complexity The first factor, which is decisive for the process-related virtualization potential, is the complexity of the consulting service. The process-related virtualization potential of a consulting service is determined by the sensory, relationship-related, synchronicity-related and the control-related features of the process. The complexity of the consulting service has a determining influence on this virtualization potential. Complex consulting services can be

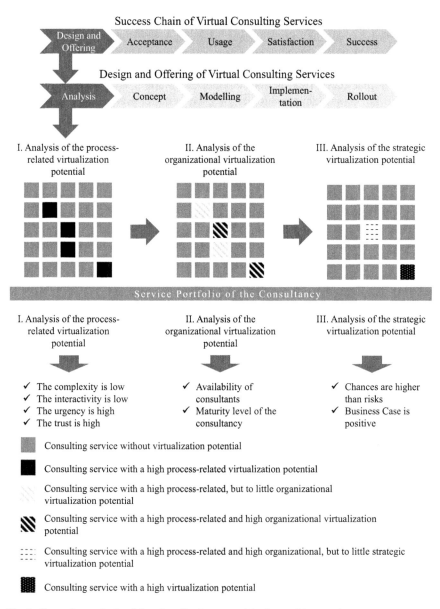

Fig. 1 Step-wise analysis of the virtualization potential of consulting services

distinguished by numerous heterogeneous objectives of the project, a multitude of stakeholders, project sites and technologies. A high complexity has a negative influence on the virtualization potential. In complex consulting scenarios, the requirements, which the consulting process imposes on the relationship between the consultant and the client, are high. A strong consultant-client relationship is necessary, which can guarantee the cooperation, even in critical phases, within the project. Furthermore, the criticality and the risk potential of the project, need to receive attention. Even though a clear connection between the project complexity and project risk could, so far, not be found in the literature, there is a widespread assumption that these two aspects are linked (Marle 2014). The complexity, moreover, imposes high synchronicity-related requirements on the consulting process. The solution of complex problems with a variety of heterogeneous information often requires that work is carried out together synchronously. That means that problems and solutions are, for example, cooperatively investigated and generated in workshops. Furthermore, high sensory requirements are revealed, when most diverse information types have to be processed. These include language information, as well as graphs or texts, and in particular the countenance and gestures of the various actors. Complex consulting services presuppose that it is known who has just interacted with whom.

Influence of the interactivity The second factor, which is decisive for the analysis of the process-related virtualization potential, is the interactivity of the consulting service. The interactivity of the consulting service includes the type, duration and frequency of the interaction between the client and consultant, as well as among consultants in the project. A high interactivity implies high sensory and synchronicity-related requirements, as well as increased control- and identification related requirements. A high interactivity therefore restricts the virtualization potential. This can be partly compensated by choosing suitable media and technologies. The analysis of the responses of the study participants showed that the interactivity should, by tendency, be medially pronounced at the most, to consider the virtualization potential high. This result agrees well with the findings obtained during the research on service modularization. Carlborg and Kindström (2014) e.g. point out that the perspective of the co-creation of service companies and clients should not be neglected. From the perspective of the service modularization strong interaction requirements can also lead to obstacles.

Interaction within consulting services should be analyzed thoroughly as it includes a broad spectrum of types: direct personal interaction, medial respectively indirect interaction or automated interaction. Frequent direct, personal interaction between the consultant and the client indicates that here is a virtualization potential for synchronous technologies, such as conference systems (Büttgen 2007).

Influence of the urgency The urgency of the consulting service, to which the priority from the client's perspective also belongs, has a positive influence on the virtualization potential in the case of a concrete project. The implementation of technology to contribute to the local independency of collaboration has temporal advantages, which, by tendency, have a positive influence on urgent problems. The local independence, which is achieved by the implementation of suitable collaboration tools, facilitates the fast and flexible collaboration of various locally spread project members, and allows a rapid exchange of information, which may be necessary for the solution of critical problems.

Influence of trust The trust between the consultant and the client is one of the core criteria for the evaluation of the consulting quality. The virtualization of consulting services leads to a changed consulting process, which reduces the direct contact between the consultant and the client. A risk, concerning the quality of the relationship, and, in particular, the trust of the client, results from this change (Nissen et al. 2015). From the client's perspective trust is especially important, because in the case of a traditional, as well as a virtual consulting service, there is a service specific quality risk—respectively information insecurity, as at that moment when the service is used, the client only has the service promise of the consulting provider (Nissen et al. 2015). Significant trust in the consulting partner, on the one side in the consulting firm as an organization, and on the other side in the specific consultant as a person, has a positive influence on the process-related virtualization potential. For the virtualizability of consulting services it is decisive, that in the case of established trustful collaboration between the consultant and client, the relationship- and control-related requirements of the involved consulting process are rather minor, as a corresponding consultant-client relationship does already exist. Thus, the actors of the consulting process only infrequently need to interact synchronously with each other or use regular controls of their collaboration. In the case of strongly virtualized consulting services the trust on an organizational level, therefore in the consulting company, plays an important role. Here the reputation management of the consulting provider can make an important contribution (Hüttl 2005).

It becomes clear that merely the PVT is insufficient to evaluate the virtualization potential practice-oriented and in a useful way. However, the criteria of PVT allow a first assessment of the fundamental suitability of a consulting service for virtualization. In the next step, it is necessary to build upon this first result and to consider the company-specific circumstances as well as the expectations of the clients.

3.3   Analysis of the Organizational Virtualization Potential

Influence of the maturity-level of the consulting organization The maturity of the consulting provider referring to the virtualization of consulting services is of great significance for determining the virtualization potential on a company-level. A high virtualization-related maturity of a consulting provider has a positive influence on the virtualization potential in concrete individual cases. When a consulting company has a high maturity level, it implies that they have experience and know-how of the digitalization of their own company processes and the processes of the client. This know-how is beneficial for the development of further virtual consulting products. Companies with a high maturity level can decide for or against the virtualization of individual processes/process steps, based on their already existing experience. This makes it easier to correctly assess the virtualization potential of individual services according to the above stipulated influencing factors.

Influence of the availability of suitable consultants Should virtual consulting services be implemented, the concerned employees have to meet certain qualification requirements. Virtual consulting services require, besides the social and professional capabilities, in particular, the knowledge to select suitable information and communication technologies, as well as the know-how of forms and features of the virtual collaboration. So that the process-related virtualization potential can be fully exploited, consultants have to select suitable media and tools by considering the previously described procedural factors. As there are several technologies available, it is necessary to have a founded knowledge for this purpose. Consequently, the consultant has to be in a position to select the right technology for the right process step at a client. If a consulting provider has employees, who fulfil these requirements, it will have a positive influence on the assessment of the virtualization potential. If this is not the case, it would be sensible to invest in the construction of such resources.

3.4 Analysis of the Strategic Virtualization Potential

The strategic fit regarding the current service portfolio of the consulting provider is important for the virtualization of consulting services (Wurdack 2001). The virtualization potential has so far been identified in two steps. In the third analysis step the providers have to test the strategic relevance and fit. A high strategic fit has a positive influence on the virtualization potential. The idea to determine the strategic virtualization potential is based on the approach of strategic service portfolio management, and aims at testing new consulting services in view of their strategic fit to the service portfolio of the consulting company. This is done to newly align the consulting service and/or the portfolio (Leimeister 2012).

Research on service modularization emphasizes that it is essential for the provider to understand the client's wishes and to already include them during the service development (Rahikka et al. 2011). For a decision in the concrete individual case, it is therefore necessary not only to keep the advantages of virtualization in mind, but in particular also their risks from the client's but also the consulting provider's perspective. The total verdict should be objectified as far as possible, by a business case, which shows the short-term and long-term potentials of virtualization. The significance of this strategic evaluation step also becomes clear via the analysis of the obstacles of virtualization. Of the questioned participants in the survey, 34% stated that the lack of a strategic fit was an obstacle for the virtualization of consulting (n = 493) (Nissen and Seifert 2016).

3.5 The Client's Quality Requirements for a Virtualized Consulting

Finally, the consulting client's perspective should be considered once more. Consulting firms market service promises in fields, which are generally of great significance and can bring along substantial risks for the client. A virtualized consulting offer can only then be successful over a long period when the quality of the service fulfills the client's expectations. It is therefore necessary to have a quality measure. Then it can be tested whether the client's expectations were not met, satisfied or even exceeded, which means that the consulting service was either successfully virtualized or not so. In the latter case one should critically evaluate whether the virtualization was generally inappropriate, or whether an improved virtualization mechanism should be found.

The investigation on the client's quality expectations, referring to virtualized consulting services was done by Nissen et al. (2015) by means of a structured literature review as well as a following client-related Delphi-study. The conducted evaluation and prioritization by experts resulted in an integrated criteria catalogue, which combines the quality criteria of classical consulting with those of electronic services. The Delphi-study also showed that the significance of the quality criteria for the client's total satisfaction varies, depending on the level of virtualization. Thus, the quality of a highly virtualized consulting service is more strongly measured by means of the criteria of the quality of electronic services, whereas a service with a lower level of virtualization is more strongly evaluated by quality criteria of traditional consulting services.

4 Conclusion and Outlook

The acceptance, usage and satisfaction of a virtual consulting service are, according to Overby (2008, 2012), the decisive (*ex post*) indicators for the virtualizability of a traditional consulting service. Hence, it is assumed that the virtual consulting service is already developed and implemented. If consulting services still need to be designed, it is difficult to determine the expected success. Therefore, it needs indicators and an analytical procedure for the *ex ante* determination of the virtualization potential of individual services or process steps.

The presented three-step procedure is a theoretical and empirical founded proposal, which still has to prove itself in a practical implementation. For this purpose, cooperation projects were started with consulting partners, which will, before long, lead to first concrete products. Case studies will be conducted in order to test the practical value of the presented method in varying consulting contexts. It will also have to be determined to what extent the procedure has to be company- or project-specifically customized to attain the largest usage.

The results of this contribution are in so far restricted as the sample only considered the German consulting market. The results of the quoted Delphi-study are to be relativized to the extent that they indeed reach the required method-specific number of participants. However, they only reflect the opinion of a manageable group of consultants and clients. These results should be further deepened in a larger study in future. In a theoretical regard, it seems to be worthwhile, once more, to take up the topics standardization and modularization of consulting services in the context of virtualization. Thereby interesting lateral relationships are found, in particular for the topic service modularity (Carlborg and Kindström 2014; Dörbecker and Böhmann 2013; Rahikka et al. 2011), where applicable results are already present.

Virtualized consulting services will not generally replace conventional on-site consulting. They should, however, following the presented decision process for or against virtualization, be seen as a possible supplement for the portfolio of consulting providers, and should be profoundly analyzed.

References

Atteslander P (2010) Methoden der empirischen Sozialforschung, 13th edn. Erich Schmidt Verlag, Berlin

Bagozzi RP (2007) The legacy of the technology acceptance model and a proposal for a paradigm shift. J AIS 8(4):244–254

Balci B, Rosenkranz C (2014) Virtual or material, what do you prefer? A study of process virtualization theory. In: Proceedings of ECIS 2014, Tel Aviv

Bartlett MS (1951) The effect of standardization on a chi square approximation in factor analysis. Biometrika 38(3/4):337–344

Bruhn M (2002) E-Services—eine Einführung in die theoretischen und praktischen Probleme. In: Bruhn M, Stauss B (eds) Electronic services. Gabler Verlag, Wiesbaden, pp 3–41

Büttgen M (2007) Kundenintegration in den Dienstleistungsprozess: Eine verhaltenswissen-schaftliche Untersuchung. Springer, Wiesbaden

Carlborg P, Kindström D (2014) Service process modularization and modular strategies. J Bus Ind Market 29(4):313–323

Churchill GA (1979) A paradigm for developing better measures of marketing constructs. J Mark Res 16(1):64–73

Cleff T (2015) Deskriptive Statistik und Explorative Datenanalyse: Eine computergestützte Einführung mit Excel, SPSS und STATA. Gabler, Wiesbaden

Dichtl M (1998) Standardisierung von Beratungsleistungen. DUV, Wiesbaden

Dörbecker R, Böhmann T (2013) The concept and effects of service modularity—a literature review. In: Proceedings of 46th Hawaii international conference on system sciences 2013, IEEE, Piscataway, NJ, pp 1357–1366

Döring N, Bortz J (2015) Forschungsmethoden und Evaluation für Human- und Sozialwissenschaftler, 5th edn. Springer, Berlin

Greff T, Werth D (2015) Auf dem Weg zur digitalen Unternehmensberatung. IM+ io - Magazin für Innovation, Organisation und Management. IMC, Saarbücken, pp 30–34

Hüttl M (2005) Der gute Ruf als Erfolgsgröße. Erich Schmidt, Berlin

Leimeister JM (2012) Dienstleistungsengineering und -management, 2nd edn. Springer, Berlin

Marle F (2014) A structured process to managing complex interactions between project risks. Int J Project Organ Manage 6(1):4–32

Nissen V (2017) Digital transformation of the consulting industry—introduction and overview. In this volume

Nissen V, Seifert H (2016) Virtualisierung in der Unternehmensberatung. Eine Studie im deutschen Beratungsmarkt. BDU, Bonn

Nissen V, Seifert H (2017) Ermittlung des Virtualisierungspotenzials von Beratungsleistungen im Consulting. In: Leimeister JM, Brenner W (eds) Proceedings of 13rd International Conference on Wirtschaftsinformatik, WI2017, St. Gallen, pp 1348–1362

Nissen V, Seifert H, Blumenstein M (2015) Virtualisierung von Beratungsleistungen: Qualitätsanforderungen, Chancen und Risiken der digitalen Transformation in der Unternehmensberatung aus der Klientenperspektive. In: Deelmann T, Ockel DM (eds) Handbuch der Unternehmensberatung, 25th edn. Erich Schmidt Verlag, Berlin

Overby E (2008) Process virtualization theory and the impact of information technology. Organ Sci 19(2):277–291

Overby E (2012) Migrating processes from physical to virtual environments: process virtualization theory. In: Dwivedi YK, Wade MR, Schneberger SL (eds) Information systems theory. Explaining and predicting our digital society. Springer, New York, pp 107–124

Rahikka E, Ulkuniemi P, Pekkarinen S (2011) Developing the value perception of the business customer through service modularity. J Bus Ind Mark 26(5):357–367

Seifert H, Nissen V (2016) Virtualisierung von Beratungsleistungen: Stand der Forschung zur digitalen Transformation in der Unternehmensberatung und weiterer Forschungsbedarf. In: Nissen V, Stelzer D, Straßburger S, Fischer D (eds) Proceedings of MKWI2016. Ilmedia, Ilmenau, pp 1031–1040

Webster J, Watson R (2002) Analyzing the past to prepare for the future: writing a literature review. MIS Q 26(2):13–23

Wurdack A (2001) E-Consulting - Entwicklung eines Rahmenkonzeptes: Aufbau und Darstellung einer E-Consulting-Lösung im Beratungsunternehmen der Zukunft. Dissertation, University Mannheim

Author Biographies

Volker Nissen holds the Chair of Information Systems Engineering in Services at Technische Universität Ilmenau, Germany, since 2005. Prior to this, he pursued a consulting career, including positions as manager at IDS Scheer AG, director at DHC GmbH, and CEO of NISSCON Ltd., Germany. In 1994 he received a Ph.D. degree in Economic Sciences with distinction from the University of Goettingen, Germany. His current research interests include the digital transformation of the consulting industry, the management of IT-agility, metaheuristic optimization, and process acceptance research. He is author and editor of 19 books and some 200 other publications, including papers in Business & Information Systems Engineering, Information Systems Frontiers, IEEE Transactions on EC, IEEE Transactions on NN, and Annals of OR.

Henry Seifert is a graduate engineer for media technology and since 2011 working as a management consultant. His main focus is on the automotive industry and artificial intelligence, analytics, process optimization and requirements management. He works in projects in the area of sales and after sales processes as well as professional learning. As doctoral candidate at the Group for Information Systems Engineering in Services at Technische Universität Ilmenau, he examines the digital transformation in the consulting industry. The goal of his dissertation is to demonstrate the opportunities and limitations of virtualization, as well as the design of artifacts that enable the realization of virtual consulting services.

A Process Model for the Virtualization of Consulting Services

Volker Nissen, Henry Seifert and Mats-Niklas Ackert

Abstract The virtualization of consulting services is a promising opportunity to extend and optimize the consulting portfolio. Before these benefits can be realized, traditional consulting processes need to be migrated to the virtual world. A suitable procedure is needed to successfully solve this task. Based on an analysis of existing process models and a survey among consulting experts, a process model for the virtualization of consulting services is proposed.

1 Introduction

1.1 Motivation

The virtualization of individual consulting tasks or whole consulting services is a complex project. In consulting, virtualization is understood as a spectrum of possible services, where the extreme points of these services are determined, on the one hand by a mere supportive use and on the other hand by an exclusive use of information and communication technology (Nissen 2017). Examples from this wide spectrum include a coaching-app that clients of a consulting provider receive to optimize their project management, an online consulting store, which allows the client to purchase studies, concepts and consulting products, and a consulting platform on which clients, partners and consultants work together. These examples for virtual consulting services require a methodical procedure, which means a structured process from the first idea to economic success.

V. Nissen (✉) · H. Seifert · M.-N. Ackert
Technische Universität Ilmenau, Ilmenau, Germany
e-mail: volker.nissen@tu-ilmenau.de

H. Seifert
e-mail: henry.seifert@infosysconsulting.com

M.-N. Ackert
e-mail: mats-niklas.ackert@tu-ilmenau.de

© Springer International Publishing AG 2018
V. Nissen (ed.), *Digital Transformation of the Consulting Industry*,
Progress in IS, https://doi.org/10.1007/978-3-319-70491-3_9

A virtualization project can be implemented in most diverse manners. Clients can participate, but they do not have to take part (Nissen and Seifert 2016). Furthermore, the virtualization can be subject of an internal project or part of a consulting project. Besides different forms of organization, the circumstances of such a project can also vary. The consulting provider may be large or small with associated differences in available resources. Furthermore, the consulting firm may be technology-oriented or from a technology-foreign consulting field. The client characteristics can also vary. Despite these different contexts, the procedure (process model) to be devised in this contribution should be equally standardized and flexible to accommodate for these varying situations. It will support different kinds of consulting firms in their struggle to successfully develop and implement virtual consulting services.

Currently such a comprehensive process model is not available (Seifert and Nissen 2016). In a large survey of the German consulting market, providers stated though, that exactly such know-how is an important prerequisite for successful virtualization (Nissen and Seifert 2016). Consequently, this contribution subsequently aims to answer the following research question: *How should a process model for the virtualization of consulting services be designed?*

This research is considered an example of consulting research (Nissen 2007), as an artefact (process model) will be designed, applying scientific research methods, that aims to support consulting firms to improve their performance in their own digital transformation. The suggested procedure builds on our previous research, where quality criteria as well as chances and risks of digital transformation in consulting have already been investigated, a method was developed to evaluate the virtualization potential (ex ante) of existing consulting processes, and an approach was suggested to choose a fitting technology in the course of a virtualization project. To integrate and extend this existing groundwork, it is necessary to create a methodical framework. This framework will support consulting companies to apply the existing know-how for virtualization in practice (Nissen et al. 2015, 2017a, b, c; Nissen and Seifert 2016; 2017a, b; Seifert and Nissen 2016).

1.2 Methodology and Structure of the Contribution

Design Science was chosen as the methodical approach for this research project as it focuses on the design of artefacts such as models or methods (Hevner et al. 2004). The artefact primarily functions as the solution to a relevant business problem (Peffers et al. 2007). From a scientific and practical perspective, Design Science is a resilient design process, which basically includes the design of the artefact; its evaluation as well as publishing the results (Hevner et al. 2004).

More specifically, the Design Science Research Methodology (DSRM) Process Model, developed by Peffers et al. (2007), is employed here in the construction of a process model for the virtualization of consulting services. For this purpose, specifically, the design and development phase of the DSRM was adapted according to established reference procedures for modeling (vom Brocke and Buddendick 2004; Rosemann and Schütte 1997). Initially, existing process models from other fields of services are investigated and evaluated in the scope of a literature review. Subsequently, an existing model is selected and adapted to the current task. In particular, the process model is modified and extended in the design and development phase. For this purpose, existing elements of the investigated model were used and artefacts of preceding virtualization research were supplemented. Subsequently a series of interviews amongst experienced consultants delivered important expectations and practical requirements which were then integrated into the process model.

2 Literature Search and Analysis of Existing Process Models

2.1 Approach to Literature Review

In this section, possibly relevant process models are identified on the basis of the available literature. Components of these models will be used for the initial design of the process model for the virtualization of consulting services. The literature review follows the methodology as outlined by Webster and Watson (2002) and vom Brocke et al. (2009), who describe a framework for the systematic compilation of a literature review. The objective of this search is not to compile a review article, but to identify relevant models. Therefore, the procedure is adapted to the purpose of the case at hand. For this reason, the comparison of the contributions was not done in a concept matrix, and setting up a research agenda was dispensed with. Instead the individual process models are evaluated by means of an analysis-matrix and finally a process model is selected as a basis for further development.

2.2 Literature Search

In the first step, suitable search terms for the search in databases were determined to allow the identification of relevant models. For this purpose, it was initially necessary to identify the research fields from which existing process models could be transferred to the context of the virtualization of consulting services. Seifert and Nissen (2016) suggest the analysis of process models from the fields of Service or Software Engineering. Service Engineering deals with the professional "[...] development and design of service products by using suitable process-models, methods and tools [...]" (Bullinger 1999), and draws parallels to engineering physical products. The investigation of process models from the field of Service Engineering is indispensable for the virtualization of consulting services as a

Table 1 Search terms used in literature review

#	Search string (German)	#	Search string (English)
1	Vorgehensmodell AND Service	7	Process Model AND Service
2	Vorgehensmodell AND Dienstleistung	8	Reference Model AND Service
3	Referenzmodell AND Service	9	Framework AND Service
4	Referenzmodell AND Dienstleistung	10	Frame of Reference AND Service
5	Prozessmodell AND Service		
6	Prozessmodell AND Dienstleistung		

professional service. In the Anglo-American literature, the concepts New Service Development or Service Design are used, which are more marketing-oriented than Service Engineering. These research fields also deal with the development and design of services and thus have the potential to yield relevant contributions for the development of a process model (Daun and Klein 2004; Schneider et al. 2006).

The prevalent virtualization mechanism is digitalization and hence the usage of the Internet and corresponding IT (Nissen and Seifert 2016; Overby 2008). Therefore, it is necessary to consider existing process models and standards of electronic services on the one side and the analysis of standards and semi-standards of IT-Service Management on the other side. IT-services are composed of persons, processes and technology (Leimeister 2012). Finally, Table 1 lists the key-terms used in the course of our literature review of the mentioned research fields.

Databases for the investigation were selected according to the journals contained by them. Scientific databases were searched which contained at least one journal, evaluated in the sub-rating business informatics with A+ or A in the established German journal ranking 'VHB-JOURQUAL 3' or rated in the sub-rating service- and commercial management. Additionally, the database IEEE Xplore was selected due to the many important conferences contained, and the database EBSCOhost due to its extensive content and broad utilization. To find relevant process models, the titles, abstracts and keywords of entries were searched. Only German and English articles, which were published after the year 1990 were considered. The databases Informs, Taylor & Francis Online, AIS eLibrary, Emerald Insight, Springer Link, Science Direct, SIAM Online, Wiley Online Library, JSTOR, IEEExplore and EBSCOhost[1] were also included in the search for relevant models. This investigation was done between 2nd and 13th of January 2017.

By analyzing the titles and abstracts 27 potentially relevant articles could be identified. After a more detailed analysis of these articles they were reduced to 13 relevant contributions. During the detailed analysis, the complete texts of the contributions were checked to find whether a process model was adequately described and whether a relation to service design and development could be

---

[1]The Databases 'Business Source Premier' and 'eBook Collection (EBSCOhost)' were searched with EBSCOhost.

established. Contributions, which were remote to the topic or otherwise out of focus, were sorted out.

Selected primary investigations on process models are summarized in five of the relevant contributions and can be used to identify further process models.

During the following backwards search, the references of the 13 articles, classified as relevant, were investigated. This was followed by a forward investigation of the contributions, which cited those that were identified in the previous steps (Webster and Watson 2002). In this way, a total of 22 process models, classified as relevant, form the basis for the conducted literature assessment and synthesis in the following section.

2.3 Literature Analysis and Synthesis

In the following, the suitability of each identified contribution is investigated to find out whether it can be used as a template for the virtualization of consulting services. The concept-matrix suggested by Webster and Watson (2002) can be supportive for comparing these considering the respective contained concepts. The identified contributions though come from various areas. They are very much distinguished in their comprehensiveness and level of detail and focus on different areas. For this reason, the process models are assessed according to the following criteria and are contrasted in a table.

The criteria are derived from the Design Science Research (DSR) literature and are transferred to the context of the virtualization of consulting services. Evaluation is of vital importance in the DSR literature (Hevner et al. 2004). As in the model of Peffers et al. (2007), the evaluation usually follows ex post, which means after the design of the artefact (vom Brocke et al. 2009; Pries-Heje et al. 2008). The decision on the selection of a particular process models, as the origin of the artefact (virtual consulting service), can be seen as an evaluation of the model versus our research objective. Thus, the selection of the template is a design decision and an ex ante assessment in the *build* phase of the DSR-process. For the ex ante evaluation vom Brocke et al. (2009) summarize criteria which are used to orient the criteria catalogue for the qualitative assessment of the process models accordingly. These are supposed to give indications about the suitability and significance as well as the convenience and correctness of the construction (Sonnenberg and vom Brocke 2012).

In the following step, the process models, identified in the previous section, are assessed according to the determined criteria. The assessment is done in three different increments and is visualized via so-called Harvey Balls. The derived evaluation criteria and assessment options are summarized in Table 2.

Table 3 shows a section of the assessment according to the in Table 2 defined criteria with ten process models, which best fit the defined requirements. The given

Table 2 Evaluation criteria and assessment options for process models

#	Evaluation criteria	Assessment options		
		O	◐	●
1	Completeness of content of the process model	A systematic procedure is missing, and thus a plan for the virtualization of consulting services	The process model contains systematics, though individual elements for support are not available	The process model has all the elements necessary for the virtualization of consulting services
2	Formal completeness of the process model	Key-elements such as activities, results or responsibilities are missing	Merely the general framework is not available	All elements for a process model are there. They are presented in detail
3	Theoretical foundation of process model	There is not any theoretical foundation	There are cross references to selected theories and principles	The method is based on a theory or principles and was derived from this theory in an understandable way
4	Availability of a supporting tool/ software	There is no tool and no software, which simplify the application of the process model	There are merely simple tools, such as a check list, which can be used as support	There is a tailored tool in the form of a software, which can be used
5	Practical relevance of the process model	The model was not used in practice and was developed without the integration of practice partners	The model was used in practice or was developed with the integration of practice partners	The model was used in practice and was developed with the integration of practice partners
6	Reference to the virtualization of consulting services	No reference to the virtualization of consulting services	Minor reference to the virtualization of consulting services	Reference to the virtualization of consulting services
7	Transferability of the process model to the context for the virtualization of consulting services	The model is not transferable to the context for the virtualization of consulting services	The model is in its basic considerations transferable. However, it has to be adapted significantly	With a few adaptions, the model can be used in the context for the virtualization of consulting services

score in the table is the mean value of the individual assessments, whereas an empty Harvey Ball has the value 0, a half-full Harvey Ball has the value 0.5 and a full Harvey Ball has the value 1.

The assessment shows that the framework for service engineering and -management, developed by Leimeister (2012), best satisfies the compiled criteria. Leimeister (2012) suggests a process model that can be used as a starting point for the virtualization of consulting services. In the model, both, the development of services and the management of existing services are considered. Thus, Leimeister

Table 3 Assessment of selected (best fitting) process models according to the compiled criteria catalogue

Process model	Criteria							Total	Score
	1	2	3	4	5	6	7		
Lin and Hsieh (2011)	●	◐	●	●	○	○	◐	◐	0.57
Kunau et al. (2005)	◐	◐	●	◐	●	○	◐	◐	0.57
Suhardi et al. (2014)	◐	◐	◐	●	○	◐	◐	◐	0.50
Yang (2007)	◐	◐	●	◐	◐	○	◐	◐	0.50
Leimeister (2012)	●	●	●	●	◐	◐	◐	◕	0.79
Jaschinski (1998)	◐	◐	●	◐	◐	○	◐	◐	0.50
Schneider and Scheer (2003)	◐	◐	◐	●	◐	○	◐	◐	0.50
Graupner (2010)	◐	◐	●	●	●	◐	◐	◕	0.71
Boughzala et al. (2010)	◐	○	●	◐	●	◐	◐	◐	0.57
Meiren and Barth (2002)	◐	●	◐	◐	◐	○	◐	◐	0.50

(2012) describes the complete lifecycle of services. Amongst others, the process model is positively characterized by its completeness. Furthermore, the decisive factor for choosing this model is the focus on the importance of IT during the development of services. As the selection and the design of IT have a decisive role during virtualization, the sought-after process model can be adapted from this framework. Corresponding adaptions are necessary in the phases where the features of consulting are in the foreground, for example the selection of the service that will be virtualized and the design activities during virtualization.

3 Design of the Process Model for the Virtualization of Consulting Services

3.1 Further Requirements w.r.t. the Model

In the previous section, criteria for the evaluation of existing process models were compiled. In the following, these will be expanded by further requirements for the virtualization process model, resulting from its intended use.

The process model will be developed as a reference model for the virtualization of consulting services. Reference models are often defined by constitutive features, whereas the features general validity and recommendatory character are in the foreground (vom Brocke 2003; Thomas 2006). The general validity applies to a class of application cases for which the model has a recommendatory character. Even when the characterization according to the mentioned constitutive features is controversial, it is appropriate to describe cases of application for which the process model can be used (Thomas 2006). The cases for application are determined by the requirements presented in Table 4. These requirements are explained in more detail below.

Table 4 Further requirements w.r.t. the virtualization process model

#	Requirements for the sought-after process model
1	Supports consulting providers during the realization of a broad spectrum of virtual consulting services
2	Supports central as well as decentralized organization, management and control of virtualization projects
3	Is applicable to small, medium and large consultancy firms during the implementation of their virtualization project
4	Supports the integration of the client into the virtualization process
5	Supports the time-flexible assignment of consultants
6	Allows for the integration of partner-companies
7	Supports the integration of the virtualization process into the consulting process as well as the synchronous implementation of a virtualization- and consulting project
8	Considers inter-department, -sector and -division cooperation
9	Takes into account the varying capacity utilization of consulting providers
10	Allows for the virtualization in different consulting fields
11	Supports the investigation of virtualization potentials and the virtualization project itself within every consulting approach (type)
12	Supports the virtualization of the consulting process, both from an ideal-typical and a real-typical perspective
13	Supports the analysis and virtualization of projects with various complexities
14	Considers the processes within the consulting process reference model "Consulting C" (Nissen and Seifert 2008) and supports their analysis and virtualization
15	Considers the dominant knowledge management strategy of the consultancy firm
16	Secures the optimal deployment of the critical resources of a consulting provider
17	Allows the design of new business models, based on virtualization
18	Promotes creativity during digital transformation
19	Includes roles and responsibilities for virtualization
20	Allows for an agile and design-thinking-oriented procedure

Level of Virtualization The virtualization of consulting services can result in a broad spectrum of heterogeneous services with varying degree of virtualization. A consulting service with a very low level of virtualization is distinguished by a merely supportive use of technology and predominantly by the direct interaction among actors. Typical technologies used here, include e-mails as well as web conference- and chat applications. A consulting service with a specifically high level of virtualization cannot be realized without technology and contains concepts such as *self-service consulting* or *automatic consulting*. For design and implementation of the latter concepts, the associated projects are complex.

Requirement 1: The process model, which will be constructed, should support consulting providers during the realization of a broad spectrum of virtualized consulting services.

Organization and Management of Virtualization Activities The organization and management of individual virtualization activities can be accounted for by an own product-development- or innovation team (Polster 2012). This would be termed a central management of the virtualization activities. An advantage of this kind of management is the assignment of dedicated resources for virtualization, which might ease planning and management. Furthermore, an own entity can be created to control the virtualization progress, the virtualization costs and the quality. Disadvantages for this kind of management are the need for resources as well as possible obstacles concerning the legitimacy of virtualization activities as this entity may be too remote from the consulting practice and value creating processes (Polster 2012). Decentralized management occurs when there is no formalized product development or innovation management. Here, the responsibility for virtualization is distributed to single persons (manager or partner of the consulting firm). The responsibility for planning, organizing and controlling of virtualization activities lies with these persons, who usually have leading functions within various consulting projects (Polster 2012). The advantage of this kind of management is the proximity to the actual consulting process and thus to the client. This can be helpful for the legitimacy of virtualization activities (Polster 2012; Wurdack 2001). However, a decentralized approach to virtualization can be unfavourable for the pace and the integration of other stakeholders of the virtualization project.

Requirement 2: The process model, which will be constructed, should support both the central and decentralized organization, management and controlling of the virtualization project.

Size of the Consulting Firm Virtualization provides chances for consulting providers, no matter their size (Nissen and Seifert 2016). However, the size of the consulting firm does have an influence on the availability of resources, scaling effects that should be attained by virtualization, as well as the risk, which is associated with the implementation of modified or new consulting services. In the worst case, an abortive virtualization project can mean the loss of a client. This loss is much more difficult to compensate for in smaller and medium firms than in the case of large consulting companies. Furthermore, it is particularly difficult to free single consultants for the implementation of virtualization projects. Basically, the capacities for the realization of the virtualization project and the number of possible pilot-clients are smaller in small and medium consulting firms. On the positive side, smaller consulting providers have a shallower hierarchy, so that virtualization projects can be legitimated in a faster and simpler way. But larger consulting firms have more resources, which can be made available.

Requirement 3: The process model must support small, medium and large consulting companies during the implementation of virtualization projects.

Integration of the Client The participation of the client during the development phase of virtual consulting services is a critical success factor (Wurdack 2001; Schuster 2005; Polster 2012; Leimeister 2012; Neuert 1990). The future demanders of virtual consulting services ideally should be involved in all phases from the design to the market launch of the virtual consulting product, in order to legitimate the service and integrate the client's demands and expectations. It is very important to involve clients of strategic significance and to realize corresponding pilot projects with them (Polster 2012; Wurdack 2001; Leimeister 2012). Thus, the process model should allow the integration of the client during the development. Clearly, it is a risk to integrate the client in the design process as problems may occur or the project may fail. This would sustainably sour the relationship with the client and would compromise one's own reputation. Basically, there are extensive design options to integrate the client in the virtualization process. For example, the kind of client-input, the integration duration, the point of integration as well as the role of the client can vary (Bruhn and Stauss 2009).

Requirement 4: The process model for virtualization must support the integration of the client in the virtualization process.

Assignment of the Consultants Based on the individual resource situation of every consulting provider, it has to be accepted that for the realization of the virtualization project a particular consultant is either completely assigned, or the virtualization only occupies a part of his/her time (Polster 2012). Depending on the workload situation as well as the individual experiences and competences, one or several consultants are assigned to the corresponding virtualization activities. The part-time assignment of consultants for a virtualization project may bear risks when other projects are prioritized (Polster 2012; Wurdack 2001).

Requirement 5: The process model for virtualization has to support the time-flexible assignments of consultants.

Integration of External Partners Besides the participation of clients in the virtualization process, other partners such as complementary service providers and software producers can also be integrated (Wurdack 2001). For instance, cooperative consulting firms can be involved in the creation of a consulting portal and help to define and test virtual processes and special integration scenarios.

Requirement 6: The process model, which will be constructed, should allow for the integration of partner-companies.

Integration in the Consulting Project Impulses and ideas for the development of virtual consulting services often come from ongoing client projects, or from the experiences gained through completed projects. Thus, it can be assumed that virtualization projects will be integrated in existing or future consulting projects. In this way, a solution for a client specific problem is acquired and simultaneously new forms of service provisions are developed by generalizing results. Advantages of this procedure are the securing of practical relevance and the utilization of the already assigned resources. The evaluation of the consulting project by the client and the overall success of the project should equally allow the drawing of conclusions on the quality of virtual consulting services. The integration of the virtualization project in a client project can be disadvantageous, though, when the quality, the costs and the duration of the consulting project suffer in comparison to a traditional consulting project. Consequently, the factors costs, time, quality and risks should get special attention by suitable project management. According to a survey in the German consulting market by Nissen and Seifert (2016), the transformation of classical into virtual consulting services takes place, both to a large extent in coherence with a concrete client project, and also to about 29% in own internal projects. To be generally valid, the process model should be able to be utilized in both virtualization approaches in independent (internal) projects and also in a (client) project-supporting role.

Requirement 7: The process model has to support the integration of the virtualization process and the synchronous processing of a virtualization- and consulting project.

Cooperation between Internal Units Depending on the size of the consulting firm, the coordination of virtualization activities between different organizational units can have significance. Large consulting firms are subdivided into divisions and sections, which are specialized in specific industries or functional services. If virtualization is realized in one part of the company, it is very important that an exchange of knowledge occurs among the divisions. Ideally, impulses can be generated in other organizational units, which may promote further virtualization initiatives.

Requirement 8: The process model for virtualization should support the cooperation between different internal organizational units of the consulting provider.

Capacity Utilization Depending on the economic situation and the size of the consulting provider, the individual consultants will be more or less deployed in current projects. Specifically at times when the workload is large, there will be a challenge to take consultants away from client projects and assign them to specific virtualization projects. Here some legitimacy efforts are necessary. When the workload is less, potential resources for virtualization are allocable, but projects and clients who can test and evaluate the results, might not be available at this time.

Requirement 9: The process model has to consider the various workload situations in the consulting company.

Consulting Field The Association of German Business Consultants (BDU e.V.) distinguishes the consulting fields strategy-, organization-/process-, IT-, and human resources consulting. The objective here is to establish virtualization as innovative strategy for the sustainable optimization of suitable consulting services in all fields of consulting.

Requirement 10: The process model has to allow virtualization in various consulting fields.

Consulting Approach (Type) Walger (1995) distinguishes expert consulting, advisory consulting, organization development and systemic consulting. These different approaches (types) of consulting have distinctly different features. The level and goal of interaction between the consultant and the client are, for example, characteristics, which can be used to differentiate among the types of consulting. Moreover, the various types of consulting are associated with different virtualization potentials. Advisory consulting, for instance, lends itself easily to automatic consulting solutions (see the contribution on the tool ProMAT in this volume by Nissen et al. 2017a). The sought-after process model for virtualization should be able to accommodate every kind of consulting.

Requirement 11: The process model should allow the investigation of the virtualization potential and the design and implementation of virtualization within every type of consulting.

Consulting Process The decisive business process in the framework of a consulting company encompasses the actual processing and solution of the client problem. Ideally, the consulting process can be subdivided into four elementary phases: preparation, problem analysis, problem solution and implementation (Nissen 2005). This rudimentary consulting process can be understood as the basis of most consulting services. Looking at consulting processes in practice, though, requires the examination of both ideal- and real-typical processes (Kraus and Mohe 2007). Ideal-typical processes can be described as a suggested succession of process phases, which have fixed starting- and end points. This ideal succession is preceded by a detailed planning with phase-related results. In contrast, real-typical consulting processes do not have a linear, rational structure, but instead have an evolutionary character. A subdivision into clearly separated phases is difficult or impossible under the real-typical perspective and by the given dynamics of the consulting process. Activities repeat themselves and overlap, they are interactively processed by various people and take place in a continuously changing organizational context (Kraus and Mohe 2007).

Requirement 12: The process model should support the virtualization of a consulting process/task, both from the ideal-typical and from the real-typical perspective.

Complexity of the Projects Maister (2007) defines three typical kinds of projects considering their different complexity. *Brain projects* show a very high level of complexity. The problem that has to be solved is rather unique. For the solution of this problem a high level of creativity and innovative approaches are necessary Therefore, highly talented consultants and specialists have to be used. *Grey hair* projects need less creativity and innovation, as existing solutions can be adapted to individual requirements and new projects of clients. The focus is on experience in similar but not necessarily identical contexts. Tasks and goals in *procedure projects* are well known, and corresponding solutions already exist. The focus here is on efficiency.

Requirement 13: The process model should support the analysis and virtualization in consulting projects of various complexities.

Consider Business Processes of the Reference Model "Consulting C" Nissen and Seifert (2008) shaped the *Consulting C* as a framework for business processes of a consulting firm. In this reference model, the leading-, main- and support processes of a consulting provider are logically sorted, modelled and described. Moreover, their mutual relationship is characterized. The framework is a helpful guidance for the virtualization of consulting services, also when the internal processes of the consulting provider are considered, such as innovation, knowledge management and product development. On a general level, the *Consulting C* framework provides the activities in the scope of the reference processes that are potentially relevant in the virtualization procedure. In addition, the roles and responsibilities in these business processes of a consulting provider are indicated.

Requirement 14: The process model should consider the business processes contained in the "Consulting C" framework and support their analysis and virtualization.

Knowledge Management Approach Knowledge is a critical resource in consulting (Nissen and Dauer 2007; Deelmann 2009; Ringlstetter et al. 2007). Consequently, knowledge management should be of primary importance in consulting firms. Two knowledge management approaches can be differentiated. On the one side, there is the codification strategy with the objective to explicate knowledge and to distribute it with the help of documents and tools. On the other side, there is the personalization strategy, which focuses more on implicit knowledge, embodied in employees. In this strategy, knowledge can best be distributed through personal contact and cooperation. Depending on the consulting field, one of the two strategies is frequently defined as prevalent knowledge management strategy. IT-oriented consulting follows more often a codification strategy, whereas strategy consulting rather uses a personalization strategy (Nissen and Kinne 2008). For the virtualization of consulting services, it is thus decisive that explicit as well as implicit knowledge is integrated into the virtualization process. Accordingly, both the experts and the system and media of the knowledge management of a consulting have to be considered in the process of virtualization. If, for example, there already is a knowledge management system in the form of a database, document management system, WIKI or something similar, then a virtual consulting platform for the clients, which is under development, should be integrated into this existing systems landscape (Wurdack 2001; Schuster 2005).

Requirement 15: The process model should consider the prevalent knowledge management approach of the consulting provider.

Critical Resources Critical resources of professional services are resources that are decisive for successful service provision. The management of critical resources will decide on the competitive advantage of a company in the market (Bürger 2005). Based on the characteristics of consulting, three critical resources can be identified in this domain: knowledge, reputation and relationship competence (Nissen and Dauer 2007; Ringlstetter et al. 2007; Deelmann 2009). Management must ensure that the individual resource carriers are available, organized and adequately used for the company objectives and client demands. The critical resources are of decisive significance for the virtualization of consulting services and the process model, to be constructed, as by virtualization their use and market impact should be optimized.

Requirement 16: The process model for virtualization has to secure the optimal utilization of critical resources in consulting.

Business Models Werth and Greff (2017) state that the most important success factor of a digital business model is that it scales well, and thus allows growth without raising cost at similar level (Werth and Greff 2017; Stampfl et al. 2013). Based on the four approaches *separation of information-based parts, leveraging assets and sharing economy, enabling customers and partners* and *automation and algorithmic processing*, which allow the scalability of digital business models, Werth and Greff describe four virtual business models: core-only-consulting, platform consulting, self-service consulting and algorithmic consulting. The process model should consider these different digital business models and allow their creation in a particular company.

Requirement 17: The process model should allow the design of new business models, based on virtualization.

Creativity In addition to digital transformation, a cultural transformation is also taking place in the western world, in which the wish and the demand for creativity is reflected. This demand is transferred to working life, where creativity has become an economic requirement. This demand also became clear during the evaluation of the process model by way of an expert survey (Sect. 4.3). The process model should indeed have a clear structure during the development of virtual consulting services. The demand for creativity though, should also be considered.

Requirement 18: The process model of virtualization should promote creativity in digital transformation.

Responsibilities A process model should document project procedures, project structures and project responsibilities (Bullinger and Meiren 2001). It is therefore also important to suggest roles and responsibilities in the virtualization process model. In addition, specifically existing methods for the virtualization of consulting services should also be integrated.

Requirement 19: The process model of virtualization should include roles & responsibilities for virtualization.

Agility and Design Thinking The process model should follow a clear structure from the idea up to the implementation of a virtual consulting service. The development of software and services are currently often realized in an agile way in practice. Prototypes and minimum viable products are produced in very short development times. In design thinking for example, new products are worked on in a client-centred way with the objective to bring new products and services to the clients quickly. An agile procedure should not present a contradiction to the process model. The phases and activities of the process model serve as an orientation for which steps should be completed to maximize the chances for a successful virtual consulting service. In this process, it is in no way determined how long a specific phase should be and which scope of services will be available at the end of a phase. The whole process or parts of it could be re-iterated to expand the product successfully. In this way, a virtual consulting product could be brought onto the market rapidly. Results and feedback could then be used for further improvements. The basic idea of the design thinking approach is specifically taken up in the design phase, where ideas are generated, implemented into prototypes and the results are evaluated.

Requirement 20: The process model of virtualization should allow an agile and design thinking-oriented process.

3.2   Overview of the Process Model

The process model consists of eight phases: analysis, rough conception, modeling and specification, implementation and tests, market launch, management and operations, performance and quality measurements and consulting service

Fig. 1 Process model for the development and management of virtual consulting services, adapted from Leimeister (2012)

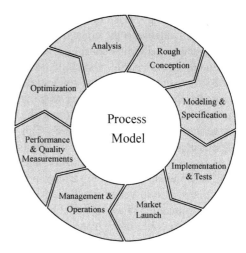

optimization. The selection of the phases orients itself on the framework of Leimeister (2012), who derived these phases from the strengths and weaknesses of existing process models. The process model addresses the management of existing virtual services as well as the development of new virtual consulting services. The fundamental structure of the work of Leimeister (2012) was adopted. Adaptions were especially needed where the characteristics of consulting are important, such as in analysis and design. The process model has an iterative character, which means that recursions between the phases and also within an individual phase are allowed and explicitly desired. Thus, the process model can be flexibly used and adaptions to different situational conditions are allowed. In Fig. 1, the procedure for the development and management of virtual consulting services is illustrated.

In the phase analysis, the creation of a virtualization strategy as well as the definition of the virtualization project are in focus. An important component of this phase is the evaluation of the virtualization potential of consulting processes and tasks. After a virtualization project has been defined in the analysis phase, the virtual consulting services are more concretely shaped during the rough conception phase. For this purpose, requirements for the consulting service, to be virtualized, need to be defined. Subsequently solutions are developed and evaluated. At this point, the selection of a suitable virtualization technology is a decisive factor. If a matching solution for the requirements has been identified, the development proceeds to the phase of modeling and specification where the solution is shaped in detail. In the sense of business process modeling, the documentation and design of the virtual consulting process is done. Furthermore, the detailed specification of the software solution takes place in this phase. In the phase implementation and tests, the solution is subsequently implemented, and tested whether the requirements are met. If the solution can fulfil the requirements, the market launch takes place. During this phase, all activities, which are necessary for the systematic launch of the virtual consulting service in the market, are performed. Now the virtual consulting service is available to the clients.

Thereafter, the virtual consulting service migrates to management and operations for continued successful availability. This phase includes all activities, which are necessary for the lasting provision and performance of a virtual consulting service. Basically, the activities necessary to guarantee the profitability, client retention and the satisfaction of employees during the provision of the consulting service are sorted into this phase (Nissen 2005). This includes, for example, the establishment of contact points for consultants as well as clients with respect to the virtual service in question. The phase performance and quality measurements aims, on the one side, at the evaluation of the service in a controlling sense. On the other side, the objective is also to determine the service quality in the sense of client satisfaction. In the optimization phase, the continuous examination of requirements, imposed on the virtual service, takes place. Building onto results from the preceding phase, optimization measures are derived and implemented.

In the following section the activities of the process model, relevant for the virtualization of consulting services are presented phase by phase in more detail.

3.3 Detailed Presentation of the Virtualization Process Model

3.3.1 Analysis

The analysis phase (Fig. 2) is the starting phase of the process model and should be run through at the beginning of every virtualization project. In this phase, a virtualization strategy is devised and a particular virtualization project is defined. An important component is the determination of the virtualization potential by means of a method by Nissen and Seifert (2017a, b).

On a general level, strategies represent long-term plans and means to achieve the set targets and objectives (Bruhn and Meffert 2012). Thus, the virtualization strategy contains a long-term plan, objectives and measures for the digital transformation of a consulting provider. The formulation of the strategy is based on a careful situation analysis which includes a detailed competitive-, company- and market analysis.

Strategies should secure the lasting success of a company and they do not refer to individual concrete actions within the company or in the market (Hungenberg 2012). Thus, the strategy formulation is not run through for a single virtualization project, but after the company has decided on creating virtual consulting services systematically. It is the responsibility of the company management to adapt the virtualization strategy, if necessary, during the strategic planning process.

The assessment of one's own virtualization status also belongs to the assessment of the initial situation. A helpful orientation is presented in the form of a Consulting

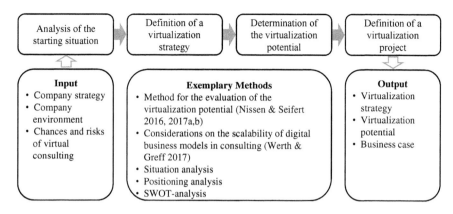

Fig. 2 Procedure in the analysis phase

Virtualization Maturity Model by Nissen and Seifert (2016), which defines four maturity levels. It allows the individual classification of a company's maturity level of virtualization and is, thus, an opportunity to assess one's own potentials. Only digital business models should be developed, which are lasting and grow with increasing profits (Werth and Greff 2017). The strategy for virtualization should be oriented accordingly.

The identification of virtualization potentials is necessary to allow the management of consulting firms to make decisions on possible virtualization projects. A method for the evaluation of virtualization potential for a given consulting service or task by Nissen and Seifert (2016, 2017a, b) supports this process. It contains three separate sub-steps for the assessment of the virtualization potential in the realm of consulting:

(1) Analysis of the process-related virtualization potential,
(2) Analysis of the company-related virtualization potential,
(3) Analysis of the strategic virtualization potential.

The evaluation process starts with an analysis of the process-related virtualization potential and continuously becomes more specific during the ongoing process, until it turns into a business case. In the realm of the business case, the chances and risks of virtualization are investigated, from the perspective of clients and consultants. Correspondingly, the analysis of the virtualization potential is the starting point of each individual virtualization project. This is triggered by an idea, which comes up during the preparation of a client project, respectively during the realization of such a project, or the idea comes from a concrete client demand. In every case, the phase is completed with the definition of a virtualization project. The definition includes which kind of virtual consulting service, according to the differentiation of Werth and Greff (2017) should be developed, emphasizing its scalability.

Particularly in the scope of the strategic analysis, classical methods such as SWOT-analysis or positioning analysis can be implemented. Nissen et al. (2015, 2017b) identify chances and risks of virtual consulting services, from the clients' and consultants' perspective. These can be taken up in the scope of strategy formulation.

Another decisive problem of the analysis phase is the selection of suitable clients. If virtualization is supposed to be successfully developed, the constant participation of clients is necessary. In this way important information on the design, development, market launch and operation of virtual consulting services can be gained. A good integration of clients into the development- and implementation process must be devised to ensure optimal input.

3.3.2 Rough Conception

After concrete virtualization potentials have been defined during the analysis phase, ideas for the implementation are collected and evaluated during the rough conception phase (Fig. 3).

Should suitable ideas for the implementation be found, these will be worked on in more detail, before they proceed to the phase modeling and specification. At any point of time during the conception, the further development can be broken off, due to a lack of resources or for economic reasons (Nissen 2005).

Again, the integration of clients in the conception and development of virtual consulting services is very important for the success of the endeavour. A good virtualization design concept hence considers the requirements and expectations of the clients from the beginning and puts these into the center of its assumptions. On a general level, the following aspects have to be considered to successfully develop consulting services:

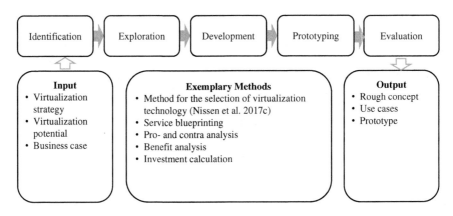

Fig. 3 Procedure in the rough conception phase

- Consulting clients (underlying problems, requirements, risks, added-value, needed competences, acceptable technologies)
- Framing conditions of the service provision (legal-, political-, social-, technical factors)
- Consulting resources (manpower, knowledge, reputation, relationship competence, technology competence, available tools and infrastructure).

In addition to the client-orientation, attention has to be paid that the virtualization concept allows an effective and efficient, and thus from a cost perspective, an attractive provision of the service (Leimeister 2012).

In the *identification subphase*, the framing conditions and constraints for virtualization are identified (Leimeister 2012). These include the localization of possible technologies as well as the preceding selection of suitable consulting sub-processes and activities. Additionally, there are pre-settings, which refer to the possible target group of the virtual consulting service. It should be specified here, which clients, consultants and partners will later be the users of the virtual consulting service. On this basis, first inputs for the design of the service are compiled. The *exploration subphase* ties in at this point and tries to compile detailed information on the expectations and the behaviour of the clients. Thus, the clients should be involved in the design process not later than at this stage.

The gained information have to be analyzed, structured and interpreted in the following step. In the *development subphase* the information on the needs of the clients, relevant constraints and the pre-set choices are simultaneously processed so that ideas for suitable virtualization mechanisms can be compiled. This is a decisive moment in the virtualization process because at this point, possible technologies, systems and tools are evaluated and their suitability for the implementation in virtualization is tested. Basically, a variety of solutions are available at this stage. Consulting processes, and most of all the interaction with clients, can be supported by various tools. The challenge now is the selection of suitable tools for the virtualization of a consulting phase or activity. The technology selection method described by Nissen et al. (2017c) in this volume can be helpful here.

In the *prototyping subphase*, the most promising ideas can be first-time realized. The prototype is used to check if the requirements and expectations are met by an initial testing of specific functions or components of the solution. Additionally, the prototype is used to evaluate solution alternatives and select suitable options. The objective must be to demonstrate the added-value, related to the virtualization of a consulting service, in the prototyping phase already.

The *subphase evaluation* includes the assessment of various ideas and solution versions regarding their suitability to fulfil the objectives set at the beginning of the virtualization project.

In the rough conception phase the focus is on the analysis of client needs and the creation of ideas and prototypes according to the Design Thinking approach (Uebernickel et al. 2015). According to this approach, the demonstrated procedure is not traversed only once, but is understood as a cycle, in which the objective—i.e. the development of a virtual consulting service—is approximated step-wise.

Design Thinking is a promising approach to support virtualization because it emphasizes the importance of the actors of a virtual service. So the expectations and requirements of both clients and consultants are assessed thoroughly and then corresponding solutions will be created using creative methods. For example, a *Customer Journey Map* could be designed that represents the future customer journey within a virtual consulting service.

3.3.3 Modeling and Specification

The basic objective of the modeling and specification phase (Fig. 4) is the modeling of virtual consulting processes and the development of a virtualization concept, which provides the basis for the development of innovative consulting tools.

Thereby all activities must be documented, which are traditionally or virtually conducted in the scope of the virtualized consulting process. A process model to be developed for virtual consulting services forms a decisive basis to specify the functions of a consulting application. According to Nissen (2005) the designed process models can be used as follows:

- Determination of the current state of the consulting process and documentation of the virtualized target process, based on process modeling and process measurements.
- Comparison of the traditional consulting service with the virtualized consulting service, and/or with the services of competing consulting providers.
- Analysis of management practices, process structures, supporting IT-systems and other components in the leading consulting companies, in particular regarding virtualization and usage of digital consulting tools.
- Deduction of internal objectives to improve the process (in particular by virtualization) on the basis of these best practices.

An important result at this stage is the detailed virtualization concept, which documents the future consulting process on a detailed level. Thus, individual tasks within the consulting process can be analyzed, and their future features can be specified. The objective of the detailed concept is to provide both clients and consultants, business as well as IT specialists, with adequate information on the

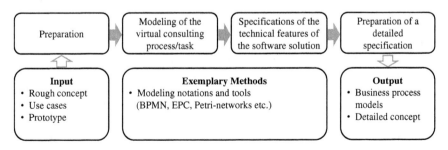

Fig. 4 Procedure in the phase modeling and specification

target state. The IT-concept of the virtualization reflects the data processing perspective and concentrates on the technical specifications of the future consulting tool. It provides the technical and system-related specifications, which are necessary to implement the consulting tool.

3.3.4 Implementation and Tests

In the phase implementation and tests (Fig. 5), the solution is subsequently implemented and it is tested whether the requirements of the virtualized consulting process are met (Meiren and Barth 2002; Ganz and Meiren 2010; Leimeister 2012).
The tests include:

- Conceptual tests for testing the consistency and credibility of the consulting service,
- Usability tests for testing the user-friendly design of applications,
- Practical-/user-tests for testing new consulting services via pilot clients, and
- Acceptance tests for testing the internal company acceptance of the virtualized consulting service.

Furthermore, a comparison with existing consulting services and an analysis of the employee- and client-feedback should be performed.

3.3.5 Market Launch

The market launch phase (Fig. 6) encompasses all the activities that are necessary to offer the newly developed consulting service in the market.
Depending on the level of virtualization and the used technologies, various measures should be conducted. Highly virtualized services, such as the launch of a consulting portal, similar as the introduction of automated consulting solutions, require more measures than, for example, the first deployment of chat applications

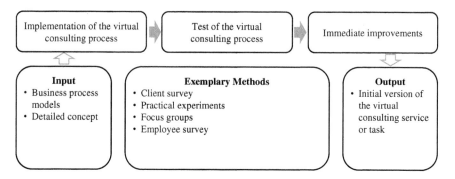

Fig. 5 Procedure in the phase implementation and test

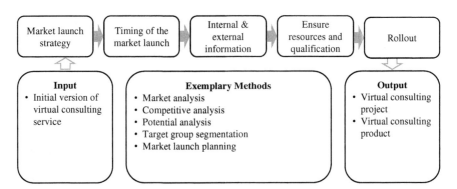

Fig. 6 Procedure in the phase market launch

and video-conference tools. A market launch strategy has to be defined for virtu-alized consulting products, which means that it has to be exactly specified when which market and which client group should have access to the new solution for the first time. It is also necessary to define whether there is one or more pilot-market(s), where the new service can be tested.

Tied to this, it should be tested when the time is optimal for the launch of the new consulting service. When the extent and time of the launch is known, it is necessary to perform internal communication in the sense of change management, and external communication in the sense of the previously defined marketing strategy. In the scope of suitable information measures, clients and consultants must be informed about the features and advantages of the new consulting solution. It is furthermore necessary to inform project managers how they can implement virtualized consulting services in their projects usefully. The qualification of those consultants, who were so far not involved in the virtualization project, and the qualification of employees, who are concerned with internal support processes are important aspects of the implementation and market launch phases. Particularly in the case of (semi) auto-mated consulting solutions, the consultants must be qualified to implement the applications in the correct position within a consulting project. The consultant also has to realize the appropriate problem for the solution via this application.

3.3.6 Management and Operations

The phase management and operations of the process model (Fig. 7) aims at the setting up of all activities, which are necessary for the lasting provision and per-formance of a virtual consulting service.

Basically, three important objectives should be considered (Wurdack 2001; Nissen 2005). Firstly, an optimal competitive position in relation to the client needs and the services of the competition should be achieved and continuously secured by the virtual consulting services. Secondly, an optimal profit should be reached. Thirdly, a good support of the virtual consulting service by the consulting

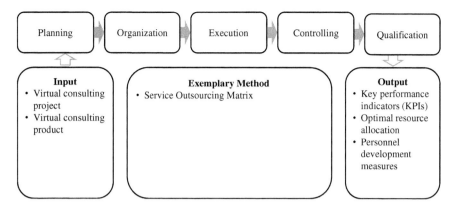

Fig. 7 Procedure in the phase management and operations

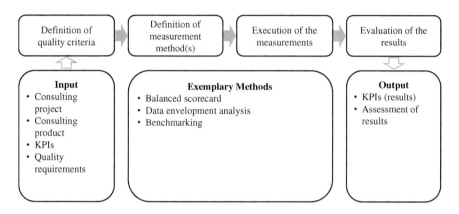

Fig. 8 Procedure in the phase performance and quality measurements

organization and its internal business processes must take place. To achieve these objectives an active management of virtual consulting services is necessary. Primarily this requires a consulting process management, which includes planning, organization and control of all the activities necessary for a (virtualized) consulting project. An important part is the resource planning and staffing, which means the planning, management, and qualification of those consultants, who take part in the corresponding projects.

3.3.7 Performance and Quality Measurements

The phase performance and quality measurements (Fig. 8) aims, on the one side, at the evaluation of services in a controlling sense, and on the other side at the determination of the quality in the sense of client satisfaction.

Change in Importance with Rising Degree of Virtualization

Professional competencies of consultants	↘
Social competencies of consultants	↘
Quality of the relationship	↘
Clients' integration	↘
Reputation of consulting provider	→
Achieving objectives	→
Consulting process quality	→
Reaction capability	↗
Efficiency	↗
System availability	↗
Fulfilment	↗
Privacy	↗
Compensation	↗
Contact	↗
Aesthetics	↗

↘ Importance goes down   → Importance stays constant   ↗ Importance goes up

Fig. 9 Importance shift of the clients' quality criteria for consulting services with rising degree of virtualization (Nissen et al. (2015) in source: Deelmann T, Ockel DM, in collaboration with BDU e.V. (eds) Handbuch der Unternehmensberatung, loose-leaf book, state 2017, KZ. 7311, courtesy of Erich Schmidt Verlag GmbH & Co. KG, Berlin 2017, more about the loose-leaf book at http://www.esv.info/978-3-503-07846-2)

To notice critical developments during the market launch and repeated conduction of virtual consulting services at an early stage, and to introduce corresponding counter-measures, service indicators (key figures) should be used. Typical key figures during the provision of virtual, as well as traditional consulting services are the marginal return and the degree of utilization of the consultants. Other important indicators can be the amount of client requests for quotes (number of opportunities) as well as the rate of follow-up projects. According to Nissen et al. (2015, 2017b) the quality of the virtual consulting service itself, can be determined by the criteria listed in Fig. 9. This figure also shows how the importance of individual quality criteria of consulting services shifts with a rising degree of virtualization.

If the quality of a virtual consulting service should be determined in this phase, these criteria have to be applied by suitable measures and measurement methods. Based on a first set of indicators, a filtering must be conducted that excludes those indicators, which cannot be measured sufficiently. The set of key figures, defined this way, has to be measured in the following step. Depending on the kind of indicators, the data can be drawn from existing IT-systems, or they have to be collected by quantitative or qualitative methods. Depending on the kind of data and data sources, these have to be appropriately structured and processed for later analyses. Here it is particularly important to optimize the various qualities of individual information items so that a homogeneous and understandable set of information can be generated.

According to Ennsfellner et al. (2014) procedures such as self-evaluation from the perspective of the consultant, the mutual evaluation of the consultant and client, the external evaluation by people outside the project, or hybrid forms can be used to determine consulting quality. Furthermore, referring to Ennsfellner et al. (2014), methods such as checklists, interviews or workshops can be used for measurements. A recurring quality measurement is the basis for the adjustment of consulting services when client requirements change over time.

3.3.8 Consulting Service Optimization

The systematic optimization of virtual consulting services (Fig. 10) is based on the concept of continual service improvement (Wurdack 2001) and the measurements of the previous phase.

With reference to Leimeister (2012) the continual service improvement, and thus the optimization phase has the following objectives:

- Testing, analyzing and recommending of improvement opportunities in every phase of the process model for the virtualization of consulting services,
- Testing and analyzing of the reached consulting quality,
- Identification and implementation of activities to improve consulting quality,
- Identification and implementation of activities to optimize the efficiency and effectiveness of virtual consulting services,
- Optimization of the profitability during the provision of virtual consulting services without losing out on the quality,
- Ensuring the use of suitable quality management methods.

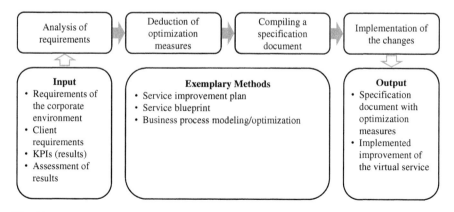

Fig. 10 Procedure in the consulting service optimization phase

Based on the results of the quality measurements in the previous phase, action fields for the optimization of the consulting service should now be determined and measures for improvement specified in detail. Ideally, the decisive action options for reaching the optimization targets are released and their implementation is started. These measures must now be considered in every virtualization project that uses the respective consulting service.

3.3.9   Roles and Responsibilities Within the Process Model

The suggested allocation of individual responsibilities within the phases of this virtualization process model is visualized in the form of a RACI chart in Table 5. According to Lloyd et al. (2007), the abbreviation stands for:

- Responsible. One or more persons, who are responsible for the conduction of this activity.
- Accountable: The one person, who is held economically responsible for it.
- Consulted: Person groups, who are consulted, respectively, who are asked to give their opinion.
- Informed: Person groups, who are informed on the actual status.

The suggested roles and responsibilities may be adapted in practice, based on the different individual situation of consulting providers (for instance, due to varying company size).

4   Evaluation of the Process Model

4.1   Concept of the Evaluation

The process model should support the consulting practice during the virtualization of consulting services. The systematic derivation of the model based on a literature review and requirements deduced from its intended use particularly account for the rigor demands of the artefact. The practical relevance of the process model must, however, preferably be ensured via the integration of consultants (and eventually clients) in the design process. The questioning of later users can give important insights. Therefore, an expert survey was conducted that aims at the acquisition of requirements and expectations of consultants in the context of digital transformation. Simultaneously, the survey was used to evaluate the quality of the existing artefact (process model) at that stage.

In this research project, a standardized questionnaire was employed, as only a limited number of experts should be questioned. A large scale empirical evaluation of the process model is postponed as future research. An expert in our sense is a person, who works in a consulting company and has at least three years of

Table 5 Suggested RACI chart for roles and responsibilities within the process model

Phases of virtualization process model	Roles and responsibilities									
	Company management	Virtualization project manager	Product development	Subject matter experts	Consultants	Controlling	Quality management	Project managers	Sales and marketing	Clients
Analysis	A	R	C	C	C/I		C	I	C	C
Rough conception	A	R	C	C	C/I		C	I	I	C
Modeling and specification	A	R	C	C	C/I		C	I	I	C
Implementation and tests	A	R	C	C	C/I		C	I	I	C
Marked launch	A	C	C	I	I	I	I	C	R	I
Management and operations	A	I	I		C/I	I	C	R	C	C
Performance and quality measurements	A	I	I	C	C/I	C	R	C	I	I
Service optimization	A	I	C	C	C	C	R	C	I	C

consulting experience. Most participants exceeded this requirement by far. In this way, it is ensured that participants are conversant with the consulting processes. "The expert has technical-, process- and interpretation know-how, which refers to his specific professional or occupational action field [...]" (Bogner et al. 2002, translated). Three experts were asked for an additional follow-up interview. They were interviewed over the telephone during the ongoing design of the process model. This made a more in-depth analysis and exploration of expert opinions and expectations possible.

4.2 Preparation and Expert Panel

The usage of MS Excel-VBA allows for the implementation of a clickable process model through which the respective expert can navigate (even offline) without any previous knowledge. At the same time, a standardized questionnaire was integrated. Every participant could click on the overview of the process model and on single phases in detail, and evaluate them in the questionnaire.

The questionnaire starts with a brief introduction on the topic *digital transformation in consulting* to make sure all participants have a basic understanding of the subject. Classification questions follow, concerning e.g. the participants work experience or the size of the respective consulting company. In the subsequent section of the questionnaire, the actual assessment of the process model is done, which encompasses standardized answer options as well as open questions.

In the standardized part, amongst others, questions are asked on the practicability, consistency and completeness of the process model. The assessment is done by an ordinal scale with the valuation options *applies fully*, *applies rather*, *applies less* and *does not apply*. A straight scale with the four valuation possibilities was chosen, to avoid the *flight to the middle*, where the questioned persons have problems to decide for the one or the other side of the scale (Porst 2014). This section of the questionnaire should assess the developmental status of the process model, and demonstrate improvement potential. In the following section with open questions, concrete optimization suggestions are requested.

The survey took place between 25/03/2017 and 10/04/2017. Table 6 gives an overview on the participants of the survey. It demonstrates that consultants with various backgrounds were involved in the evaluation. This is particularly important because the process model should be equally useful in different fields of consulting and companies of different size.

4.3 Results and Discussion

The experts overall positively evaluated the proposed process model for the virtualization of consulting services, though there are still some improvement options.

Table 6 Composition of the expert panel

#	Work experience (years)	Position	Professional focus	Size of the consultancy (number of employees)	Experience with virtualization of consulting services (1 = none/ 4 = much)	Experience with virtualization in general (1 = none/ 4 = much)
1	6	Manager	CIO/CDO advisory	2000	2	2
2	3	Senior consultant	Retail	1800	3	3
3	14	Consultant	Retail	2000	2	2
4	5	Senior consultant	Customer experience management	1500	1	2
5	6	Manager	CIO/CDO advisory	2000	2	2
6	3	Consultant	Agile business transformation	70	1	1
7	20	Senior manager	Banking	2000	2	2
8	18	Senior manager	Banking/ business consulting	38,000	2	1
9	18	Senior manager	Business consulting	40,000	2	2

Table 7 Assessment of the developed process model in the expert survey (frequency of answers, n = 9)

The presented process model	Applies fully	Applies rather	Applies less	Does not apply
...is complete	3	5	1	0
...is understandable	2	6	1	0
...is practicable	1	7	1	0
...has an appropriate level of detail	2	3	4	0
...is consistent	3	4	2	0
...is useful	1	6	2	0

Most questions were answered with *rather applies* or *applies fully*. The frequency of the answers is presented in Table 7.

The process model's level of detail was evaluated worse than other aspects as can be seen in Table 7. However, the presentation of the process model was shortened for the experts, because of its magnitude in the presentation. During the development of a supporting tool, which is used for the application of the process model, it should be ensured that basic elements of the model are described succinctly, and that the methods included in it, are further elaborated. Some experts suggested to give examples of the used tools and to describe them further. During the development of a supporting tool for the process model, templates for individual methods can be created that would ease their later use in practice.

Another expert identified the analysis phase as the basis for further work and suggested a more precise description of this phase. Further improvement potentials were identified in the delimitation of single phases of one another. Two experts stated that the phase *implementation and tests* and the *market launch* can be consolidated. At this point, the two phases were more clearly separated from each other in the process model specification. It was also explained that the phase *market launch* is used to make the service available to the market. Moreover, some renaming of phases took place to underline their respective focus. Also, some activities were shifted between adjacent phases, to adhere more closely to their respective focus.

One expert criticized that the process model is lacking something *new*, such as for example a method, which supports the development of digital business models. In fact, in our view, the process model integrates quite a few new approaches, such as the method to evaluate the virtualization potential of a particular consulting service or task, or the method to determine a fitting technology for a virtualization project. However, at this point, the work of Werth and Greff (2017) was integrated into the process model, which describes four possible digital business models in consulting. This consideration does not lead to a new method for the development of digital business models. It does, however, provide reference points, which business models, depending on the respective level of virtualization of the consulting service can be pursued.

Basically, the approach pursued in the process model is to identify virtualization potentials in the service portfolio of the consulting company, and to develop virtual consulting products so that these potentials are used. Virtualization thereby provides the basic "approach for the design of new business models of consulting" (Nissen and Seifert 2016). Thus, the development of new digital business models indeed requires the development of virtual services; respectively new business models are possible through using virtualization. But, the invention of new digital business models does not take place in the scope of the development of virtual consulting services, and it is therefore not a component of the proposed process model.

Finally, some remarks on the surplus value and adaption compared to existing models, in particular the generic process model of Leimeister (2012). Because of its focus on the role of IT, the process model of Leimeister (2012) was a good starting point for our own considerations, as IT is of paramount importance in virtualizing consulting processes. The surplus value of our process model in the given consulting domain is created by both the integration of existing methods and knowledge on the virtualization of consulting services, and by considering the specific characteristics of consulting in individual phases of the process model.

4.4 Limitations

The expert survey and the evaluation of the process model are not based on an implementation of the process model in consulting practice. This certainly limits the significance of the results. Assessments of the consultants are based on their experience and their vision, how a virtualization project could be conducted. The real conduction of the phases and activities in a real virtualization project could provide detailed information and feedback on the strengths and weaknesses of the proposed process model.

Another weak point is the fact that it cannot be definitely said, whether all the participants correctly understood the content of the process model, even though it was tried to make its content and targeted use as clear as possible. The visualization of the process model by means of Excel-VBA moreover presents a form of reduction. Due to the sheer size of the model content, not all of the aspects of the process model were presented in detail to the experts. This would have overloaded the participants, but might influence the assessment results. The standardized survey considerably limited the opportunities to scrutinize detailed aspects of a phase. The validity of this evaluation may further be limited by the composition of the panel. In the future, repeating the evaluation with a larger und even more diverse panel of consulting experts, maybe also integrating clients, appears desirable. The model should also be used and evaluated in the course of practical projects where virtual consulting services are designed and implemented.

5 Conclusions and Outlook

The development of successful, innovative consulting products requires a systematic approach. A process model should support consulting providers to generate ideas, to adequately implement them and to launch and operate them successfully. Virtualization projects in the consulting industry are influenced by various constraints and framing conditions. The size of the firm, the consulting field and approach, as well as the individual virtualization-related maturity level of the company is of importance.

The proposed process model is intended as an orientation for future virtualization projects in the consulting industry. For this reason, existing process models of service- and software-engineering, new service development, service designs and of IT service-management were initially analyzed and a process model was selected as a template. This process model was then adapted to the specific domain of virtualization in consulting. The next step involved the evaluation of the process model by nine experienced consultants and project managers, while simultaneously new requirements and ideas for improving the model were generated.

As a result, a process model as an artefact with eight phases was designed for the virtualization of consulting services. It consists of the phases analysis, rough conception, modeling and specification, implementation and tests, market launch, management and operations, performance and quality measurements, and consulting service optimization. This model represents a first proposal that should now be applied, broadly evaluated, and optimized in the course of practical virtualization projects.

References

Bogner A, Littig B, Menz W (2002) Das Experteninterview. VS Verlag für Sozialwissenschaften, Wiesbaden

Boughzala I, Assar S, Romano NC Jr (2010) An E-government field study of process virtualization modeling. Group Decis Negot 154:32–47

Bullinger HJ (ed) (1999) Entwicklung innovativer Dienstleistungen. In: Dienstleistungen - Innovation für Wachstum und Beschäftigung: Herausforderungen des internationalen Wettbewerbs. Gabler Verlag, Wiesbaden, pp 49–65

Bullinger HJ, Meiren T (2001) Service Engineering – Entwicklung und Gestaltung von Dienstleistungen. In: Bruhn M, Meffert H (eds) Handbuch Dienstleistungsmanagement: Von der strategischen Konzeption zur praktischen Umsetzung, 2nd edn. Gabler, Wiesbaden, pp 149–175

Bruhn M, Meffert H (2012) Handbuch Dienstleistungsmarketing - Planung - Umsetzung - Kontrolle. Springer Gabler, Wiesbaden

Bruhn M, Stauss B (2009) Kundenintegration im Dienstleistungsmanagement - Eine Einführung in die theoretischen und praktischen Problemstellungen. Springer, Wiesbaden

Bürger B (2005) Aspekte der Führung und der strategischen Entwicklung von Professional Service Firms: der Leverage von Ressourcen als Ausgangspunkt einer differenzierten Betrachtung. Springer, Wiesbaden

Daun C, Klein R (2004) Vorgehensweisen zur systematischen Entwicklung von Dienstleistungen im Überblick. In: Klein R, Herrmann K, Scheer AW, Spath D (eds) Computer aided service engineering. Springer, Berlin Heidelberg, pp 43–67

Deelmann T (2009) Internetberatung - Einige Überlegungen zu Möglichkeiten einer sinnhaften Vollautomation von Beratungsleistungen. In: Fischer S (ed) Informatik 2009. Im Focus das Leben - Beiträge der 39. Jahrestagung der Gesellschaft für Informatik e.V. (GI), Bonn, pp 3745–3759

Ennsfellner I, Bodenstein R, Herget J (eds) (2014) Exzellenz in der Unternehmensberatung - Qualitätsstandards für die Praxis. Springer Gabler, Wiesbaden

Ganz W, Meiren T (2010) Testing of new services. In: International conference on service sciences (ICSS), Institute of Electrical and Electronics Engineers. China, Hangzhou, 13–14 May 2010

Graupner TD (2010) Vorgehensmodell zur Gestaltung internetbasierter Mehrwertdienste für den Maschinen- und Anlagenbau. Dissertation, Karlsruhe University. Series IPA-IAO-Forschung und Praxis, no. 493

Hevner AR, March ST, Park J, Ram S (2004) Design Science in information systems research. MIS Q 28(1):75–105

Hungenberg H (2012) Strategisches Management in Unternehmen, 7th edn. Springer, Berlin

Jaschinski C (1998) Qualitätsorientiertes Redesign von Dienstleistungen. Dissertation, Aachen University. Shaker, Aachen

Kraus S, Mohe M (2007) Zur Divergenz ideal-und realtypischer Beratungsprozesse. In: Nissen V (ed) Consulting Research. Unternehmensberatung aus wissenschaftlicher Perspektive. DUV, Wiesbaden, pp 263–279

Kunau G, Junginger M, Herrmann T, Krcmar H (2005) Ein Referenzmodell für das Service Engineering mit multiperspektivischem Ansatz. In: Herrmann T, Kleinbeck U, Krcmar H (eds) Konzepte für das Service Engineering. Physica-Verlag, pp 187–216

Leimeister JM (2012) Dienstleistungsengineering und -management, 2nd edn. Springer, Berlin

Lin FR, Hsieh PS (2011) A sat view on new service development. Serv Sci 3(2):141–157

Lloyd V, Rudd C, Taylor S (2007) ITIL: [IT service management practices; ITIL v3 core publications], 2. impr. with corr. TSO, London

Maister DH (2007) Managing the professional service firm. Simon & Schuster

Meiren T, Barth T (2002) Service Engineering in Unternehmen umsetzen. Leitfaden für die Entwicklung von Dienstleistungen. Technical Report. Fraunhofer-IRB, Stuttgart

Neuert UW (1990) Computergestützte Unternehmensberatung; Möglichkeiten und Grenzen der Computerunterstützung unter besonderer Berücksichtigung der Strategieberatung. Dissertation, Universität Marburg

Nissen V (2005) Entwurf eines Prozessmodells für Beratungsunternehmen. Forschungsberichte zur Unternehmensberatung, vol 2005-01

Nissen V (ed) (2007) Consulting Research—Eine Einführung. In: Consulting Research. Unternehmensberatung aus wissenschaftlicher Perspektive. DUV, Wiesbaden, pp 3–38

Nissen V (2017) Digital transformation of the consulting industry—introduction and overview. In this volume

Nissen V, Dauer D (2007) Wissensmanagement in Beratungsunternehmen - Ergebnisse einer empirischen Untersuchung deutscher Unternehmensberatungen. Ilmedia, Ilmenau

Nissen V, Kinne S (2008) IV-und Strategieberatung: eine Gegenüberstellung. Proceedings der Teilkonferenz „IT-Beratung "der Multikonferenz Wirtschaftsinformatik, pp 89–106

Nissen V, Kuhl J, Kraeft H, Seifert H, Reiter J, Eidmann J (2017a) ProMAT—a project management assessment tool for virtual consulting. In this volume

Nissen V, Seifert M (2008) Das Consulting C – Grundzüge eines Prozessreferenzmodells für IV-Beratungsunternehmen. In: Bichler M, Hess T, Krcmar H Lechner U, Matthes F, Picot A, Speitkamp B, Wolf P (eds) Multikonferenz Wirtschaftsinformatik, Proceedings of REFMOD 2008. GITO, Berlin, pp 1661–1674

Nissen V, Seifert H (2016) Virtualisierung in der Unternehmensberatung. Eine Studie im deutschen Beratungsmarkt. BDU, Bonn

Nissen V, Seifert H (2017a) Ermittlung des Virtualisierungspotenzials von Beratungsleistungen im Consulting. In: Leimeister JM, Brenner W (eds) Proceedings of 13rd International Conference on Wirtschaftsinformatik, WI2017, St. Gallen, pp 1348–1362

Nissen V, Seifert H (2017b) Evaluating the virtualization potential of consulting services. In this volume

Nissen V, Seifert H, Blumenstein M (2015) Virtualisierung von Beratungsleistungen: Qualitätsanforderungen, Chancen und Risiken der digitalen Transformation in der Unternehmensberatung aus der Klientenperspektive. In: Deelmann T, Ockel DM (eds) Handbuch der Unternehmensberatung, 25th edn. Erich Schmidt Verlag, Berlin

Nissen V, Seifert H, Blumenstein M (2017b) Chances, risks and quality criteria of virtual consulting. In this volume

Nissen V, Seifert H, Blumenstein M (2017c) A method to support the selection of technologies for the virtualization of consulting services. In this volume

Overby E (2008) Process virtualization theory and the impact of information technology. Organ Sci 19(2):277–291

Peffers K, Tuunanen T, Rothenberger MA, Chatterjee S (2007) A design science research methodology for information systems research. J Manage Inf Syst 24(3):45–77

Polster T (2012) Innovation in Beratungsunternehmen. Gabler Verlag, Wiesbaden

Porst R (2014) Fragebogen. Springer Fachmedien, Wiesbaden

Pries-Heje J, Baskerville R, Venable J (2008) Strategies for design science research evaluation. In: Proceedings of the 16th European conference on information systems (ECIS), Galway

Ringlstetter M, Kaiser S, Kampe T (2007) Strategische Entwicklung von Unternehmensberatungen - Ein Beitrag aus Sicht der Professional Services Firms Forschung. In: Nissen V (ed) Consulting Research. Unternehmensberatung aus wissenschaftlicher Perspektive. DUV, Wiesbaden, pp 179–195

Rosemann M, Schütte R (1997) Grundsätze ordnungsmäßiger Referenzmodellierung. Entwicklungsstand und Entwicklungsperspektiven der Referenzmodellierung 32:16–33

Schneider K, Daun C, Behrens H, Wagner D (2006) Vorgehensmodelle und Standards zur systematischen Entwicklung von Dienstleistungen. In: Bullinger HJ, Scheer AW (eds) Service engineering. Springer, Berlin, Heidelberg, pp 113–138

Schneider K, Scheer AW (2003) Konzept zur systematischen und kundenorientierten Entwicklung von Dienstleistungen. Technical report. Saarland University, DFKI, no. 175

Schuster K (2005) E-Consulting; Chancen und Risiken. Dissertation, University of Mannheim

Seifert H, Nissen V (2016) Virtualisierung von Beratungsleistungen: Stand der Forschung zur digitalen Transformation in der Unternehmensberatung und weiterer Forschungsbedarf. In: Nissen V, Stelzer D, Straßburger S, Fischer D (eds) Proceedings of MKWI2016. Ilmedia, Ilmenau, pp 1031–1040

Sonnenberg C, vom Brocke J (2012) Evaluations in the science of the artificial—reconsidering the build-evaluate pattern in design science research. In: Hutchison D, Kanade T, Kittler J, Kleinberg JM, Mattern F, Mitchell JC, Naor M, Nierstrasz O, Pandu Rangan C, Steffen B, Sudan M, Terzopoulos D, Tygar D, Vardi MY, Weikum G, Peffers K, Rothenberger M, Kuechler B (eds) Design science research in information systems. Advances in theory and practice. Springer, Berlin, Heidelberg, vol 7286, pp 381–397

Stampfl G, Prügl R, Osterloh V (2013) An explorative model of business model scalability. Int J Prod Dev 18(3–4):226–248

Suhardi, BPM, Yustianto P (2014) Service engineering framework: a simple approach. In: Proceedings of 2014 international conference on information technology systems and innovation (ICITSI). Piscataway, NJ, pp 130–134

Thomas O (2006) Das Referenzmodellverständnis in der Wirtschaftsinformatik: Historie, Literaturanalyse und Begriffsexplikation. http://scidok.sulb.uni-saarland.de/volltexte/2006/636/pdf/IWi-Heft_187.pdf. Accessed 20 Apr 2017

Uebernickel F, Brenner W, Pukall B, Naef T, Schindlholzer B (2015) Design Thinking: Das Handbuch, 1st edn. Frankfurter Allgemeine Buch, Frankfurt am Main

vom Brocke J (2003) Referenzmodellierung: Gestaltung und Verteilung von Konstruktionsprozessen. Advances in Information Systems and Management Science, vol 4. Logos, Berlin

vom Brocke J, Buddendick C (2004) Konstruktionstechniken für die Referenzmodellierung - Systematisierung, Sprachgestaltung und Werkzeugunterstützung. In: Becker J, Delfmann P (eds) Referenzmodellierung: Grundlagen, Techniken und domänenbezogene Anwendung. Physica-Verlag HD, Heidelberg, pp 19–49

vom Brocke J, Simons A, Niehaves B, Riemer K, Plattfaut R, Cleven A (2009) Reconstructing the giant: On the importance of rigour in documenting the literature search process. In: Proceedings of European conference on information systems, ECIS 2009, Verona, pp 2206–2217

Walger G (ed) (1995) Idealtypen der Unternehmensberatung. In: Formen der Unternehmensberatung: Systemische Unternehmensberatung, Organisationsabwicklung, Expertenberatung und gutachterliche Beratungstätigkeit in Theorie und Praxis. Otto Schmidt, Cologne, pp 1–18

Webster J, Watson R (2002) Analyzing the past to prepare for the future: writing a literature review. MIS Q 26(2):13–23

Werth D, Greff T (2017) Scalability in consulting: insights into the scaling capabilities of business models by digital technologies in consulting industry. In this volume

Wurdack A (2001) E-Consulting - Entwicklung eines Rahmenkonzeptes: Aufbau und Darstellung einer E-Consulting-Lösung im Beratungsunternehmen der Zukunft. Dissertation, University Mannheim

Yang CC (2007) A systems approach to service development in a concurrent engineering environment. Serv Ind J 27(5):635–652

Author Biographies

Volker Nissen holds the Chair of Information Systems Engineering in Services at Technische Universität Ilmenau, Germany, since 2005. Prior to this, he pursued a consulting career, including positions as manager at IDS Scheer AG, director at DHC GmbH, and CEO of NISSCON Ltd., Germany. In 1994 he received a Ph.D. degree in Economic Sciences with distinction from the University of Goettingen, Germany. His current research interests include the digital transformation of the consulting industry, the management of IT-agility, metaheuristic optimization, and process acceptance research. He is author and editor of 19 books and some 200 other publications, including papers in Business & Information Systems Engineering, Information Systems Frontiers, IEEE Transactions on EC, IEEE Transactions on NN, and Annals of OR.

Henry Seifert is a graduate engineer for media technology and since 2011 working as a management consultant. His main focus is on the automotive industry and artificial intelligence, analytics, process optimization and requirements management. He works in projects in the area of sales and after sales processes as well as professional learning. As doctoral candidate at the Group for Information Systems Engineering in Services at Technische Universität Ilmenau, he examines the digital transformation in the consulting industry. The goal of his dissertation is to demonstrate the opportunities and limitations of virtualization, as well as the design of artifacts that enable the realization of virtual consulting services.

Mats-Niklas Ackert is a consultant at Sopra Steria Consulting, a technology and management consultancy with focus on digital transformation. He completed his Master degree in industrial engineering and management with specialisation in automation and strategic management at Technische Universität Ilmenau, Germany and wrote his Master thesis about the virtualization of consulting at the Institute for Business Information Systems Engineering.

A Method to Support the Selection of Technologies for the Virtualization of Consulting Services

Volker Nissen, Henry Seifert and Marco Blumenstein

Abstract Digital transformation in consulting and the virtualization of consulting services are based on the use of information- and communication technologies, such as data mining software, collaboration tools or smartphone apps. There is a pool of possible technologies and tools from which the most appropriate combination can be selected for the consulting process or individual task to be virtualized. So far, though, there is a lack of suitable methods and tools to perform this selection. In this chapter, we propose using a combination of the Analytical Hierarchy Process (AHP) and core ideas from Quality Function Deployment (QFD) to address this issue successfully. This suggested method is based on an extensive literature review, and the analysis of existing virtualization initiatives. It aims to support consulting companies in determining appropriate technologies and tools for the virtualization of consulting services. An example illustrates its application in a practical consulting context. The devised method is part of the virtualization process model, described in detail in a different chapter of this volume. The method belongs to the design-oriented parts of the process model and builds on the virtualization potential of individual consulting services, as determined in the initial analysis phase of the process model.

V. Nissen (✉) · H. Seifert · M. Blumenstein
Technische Universität Ilmenau, Ilmenau, Germany
e-mail: volker.nissen@tu-ilmenau.de

H. Seifert
e-mail: henry.seifert@infosysconsulting.com

M. Blumenstein
e-mail: marco.blumenstein@x-case.de

© Springer International Publishing AG 2018
V. Nissen (ed.), *Digital Transformation of the Consulting Industry*,
Progress in IS, https://doi.org/10.1007/978-3-319-70491-3_10

243

1 Problem, Objective and Research Method

1.1 Problem

Virtualization (Overby 2008) in consulting means the transformation of classical face-to-face consulting processes or tasks into the digital world by adequate use of information- and communication technologies (ICT). Various ICT can be used for this digital transformation. Thus, consulting providers must identify suitable technologies and employ them according to individual objectives. For this purpose, it needs knowledge on which ICT are currently available and how these should be selected for the virtualization of consulting services.

In a study on the status quo of virtualization in the German consulting market 25% of the consultants questioned, reported that this knowledge is missing and therefore it presents a barrier for virtualization (Nissen and Seifert 2016b). Furthermore, an analysis of the present literature on the virtualization of consulting services shows that the selection and systematic application of suitable ICT for the transformation process has so far been insufficiently discussed (Seifert and Nissen 2016).

Some contributions on virtualization in the consulting industry introduce various typologies of ICT. In particular, functional and task- related technology classifications are used (Najda 2001; Schuster 2005; Werth et al. 2016). When ICT must be selected for the use in a consulting virtualization initiative, this choice should be based on requirements of the respective consulting task or process to be virtualized. This is complemented by determinants that are concerned with the concrete development and usage of specific technologies, such as costs, performance and security.

So far, aspects, such as the organization and the actual process of selecting the right technology, as well as the evaluation of specific tools, are not covered by the literature on virtualization (Seifert and Nissen 2016).

1.2 Objective of Research

To support consulting organizations during virtualization, a tool-supported method for the systematic selection of virtualization technology will be constructed. The method aims at the determination of suitable ICT in the conception phase of the virtualization project. At this point of time, it should be known which range of functions and which quality of the virtual consulting service the future user is basically expecting. Moreover, it can be assumed in this phase, that first suggestions on technology components, which may be used, already exist and can be integrated into the method. Furthermore, the method should supply the basis for the detailed specification of the later solution (detailed concept, functional specification document). Thus, it is necessary to find an abstraction level, which allows the profound selection of specific ICT, without having a detailed specification of the desired virtual consulting service. The method should allow for a comprehensible decision on the technical parts of virtualization. In this way, subjective and predominantly cost-oriented decisions can be avoided.

To embed the method into the present research of virtualization, it will be briefly illustrated how various virtualization projects can be classified and which types will be supported by this method. According to Nissen et al. (2015), virtualization of consulting services can be fundamentally understood as a continuum with different virtualization degrees. The spectrum ranges from little to fully virtualized consulting services (Nissen et al. 2015). Werth et al. (2016) build onto these characteristic forms and divide virtualized consulting services into four categories:

- *Computer Supported Consulting* describes the issue that domain neutral software tools are used to support single tasks of a consultant. Typical examples are text processors or spreadsheets.
- In contrast, *Computer Assisted Consulting* includes such software tools, which were specifically developed for the consulting industry. These tools support single tasks in the consulting domain, such as business process modeling.
- *Computer Controlled Consulting* focusses not on individual tasks and functions as before, but rather the whole consulting process is supported.
- *Computer Executed Consulting* finally aims less at the consultant support, than at the substitution of the consultant by a software system. It is the application itself, which (at least partly) executes the consulting service.

The consulting services developed within these virtualization classes, will later be made accessible to the client in the context of consulting business models. Werth and Greff (2017) subdivide such digital business models into core-only-consulting, platform consulting, self-service consulting and algorithmic consulting. The following figure displays this differentiation and also which elements are primarily covered by the technology selection method proposed in this chapter (Fig. 1).

In the current stage, the method focuses on computer supported and computer assisted consulting, i.e. it has a functional focus. The more complex scenarios computer controlled and computer executed consulting refer to large-size software development projects, where generally a technical solution for the virtualized services will be designed from scratch. However, future versions of the technology selection method presented here will also address these application areas as well.

1.3 Methodology

The procedure for the construction of a suitable method is based on the Design Science procedure model of Peffers et al. (2007). The objective of the research has already been described and justified above. In the next section, the requirements for the method, which is to be developed, are specified as part of the design activities.

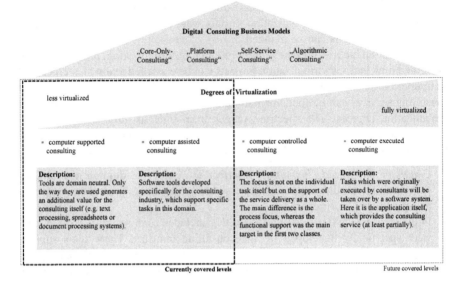

Fig. 1 Application areas of the technology selection method proposed in this chapter

Subsequently, a literature review is conducted, which supports the identification of suitable methods to base the design on. Thereafter, the design and development of the actual method is highlighted. This is followed by a demonstration. A practical example is used to show how the method is applied and that is generates useful output. Finally, the method is summarized, critically evaluated, and an outlook on further avenues of research in this context is provided.

In the scope of this contribution, the term *technology* should be understood as an application-oriented product, which is defined in the form of a concrete software solution (following Corsten et al. 2016). To simplify the wording, a concrete ICT-product (e.g. process modelling software) can also be considered as technology. Furthermore, the term technology bundle is used. A technology bundle reflects a number of specific ICT-products with similar functionality, which can also be referred to as an ICT-class, such as *information search* or *presentation support*.

2 Design and Development

2.1 Requirements on the Method

For the development of the method, it is initially necessary to define valid requirements. These requirements are composed of the fundamental requirements for methods in general, as well as specific requirements for virtualization. As the method is supposed to be developed as an artefact according to the scheme of

Design Science, evaluation criteria from Design Science are also considered. On the basis of a structured literature review, Greiffenberg (2004) establishes significant requirements for the development of methods in general. His literature analysis was used as the foundation for the underlying research project of this chapter. Before using Greiffenberg's analysis, an additional investigation tested it for its completeness and transferability to the virtualization context. Furthermore, it was ensured that additional practice-relevant criteria from the consulting industry enter the requirements.

The first requirements are derived from the description patterns of methods from Hess and Brecht (1996). They describe the categories objective, procedure and results, techniques, roles, embedding, application area and tool support. Sonnenberg and vom Brocke (2012) mention, without a particular recommendation, possible evaluation criteria at different points in the process of creating an artefact in Design Science. To show that the artefact is both applicable and useful in practice, they list the criteria applicability, effectiveness, efficiency, accordance with real world phenomenon, generality, impact on artefact environment and user, internal consistency, or external consistency.

Offermann et al. (2010) additionally suggest systematics, principle-orientation, theoretical profound knowledge and testable possibilities (practical examples) as necessary criteria during the development of methods. The descriptions of input/output variables of the processes, as well as the relationships of all process fragments with each other, are further requirements for the evaluation of the completeness of a method (van Hillegersberg and Kumar 1999).

Initially this is only a loose collection of possible requirements for the technology selection method to be developed. In total, there is an unstructured amount of criteria that are only partly quantifiable and hence also measurable. Greiffenberg (2004) approached this problem and provided a structuring of the (many) evaluation criteria for methods he analyzed. This structuring can be classified into the field of Method Engineering (ME). It is useful to apply his results to the case discussed here. Thus, the structuring was used as basis for the list of requirements related to our own method.

Figure 2 demonstrates the systematization of the identified requirements according to Greiffenberg. The figure includes the quality features as well as a description of the associated requirements. It is subdivided into three categories. The first category is the completeness of the method, which particularly highlights the descriptive requirements. The second category is purpose related, which proves the practical significance of the method and the third category is consistency, which establishes the criteria for consistency and consequently the foundation of the method elements. This sub-division made it possible to classify the previously mentioned requirements. Subsequently these requirements will be used to investigate suitable methods for supporting technology selection in the literature. Finally, they will be re-used to evaluate the technology selection method devised in the course of this contribution.

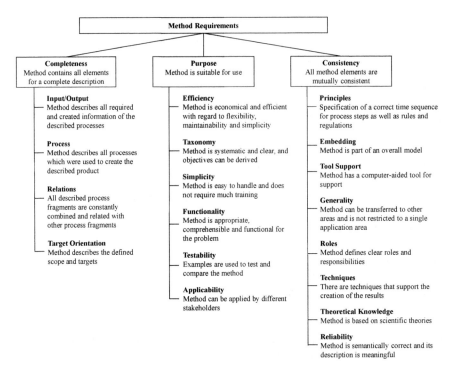

Fig. 2 Requirements related to methods (adapted from Greiffenberg 2004)

2.2 Literature Review

The construction process underlies a literature review that was conducted according to Webster and Watson (2002) and vom Brocke et al. (2009). The objective was the identification of existing methods, which could be used for the method to be constructed. The selection of scientific databases, which were used for the investigation, was based on the ranking of the German Academic Association of Business Research. Those databases were used, which included at least one of the top ten journals of business informatics.

Altogether 81 contributions were identified. They were analyzed in detail and tested for their relevance in the literature review. The contributions, which did not discuss a method for technology selection or which presented a method which could not be transferred to the presented use case in this project, were excluded. This selection process lead to 13 relevant contributions. Subsequently the so-far results were presented and discussed in our research group. During the discussion, another three fitting contributions were identified that had previously not been considered because they were outside the employed journal ranking. These 16 contributions then served as a basis for a forward and backward research according to Webster and Watson (2002), which yielded a further three new contributions.

Table 1 Criteria for the transition into the concept matrix

#	Criterion
1	Reference to virtualization of consulting services
2	Completeness of contents of the method
3	Formal completeness of the method
4	Theoretical foundation of the method
5	Availability of a tool/software
6	Practical relevance of the method
7	Transferability of the method into the context of virtualization in consulting

The 19 contributions found, come from all kinds of research fields. For instance, papers from service management, quality function deployment as well as production planning and investment management, were considered in the analysis. Seventeen of the 19 contributions were in English. Five of 19 contributions come from A and A+ journals, while the remaining contributions come from either B or C journals or were not included in the journal ranking. As a whole, we consider this set of contributions as a reasonably complete basis for our synthesis. However, only papers in German and English of the past 20 years were considered. The criteria (Table 1), which were subsequently used for the evaluation of the methods found, were derived from the requirements discussed in Sect. 2.1.

For each of the 19 contributions it was now checked how well or how poorly the respective criterion was fulfilled. Merely two of the 19 contributions have a direct connection to the virtualization of consulting services. All the other contributions come from application fields, which are somewhat related to the addressed topic. On the basis of the created concept matrix five contributions could be identified, which appeared useful to support the conception of a method for technology selection in the field of consulting virtualization.

In particular, the practical relevance and the transferability of the method into the field of consulting virtualization are of great significance when creating an own method. Each of these five contributions was evaluated as good or very good by these criteria. Thus, they represent a good foundation for the further design steps. It turned out that for the development of our own method the contributions of Kim et al. (2000), Cochran (2009), Starzyńska and Hambrol (2013) are of particular importance. Kim et al. and Starzyńska recommend methods from quality function deployment, and describe an explicit procedure during the conception of their methods. Cochran is a representative of the technology selection model (TSM). This model shall serve as the theoretical basis for the conception of our own method, as it presents crucial elements and frame conditions in the context of technology selection. To ensure the practical significance of the method, the contributions of Najda (2001) and Schuster (2005) also enter the construction of our method. In these contributions, profound recommendations, instead of a complete method, for the selection of appropriate ICT-support are presented and transferred to the classical, and also virtual consulting process.

2.3 Theoretical Concepts and Fundamental Considerations

2.3.1 Input from Quality Function Deployment (QFD)

Quality function deployment (QDF) was developed by Yoji Akao in Japan in 1966. It refers to a compositional method for the systematic and client-oriented development of products. The objective is to compile client's requirements and other influencing variables within the phases of product planning, development and the creation of the final product (Akao 1990). With QFD the extracted client's requirements can be linked to measurable technical features of a product. The basis for the QFD-process is formed by a series of planning matrices, which are put together into the so-called House of Quality (HoQ). Kim et al. (2000) have used this method for the investigation of the optimal path for IT-investments. They also used QFD for business-IT alignment. Thereby the product, to be developed, is an investment decision path, which is formed on the basis of the factors flexibility, efficiency and alignment between business strategy and IT investments. In this process, Kim et al. use only general principles of QFD as an instrument to support the decision-making for an IT investment. For that reason, the relations between the company vision and business strategy, business strategy and critical success factors, as well as critical success factors and flexibility as well as efficiency are established. Subsequently the factors of flexibility and efficiency are confronted with a set of technical requirements. By means of the HoQ-process, a value for the flexibility and efficiency can respectively be determined for an IT-application.

2.3.2 Input from Technology Selection Model (TSM)

The technology selection model deals with the transition of an actual technology to a new technology. Cochran (2009) starts from the observation that organizations will have implemented technology-based applications that direct the business processes. The objective of the TSM is to support the ICT-selection in this context. In previous approaches for supporting the selection decision, not all of the human interaction specifics were addressed. There are additional factors, which were not considered in previous theories such as the *Theories of Reasoned Action* (TRA) (Fishbein and Ajzen 1975) or the *Technology Acceptance Model* (TAM) (Davis 1986). The TSM tries to fill this gap and contains other dimensions, which should be considered during the evaluation of technologies. The model is supported by the purchase pattern theory and was empirically evaluated in a positive way (Cochran 2009). It builds upon the theories of TRA and of TAM, and particularly extends the factors of TRA with additional dimensions.

Conceptionally the TSM contains three groups of influences: TRA-factors (costs, benefits and preconceived notions), external influencing factors (peer/market information or evaluations, effort for vendor-marketing) and internal influencing factors (the fulfilment of requirements (satisficing), technical evaluation, and organizational fit).

The TSM provides domain neutral criteria for the selection of technology, which are an important input for the development of our own more specific method. From previous studies on the virtualization of consulting services, consulting-specific criteria could be determined which can be assigned to the TSM suggested influences. Besides the costs- and benefits aspects, as well as the preconceived notions against virtualized consulting services (TRA factors), chances and risks of virtualization are highlighted in Nissen et al. (2015). These can be assigned to the external factors of influence. They are complemented with the barriers of virtualization (Nissen and Seifert 2016a).

Besides the technical evaluation, the internal influencing factors explicitly address the adequacy for the client as well as for the providers own organization. At this point, the quality criteria related to virtual consulting services, empirically identified in Nissen et al. (2015), have an impact on the selection of the technology. They answer the question how a virtualized consulting service should be designed and presented to the client.

The discussed criteria, integrated into the TSM-model, are a foundation for the selection of a suitable virtualization technology with the help of QFD. What is still lacking at this point of the argumentation is a weighting of the respective criteria in a concrete decision situation. This issue will be solved by applying the Analytical Hierarchy Process, as will be outlined in Sect. 2.4.

2.3.3 Classifying ICT Products in More Abstract Technology Bundles

Even today, there is an ever increasing amount of ICT-products, which are employed by consultants in their daily routine. To reduce complexity, and support consultants in their choice of a suitable ICT-product for virtualization, it is necessary to form ICT-classes. An assignment of the available technology products on the market to individual consulting tasks or consulting process phases could only have an exemplary character, as the products can barely be meaningfully compared with each other because of their divergent range and functions. They are also frequently composed of several smaller technology products. Moreover, technologies change rapidly and continuously due to short technology development cycles, or else they are taken off the market, so that an assignment on the product level would be hardly enduring. Therefore, a suitable classification of concrete ICT-products seems to be inevitable. On the basis of a broad review of available approaches, Najda (2001) suggested a function-oriented classification. According to him, the lowest functional class of ICT are so-called technology bundles. In every technology bundle, various ICT-products with comparable functionalities are subsequently combined. Moreover, every ICT-product presents an application related

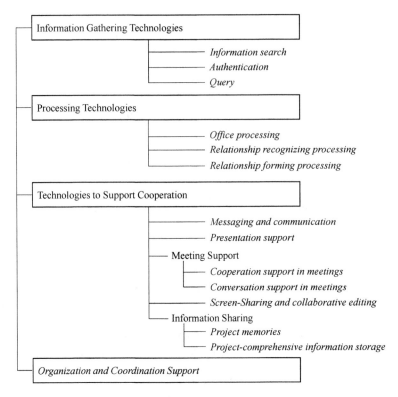

Fig. 3 ICT-classes in consulting as defined by Najda (2001)

combination of basis technologies, which can be assigned to the basic functions *processing*, *communication* and *storage of information* (Krcmar 2015).

With respect to business consulting, Najda (2001) distinguishes 14 function-oriented technology bundles, which are divided into four major classes (text-boxes in Fig. 3) and two connection classes (meeting-support and information sharing). In Fig. 3, the technology bundles are printed in italics.

The overall functions of ICT-classes are not free of overlapping but are partly closely linked. For example, the software from the technology bundle *office processing* can be used by means of application sharing also in various technology bundles concerning the collaboration of people (Najda 2001). An assignment of concrete ICT-products into this classification is therefore not completely unambiguous. Additionally, it is made more difficult as the technology products may fulfil different functions.

Nevertheless, the classification according to Najda presents an important element in the conception of our own method for technology selection. An assignment of particular ICT-products will be done on technology bundle level, by means of a database. An important aspect, which is thereby addressed, is the requirement for updatability and flexibility of the method. The consultant should be allowed to continuously expand his set of ICT-products.

2.4 Conception of the Method for the Selection of Technologies

2.4.1 Overview

With the objective to support the technology selection for virtualized consulting services, the theoretical input in Sect. 2.3 is now used to develop a dedicated selection method. The fundamental procedure of the method broadly follows Kim et al. (2000) and employs basic elements of QFD. The preselection of technologies, which qualify for a closer evaluation, will be done according to Najda's (2001) technology bundles.

The criteria used within QFD to establish the suitability of different technologies in the context of a virtualization project are based on the criteria outlined in Sect. 2.3.2. The resulting method delivers transparency and orientation to the consultants confronted with the necessity to make an informed technology choice in a concrete project situation. It provides a ranking of various potential technologies subject to the consulting virtualization task. Moreover, this ranking provides a specification of the respective technologies as well as key features of the consulting task from an abstract perspective (Fig. 4).

2.4.2 Integration of the Method into the Process Model of Virtual Consulting Services

The method can be assigned to the *rough conception* phase (Fig. 5) of the process model of virtual consulting services (Nissen et al. 2017). The method is a foundation for the detailed modelling and specification of a particular virtual consulting service. At the same time, the method is depending on the preceding analysis phase. In this analysis phase, the virtualization potentials are identified and possible virtualization projects are defined.

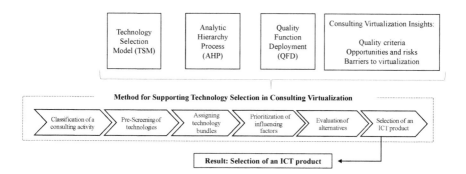

Fig. 4 Basic elements of the proposed method for technology selection

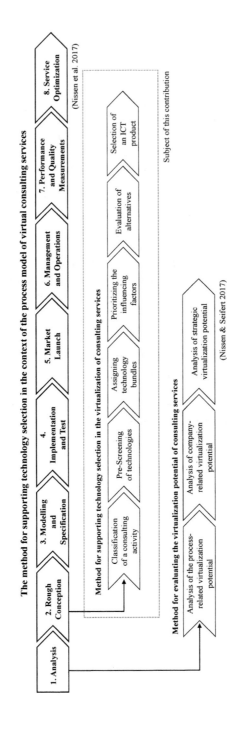

Fig. 5 Process model of virtual consulting services (Nissen et al. 2017). The phase that integrates the proposed technology selection method is the second (rough conception)

If a useful consulting service for virtualization was identified, a first idea and a rough concept should be defined at the beginning of the rough conception phase. Following this activity, the here presented method can be used to determine suitable technologies for this particular virtualization.

The method used to support the technology selection has six phases (Fig. 6). After the selection of a consulting task, a pre-screening on possible technology-alternatives follows. Subsequently an assignment of potentially relevant technologies to defined technology bundles can follow. Eventually a prioritization of influencing factors is conducted, which presents the basis for the actual evaluation. The method ends with the final selection of the technology by the consultant. Up to this step, the development of virtualized consulting products can mostly happen without the client. Nevertheless, it will be necessary to undertake client-related adaptions when the virtualized solution is implemented in the context of a customer project. For this reason, it is recommended to already integrate the client during the development of virtualized consulting services and hence, also during the technology selection. In the following, these phases are described in more detail.

Figure 6 explains the phases of the method and presents the applied methodology, the client's integration and whether the activity is explicitly supported by the method. Depending on the organization of the project, the client's integration may vary. Basically, there are two application cases of our method. In the first case, a new virtualized consulting service is designed and developed. In this process, a pilot client should be integrated at an early stage. The second case covers a virtual consulting product that is basically already available in the consulting firm. When this product is used within a client project, an adaption (also in the field of technology) for this particular client might be necessary.

2.4.3 Classification of the Consulting Activity

The first phase of the method is distinguished by the initial classification of the underlying consulting activity in focus. In the virtualization project, the responsible consultant determines which consulting activity should be executed with technology support. This also means that complex services might be divided into sub-services and smaller service-modules in order to be able to classify them properly. Depending on the selection, available options are limited in the further course of the method. At this point, the consultant needs full information and characteristics on every activity in the course of the consulting service to avoid misunderstandings. The method must provide useful classifications, so that it is clear for the consultant which kind of activity he looks at. We follow the classification of consulting activities suggested by Schuster (2005). Then, the selection of a fitting technology should be possible without great effort. The output of this phase is the selection of a specific consulting activity for further processing. It presents the input for the following process step.

Method to support the selection of a virtualization technology

Phases	Classification of a consulting activity	Pre-Screening of technologies	Assigning technology bundles	Prioritizing the influencing factors	Evaluation of alternatives	Selection of an ICT product
Characteristics	• Information Gathering • Analysis • Creative Activities • Information Presentation • Information Storage • Decision Making • Discussion • Cohesion • Organization • Coordination • Administration	• Existing ICT products • In-house developments	• Information gathering technologies • Processing technologies • Technologies to support cooperation • Technologies to support organization and coordination	• Opportunities • Risks • Costs • Benefits • Assumptions • Quality requirements • Barriers	• Usage of Quality Function Deployment	
Methods	Classification	Workshop	Classification	AHP	QFD	QFD
Customer Integration	not necessary	not necessary	not necessary	suggested	possible	suggested
Supported?	Yes	No	Yes	Yes	Yes	Yes

Fig. 6 Steps of the technology selection method in detail

2.4.4 Pre-screening of Technologies

To limit the selection of available technologies to a realistic and rateable measure, it is recommended to conduct a pre-screening of potentially relevant technologies. In the scope of the pre-screening, tools and technologies, which are available in the respective consulting firm, because they were either developed in earlier projects or were externally purchased, are pre-selected for further examination in the course of virtualization projects. As it is almost impossible to provide a complete selection of technologies (Najda 2001) and to integrate them into the method, it is reasonable to include this step. During pre-screening a concrete selection of technologies for a virtualization project does not take place. Instead, it results in a loose collection of potentially useful technology-alternatives, which have to be evaluated systematically and in detail in the face of a given virtualization initiative. For this reason, pre-screening can be conducted in the form of a workshop, a brainstorming-session or other creative techniques. At this point, earlier experiences in virtualization can already be integrated by the project team. In the same way, appropriate in-house developments can also be considered.

2.4.5 Assigning Technology Bundles

The objective of this phase is to ascertain the assignment of the consulting activities, ICT-classes and ICT-products. In future, this step will be semi-automatically realized by a Web-application with a corresponding database, which is currently under development. It will be further explained in the case study of Sect. 3.

After the consultant has indicated his actual consulting activity, a mapping between the consulting activity and the technology bundles, established in Fig. 3, follows. This step is automatically conducted in the background. In this phase, the database with all technology bundles and a set of associated ICT-products, which were initially added to the technology bundles, makes sure that the consultant gets an overview of available technologies. To conduct this phase, it is important to maintain a consistent and reasonably filled database of relevant technologies. At this point, the consultant will also be able to include his own tools and software that was previously developed in-house, so that it can also be considered during the selection of technologies. The technologies which were determined in a foregone pre-screening can hence directly be included in the database. It should be possible to add extra technologies to the database and to assign these to various technology bundles without great effort. For a first prototype, the objective was to provide respectively three technology alternatives for each of the technology bundles. The technologies included in the database represent master data for the method, which can be used in the following phases.

If a consultant thinks that the database is adequately maintained, a first selection of technologies can be done as part of this phase. The consultant is offered a set of technology bundles according to his initially selected consulting task. At this point, he already has an opportunity to exclude technologies from further evaluation, in order to integrate existing experience or personal preferences, or shorten the upcoming detailed evaluation. The underlying mapping is based on the classification of Najda (2001), and an associated relevance of technology bundles with respect to abstract consulting activities. The result is a list of technologies, selected by the consultant, which enter the upcoming detailed evaluation.

2.4.6 Selection and Prioritization of the Influencing Criteria

The selection of suitable factors for the evaluation of available technologies and tools is based on the discussion in Sect. 2.3.2. Basically, criteria of the Technology Selection Model (Cochran 2009) and insights from current research into the virtualization of consulting services are combined. The consolidation of these various criteria results in an initially unsorted set of 52 criteria. To meet the requirements of efficiency and practicability, these criteria were tested on substantial overlapping and their aptness for the evaluation of technologies. By means of this process, the set could be reduced to five major criteria with a total of 19 sub-criteria, which are illustrated in Fig. 7.

In order to apply the criteria meaningfully in the scope of QFD, a prioritization is undertaken. When the ranking of the criteria is determined, various procedures can be used such as a conjoint analysis (Green and Srinivasan 1990). The creation of stimuli[1] and the following evaluation by means of the conjoint analysis would only be helpful to a limited extent in our application. The number of stimuli is too large for a realization. Furthermore, the inclusion of preference statements such as 'twice as good' or 'barely worse' is theoretically difficult for the model. The simple evaluation by means of a questionnaire is also not recommended, as a scale-evaluation does not allow any preferences and dependencies of the criteria among each other (Döring and Bortz 2015). On the basis of a questionnaire many criteria would be equally weighted, which would lead to inaccuracies in the evaluation phase. For this reason, other procedures were investigated to meet the requirements of this problem. During the literature review of methods supporting technology selection, the Analytical Hierarchy Process (AHP) technique was increasingly suggested (Houseman et al. 2004; Chuang et al. 2009; Frank et al. 2013; Yu and Lee 2013). AHP is a technique used to solve multi-criteria decision problems. It finds numerous applications in research fields with many influencing quantities and requirements (Saaty 2000; Saaty and Vargas 2012).

As AHP has already been used in technology selection, and covers many requirements for a needed prioritization (multi-criteria problem, categorized and comparable requirements), it was used as the methodology for the prioritization of the influencing criteria here. AHP is based on paired comparisons, which are

---

[1]A stimulus describes a certain combination of the individual criteria expressions of a possible technology (Green and Srinivasan 1990).

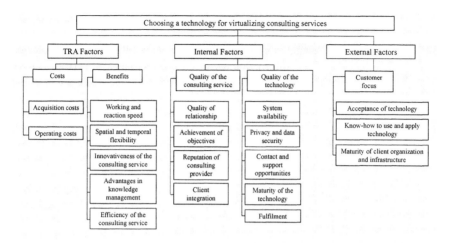

Fig. 7 Structured factors of influence on technology selection during the virtualization of consulting services

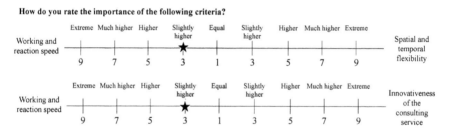

Fig. 8 Examples of the preference determination of the consultant. In both cases, the criterion on the left is weighted slightly higher than the criterion on the right

conducted on various hierarchical levels. The individual paired comparison of two criteria is conducted by the consultant by means of the scale presented in Fig. 8.

The results of the pairwise comparisons of criteria and sub-criteria are subsequently summarized in matrices and are used for the determination of the absolute judgement.

In the end, AHP provides a weighting for every criterion and every sub-criterion, which finds an application in the HoQ of QFD. It means that the consultant decides how important each factor is for the method to determine the fitting virtualization technology. In the case of external client projects, the client should be included during prioritization. QFD would only be partly usable without this initial AHP-generated weighting, as all criteria were then supposed to be of equal weight.

2.4.7 Evaluation of the Technologies

Subsequently the actual evaluation of the technologies can follow. With the selected set of technologies and the prioritization by the questionnaire, the HoQ can be filled. Thereby the methodology of QFD is considered for the calculation of the overall assessment. Within the HoQ, the weighting of individual influencing factors is multiplied with the corresponding evaluation of ICT-products, and then subsequently summarized by forming a column sum, which presents the overall assessment. In this process, QFD is used as a pure evaluation technique and other functionalities of this methodology, for example the determination of competitive comparisons, are dispensed with (similar in spirit to Kim et al. 2000).

The result of this phase presents an evaluated ranking of technologies according to the HoQ. On the basis of this evaluation the actual selection of the technology can subsequently follow.

2.4.8 Selection of the Technology

By means of the technology-ranking, the responsible consultant can finally select a concrete ICT-product for his virtualization task. In addition to the simple description of the respective ICT, it is planned to provide a technical description of the product as well as a description of the characteristic features of the considered consulting activity. This additional information will support the consultant during the following application of the chosen technology.

3 Demonstration

3.1 Description of the Use Case

The case study we use to demonstrate the usability and utility of the proposed technology selection method is related to roughly similar real-world consulting projects. However, as it serves only demonstrative purposes, we use a relatively simple case where a merely supportive use of technology is sought. The client is an international bicycle manufacturer who wants to supply a smartphone-app to his customers to find bicycle repair shops. This development project is conducted with the help of a consulting firm, and in particular the project management is accounted for by the consulting provider. The objective in terms of consulting service virtualization in this case is to identify a supportive tool for the controlling of the rollout project for this bicycle manufacturer.

The key data of the consulting project are summarized in Table 2. After analyzing the virtualization potential, the consulting provider has decided to implement supportive technology for this sub-aspect of the consulting project. Here, in

Table 2 Characteristics of the sample case study

Feature	Virtualization project (simple case of supportive technology)
Size of the consulting firm	500 employees
Consulting field	IT consulting
Objective of the project	An IT-based controlling tool is sought, which will support all phases of the client project
Size of the project team	Five team members
Participation of the clients	Yes
Actual state of the project	Virtualization project has only started

particular, the cost minimizing potential and the opportunity to increase the quality of the consulting service by an approved control of the consulting activities are in the foreground. After the decision was taken, use cases were defined and a rough concept described, where it was specified which requirements the consulting service, and thus a tool, needs to fulfil. For the next step, a suitable technology must then be determined that helps to fulfil the requirements of the rough concept. Following the selection of the technology, a detailed concept of the service will be created.

3.2 Application of the Method

For the execution of the method, the process steps, presented in Sect. 2.4, are carried out. With the aid of initial mock-up examples, it will be explained what a tool supported implementation of the method may look like in practice. Such a tool is currently under development at our chair in the form of a web-based evaluation platform. It can be supposed that in the future consulting providers have their own platforms with re-usable services for the virtualization of their respective portfolios.

A registration at the web-based platform is necessary, before the method can be used (Fig. 9). This step allows the saving of master data into the database.

The client rollout project consists of different phases that reach from the problem analysis to the go live and follow-up tasks. In these phases, various consulting activities are conducted. The project controlling which is the focus here runs parallel to the rollout phases. One can thus describe it as a cross-cutting *organization- and coordination activity*. The consultant should then exactly select this activity in the method.

Figure 10 explains this selection within a tool-supported solution for the technology selection. The division of the various consulting activities goes back to the classification by Schuster (2005). Ten consulting activities were defined, which are

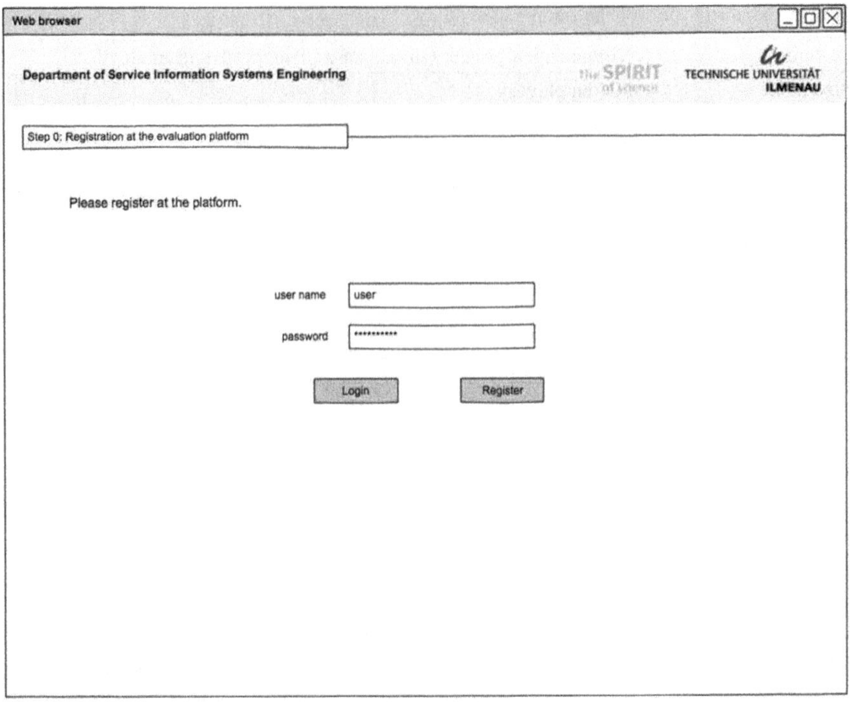

Fig. 9 Registration at the platform

of great practical significance. A detailed description of the different consulting activities and associated ICT classes can be found in Table 6, in the Appendix of this chapter. For a further virtualization of this project, our method could be repeatedly used. One could, for example, test whether the training of client employees as part of the rollout could be virtualized.

Within the pre-screening a first set of available technologies to support the virtualization initiative, can be assembled by means of a workshop with all five project team members. As already recognized by Najda (2001), the market of ICT-products is too dynamic and large to summarize it to an adequate measure in a single method or tool. For this reason, the step of pre-screening is recommended. This additionally ensures that knowledge and experience of the project team are included at an early stage. Table 3 lists some exemplary technologies (software), which were acquired in the scope of the workshop. They can now be entered into the database of the technology selection tool (Fig. 11). It should be noted that the pre-screening step maybe omitted when the database is sufficiently filled and maintained.

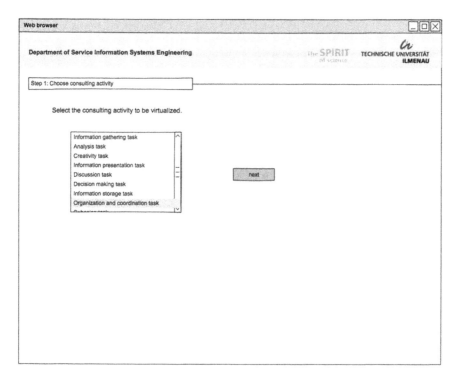

Fig. 10 Selection of the consulting activity

Table 3 Exemplary technologies (ICT products) as a result of the pre-screening workshop

Technology (supplemented by further information/web links)
Microsoft Project 2016
Oracle Primavera P6 Professional Project Management
Asta Powerproject 14
PACS Projectcontrolling-Software
Inloox PM

Subsequently these software solutions are assigned to one or more technology bundles. They are then evaluated and stored in the database. The project controlling can be assigned to the technology bundle *organization- and coordination support*. The objective of this bundle is the organization, planning, steering and control of the administration. Associated technologies can, for example, be project management systems, electronic group appointment calendars or workflow-systems (Vöhringer 2004). Finally, each software solution is rated with respect to the 19 criteria from Sect. 2.4.6, and the results are stored in the database. The criteria are evaluated according to the three possible levels (weak = 1; medium = 3; strong = 9). They represent the influencing criteria on the second sub-criteria level of the AHP-hierarchy.

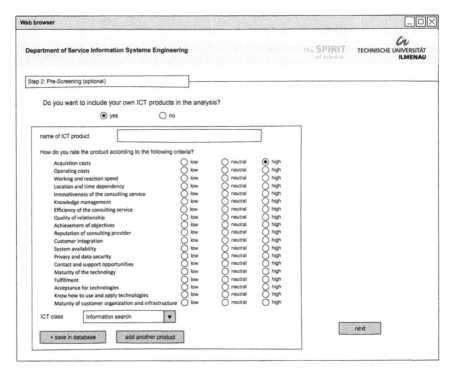

Fig. 11 Pre-screening and the adding of ICT-products (optional) in the database

In the next step of the method (Fig. 12) the consultant is shown those ICT-classes which are associated with the consulting activity (here: *organization and coordination*) in question. In our case, three ICT-classes were automatically identified in the database. The consultant now selects the appropriate class. To avoid any ambiguities referring to the terminology, the system can provide closer elucidations on every identified ICT-class by information fields.

The responsible consultant selects the technology bundle *organization and coordination support* as the relevant one. Thereafter, the actual prioritization and evaluation of the technologies can begin. Initially, the project team, as user of the method, will undertake a prioritization of the criteria for the AHP-technique. With the aid of the presented slide bar (Fig. 8), paired comparison matrices are generated for the calculation of AHP-values at different levels of the criteria hierarchy as visualized in Fig. 13. The values chosen there are only of a demonstrative character.

In order to explain the criteria comparisons in more detail, the paired comparison matrix in our example for the sub-criteria of the group *benefits* from Fig. 7 is illustrated in Table 4.

The value 3 in the 1st column of the fifth line indicates that a slightly higher significance is assigned to the criterion *efficiency of the consulting service*, than to the criterion *working and reaction speed*. The judgements in the matrix are

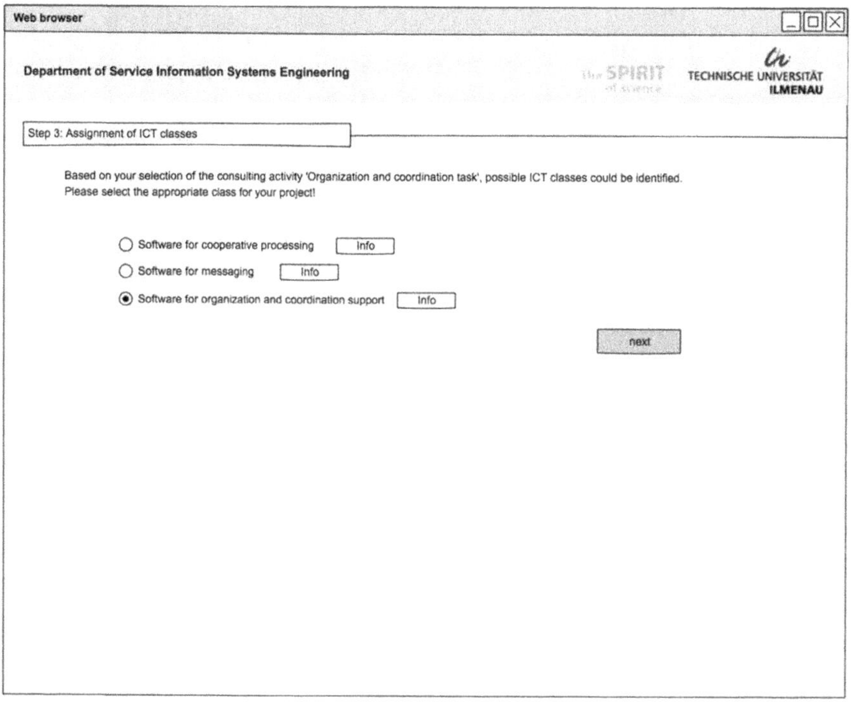

Fig. 12 Selection and classification of the ICT-classes (technology bundles)

subsequently tested on their consistency by means of the AHP-technique, and the matrix is adapted if necessary. The presented matrix in Table 4 has a consistency value equal to zero. This means that the paired comparison judgements in the matrix are consistent, so that the matrix does not need to be revised (Peters and Zelewski 2002). As a further result derived from the matrix, AHP calculates priority values for all criteria as shown in Table 5. Thus, from the point of view of the project team, efficiency of the consulting service is the criterion with highest priority when selecting a fitting technology. As AHP is documented well in the literature, and the calculations can be conducted with the aid of a tool, a detailed description of the calculation will not be given here.

The result from the AHP-algorithm is subsequently transmitted to the HoQ, and is combined with the evaluation of relevant technologies w.r.t. the 19 criteria in the database. The final HoQ for our example is given in Fig. 14. The weightings of the criteria, presented on the left side of the HoQ, were determined by means of the AHP-technique and the processing of input from the project team. The evaluation of the technologies, in the center of the HoQ, stems from master data in the database. If new ICT-products are added to the database within the pre-screening step, their initial evaluation, referring to the 19 influencing criteria, creates this master data. Subsequently weighted average values, respectively overall

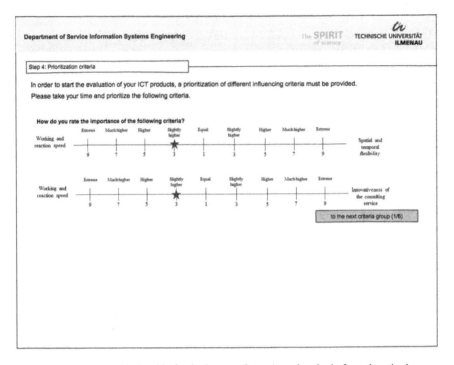

Fig. 13 Prioritization with the aid of paired comparisons (sample criteria from the criteria group *benefits*)

Table 4 Paired comparison matrix for the sub-criteria of group 'benefits' from Fig. 7 (fictitious example)

Sub-criteria within group *benefits*	(A) Working and reaction speed	(B) Spatial and temporal flexibility	(C) Innovative-ness of the consulting service	(D) Advantages in knowledge management	(E) Efficiency of consulting service
(A) Working and reaction speed	1	3	3	9	$\frac{1}{3}$
(B) Spatial and temporal flexibility	$\frac{1}{3}$	1	1	1	$\frac{1}{7}$
(C) Innovativeness of the consulting service	$\frac{1}{3}$	1	1	3	$\frac{1}{3}$
(D) Advantages in knowledge management	$\frac{1}{9}$	1	$\frac{1}{3}$	1	$\frac{1}{9}$
(E) Efficiency of consulting service	3	7	3	9	1

Table 5 Priority values of the 19 criteria in Fig. 7 for the present case (values sorted in ascending order, minor rounding errors may occur)

Criterion	Priority value
Advantages in knowledge management	0.007
Reputation of the consulting provider	0.007
Contact- and support opportunities	0.017
Acceptance of the technology	0.02
Know-how to use and apply technology	0.027
Spatial and temporal flexibility	0.028
Client integration	0.028
Quality of relationship	0.033
Maturity of the technology	0.038
Operating costs	0.037
Achieving objectives	0.047
Maturity of the client organization and infrastructure	0.047
Innovativeness of the consulting service	0.05
Fulfilment	0.083
Working- and reaction speed	0.087
System availability	0.087
Privacy and data security	0.111
Acquisition costs	0.117
Efficiency of the consulting service	0.128

judgements can be formed from the combination of prioritized influencing criteria on the left side and the evaluated technologies in the center.

The result of the method can be selected from the HoQ. On the basis of technology evaluation from the pre-screening workshop and the prioritization of influencing criteria, the consultant is advised to use Microsoft Project 2016 for the support of controlling in the client project.

During the first-time conduction of the technology selection method, some important information, e.g. the priorities of influencing criteria, were filed for future technology decisions. This has the advantage that future decisions can be realized more rapidly, and master data maintenance effort is considerably reduced.

4   Conclusions, Limitations and Outlook

In this contribution, a method for the systematic selection of suitable technologies and tools for the virtualization of consulting services was proposed, following the Design Science process model by Peffers et al. (2007). So far, such a procedure was missing and therewith a decisive component to support virtualization initiatives in the consulting industry. Initially the actual state of research was analyzed and

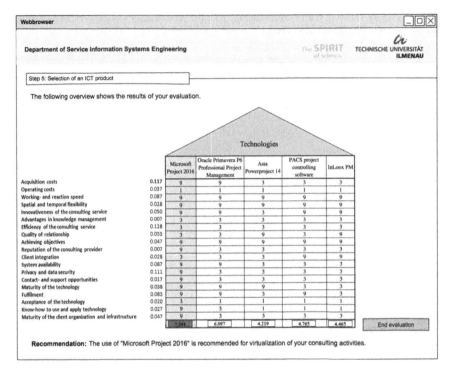

Fig. 14 Evaluation of the technology-alternatives by means of HoQ

literature on software and service engineering was reviewed to lay the foundations for the construction of this method. Two particularly relevant methodical contributions (TSM and QFD) could be identified. They supplement the results of the preceding research on digital transformation and form the foundation of the method. Thereafter, technology bundles and 19 decision criteria for the evaluation of virtualization technologies were defined.

The method was then presented in six steps, and subsequently applied in a demonstrative case study to show its usability and benefits. Even though a relatively simple case was looked at for reasons of clarity, the demonstration nevertheless shows that the method is basically suitable to select a technology from a bundle of possible technologies, using specified weighted evaluation criteria. In the following, the initially determined requirements of a 'good method', i.e. completeness, purpose, and consistency are taken up again and the respective compliance of our method is evaluated.

First, the aspect of *completeness* will be discussed. The method includes all phases of a systematic selection of technologies and integrates the acquisition of entry information (e.g. consulting activity at hand) and the presentation of results (e.g. priorities of evaluation criteria). The method also includes a pre-screening of technologies, which allows additional technologies to enter the evaluation.

The objective of the method was made clear. The relation between the different phases was emphasized and the decision process gradually deduced.

The *purpose* fulfilment of the method appears to be a little restricted, because the ICT-products, which are deposited in the method (or a tool implementing the method) are continuously actualized. Thus, functions and product features, which exist today, may be gone tomorrow or exist in a changed form. If one is working with a concrete ICT-product (and not with a more general ICT-class) a regular update of the master data concerning ICT products/technologies seems required. The proposed procedure was explicitly developed for the selection of technologies in the context of consulting virtualization. It is though conceivable that the method is used in the context of other professional services, such as legal advice or auditing.

The method was constructed in such a way that it can be used by experienced and inexperienced consultants. When looking at the prioritization of the influencing criteria, it is though recommended that the consultant has a direct relation to the client project, respectively that the consultant is experienced. Specific fore-knowledge for the use of the method is not necessary. Therefore, it is not necessary (but certainly helpful) to become acquainted with the AHP-technique and to understand it. In this contribution, an example shows how the technology selection method should be applied, which will help to implement the method correctly in consulting.

The third key aspect of a 'good method' is *consistency*. The defined process step for the selection of the technology and the rules for a prioritization and evaluation by means of the AHP-technique were clearly defined. An embedding in the entire virtualization project was indicated, but not detailed. For instance, currently a definition of the roles and responsibilities concerning the evaluation and selection process are still missing. Together with consulting practice, it should be evaluated which roles, within the consulting firm or client project, will ideally be responsible for the prioritization of evaluation criteria and selection of technologies.

A tool support is only available as a first prototype today. The method should be available in the future as part of an IT-platform solution that supports virtualization projects in consulting. Smaller consulting firms can thus access a web-based on-demand solution. This would be cost-saving for them, and still allow to professionally expand and complement their product portfolio with digital offerings.

Only the complete transfer into a tool-based solution will illustrate the full potential of the technology selection method proposed in this chapter. In particular, the benefits, acceptance and usability of the method can only rightfully be assessed w.r.t an IT-implementation of the method. To date, the method has been implemented in a first MS Excel prototype and can be carried out with the help of this.

The generalization demand of the method is basically fulfilled, because activities of various consulting fields can be object of the technology selection. The method is theoretically profound and is based on already tested approaches for the selection of technologies. The reliability of the method can currently only be assessed to a limited extent and needs more testing in practice. Referring to the used methodology in the scope of the Design Science procedure according to Peffers et al. (2007), a broad evaluation of the method should subsequently follow. This can be done in the form of case studies, expert interviews or other empirical research approaches. For this purpose, it appears useful to evaluate the method, but also its implementation in one step.

The actual state of development of the method is an important starting point for the use in consulting practice, even though it is not the final state. It is important to continuously optimize the selection process and evaluation criteria by the repeated usage in practice, and to possibly adapt practice-related features. We encourage researchers and consultants to use and possibly extend the here proposed method in the course of virtualization projects. In this way, simultaneously with improving the existing artefact, know-how on its application would be generated while virtualization projects in the consulting industry are effectively supported. By means of additional research projects, our own goal in the long run is to establish a digital platform-consulting solution to support virtualization initiatives in consulting practice.

Appendix

See Table 6

Table 6 Characteristics of categorized consulting activities and support by ICT-classes

Activity category	Characteristic of the activity	
	Activity content	Support by ICT-class
Information procurement activity	• Search in a narrower sense • Agreements on the access to information • Information access	• Information search • Authentication • Query • Communication • Meeting-support • Ancillary: project memory, project overlapping information storage
Analysis activity	• Derivation of structures and coherences • Information transformation/translation	• Relation recognizing processing • Ancillary: communication, presentation support, meeting support • Screen-sharing and mutual editing, project memory
Creativity activity	• To reinterpret coherences and develop new purpose-means-links • To abstract from interpretation- and solution patterns • Use of creativity techniques	• Relation creating processing • Collaboration support in sessions • Ancillary: communication, presentation support • Meeting-support, screen-sharing and mutual editing, project memory

(continued)

Table 6 (continued)

Activity category	Characteristic of the activity	
	Activity content	Support by ICT-class
Information presentation activity	• Information preparation • Active or passive one-sided information mediation	• Office processing • Relation recognizing processing • Relation creating processing • Communication • Presentation support • Collaboration support in sessions • Screen-sharing and mutual support
Discussion activity	• Reciprocal clarification of issues • Exchange of opinions for the purpose of evaluation and approach of conclusions • Mutual collection of ideas	• Communication • Meeting-support • Screen-sharing and mutual editing
Decision activity	• Explicit or implicit selection of one or more alternatives • Various forms of agreement/voting	• Relation recognizing processing • Communication • Meeting-support
Information deposition activity	• Project related information storage • Project overlapping information storage (knowledge management)	• Project memory • Project overlapping information storage
Organization- and coordination activity	• Creation of a project environment • Alignment of activities on the project objective by the use of coordination instruments	• Organization- and coordination activity • Communication • Presentation support • Conversation support in sessions • Project memory
Supportive and administrative activity	• Activities as services for the participating persons of a project (without any content work)	• Information procurement technologies • Processing technologies • Technologies to support the collaboration • Organization- and coordination support
Cohesion activity	• Creation and looking after of social relationships • Definition of personal objectives attitudes, skills and influencing potentials of the participants • Agreement on the social roles • Living of the social roles in the communication	• Communication • Conversation support in sessions

References

Akao Y (1990) Quality function deployment: integrating customer requirements into product design. Productivity Press, New York

Chuang M, Yang YS, Lin CT (2009) Production technology selection: deploying market requirements, competitive and operational strategies, and manufacturing attributes. Int J Comput Integr Manuf 22(4):345–355

Cochran M (2009) Introduction of a technology selection model. In: HICCS 2009—42nd Hawaii international conference on system sciences. Waikoloa, pp 1–10

Corsten H, Gössinger R, Müller-Seitz G, Schneider G (eds) (2016) Grundlagen des technologie- und innovations managements, 2nd edn. Vahlen, Munich

Davis FD (1986) A technology acceptance model for empirically testing new end-user information systems: theory and results. Dissertation, Massachusetts Institute of Technology

Döring N, Bortz J (2015) Forschungsmethoden und Evaluation für Human- und Sozialwissenschaftler, 5th edn. Springer, Berlin

Fishbein M, Ajzen I (1975) Belief, attitude, intention, and behavior: an introduction to theory and research. J Bus Ventur 5:177–189

Frank AG, Souza DVSd, Ribeiro JLD, Echeveste ME (2013) A framework for decision-making in investment alternatives selection. Int J Prod Res 51(19):5866–5883

Green PE, Srinivasan V (1990) Conjoint analysis in marketing. New developments with implications for research and practice. J Mark 54(4):3

Greiffenberg S (2004) Methodenentwicklung in Wirtschaft und Verwaltung. Kovač, Hamburg

Hess T, Brecht L (1996) State of the art des business process redesign: Darstellung und Vergleich bestehender Methoden, 2nd edn. Gabler, Wiesbaden

Houseman O, Tiwari A, Roy R (2004) A methodology for the selection of new technologies in the aviation industry. Cranfield University, Bedfordshire

Kim SH, Jang DH, Lee DH, Cho SH (2000) A methodology of constructing a decision path for IT investment. J Strateg Inf Syst 9(1):17–38

Krcmar H (2015) Informationsmanagement. Springer, Berlin

Najda L (2001) Informations- und Kommunikationstechnologie in der Unternehmensberatung: Möglichkeiten, Wirkungen und Gestaltung des Einsatzes. Dissertation, University of Hohenheim

Nissen V, Seifert H (2016a) Digitale Transformation in der Unternehmensberatung: Status Quo in Deutschland. In: Deelmann T, Ockel DM (eds) Handbuch der Unternehmensberatung. Erich Schmidt Verlag, Berlin, pp 7312–7319

Nissen V, Seifert H (2016b) Virtualisierung in der Unternehmensberatung. Eine Studie im deutschen Beratungsmarkt, BDU, Bonn

Nissen V, Seifert H (2017) Ermittlung des Virtualisierungspotenzials von Beratungsleistungen im Consulting. In: Leimeister JM, Brenner W (eds) Proceedings of the 13th International Conference on Wirtschaftsinformatik, WI2017, St. Gallen, pp 1348–1362

Nissen V, Seifert H, Ackert MN (2017) A process model for the virtualization of consulting services. In this volume

Nissen V, Seifert H, Blumenstein M (2015) Virtualisierung von Beratungsleistungen: Qualitätsanforderungen, Chancen und Risiken der digitalen Transformation in der Unternehmensberatung aus der Klientenperspektive. In: Deelmann T, Ockel DM (eds) Handbuch der Unternehmensberatung, 25th edn. Erich Schmidt Verlag, Berlin

Offermann P, Blom S, Levina O, Bub U (2010) Proposal for components of method design theories. Bus Inf Syst Eng 2(5):295–304

Overby E (2008) Process virtualization theory and the impact of information technology. Organ Sci 19(2):277–291

Peffers K, Tuunanen T, Rothenberger MA, Chatterjee S (2007) A design science research methodology for information systems research. J Manage Inf Syst 24(3):45–77

Peters ML, Zelewski S (2002) Analytical hierarchy process (AHP): Dargestellt am Beispiel der Auswahl von Projektmanagement-Software zum Multiprojektmanagement. Technical Report 2002–14, Universität Essen

Saaty TL (2000) Fundamentals of decision making and priority theory with the analytic hierarchy process. Technical Report 2000–6, University of Pittsburgh

Saaty TL, Vargas LG (2012) Models, methods, concepts & applications of the analytic hierarchy process. Springer, Boston

Schuster K (2005) E-Consulting; Chancen und Risiken. Dissertation, University of Mannheim

Seifert H, Nissen V (2016) Virtualisierung von Beratungsleistungen: Stand der Forschung zur digitalen Transformation in der Unternehmensberatung und weiterer Forschungsbedarf. In: Nissen V, Stelzer D, Straßburger S, Fischer D (eds) Proceedings of MKWI2016. Ilmedia, Ilmenau, pp 1031–1040

Sonnenberg C, vom Brocke J (2012) Evaluation patterns for design science research artefacts. In: Helfert M, Donnellan B (eds) Practical aspects of design science. Springer, Berlin, pp 71–83

Starzyńska B, Hamrol A (2013) Excellence toolbox: decision support system for quality tools and techniques selection and application. Total Qual Manage Bus Excellence 24(5–6):577–595

van Hillegersberg J, Kumar K (1999) Using metamodeling to integrate object-oriented analysis, design and programming concepts. Inf Syst 24(2):113–129

Vöhringer B (2004) Computerunterstützte Führung in Kommunalverwaltung und -politik: Steuerung mit New Public Management und Informationstechnologie. DUV, Wiesbaden

vom Brocke J, Simons A, Niehaves B, Riemer K, Plattfaut R, Cleven A (2009) Reconstructing the giant: on the importance of rigour in documenting the literature search process. In: ECIS 2009 proceedings of European conference on information systems, Verona, pp 2206–2217

Webster J, Watson R (2002) Analyzing the past to prepare for the future: writing a literature review. MIS Q 26(2):13–23

Werth D, Greff T (2017) Scalability in consulting: insights into the scaling capabilities of business models by digital technologies in consulting industry. In this volume

Werth D, Greff T, Scheer AW (2016) Consulting 4.0—Die Digitalisierung der Unternehmensberatung. HMD Praxis der Wirtschaftsinformatik 53(1):55–70

Yu P, Lee HJ (2013) Optimal technology selection considering input levels of resource. Ind Manage Data Syst 113(1):57–76

Author Biographies

Volker Nissen holds the Chair of Information Systems Engineering in Services at Technische Universität Ilmenau, Germany, since 2005. Prior to this, he pursued a consulting career, including positions as manager at IDS Scheer AG, director at DHC GmbH, and CEO of NISSCON Ltd., Germany. In 1994 he received a Ph.D. degree in Economic Sciences with distinction from the University of Goettingen, Germany. His current research interests include the digital transformation of the consulting industry, the management of IT-agility, metaheuristic optimization, and process acceptance research. He is author and editor of 19 books and some 200 other publications, including papers in Business & Information Systems Engineering, Information Systems Frontiers, IEEE Transactions on EC, IEEE Transactions on NN, and Annals of OR.

Henry Seifert is a graduate engineer for media technology and since 2011 working as a management consultant. His main focus is on the automotive industry and artificial intelligence, analytics, process optimization and requirements management. He works in projects in the area of sales and after sales processes as well as professional learning. As doctoral candidate at the Group for Information Systems Engineering in Services at Technische Universität Ilmenau, he examines the digital transformation in the consulting industry. The goal of his dissertation is to demonstrate the opportunities and limitations of virtualization, as well as the design of artifacts that enable the realization of virtual consulting services.

Marco Blumenstein has studied Business Information Systems Engineering at Technische Universität Ilmenau, Germany. There he was also involved in a research project on the virtualization of consulting services and specifically examined the expectations of consulting clients and developed a method to support the selection of a particular virtualization technology. He graduated as a Master of Science in 2017. Since 2013, he has been working as a working student at X-CASE GmbH, in the area of SAP ERP consulting. Since 2017, he is a SAP Consultant focused on logistics and e-commerce processes within the SAP ERP.

Part II
Applied Digitalization in the Consulting Industry

Improving Business Development Through Crowdsourcing Supported Consulting—A Methodical Approach

Oliver Christ, Michael Czarniecki and Lukas Andreas Scherer

Abstract This paper deals with the issue on how organizations can use crowd-sourcing effectively for business development. The result is that crowdsourcing needs to be designed in an iterative fashion in order to have organizational impact. Organizations resist change and an iterative approach is necessary in order to enhance the maturity of the crowdsourced solution. We call this type of crowd-sourcing K-crowdsourcing, based on an analogy from parental biology, which distinguishes between r- and K-strategists. Using this analogy, today's understanding of crowdsourcing is mostly r-crowdsourcing: resulting in a large amount of solutions. On the contrary, using K-crowdsourcing you will have fewer solutions, but they are more easily implemented in the organization. The role of the consulting firm changes in a K-crowdsourcing setting. The traditional stakeholder of the consultant is the client. In a K-crowdsourcing setting, the client as well as the crowd are equally important. By using the crowd, the consultant is able to deliver better quality. In some strategic settings, choosing the right strategy is vital for the long-term survival of the client.

1 Introduction

Crowdsourcing offers companies effective and efficient options for harnessing the collective intelligence of internal or external groups to support innovation management. By using digital crowdsourcing platforms, open calls can be made scalable and organized globally, and integrated into organizations' innovation processes. Conventional crowdsourcing usually involves sending a structured

O. Christ (✉) · M. Czarniecki · L. A. Scherer
FHS University of Applied Sciences, St. Gallen, Switzerland
e-mail: oliver.christ@fhsg.ch

M. Czarniecki
e-mail: michael.czarniecki@fhsg.ch

L. A. Scherer
e-mail: lukas.scherer@fhsg.ch

© Springer International Publishing AG 2018
V. Nissen (ed.), *Digital Transformation of the Consulting Industry*,
Progress in IS, https://doi.org/10.1007/978-3-319-70491-3_11

request to a selected or unknown group of potential providers of ideas, consciously results in a large number of ideas being generated outside the organization, and a decision on whether to use ideas is taken once the submission period has expired (Gassmann 2012). This conventional process is very well suited to developing ideas for new products and services, but is limited if the aim relates to transforming the core of a company's business and its business model, strategy or organizational structure. Externally generated ideas for such aspects are usually not mature enough to change a company's complex structures. Organizations are unwilling to provide an anonymous crowd with all of the information required for the solution, while objectively successful solutions are blocked by the organizational immune system, without being systematically assessed or fine-tuned. In order to capitalise on the potential of crowdsourcing for such activities, the authors have developed a methodical approach that systematically overcomes these weaknesses. External development of solutions is supported for a longer period and by means of iteration between the crowd, the consultant applying the method and the company looking to implement innovation, until the solution gradually moves closer to the core of the company. In this way, solutions reach a higher degree of maturity and are able to hold their own against the organizational immune system.

This article investigates the potential and limitations of crowdsourcing in relation to supporting business development and business model innovation, and demonstrates how a considered combination of consulting and crowdsourcing could be used to support the transformation of companies or organizations. To this end, Sect. 2 describes the potential and limitations that become apparent when systems theory models are applied to the transformation of organizations and business model innovation, how effective development of companies should be designed, and the challenges specifically related to innovation management of entire companies or individual lines of business. Section 3 examines the potential and challenges of crowdsourcing with respect to business development. Following a clarification of the concept of crowdsourcing, the weaknesses of conventional crowdsourcing methods in the context of organizational transformation are investigated. Based on these insights, Sect. 4 then presents a methodical approach to minimising the present weaknesses and limitations of crowdsourcing with a view to exploiting it for business development and business model innovation. Finally, the potential ways of combining crowdsourcing and consulting in the context of business development are analysed and the altered role of management consultancy is explored. Methodically, this article applies theoretical models of systems management and systems organizational theory, linking them with hands-on experience and findings of the authors' own applied research.

2 Sustainable Transformation of Complex Systems

In recent years, in addition to product and service innovation, business model innovation has come into sharper focus. Companies were no longer satisfied simply with launching new products on the market, but began trying to renew the way they run their businesses—their whole business model. A business model describes the essential functions of a company and the means by which it generates profit and value (Osterwalder and Pigneur 2011). Business model innovation has impacts on the entire company or individual lines of business and it must take account of the company's specific situation, as well as current environmental factors and trends (Osterwalder and Pigneur 2011, 2015; Rüegg-Stürm and Grand 2015; Rüegg-Stürm 1989; Blohm et al. 2013; Bleicher 1980). There is a strong dependency between business model innovation and effective business development, as sound innovation of a company's business model only creates value if the organization has been transformed into a sustainable, appropriate form. Bleicher defines business development as "the evolution of an economically-orientated social system in the conflict between the demands and possibilities of the internal and external environments" (Bleicher 1980). The factors that have a decisive influence on the development of a business are its specific situation, its environment and the dynamics of its development. The dimension of time is also taken into account: the current and future situations of the organization and the environment must be adequately reflected (Bleicher 1980). Sound business development identifies and analyses a business's reality and current areas of conflict and potential, as part of the continuous analysis of the business's specific situation and the environmental situation. It systematically develops a new, evidence-based form by which opportunities can be acted on and areas of conflict removed (Bleicher 1980; Rüegg-Stürm 1989; Rüegg-Stürm and Grand 2015). This situation, which is complex in comparison with that of purely generating ideas for new products and services, gives rise to particular challenges for the design of effective methodologies for business model innovation aimed at promoting business development. It raises the question of whether new instruments and techniques are necessary for this area of application and how they should be organized.

In this study, organizations are understood from a systems theory perspective; companies and organizations are viewed as complex social systems that are self-regulating and cannot be directly influenced by external factors. In order to determine the specific challenges relating to the transformation of organizations, the next section describes some of the relevant models of the new systems theory and their implications for the transformation of complex systems.

2.1 Organizations as Social Systems

For a long time, many organizational and management models have been based on a systemic understanding of companies and organizations. These models have increasingly incorporated models and theories from the new systems theory, adapting them for application in these areas. Examples of widely used systems organizational models are the St. Gallen Management Model (Rüegg-Stürm and Grand 2015) or Stafford Beer's Viable Systems Model (Beer 1995). Systems were classically understood as a collection of interrelated elements, i.e. as stable entities, and their actual or possible connection in terms of an ontological paradigm, which, as a rule, views change as an exception (Simon 2007). New systems theory, which was comprehensively formulated by Niklas Luhmann, methodically shifted systems thinking and the concept of a system to an operational paradigm, which is permeated by the idea of differentiation as the central logical distinction. For Luhmann the idea of differentiation is the defining characteristic of a system (Simon 2007). A system does not come into existence until a difference is defined, namely the difference between the system and the environment, which creates a boundary between the system itself and everything else that does not belong to the system—the environment (Luhmann and Baecker 2009). Therefore, for a system, other systems are equivalent to the environment. For a long time, systems were understood ontologically, but the new systems theory views them as radical operational. Systems set the boundaries to their environments by means of their operations (Luhmann and Baecker 2009). Luhmann argued that systems conform to the concept of autopoiesis (Luhmann 1996), borrowing that term for his systems theory from neurobiologists Humberto Maturana and Francisco Varela. The concept refers to the process by which biological systems maintain and reproduce themselves. Autopoietic systems are operationally closed units that reproduce themselves by building their components with the aid of their existing components (Maturana et al. 1980). Luhmann adapted the biological concept of autopoiesis to apply it to psychological and social systems (society, interactions and organizations). Social systems are exclusively made up of their basic operation, which is communication (or decisions as a specific form of communication in the case of organizations) and operate autopoietically as communication always connects to new communication and decisions always connect to new decisions. A crucial aspect here is that on the level of its own operations, there is no direct contact with the environment or with other systems within the environment, as according to the system/environment difference, a system is always closed off from its environment (Luhmann and Baecker 2009). This also determines the scope of influence: the system cannot influence the operations of other systems, and cannot be directly influenced by other systems in terms of a causal effect. The system therefore relies on self-organization, as its own structures can only be created by means of its own operations (Luhmann 1996). Using their system-intrinsic operations, social systems such as organizations develop a kind of immune system and a highly selective susceptibility to failure, making them extremely stable and robust, particularly in the case of organizations (Luhmann and Baecker 2009).

This poses a relevant question for this analysis: the question of how systems can influence each other without abandoning the concept of autopoiesis and operational closure. According to Luhmann this occurs via structural coupling (Luhmann and Baecker 2009). Structural coupling means that events in a system's environment and therefore events from other systems are observed by the system and processed via its own operations. In this way, two systems can interact with each other, without having to abandon the principles of autopoiesis and operational closure. Through the coupling of different systems, for example in the context of organizations, the sensitivity for dedicated irritations in the sense of stimulating (not causal) challenges rises. This impetus will increase the probability for system reaction according to these irritations (Simon 2014). In the context of business development and business model innovation the crucial area of activity is the compatible coupling of different systems to achieve co-evolution of the external influencing system and the target system.

2.2 Challenges for Business Development

As described, in many social systems—including companies—perception of the environment is often highly selective. In combination with highly closed operations and a selective supply of information to reduce complexity, companies form a kind of organizational immune system, which translates only small amounts of stimuli from the environment into effective knowledge that leads to changes within the organization (Blohm et al. 2013; Luhmann 1996; Simon 2014). This is true of individual companies, and their customers and suppliers. Selective perception and the organizational immune system help to ensure stability, continuity and cohesion, thereby contributing to the business's success. However, in the context of innovation management, an organization that is too closed runs a high risk of failing to identify opportunities or identifying them too late, and of delayed reactions to changes in the environment—risks that can lead to critical situations for the business in a competitive environment that is increasingly globalised and strongly defined by differentiation through product and service innovations.

For business development activities, this results in a contradiction: An organization creates order within itself, thereby reducing the complexity of its environment (Simon 2014; Luhmann 1996). In contrast, an organization that makes use of business development approaches increases its variety and, especially when the core of the organization is affected, blocks new ideas as unsuitable due to the closed operation of the system. It is difficult to change protected and highly closed areas such as strategy, organizational structure and culture using conventional forms of open innovation.

So how does effective business development needs to be designed and embedded in an organization, so that external perspectives and disruptions from the organization's environment can influence its core, without coming up against resistance?

In order to effectively bring about a lasting change to an organization by means of its environment (e.g. through external or internal consultants), the following challenges in particular must be taken into account and systematically overcome.

(a) *Time for co-evolution*: Effective development of an appropriate new business model that is accepted and sustainably embedded in the organization takes time, and necessitates significantly closer collaboration than, for example the development of product or service ideas. In contrast to the improvement of innovation in isolated areas of the organization (e.g. processes, tasks, specific ICT systems) or the development of product ideas, the complex and sensitive topic of business development requires structural coupling between the company and its transforming environment, in order to stimulate their co-evolution and transformation. The co-evolution of structurally coupled systems takes time, increased willingness to accept irritations (or disruptions) and iterative development cycles, which must be taken into account in the organization of business development.

(b) *Conflict between confidentiality and necessary knowledge of company-specific details*: Sound analysis and development of a company's business model requires knowledge of the internal starting position in relation to the demands and opportunities in the company's environment. Most businesses do not want to publish these details nor make their change plans transparent. Companies will either refrain completely from releasing such information and not make use of the potential of collective intelligence for development of their business model, or only supply insufficient information. Thereby they are running the risk that only useless ideas with no potential for implementation will be generated. Furthermore, and related to the critical aspect of confidentiality, development of a new business model requires knowledge of the company's specific situation, which cannot be simply established or simulated in an isolated problem-solving or creativity process that is completely detached from the company itself. Fundamental and effective business development requires that the people analysing the business are able to acquire sufficient knowledge about the current situation and company-specific environmental factors, which cannot be simply acquired without the support of experts—normally experienced employees of the company. There is a danger that many useless and unrealistic ideas are generated, which just absorb time and money.

(c) *Overcoming the organizational immune system*: As discussed above, companies as socioeconomic systems generally take a highly selective view of their environments, and process information according to their own rules and criteria (Simon 2007). The possibilities for change, especially in their fundamental organizational approach, are therefore very limited, performing an important protective function which results in stability and cohesion. Business development focuses on precisely this point—it attempts to identify potential in existing situations, and to understand, strengthen or attenuate tendencies in the company's development. As a result it is probable that ideas which apply to the foundations of the business and its evolution do not penetrate the organizational immune system and are discarded without being examined or after only superficial consideration, because they fail to see the reality of the business from the perspective of its internal representatives, and develop (apparent) potential without regard to fundamental aspects of the business. There is also a risk for the company that due to its selective perception, i.e. its operational blindness, it will overlook crucial opportunities and risks. This set of problems can be overcome by means of a systematically controlled interface between external idea generation and the internal organization. The next section outlines the relevance of the innovator's dilemma. Especially potentials and limitations of existing crowdsourcing methods in the context of business development are discussed.

3 Crowdsourcing for Improved Innovation Management and Business Development

3.1 Concept, Methods and Applications of Crowdsourcing

The term crowdsourcing, a neologism that combines the words crowd and outsourcing, became established at a relatively late stage, originating in an article by Jeff Howe in Wired magazine in 2006. Howe describes the concept of crowdsourcing as "the act of a company or an institution taking a function once performed by employees and outsourcing it to an undefined (and generally large) network of people in the form of an open call" (Howe 2006). The outsourcing of tasks by an organization to an internal group, or an external group of potentially interested people by way of an open call, forms the decisive feature of crowdsourcing (Durward et al. 2016). There is a long history of attempts to exploit the potential intelligence, creativity and problem-solving skills of a large, anonymous group of people to develop new solutions efficiently and effectively, and such approaches were used before the invention and spread of modern information and communications technology (Gassmann 2012).

The development of more powerful information systems, and especially the worldwide connection of these systems using standardised internet-based protocols, have opened up new possibilities for using the potential collective intelligence of anonymous groups globally and integrating the results of online calls for contributions directly into organizational and innovation processes. Thanks to digitalisation and automation, individual assignments and calls can be launched and implemented efficiently, scalably and very flexibly, in principle reaching all internet users regardless of location, via web-based platforms. The open call is normally made via internet-based platforms that are provided and administrated by crowd-sourcing intermediaries or by the organization itself. Crowdsourcing platforms allow organizations to assign tasks that have previously been taken care of internally—or in extreme cases have not been tackled at all. Such tasks may vary greatly in terms of their complexity and area of application. The spectrum ranges from simple, routine tasks (e.g. use of Captcha validation, which was originally developed to identify human users on websites for the systematic, incremental improvement of semi-automated digitisation of books and newspapers), to complex, open-ended projects (such as the development of new product ideas or service improvements using platforms like Innocentive or Atizo), to outsourcing creative assignments to anonymous groups (e.g. organising design competitions via platforms including Wilogo/Fotolia and Crowdspring) (Simula and Ahola 2014; Gassmann 2012).

A large number of crowdsourcing platforms are now established on the market, using a variety of methods to pursue a range of different goals, and addressing the needs of diverse organizations and users in a highly targeted way. Over time, an increasingly differentiated market has developed, as has more and more sophisticated conceptualisation and categorisation of crowdsourcing services, applications and methods. Durward et al. (2016) and Gassmann (2012) provide a detailed overview of the available crowdsourcing services, application scenarios, platforms and methods. Many companies use crowdsourcing to supplement internal innovation management or as an alternative to it. Crowdsourcing in particular exalts the chance to overcome organizational blindness and perceptions of its environment that are usually highly selective, expanding them with an intentionally broader external perspective. In the context of innovation development, crowdsourcing can be viewed as part of an open innovation approach (Gassmann 2012). This concept involves integrating external partners to an organization, such as academic institutions, customers or suppliers, into the company's innovation process so that products, services or processes can be improved collaboratively (Sloane 2011; Gassmann 2012). Integration of key customers and suppliers into the innovation process has been established in many companies for a long time. Crowdsourcing platforms designed specifically for innovation development now offer companies efficient and effective opportunities to expand the circle of innovation partners to people outside the sector, going beyond the limited perspective of the company and its established partners.

3.2 Limitations of Crowdsourcing for Business Development—Overcoming the "Innovator's Dilemma"

As presented, among others, by Clayton Christensen in his book 'The Innovator's Dilemma' (Christensen 2003), established organizations face the problem that they do not take new and potentially "disruptive" market participants seriously or recognise them as potential competitors, because at first glance a company with an innovative but immature product is not a realistic competitor for an organization focused on excellence. As Christensen has repeatedly emphasised in various publications (Christensen 2003; Christensen et al. 2008; Christensen and Raynor 2017), the problem of disruptive innovation is not that a technology emerges out of the blue and disrupts entire industries, but that internal innovators frequently do not manage to integrate an immature solution into organizations that are already focused on excellence and operate on the basis of highly selective and standardised operations. Because potentially disruptive companies initially perform very poorly by industry standards and therefore only occupy niche markets in which quality plays a less important role, the established business retreats from these niches— which are in any case unprofitable in its view—opening a bridgehead for the disruptor. And when the disruptor has developed further, it is too late for the established business to come up with a response that is suitable strategically and structurally, not to mention culturally.

A similar problem arises when crowdsourcing is used for innovation at the nucleus of the organization. Ideas generated by crowdsourcing are not mature, and are frequently not sufficiently thought through, which is not a problem in many areas of application. This is why crowdsourcing works well when applied to product innovation, technical scouting or design questions. In such cases, the external ideas can be built into the organization's innovation processes, refined by these processes and developed to maturity. However, up to now, the mechanism through which crowdsourcing has an effect has not managed to breach the core of organizations. One solution is analogous to the process of "disruptive innovation" as originally understood by Christensen: provide a "bridgehead" for the ideas aimed at the core of the organization that are generated by crowdsourcing to ensure that they can be integrated. The solutions can be developed to maturity on this bridgehead using an iterative approach, and infiltrate the core of the organization later on.

The following section sets out the theoretical foundation of a methodical approach to overcoming the challenges mentioned above in the context of business development, which is presented together with an already implemented and validated innovative method of crowdsourcing.

4 A Crowdsourcing Approach Exploiting Collective Intelligence for Business Development

4.1 r and K-Crowdsourcing: An Analogy from Reproduction and Raising Offspring

As discussed in the previous section, a crowdsourcing approach that advances external perspectives to the core of organization development must overcome several barriers. This section presents an analogy between crowdsourcing and parenting as a way of overcoming the following obstacles to applying crowdsourcing in the context of business development:

- The barrier of **time for co-evolution**: Human children are not left to fend for themselves in the environment immediately after birth. They are prepared for the environment through a nurturing process that lasts many years. When viewed objectively this is alarming; a baby is unable to survive alone and has very poor mechanical and cognitive skills. However, a non-pathological family sees this as an opportunity to bring up a child its own way, and not as a reason to abandon it. This is how biological systems solve the innovator's dilemma, namely not taking new-borns seriously because of their low maturity.
- The barrier of **confidentiality**: Parents form a "parenting organization" which views their children as a part of "their system" (the family). The organization wishes to support and challenge its children and has an intrinsic need to guarantee them the foundations for their future survival in the environment. To this end, family secrets are selectively shared with the children at appropriate stages of maturity.
- The barrier of **overcoming the immune system**: The parents get to know their children by nourishing them. They are able to pass on their values and their cultural heritage. This makes the children a part of the system, because barriers to the outside world are now defined by the communities.

An analogy with generational change will help to better illustrate these three barriers.

Drawing analogies between business development and reproductive biology is not new. For instance in Ahlstrom and Bruton (2010) an analogy with marriage was made in the context of joint venture. Literature, which subscribes to the evolutionary view increasingly refers to spin-offs as children of existing organizations (Agarwal et al. 2004). The child is in a position to adapt to changing environmental conditions and opportunities which the parent organization is not in a position to exploit because it was created for a world "of the past".

We want to continue this tradition of drawing such analogies and apply it to crowdsourcing. In crowdsourcing, foreign "DNA" penetrates the existing organization, similar to the way it does in a joint venture (the "child" resulting from a "marriage"). In this context, a joint venture is a separate business entity, which is created by its parent companies. In the case of joint ventures, several stages are usually described: from "strategic fit", "partner selection" and "negotiations" to "management of joint ventures" and "exit strategies" (Yan 2016). These stages describe the entire lifespan of a joint venture: from "partner selection" to transitioning the joint venture to independent existence in its own environment. In this way, joint venture projects focus more on quality than on quantity. Few joint ventures are established, but they must work. Therefore, joint ventures are usually strategically organized and typically an activity carried out by the organization's senior management (i.e. formulated at the strategic level). A joint venture is thus an example of a business strategy, described as a "parental strategy". "Parental strategies" usually involve a high degree of involvement on the C-level of a company. Other examples involve spin-offs, spin-ins and similar merger and acquisition activities.

In the case of crowdsourcing, however, quantity is a higher priority than quality. The organization is confronted with many ideas, which cause disturbances in the pattern of thinking, and therefore in most cases promote innovation on the operational level, such as product innovation. The approach is: the more the better, and with luck there will be some success. The C-level usually is not involved in the active management of these solutions, rather they are assessed in the operations of a corporation.

r and K-strategies The difference between parental strategies like joint ventures and crowdsourcing can be compared with two different reproductive strategies found in biology: the r-strategy and the K-strategy for raising offspring.

While r-strategists, for example mice, focus on quantity and producing as many progeny as possible, K-strategists, for example elephants, produce fewer offspring in which they invest more, and quality plays an important role (Pianka 1970; Parry 1981). The resources of K-strategists are primarily invested in raising offspring, while those of r-strategists are invested in the quantity of progeny. The parents of an elephant—K-strategists—pass on their knowledge and experience, so that today's elephants are literally "standing on the shoulders of giants". Our own species, homo sapiens, are also biological K-strategists. In contrast, frogs lay hundreds of eggs, and only a few young tadpoles are able to find their way independently, while the vast majority do not survive. Frog parents do not invest any energy in raising their children, and information about them does not reach them. In crowdsourcing, too, only a very small number of ideas "survive", and as illustrated in the section above, most crowdsourced proposals do not penetrate the parent organization—let alone become nurtured by it. As demonstrated above, crowdsourcing disrupts the thinking of employees involved in processes on the operational level, such as product development. But the innovation process remains an internal, operational one (Table 1).

Table 1 The analogy between business development and parenting

	Biology	Business development	Involvement of parents (parental organizations)
K-strategy	Few offspring with a higher probability of individual survival	Organization of a small number of entities at strategic level like joint ventures, spin-offs and M&A's (parental strategy)	Active development of survival strategies for offspring
r-strategy	Many offspring with a low probability of individual survival	Crowdsourcing for products and designs on the operational level	Passive attitude at the strategic level

In both organization development and in the natural world, there is a trade-off between quality and quantity. Successful adaptation to the environment directly depends upon the number of progeny and how well the child can exploit the potential offered by new environmental conditions. The greater the number of offspring and the better prepared they are, the more the parent organization is able to pass on its DNA. The long-term success of an organization could therefore be described mathematically using a Lagrange multiplier. Maximum success in passing on DNA = quality x quantity of progeny—cost of creation and raising offspring, with the constraint that resources are limited. In a world without limited resources, organizations would carry out crowdsourcing and create a joint venture out of every single idea generated by the crowd that had potential for success. However, in our world resources are limited.

Influence of ICT on the model A child's upbringing depends heavily on how communication between the old generation and the new is organized. Active nurturing (in the K-strategy) involves a lot of communication. Whether through example or intervention in behaviour by parents, or imitation and reception of feedback by the child, communication between parents and children is the most important thing (perhaps besides love) in the nurturing process. Communication has become less expensive and easier with the development of information and communication technologies (ICT). This slackens the Lagrange constraint of limited resources. The less these cost, the more a third way is made possible—something between crowdsourcing and forming joint ventures.

The third way: K-crowdsourcing When the cost of ICT comes down, the constraint of limited resources described above in the Lagrange multiplier can be relaxed. More communication is possible, and more information can flow, without using more resources. This gives rise to a third path for offspring development, between the two extremes of parental strategy on the one hand and crowdsourcing on the other: crowdsourcing combined with ICT-supported feedback mechanisms (quality), so that the best can be taken from both worlds. We call this third way K-crowdsourcing. K-crowdsourcing is distinct from r-crowdsourcing in that r-crowdsourcing takes a problem from the operational part of the business and presents it alone to a mass of contributors, asking for a solution. A parental strategy is conducted purely at the strategic level and the focus is on the quality of a small number of projects. K-crowdsourcing combines the reproductive strategies of mice and elephants, so to speak.

As is shown in Table 2, K-crowdsourcing (with iterations) reaches through to the strategic level. The next section presents an innovative crowdsourcing methodology, demonstrating how the three problems described above could be solved using K-crowdsourcing.

Table 2 Quality and quantity trade-off in business development

	Normative level	Information flow to "offspring"	Quantity	Examples of application
Parental strategies	Strategic, structural and cultural	Close collaboration between partners and offspring organization	Small number of joint ventures, spin-offs and projects	Incorporation of a technology firm to improve the product portfolio
K-crowdsourcing	Strategic, structural and cultural	Feedback mechanisms using ICT's	Many teams	Crowdsourcing a new business model
r-crowdsourcing	Operational	Problem presentation and challenge, without iterations	Many individual opinions	Crowdsourcing product ideas or designs

4.2 K-Crowdsourcing Using the BeeUp Method

BeeUp is a K-crowdsourcing-based innovation method geared towards business development. BeeUp was developed at the University of St. Gallen and the University of Applied Sciences in St. Gallen. The motivation for the research project was the less-then-satisfactory experience with r-crowdsourcing services for the purpose of business development. To their credit, r-crowdsourcing services are very creative, innovative and foster out-of-the-box thinking. But the generated ideas were not implementable and were nowhere near the maturity which is necessary to overcome the organizational immune systems.

The aim of the BeeUp method is to take advantage of growth opportunities in a changing environment in a way that (a) fits current core competencies, (b) generates innovative ideas and (c) identifies and systematically develops individuals with a talent for implementing solutions. The first step involves analysing a company's or department's core competencies. Based on this analysis, the consultant develops anonymised case studies which describe the company's situation and current problems. Next, the case studies are published on BeeUp's online platform (www. beeup.com) where they can be studied by groups, or crowds. Crowds are motivated by the learning incentives offered by the platform and the participating educational institutions.

The individual steps in the method are described below and assessed in terms of their suitability for application in connection with business development (Fig. 1).

Step 1: Problem or task The problem or task comes from a company. At this stage, it is important to formulate the problem accurately. The challenge lies in getting to the heart of the problem. Superficial descriptions of tensions are often symptoms of deeper-seated problems. Experience shows that poorly defined problems do not lead to a satisfactory solution.

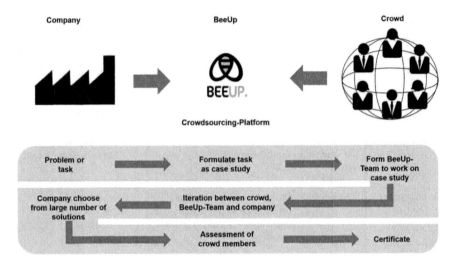

Fig. 1 The BeeUp method

Step 2: Formulating the task as case study A case study is prepared on the basis of the problem. The anonymised study includes the problem and a description of the company's culture. The information contained in the case study is not sufficient to come up with a solution, but simply serves as a starting point for the iteration process. In addition to the problem, the case study is enriched by means of incentives. On BeeUp, the incentive is access to free qualifications, in the shape of certificates related to particular methods. For example, the certificate for "Business Model Canvas" refers to the method of the same name developed by Osterwalder and Pigneur. If a user wants to learn about business model innovation, he or she solves a case study and earns the corresponding certificate, which provides proof of their experience in using a particular method.

Step 3: Form BeeUp teams to work on case study Users form BeeUp teams to look at different aspects of the case study, and together the teams make up the crowd. Participants benefit by learning from their colleagues and supporting one another. A consultant follows the discussions and solutions, and can give the entire team targeted feedback. Every BeeUp team signs a non-disclosure agreement (NDA), which obliges the team members to keep information they receive from the consultant and the company confidential. Teams are not allowed to share information with each other.

Step 4: Iteration between crowd, BeeUp-Team and company Teams receive feedback after they make their first contribution. The better the team's proposal, the more time the consultant puts into the team's training and development by means of repeated rounds of coaching and feedback. Once a high level of quality has been achieved, the solution is presented to the company, followed by feedback from the real-life corporate environment. In a manner of speaking, the consultant primarily introduces the team to the company, with which the consultant is familiar but the team is not. In this way, the solution matures in line with the company's needs, while the company also provides targeted and protected information to the team. The solution matures as follows:

- Initial exploratory proposals based on a verified understanding of the company.
- Generating large numbers of non-implementable ideas for solving the problem.
- Selecting a few ideas with the help of a consultant who is familiar with the company; these ideas are then prepared for implementation.
- Presenting these few ideas in full accordance with the methods applied and preparing reasoned, fact-based lines of argumentation to defend against early-stage counterarguments from the company.
- Incorporating company feedback into the solution.

In this way, companies can integrate complex and mature solutions into their organizational structures. The role of the consultant, following the above-introduced analogy, is a parental one. He or she is responsible to give the BeeUp-teams the chance to mature, before they confront the "real world" and are left to fend off for themselves with real companies. This is why we are calling BeeUp crowdsourcing of the K-type.

Step 5: Choose from large number of solutions In the final stage of the method, the company chooses one or two teams, or alternatively solutions without the related teams. Typically, companies are very interested in the team that generated the solution, as well as the solution itself. In this way, BeeUp opens up new opportunities in HR management: teams do not apply to an organization, but shape the organization's future. As a result, the company integrates talents required in future into the current organization. In turn, these external teams directly shape the company's culture. In this context, integrating a solution that has developed and matured in a different environment into the organization is an important factor.

Step 6: Evaluating solutions, and certification Even if a team is not successful, its solution is assessed and feedback given. This is the incentive, which is promised to the crowd. Software measures each user's level of activity and the degree to which he or she is capable of forming connections with others. Additionally, the evaluation influences the specialist competencies that are described in the aforementioned certificates.

The K-type nature of crowdsourcing is thus seen by three distinct properties of the method:

- Time for Co-evolution: The consultant is actively coaching the crowd and enabling it to achieve better solutions. He or she is also responsible to defend the crowd's solution before the client and thus nurturing the otherwise resistant organization. With this iterative approach, the crowd becomes more a part of an organization, the more iterations between the crowd, the consultant and the company.
- Confidentiality: For better or worse, you do no tell your children going to kindergarten the peculiarities of your family finances. It is the same approach in K-crowdsourcing. The consultant does not disclose all information to fresh

BeeUp-teams, though they have signed an NDA. Once the maturity of the solution increases and a trustworthy relationship is established, the consultant can share more information and the maturity will increase by this action.

- Overcoming the organizational immune system: It is very crucial to answer this question even before the project is started. It is the consultant's role to access what kinds of implementation practises are envisioned by its client before the start of a project. The consultants assess critically the abilities of the organization at step one, and based on this assessment, selectively and promotionally adopt the feedback in the iterative loops to the crowd.

4.3   K-Crowdsourcing in Practice

Two examples from different fields of application are presented below in order to illustrate the practical suitability and benefits of the iterative crowdsourcing approach for business development.

Marketing in the aviation and aerospace sector A company in the aviation and aerospace industry (which engineers custom parts) was looking to develop an effective new B2B marketing strategy. The company was faced with the problem that important potential customers all over the world were looking for solutions that the company's industrial services could provide, but the prospects were not aware of this. The aim of the project was to ensure that engineers in decision-making positions thought of the company at the vital moment and requested a quote.

A BeeUp team of business administration students developed an innovative inbound marketing strategy supported by the internet of things, which could potentially result in increased differentiation compared to the usual search engine optimisation tools and blog posts. The iteration between the team and the consultant went as follows: to begin with, the team was overwhelmed by the complexity of the case and had no idea how to approach the process of finding a solution. This commonly occurs with case studies that only describe the problem and the corporate culture. Pressure from the team signalised its willingness to make a valuable contribution to the problem-solving process. With support from the consultant, the team succeeded in visualising the problem, which consisted of overcoming three barriers: the prospect's location, finding out when prospects take decisions, and identifying the relevant positions in the target organization's hierarchy. By building on its visualisation, the team was in a position to devise solutions for the various sub-problems and synthesise them to form a coherent overall solution. At the time when this article went to review, the team works for the company and is responsible for implementing the solution and is answerable only to the CEO.

Such deep penetration into marketing strategy would not have been possible without the help from the consultant. It is also clear that the consultant would not have had the ideas on his own on how to solve the problem at hand. His input was very crucial in the beginning for problem definition. Later on, his feedback was useful for the team in order to mature the solution.

Strategy of a pharmaceutical company The customer is a pharmaceutical company and its core competency is distributing pharmaceutical products. Its main customers are chemist's and health and beauty retailers. According to the problem description, the aim was to bypass the main customers and reach consumers directly using digital methods. Another aim was to get the pharmaceutical company's business model in shape for the digital future.

The case was distributed among teams, each with five members with a background in engineering, and among secondary school pupils (aged around 16), spread among various teams. During the iteration process, the biggest challenge facing the teams of engineers was focusing on customer benefits. Initially, they concentrated too much on technical feasibility. When the solution had reached a high level of maturity, the next problem involved integrating the customer's legal circumstances into the solution. The successful BeeUp team mainly comprised engineers. The team spokesman and head of the BeeUp team was an engineer participating in vocational training. At that stage, he had had nothing to do with the pharmaceutical industry. He is now implementing the solution in combination with completing a doctorate. In order to ensure that the existing structure's immune system does not nip the new strategy in the bud, the company's future structure will be implemented outside the current one.

With the school pupils, the consultant's job was to steer their initially very unconventional and partly unrealistic ideas in a more realistic direction. The second problem was structuring the solutions in such a way that they could be presented to the end customer. Eventually, one team (comprising 15- and 16-year-old girls) convinced the management to adopt a very innovative, digital-media-based marketing plan aimed at young women. The group's personal association with the subject was again a significant advantage in developing the solution. There was actually a problem with the company's structure and culture obstructing implementation of the solution. The entire company was geared towards selling products for chemist's and health and beauty retailers, but new groups (end users, young women) were integrated into the new solution, meaning that sales intermediaries could be bypassed in the long term. This opened the door to a new business model for the pharmaceutical company.

From the consultant's perspective, K-crowdsourcing entails some workload changes: On the downside, the iterations with the crowd result in a higher virtual workload for the consultant. As one remedy to this higher workload, we have used a "first layer coach" for all teams, so that the consultant needs only to bother with the high-performing teams. On the upside, the organizational burden to organize workshops internally decreases: virtual teams are easier to handle. The crowd also delivers high value content, which the consultant can adopt for his or her purpose without creating all the content from scratch.

In total, the workload tends to decrease for the high-paid consultant but increases for the people who are in charge of the first layer coaching activities.

The following section addresses the question of what the function of the consultant will look like in future, considering the incorporation of K-crowdsourcing. The section is divided into two parts. The first part describes the functions of a consultant. The second part presents the "reinvented" consultant, who with the aid of crowdsourcing can bring their skills into play to a greater degree than previously possible.

5 Role of the Consultant in the System Using K-Crowdsourcing

According to United Nations Industrial Development Organization (1974), external consultants perform four distinct functions:

1. Reducing the time required for implementation,
2. Appropriation of knowledge and skills,
3. An external view: new approaches to established practices,
4. Independent perspective.

While point four, can be reduced to sociological functions (e.g. an independent arbiter is needed), the first three functions are essential for the purposes of business development. In summary, all three functions introduce knowledge to the organization, whether implementation knowledge, specialist expertise or outside-the-box thinking.

K-crowdsourcing, when applied correctly, transfers decentralised information into knowledge in the strategic, structural or even the organizational core of an organization. This means that at first glance, K-crowdsourcing has the potential to substitute functions 2 and 3 of a consultant. According to Brynjolfsson and McAfee (2016), tasks with a routine character are at the most risk of being replaced by digitalised methods. However, our experience with BeeUp has shown that coaching the crowd (as well as nurturing a child) is not a routine task. This means the duties of the consultant change when K-crowdsourcing is used, but they do not decrease.

When using the BeeUp method, a considerable portion of the quality of the result depends upon the respective crowd coach—a role played by the consultant. The most important skills are understanding the problem posed by the client, correct didactic and content guidance of the crowd, and the art of strengthening input from the crowd in the right way. These activities are all organized virtually, which does not make the coach's job any simpler. This is a highly demanding profile, especially since the timing of crowd contributions is distributed randomly.

The activities cannot be automated and do not differ significantly from the traditional tasks of a consultant. The difference when it comes to K-crowdsourcing is that for the consultant, the crowd are stakeholders, and therefore the consultant's market is two-sided (King 2013). While traditional consultants provide these skills to the client side, a consultant for K-crowdsourcing uses their expertise to support the client side and the crowd side. The consultant's value proposition to the client increases in a K-Crowdsourced setup. The reason is that the consultant is able to bring in more views on a given problem. The source of these views are either internal (within the client's organization) or external (from various sources and users of the crowdsourcing platform). Thus, more knowledge is integrated into the problem solving procedure, which increases the likelihood of a good solution and decreases the likelihood of a bad one. In comparison to the traditional consultant-client setup, the type of knowledge which is integrated is thus the knowledge which is usually not considered by neither party. By using K-crowdsourcing, companies are able to surface the unconscious parts of an organization to the consulting-process. As one CEO of a pharmaceutical business put it after seeing the results of a BeeUp-project: "We knew that digitalisation is going to affect us in one way or another, but we were not aware on its massive impacts on our clients—the drugstores. If the business models which the crowd proposes will come true, they will simply disappear in the next 20 years." The company, however, has based their long-term digitalisation strategy on wrong assumptions. The external crowd was able to show how wrong these assumptions were in due time. This knowledge surfaced to consciousness.

By using K-crowdsourcing internally in an organization, companies will get to know what their own employees really think about the common organization, which, by the way, might not be the most pleasant thing to know. Nonetheless, it is a very valuable resource. For example, a company which was engaged in a highly regulated market learned by internally crowdsourcing, that they are trapped in a strategic trilemma: Of the three strategic goals which the management was pursuing, only a pair of two were implementable in the organization. This resulted in dissatisfaction in certain functional departments. The management was aware of the dissatisfaction, but not of the root cause. The internal K-crowdsourcing activities gave the management the necessary information to argue before the board that at least one strategic goal must be set aside. Had this information within their own organization not surfaced to the consciousness of the managers, they would have kept on their three-goal-strategy, which was doomed conceptually. The internal crowd thus prevailed the managers to plan an impossible task and thus saved the organization from internal turmoil. In a K-crowdsourced setup, the client gains from the consultant's value proposition as described above, because more knowledge is brought to bear on a problem and more carriers of knowledge are integrated into a project. Consultants are in a better position to fulfil their role, as they have more knowledge themselves.

In summary, the consultant who manages the K-crowd can give recommendations of a much higher quality for a given price. Because strategic decisions are high stakes, and errors can lead to disaster, it is worthwhile to allocate resources to nurture the crowd and treat the crowd members as your next generation. Nevertheless projects involving K-crowdsourcing do need more time and attention than either r-crowdsourcing or conventional consulting projects and the complexity of the projects increases. The iterations with the crowd do cost time and attention the same way parenting does. Therefore, a careful evaluation of scope, target and timeline of the dedicated project is necessary. As we described above, conventional crowdsourcing delivers in many cases satisfying results in a flexible and efficient manner.

6 Summary

This article argues that crowdsourcing offers access to more and diverse information. This information can be transformed to knowledge if the process for doing so is well-designed. From a systemic point of view, crowdsourcing irritates an otherwise to stabilization tending organization. Organizations are systems, which have been built for stabilization. When you thus crowdsource a new strategy, the current organization will find ways to resist your proposed change. It is therefore good practise for organizations to venture-out new business models or otherwise radically innovative projects. We introduced therefore two types of crowdsourcing, which follow the analogy from biology: r- and K-Crowdsourcing. R-crowdsourcing is generation of many ideas without caring for the ideas and the people behind the idea. Whereas r-crowdsourcing generates many ideas and takes this idea into pre-defined innovation processes, K-Crowdsourcing generates new processes, business models and strategies. The latter does so by building up an iterative process between the crowd, the consultant and the client at hand. There are fewer crowdsourced solutions, but these are more advanced and more thought-trough. In essence, whereas r-crowdsourcing is useful for generating ideas which you can use in your operations, K-crowdsourcing is useful for identifying business models and allocate people to the new tasks arising from the new business models. It makes thus the organization more agile.

By K-crowdsourcing solutions, the role of the consultant changes. By increasing the quality of the service, the consultant is able to provide value to the company. We have argued that while the consultant usually had the role of helping the client with conscious competence, K-crowdsourcing opens new perspectives and discloses unconscious fields of knowledge, namely the unconscious competence and unconscious incompetence. While the former can be addressed by applying K-crowdsourcing on the internal crowd, the latter is revealed by using an external K-crowd. Therefore, we think that the consulting markets is going to grow, because with cheaper and better information and communication technologies much more knowledge—one of the main functions of consulting—can be allocated to organizational problems. More knowledge for problem solving substantiates the value proposition of consulting.

References

Agarwal R, Echambadi R, Franco AM, Sarkar M (2004) Knowledge transfer through inheritance: spin-out generation, development, and survival. Acad Manage J 47(4):501–522

Ahlstrom D, Bruton GD (2010) International management: strategy and culture in the emerging world, International edn. South-Western/Cengage Learning, Mason, Ohio

Beer S (1995) Brain of the firm, 2nd edn. In: The managerial cybernetics of organization. Wiley, Chichester

Bleicher K (1980) Unternehmensentwicklung und organisatorische Gestaltung: Arbeitsbuch zu Unternehmensentwicklung und organisatorische Gestaltung. Grundwissen der Ökonomik. Fischer, Stuttgart

Blohm I, Leimeister JM, Krcmar H (2013) Crowdsourcing: how to benefit from (too) many great ideas. MIS Q Executive Res J Devoted Improving Pract 12(4):199–211

Brynjolfsson E, McAfee A (2016) The second machine age: work, progress, and prosperity in a time of brilliant technologies. Paperback edn. W.W. Norton & Company, New York

Christensen CM (2003) The innovator''s dilemma. In: When new technologies cause great firms to fail. Harvard Business School Press, Boston

Christensen CM, Johnson C, Horn M (2008) Disrupting class. How disruptive innovation will change the way the world learns. McGraw-Hill, New York

Christensen CM, Raynor M (2017) The Innovator's Solution. Warum manche Unternehmen erfolgreicher wachsen als andere. Vahlen, Munich

Durward D, Blohm I, Leimeister JM (2016) Crowd work. Bus Inf Syst Eng BISE 58(4):281–286

Gassmann O (2012) Crowdsourcing - Innovationsmanagement mit Schwarmintelligenz: -Interaktiv Ideen finden - Kollektives Wissen effektiv nutzen - Mit Fallbeispielen und Checklisten. Hanser Carl, München

Howe J (2006) The rise of crowdsourcing. Wired Magazine, June 2006

King SP (2013) Two-sided markets. Aust Econ Rev 46(2):247–258

Luhmann N (1996) Soziale Systeme: Grundlagen einer allgemeinen Theorie. Suhrkamp Taschenbuch Wissenschaft. Suhrkamp, Frankfurt am Main

Luhmann N, Baecker D (eds) (2009) Einführung in die Systemtheorie, 5th edn. Lizenzausg. Wiss. Buchges, Darmstadt

Maturana HR, Varela FJ, Beer S (1980) Autopoiesis and cognition: the realization of the living. Boston studies in the philosophy of science, vol 42. Reidel, Dordrecht

Osterwalder A, Pigneur Y (2011) Business Model Generation: Ein Handbuch für Visionäre, Spielveränderer und Herausforderer. Campus, Frankfurt am Main

Osterwalder A, Pigneur Y (2015) Value Proposition Design: Entwickeln Sie Produkte und Services, die Ihre Kunden wirklich wollen. Beginnen Sie mit ... [Die Fortsetzung des Bestsellers Business Model Generation!]. Campus, Frankfurt am Main

Parry GD (1981) The meanings of r- and K-selection. Oecologia 48(2):260–264

Pianka ER (1970) On r- and K-selection. Am Nat 104(940):592–597

Rüegg-Stürm J (1989) Unternehmensentwicklung im Spannungsfeld von Komplexität und Ethik: Eine permanente Herausforderung für ein ganzheitliches Management. Veröffentlichungen der Hochschule St. Gallen für Wirtschafts-, Rechts- und Sozialwissenschaften. Schriftenreihe Betriebswirtschaft, vol. 15. Haupt, Bern

Rüegg-Stürm J, Grand S (2015) Das St. Galler management-modell, 2nd edn. Haupt, Bern

Simon FB (2007) Einführung in Systemtheorie und Konstruktivismus, 2nd edn. Carl-Auer Systeme Verlag, Heidelberg

Simon FB (2014) Einführung in die (System-)Theorie der Beratung. Carl-Auer Compact. Carl Auer, Heidelberg

Simula H, Ahola T (2014) A network perspective on idea and innovation crowdsourcing in industrial firms. Ind Mark Manage Int J Ind High-tech Firms 43(3):400–408

Sloane P (ed) (2011) A guide to open innovation and crowdsourcing: expert tips and advice, 1st edn. Kogan Page, London, Philadelphia

United Nations Industrial Development Organization (1974) Consulting roles and sources. Int Stud Manag Organ 4(3):79–92

Yan A (2016) International joint ventures: theory and practice. Taylor and Francis, Florence

Author Biographies

Oliver Christ is a lecturer and senior researcher at the Institute for Quality Management and Business Administration (IQB) at the FHS University of Applied Sciences St. Gallen, Switzerland (FHS). After studying business administration, Oliver Christ worked as research assistant at the University of St. Gallen and finished his Ph.D. in 2001. For 10 years, he was employed by SAP, first as assistant to the CEO and commencing 2006 as Research Director SAP Switzerland, where he established the local research organization and managed the distributed organization with 3 locations including a team of +40 international researchers. Over the last 18 years, Oliver Christ worked as lecturer and researcher with different Swiss Universities and teaches courses on bachelor and master level on Enterprise Systems, Business Intelligence, Business Process Management, Emerging Technologies and Organizational Theories.

Michael Czarniecki is a lecturer and project manager at the Institute for Quality Management and Business Administration (IQB) at the FHS University of Applied Sciences St. Gallen, Switzerland (FHS). He worked on projects in Switzerland and abroad for private and public institutions. The projects involved maturity development, market introduction and market research projects. Michael Czarniecki is co-founder and member of the Management Board of Solid Chemicals GmbH since 2001 and was Managing Director from 2007 to 2011. Michael Czarniecki is also the co-founder of BeeUp GmbH. Michael Czarniecki holds both a M.A. in economics and teaching degree at the University of St. Gallen as well as a CAS in management in the life sciences of the EPFL in Lausanne.

Lukas Andreas Scherer is the managing director of the Institute for Quality Management and Business Administration (IQB) and professor at the FHS University of Applied Sciences St. Gallen, Switzerland (FHS). As lecturer, researcher and consultant he focusses on strategic management and entrepreneurship in SME and multinationals. After studies of Business Administration at the University of St. Gallen and at the Stockholm School of Economics (University Stockholm) and the PhD at the University of St. Gallen he was business consultant for private and public organisations. In 1998 he joined the first private university in Switzerland as Dean and CEO. Besides these business activities he is engaged in several non-profit organisations.

Crowd Workplace—A Case Study on the Digital Transformation Within IT- and Management-Consulting

Henry Seifert and Volker Nissen

Abstract The digital transformation of consulting is a phenomenon that can affect both external and internal processes of a consulting firm. Consequently, consulting firms should analyze and monitor not only customer-faced processes but also processes that occur in back offices and without any client interaction. The following case study addresses two issues. First, it gives insights of the status of the digital transformation of a German IT- and Management-Consulting firm with more than 1500 employees. It applies the current knowledge about the virtualization of consulting services in a real life setting. Second, the case study describes, how internal processes can be virtualized and digitally transformed via the implementation of a digital platform that will enable a crowd workplace. The paper concludes with implications for practitioners and future research.

1 Introduction

1.1 Background and Motivation

The consulting industry, just as basically all other industries, is affected by the mega-trend *Digitalization*. Consequently, researchers and practitioners are interested in the different dimensions of this important phenomenon. One especially interesting aspect is the current state of the digitalization of consulting firms, as currently only few information exists how digitalization and thus virtualization of consulting processes is realized. Furthermore, researchers and practitioners are eager to find out what impacts this has trend both on internal and external processes of consulting organizations. The term internal thereby addresses all processes that do not involve clients but are nevertheless necessary to run a consulting firm

H. Seifert (✉) · V. Nissen
Technische Universität Ilmenau, Ilmenau, Germany
e-mail: henry.seifert@infosysconsulting.com

V. Nissen
e-mail: volker.nissen@tu-ilmenau.de

© Springer International Publishing AG 2018
V. Nissen (ed.), *Digital Transformation of the Consulting Industry*,
Progress in IS, https://doi.org/10.1007/978-3-319-70491-3_12

(e.g. the human resources or accounting processes). The term external processes on the other hand covers the processes that are client-faced and that typically represent the actual consulting service. The overall scientific target of research in this field is to get a better understanding of the digital transformation of consulting in order to create artefacts that can support consulting firms dealing with this mega-trend. Practitioners are interested in knowledge about use cases and best practices of virtual consulting as well as concepts that help them planning and realizing their individual transformation initiatives.

This paper addresses both researchers and practitioners, and aims at fulfilling both scientific and practical expectations. At first, the theoretical foundation is presented and an overview about the current knowledge base is given. Following this, the concept of the case study is presented according to the methodological framework of Yin (2014). Then, as the first part of the case study, an analysis of the general status of the digital transformation for a specific consulting provider is performed. Thereafter, the *crowd workplace* as an example for one specific virtualization initiative in this company is described. The paper concludes with a short summary and some implications for researchers and practitioners.

1.2 Morphological Framework of the Digital Transformation

In this section, a morphological framework will be derived that helps to identify important aspects of digital transformation projects in the consulting industry. For this, we build upon the results of other contributions, where fundamental issues, such as the expectations of consultants and clients w.r.t. virtual consulting services, quality criteria of virtualized consulting, barriers of virtualization, as well as respective benefits and risks have already been investigated (Nissen et al. 2015; Nissen and Seifert 2016).

These findings and artefacts form the theoretical pre-understanding (Gassmann 1999) and will later be compared to the real-life information gathered from our case study. More precisely, the framework will be used to examine how the theoretical findings can be applied to a particular case and whether the results help to understand the digital transformation in the consulting industry.

As a first theoretical input, the Success Chain of Virtual Consulting Services (Fig. 1) briefly describes the steps that need to be passed in order to achieve success, when applying virtualization in the field of consulting. It is a mental construct that helps sorting various factors and aspects along a logical chain of internal and external factors (e.g. the criteria for acceptance and success of virtual

Fig. 1 Success chain of (virtualized) consulting services

consulting products). In the first phase of the chain *Design and Offering*, the consulting firm assesses the overall potential of virtual consulting services. If adequate potential was identified the consulting firm would start to design and implement the new, innovative consulting service. If this service has been developed properly and the major success factors have been considered, clients theoretically should accept the new service and thereby reach the next phase *Acceptance*. Once a new service has been accepted, the client will use this consulting service to solve a specific business problem (phase *Usage*). Thereafter, the *Satisfaction*-phase of the success chain then describes whether a client is or is not satisfied with the quality of the consulting service or product. If the client is satisfied and multiple clients are also eager to use the service and the economic factors (e.g. concerning competitors) are positive, then the final phase, called *Success*, will be reached. The success chain can help to structure the virtualization initiative of a specific consulting firm and thus provide orientation.

Another important aspect of the digital transformation in consulting is the *size of the consulting firm*. Within an empirical study on the state-of-practice within the consulting industry, it was discovered that the size of the firm does have an influence on the digital transformation (Nissen and Seifert 2016).

Besides the size of the firm, the *consulting field* (Strategy-, Organization-, Information Technology- and Human Resources-Consulting) and the *consulting type* are characteristics that have an impact on the digital transformation as well (Nissen and Seifert 2016). Both aspects will be taken up within the actual case study.

The virtualization of the consulting process affects various idealistic *phases of the consulting process* in different ways. The following phases may be distinguished: Acquisition, Preparation, Analysis, Solution, Implementation and Follow-up. These phases represent an ideal approach to the understanding of a consulting service. Depending on the specific project, some phases may not be relevant or additional phases may need to be added.

Furthermore, it will be interesting to examine the overall *maturity level of the digital transformation* that represents the level of individual virtualization progress of the investigated consulting firm. Four maturity levels can be differentiated as outlined in the contribution of Nissen and Seifert (2016) on the status quo of virtualization in this volume. They provide orientation in this challenging transformation process.

The digital transformation in consulting requires the organizations to overcome various *barriers*. These barriers can be classified into client- and knowledge-related, technological, legal, political and organizational barriers (Nissen and Seifert 2016). Depending on the current situation and profile of the consulting firm one type of barrier may be more relevant than the other.

The virtualization of consulting processes and the digital transformation of consulting services will lead to different types of applications and use cases. Typical examples include *Virtual Assessment, Remote Analysis, Virtual Collaboration, Virtual Communication, Online Knowledge Management, Virtual Coaching,*

Phase of the Success Chain	Design and Offer	Acceptance	Use	Satisfaction	Success		
Size of the Consulting Firm	Small		Medium		Large		
Field of Consulting	Strategy	Organization	IT	HR			
Type of Consulting	Expert	Advisory	Organizational Development	Systemic			
Phase of the Consulting Process	Acquisition	Preparation	Analysis	Solution	Implementation	Follow-up	
Maturity of Digital Transformation	1. Level	2. Level	3. Level	4. Level			
Virtualizability of the Consulting Process	Very Low	Low	Medium	High	Very High		
Degree of Virtualization of the Consulting Process	Very Low	Low	Medium	High	Very High		
Project Context of Virtualization Initiative	Before	While	After	Without			
Integration of the Client	Yes	No					
Barriers	Client-related	Knowledge-based	Technological	Legal	Political	Organizational	
Virtualization Applications	Virtual Assessment	Remote Testing	Remote Analysis	Virtual Collaboration	Virtual Communication	Online Knowledge Management	Virtual Coaching
	E-Learning	Virtual Project Management	Knowledge Sharing	Knowledge Seeking	Online Marketing	Network Building	Other
Benefits (Categories)	Time	Costs	Quality	Flexibility and Availability	Reputation	Knowledge and Cooperation	Work-Life-Balance
Risks (Categories)	Time	Costs	Quality	Technology Dependency	Reputation	Data Misuse	Relationship
Virtualization Technology	Audio and Video	Groupware and Knowledge	Social Software	Data/Process	Web Platforms	Virtual Reality	Other

Fig. 2 Morphological framework (box) of the digital transformation in consulting

E-Learning, Virtual Project Management, Online Marketing, Network Building as well as *Remote Testing* (Nissen and Seifert 2016).

The digital transformation comes with risks and chances, which are expected (with some differences in focus) by both clients and consultants. These refer to the dimensions time, costs, quality, and reputation (Nissen et al. 2015).

The virtualization of consulting processes is strongly based on the usage of adequate technologies (Nissen and Seifert 2016; Werth et al. 2016). Although there is a vast number of available technologies, the digital transformation in the consulting industry will mainly depend on technologies like audio- and video-tools, groupware, social software, data and process mining tools, voting tools, presentation tools and websites (Nissen and Seifert 2016).

Figure 2 summarizes and complements these facets of the digital transformation in the form of a morphological framework (box).

1.3 Subsumption Under Consulting Research

The research discussed here is attributable to Consulting Research (Nissen 2007), which includes the scientific investigation of consulting services, consulting firms and the consulting market with its various participants on the supplier and the buyer side. Consulting Research has two concerns: Firstly, the scientific penetration of the topic of consulting, with the focus on the scientific knowledge being abstracted from individual consulting projects. Secondly, the transfer of scientific theories, knowledge and methods to consulting practice with the aim of better solving consulting tasks. The present paper concentrates on the first core concern of consulting research, since the understanding of the digital transformation in consulting shall be enhanced. Additionally, we aim to enhance the creation of artefacts that can support consulting firms within their individual virtualization initiatives.

2 Case Study

2.1 Case Study Design

This case study describes for a specific consulting provider how virtualization is implemented in the field of information technology (IT) and management consulting. The questions to be answered with the help of this case study are:

1. Is the morphological framework developed in the previous section helpful in adequately explaining the current situation of digital transformation in the consulting practice?
2. How is the digital transformation conducted in an actual consulting firm?

According to Yin (2014), these questions form the starting point for the planning, implementation and evaluation of the case study. The structure of the case study presented in this section is based on the requirements of Yin (2014). At the outset, the company of the case and the scope of the case are presented. Then a detailed analysis of the current state of development of the digital transformation for this consulting provider is presented, using the structure developed in the previous section. Based on this, a particular transformation initiative of the consulting firm will be presented. The case study concludes with a summary and critical reflection of the suggested framework of the digital transformation.

The case study was conducted during the period from January 2016 to April 2017. In order to obtain a comprehensive picture of the case considered, various sources of information were studied. In addition to the analysis of company-specific documents such as PowerPoint presentations, Excel sheets or Word documents, contributions of the internal blog of the virtualization initiative were taken into account. Over 40 documents have been analysed. In addition, personal and telephone interviews were conducted with representatives of the initiative, such as the project manager, the head of the business development and various heads of other departments. Moreover, important information on virtualization in the firm could be gathered through the participation in internal workshops.

2.2 Facts About the Consulting Firm

The consulting firm of the case study is a Management- and IT-Consulting firm based in the southern part of Germany and one of the leading consulting firms in this country. This consulting provider optimizes the processes of its clients across the entire value chain. Currently, the company has significantly more than 1500 employees at several locations worldwide and over 300 clients from different industries, such as automotive and aviation. In 2015, the firm recorded a turnover of well over 200 million Euro.

2.3 Status of the Digital Transformation in the Studied Company

2.3.1 Overview

In order to secure the future success of the company, the consulting firm has developed a strategy that targets strategic objectives and measures for the year 2018 and further. From this entrepreneurial strategy, a strategic initiative has been launched, which takes on the digital transformation of the company. The next section describes briefly, what the current status in respect to the digital transformation at the consulting firm is. The different fundamentals of the digital transformation that have been summarized in the morphological framework will be applied in this chapter. First, opportunities, threats and barriers of the digital transformation will be discussed. Second, the maturity level of the firm in respect of the digital transformation will be evaluated. Finally, the characteristics of the company-wide transformation initiative will be summarized. It has to be stressed that the discussion of digitalization in this case study always refers to the situation of the service provider, not its clients.

2.3.2 Opportunities, Threats and Barriers of the Digital Transformation

In the perception of the consulting firm, the mega-trend digitalization plays an important role, as digitization causes a fundamental change in organizations, processes and products of partners and competitors. Consequently, the consulting firm needs to evaluate the future requirements of cooperation within the organization, with clients and with partners. Following these dramatic changes, the consulting firm tries to assess the consequences of digitization and to derive appropriate measures. In order to define an own vision and strategy, the consulting firm evaluated the importance of virtualization for its organization and whether it is a threat or opportunity.

Regarding the opportunities, the consulting firm expects three major benefits. First, the virtualization of business processes can help to develop and test innovative solutions for problems of existing or future clients. The opportunity to build lighthouse projects within the consulting firm within the framework of virtualization and to create a reputation gain as well as new references are motivators for virtualization at the consulting firm. Virtualization also creates the opportunity for the firm to become a pioneer in terms of digitalization within the parent group. The targeted gain in reputation addresses a benefit that was not explicitly mentioned in a previous study on benefits and risks of virtualization in consulting (Nissen et al. 2015).

Secondly, there is a very high cost pressure in the area of commodity and standardized consulting services, mainly from the IT consulting field. Rates for consulting services, such as the conception and implementation of ERP systems, are more and more decreasing. These low day rates are jeopardizing the goal of economic viability and require new consulting concepts that allow for more favourable cost conditions with comparable quality. At this point, the firm sees the opportunity to offer consulting services more cost-effectively. For example, standardization and automation potentials are to be exploited by virtualization, where the price pressure at the consulting firm is greatest. This chance to safe costs and increase efficiency is a known core benefit of virtualization (Nissen et al. 2015).

Thirdly, the compliance conditions of employee assignment for consulting projects gained importance. To prevent complaints about compliance violations many clients are limiting the direct contact of consultants to their employees as well as the time that consultants can spent in their offices. Virtualization offers the consulting firm the possibility to provide consulting services remotely and thus fulfil the requirements of compliance. This opportunity has not been mentioned so far in the literature. It shows that virtualization can be a tool to abide regulatory requirements.

In addition to these opportunities, there are also threats that are expected to come along with the digital transformation.

First, the risk, that the standardization or automation could reduce the need for consultants and thus lowers the capacity utilization of employees. The consulting firm questions whether the current business model would support such automation and standardization, as it is strongly based on the billing of man-hours and man-days. This conforms to the barrier of "limited strategic fit" that was identified as an important prerequisite for any virtualization project in the market study of Nissen and Seifert (2016).

There is also the concern that virtual consulting services are more easily imitated by competitors. The fear is that the required standardization and modularization of consulting services in the course of virtualization may increase the service comparability and thus endangers the knowledge leadership of the company. Furthermore, the risk of weaker client-consultant-relationships is anticipated. These risks were mentioned in the literature before (Nissen et al. 2015). Moreover, the firm sees a risk that the majority of their consultants will not be convinced of the digital transformation and, thus, resistance to the virtualization of services will grow. Furthermore, it could happen that the efforts that come along with a broad virtualization initiative would not be endured. Consequently, the initiative could fail.

2.3.3 Maturity of the Digital Transformation in the Respective Company

Virtualization is initially operated in trivial form through the use of common communication media (e-mail, chat, Skype and telephone). Furthermore, a near-shore model is used, e.g. the processing of individual project work packages by teams in Romania. The firm also has a share point server, which provides internal information about the organization, departments, business processes, employees and projects. The consulting firm also produces podcasts and e-books for the distribution of knowledge to customers as well as employees. However, there are no forms of higher virtualization, such as a consulting shop, online coaching or self-service consulting. This observation is consistent with the results of the study on virtualization in the German consulting market by Nissen and Seifert (2016). There is also a lack of technology-based networking with clients and partners in the respective company.

The consulting firm can be classified on the second level of the maturity model suggested in the previous section. This seems to be a little behind the peer group, considering results of the study by Nissen and Seifert (2016), who indicated that virtualization is relatively well established in large consulting firms, particularly in the areas of IT and HR consulting. The discussed company offers consulting services from all fields of consulting, although the proportion of process and IT consulting services predominates. However, the fact that the consulting firm operates a digitization initiative and acknowledges the opportunities of virtualization is certainly due to its technology orientation, which is characteristic for this consulting firm. The company's size (>1500 employees/ >EUR 200 million turnover) also underlines the thesis that major consulting companies are more likely to engage in the virtualization process and continue to do so (Nissen and Seifert 2016).

In the study on the German consulting market (Nissen and Seifert 2016) it was also shown that virtualization predominantly takes place in the consulting project phases *preparation, problem analysis* and *project wrap-up*. At the consulting firm of this study, simple information and communications technology (ICT)s are used at every stage of the consultation process in order to work locally distributed. However, more complex technologies and solutions for the (partial) automatic analysis and solving of the client problems are not used. The degree of virtualization also depends heavily on the respective department and the individual project. For example, teams of application management or teams who are involved in the testing of software work more often with clients in a virtualized way.

2.3.4 Company-Wide Virtualization Initiative

A company-wide initiative (Fig. 3) was initiated to promote the digital transformation of the business model. An internal project, which is independent of actual consulting projects, was started. The virtualization initiative began with the development of six digital mission statements:

First, a cross-company network of data, processes and organizations should be created. Second, the productivity should be increased by focusing on the use of virtual consulting applications. Third, creative thinking should enable new approaches and solutions for internal and client-faced processes. Fourth, data that is generated within internal and client-faced processes (e.g. client master data, sales data or tickets of the internal helpdesk and employee-support) should be seen as a treasure and therefore be utilized. Fifth, digital offers should be created that lead to interest and participation among clients as well as employees. Sixth, cross-company collaboration and automated knowledge management should be enabled.

Then the project team started to develop key aspects of the digital transformation in order to create a common understanding:

- Through the application of innovative technologies, digitized, lean processes should be created.
- The introduction of a new collaboration model was targeted and the release of crowd mechanisms such as self-forming networks, virtual, constructive discussions and virtual collaboration were aimed for.
- The ultimate goal is a digital identity and culture—in this way, digital trends are to enter the company and actively shape the workplace of the future.
- The cooperation is to be networked and project-oriented.

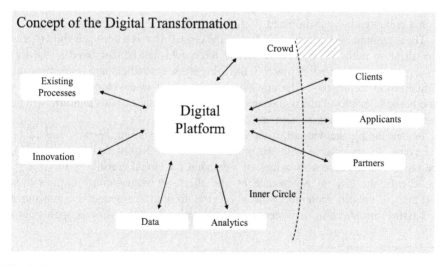

Fig. 3 Concept of the digital transformation initiative (inner circle = all employees of the consulting firm)

- Innovation should be realized more quickly, thus teams are built for fast, creative solutions.
- The individual employee is to be perceived and encouraged as an individual.
- New business models are to be developed, which are based on the linking and analysis of internal data, which should enable the uncovering of potential for improvement.

The objective here is to increase the efficiency and the profit—key benefits of the digital transformation that have been summarized in the morphological framework. From a technical perspective, customers, applicants and external partners are brought closer to the consulting company by means of a web-based IT-platform. An end-to-end networking with the customer is pursued. The consulting firm imagines that in the future, and with the support of a web-based IT-platform, it could be possible to directly connect employees of the client with consultants. Therefore, employees of the client organization and of the consulting firm would interact with each other on the shared platform, the digital workplace. Furthermore, not only people but also systems such as the client's CRM-system and dedicated applications of the consulting firm (e.g. Business Intelligence System) could be connected to exchange data in real-time and to enable the identification as well as processing of client-specific problems.

The ideas and input of the task force on digital work at the company were then presented and discussed at the company level. In the next phase, a company-wide identification of company digital use cases and end-to-end processes that could be relevant for the virtualization was begun. They identified use cases within the actual project procedure models, the recruiting process as well as other internal processes. Afterwards the conception of the digital governance and the priorities were in focus. Responsibilities were assigned to each digitalization use case.

Once that was done, the development of an evolving internal community for digital collaboration was initiated (Fig. 4).

These communities were a key part of the crowd[1] that is a core principle of this virtualization initiative. Further details of the crowd will be discussed in the following section. The next step within the initiative was to select and implement the virtualization technology. The consulting firm started to develop a concept of a web-based IT-platform that could support the crowd. Details of this platform will be present in the following section as well.

In developing the virtualization initiative further, various barriers had to be overcome. In accordance with the empirical study of Nissen and Seifert (2016), the biggest issues here were a lack of a demand for virtual consulting services by the clients, the lack of acceptance by the client for virtual consulting services and the still unclear economic benefits of virtualization. Consequently, to achieve successful virtualization, it is necessary to examine how the various applications

---

[1]Kittur et al. (2013) define crowd work as "[…] paid, online crowd work, which we define here as the performance of tasks online by distributed crowd workers who are financially compensated by requesters (individuals, groups, or organizations)."

Fig. 4 Screenshot of the starting page of the consulting firms share point with the different communities, including the digital transformation community

(digital cases) can have an economic importance and positive impact. As the consulting firm of this study is very experienced in the transformation of processes and the implementation of IT-systems, most of the knowledge necessary to create the digital consulting solutions is available. Knowledge that is missing is concerning the future demand and acceptance of the clients. Technical and organizational barriers are present in the form of parent group IT restrictions that affect most internal IT projects of the consulting firm.

The virtualization initiative, including the crowd work concept, focuses on the internal aspects of the digital transformation, such as optimizing internal processes like the project staffing or the company car management. At the moment, it only briefly addresses the virtualization of actual (client-faced) consulting services. Thus, innovating the integration of the client is at the moment not the key issue; consequently clients are not involved in the initiative. According to Nissen and

Seifert (2016), the transformation of client-faced process would require the integration of one or more clients in the initiative, which is currently not the case. Client-integration however is an important condition for the success of an innovative consulting service and should therefore be considered. The consulting firm is currently concentrating on the optimization and virtualization of the internal collaboration processes, discussed in the next section. For this, the consulting firm utilizes various social software and groupware as key technologies in the virtualization of its business processes and internal consulting organization (Martensen 2014). This of cause is just a small portion of the possible technologies of virtualization that have been summarized in the morphological framework.

For the internal project marketing of the virtualization initiative, so far five internal events called Quick Wins were conducted by the project leader and members of the project team. These short, internal information events often take place virtually (via video-conference) and in the evening. They can be joined by every employee of the consulting firm (both consultants and back-office staff). In this way, employees can be informed about the objectives, the members and the current progress of the virtualization initiative. This measure is especially important as it communicates the key aspects of the digital transformation project across the consulting firm. It helps to win consultants and other employees for the project or at least to activate them to share expectations and experiences in the context of the digital transformation.

2.4   Implementation of a Crowd Workplace

2.4.1   Overview

This section describes how a crowd workplace was implemented at the consulting firm of this case study. First, the general process of crowd working and the approach of this consulting firm are shown. Second, the technological perspective of the crowd working initiative is presented. Both sections cover the comparison of the real-life-situation and the theoretical aspects of the digital transformation.

2.4.2   Crowd Working Process

The first digital case of the consulting firm, which is implemented in the course of the virtualization initiative, is the *crowd workplace*. Crowd work is seen by the firm as an innovative working model in the age of digitalization. The company assumes that the Internet offers the chance to create a large pool of potential workers, that can be accessed quickly and for specific tasks. Novel Internet platforms enable companies like the one presented here to connect and distribute tasks to a large number of people or Internet users, the so-called *crowd*. Internet users act as workers and perform outsourced activities through their personal devices. The idea of the crowd is that innovative thoughts, information and solutions are collected and made available by people potentially from all over the world. The crowd members work as remote digital workers, crowded through the appropriate IT-platforms. Crowd Sourcers[2] search for crowd workers to solve their tasks. Compared to classical cooperation within a company, fundamental changes in communication and coordination processes, as well as the way in which tasks are handled occur. Examples of crowd platforms are Amazon Mechanical Turk,[3] Spreadshirt[4] or InnoCentive.[5]

For the consulting firm, the question arises as to which level internal activities can be virtualized and integrated into the crowd. In order to use the crowd, work packages must be defined in detail, described in detail and they usually need to be divided into small units. In addition, the crowd working process must be managed. The management process should, in the opinion of the consulting firm, specifically concern skill and project management. In Skill Management, the right knowledge, abilities, experiences and references have to be provided at the right time in the right place at the right price. In the discussed company, it is furthermore believed that projects should be available digitally and globally through valid standards for software development, project management, rollouts and accounting. Regardless of these preconditions, the consulting firm started to investigate more details of crowd working.

The crowd working process (Fig. 5) begins with the selection and specification of a corresponding task (phase 1). This is followed by the selection of the crowd workers, a mapping which is based on the respective skills, availability and costs (phase 2) of potential candidates. The next step involves the actual processing of the task and the solution to the problem (phase 3). In this step, for example, a constructive competition to find the best solution is initiated, thus using gamification to foster better results. In the subsequent phase, the individual solutions are either compared with one another and the best solution is selected or solutions are combined and a new and appropriate solution is created (phase 4). The final phase of the crowd working process includes the completion of the assignment (phase 5).

---

[2]Leimeister et al. 2015 define crowd sourcing as follows: "*In crowdsourcing, a crowd sourcer who can be a business, organization, group or individual, proposes an open call to an undefined set of potential contributors (crowdsources or crowd workers). These crowd workers, who can be individuals, formal or informal groups, organizations or companies, will take over the task. The following interaction process takes place via IT-supported crowdsourcing platforms. The performance of crowdsourcing lies in the aggregation of multitude knowledge and resources of different and independent contributors as well as in the possibilities of decomposition, distribution, parallelization, standardization and automation as well as subsequent aggregation of partial tasks.*"

[3]https://www.mturk.com/mturk/welcome (last visit 27-April-2017).

[4]https://www.spreadshirt.de/ (last visit 27-April-2017).

[5]https://www.innocentive.com/ (last visit 27-April-2017).

Crowd Work Process

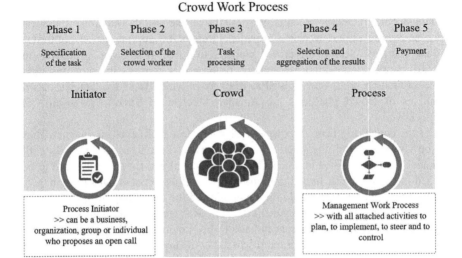

Fig. 5 The crowd working process as a part of the digital transformation concept

With the introduction of crowd working and virtual collaboration, the consulting firm is confronted with both opportunities and risks. Benefits that are expected to occur for the crowd sourcer (consulting provider), are:

- *Access to an enormous knowledge pool,*
- *The acquisition of innovative solutions,*
- *Faster solving of task,*
- *Lower costs,*
- *Increase in flexibility and scalability by demand-oriented use,*
- *Concentration on core competencies,*
- *Increase of acceptance in the market through integration of (potential clients) in the problem-solving process.*

For the crowd worker (which, in the first step, would be a consultant and in a later phase, could be an external partner or a designated employee of the client) the following benefits may arise:

- *Increased motivation as crowd workers can focus on the tasks that match their personal profile most,*
- *The chance to work on different tasks with a greater task variety,*
- *More autonomy with respect to the individual tasks,*
- *Higher flexibility as tasks can be accepted or declined,*
- *Easier communication between crowd workers through the shared platform.*

The comparison of these chances and the opportunities that have been identified for the virtualization of consulting delivers a clear consensus. However, the crowd working principle comes with risks that need to be considered too. In respect to the crowd sourcer, the following risks have been identified:

- *Additional effort as tasks need to be precisely defined in order to assign them in the crowd,*
- *The difficulty to calculate the overall costs of the crowd working,*
- *The danger of losing control over the process,*
- *The effort to create incentive structures,*
- *A certain risk to make confidential details of the consulting task publically available,*
- *The danger of losing important know-how to external crowd workers,*
- *The risk of resistance of the internal staff.*

For the crowd worker, the following risks should be considered:

- *A risk of lower income as crowd workers from low-income countries compete,*
- *An intensive competition with other crowd workers,*
- *The small scope of individual tasks that makes it difficult to see the value of one's own contribution,*
- *The danger of continuous surveillance through the crowd platform,*
- *Problems associated with the legal framework (labour law questions).*

Some risks of crowd working coincide with risks of virtualization in general that have been summarized in the morphological framework. Together with the previously mentioned overlap of the benefits, this emphasises the relevance of crowd working for the digital transformation of consulting. Crowd working can be a concept that covers various aspects of virtualization, such as standardization, automation and virtual collaboration. Nevertheless, the crowd work concept as well as the digital transformation itself, are very demanding in terms of the use of technology and the definition of processes as well as their management and continual improvement. Whether crowd working is a promising approach or not, may be systematically analyzed as it is being proposed in the chapter on evaluating the virtualizability of consulting processes by Nissen and Seifert (2017) in this volume. Nevertheless, the authors assume that the evaluation process needs to be adapted in order to fit to this special crowd-use case. So maybe additional or different evaluation criteria will be needed.

To summarize, crowd working seems to be an interesting "variant" of virtualization that focusses on the integration of a vast group of qualified people, that can be part of the same organization but may also be external, and potentially from all parts of the world.

2.4.3 Crowd Working Platform

The consulting firm decided to put more effort in the crowd work concept and to develop a digital platform to enable crowd work and support the digital

High Level Architecture

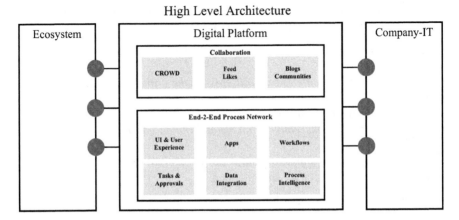

Fig. 6 High-level architecture of the digital crowd platform (UI = user interface)

transformation of its organization. This section summarizes the implementation project of the digital platform[6] (Fig. 6).

At first, the business requirements for the platform were defined by members of the virtualization initiative and members of the internal IT-department. Additionally, requirements were gathered through discussions of employees that took place in the internal community.

One major requirement stated that the future platform should cover the complete crowd working process as well as the virtualized internal processes of the consulting firm. Moreover, the data that will be created conducting those processes should be captured permanently and stored for further analysis. Redundant data storage should be avoided in order to create a seamless data profile of the workflows and processes that happen in the consulting firm. Furthermore, the platform should offer an appealing user interface that is accessible from any device at any time. The platform should be developed with a focus on usability and strategy alignment. Moreover, the platform should be flexible enough to grow incrementally. It should be "intelligent" in the sense that it informs the crowd workers proactively about new tasks based on data processing. In order to make most of the platform and the process, data should be stored along all process phases. The target here is to be able to create future use cases based on new insights that can be derived from the data. The platform should furthermore support the development of a community, so people can communicate and collaborate across the different departments of the consulting firm in the first step. Later it could be possible to open

---

[6]Crowdsourcing platforms take over the IT-supported coordination of crowdsourcing initiatives and bring together the crowd sourcer with the crowd (Leimeister et al. 2016; Martin et al. 2008). They thus represent the framework and stage for crowdsourcing activities. A distinction can be made between company-owned and external platforms (Leimeister et al. 2016).

the communities or to create new opportunities for clients and partners. Thus, the borders of the consulting firm could be crossed by the use of one shared virtual workplace.

If possible, the platform should enable the use of gamification. So competitions and creative challenges could be realized in order to find the best solution for any given problem. Predictive analyses that could increase the efficiency and overall benefit of the internal organization should be another feature of the future digital platform.

By fulfilling these key requirements, the consulting firm hopes to create certain benefits. These include, in particular, a cost reduction and optimization, as already described in the beginning of this paper. An increase in efficiency and the shaping of a competitive advantage are also targets of the consulting firm. Furthermore, the consulting firm expects to improve the overall quality of internal and external processes as well as to minimize risks that can occur in consulting services. This means that the consulting firm aims precisely at the opportunities that were identified in the survey on the expectations of consultants towards virtualization in the German consulting market (Nissen and Seifert 2015). The question then arises as to how the consulting firm addresses the risks of virtualization and the risks of implementing such a platform. Since this is a virtualization project that predominantly focusses on the internal processes and the internal use of crowd working, client-specific risks can initially be neglected. Risks that should be taken into account are primarily risks relating to the quality of communication, collaboration and coordination (Nissen and Seifert 2015). Those risks were not explicitly named by the consulting firm in the context of the workplace. However, the consulting firm investigated the risks of crowding and also identified risks through a SWOT analysis. The identified risks are in line with the virtualization risks already presented in Nissen and Seifert (2015).

To ensure the quality of the digital platform, the consulting firm intends to monitor and automatically measure process performance on the platform. For this purpose, the project team created a set of process-related KPIs. To evaluate the quality of the platform and its processes, one might refer to the quality criteria suggested by Nissen and Seifert (2015) for virtual consulting services (see the morphological framework in the beginning of this contribution). Although these criteria aim at client-faced processes, they can also serve as a point of orientation for the quality-assessment of internal processes on this platform.

Before technically implementing the digital platform, the technical requirements were defined and the existing application systems landscape of the firm was analyzed. The next step was to select a technology that is suitable to serve as a starting point for the platform development. Within the requirements definition, the following key factors for the evaluation of possible technologies for the platform emerged:

- *The possibility to integrate both Microsoft SharePoint and SAP-systems (CRM, ERP and BI),*
- *The possibility to displace current Excel-based solutions,*
- *The chance to implement true end-to-end-processes.*

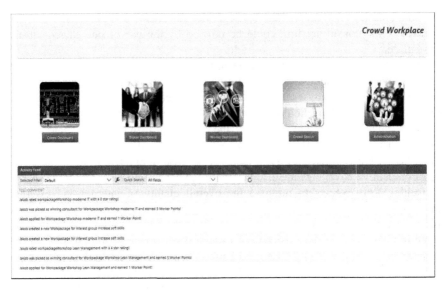

Fig. 7 Screenshot of the platform prototype with the crowd workplace

Thereafter, possible integration points were defined and available platforms were evaluated. Solutions considered were SAP- or IBM-based. Moreover, products of platform providers like K2 and Nintex were also included in the evaluation process. Finally, a K2-low-code[7]-platform was selected. The decisive criteria were:

- *Process-focus of the tool,*
- *Chance to connect the SAP-landscape,*
- *Good Microsoft SharePoint integration,*
- *High development speed,*
- *Simple governance,*
- *Low preparation time,*
- *Low complexity and maintainability,*
- *Good mobile support.*

Within a short programming session, a first prototype was implemented within a demo-environment to emphasize the appropriateness of the solution (Fig. 7). After the decision was taken in favour of the low-code platform, the first training courses were carried out to get to know the platform and its' basic components. The next step was to install the system, provide the infrastructure and configure the

---

[7]Rymer et al. (2016) define low-code platforms as follows: "*Platforms enable rapid delivery of business applications with a minimum of hand-coding and minimal upfront investment in setup, training and deployment.*" Key features of the low-code approach are: a large number of development and design tools are provided, which drastically reduce programming effort; processes and standards of software development are fully supported from the outset; access to prototypes and experimental platforms is comprehensive and often free of charge.

development and production system. This was followed by the integration of the corporate share point. The definition of the platform concept followed, including the clarification of platform responsibilities, the backup strategy of the system, the definition of central data objects and most important, the integration of the company-specific processes.

2.4.4 Outlook

The implementation of the crowd workplace is going on after the successful installation of the platform environment in February 2017. Furthermore, the responsibilities for the platform from business and technical perspective have been clarified. Now, one major target is the integration of existing systems like a SAP ERP and CRM. Additionally, first trainings for the core team in key software features were conducted. Moreover, the operation manual was created. While the technical tasks are being completed, the digital transformation as well as the digital platform community progresses. The community wishes to exchange more ideas and experience that can shape the future platform and crowd. The next phase in the project targets the implementation of the first productive version of the platform with the first actual virtualized internal process. The first use case that is going to be implemented within the crowd workplace is the *Company Car Cockpit*. The Company Car Cockpit covers the management of company car orders and other requests that are connected to the employees' cars. Further internal processes like the staffing and sourcing process or processes that cover the activity reporting will follow.

3 Conclusions, Limitations, and Perspectives

The example of a German consulting firm illustrated the importance of virtualization in the majority of German consulting firms (Nissen and Seifert 2016). The case also underlined that virtualization is a concept that affects virtually all processes and departments of a consulting firm. The discussed consulting firm is on the verge to a higher level of virtualization. In order to push the digitalization of the organization, principles of crowd working are used and a digital platform for the virtualization and automation of internal processes is currently being implemented with a productive solution to be expected in the middle of 2017. It remains exciting to see how far the particular consulting firm investigated here is driving virtualization and how innovative and how much virtualized the future organization will be.

The transparency of our case study is limited, as the documents that were sources for the data analysis are not to be made publically available. Consequently, details of the analysed information cannot be published. Additionally, these documents were inspected only by the first author, which may have introduced a certain interpretation bias.

Generally, acknowledged weaknesses and challenges of the case study method are insufficient structure and reliability, insufficient transparency, objectivity and generalizability, and a high effort in relation to a questionable relevance (Yin 2014; Eisenhardt 1989). Consequently, the presented results should be generalized with care.

Nevertheless, the authors believe that the findings can be tentatively applied to other consulting firms, especially consulting firms of roughly the same size and the same consulting sector. Service providers of different fields as well as smaller consulting firms may show different results when studied.

The discussed case gave insights into the digital transformation at a Management- and IT-Consulting firm (Fig. 8). It showed how a consulting firm defined its vision of a 'digital consulting firm' and that virtualization should affect not only the core process of consulting. Thus, the case study can serve as an impulse for other consulting firms to consider not only the consulting process itself but also the vast amount of internal, back-office processes behind the value chain of a consulting firm. Virtualization here would contribute to a substantial efficiency improvement and, thus, offer great economic potential. Additionally, the virtualization of internal processes can help to prepare the digital transformation of the actual consulting processes.

Focusing on internal processes, as presented in the case study, should not discourage consulting firms from integrating clients into the transformation process. For the importance and acceptance of the virtualization project in the consulting

Key Insights of the Case Study

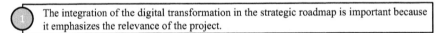

1. The integration of the digital transformation in the strategic roadmap is important because it emphasizes the relevance of the project.

2. Setting up a company-wide digital transformation initiative requires resources from almost all departments of the consulting organization (e.g. HR department).

3. Setting up a distinct project organization helps allocating the necessary resources and the realization of the projects goals.

4. Crowd work requires the digital transformation, at the same time, the digital transformation benefits from knowledge and experiences that are created in crowd work.

5. Innovative concepts like crowd work require a change in thinking as well as innovative and integrated technological solutions.

6. The greatest barriers as well as promoters of the digital transformation and virtualization of consulting processes are the clients.

7. Virtual collaboration and communities as well as project marketing measures can help to decrease internal barriers.

Fig. 8 Key insights of the case study

firm, the involvement of a suitable client can be of major importance. The results of the case study suggest that business consultants should not shy away from building their own virtualization projects and bundle as much capacity as possible when organizing such projects—regardless of the often highly prioritized day-to-day business.

It is clearly of paramount importance to establish clear roles and responsibilities as well as primary contacts in the course of a digital transformation initiative. Moreover, a strategic vision how digitalization will amend the existing business model is called for. As virtually all processes are affected by the digital transformation, it also seems sensible to create a network that includes experts from the classic consulting business as well as experts from internal, non-customer-faced processes. In this way, a corresponding knowledge transfer between internal and client-faced, as well as classical and virtual areas of the organization can be ensured. Consulting firms should communicate widely and openly about objectives and procedures of digital transformation, its components, opportunities and threats, and risk-minimizing measures in order to counter possible internal barriers, and to increase the willingness to cooperate in virtualization projects.

In view of the authors, two major implications follow from our case study. First, the case offers some profound insight into the digital transformation of a large management and IT consulting organization. This will hopefully result in new impulses for ongoing and future research projects. Practitioners now have the opportunity to compare their own progress in digital transformation with the progress described in the presented organization. Nevertheless, the relevance as well as the external validity of the case study could be enhanced by including more than one consulting firm in the analysis as well as more researchers (Yin 2014).

With regard to research question one and the digital transformation in consulting, the authors argue that the morphological framework serves as a proper structure for the analysis of a real-life virtualization initiative. Building on existing knowledge about digital transformation this way, supports the assessment and planning of digital transformation initiatives in consulting. However, in determining the different aspects and characteristics of the morphological box a degree of subjectivity is present. But as the content of the framework is a compilation of characteristics and theoretical considerations presented in the literature, the appropriateness for the current research seems given.

What is missing is a better understanding of the internal processes and how the digital transformation will affect these processes and parts of the consulting organization. For consulting researchers our contribution and case study offers many starting points for further investigation. For instance, it appears worthwhile to analyze whether opportunities and threats identified in the literature for the digital transformation of consulting actually materialize in practice, and how consulting providers cope with the risks.

The case study supports the presented virtualization maturity model in consulting. Although the individual situation of a consulting firm may not fit 100% to one of the four levels, the model helps to characterize the situation in a specific firm. Further research could investigate how a consulting firm moves from one level to the next and why maybe the fourth and highest level, for some companies, is not desirable.

The case study showed that internal processes are as much a part of the digital transformation as the actual consulting and sales processes. Future research projects could explore which sequence is the most favourable, when transforming a consulting firm. Is it better to first virtualize the internal and then the external processes or vice versa? We also suggest analyzing more case studies of digital transformation in consulting with providers of varying size, consulting focus and regional mapping. As a consequence, our understanding will be elevated and transformation projects in practice can benefit from the knowledge that is thus generated.

References

Eisenhardt KM (1989) Building theories from case study research. Acad Manag Rev 14(4): 532–550

Gassmann O (1999) Praxisnähe mit Fallstudienforschung. Wissenschaftsmanagement 5(3):11–16

Kittur A, Nickerson JV, Bernstein M, Gerber E, Shaw A, Zimmerman J, Horton J (2013) The future of crowd work. In: Proceedings of the 2013 conference on computer supported cooperative work. ACM, pp 1301–1318

Leimeister JM, Zogaj S, Durward D, Blohm I (2015) Crowdsourcing und Crowd Work – Neue Formen digitaler Arbeit. In: Bullinger A (ed) Mensch 2020 – transdisziplinäre Perspektiven. Chemnitz, pp 119–124

Leimeister JM, Zogaj S, Durward D, Blohm I (2016) Systematisierung und Analyse von Crowd-Sourcing-Anbietern und Crowd-Work-Projekten. Study der Hans-Böckler-Stiftung

Martensen M (2014) Einsatz von Social Software durch Unternehmensberater: Akzeptanz, Präferenzen. Nutzungsarten, Springer, Wiesbaden

Martin N, Lessmann S, Voß S (2008) Crowdsourcing: Systematisierung praktischer Ausprägungen und verwandter Konzepte. Proc. MKWI 2008. GITO, Berlin, pp 273–274

Nissen V (ed) (2007) Consulting Research. Unternehmensberatung aus wissenschaftlicher Perspektive, DUV, Wiesbaden

Nissen V, Seifert H (2015) Virtualization of Consulting – Benefits, Risks and a Suggested Decision Process. In: Pavlou P, Saunders C (eds) Proceedings of AMCIS 2015, vol. 2, Puerto Rico, pp 1380–1391

Nissen V, Seifert H (2016) Virtualisierung in der Unternehmensberatung. Eine Studie im deutschen Beratungsmarkt, BDU, Bonn

Nissen V, Seifert H (2017) Evaluating the virtualization potential of consulting services. In this volume

Nissen V, Seifert H, Blumenstein M (2015) Virtualisierung von Beratungsleistungen: Qualitätsanforderungen, Chancen und Risiken der digitalen Transformation in der Unternehmensberatung aus der Klientenperspektive. In: Deelmann T, Ockel DM (eds) Handbuch der Unternehmensberatung, 25th edn. Erich Schmidt Verlag, Berlin

Rymer JR, Richardson C, Mines Ch, Tajima C (2016) The Forrester wave: low-code-development platforms. The 14 providers that matter the most and how they stack up. Forrester

Werth D, Greff T, Scheer AW (2016) Consulting 4.0 - Die Digitalisierung der Unternehmensberatung. HMD Praxis der Wirtschaftsinformatik 53(1):55–70

Yin RK (2014) Case study research: design and methods, 5th edn. SAGE Publications, Inc., Thousand Oaks

Author Biographies

Henry Seifert is a graduate engineer for media technology and since 2011 working as a management consultant. His main focus is on the automotive industry and artificial intelligence, analytics, process optimization and requirements management. He works in projects in the area of sales and after sales processes as well as professional learning. As doctoral candidate at the Group for Information Systems Engineering in Services at Technische Universität Ilmenau, he examines the digital transformation in the consulting industry. The goal of his dissertation is to demonstrate the opportunities and limitations of virtualization, as well as the design of artifacts that enable the realization of virtual consulting services.

Volker Nissen holds the Chair of Information Systems Engineering in Services at Technische Universität Ilmenau, Germany, since 2005. Prior to this, he pursued a consulting career, including positions as manager at IDS Scheer AG, director at DHC GmbH, and CEO of NISSCON Ltd., Germany. In 1994 he received a PhD degree in Economic Sciences with distinction from the University of Goettingen, Germany. His current research interests include the digital transformation of the consulting industry, the management of IT-agility, metaheuristic optimization, and process acceptance research. He is author and editor of 19 books and some 200 other publications, including papers in Business & Information Systems Engineering, Information Systems Frontiers, IEEE Transactions on EC, IEEE Transactions on NN, and Annals of OR.

A Reasoning Based Knowledge Model for Business Process Analysis

Anne Füßl, Franz Felix Füßl, Volker Nissen and Detlef Streitferdt

Abstract The article presents the ontology based knowledge model iKnow that can automatically draw conclusions and integrate aspects of machine learning. Due to the knowledge-intensive nature of the consulting industry, the abstract reasoning based knowledge model can be used specifically for knowledge processing and decision support within a consulting project. There is a multitude of potential applications for iKnow in the realm of consulting. Business process analysis was chosen as a pilot application, since many consulting projects in the problem analysis and problem solving phase, require a comprehensive knowledge of business processes. In this paper it is outlined how iKnow can be used for an automated analysis of business process models. We describe the basic structure of the knowledge model as a business process analyzing tool and present a suitable demonstration. It is worth mentioning that iKnow does not necessarily rely on log-files or other data input from process-supporting IT-systems. In this way, and through the generality of its ontology based structure and reasoning capabilities, it is far more broadly applicable than current process mining solutions.

A. Füßl (✉) · V. Nissen · D. Streitferdt
Technische Universität Ilmenau, Ilmenau, Germany
e-mail: anne.fuessl@tu-ilmenau.de

V. Nissen
e-mail: volker.nissen@tu-ilmenau.de

D. Streitferdt
e-mail: detlef.streitferdt@tu-ilmenau.de

F. F. Füßl
iTech Solutions—Internet Technology Franz Felix Füßl, Geschwenda, Germany
e-mail: franz.fuessl@itech-solutions.de

© Springer International Publishing AG 2018
V. Nissen (ed.), *Digital Transformation of the Consulting Industry*,
Progress in IS, https://doi.org/10.1007/978-3-319-70491-3_13

1 Motivation of iKnow Using in the Consulting Industry

iKnow is an abstract model for the application of inference-capable ontologies and is intended to be used for information technology (IT)-supported decision-making (Füßl 2016). In general, it aims to acquire, to structure and to visualize knowledge for deductive reasoning under the influence of variable factors using machine learning approaches. Based on this premise, iKnow is considered as a knowledge-based tool for supporting consulting services, especially during the problem analysis and problem solving phases.

The present paper will especially examine how iKnow can be used for the analysis of business processes. For this purpose, the authors are guided by the design oriented research approach and use the design science research methodology of Peffers et al. (2007). For the conceptual design of iKnow as a business process analyzing tool, iKnow has to be understood in a holistic way. Furthermore, we describe its method of operation through an illustrative example. On the basis of the principal structure of iKnow, the design concept of iKnow as business process analyzing tool is subsequently developed and demonstrated.

The article is structured in five parts. Following the research motivation, essential definitions concerning consulting projects as well as fundamentals about process analysis are given. Section three describes the abstract model iKnow with its basic elements, deductive reasoning algorithms and machine learning approaches. An illustrative use case, choosing the best technology for a specific application situation, is also presented. Thereafter, the use of iKnow as a business process analyzing tool is highlighted. For this purpose, preliminary considerations of the tool, the conceptual approach and its practical demonstration are described. The paper concludes with some reflections and avenues for continued research.

2 Terms and Definitions

2.1 Consulting Project

For the concept to be developed the present paper will only consider expert consulting (based on the consulting concept of Jeschke (2004) and Walger (1995)) and its procedure of a consulting project. Based on (Kubr 2005) the typical consulting process during a consulting project can be structured into six phases. The following Fig. 1 shows these six phases.

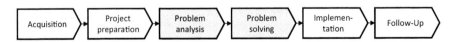

Fig. 1 Typical process phases during a consulting project

This paper focuses on the grey part in Fig. 1, the problem analysis as well as the problem solving phase, where collecting and analyzing data represents the main task at this stage. The objective of the problem analysis phase is to investigate the problem handled and to identify the issues that are causing and influencing the problem (Kubr 2005; Jeschke 2004). That requires a preparation of all information and data that are involved in the current state. For this purpose, in addition to data analyzing approaches, process analysis is used for determining information and knowledge coherences that are connected to the existing problem (Emrany and Boßlet 2001; Gadatsch 2008). In the following section, process analysis will be described in more detail.

2.2 Process Analysis

In general, process analysis is the systematic investigation of processes and the decomposition into its parts in order to gain an understanding of the process and to recognize weak points and potential for improvement (Miebach 2009). There are different types of processes to be analyzed. With regard to the present article, business processes will be considered. According to Gadatsch (2008) a business process is a goal-oriented, chronological sequence of tasks which can be carried out by several organizations or organizational units using information and communication technologies. It is used to generate services according to the given process objectives derived from the company strategy. Generally, processes consist of activities that lead to output through the processing of input and contribute to business value creation (Palleduhn and Neuendorf 2013).

The analysis of business processes includes the documentation respectively the modeling, analyzing and improvement of a current state (Gadatsch 2008). The starting point is the documentation and modeling of the actual as-is business processes, including the sequence of activities, roles and responsibilities, related documents and systems etc. For modeling the current state, a formal detailed description is required. Based on ARIS[1] (Architecture of Integrated Information Systems) there are two main notations for modeling business processes: with the aid of EPC (Event-driven Process Chain) and BPMN (Business Process Model and Notation). Subsequently the processes are subjected to an analysis with regard to their effectiveness and efficiency, also taking into account the business process objectives derived from the business strategy. For instance, unproductive or superfluous tasks or business processes, unnecessary loops, inadequate roles and responsibilities, suboptimal IT-support, and similar deficiencies will be identified with the aim to improve and optimize the existing business processes. Possible indicators that can be used to identify such unproductive parts and weaknesses in a

---

[1]The ARIS concept is process-oriented and recommends the perception of operational reality as a goal-oriented cooperation of business processes (Staud 2006).

business process can be e.g. capacity utilization, lead times or process costs. For the operational identification of such weaknesses and execution of the process improvement, an individual elaboration of an analyzing checklist is recommended by Staud (2006) and Gadatsch (2008).

With each business process model in form of an EPC or BPMN, information and knowledge constructs of a current state or a problem situation are formally described. Information systems and tailored methods are available for the documentation and analysis of the current process state in the course of a consulting project. A prominent example is process mining. This technique allows reconstructing and analyzing business processes based on digital traces in IT-systems (van der Aalst 2016). The individual steps of the process stored in the systems are merged and the process as a whole is visualized. This approach aims to highlight implicit, hidden process characteristics that are contained in data. However, process mining is only applicable if log-data on the respective processes does exist. Another approach is business process simulation for assessing the dynamic behavior of processes (Jochem and Balzert 2010). This results in findings that lead to decisions on improved procedures in the interaction of people, equipment, materials and information. The results of business process simulation comprise quantitative time-based and cost-related data about the process execution. In both approaches, soft influencing variables, such as customer satisfaction or employee motivation, as well as implicit process knowledge of the interacting people cannot be considered. The analysis can only be carried out on the basis of existing data of IT-systems or process models. Moreover, there is currently little support in the interpretation of results or the decision for process improvements.

In order to overcome these drawbacks, and enrich automated process analysis with context-related information as well as expert knowledge, the AI-based knowledge model *iKnow* is presented in the next section of this contribution.

3   The Abstract Knowledge Model iKnow[2]

3.1   *Elements and Associations*

The model can be described as a four-level architecture. These levels result from an input, a data transfer, an information processing and an abstraction layer. They represent different levels of content, whereby knowledge can be stored and processed in different depths of detail (Fig. 2).

Feature and *Data Source* elements serve as application layers for the communication with users or for integration of content, such as process models. *Data Sources* capture elementary facts through a simple request-response principle.

---

[2]The description of the abstract model iKnow in the Sects. 3.1, 3.2, 3.3 and 3.4 bases on the Ph.D. thesis in Füßl (2016).

 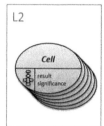 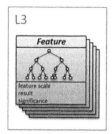 

Fig. 2 Overview of iKnow elements (Füßl 2016)

In this way, for example, the current state of a project environment can be recorded. *Data Source* elements can transfer various data into the model through user queries, measuring instruments or sensors. Each *Feature* can be understood as an influencing variable to a particular situation. Examples are project budget, personal motivation or experience with a process model.

A *Feature* is associated with at least one *Cell* (or *Item*). According to Hasenkamp and Roßbach (1998), *Cells* could be understood as semantic building blocks and, according to Landauer (1998), as context blocks. They collect data by analyzing their associations and convert this data into information. *Cells* represent the basis for generating knowledge. By linking to each other, they can specifically evaluate adjacent *Features* and access information from other *Cells* to include them in their own results.

The information stored in *Cells* is used by so-called *Items*. Each *Item* contains an abstract component, which have to be examined in detail how they effect for example the success of a consulting project. They can be used in various project sections and to accomplish various tasks. For example, "current process" can be symbolized as an *Item*. It is an essential part of "process management" and necessary to successfully complete consulting projects with focus on process optimization.

For a better understanding of what *Items* and *Cells* are: *Items* are used as a descriptive point of view on the knowledge stored in a model, while *Cells* build a crucial viewpoint with concrete instances. *Cells* therefore refer to something concrete, where *Items* represent something general, abstract or classifying.

In order to integrate tasks, functions or actions into a knowledge base, the model provides so-called *Activities*. In the first place, they integrate executable actions, which can be performed by a role, an individual or a subject. *Activities* embody an implicit behavioral pattern. They can become subject of inference. In addition, they could be provided with explicit behavioral patterns to automate specific functions. Explicit behavioral patterns can contain for example circuit sequences, business processes, algorithms, motion sequences or the initialization of measurement and sensor techniques. *Activities* can be classified as active or passive, which depends strongly on the perception of a modeler (mental model). *Speak* (active) is uniquely connected with a certain behavioral pattern in every human being, which offers little

Fig. 3 Combinings (adapted from Füßl 2016)

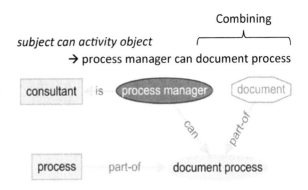

scope for interpretation. *Organize* (passive), on the other hand, may be associated with different behavior depending on the subject.

In contrast combining *organize* with additional information, such as *organize requirements*, is connected to a (largely) common mental model. Therefore, linking an object to a passive activity usually leads to information enrichment. For this purpose the model provides so-called *Combinings*. One *Combining* is a composition of at least two elements: for example, the linking of a passive activity to an object. It is also possible to link a property to a subject or to connect properties and objects.

Figure 3 illustrates usage of *Combinings*, using the example of the ability of a process manager to document processes. There are two *Items* ("consultant", "process"), a *Cell* ("process manager"), an *Activity* ("document") and a *Combining* ("document process"). If Fig. 3 were to be formulated in natural language, this would be as follows: Process manager is a consultant. Process manager can document process.

Ontologies are a form of knowledge representation and a part of artificial intelligence. They offer the possibility to create associations between terminologies (Arp et al. 2015; Brewster and Wilks 2004). Task of these relations is the description of contexts. They can be defined in any way. Through this free definition of relations, a uniform traversing on paths within the ontology graph to draw complex conclusions in a simple way is made more difficult. Reason for this is the lack of formalization in the creation of concepts. To circumvent this drawback, iKnow uses a number of predefined connection types, referred to as association classes. In contrast to conventional ontologies, where contexts with activity characteristics are expressed by edges, this model uses nodes to represent this knowledge. In this way, the integration of inference algorithms, for example for deduction, can be much simplified. The following sections describe the current association classes in more detail, referring to examples of their application.

The *Is* association (Fig. 4a) is used to integrate inheritance structures, classifications or instances into the model. For example, the relationship between "MS Visio" and "Software" could be illustrated with an *Is* association: "MS Visio is Software".

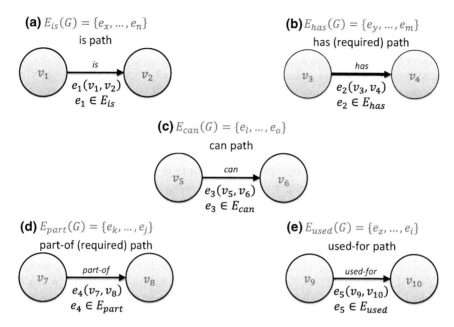

Fig. 4 Main association classes (Füßl et al. 2015)

The *Has* association (Fig. 4b) is used to model properties, for specifying elements more precisely and assign attributes or characteristics to them. For example, each software has a price and an installation type.

Figure 4d represents another association class, the *Part-Of* association. This class is used to model part-whole relationships. In contrast to the *Has* association, in which the linked elements can exist individually, *Part-Of* illustrates a binding relationship. Consequently, v_7 can exist only if v_8 exists. An example is the partial whole relationship between display and notebook: "Display is part-of Notebook".

The *Can* association (Fig. 4c) aims at modeling the capabilities of an object or subject and is the most common link type between *Cells* and *Activities* or *Combinings*. This class can, for example, assign certain tasks to roles, different qualifications to subjects, or functions and skills to objects, for example: "Human can think.", "Light can light up.", "Google can search.", "Product owner can prioritize requirements".

The last main association class is the *Used-For* association. It is used to make *Activities* of certain objects or subjects executable. The relationship between the two elements in Fig. 4e can be formulated as: element v_9 can be used to activate or execute element v_{10}, for example "MS Word is used-for Text Processing".

It is possible to extend the model by further types of associations. To integrate more complex knowledge structures, five further types of associations have been found, which are not addressed in this paper.

3.2   Constraints and Deductive Element Pruning

In order to integrate reasoning into an ontology, different approaches exist. Most are based on a so-called reasoner, which uses axioms and other calculation bases to provide problem solutions (Fernández-López et al. 1997). In this model as well, inferences should be drawn on the basis of knowledge contained in the model. Therefore, each node has a specific result, which can require its neighbor elements. To create such a result a boolean *Result Expression* has to be calculated, composed of so called *Negative* and *Positive Constraints*. Goal of integrating constraints is to make the knowledge graph more efficient by performing the processing of elements intelligently and thus deriving results with a smaller number of deduction steps. Processing of an element is only necessary if all its constraints are fulfilled.

Constraints can be understood as bounds, which are used to exclude a path within the knowledge graph from the set of all paths. If just one *Negative Constraint* of an element is true, the element can be excluded from the set of all nodes relevant for a possible deduction. The difference to *Positive Constraints* lies in the linking of the expressions: Even a single fulfillment of a *Negative Constraint* results in the negation (false) of the element. In contrast, all *Positive Constraints* must be fulfilled to turn the result of the node to true. As negation of the last sentence just one non-fulfillment of a *Positive Constraint* leads to a negation of the element.

This process of node reduction is referred to as *Deductive Reasoning Element Pruning* (DREP). Element pruning is a term known from the literature, for example for selection algorithms (Dor and Zwick 1999; Dor 1995; Anand and Gupta 1998), or from clustering methods as in (Bisson et al. 2000) or (Fernandes and García 2012). DREP is therefore an improvement measure during the deduction, which can reduce the number of residue elements to be traversed on the basis of *Constraints*.

Generating results depends on the class of the element whose result is required. Additional conditions defined by *Negative* or *Positive Constraints* also affect the generation of results. The following listing contains the core methodologies used to generate results:

- Results of *Items* and *Cells* are boolean values (true, false, 0, 1) or empty.
- *Items* are true if at least one of the adjacent *Is*-predecessors is true.
- Boolean expressions are used to create results of elements. These *Result Expressions* depend on the *Negative* and *Positive Constraints* assigned to the element.
- Thus, elements are true if the result of each *Negative Constraint* successor is false and the result of each *Positive Constraint* successor is true.
- Furthermore, the result of an input *Feature* can be any possible input value. A choice *Feature* can set the result of each adjacent *Cell*, as long as it is *Part-Of*-predecessor to this *Feature*.
- *Questions*, as a special form of a *Data Source* elements, have no result. They are only used to output a questionnaire in order to be able to query user inputs more precisely.

3.3 Deductive Reasoning

The knowledge base consists of elements which must be combined in a meaningful way to derive knowledge. There are information fragments of different abstraction depths, data and association types. In addition, the basic architecture provides two views on the knowledge system: a descriptive view that can generate knowledge independently of the viewer, and a crucial view that generates knowledge based on external influences. It is also possible to mix the two views in order to uniquely identify descriptive elements under the influence of different parameters. In order to be able to derive knowledge using views and elements, different algorithm-based deductions are necessary. The different association and element classes of the model form the basis for these deductive reasoning algorithms. The goal is to be able to derive conclusions from given facts which relate specifically to a sought set of elements and depend on variable influencing factors. For example the influence of employee motivation on project success.

The following generalized problems can be derived from the objectives of the model and the questions contained therein:

(1) Is it an object/subject of a given variety?
(2) What kind of object/subject is it?
(3) What does a certain object/subject consist of?
(4) What are the characteristics of a certain object/subject?
(5) Find elements of a particular class to fulfill a given purpose!

While questions (2–5) must include at least one element in their answer, the answer to question (1) leads to a simple yes or no, which makes the deductive reasoning algorithm easy. The algorithm for clarifying problem type (1) is called *Isn't-It?* and corresponds to the solution of a simple decision-making problem. Concrete examples are: "Is it Scrum?", "Is it a successful consulting project?" or "Is Mrs. Smith a project management expert?".

As mentioned above, the *Isn't-It?* algorithm can be described as a simple decision-making process by which the result of the searched element is generated and checked to true or false, taking into account all influences which are present on the result path.

While the *Isn't-It?* algorithm tests an element for its pure existence, the *Kind-Of?* algorithm also finds instances of an element. This is intended to answer problem (2): "What kind of object/subject is it?". Examples include "Who is an experienced process manager?" or "Which documents are needed for a well-documented process?". For this purpose, in the first iteration step, the previously described *Isn't-It?* algorithm is executed to output all *Is*-children that have the result *true*.

Problem (3) is the goal of the third algorithm, the *Part-Of?* algorithm. It primarily serves to search for part-whole relationships in order to answer questions, such as: "What does software engineering consist of?". Only one step is required to solve the problem. Reason is the model itself, which already provides its own association class *Part-Of* for part-whole relations. As an extension of this algorithm, the solution can be filtered using element classes. In this way you can, for example, find specific tasks or abilities of an object: "What tasks are connected with requirements engineering?" or "What tasks have to be finished to complete the problem analysis phase of a project?".

The *Characteristics?* algorithm finds properties of elements and is therefore used to solve problem (4). Its execution answers questions such as: "What are the qualities of a good change manager?", "What are the properties of Konrad Zuse?" or "What is Scrum?".

The most comprehensive and at the same time most powerful algorithm of iKnow is the *Find!* algorithm. It serves as a solution for the problem (5), for instance "Finding software to describe requirements". In this case, "software" is a prescribed classification of the solution elements. "Describe requirements" is the goal, in this case, a combination of object and activity.

3.4 Machine Learning—Initial Approaches

3.4.1 Learning by Syntax and Semantics

An essential component of the knowledge acquisition is the transfer of knowledge from natural language into the formal structure of the model. This transformation can be done manually by a human modeler who is familiar with the components of the model with all its element and association classes. An approach with more practical appeal is to automatically extract knowledge from text modules or other sources of input (e.g. XML-formats of BPMNs) and transfer it into the knowledge base. For this purpose, keywords as sources for knowledge connections and transfer algorithms (methods for the correct storage of the knowledge artifacts) must be known to an automation mechanism. These keywords are dependent on the language (such as German, English, French, etc.). For this reason, distributing keywords into different "language systems" is essential when learning through syntax and semantics.

The general procedure is explained in the examples below. Initial keywords "a", "each", and "all" always lead to some general or classifying. In the purpose of the model they are followed by an *Item*. On the other hand, the keyword "the" points to something concrete, a *Cell*. Subject-object relationships are made clear by keywords "can", "is", "used", "has," "must", "should" or "same as" resulting from the association classes. Specific application examples for the transfer of model-based knowledge from natural language are given by the following list:

- Each consultant can think.
- A management consultant is a consultant.
- Management consultant is a consultant.
- John is a management consultant.
- Smith is the last-name of John.

In the first example, the keyword each suggests that "consultant" is an abstract class, which is an *Item*. Can indicates the Activity "think". An association between "consultant" and "think" can be formed. The second sentence illustrates a structure of inheritance between "management consultant" and "consultant". The keyword "a" also turns "management consultant" into an abstract *Item*. In contrast, "management consultant" would be modeled as a concrete instance of "consultant" if the third sentence is considered. In the fourth example, "John" is created as a *Cell*. If at this time "*management* consultant" is also a *Cell*, it is automatically changed to an *Item* because an instance cannot form the class of another instance. The last example involves more complex knowledge connections. A *Cell* "Smith" and an *Item* "last-name" are generated. "Smith" is an instance of "last-name". In addition, the link between "John" and "Smith" is performed by a *Positive Constraint*. At this point it is unclear whether each "management consultant" has a "last-name". Since "John" is the instance of a "management consultant", this conclusion is obvious. Therefore, a systematic query might lead to a *Has* association between "management consultant" and "last-name", for which a user must answer the question "Has each management consultant a last-name?" with yes. This learning behavior, according to user feedback, will be examined in more detail in the following section.

3.4.2 Learning by Inductive Reasoning

This section considers some essential rules of reasoning, based on the link between a class and its concretization.

Transmission of Characteristics of an Abstraction to a Concretization
Something concrete, which is related by an *Is* association with something abstract, inherits the characteristics of the abstract. If the inheriting element is a *Cell*, it may not be possible to exactly predict the concrete expression of the abstract property to be inherited. A common approach to tackling this problem is the inclusion of weights, probabilities and interactions.

Each *Item* with *Is* association to another *Item* inherits the properties of the parent element. In addition to abstract characteristics such as "duration" or "length", *Items* can also have specific properties. For example, each "media break" has the "ineffective" property, which is a concrete instance of "quality lack". In this case, the concrete characteristic would also be inherited to all abstract classes of "media break".

Also *Features* can be inherited to child elements. If they are modeled as a property of an abstract object, they represent a transferable component for data acquisition. For example, each software has a price that must be recorded as soon as a new software instance is integrated in the knowledge base. A "Software" *Item* therefore has the property "Price", which is modeled as an input *Feature*. When a new *Cell* "MS Visio" will be created, data entry is required for the "Price". This input will be stored as a *Cell* and associated with a *Positive Constraint* of "MS Visio".

Weightings Conflicts may occur when a concretization algorithm is executed. For example, the input of a *Feature* can be applied to different *Positive Constraints* of different elements. These conflicts lead to the fact that answering a problem cannot be made unambiguously, which may prevent system decision-making.

One solution to solve this problem lies in the integration of weightings and probabilities, as well as in the interaction with users. Weights are used to deal with conflicts, in order to decide, which concrete instance of a parental property on the child applies. The following is an example: Each software is subject to a cost category, for example "open source", "one-time cost", "license fee", etc. If a new ERP system is detected during the analysis of a process, which is not already present in the generic knowledge base, various properties are assigned to it in order to store it. ERP systems are mostly proprietary. When allocating the cost category, "open source" can therefore be weighted less than "license fee" and "one-time cost".

It is also possible to make the routing of the deduction paths more efficient by prioritizing the associations. The weighting is performed by assigning an edge weight to each edge and a node weight to each node. The weights are simplified by integers. Edge weights are composed of the degree of an adjacent node and a factor calculated by the system during learning. If an edge has already received a higher weight, it retains its original weight.

Trial and Error: Chance, Probabilities and User Interaction For the long-term storage of the knowledge based on weighting, the model has two abstract storage centers: a short-term memory (STM) for the short-term storage of learned weights and a long-term memory (LTM) to store it for a long period. The behavior of the two knowledge stores is based on human knowledge processing. Knowledge is stored in human brains in the long term if it is associated with an emotion or the information has been repeated often enough.

The STM contains elements that are entirely new or already present in the LTM but have received new weights. Each element of the STM has an expiration time and the number of selections of this element in previous user decisions, which have resulted from interaction with users in the event of a conflict. The expiration date of an element is reset with each selection. After seven selections, the element and all its associations are stored in the LTM for a long time. Each element of the LTM has an expiration time which behaves analogously to the STM but has a significantly higher value. An element whose expiration time has passed loses its weight. All adjacent edges lose their weight to null. Contents of elements are not deleted. This means that, once the element has been selected again, only the weights have to be renewed. The element itself does not have to be recreated. In this way, the prioritization during the deduction is placed under a temporal influence without loss of knowledge. Thus, machine learning is supplemented by machine forgetting.

The following example demonstrates the procedure of storing knowledge in STM and LTM. It is assumed that a certain conflict occurs for the first time. Now the model has three different ways to solve the problem:

- The model randomly chooses a conflicted element and then asks the user if the selection was correct. Subsequently, the user's response is integrated into the relevant elements by updating the STM.
- The model uses pre-modeled probabilities to decide which element to choose. As before, the automated selection is followed by a user query where the answer changes and stores the probabilities in the STM.
- The model lets the user decide directly and saves the selection by weighting in the STM.

If this conflict occurs again, the procedure is repeated, taking into account the information stored in the STM. After the same element has been selected seven times, all data associated with the conflict are stored in the LTM.

3.5   Use Case in the Consulting Industry

iKnow has already been applied in form of a first prototype in the area of virtu- alization of consulting services (Nissen et al. 2017). The aim of this application was to systematically determine an appropriate technology for the virtualization of a particular consulting service. The aim of virtualization is to reduce the amount of face-to-face interaction between consultant and client by the suitable implementa- tion of information and communication technologies (ICT) (Greff and Werth 2015; Nissen et al. 2015). It can thus be referred to as the strategy for digital transfor- mation of the consulting business.

In order to support the consulting organizations in the virtualization of their ser- vices, a tool-based method to systematically select adequate virtualization tech- nologies is sought. Depending on the respective consulting activity (e.g. "information gathering activity", "analyzing activity", "creative activity", etc.) and the prioritiza- tion of influencing criteria, such as "working speed and reaction rate" or "dependence of location and time", as well as the rating values of the technologies based on the QFD[3] method, suitable virtualization technologies are to be chosen (Nissen et al. 2017). In doing this, it should be possible to expand, modify and automatically develop new knowledge constructs on which the decision is based.

As a starting point, the method how an appropriate technology can be identified for virtualizing a particular consulting task was already available. It then had to be transferred to the prototype of the abstract model iKnow in the form of a knowledge base. Figure 5 shows a small part of the modeled knowledge base for this appli- cation in order to convey an impression.

In this knowledge transfer process to iKnow, which at this stage of the prototype had to be done manually, consulting activities (such as information gathering) and specific ICT classes[4] are represented as *Items* (rectangles) and linked to the

---

[3]Quality Function Deployment, see Nissen et al. (2017).

[4]An ICT class represents a group of certain technologies, see Nissen et al. (2017) in this volume.

Fig. 5 iKnow extract of the modeled knowledge base for the use case

Used-For association (see Fig. 5 "search for information is *Used-For* information gathering activity"). And, "search for information" is a type of the generic *Item* "ICT class". An ICT product as such was modeled in form of a *Cell* (ovals) and associated with the *Is* association to an ICT class. The core of the modeling is the assignment of the influence criteria on the right-hand side of the image (shown by *Features* as squares, e.g. k1 in Fig. 5), which significantly affects the solution of the decision-making problem. In order to assign these to a specific ICT product, a *Result Expression*, that is defined as *Positive Constraints* (shown as association between *Cells* (e.g. tool_a1) and *Features* (eg. k1, k2)), was specified for each ICT product (each *Cell*) as a function of the respective influencing criterion. Therefore on the one hand, the weighting of the ICT product with respect to a criterion (QFD[5] values), as well as the prioritization of the influencing criteria by the AHP[6] algorithm, are included in the calculation of the *Result Expression*. Every *Result Expression* of every *Cell* resp. every ICT product of a certain ICT class has to be defined in the following way:

$$r(a_x) > (r(a_{x+1}) \ AND \ \dots \ AND \ r(a_{x+n}))$$

- r: *Result Expression*, that expresses a boolean value
- a_x: a specific *Cell*.

The *Result Expression* checks if the value of $r(a_x)$ that represents a *Cell* of an ICT product is larger than a respective *Result Expression* value of all other *Cells* ($r(a_{x+n})$) that are associated to the same *Item* (a certain ICT class).

In a more specific way, the concrete *Result Expression* for the ICT product (*Cell*) "tool_a1" of the ICT class "search for information" of the presented example in Fig. 5 is as follows:

$$\sum_{y=1}^{n} r(k_y) * QFD(a_1 k_y) > \left(\sum_{y=1}^{n} r(k_y) * QFD(a_2 k_y) \quad AND \quad \sum_{y=1}^{n} r(k_y) * QFD(a_3 k_y) \right)$$

---

[5]In this case the QFD (Quality Function Deployment) values 3-5-9 may apply.

[6]The AHP (Analytic Hierarchy Process) algorithm was used for weighting the criteria that were prioritized by a user resp. consultant. For a detailed description of the developed method, see Nissen et al. (2017) in this volume.

- k: a criterion resp. *Feature*,
- n: number of criteria,
- y: variable of a certain criterion,
- a: the ICT products resp. the specific *Cells* of the ICT class "search for information",
- r(ky): *Result Expression* of a criterion resp. of a *Feature* (in this case it expresses the respective input value (between 0 and 1) of an prioritized influencing criterion based on AHP),
- QFD: value (3, 5 or 9) of a certain ICT product (a1, a2, a3) depending on their criteria.

As result of all *Result Expression* of the *Cells,* there will be generated *Positive Constraints* (from a *Cell* to each dependent criterion resp. *Feature*) with the boolean values "true" or "false", that indicates whether an ICT product is suitable depending on its prioritized influencing criteria (*Features*).

Finally, *Data Source* elements in the form of an input (rhombuses on the right) are added to each criterion in order to integrate the determined AHP values of the individual influencing criteria into the prototype.

The first step of the method is selecting the consulting activity from which a choice of the ICT class (technology group) must be made in the next step. The *Find!* algorithm can be used to perform this step. This algorithm serves as a solution approach of the problem: "Find all elements of a certain class for the fulfillment of a given purpose!" (Füßl 2016). In relation to the application example, one possible task is: "Find all ICT classes to support the selected consulting activity". While the *Find!* algorithm has been executed, the prototype of iKnow will ask for the element you are looking for (resp. what should be found, Fig. 6: What kind of element are you looking for?) and what consulting activity it is (Fig. 6: What should it be used for?). As a result, the user resp. a consultant will receive an overview of the ICT classes that are relevant to the chosen consulting activity and that are modeled within the knowledge base (see Fig. 6 on the right: "Result: The following ict-classes...."). This assignment was created using the *Used-For* association in the modeling (cf. Fig. 5: "search for information *Used-For* information gathering activity").

The second step has to determine the best ICT product of each ICT class. For this request the *Kind-Of?* algorithm is required. This algorithm can find instances or expressions of an element and answer the problem: which element (ICT product) is fitting (Füßl 2016). During the *Kind-Of?* algorithm, the *Result Expression*s of each ICT product (each *Cell*) within an ICT class is addressed and the evaluation of the various product alternatives of each ICT class is carried out. As a result, the consultant is offered the best ICT product of each ICT class, which was determined based on the prioritization of the influence criteria by means of AHP and his selection of a consulting activity during the first step.

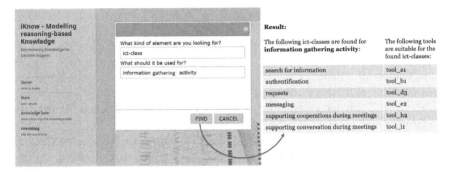

Fig. 6 Find! algorithm for selecting the activity that needs to be examined

With the aid of the prototype of iKnow the main functionality developed in the method are shown. The paths of the modeled knowledge base are called with each application of the decision-making process. A further development is intended to provide the opportunity for adding automatically further criteria or technologies in the decision-making process. For this purpose, additional criteria and technologies must be entered and the elements of the knowledge base to be modeled must be created automatically. In addition, context-related information about the dependence of consulting activities or for example about ICT classes and their characteristics can also be included in the knowledge base. This will influence the decision-making path. Therefore it will be necessary to include for example weightings to particular *Result Expressions*. If the decision-making process has led to a false result, it should be possible to include the right solution based on expert knowledge into the relevant *Result Expression*, which also changes the decision-making path. In this way, the machine learning of the model can be supported.

In addition to a fixed knowledge base and its *Result Expressions* for analyzing, context-related information as well as expert knowledge are also incorporated into the decision-making process. This is intended to continuously improve the decision-making process and try to always lead context-dependently to the right decision.

4 iKnow as a Tool for Business Process Analysis

4.1 Preliminary Considerations

With regard to a standardized procedure for business process analysis and in order to design iKnow as a learning and decision-making tool, a comprehensive investigation of possible weak points of processes is required. Gadatsch (2008) recommends the use of a checklist of analysis criteria for each weak point (cf. Sect. 2.2). In order to identify not only deficiencies, but also to determine fitting measures of process improvement, all contextual appropriate measures must be assigned to each weak point. In addition, a modeled business process has to be in form of a suitable modeling notation (e.g. EPC or BPMN) to investigate a specific process. In the course of this section, the conceptual design of iKnow as a tool for business process analysis is presented, followed by a demonstration of the concept. In this paper, a comprehensive analysis and recommendation of improvement measures is not provided. Rather, the focus is on designing the model iKnow for this purpose.

4.2   Development of the Conceptual Approach

iKnow documents, structures and visualizes knowledge as knowledge base in form of elements and associations. The visual design is used to ensure that conclusions by use of the decision-making process of iKnow are always comprehensible (Füßl 2016).

In contrast to previous process analyzing methods, iKnow integrates not only existing process models but also knowledge about the underlying process elements. In this way, it is possible to integrate generic knowledge structures into decision-making processes and to reuse the results of this analysis in subsequent analyses. In this context, new business process models to be examined can be supplemented by generic knowledge.

The following figure illustrates the developed conceptual approach of iKnow as a process analyzing tool. To be able to draw conclusions, a knowledge base must exist in iKnow. As precondition for analyzing business process models through iKnow, knowledge about applicable process analysis criteria, weak points and potential process improvement measures must therefore be integrated initially as explicit knowledge into iKnow (see Fig. 7: Foundation for Reasoning). This knowledge represents the knowledge base of iKnow.

For analyzing an individual business process in iKnow, it is necessary to convert the content of the business process model into the form of the model iKnow (see Fig. 7: Input), so that values of the process analysis criteria can be identified through pattern matching. When transferring a business process model, it should be possible for example to identify the number of organizational units involved or a switch between analog and electronic tasks in this business process. In iKnow, the element *Data Source* of the application layer performs the input (see the rhombus in Fig. 7) and represents the interface for the integration of content (Füßl 2016). In order to communicate with this interface, the business processes to be integrated must be in a format that can be converted in the required iKnow format. Within the prototype, the knowledge base is defined using JSON. Business process models are mostly available as XML. A technical interface that automatically converts a XML file of the business process model to the required JSON format of iKnow should be used.

In order to check the business process with respect to the applicable analysis criteria and process improvement measures, the following questions must be answered:

- Which weak points exist in the process?

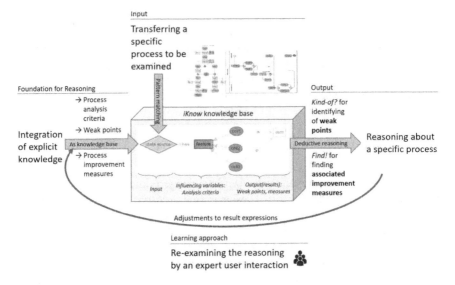

Fig. 7 Concept of iKnow for process analysis

- Which improvement measures must be taken to remove the deficiencies resp. to improve the existing process?

For answering the first question, the associations which analysis criteria indicate which weak points must exists within the knowledge base. According to iKnow, the deductive reasoning algorithm *Kind-Of?* detects first whether a concrete weak point is identified (first question). The ascertainment, whether a particular weak point exists or not, takes place through the *Result Expression* of the *Cell* of the respective weak point. For example, if five organizational units involved are identified within a process and the *Result Expression* of a *Cell* "organizational break" identifies that an "organizational break" exists, the *Kind-Of?* algorithm will activate the *Cell* "organizational break". In case of a weak point, the *Find!* algorithm will further determine associated improvement measures to be derived (second question). Therefore, in the knowledge base, associations between weak points and their improvement measures also have to be included. In this way, answering both questions through the iKnow reasoning algorithms represents the decision-making process. The weak points and their improvement measures represent the output (see Fig. 7: Output). In a technical manner, through the processing of the algorithms, the decision-making paths of the knowledge base will be activated and are traceable for understanding (or even explaining) a particular output.

After successfully completing the deductive reasoning, the machine learning component, which is described in more detail in Sect. 3.4, would now ask the user of iKnow (or an expert) to examine whether the generated result appears to be the right solution (see Fig. 7: Learning approach). If not, on the one hand, it should be possible to select the correct measure of the analyzed process. On the other hand, in case of new improvement measures, that are still not part of the knowledge base, but are relevant for the given process, the additional improvement measure should be integrated in the knowledge base. In both cases, the individual *Result Expressions* will be modified and other decision-making paths will be activated. The more application cases resp. processes are analyzed, the better the model is trained, consequently the model can generate better analyses and suggest more adequate improvement measures to optimize the business process at hand.

4.3 Demonstration of the Conceptual Approach

4.3.1 Description of the Case

In the following, the approach described above is applied to a particular business process that displays the following weak points: "data redundancy", "organizational break", "media break" and "system break". In that respect, it is first determined which analysis criteria are part of the checklist to identify the chosen deficiencies. In addition, appropriate improvement measures must be defined for each weak point. The following assumptions in Table 1 are made for the demonstration.

Table 1 Weak points, their analysis criteria and associated improvement measures

Weak point	Analysis criteria	Improvement measures
Data redundancy	Data inconsistencies	Find duplicated data storage
	Same data in several places	Delete duplicated data storage
		Integrate systems
		Implement ERP systems
		Implement workflow management systems
Organizational break	Number of organizational units involved in the same process	Keep processes as much as possible within an organizational unit
		Determining of process owners Introducing of process teams
Media break	Switch between documents/ forms	Automating analogous processes
	Switch between ICT and paper	Improving communication and coordination through groupware systems, enterprise social network
		Introducing ERP systems and workflow management systems
System break	Switch between different IT systems	Integrating of different systems
	Switch between non-integrated IT systems	Introducing ERP systems

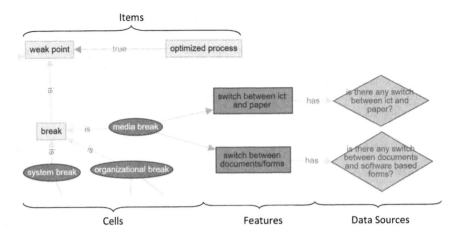

Fig. 8 Example of integrating potential process deficiencies and associated analysis criteria as a knowledge base

4.3.2 Integration of Explicit Knowledge (Foundation for Reasoning)

First, basic knowledge about potential process deficiencies, associated analysis criteria and improvement measures must be integrated into the knowledge base of iKnow. According to the basic elements of iKnow, the analysis criteria, whose values could impact the process analysis, must be created as influencing variables in the form of *Features* in iKnow. In context of the business process analysis tool to be developed, output values are always defined as *Cells* in iKnow (see Fig. 7, inside the cube). All possible values of an analysis criterion must be integrated and connected to the *Feature*. The check of the values of an analysis criterion, whether it is *true* or *false*, is defined as *Result Expression* in the respective *Cell*. By way of example, for the weak point "media break", the analysis criteria "switch between documents/forms" and "switch between ICT and paper" are defined within the *Result Expression* of the *Cell* "media break" (see Fig. 8: *Cell* "media break" and Features "switch between documents" and "switch between ICT and paper"). The arrows between the *Features* and the *Cell* "media break" denote that the *Result Expression* of the *Cell* "media break" is specified through values of both *Features*. Whereas *Result Expressions* express boolean values, the arrows are *Positive Constraints* due to the defining whether any switch, that causes a media break, exists resp. is identified as *true* (cf. Sect. 3.2). The respective *Result Expression* for the *Cell* "media break" is determined as follows:

$$r(switch\ between\ ict\ and\ paper) \quad OR \quad r(switch\ between\ documents/forms)$$

Since there is a "organizational" and "system break" in addition to the media break, all three weak points can be assigned to a higher-ranking *Item*, that constitutes content-related information (see Fig. 8: "breaks"). In iKnow, this generic

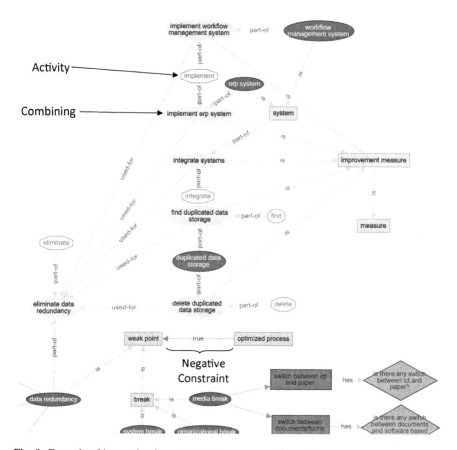

Fig. 9 Example of integrating improvement measures as a knowledge base

knowledge construct can be linked to an *Is* association, which leads to the deductive reasoning with the *Kind-Of?* algorithm: "organizational break is (of the type) break" or "media break is break" or "system break is break" (cf. Sect. 3.4.1). Therefore, if a media break exists and consequently no optimized process exists, this can be modeled using a *Negative Constraint* between an *Item* "optimized process" and an *Item* "break" (cf. Sect. 3.2). Further analysis criteria of the weak points "organizational" and "system break" can be integrated as a knowledge base in the same way.

Ultimately, for each weak point in a process the corresponding improvement measure has to be included in the knowledge base. Since the output values represent, beside the weak points, the improvement measures, these have to be modeled as *Cells* in iKnow. A specialty of *Cells* in iKnow is a *Combining* (see Sect. 3.1). In order to express activities, the improvement measures are presented as *Combinings*. In the illustrated example, the improvement measures of the weak point "data redundancy" are integrated as *Combinings* into the knowledge base as shown in Fig. 9. For each verb (find, delete, integrate, and implement) of the improvement measures of the weak point data redundancy (cf. Table 1), an *Activity* is modeled (see Fig. 9).

Moreover, each object, which is connected to the improvement measure, is integrated as *Cell* or *Item* according to *Combining*. By means of the *Used-For* association, it is shown that all concrete measures contribute on the basis of given analysis criteria to the elimination of the weak point data redundancy. In this case, the *Used-For* association is interpreted by the *Find!* algorithm for identifying all applicable improvement measures. In addition, to define what the *Find!* algorithm is intended to find exactly, it is important to create a higher-level *Item* "improvement measures", which is itself of type "measure" (*Item*). The modeled integration of this knowledge construct within iKnow can be visualized as shown in Fig. 9. By way for example, "implement erp system" is a *Combining* that consists of the *Activity* "implement" and the object "erp system". This *Combining* is an "improvement measure" and simultaneously a "measure", because "improvement measure" is a "measure". Furthermore, "implement erp system" is *Used-For* the *Combining* "eliminate data redundancy" which consists of the *Activity* "eliminate" and the object "data redundancy" that displays simultaneously a weak point ("data redundancy" is "weak point").

In order to check the initial situation, whether or not weak points exist, a *Negative Constraint* is also required from the *Item* "optimized process" to the superordinate *Item* "weak point". The *Result Expression* of the *Item* "optimized process", that is designed as follows "!r(weak_point)", defines if a weak point exists there is no optimized process.

Such modeling depicts the knowledge base in iKnow to document and structure knowledge connections. This makes it possible to identify weak points during the analysis of a business process and consequently to draw conclusions which improvement measures are best suited for the analyzed weak points of the process to be checked.

Transferring a specific process (see Fig. 7: Input) and the necessary pattern matching algorithms for detecting the values of *Result Expressions* are not considered in the paper. The automated transfer of business process models to the knowledge base of iKnow is not yet possible at the moment. For the transfer of a business process model as EPC or BPMN, in the present example the *Data Sources* are used, that integrate the necessary content for the examination of a process by means of user interaction.

4.3.3 Reasoning About a Specific Process (Generating Analysis Output)

The aim of automatic decision-making in the present application is to analyze a process for deficiencies and to suggest improvement measures. On the basis of the underlying knowledge base, different conclusions can be drawn:

(1) Is it an optimized process?
(2) Are there any weak points in the process?
(3) What are the weak point of a process?
(4) What measures can be taken to remove a particular weak point?

In order to carry out these automatic conclusions, the reasoning algorithms described in Sect. 3.3, the algorithms *Isn't-It?*, *Kind-Of?* and *Find!* are used. The answers to questions (1) and (2) are carried out by the *Isn't-It?* algorithm. Starting from the *Cell* "weak point" or "optimized process", all predecessors required for the deduction are checked for the presence of their result. If there is no result, the system switches to the next predecessor level. This procedure is repeated until all the results required for decision-making are available. When integrating user interaction, during this deduction phase, *Features* and *Data Sources* in form of *Questions*, which must be answered by users (process specialists/experts), are inevitably involved. The respective answers require the results of elements (*Cells* and *Items*). If all necessary answers and results are available, the *Isn't-It?* algorithm outputs the corresponding result.

Question (3) requires the execution of the *Kind-Of?* algorithm. It indicates all weak points that have been identified as being true during an *Isn't-It?* deduction and outputs the corresponding elements. In this way, a process analyst receives exactly the deficiencies contained in the knowledge base and which apply to the examined process. In order to continue the process analysis, appropriate measures have to be proposed, which lead to the elimination of identified process deficiencies. This is the starting point to answer question (4).

The *Find!* algorithm is used for automatic search for suitable measures. The algorithm searches extensively for appropriate improvement measures, which were modeled in the knowledge base and apply to a present process deficiency (for example "data redundancy"). In the example (see Fig. 9), the algorithm finds five measures in form of *Combinings* that can be used to "eliminate data redundancy" (realized with the *Used-For* association): "delete duplicated data storage", "find duplicated data storage", "integrate systems", "implement erp system" and "implement workflow management system". To check how useful individual measures are and how easily they can be implemented, all influencing factors, such as budget, experience or project duration, have to be included in the decision-making process. Because this example mainly serves the purpose to illustrate decision-making in iKnow, these influencing factors are not further analyzed in the present example. As described above, iKnow provides the ability to add descriptive knowledge to modeled elements. The present knowledge base contains, for example, information that "erp system" and "workflow management system" are instances of "system" and that "improvement measure" is a specialization of "measure". A further detailing of the knowledge elements would be possible at this point in order to allow more specific conclusions in the entire process analysis.

4.3.4   Re-examining the Reasoning (Learning Approach in iKnow)

In Sect. 3.4.2, a machine learning approach based on weighting and conflict resolution was presented. As shown above, the search for suitable measures to eliminate process deficiencies can produce a plurality of results. A manual analysis of
these measures usually leads to a singular selection of a result, since parallel execution of all measures might not be effective or inefficient. For example, the
implementation of an ERP system ("implement erp system") can change the process in such a way that the consideration of all further measures is no longer
required.

In such a conflict, iKnow will initially output all the results but then ask a
process specialist or expert what measure he or she would choose. In order to be
able to learn from this decision, the resulting knowledge must be returned automatically into the knowledge base by means of machine learning algorithms and the
user selection will be weighted higher. A further interaction takes place to determine whether the process will be fault-free following this one measure. If the
chosen measure always leads to a defect-free process, further measures must no
longer be proposed by the system. According to Sect. 3.4.2, this procedure is
repeated several times in the short-term memory of the model (STM) until a
long-term storage (LTM) of the weighting is performed.

Section 3.4.2 also describes a decisive factor to ensure the timeliness of weights
from long-term storage: machine forgetting. Highly-weighted measures can lead to
mistakes when new measures or associations, such as IT systems, are applied with a
lighter weighting. If, for example, a new ERP system is detected during the analysis
of a process, it must be determined whether this system is more suitable as
application in "implement ERP system" than the previously modeled ones. All
influencing variables such as budget, experience or time, which are associated to
"implement erp system" have to be considered in detail for each new ERP system.
Therefore, every time when new knowledge is created, that relates to existing
knowledge and their weights, it has to be verified by use of pattern matching
algorithms which generic knowledge constructs can be activated, and how the
previous weights still have their validity.

5   Conclusion and Further Researches

The present paper shows how the knowledge-based model iKnow is applicable not
only to the selection of technology for virtualizing consulting tasks (Sect. 3.5) but
also as a tool for automated process analysis during a consulting project. The
advantage of iKnow is the comprehensive integration and processing of process
knowledge as well as additional knowledge that is not modeled in the process
model, for example the usage of a workflow management system is associated to
reducing costs in case of inefficient tasks. The opportunity of user interaction makes
it possible to integrate additional expert knowledge for analysis purposes and thus

to implement a comprehensive process analysis. Moreover, process data stored in IT systems (such as process logs used in process mining) could be integrated as a knowledge source in iKnow to further improve the quality of the analysis. Due to the ontology-based basic structure of iKnow, the process knowledge relevant for a given business process can be unambiguously identified and improvement measures can be detected based on this.

It is conceivable to use iKnow as an automation device in consulting projects in order to support the problem analysis and problem solving phase. Based on a fully configured data base in iKnow, business process models could be analyzed automatically to provide a starting point for the consultants. The machine learning approach available in iKnow helps to improve the knowledge base and extend it by additional knowledge of experts entered through user queries. The question remains whether it is sensible to develop a uniform knowledge base for process analysis independent of the consulting company. If such knowledge was considered company-specific, issues of data protection and data security would have to be discussed. In a later phase, it is also conceivable to provide the tool as a self-service consulting application for clients. Clients would then be in a position to analyze their own process models and to uncover potential improvement measures without a consultant.

iKnow as process analyzing tool can be classified according to the conceptual model of the consulting industry of Werth and Greff (2017) as *algorithmic consulting*.

A hot spot of our current research, and the next step for the technical implementation of iKnow as business process analysis tool, is the automated transfer of business process models. This substantially speeds up the analysis and improvement of business processes. A further research stream concerns the broad evaluation of iKnow in consulting practice, as the examples presented in this contribution were either of a demonstrative nature or not fully implemented, yet. However, in our view, the machine-learning based approach of iKnow has great potential to assist consultants or even automate the execution of complex and frequent tasks in process optimization, even if no log-data or similar input from IT systems is available.

References

Anand T, Gupta P (1998) A selection algorithm for X + Y on Mesh. Parallel Process 8(3): 363–470

Arp R, Smith B, Spear A (2015) Building ontologies with basic formal ontology. MIT press, Cambridge, MA

Bisson G, Nédellec C, Canamero D (2000) Designing clustering methods for ontology building - The Mo'K workbench. In: ECAI workshop on ontology learning, vol 31

Brewster C, Wilks Y (2004) Ontologies, taxonomies, thesauri: learning from texts. In: Proceedings of the Use of Computational Linguistics in the Extraction of Keyword Information from Digital Library Content Workshop

Dor D (1995) Selection algorithms. Dissertation, Tel Aviv University

Dor D, Zwick U (1999) Selecting the median. SIAM J Comput 28(5):1722–1758

Emrany S, Boßlet K (2001) Prozess-Beratung. In: Scheer A-W, Köppen A (eds) Consulting. Springer, Berlin, pp 153–180

Fernandes L, García A (2012) Association rule visualization and pruning through response-style data organization and clustering. In: Hutchison D, Kanade T, Kittler J, Kleinberg JM, Mattern F, Mitchell CJ (eds) Advances in artificial intelligence - IBERAMIA 2012, vol 7637. Springer, Heidelberg, pp 71–80

Fernández-López M, Gómez-Pérez A, Juristo N (1997) Methontology: ontological art towards ontological engineering. In: Proceedings of the ontological engineering. Spring symposium series, pp 33–40

Füßl FF (2016) Entwicklung eines Modells zur Anwendung inferenzfähiger Ontologien im Software Engineering. Dissertation, Technische Universität Ilmenau

Füßl FF, Streitferdt D, Shang W, Triebel A (2015) Introducing a method for modeling knowledge bases in expert systems using the example of large software development projects. Int J Adv Comput Sci Appl 6(12):1–17

Gadatsch A (2008) Grundkurs Geschäftsprozess-Management. Methoden und Werkzeuge für die IT-Praxis: Eine Einführung für Studenten und Praktiker. 5th edn. Friedr. Vieweg & Sohn, GWV Fachverlage GmbH, Wiesbaden

Greff T, Werth D (2015) Auf dem Weg zur digitalen Unternehmensberatung. IM+io - Magazin für Innovation, Organisation und Management. IMC, Saarbücken, pp 30–34

Hasenkamp U, Roßbach P (1998) Wissensmanagement. WISU (Das Wirtschaftsstudium) 27(8–9): 956–964

Jeschke K (2004) Marketing für Beratungsleistungen. Marketing ZFP 26(2):159–173

Jochem R, Balzert S (2010) Prozessmanagement. Strategien, Methoden, Umsetzung. Symposion, Dusseldorf

Kubr M (2005) Management consulting. A guide to the profession. 4th edn. Bookwell, New Delhi

Landauer C (1998) Data, information, knowledge, understanding: computing up the meaning hierarchy. In: SCM'98 conference proceedings IEEE international conference on systems, man, and cybernetics. San Diego, pp 2255–2260

Miebach B (2009) Methoden der Prozessanalyse. In: Miebach B (ed) Prozesstheorie. VS Verlag für Sozialwissenschaften, Wiesbaden, pp 125–178

Nissen V, Seifert H, Blumenstein M (2015) Virtualisierung von Beratungsleistungen: Qualitätsanforderungen, Chancen und Risiken der digitalen Transformation in der Unternehmensberatung aus der Klientenperspektive. In: Deelmann T, Ockel DM (eds) Handbuch der Unternehmensberatung, 25th edn. Erich Schmidt Verlag, Berlin

Nissen V, Seifert H, Blumenstein M (2017) A Method to Support the Selection of Technologies for the Virtualization of Consulting Services. In this volume

Palleduhn DU, Neuendorf H (2013) Geschäftsprozessmanagement und integrierte Informationsverarbeitung. Oldenbourg, Munich

Peffers K, Tuunanen T, Rothenberger MA, Chatterjee S (2007) A design science research methodology for information systems research. J Manag Inf Syst 24(3):45–77

Staud JL (2006) Geschäftsprozessanalyse. Ereignisgesteuerte Prozessketten und objektorientierte Geschäftsprozessmodellierung für Betriebswirtschaftliche Standardsoftware. Springer, Dordrecht

van der Aalst W (2016) Process mining. Data science in action. 2nd edn. Springer, Berlin

Walger G (1995) Unternehmensführung und Unternehmensberatung als Aufgabe der Betriebswirtschaftslehre. In: Wächter H (ed) Selbstverständnis betriebswirtschaftlicher Forschung und Lehre. Gabler, Wiesbaden, pp 125–146

Werth D, Greff T (2017) Scalability in Consulting: Insights into the Scaling Capabilities of Business Models by Digital Technologies in Consulting Industry. In this volume

Author Biographies

Anne Füßl is a doctoral candidate at the Chair of Information Systems Engineering in Services at Technische Universität Ilmenau, Germany. Her research interests focus on the development of a learning and decision-making knowledge model (iKnow) to support consulting services in the context of digital transformation. In 2015, Anne has already contributed to the research and development of the knowledge model iKnow in two publications. She holds a Master's degree in Business Information Systems Engineering, was a student assistant and worked as product manager at Magnitude Internet GmbH for an online portal.

Franz Felix Füßl is a consultant in Software Engineering and holds a Dr.-Ing. (2016) in Computer Engineering from Technische Universität Ilmenau, Germany. He gained his expertise mainly in the field of software engineering, especially in the area of web development and software architecture. During his doctorate, he dealt with learning systems and computer-assisted decision-making. Today, he is working on web-based software systems to increase the efficiency of processes in industrial production, production automation and key figure analysis.

Volker Nissen holds the Chair of Information Systems Engineering in Services at Technische Universität Ilmenau, Germany, since 2005. Prior to this, he pursued a consulting career, including positions as manager at IDS Scheer AG, director at DHC GmbH, and CEO of NISSCON Ltd., Germany. In 1994 he received a Ph.D. degree in Economic Sciences with distinction from the University of Goettingen, Germany. His current research interests include the digital transformation of the consulting industry, the management of IT-agility, metaheuristic optimization, and process acceptance research. He is author and editor of 19 books and some 200 other publications, including papers in Business & Information Systems Engineering, Information Systems Frontiers, IEEE Transactions on EC, IEEE Transactions on NN, and Annals of OR.

Detlef Streitferdt is currently senior researcher at Technische Universität Ilmenau heading the research group Software Architectures and Product Lines since 2010. The research fields are the efficient development of software architectures and product lines, their analysis and their assessment as well as software development processes and model-driven development. Before returning to the University he was Principal Scientist at the ABB AG Corporate Research Center in Ladenburg, Germany. He was working in the field of software development for embedded systems. He received his doctoral degree from Technische Universität Ilmenau in the field of requirements engineering for product line software development in 2004.

ProMAT—A Project Management Assessment Tool for Virtual Consulting

Volker Nissen, Jochen Kuhl, Hendrik Kräft, Henry Seifert,
Jakob Reiter and Jim Eidmann

Abstract Advisory consulting is a good application for virtual consulting products, as only limited and well-structured communication between client and consultant is required. In this paper we describe the design and development of a tool to create virtual expert assessments in basically arbitrary areas of expertise. We also report on its first practical usage in the area of assessing the quality of project management at clients.

1 Introduction and Related Work

Four different types of business consulting can be differentiated: advisory consulting, expert consulting, organizational development/coaching and systemic consulting (Deelmann 2012). The focus of this paper is on advisory consulting, which presents a form of content-oriented consulting, where a consultant, based on specific knowledge, suggests a solution to a client problem in the form of a report (Bamberger and Wrona 2012). The consultant acts as an external and neutral expert. Initially, he gathers information, analyzes it, and develops one or more alternatives

V. Nissen (✉) · H. Seifert · J. Reiter
Technische Universität Ilmenau, Ilmenau, Germany
e-mail: volker.nissen@tu-ilmenau.de

H. Seifert
e-mail: henry.seifert@infosysconsulting.com

J. Reiter
e-mail: jakob.reiter@tu-ilmenau.de

J. Kuhl · H. Kräft · J. Eidmann
Dr. Kuhl Unternehmensberatung, Hardegsen, Germany
e-mail: JKuhl@DK-UB.de

H. Kräft
e-mail: HKraeft@DK-UB.de

J. Eidmann
e-mail: JEidmann@DK-UB.de

© Springer International Publishing AG 2018
V. Nissen (ed.), *Digital Transformation of the Consulting Industry*,
Progress in IS, https://doi.org/10.1007/978-3-319-70491-3_14

for solving the client problem in the form of textual elaboration. The concerned employees usually do not take part in the final expert report for decision-making (Lippold 2016). On the other hand, the consultant is usually not involved during the (optional) implementation of these proposals.

Advisory consulting is marked by relatively little interaction between the client and the consultant. The consultant here takes "the role of an expert third party" (Deelmann 2012) and aims to transfer expert know-how to the client. The scarce human interaction within this process makes advisory consulting to an ideal test case for the virtualization of consulting services.

As is highlighted in other contributions of this volume, the current state of practice with respect to higher degrees of virtualization is currently not very advanced (Nissen and Seifert 2016, 2017). However, in the literature are some contributions that describe the concept or even implementation of digital tools in virtual consulting. These include Strehlau and Sieper (2009), who designed a tool for the optimization of business fields. This tool can be used in consulting projects to collect the opinion of a client's customers via an online-survey. It also includes methods to analyze the data subsequently in order to optimize the business model and services of the respective client. A different approach is pursued by König (2009). In his work, he develops a Wiki-based process model for business intelligence projects. This can be seen as a form of advisory consulting since one of the objectives is to support companies in setting up and conducting business intelligence projects successfully. Furthermore, the works of Allegra et al. (2000), Fulantelli et al. (2001), and Fulantelli and Allegra (2003) deal with virtual consulting tools. Here the focus of investigation is on the client acceptance of virtual business consulting, particularly online coaching and distance training through the use of telemedia in smaller companies. Finally, Werth et al. (2016) develop a prototype of an online shop for virtual consulting services.

On the practical side, the website www.bestprax.de offers advisory consulting to dentists—a group of clients that would usually not be seen as a primary target for consulting providers. Dr. C. Stummeyer, a former BCG strategy consultant, realized a concept of fully virtualized strategy consulting that exploits the generally bad management knowledge of medical doctors, here dentists. Since the practice of a dentist can have a considerable number of patients and yearly turnover, an active management of the business aspects of such a medical practice is demanded. Few dentists are in a position to do this sufficiently since they lack the necessary qualification. Here the digital assessment of bestprax.de offers help in identifying potential business improvements. Customers first fill in an online questionnaire, giving information that is subsequently used in an automated analysis to reveal the relative market position of the practice in relation to similar medical practices. Essentially, some form of benchmarking is provided that helps the dentist to better understand the strength and weaknesses of his practice. The analysis in turn is then used to advise on potential measures to improve the situation of the medical practice.

The virtual consulting application presented in the present contribution is similar in spirit to the basic concept of bestprax.de. The details will be outlined in the following sections. First, the addressed research question and associated methods to it are highlighted. Then we describe the successive steps in our design-science oriented approach to develop a virtual assessment tool. We demonstrate its' use for assessing the quality of project management at a consulting client. Some avenues for future research conclude this article.

2 Research Objectives and Method

In the present contribution, we wish to design and implement a technical framework that allows the straightforward provision of fully virtualized assessment products for a range of different themes. Assessments are a form of advisory consulting and particularly suited for virtualization as they rely only on a structured low level interaction with the client (Deelmann 2012).

To simplify the conception, and to be able to focus on details of the system design as well as its implementation, the first consulting application chosen was a virtual expert assessment of project management. This development project was done in close collaboration between the chair of information systems engineering in services (WID) at the University of Technology Ilmenau, Germany, and the Dr. Kuhl Unternehmensberatung (DKUB), Hardegsen, Germany, a consulting provider of project management expertise, amongst other topics. This consulting firm has specialized on small and medium-sized customers and exists since 2003. From the perspective of DKUB, the practical goal is to extend the consulting service portfolio with a virtual project management service that complements the classical face-to-face consulting usually provided to clients of DKUB. For WID the objective is to put scientific results on the virtualization of consulting services into practice and scientifically accompany the usage thereof by clients and consultants.

Since a software system should be created, an artefact in the sense of Hevner et al. (2004); Hevner and Chatterjee 2010), a design-science (DS) approach was chosen for this study. More specifically, we follow the DS process model suggested by Peffers et al. (2007). This process model consists of six steps: (1) Identify problem & motivate, (2) Define objectives of a solution, (3) Design and development, (4) Demonstration, (5) Evaluation and (6) Communication of the results. These steps serve as an orientation and the model can be started at various points. Furthermore steps 2–6 are parts of an iterative process.

The structure of this contribution is basically derived from the DS process model. The focus is especially on the design and development, as well on as the demonstration of the usability and usefulness of the artefact. The broad evaluation of the virtual consulting product is not covered in this paper. It will be a focus of future research. However, the project management assessment is currently being adapted for a German DAX 30 company, which serves as a testimony of its practical value.

Requirements engineering procedures are employed to determine the system requirements. In the process, functional and non-functional requirements should be differentiated (Patig and Dibbern 2016). Functional requirements describe the desired functions and the behavior of a system, whereas non-functional requirements are rather of a qualitative nature, and describe the total system (Pohl 2008; Sommerville 2011).

The requirements are initially collected from various sources. These include a current requirement specification, a study on the quality requirements of a virtual consulting service and general features of advisory consulting. The requirements are then described in natural language, and are brought into a uniform overview. Subsequently the critical requirements of the initial prototype are identified, and are prioritized for the implementation later. Finally, the requirements are classified into three categories. These categories are derived from various views of the prototype. The category "user front end" describes every requirement, which deals directly with the later visible user experience. The category "data storage and maintenance" collects every internal requirement and the category "administration" collects all requirements of the administration and maintainability of future systems. Afterwards vague or still indefinite requirements are identified and described more accurately, and are also validated by discussion with the practice partner DKUB. In this process, some requirements can be shifted to a future version, but the priority of some requirements can also be changed.

Subsequently the system design and the implementation of the requirements within a prototype take place. The prototype-oriented process model chosen for implementation allows to quickly create first versions of the future IT system. Moreover, after validating the given prototype the model allows for iterations of phases and backward steps in the overall procedure (Bunse and von Knethen 2008; Balzert et al. 2009).

In the context of the given objective, a prototype-oriented process model seems to be reasonable, as several obscurities regarding the system design are initially present, which can be quickly clarified by suitable prototypes. Three kinds of prototypes can generally be differentiated: Demonstrators, laboratory prototypes and pilot systems. Demonstrators provide an initial view on the finished system. They do, however, have little functionality. Pilot systems are validated by means of the later users, and come relatively close to the finished software. The laboratory prototype is used to test technical aspects (Kuhrmann 2012). As the practice partner should also be integrated, pilot systems are targeted in our case. If technical obscurities exist, laboratory prototypes can also be used.

3 Requirements Analysis

In the scope of this research project, the requirements analysis took place without a particular client. Instead, the basis for this project was an already existing business concept, which was developed jointly by our research group at the University of Technology Ilmenau, and our cooperating consulting partner, the Dr. Kuhl Unternehmensberatung, Hardegsen, Germany. Furthermore a study of

Nissen et al. (2015) on quality requirements for virtual consulting services was used, and the general features of advisory consulting were considered.

The process within the prototype should roughly reproduce an expert report by having the opportunity to gather data from the client's company as well as linking these with expert knowledge to finally produce a well-founded assessment on the given subject.

A rough system draft was already outlined in the business concept, which served as basis for the design of the prototype. Thus, this system is supposed to have a survey function, which makes it possible to conduct online surveys. In the course of these surveys different question formats, such as e.g. open questions or scale-based questions, as well as a branching out of questions, should be possible. A further component of this system is the user account, which is necessary for the authentication and registration of a client and can store the required information on him. The data storage and data processing components include the evaluation of survey data, logics on the selection of a recommendation for action and the opportunity to define these logics by means of formulae.

Furthermore, all the required data to issue an expert report, should be stored in a structured way. At the end of the survey, these data should be presented to the user in an edited form, so that the user gets an overview of the key figures and recommendations for action. This generated report can be printed or saved. Moreover, the opportunity to export the raw data from the system should exist, so that the gathered data can be re-used in other software tools.

The concrete requirements are divided into different categories. Initially, however, the requirements were gathered in a uniform, tabular structure without categorization. The category user administration includes some requirements of the user account, as an anonymized participation and the function to add several participants are necessary. The requirements in the field of data collection especially refer to the survey. For example, it should be possible to collect these data either by an external or an internal survey, and to consolidate the results of questionnaires from different participants (with possibly different roles) for the evaluation. The category data import describes requirements of the manual import of survey data, which can subsequently be assigned to a user. In the category data processing, key figures must be calculated on the basis of survey data and recommendations for action should be selected. Furthermore, all the required data, such as questionnaire, survey —and evaluation results, as well as user data should be permanently stored. Moreover, the evaluation results should be presented in a simple and clear way to the client, and it must be possible to print and save them. Furthermore, proposals for a data—and authorization model, as well as for the definition of suitable interfaces were part of the business concept. These will be elaborated on later in this contribution.

Further requirements were derived from a study by Nissen et al. (2015). In this study, the quality criteria of virtualized consulting services were initially determined by a literature review, and subsequently evaluated by an expert group in a Delphi-study. In doing so, a set of quality criteria were defined. We will focus on those that particularly apply to fully virtualized consulting services, and are relevant for application development in this context. More details on quality criteria can also be found in the paper on chances, risks and quality criteria of virtual consulting (Nissen et al. 2017) in this volume.

We will briefly explain these quality criteria in a descending order of importance. These include the general system availability of the virtualized consulting process, as well as the actuality of the gathered data. The criterion, fulfillment, describes the expectations of the client, that the promised and expected service correlates with the resulting solution of the consulting process. In the case of mistakes or problems, the efficiency of the process, as well as the reaction capability of the responsible business consulting, is also important. Moreover, the most sensitive company data should be adequately protected, and a simple way to contact the business consulting should be given. The chance of compensation should also be provided when there are deficiencies in the process. Furthermore, the solution should have an appealing appearance and it should be possible to use the consulting service easily.

Every requirement was then transferred into a uniform tabular structure, to be able to get a complete overview on all requirements. In these tables, requirements were either classified as functional or non-functional requirements, and sorted into one of three categories (user interface, administration and data processing). Subsequently a prioritization of the requirements took place according to their significance for the fundamental functions of the prototype and the benefit, which can be expected, when they are implemented. A mere scale from 0 to 3 was used here:

- 0—Implementation does not take place in the context of a prototype
- 1—minor significance for the implementation
- 2—medium significance for the implementation
- 3—high significance for the implementation

Subsequently ambiguous requirements were specified more accurately. This happened by interviewing the consulting partner since the targeted application would later complement the classical face-to-face project management services of this company. More accurate specifications were needed for the above described service quality requirements as these had to be adapted and formulated on the concrete case of application. Furthermore, central elements were conceptually defined, to attain a uniform understanding. The term 'consulting product' was given to the central element of the prototype, the gathering of data and preparation of an expert report.

In the following, a concrete consulting project, acquired by the client, will be described as an assessment. Moreover, two groups of persons must be differentiated. On the one side is the client, who acquires the assessment. He may invite different persons to enter data, and he finally receives the expert report afterwards. On the other side is the participant, who needs to be invited by the client and only partly gains access to the data gathering. Questionnaires with corresponding answer options are crucial for gathering data. When the collection of data has been completed, a report with recommendations for action and explanatory text blocks is generated.

The list, which was now completed, was finally validated in collaboration with the research group WID at Ilmenau and the consulting partner DKUB. In this process, some requirements were prioritized differently than before. As a result, some requirements are omitted and others attain a greater significance during implementation. For example, the opportunity to add more participants to a survey was more strongly prioritized. In doing so the virtual processes of advisory consulting were specifically considered in the prototype while other necessary functions for commercial use, such as web shop integration, were initially less in focus.

In the following section, based on these requirements, the system design with the development of a data model and software architecture is highlighted. Subsequently the implementation of the requirements is presented by means of various components in the prototype. Then a case study exemplifies how the system is used. Due to non-disclosure considerations, not all details of the real system will be presented. However, the description should give a clear picture of the tasks in developing an online assessment as well as its working in a practical setting.

4　Design and Development

After all the requirements for a prototype have been gathered and specified, the system design and details on the concrete implementation follow. The requirements implicitly refer to a web-based solution, so that web-technologies were specifically chosen. Furthermore, the system design of the prototype should possibly be flexible and extensible, to allow a simple advancement.

4.1　Process Design

Initially the central processes of the prototype were defined to get an impression of the future user experience. The basis for this design was, in turn, the collected requirements, and a first outline of the processes within the business concept.

The first process deals with acquiring an assessment (Fig. 1). For this purpose, the client uses an online-shop, the accurate details of which will not be part of this contribution. There he chooses a consulting product and consequently receives an assessment. Afterwards this acquired assessment is shown to him on an overview page. Every assessment has a detailed view, which lists some details and provides the opportunity to invite any number of participants. The participants are notified by e-mails and with a link within the e-mail they can call up the survey.

The second process deals with the participation in a survey (Fig. 2). In this case, it is necessary to differentiate between the client and the participant, who was invited by e-mail. Whilst a participant receives the link for participating in a survey via e-mail, the client can directly access the survey from the assessment detail page. Afterwards the process is the same again for both user groups. The retrieved data

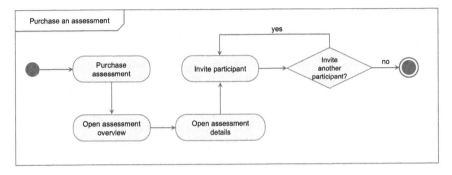

Fig. 1 Illustration of the processes needed to acquire an assessment

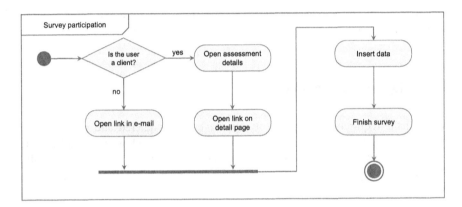

Fig. 2 Illustration of the processes needed for the participation of a survey

Fig. 3 Illustration of the process to call up an expert report

are entered into the online-survey and finally the data are saved, after completing the survey.

The third central process is calling up the expert report after completing the survey (Fig. 3). In this process, the client opens the assessment in his assessment overview once more, chooses the particular assessment, and opens its detailed view. Within the detailed view the user can then call up the expert report and display it in the browser. Furthermore, there is the opportunity to save and print the expert report.

There are several additional processes, for example the process used to create a user account. As this process is, however, generically constructed, according to general known procedures, a detailed modelling was dispensed with. Moreover, there are processes to maintain the templates and for the preparation of new consulting projects, which will be described in detail in the following chapters.

4.2 Data Model

During the development of the data model, several requirements, as well as a preliminary data model from the business concept, and suggestions of the practice partner, were considered. Furthermore, the data model should have the flexibility for an arbitrary focus area of the consulting product, and should provide the opportunity for future expansions. For that reason, the data model is more extensive than the original design in the business concept.

The data model includes four different areas for all the data of a potential consulting product: client data, survey templates, report templates and report data. Within the client data, the entities user and participant are found. According to the requirements, a user is a client, who acquired the product. A participant is a person, who takes part in a survey. For every client who takes part in the survey, a participant is also generated. Furthermore, the entity assessment exists. This entity represents a single purchase of the consulting product and can be assigned to a user. The entity answer saves all the participant's responses of a survey.

The survey template contains all the data, which are needed to compile a survey for a consulting product. Here there is the entity survey that describes the scope of a survey and can be assigned to a product. It also contains the entity section, which groups individual questions under a common title. Furthermore, the entity question exists, which contains the text for a concrete question and more information on the processing within an expert report. Several entities of the type option can be assigned to a question. These present individual answer options for the questions.

A similar purpose is accomplished by the report template, where all data are saved to provide a basic frame for an expert report of a consulting product. Every consulting product has a template, which describes the basic features of the expert report. This expert report is composed of several entities of the type block, which represent individual building blocks of the expert report. This entity can accept various types, and can derive more accurate details from the entity text-input or graph-input, which either describes text or a graphical building block. The differentiation was made here, because text building blocks need less information than a graphical element.

Finally, to issue an expert report, calculated key figures have to enter into the template and afterwards a completed report can be presented. For this purpose the report data is available, which saves the concrete expert report as the entity report. In the report template variables are used, which are individually calculated from the client data, for each expert report. For this reason, the entity value is assigned to the report. The linking between the expert report and the template is presented by the entity entry, which represents a single part of the expert report. To every entry another entity calculation can be assigned, which intermediately stores the results for the graphical elements.

Beyond this core data model, there are more data structures, which, however, were outsourced. These include the data of the authentication of the client, as well as the intermediate stored survey data, which were already implemented in the used third-party survey software LimeSurvey.

4.3 System Architecture

4.3.1 General Approach

Amongst the requirements to the system architecture a high flexibility stands out, in order to be able to react to different application areas in terms of consulting content, changed requirements or new insights in the development process. By choosing prototyping as a model for the development, the requirements arose, that on the one hand, the opportunity for experimenting should be given to be able to validate compiled hypotheses quickly. On the other hand, a certain independency of the programming language should be guaranteed, so that the decision for a programming language can be made dependent on its suitability for the intended use.

The simplest form of structuring an application often is the monolithic architecture, where the complete software is implemented within a single component (Vogel et al. 2011). The advantage of the choice of this architecture style is the increased pace at the beginning of the development, as the system- and developing environment only needs to be established once. A decisive disadvantage of such an application is, however, the inflexibility, as only one programming language can be used. The integration of third-party providing software can also be complicated.

Alternatively, there are flexible architecture styles, such as the approach of service-oriented architecture. Service-oriented architecture describes a collection of services, communicating with each other (Barry 2013). They can be addressed via an interface and can either only exchange simple data, or allow for complex activities among various services (Zdun et al. 2006). The services are reusable, loosely linked, and have a standardized interface (Vogel et al. 2011). As a special case of service-oriented architecture, there is the concept of microservices, where the individual components of the software can be disassembled in even smaller sub-components. These also communicate with each other by a language independent interface via a network (Namiot and Sneps-Sneppe 2014; Newman 2015; Kuchen 2016). The advantage of such architecture is a higher flexibility because, in contrast to the monolithical developing approach, services can be quickly changed or even replaced. Furthermore, the architecture style provides a high modularity so that individual tasks can be conducted in an isolated way. Another advantage is the higher serviceability, as changes in the fundamental development or framework, only affect a small part of the software (Dragoni et al. 2017).

For the implementation of the prototype, a simple form of service-oriented architecture was chosen, which, however, also shows aspects from the microservice concept. After the first outline, the services were roughly structured according to the required functions of the software. Initially three services were developed, which can be complemented by more services in future expansions. As the extent of the in-house development of a survey function was too large for this scope, a service for this work task was established within the system architecture. The implementation of functionality for the user administration and display of web pages also seemed too comprehensive. Therefore, these functions were also outsourced into their own services.

4.3.2 Architectural Components

The backend-service required the major effort during the development, as this had to be implemented from scratch. It represents the core component of the architecture, as the coordination of the other services, data storage and data processing takes place there. Python was chosen as programming language. This language is suitable for a rapid development and provides efficient libraries to analyze data. The decision to use Python was due to the simple syntax, so that a third party can understand the program code quickly and easily. Despite this simple syntax, it is possible to develop complex systems. The reusability and the opportunity of object-orientation also contributed to this decision. Furthermore, Python provides an accelerated developing process, as it is an interpreted language (Theis 2011).

In the backend, the delivered data for an assessment and the corresponding questionnaire as well as the expert report are processed. These data are transmitted by means of a standardized Excel-file. The Excel-file is read, the data are copied into the database and afterwards they are transmitted to the survey-service via the SOAP-interface. This component was used to implement the requirements referring to the storage of formulae for the calculation of key figures and the import and configuration of questionnaires. Figure 4 gives an overview of the system architecture.

The backend-service is closely linked to a database-service, where all the data are deposited. Communication with the frontend takes place via a REST-interface and can only be used with a correlating API-key. The survey-service is linked to a SOAP-interface, which is also secured by a password.

The front end-service provides all the services required for the graphical user interface. This includes the administration of assessments by the client. This service also takes over the authentication of the end user, and therefore provides the opportunity to create a user account. *Wordpress* is used for this process, as it contains the required functionality and is freely available. This way it is possible for the client to open up a user account, and to log on to the system with an e-mail address and a password. Furthermore, pages for an overview of all purchased

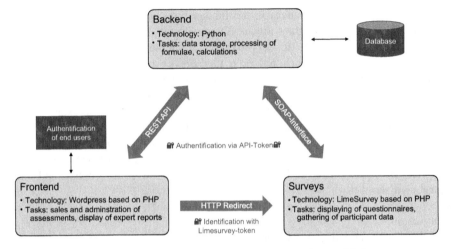

Fig. 4 Illustration of the overall system architecture with key services and links

assessments, a detailed view of a specific assessment with a display of the participants, and the opportunity to show the expert report, were implemented.

Communication with the survey-service takes place via simple HTTP-redirects, where the user is redirected within the browser. The authentication takes place via an internal token of the survey-service.

The survey-service supplies every function for the administration and implementation of the survey. LimeSurvey was chosen as the tool to conduct the survey. LimeSurvey is an extended open source survey tool and supplies various advantages compared to other solutions such as e.g. surveymonkey. In addition to the fact that this software is freely available, LimeSurvey supplies a comprehensive interface for the communication with other services within the architecture. Furthermore, it supplies good opportunities to expand the software and includes a large range of functions. LimeSurvey is based on the programming language PHP, which is widely spread in the Internet and uses MySQL as data storage. This database is within the context of this prototype only responsible for the intermediate storage of the survey data, which are transmitted to the backend, after successfully completing the survey.

The survey within LimeSurvey is automatically applied and configured by the backend-service via the SOAP-interface. Furthermore, a key is issued to every participant, which simplifies the later assignments of questions to a specific assessment and also excludes multiple use of the survey by one person. Besides, a surveillance of the progress of a participant is possible, as the surveys can be interrupted.

The administration within the prototype is initially limited to the construction of new consulting products. At some later point of time more administration functions could be implemented, which would be suitable to support the client or solve problems in consulting.

All the data for a concrete consulting product are essentially stored in an Excel-file, which consists of two different worksheets. The first worksheet contains all the data for a survey, and the second worksheet all data for the generation of the expert report for the client, after completing the survey. The supply of Excel-files takes place via a simple file transfer on the server of the backend-service. Subsequently a command line-tool has to be rendered, which stores the data in the database and releases the corresponding survey into LimeSurvey.

The non-functional requirements have already been looked at on this level, as they do not refer to individual functions of the software, but rather define common qualitative requirements. It was attempted to implement the requirement of system availability with distributed architecture, as in this way the individual services can partly operate independently from each other. The efficiency of the consulting service can be guaranteed by the chosen standard software, as this provides already known operating patterns, which supplies efficient processes for the user. Privacy will be guaranteed by the authentication concept. By using the API-token most attacks can already be barred. In the case of a future version it is advisable though, to think about data encryption. Finally, the requirements of aesthetics were considered by constructing the prototype in the design of the practice partner.

5   Demonstration

In this section the resulting software will be briefly demonstrated with various screen shots, to convey a first impression. The particular application area here is the assessment of the project management quality for a given project based on a survey amongst project stakeholders. These can have different roles, such as project manager and project worker or external project partner. Based on the role, the questionnaire used in the respective survey changes adaptively. Finally, the virtual assessment product was termed ProMAT (Project Management Assessment Tool).

The design of the user-frontend was based on the website of the practice partner, a project management consulting firm. The assessment can be bought by the client directly on the website of the consulting firm (Fig. 5).

The overview page of the consulting product gives some details about the product, its basic principles as well as its benefits. Furthermore, clients that have already used the tool have the option to give feedback via a feedback-form. Besides that, feedback and questions can be communicated via e-mail and telephone. Corresponding contact information is presented in the header of the website.

Once the client clicks on the shopping-cart-button the assessment will be stored in the personal shopping cart. If the client then clicks on "proceed to checkout" he will be forwarded to the checkout page of the assessment where he must enter basic information like his name, address or e-mail. Furthermore, the client is asked to select a payment method. Once the client clicks on "Send Order" the assessment buying process is finished and the client will be able to use the assessment product.

Fig. 5 The assessment can be bought on the website of the consulting firm (see bottom)

The assessment overview page serves the administration of an individual assessment (Fig. 6). When an assessment has been acquired, the client can administrate the participants of the survey. For this reason, there is a set form to attach participants by means of their e-mail addresses. Afterwards they can be invited to the survey per e-mail. When the client has logged himself in as a participant, he can open the survey directly from the detailed view, and participate. Furthermore, every participant is shown and whether he has already been invited, or whether he has completed the survey. Finally, the client may call up the generated expert report.

The implementation of the survey is done via an online-questionnaire, which is currently quite simply designed. The questionnaire consists of various pages with grouped questions, referring to a specific topic of project management. Figure 7 displays an exemplary illustration. At the head of the page the actual progress of the questionnaire is shown to the participant, subsequently followed by individual questions. The questions are composed of a text and the possible answer options to it. Often, only one answer can be chosen. However, in the case of multiple-choice-questions several options may be chosen. After completing the survey, the participant is directed to a page in the user-front end, where the software thanks for his participation. In the background the survey data are transferred from the survey-service to the backend-service.

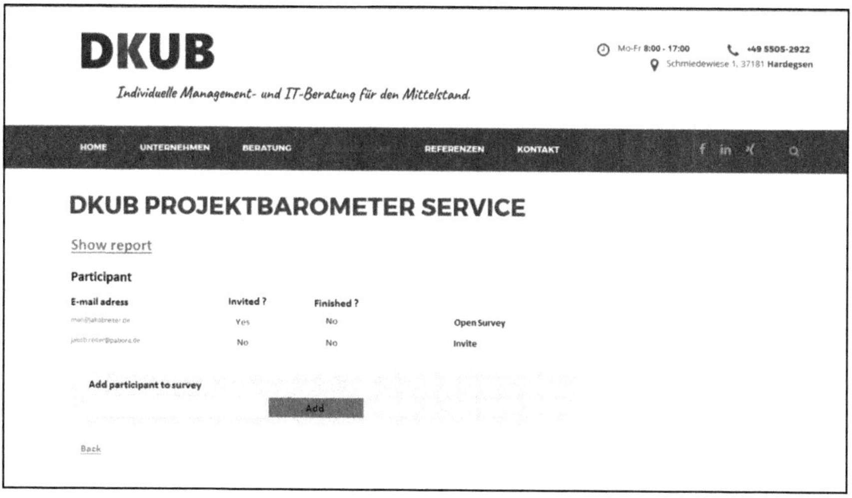

Fig. 6 Assessment overview page (translated)

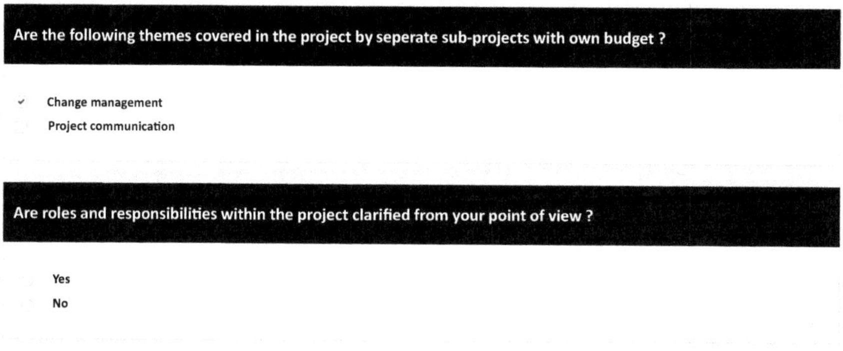

Fig. 7 Exemplary illustration of two questions in the survey-service (translated)

After all participants have successfully taken part in the survey, the client can call up an expert report via his detailed view of an assessment. Subsequently the client has the opportunity to read the expert report directly in the browser, to save it as a PDF-file, or to print it. The report is composed of an introductory radar-chart (Fig. 8), which summarizes all the key figures of the report. It is divided in six perspectives on the quality of project management.

Furthermore, the report contains various sections on these different perspectives of project management. These sections are comprised of a heading, a graph and text blocks, which are shown, depending on the answers of the participants in the survey. The key figures for the graphical elements are also generated from these data. Figure 9 shows an exemplary section on project communication.

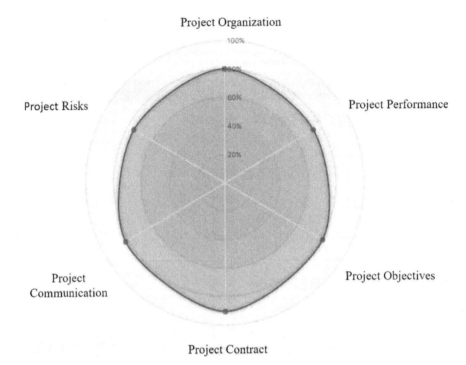

Fig. 8 Overview radar chart of expert report (translated)

Projektkommunikation

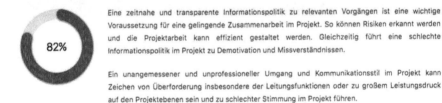

Eine zeitnahe und transparente Informationspolitik zu relevanten Vorgängen ist eine wichtige Voraussetzung für eine gelingende Zusammenarbeit im Projekt. So können Risiken erkannt werden und die Projektarbeit kann effizient gestaltet werden. Gleichzeitig führt eine schlechte Informationspolitik im Projekt zu Demotivation und Missverständnissen.

Ein unangemessener und unprofessioneller Umgang und Kommunikationsstil im Projekt kann Zeichen von Überforderung insbesondere der Leitungsfunktionen oder zu großem Leistungsdruck auf den Projektebenen sein und zu schlechter Stimmung im Projekt führen.

Bei Projekten, die einen erheblichen oder fundamentalen Wandel in der Organisation auslösen, ist ein aktives Changemanagment notwendig. So können Organisation und Mitarbeiter auf die Veränderungen vorbereitet werden und diese gelingen. Eine große Zahl von Reorganisationsprojekten sind nicht erfolgreich, obwohl es dafür weder betriebswirtschaftliche noch technische Gründe gibt. Dabei mangelt es meist nur an der Beantwortung von zwei Fragen: 1. Wie können die Mitarbeiter den neuen Strukturen angepaßt werden? 2. Wie können die alten Muster im Kopf durch neue ersetzt werden? Change Management liefert Lösungen zur Beantwortung dieser Fragen.

Fig. 9 A section on project communication from a generated expert report (in German)

The expert report gives the client an approximate overview on the status of the project management in his project. Moreover, recommendations for actions to improve the situation are given.

6 Conclusion, Limitations and Further Research

With the present system, it is possible to conduct advisory consulting on in principle an arbitrary subject in a virtualized way. For this purpose, a questionnaire for the gathering of participant data is used, and procedure to generate an expert report automatically from this data are provided. Moreover, a front-end for the client is available where he can administrate his surveys.

The focus of this contribution was mainly on the technical realization, while the content of the consulting product was not considered here in much detail. The first generated expert reports are promising. However, there is still room for improvement, and an extensive evaluation of the virtual assessment is only now starting. On the technical side, some limitations should be dealt with. For a market-ready product, the authentication concept has to be revised and different software for the front end-service may have to be implemented, as some requirements could only be realized in Wordpress with quite some difficulties.

In the future, a second consulting product from another topic area will be integrated. The practice partner has already indicated, that he would be prepared to develop the system further, and use it in a complementary way to the classical project management consulting services offered. Currently, the system is being prepared for use in a German DAX30 company to assist in continuously monitoring projects.

References

Allegra M, Fulantelli G, Chiazzese G, Stanford-Smith B, Kidd PT (2000) Distance consulting for small and medium-sized enterprises. E-business: key issues, applications and technologies. IOS press, Amsterdam, pp 953–959

Balzert H, Balzert H, Koschke R, Lämmel U, Liggesmeyer, P, Quante J (2009) Lehrbuch der Softwaretechnik: Basiskonzepte und Requirements Engineering. 3rd edn. Spektrum

Bamberger I, Wrona T (2012) Konzeptionen der strategischen Unternehmensberatung. In: Wrona T (ed) Strategische Unternehmensberatung, 6th edn. Gabler, Wiesbaden, pp 1–44

Barry DK (2013) Web services, service-oriented architectures, and cloud computing, 2nd edn. Elsevier

Bunse C, von Knethen A (2008) Vorgehensmodelle kompakt. Spektrum

Deelmann T (2012) Organisations- und Prozessberatung. In: Nissen V, Klauk B (eds) Studienführer Consulting. Gabler, Wiesbaden

Dragoni N, Giallorenzo S, Lluch-Lafuente A, Mazzara M, Montesi F, Mustafin R, Safina L (2017) Microservices: yesterday, today, and tomorrow. Present and ulterior software engineering. Springer, Berlin

Fulantelli G, Allegra M (2003) Small company attitude towards ICT based solutions: some key-elements to improve it. J Educ Technol Soc 6:45–49

Fulantelli G, Chiazzese G, Allegra M (2001) Distance training as part of a distance consulting solution ED-MEDIA 2001 world conference on educational multimedia, hypermedia & telecommunications. In: Proceedings Tampere, Finland, 25–30 June 2001, pp 527–532

Hevner A, Chatterjee S (2010) design science research in information systems—theory and practice. Springer, Berlin, pp 9–22

Hevner AR, March ST, Park J, Ram S (2004) Design science in information systems research. MIS Q 28(1):75–105

König S (2009) Ein Wiki-basiertes Vorgehensmodell für Business Intelligence Projekte. In: Baars H, Rieger B (eds) Perspektiven der betrieblichen Management-und Entscheidungs-unterstützung, pp 34–51

Kuchen H (2016) Architekturmuster. In Gronau N et al. (eds) Enzyklopädie der Wirtschaftsinformatik. 9th edn. Berlin. GITO. http://www.enzyklopaedie-der-wirtschaftsinformatik.de. Accessed 14 Dez 2016

Kuhrmann M (2012) Prototyping. In Gronau N et al. (eds) Enzyklopädie der Wirtschaftsinformatik. 9th edn. Berlin. GITO. http://www.enzyklopaedie-der-wirtschaftsinformatik.de/. Accessed 14 Dez 2016

Lippold D (2016) Grundlagen der Unternehmensberatung: Strukturen – Konzepte – Methoden. Springer Gabler, Wiesbaden

Namiot D, Sneps-Sneppe M (2014) On micro-services architecture. Intl. J Open Inf Technol 2 (9):24–27

Newman S (2015) Building microservices: designing fine-grained systems. O'Reilly Media, Sebastopol

Nissen V, Seifert H (2016) Virtualisierung in der Unternehmensberatung. Eine Studie im deutschen Beratungsmarkt. BDU e.V, Bonn

Nissen V, Seifert H (2017) Digital transformation in business consulting—status quo in Germany. In this volume

Nissen V, Seifert H, Blumenstein M (2015) Virtualisierung von Beratungsleistungen: Qualitätsanforderungen, Chancen und Risiken der digitalen Transformation in der Unternehmensberatung aus der Klientenperspektive. In: Deelmann T, Ockel DM (eds) Handbuch der Unternehmensberatung, 25th edn. Erich Schmidt Verlag, Berlin

Nissen V, Seifert H, Blumenstein M (2017) Chances. Risks and quality criteria of virtual consulting, In this volume

Patig S, Dibbern J (2016) Requirements engineering. In: Gronau N et al. (eds) Enzyklopädie der Wirtschaftsinformatik. 9th edn. Berlin. GITO. http://www.enzyklopaedie-der-wirtschaftsinformatik.de. Accessed 10 Dez 2016

Peffers K, Tuunanen T, Rothenberger MA, Chatterjee S (2007) A design science research methodology for information systems research. J Manage Inf Syst 24(3):45–77

Pohl K (2008) Requirements engineering: Grundlagen, Prinzipien, Techniken, 2nd edn. dpunkt, Heidelberg

Sommerville I (2011) Software engineering, 8th edn. Pearson Studium

Strehlau R, Sieper M (2009) E-Consulting 2.0: der Einsatz von Web 2.0 im Beratungsgeschäft. Zeitschrift der Unternehmensberatung 4(2):57–61

Theis T (2011) Einstieg in Python, 3rd edn. Galileo Press, Bonn

Vogel O, Arnold I, Chughtai A, Kehrer T (2011) Software architecture: a comprehensive framework and guide for practitioners. Springer, New York

Werth D, Greff T, Scheer AW (2016) Consulting 4.0—Die Digitalisierung der Unternehmensberatung. HMD Praxis der Wirtschaftsinformatik 53(1):55–70

Zdun U, Hentrich C, v.d.Aalst W (2006) A survey of patterns for service-oriented architectures. Internet Protoc Technol 1(3):132–143

Author Biographies

Volker Nissen holds the Chair of Information Systems Engineering in Services at Technische Universität Ilmenau, Germany, since 2005. Prior to this, he pursued a consulting career, including positions as manager at IDS Scheer AG, director at DHC GmbH, and CEO of NISSCON Ltd.,

Germany. In 1994 he received a Ph.D. degree in Economic Sciences with distinction from the University of Goettingen, Germany. His current research interests include the digital transformation of the consulting industry, the management of IT-agility, metaheuristic optimization, and process acceptance research. He is author and editor of 19 books and some 200 other publications, including papers in Business & Information Systems Engineering, Information Systems Frontiers, IEEE Transactions on EC, IEEE Transactions on NN, and Annals of OR.

Jochen Kuhl studied economics with a focus on business informatics in Braunschweig and Göttingen. He obtained his Ph.D. in Business Informatics at the University of Göttingen. Jochen is Managing Director of Dr. Kuhl Unternehmensberatung and specialized in the optimization and digitization of management and business processes in midmarket companies. Furthermore, he is Managing Director of MeyerundKuhl Spezialwäschen GmbH, which is specialized in innovative washing and impregnation processes.

Hendrik Kräft studied Social Sciences (Diplom Soz.-Wirt) with a focus on media and communication in Göttingen. He is a consultant and project manager at the Dr. Kuhl Unternehmensberatung and manages the business field of project management. His focus is the methodical development of project management and the consulting of midmarket customers in the digitization of business processes.

Henry Seifert is a graduate engineer for media technology and since 2011 working as a management consultant. His main focus is on the automotive industry and artificial intelligence, analytics, process optimization and requirements management. He works in projects in the area of sales and after sales processes as well as professional learning. As doctoral candidate at the Group for Information Systems Engineering in Services at Technische Universität Ilmenau, he examines the digital transformation in the consulting industry. The goal of his dissertation is to demonstrate the opportunities and limitations of virtualization, as well as the design of artifacts that enable the realization of virtual consulting services.

Jakob Reiter is a Master student of Business Information Systems Engineering at Technische Universität Ilmenau, Germany. He holds a Bachelor of Science and is currently finishing his Master studies with research on digitalized consulting products at the chair of Prof. Volker Nissen. Besides his study, he works as a freelance web developer.

Jim Eidmann is an apprenticeship specialist in application development at the Dr. Kuhl Unternehmensberatung. His main focus is the development of software prototypes.

Consulting Self-services—A Multi-project Management Application

Friedrich Augenstein

Abstract Consulting self-service applications are the type of digital services where consulting know-how is condensed in easy to use *apps* that require no or only small involvement of consultants in a project. App users at the client's company are enabled to solve problems in their company on their own by using professional and practice-proofed procedures implemented in the app. This article shows how such an application for (multi-) project management is working. It offers easy access to a consulting service reference model in project management by dividing the model up into several phases, and every phase into several steps. Every step is supported by a variety of tools and templates, e.g. based on Microsoft Excel or Microsoft Word. The future role of the consultant is discussed as well as the approach for the development of consulting self-service applications.

1 Classification of Self-service Applications and Research Question

In recent scientific discussions about the future of consulting several classifications of digital consulting services have been developed. One classification is derived from service management research and describes to what degree a digital consulting service fulfils the following criteria (Nissen and Seifert 2016):

- Standardization
- Integration (of internal and external resources)
- Modularization
- Interaction
- Digitalization.

Another classification describes the degree of the involvement of the client and the degree of the consultants' engagement (see Fig. 1 on the following page).

F. Augenstein (✉)
DHBW, Stuttgart, Germany
e-mail: friedrich.augenstein@dhbw-stuttgart.de

© Springer International Publishing AG 2018
V. Nissen (ed.), *Digital Transformation of the Consulting Industry*,
Progress in IS, https://doi.org/10.1007/978-3-319-70491-3_15

371

Fig. 1 Classification of digital services (Adapted from Werth et al. 2016; Johann et al. 2016)

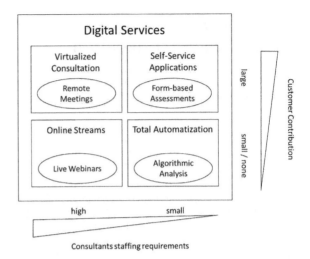

Self-service applications need only small consultant involvement, because consultants' knowledge is incorporated in these applications. This allows the clients—as the users of such an application—to work out professional solutions for a problem in their company on their own by using professional consultants' knowledge. To incorporate consultants' knowledge into these applications, solution pathways have to be standardized. As a whole consulting process is supported by information and communication technology, we classify such applications as computer controlled consulting solutions according to (Johann et al. 2016).

The research question of this article is how consulting know-how can be implemented into a self-service application in a way that allows a user—being familiar with the topic of the application—to solve a problem in his company without or only with little consultants' support by using the application.

To answer this question scientific approaches of reference modelling as well as consulting literature approaches of how to standardize consulting services are considered. This is the basis for the deduction of a standardized approach for the development of consulting self-service applications. The feasibility of this approach is shown by an application for project and multi-project management. Scenarios for the use of this application are shown and advantages for the user compared to conventional consulting services are specified. The article ends with a discussion of the impact of this approach to the consulting business and of future research to be done.

2 Scientific Background

The individual development of solution pathways for problems within a company is time and cost consuming and requires consolidated knowledge of the problem topic. Therefore, in companies often so called reference models are used to standardize typical processes in a company e.g. in accounting or human resources (Dillerup and Stoi 2016). "[...] Reference models are information models that are developed with the aim of being reused for different but similar application scenarios" (Becker and Delfmann 2007). Reference models, e.g. implemented in enterprise resource planning (ERP) software, are thus not only more cost-efficient and quicker available for companies, but often also of higher quality than self-developed solutions (Dillerup and Stoi 2016).

A development process for a reference model in project management is described in Ahlemann (2009). It consists of the following phases and corresponding activities:

- *Problem definition* phase: problem definition
- *Exploration and generation of hypotheses* phase: construction of the information system architecture, literature review/analysis of project management standards, analysis of project management software systems, construction/refinement of the reference model
- *Validation* phase: interviews with domain experts, practical application, refinement of the reference model
- *Documentation* phase: documentation.

To set up and reuse a reference model a high standardization of the underlying approach of such a model is required. For a lot of management disciplines well-structured and standardized approaches exist that show the way towards a solution to a managerial problem and that can be used in a reference model sense. Often these approaches are structured in a phase-by-phase procedure showing what particular steps have to be taken and in what sequence to work out the details of a solution. The pathway from a problem to a solution of the problem is thus shown in a transparent way. E.g. in strategic management the way towards a new strategy can be described in the following phases: development of targets—strategic analysis—target revision—strategy development—strategy implementation—strategic control (Paul and Wollny 2011). In cost management the approach of the overhead value analysis is widespread and follows a phase by phase approach as well (Van Assen 2009) that can be visualized as follows (Fig. 2).

In project management these standardized phase-wise approaches are very common. For example the PMBOK—the Project Management Body of Knowledge (PMI 2000)—shows such very common phase models like shown in Fig. 3.

So literature offers an answer to the WHY certain methods should be applied and why they should be structured in a certain way, but offers no detailed answer to the HOW TO use these methods. A hands-on *operating manual* for these methods is missing. For instance in project management in the above mentioned model the

Fig. 2 The overhead value analysis process

Project Initiation
Project Planning
Project Execution
Project Closure

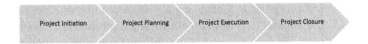

Fig. 3 The project management process

reader of a project management book is told to plan a project by setting up a work breakdown structure, but is not told in detail how to identify tasks to be done in a project, how to structure them in a work breakdown structure hierarchy etc.

Therefore, the main problem in using established management methods is the missing easy, structured access to methodical know-how in management topics. This hands-on access and the support by templates and tools would ensure a usage of those methods in an efficient and professional way.

Consultants use such standardized *operating manual* like methods for their day-to-day work (Niedereichholz 2008), but they do not offer such methods as self-service applications. And these methods are to the author's knowledge not enabling the client to use them without consultants' support.

So these approaches have to be further detailed by dividing every phase into several steps. The project management process in Fig. 3 is further detailed by the following figure that shows a project management method that has been worked out by consultants (definition phase and initialization phase are used synonymous).

Figure 4 shows the transfer of the reference model idea to consulting services. A standardized approach is developed using a phase-by-phase pathway towards the solution of a managerial problem. Every phase is detailed into several steps, every step is supported by tools (that offer analytical and calculation features like e.g. analysis tools in spreadsheet or database format) and templates (that offer proven and tested samples e.g. a form to be filled out in a text processing system).

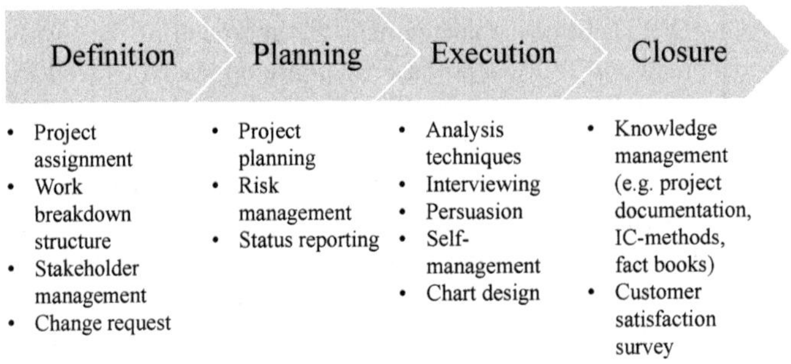

Definition
Planning
Execution
Closure
• Project assignment
• Work breakdown structure
• Stakeholder management
• Change request
• Project planning
• Risk management
• Status reporting
• Analysis techniques
• Interviewing
• Persuasion
• Self-management
• Chart design
• Knowledge management (e.g. project documentation, IC-methods, fact books)
• Customer satisfaction survey

Fig. 4 Project phases detailed by steps and templates (Adapted from: Wegmann and Winklbauer 2006)

For the application shown in this article the above mentioned project management models and standards are used. For multi-project management the above mentioned model already contains certain aspects like (cross-project) knowledge management. Further topics of multi-project management are e.g. cross-project resource management, managing project dependencies, prioritization of project proposals etc. Another important topic in project management is the project controlling (Fiedler 2010). All these topics are implemented in the application shown in this article.

3 General Approach for the Development of Consulting Self-service Applications

The objective of the approach presented here is to show how management methods— in project management, strategic management, cost management and others—can be structured transparently and to develop an intuitive, hands-on access to them. The deliverable of this approach then is a self-service application as an *operating manual* for the professional usage of a particular method.

The scientific basis laid by reference models and reference model development shown above supports this approach. Standardized phase-by-phase management methods like the ones mentioned above for strategic management, cost management and project management fulfil the preconditions for a reference model. The reference model development process shown above is the basis for the implementation of corresponding self-service applications.

Thus, from the reference model development process shown above and from the author's professional experience gained in several global consulting firms the following general approach for the development of consulting self-service applications for a particular method (e.g. for a project management application) can be derived:

1. Problem definition: define the problem domain (e.g. project management) and gain overview of the sub-topics (e.g. multi project management, project controlling).
2. Exploration and generation of hypotheses:

   a. Explore methods and phase-by-phase approaches in the selected topic (e.g. PMBOK approach, PRINCE 2 approach in project management).
   b. Derive a *best of* reference model by merging the considered approaches—the criteria of what is *best* and the discussion and decision process might be defined individually for each development process. The model should fit the requirements of a reference model (standardization, degree of coverage, reusability, and modularization).
   c. Structure the model into several phases to get an overall process for the application of this model.
   d. Divide each phase up into several steps to add more detail to the approach.

e. Describe in detail how to proceed in each step.
f. Implement the method in a web-based *click-by-click* way that offers an easy access to the phases and steps of the method. Develop a hypertext document (e.g. in MS-PowerPoint) with navigation and link features.
g. Develop tools (e.g. multi-project analysis for identifying inter-project dependencies) and templates (e.g. a project status report) in a common data format like Microsoft Excel, Microsoft Word etc. to support a particular step in the method and to give hands-on help to the user. Avoid macro programming and other *black box* items to enable an easy adoption of the model to the user's needs. Link the tools and templates to the corresponding steps of the method.

3. Validation: Test the application in pilot projects and let it be tested by experts in the topic of the app.
4. Documentation: Implement the application by exporting the hypertext document in a common format e.g. as PDF file so that it can run on several platforms. Develop a *how to implement and use* guideline for the user of the application.

The steps 1 and 2a can be done by using the models offered in literature. The next steps require expert knowledge. The issue here is to find an expert being able and willing to provide the knowledge needed for detailing the model.

4 The Self-service Application "Project Management Tool"

The self-service application *Project Management Tool* introduced in this article is based on the project management phase-by-phase approach shown above and complemented by multi-project management parts. It has been developed using the process described in the previous chapter and offers an easy *operating manual like* access to expert project management knowledge.

The application is computer-based. It can thus be classified as self-service application and as a computer controlled consulting solution in the above mentioned way. It shows a high degree of standardization, modularization and digitization according to the first classification shown above.

The target group for this application are project managers and inhouse consultants. They have the required knowledge to use the app in an appropriate way without or only little support of an external consultant. And they have the need to use well-tested and established solution pathways for the problems within their companies.

To make clear—at least for some topics—how the concepts in the chapters above are transferred into this application, the functionality of the app is illustrated exemplarily by showing the following pages of the app—with at least one page out of every phase:

• Introduction phases—Handling: Fulfilment of the last point in the development process (*documentation*).

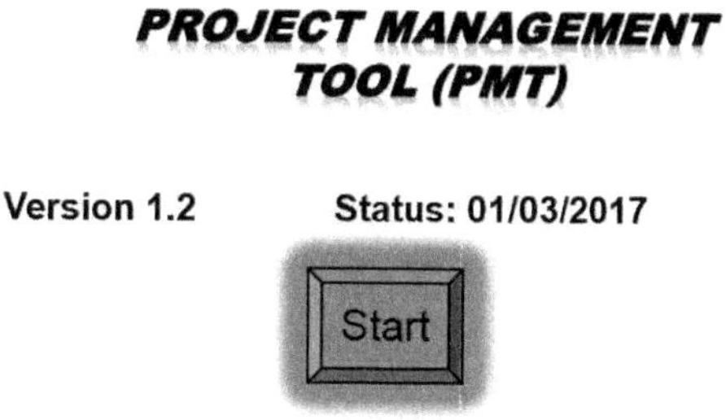

Fig. 5 The application—start
screen

**PROJECT MANAGEMENT
TOOL (PMT)**

Version 1.2   Status: 01/03/2017

- Strategic Project Portfolio Management phase—Strategic Project Portfolio Management: Illustrating the reference model and the phase-by-phase approach in the structural elements of the app, also illustrating the multi-project management functionality in the app and illustrating the analytical feasibility of the linked tools.
- Project Initialization phase—Project Charter: Illustrating single-project management functionality in the app and illustrating the sample character of the linked templates as well as the hyperlink mechanism in the app.
- Project Planning phase—Communication: Illustrating the communication planning in single-project management and illustrating the sample character of the linked templates.
- Project Execution phase—Team Development: Illustrating the integration of established and tested tools out of literature (see reference model development process, step 2).
- Project Controlling phase—Single Project Controlling: Illustrating the project controlling functionality in the app.
- Project Review and Knowledge Management phase—Overview: Illustrating the integration of consulting knowledge (see Fig. 4—the project management method developed by consultants).

The self-service application *Project Management Tool* is a PDF file that was created in Microsoft PowerPoint and then exported as PDF. When the PDF is opened the start screen appears (Fig. 5).

The user starts the app by clicking on the "Start" button. The app can be easily handled by using buttons and links. So the user can use the application like an "app" or a website. The handling of the app is well documented and made transparent to the user (Fig. 6).

The application is a reference model for project and multi-project management. The selected structure of the app is a phase-by-phase approach mainly based on the PMBOK methodology expanded by multi-project management tools. This structure is represented by the main menu bar on the left that allows a direct access to the particular phases of the application. The detailing of a particular phase is carried out by a phase-specific menu bar that appears at the upper side of the screen. Using this menu bar the user has access to the steps of a phase (see Fig. 7).

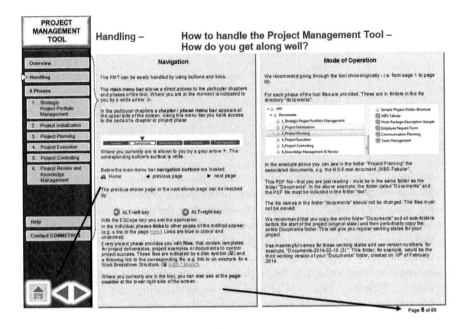

Fig. 6 The application handling is illustrated

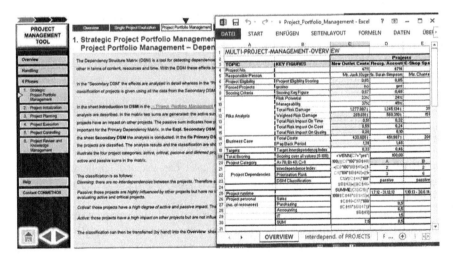

Fig. 7 The structure of the app is represented by the menu bars—here shown in the Strategic Project Portfolio Management phase and also showing the multi-project-management tool

Figure 7 shows a sample screen of the app that illustrates the menu bars representing this structure. Also the multi-project management functionality in the app and the analytical feasibility of the linked tools is shown.

The user can access the particular parts of the application by clicking the corresponding button. This is an appropriate way to use the app for experienced users looking for certain solutions for a particular problem in project management. A phase-by-phase (accessible by the menu bar at the left) and within a phase a step-by-step (accessible by the menu bar at the upper side of the screen) approach is recommended for users who want to ensure to use the consistent and complete approach of the app to set up and manage a project. They follow the structure of the underlying project management method phase by phase and step by step.

In the *Project Management Tool* application nearly 70 Word, Excel and PowerPoint documents are linked to the steps of the app. These tools and templates come out of project management literature and out of consulting knowledge the author gained in more than twenty years of consulting experience. Thus these tools and templates are well-tested and practice-proven. At the end of this chapter for every phase of the app all tools and templates are listed.

One example for such a tool is the "Project_Portfolio_Management" file shown in Fig. 7. This also is an example for some of the documents of the app that are linked to each other, so that an analytical structure is implemented containing analytical consulting knowledge. The example in Fig. 7 contains a sophisticated evaluation of the project eligibility and a resulting project rating.

The single-project management functionality in the app and the sample character of the linked templates is illustrated by the project charter template. Every step of the *Project Management Tool* provides the user with files that contain tools and templates for deliverables, examples, analytics or documents to control project success. These files are indicated by a computer symbol and a following link to the corresponding file, e.g. a link to a template for a project charter. In the example shown in the next figure when the link "Single_Project_Evaluation_Template" is clicked a template in MS-Excel format opens that can be edited by the user and contains a project charter in one sheet of the file.

In the *Project Charter* template the yellow cells can be edited, the white cells contain data out of other sheets of the Excel file and are locked (see the following Fig. 8).

In the Project Planning phase a *Communication Plan* for single-project management is developed using a template linked to that phase and here to the step Communication (Fig. 9).

The *Team Development* page out of the Project Execution phase is illustrating the integration of established and tested tools out of literature, here the Tuckman phase model of *Team Development* as shown in Fig. 10.

Another example is the set-up and controlling of a work breakdown structure. In the *Project Management Tool* a template for this is contained and the use of that template for project controlling is described in detail. When the user clicks on the link "WBS-Tabular" a excel template opens where he can set-up the work breakdown structure and type in the corresponding data in the table (see Fig. 11). The

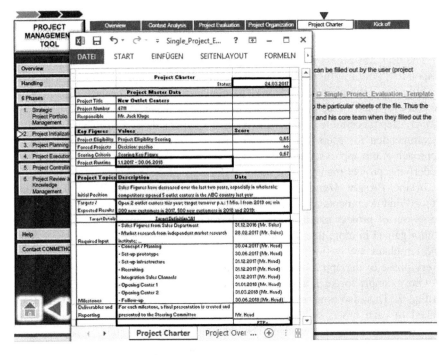

Fig. 8 The project charter template

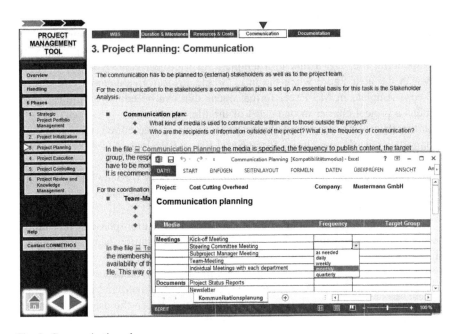

Fig. 9 Communication plan

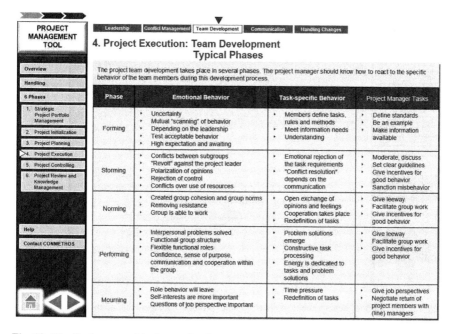

Fig. 10 The Tuckman model of team development

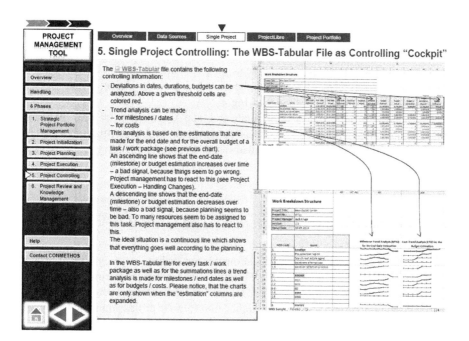

Fig. 11 Project controlling—Setting-up a work breakdown structure and using automatic evaluation functionality like milestone trend analysis

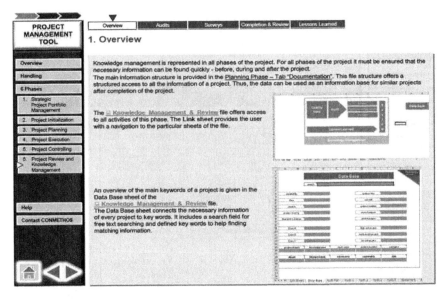

Fig. 12 Knowledge management is part of the project management method developed by consultants

template contains automatic evaluation schemes e.g. for a milestone trend analysis, a well-established controlling analysis for the adherence to schedules (Fiedler 2010).

The *Overview* page out of the Project Review and Knowledge Management phase shows how consulting knowledge is integrated into the app (see Fig. 12). The knowledge management is part of the detailed project management method developed by consultants as shown in Fig. 4.

The following tools (that offer analytical and calculation features like e.g. analysis tools in spreadsheet or database format) and templates (that offer proven and tested samples e.g. a form to be filled out in a text processing system) are used in the phases of the app (Table 1).

5   Utilization Scenarios, Experience and Critical Reflection

The *Project Management Tool* application is used mainly in postgraduate master classes in business administration at universities in Germany. The master students are all employed at a company and study in cooperative education programs. So they have the opportunity to use the application in their professional environment. They all have to work on a project during their master program and often work as consultants or inhouse consultants. So these master students are good representatives for the target group of the app.

Table 1 Tools and templates of the project management tool

Phase	Name	Category	Format	Description
Strategic project portfolio management	Project employee qualification	Template	Excel	Listing of employees in a company available for projects, for every employee qualification details are specified
	Project employee utilization	Template	Excel	Listing of employees in a company available for projects with their current utilization in line business and in projects
	Project portfolio management	Tool	Excel (7 sheets)	Overview, rating and prioritization of all projects in a company; the particular sheets in this excel file evaluate also the interdependencies of projects
	Single project evaluation template	Tool	Excel (7 sheets)	In the particular sheets of the file all characteristics of a project are collected triggers, eligibility, scoring, risks, business case, targets and organization. All the data is concentrated in the project charter
Project initialization	Context analysis	Template	Excel (2 sheets)	Listing of factors that influence the project (markets, strategies, legal requirements, technical issues etc.)
	Kick-off agenda	Template	Excel	Sample agenda for a project kick-off workshop
	Role descriptions	Template	Word (14 pages)	Sample descriptions for roles in a project
	Stakeholder analysis	Template	Excel (2 sheets)	Template for listing and classification of stakeholders, also listing of measures how to deal with them; hints for working out the analysis
Project planning	Sample project folder structure	Template	Windows explorer folders	Folder structure with up to 3 levels for a standardized documentation scheme in projects
	Communication planning	Template	Excel	Sample for a communication plan
	Employee request form	Template	Excel	Form to request employees for a particular project
	Team management	Tool	Excel (6 sheets)	Tool for the management of the project team with contact information, committee structure and participation, attendance for the project and open issues
	WBS tabular	Tool	Excel	A work breakdown structure for a project in tabular form, controlling

(continued)

Table 1 (continued)

Phase	Name	Category	Format	Description
				of schedules, budgets, earned value analysis, trend analysis
	Work package description	Tool	Excel	Work package description with start and end dates, responsibilities, targets, tasks, risks, budgets, percentage of completion and others, planned and actual figures
Project execution	Change request form	Template	Word	Form for a change request to be sent to the project manager
	Time sheet	Template	Excel	Time sheet sample for a project employee for the monthly recording of the time worked on the project separated to tasks
Project controlling	ProjectLibre test controlling	Tool	Project libre	A sample ProjectLibre file with Gantt charts and time and cost information that can be adopted to a particular project
	Status report	Template	Word	Template for a status report to be prepared by the project manager and to be presented to the project sponsor or steering committee
Knowledge management and review	Knowledge management and review	Tool	Excel (16 sheets)	A tool containing review and audit forms, forms for assessing the satisfaction of several stakeholder groups, evaluation sheets and lessons learned

The application has been distributed to more than fifty master students yet. Moreover the app has been sold to ten companies. The author had the opportunity to coach master students within the framework of their master thesis and companies in the usage of the app. Typical utilization scenarios—in each case described by an example—have emerged:

- Complete integration of the app into business processes within the user's company, e.g. within the framework of developing a project management handbook. Here at a professional training company the app was the basis for the development of a project management handbook. The app was complemented by approaches of agile project management.
- The author as an external consultant supported on-site at the user's company in three workshops—lasting for two to four hours—in the appropriate usage and enhancement of the app.
- Usage of single parts of the app, also as "spin doctor" for company specific solutions. Here a high tech professional services company uses parts of the app (e.g. work breakdown structure tool, project controlling tool) for a project to

integrate an acquired company in the business processes of the mother company. Parts of the app are used and adapted to company specific needs. The external consultant was not needed for any on-site support.

- Usage of the app and its approach to set up new consulting services. Here a subsidiary of an audit and tax consulting firm used the phase-by-phase approach and the approach of supporting tools and templates for the development of new consulting services. The author as an external consultant supported on-site at the user's firm in two half-day workshops in ensuring an appropriate transfer of the approach to new consulting services.

These utilization scenarios also confirm the intended target group of the app defined in the previous chapter—project managers and inhouse consultants. However, external consultants using the approach of the app for the development of consulting services have to be added. Findings out of these utilization scenarios that are integrated into the further development of the app are:

- An even higher integration between the analytical tools of the app would be helpful.
- New approaches like agile project management should be integrated.
- A higher integration or an interface to IT systems in the user's company (e.g. employee dispatching) would also be helpful.

But in general the perception of the scenarios described above is that the usage of the app is possible with only selective support of an external consultant and offers a clear value added to the companies at reasonable cost. In all cases, dozens of consultant days would have been needed without usage of the app.

6 General Limitations and Advantages of Self-service Applications

The previous chapter shows that there are some limitations and restrictions in using consulting self-service applications. These applications require an experienced user who has some advanced knowledge about the issues of the particular topic. The unexperienced usage of a self-service application might result in non-professional outcomes even when using the professional knowledge included in the applications. And that might also cause longer project durations—also because the (internal) project members are not full-time dedicated to the project as external consultants normally are. So consultants' support when using the app might make sense. Further limitations might be:

- The approach is rather appropriate for highly standardizable consulting services.
- Very individualized solution pathways are difficult to implement.
- The consultant has still to be available for the selection of the appropriate app or parts of the app and for on-site coaching.

The advantages of consulting self-service applications are obvious; some of them have already be named in the previous chapter. Cost savings are very probable, because the consultants' fees will definitely be higher than the license fees for the apps. Project deliverables might have a higher acceptance within the company, because own employees have developed the project results. Other advantages are the development of knowledge about the topic of the app within the organization and the reusability of the app and the included approach for similar problems and projects. Also there are no or little dependencies on external consultants (neither on their knowledge nor on their availability).

7 Integration of Consulting Know-How—The Role of the Consultant Changes

Such consulting self-service applications incorporate knowledge from management methods and several consulting projects and thus ensure knowledge transfer by externalizing this knowledge into a structured approach. Consulting know-how is integrated in the following way:

1. The structure of the application—phase by phase, step by step—ensures a professional approach towards the solution of a business problem that was tested in consulting projects.
2. The tools and templates ensure completeness and concreteness to solve a business problem.
3. The analytic procedures and functions in the templates help to find an appropriate way to reach a target.

This has some severe implications for the classical business model of consultants. Since now consultancies have no interest in giving their methodical knowledge away to their customers, because they only earn money when selling well trained consultants, but not methodical knowledge. The owners of methodical management knowledge seem not to be interested in sharing it. Many reports, articles and books discuss the barriers to sharing knowledge, e.g. McDermott and O'Dell (2001) or Mitchell (2005).

But new competitors like internet companies will enter the scene and try to standardize management methods and solutions in a more ready-to-use way they can then offer for far less money to the clients than consultants do in their consulting projects. An example for that is Amazon with Amazon Web Services (AWS) offering IT related standardized solutions in analytics, IT administration, database services and others (Amazon 2017). And even top consultancies like McKinsey went into this field of computer controlled consulting. McKinsey Solutions offers Software as a Service (SaaS) applications for nine industries (e.g. oil and gas: support for energy companies to manage uncertainty and improve performance through analysis, insights, and benchmarking) and 14 business functions (e.g. OrgLab for organizational transformations) (McKinsey 2017).

To what degree "classical" consulting business will be replaced by new digital consulting services in general and self-service applications in particular is subject to further research. For the new parts of course the new role of the consultant will be more a facilitator of knowledge transfer to the client and an enabler for the usage of these self-service applications. A suitable model might be the *Lean Consulting* approach described by Niedereichholz (2010). This approach transfers particularly analytical tasks in a project to the client, the development of concepts and implementation plans then is a joint effort where the client follows the solution pathways of the app coached by the consultant. On consultant's side this requires skills like the ability to make decisions by consensus, persuasiveness and the willingness to share intellectual property. So there will still be enough "classical" consulting tasks to perform, e.g.:

- Train the clients in the usage of these self-service applications. Although self-service applications should be self-explaining, there might be still some need of individual adaptions and support in the utilization of the app.
- Creativeness in the development of individual not standardizable solutions for the clients, e.g. in strategy development, market entry projects and corporate social responsibility initiatives—in fields where standardized approaches are not appropriate. The clients will much more expect the consultant to support the creative process to develop future scenarios and to develop strategies to survive in an ever more rapidly changing environment.

The future role of consultants and their services in a digital world, however, will be subject to further scientific research.

8 Further Examples of Consulting Self-service Applications

The self-service application approach presented in this article has been used also for developing consulting self-service applications for other management methods. Consulting self-service applications have been developed and published for:

- Strategic management (using standardized processes in strategic management),
- Cost management (using the overhead value analysis method),
- IT service management (using the IT Infrastructure Library (ITIL®) approach),
- Information security management (using norms like ISO 270002).

More information can be obtained at http://www.conmethos.com/management-tools.php.

References

Ahlemann F (2009) Towards a conceptual reference model for project management information systems. Int J Project Manag 27(1):19–30

Amazon (2017) Amazon web services. https://aws.amazon.com/?nc1=h_ls. Accessed 31 Mar 2017

Becker J, Delfmann P (2007) Reference modeling. Physica, Heidelberg

Dillerup R, Stoi R (2016) Unternehmensführung, 5th edn. Vahlen, München

Fiedler R (2010) Controlling von Projekten, 5th edn. Vieweg + Teubner, Wiesbaden

Johann D, Greff T, Werth D (2016) On the effect of digital front stores on transforming business models. AWS-Institute, Saarbrücken

McDermott R, O'Dell C (2001) Overcoming cultural barriers to sharing knowledge. J Knowl Manage 5(1):76–85

McKinsey (2017) McKinsey solutions. http://www.mckinsey.com/solutions. Accessed 09 Feb 2017

Mitchell H (2005) Knowledge sharing—the value of story telling. Int J Organ Behav 9(5):632–641

Niedereichholz C (2008) Unternehmensberatung Band 2—Auftragsdurchführung und Quali-tätssicherung, 5th edn. Oldenbourg, München

Niedereichholz C (2010) Unternehmensberatung Band 1—Beratungsmarketing und Auftrags-akquisition, 5th edn. Oldenbourg, München

Nissen V, Seifert H (2016) Virtualisierung in der Unternehmensberatung. Eine Studie im deutschen Beratungsmarkt. BDU, e.V. (ed.), Bonn

Paul H, Wollny V (2011) Instrumente des strategischen Managements. Oldenbourg, München

PMI (2000) A guide to the project management body of knowledge. Project Management Institute, Newton Square

Van Assen M (2009) Key management models, 2nd edn. Pearson Education, Harlow

Wegmann C, Winklbauer H (2006) Projektmanagement für Unternehmensberatungen. Gabler, Wiesbaden

Werth D, Greff T, Scheer A-W (2016) Consulting 4.0—Die Digitalisierung der Unternehmensberatung. HMD 53:55–70

Author Biography

Friedrich Augenstein is a Professor for Consulting and Corporate Management at the Baden-Württemberg University of Cooperative Education Stuttgart and head of department for Business Management–Services Management. He is also the owner of CONMETHOS GmbH corporation for consulting methods. He studied Business Engineering at the University of Karlsruhe, was researcher and doctorate at the Institute of Computer Science at the University of Freiburg and has more than 20 years of professional experience as a consultant (Senior Manager at KPMG, Principal at Capgemini). Since 2005, Friedrich is a full-time Professor at the Baden-Württemberg University of Cooperative Education.

The Best of Two Worlds—Digitization of Matchmaking Between Consulting Firms and Independent Consultants

Christoph Hardt

Abstract Online marketplaces for consulting are facilitating the matchmaking between independent consultants on one hand and companies on the other hand. The article describes the independent consultants' motives to work on their own as well as the reasons why consulting firms hire contractors. Furthermore it illustrates how digitalized processes shape the marketplaces' matchmaking between both parties based on two years of operational business at COMATCH. The description focuses on digital tools within sourcing, matchmaking, feedback and administrational processes. The application based paper ends with a glimpse of future opportunities but does not leave out risks and questions for further research.

1 Introduction

1.1 Independent Workforce in Consulting

4,000 applications reached COMATCH from March 2015 to March 2017. Starting an online marketplace matching independent consultants with projects could not have been timed better—as in other service industries freelancing in consulting is on the rise as well. The profession attracts people with high intrinsic drive, education and self-organisation, it promises good income prospects and offers flexible project based work—in short: It is perfectly suitable for a career as an independent.

If we look at the two biggest consulting markets in Europe the numbers are impressive: In Germany 14,000 of 107,000 consultants in total are independent (BDU 2015). In the UK the part of independent consultants (ICs) is even higher, as 55,000 of 175,000 consultants are estimated to work independently (Hill 2016). Freelancing is an attractive option also for those still employed; 42% of consultants

C. Hardt (✉)
COMATCH GmbH, Schinkestraße 20, 12047 Berlin, Germany
e-mail: c.hardt@comatch.com

© Springer International Publishing AG 2018
V. Nissen (ed.), *Digital Transformation of the Consulting Industry*,
Progress in IS, https://doi.org/10.1007/978-3-319-70491-3_16

389

can imagine a career as an independent with the number growing within the last years (Odgers Berndtson 2015).

Why is that? Since October 2014, we conducted over 2,500 interviews with independent consultants. Those 45–60 min long conversations were part two of a two-step-qualification process that guarantees high quality among the consultants in the COMATCH network. In a survey, we backed up the motives that we had identified in those conversations by numbers (COMATCH 2017):

1. For 83% it is quite or very important to decide what topics they work on,
2. For 74% it is quite or very important to work less or with more flexibility,
3. For 70% it is quite or very important to decide what clients they work with.

The time the consultants in our network had gained when they moved into freelancing was used mainly:

- To focus on family (60%)
- To facilitate their own company in consulting or other areas (64%)
- To follow hobbies like sports or travelling (53%)

In short we can sum up that independent consultants want to decide when, with and for whom they work and which projects they choose. Our survey also showed that they make use of their freedom; 86% stated that they had denied a project within the last 12 months. For many consultants freelancing has become the solution for their personal work-life dilemma, and wish for freedom and self-determination. The often quoted *Generation Y* is surely giving a large push to the trend of freelancing as well.

1.2   Consulting Firms with Demand for IC's

COMATCH is successfully working with companies of all sizes and industries, be it big corporates (e.g. by now there are contracted projects with seven of the DAX30 companies), Start-ups or SME's. Clients of the public sector are playing a minor role at this point of time but can use the service as well. In general, every project that requires strategy or management consulting or an industry expertise is potentially suitable. In this article, though I would like to focus on a certain type of clients. Since the early start of COMATCH consulting firms work with us to improve their own service for the client.

All of Europe's decisive consulting markets show respectable growth rates over the last six years and there is no reason to believe the trend will stop anytime soon (Fig. 1).

Naturally, a growing demand for consulting services comes down to a growing demand for qualified consultants. Approximately one fifth of the consultants leave a consulting firm (Batchelor 2011) as a consequence of the *up or out* principle that is widespread in the industry of management consulting. Consulting firms are very

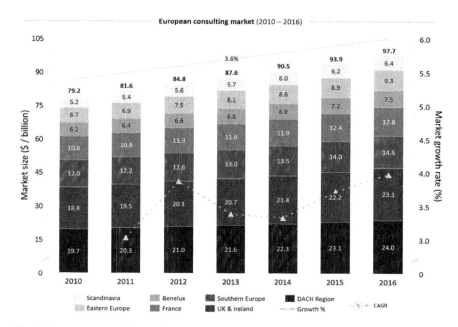

Fig. 1 European consulting market (2010–2016) (Consultancy.uk 2017)

popular employers of choice for young professionals: A recent study performed by Universum showed McKinsey and Company, Deloitte, KPMG, Ernst and Young and PwC to be among the Top Ten of dream employers of European Business students (Clark 2016). So the Top Tier and Big Four simply have to invest into recruiting to keep their business going. But the war for talents also affects consulting firms, especially the start-up world is an attractive competitor. Also, the expectations of employees of all white collar professions changed. Nowadays they consider remote work, part-time-opportunities and an academic leave or sabbatical options to be part of a standard package offered by their dream employer. Smaller consulting firms that might not be located in the capitals or do not have the brand like the bigger ones can face a lack of resources (Though big consulting houses also need additional staffing once in a while.). In our experience, consulting firms reach out for external support by independent consultants in the following three scenarios.

- Basic lack of resources: employed consultants are on projects and there is still a need to staff for new assignments.
- Lack of a very specific expertise, e.g. a specialist for the oil-gas-industry with Norwegian language skills, something that we would call a *sharp profile.*
- A specific geographical demand, e.g. someone willing to spend one year in Saudi Arabia.

Independent consultants and facilitators matching them with companies are not a new phenomenon, e.g. Eden McCallum started its international business in the year

2,000. In the last five years, though digital marketplaces, platforms and even one app changed the process of matching between the companies and the consultants. They carry the potential to speed up the matching by making it simpler and more direct. If it is combined with a quality check of the consultant's performance, it also adds trustworthiness. By doing so they can support consulting firms in their staffing at very low transaction cost. Therefore, they are able to provide better service for their clients, or even grow and exercise new fields of business.

1.3   COMATCH—The Consulting Marketplace

Dr. Jan Schächtele and the author of this article (Dr. Christoph Hardt) founded COMATCH in late 2014 in Berlin. Both of us have been consultants for many years, so we are familiar with the needs of the client—be it a consulting house or a corporate—as well as the needs of the consultants. A new business model succeeds when it jumps into the gap between reality and potential of a market, when it helps the customer by making things simpler, quicker or cheaper. In the case of online consulting marketplaces, it is the gap between the demand for consultants and the independent workforce in consulting which offers opportunities. COMATCH matches independent consultants and industry experts and companies in need of external support for projects. The website www.comatch.com was launched in March of 2015 and is now available in German, English, French, Danish, Swedish and French. In early spring 2017 the marketplace counts more than 2,000 consultants in its network (with the database growing by more or less a 100 each month) and has successfully contracted approximately 350 projects. Service is offered worldwide but focusing on the German speaking countries (DACH), the Nordic, Benelux, France and the Middle East.

2   Digital Supply Process

2.1   Sourcing and Quality Ensurance

The first consultants who applied on www.comatch.com came from our very personal professional network, often they were former colleagues. Word of mouth recommendations were and still are crucial for the growth of the community. In addition, media coverage gave us a big boost and is supported by search engine advertising (SEA) and search engine optimization (SEO) activities. To strengthen the pool selectively we are still using active sourcing: fitting candidates are approached via the business social networks. However, this method is only used if a consultant could be a good match for an actual incoming project request.

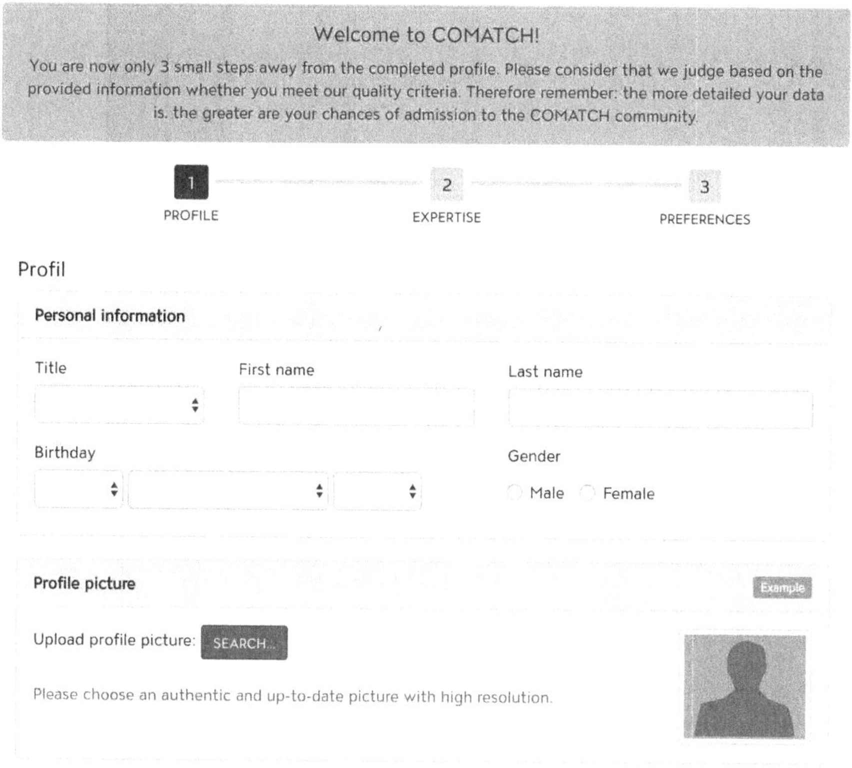

Fig. 2 Registration form for consultants on comatch.com

No matter through which channel a consultant learns about COMATCH he[1] needs to register online to be considered for admission. Three information clusters are important:

- CV,
- Expertise,
- Working preferences.

Either the consultants can fill in all the necessary data in an entry form themselves (see Fig. 2 on page before) or they simply connect their existing CV's as they are stored on Linkedin or XING via API with the COMATCH database. This takes only seconds. If multiple language versions of a CV are stored in these business social networks, it is possible to transfer those, too. In a next step the consultant needs to add more information on their functional and industrial expertise to make the profile significant. Here, COMATCH follows a matrix system

---

[1]The author uses the male language version in the article with referring about consultants of both genders. In the COMATCH network there are 87% men and 13% women.

Expertise

Industry expertise   ⓘ Please do not pick more than 5 industries

ⓘ Scroll down for more options.

☐ Agriculture & Forestry   ☐ Plant & Machinery
☐ Automotive industry   ☐ Banking
☐ Construction industry   ☐ Biotechnology
☐ Chemistry   ☐ Computer hardware
☐ Energy industry   ☐ Financial services
☐ Leisure & Tourism   ☐ Catering
☐ Household electronics   ☐ Real estate

Functional expertise   ⓘ Please do not pick more than 10 functions

ⓘ Scroll down for more options.

Organisation & IT

☐ Building leadership skills   ☐ Carve Out
☐ Change management   ☐ Company culture management
☐ Compliance   ☐ IT-architecture
☐ IT-project management   ☐ Organisational design
☐ Post merger integration   ☐ Remuneration and incentive structure
                                                           optimisation

Fig. 3 Registration form for consultants / Industry and functional expertise

where consultants can pick up to five industries and ten functional spikes in which they gathered experience throughout their career (see Fig. 3). The profile is completed by information on language, IT-skills, working preferences (place, time, willingness to travel, etc.) and the daily rate the consultants expect to receive for their services. Memberships in professional associations are not decisive for the registration.

An inherent part of the sourcing process of COMATCH and crucial to ensure quality is the already mentioned two-step-selection-process.

- Step 1—CV Check: To be admitted to the network the consultants must have at least two years of experience in a well-established consulting firm (top tier or boutique). Industry experts in our pool need to have a strong track record of at least ten years in a certain industry ideally combined with a certain functional focus.
- Step 2—Personal interview: An interview of 45–60 min with those who match the CV criteria gives insights in soft skills, leadership style, self-organisation and motivation triggers. Those interviews are often performed via Skype or on the phone. All results are filled in by the interviewers so the information is stored in our database and can be used for matching afterwards.

In particular, the interviews are a good example for what the *Best of Two Worlds* means—it is often intuition and experience next to the facts which decides whether a consultant is getting access to the pool. During this process approximately 50% of consultants' applications are denied. To carefully check a consultant's development is a major part of the facilitator. It increases transparency in a market that is non-transparent by nature: as anyone can call themselves a consultant it is hard to find the good ones.

2.2 Matching

The heart of the business, the matching between consultants and consulting firms is based on a combination of technology and personal experience.

In the first step a self-programmed algorithm scans and matches demands of clients (similar to consultants, the clients fill in their project demands online) and capabilities of the consultants. A match of at least 70% is required for candidate profiles to be selected for the request. In a first best solution the algorithm tries to find consultants based on one-to-one matches, that completely reflects the criteria of the project request. If this approach does not find enough suitable candidates, the second best solution is based on clusters of industry and functional expertise. For example if a consultant for sales in the energy sector is searched for, the algorithm knows that the telecommunication industry went through a similar phase of deregulation a couple of years ago. The goal at the end of the technology based search is that the number of the consultants in the selection goes down from about 2,000 to five to 20 suggestions.

In the second step the personal experience comes into the play to do fine-tuning within the smaller sample provided by the algorithm. For example, soft skills that were identified during the interview might influence whether a consultant is a good fit for a project request or not. How are a person's leadership skills? Where does he take his motivation from? Is he an introvert or an extrovert? After adapting the selection the responsible employee sends out project suggestions to the ten best suitable consultants—by clicking one button. The consultants in this selection process get a push notification and are asked to respond within 48 h (automated reminders after 24 h included).

As a result, a small sample of two to four candidate profiles of the consultants who accepted the suggestion will be electronically sent to the client, who then can chose if and with which consultants he would like to speak personally. The interviews between clients and consultants are often conducted via phone. When all data is given correctly and are updated on a regular basis and when the consultants quickly respond to the suggestions, they receive via email—a match can be made within a few hours (The idea to send out notifications on a new project suggestion via what's app is still being examined.). At this step of the process improvements can surely be made, but overall the whole matching works very quickly, as consultants are a very online-affine target group per se. The regular communication is 100% email based and strongly connected to the login-area of the platform, where every consultant and client has their own profile with all information necessary that is easily accessible for mobile devices as well. Of course, there is always a contact person in sales and community management people can address if there are questions or ambiguities.

The process works and by now, 95% of all project requests could be covered with candidate suggestions.

2.3 Administrational Support and Feedback

Client and consultant are fully supported with the administration of their common project. The services provided consist of contracting, time-tracking and billing as well as feedback tools.

- Contracts are closed between the consultant and COMATCH, as well as COMATCH and the client. All the important documents, contracts, general terms and conditions are available in the login area. There is no paper based contracting necessary. We can also provide a paper version upon request.
- Consultants do fill in time-trackers on a monthly basis. The status quo of those time trackers are mirrored to the client. After he released it, an invoice is automatically generated. The time trackers are, like all features, working with real-time updates
- At the end of each month and in a final note the client will evaluate the consultant he hired concerning work quality, interaction and professional behaviour. Each category contains several aspects (see picture as example for the section of work quality), space for comments and builds an overall five star rating for the consultant. The five-star model is of course very common in the online world and creates transparency. If a consultant receives two profoundly bad ratings, he or she will not be considered for further matches. The consultant also gives feedback to the client in return and both parties evaluate how satisfied they are with the COMATCH service (see Figs. 4 and 5).

3 Opportunities and Risks

The matching and staffing with a model like this guarantees quick and reliable results and enables consulting firms to react flexible to the demands of the market. The quick access to a wide range of experts with background of various knowledge, experiences, IT and language skills can be the decisive advantage towards competitive firms in times of growth. Usually consulting firms need to increase the

Category/ Attribute	1	2	3	4	5	Not relevant
	Not satisfied		Expectations met		Very satisfied	
Work quality						
Expertise	Expertise (industry / function) only partially available; selected approaches / methods did not work / worked limited; despite explicit demand / criticism no approaches / methods adapted to the situation have not been introduced	Performance is between 1 (Not Satisfied) and 3 (Expectations met)	Good expertise (industry / function); use of meaningful approaches / methods in the project process; adaptation of approaches / methods to specific situation	Performance is between 3 (Expectations met) and 5 (Very satisfied)	High expertise (industry / function) available; effective / efficient use of known approaches / methods and (selectively) of innovative concepts; targeted adaptation of approaches / methods to specific situations	
Problem solving	Core issues were not properly identified, structuring and distribution of the problem in less complex partial problems not useful / not present; link between activities and project target often unclear	Performance is between 1 (Not Satisfied) and 3 (Expectations met)	Core issues were identified; structuring and distribution of the problem in less complex partial problems; basic orientation of the activities on the project aim	Performance is between 3 (Expectations met) and 5 (Very satisfied)	Core issues were identified very quickly, very good; intuitive structuring and distribution of the problem in less complex partial problems; consistent focus of activities on project goal	
End products	Final products were partially incorrect and not always well understood; developed recommendations were not well understandable	Performance is between 1 (Not Satisfied) and 3 (Expectations met)	End products were mostly error-free, logical and understandable; developed recommendations were understandable and actionable	Performance is between 3 (Expectations met) and 5 (Very satisfied)	Final products were correct, logically structured, graphically appealing, easy to understand and compelling in the arguments; developed recommendations were very well understandable and the implementation plan reflected the general conditions	

Fig. 4 Feedback matrix for the aspect of *work quality*

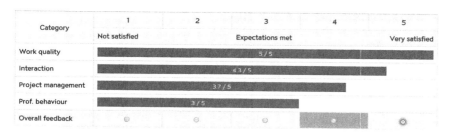

Category	1	2	3	4	5
	Not satisfied		Expectations met		Very satisfied
Work quality			5 / 5		
Interaction			4.3 / 5		
Project management		3.7 / 5			
Prof. behaviour		3 / 5			
Overall feedback				●	

Fig. 5 Feedback overview for consultants

number of projects so they can employ more consultants while they also need to hire more consultants in order to staff a higher number of projects. With external staffing consulting firms can experiment with new topics and geographical markets without risking high fixed costs for staff. As a certain percentage of freelancers is always, up to go back into a permanent positions it is not unlikely to find a match even for a longer time of cooperation. All this can be done with little capacity for planning and administration.

Consulting firms need the digital facilitators to provide human resources, the marketplaces in return also need the consulting firms: Not only are they clients, they also take a big part in the quality control of the business model of the online marketplaces. The recruiting process of the facilitators is, in a way, *outsourced to the past* as the big companies carry out assessment centres to make sure only the best and most suitable step into the industry. Therefore, big consulting firms and digital marketplaces can regard each other as connected in a symbiosis with a clear distribution of roles in the market. Consulting firms offer services that cannot be sufficiently achieved by digital approaches: They build deep relations to the clients due to the strong partner structure, they can assemble big, international teams and offer a brand name based on size and experience which is essential for certain projects. For the consultants the chances are obvious, as they can find assignments without costs and live their personal work-life balance. All involved parties benefit from a rise of transparency and flexibility in the market.

The risks of digital matchmaking in consulting is surely located in a perceived loss of control and personality. Fix employment is still associated with higher trust in confidentiality. Closely connected to this is the fear of losing the character of a *people business* as well as a company's culture. In our experience, there are measurements to lower the risk of being an anonymous online-provider: We installed regular face-to-face events like meetups in cities with high consultants' density, monthly communication through newsletters, calls or supportive affiliate programs with e.g. booking websites or rental car providers. In the end, consulting is a business between people and digitization can be a tool to make it easier but not replace it.

4   Perspective and Further Research

We believe that online marketplaces will not be a short-time trend but will receive a growing share of the consulting market in the next few years. Still, the business model of online marketplaces clearly shows that digitization, at least at this point of time, can only be a supportive mean that simplifies and fastens matching processes. But if the CV you apply with is not expressive and telling, there will be no match for you. If there are no people checking the quality of a consultant and his soft skills, project success is endangered. If there are no people to assist when difficulties during a project occur, there will be a delay in the project. This is why we understand our business model as a combination of the best of two worlds: digital technology to keep processes fast and lean and the personal character and quality promise of consulting which is known to be a classic *people business*.

Marketplaces and platforms definitely can take the role of scouts for independent consultants all over Europe or even all over the world, especially if they meet the consultant's needs for high quality project offers, a simplified handling of all administrational processes and provide friendly communication and community building services on top. In the past two years many platforms, marketplaces and even apps started business in the German speaking markets, they operate with varying pricing models, quality control demands and offer service for different target groups. While an app seems a visionary project at this point of time—we still believe that business decisions involving several thousands of Euros will not be made on mobile devices—though it might work in the future. For our own business model and algorithm we of course see opportunities for improvement. To be fit for the future the topic of automated evaluation of soft skills is important. The algorithm has to be regarded as a constant work in progress and it should be our goal to make it as intelligent as possible. With the growing importance of online matchmakers research could answer the question which factors determine success and satisfaction for both parties involved—clients and consultants.

References

Batchelor C (2011) "Up or out" is part of industry culture. Finanical Times. https://www.ft.com/content/d42434b2-6b69-11e0-a53e-00144feab49a. Accessed on 2 Feb 2017

BDU (2015) Facts & Figures zum Beratermarkt 2014/2015. BDU e.V., Bonn

Clark C (2016) The 10 companies business students in Europe want to work for the most. http://uk.businessinsider.com/companies-business-students-want-to-work-for-the-most-2016-10/#10-goldman-sachs-1. Accessed on 2 Feb 2017

COMATCH (2017) The DNA of the independent consultant. Survey among the consultants and industry experts in the COMATCH network (in press)

Consultancy.uk (2017) European Consulting Market. http://www.consultancy.uk/consulting-industry/europe. Accessed on 2 Feb 2017

Hill A (2016) When McKinsey met Uber. The gig economy comes to consulting. https://www.ft.com/content/a5419fca-7f24-11e6-bc52-0c7211ef3198. Accessed on 2 Feb 2017

Odgers Berndtson (2015) Consulting-Monitor 2015. http://www.odgersberndtson.com/media/2355/odgers_berndtson_consulting-monitor_2015.pdf. Accessed on 2 Feb 2017

Author Biography

Dr. Christoph Hardt born 1980 in Gießen is one of the two founders of COMATCH. He is an expert in B2B marketing and sales and previously worked at McKinsey & Company, Inc. as a project manager for large international companies, particularly in the chemical, energy and logistics industry for more than seven years. He studied Business Administration with the degrees in Business Studies and Dr. rer. pol. at the University of Bayreuth and the EDHEC in Nice. He holds several teaching assignments in B2B marketing and sales.

Experiences with the Digitization of the Interaction Room Method for IT Strategy Development and Software Project Scoping

Erik Hebisch, Simon Grapenthin, Matthias Book, Markus Kleffmann and Volker Gruhn

Abstract Complex software projects typically involve stakeholders from a variety of backgrounds that bring a variety of goals and expectations, but also valuable knowledge to the project. To facilitate communication and cooperation in such heterogeneous, interdisciplinary teams, we previously introduced the Interaction Room, a consulting method that uses large whiteboards to help stakeholders identify the key risk, value and effort drivers of their projects early. In this paper, we describe drawbacks of the original Interaction Room approach and show how a digitally augmented version of the method, relying on large interactive displays, was designed to improve the quality of the discussion, the long-term impact of the insights, and the inclusion of remote stakeholders. The Augmented Interaction Room is an example of how digitization can not only improve existing consulting methods, but also produce new insights and ways of collaborating with clients.

E. Hebisch · S. Grapenthin
Interaction Room GmbH, Essen, Germany
e-mail: hebisch@interaction-room.de

S. Grapenthin
e-mail: grapenthin@interaction-room.de

M. Book (✉)
Department of Computer Science, University of Iceland, Reykjavík, Iceland
e-mail: book@hi.is

M. Kleffmann · V. Gruhn
paluno – The Ruhr Institute for Software Technology,
University of Duisburg-Essen, Essen, Germany
e-mail: markus.kleffmann@paluno.uni-due.de

V. Gruhn
e-mail: volker.gruhn@paluno.uni-due.de

© Springer International Publishing AG 2018
V. Nissen (ed.), *Digital Transformation of the Consulting Industry*,
Progress in IS, https://doi.org/10.1007/978-3-319-70491-3_17

401

1 Background and Motivation

The quality of software systems has a direct impact on the quality of many services that our society relies on: information technology (IT) drives everything from communication to finances, from public safety to health care, from logistics to utilities. Faulty information systems (i.e. software that does not work properly or does not address the needs of its users and the people it affects) can be inefficient and inconvenient at best, but outright dangerous to people's health, financial assets and the environment at worst.

The causes for software faults can often be traced to software engineers' lack of understanding of the application domain at the time of software construction. To foster better communication between software engineers and application domain experts, we developed the *Interaction Room* (IR) method as a consulting approach that can be applied in organizations' IT strategy development as well as in the early scoping phases of complex software projects (Book et al. 2012).

Guided by specially trained consultants ("IR coaches"), software engineers and domain experts use large whiteboards to jointly sketch key aspects of a software system and its environment as they discuss requirements, priorities and technical solutions (Fig. 1). Each whiteboard ("canvas") is dedicated to a particular perspective on the software product and its application domain, from business processes to domain objects to the overall system landscape. By having all these perspectives on the system and its context visible simultaneously (a literal 360° view of the project), business and technical stakeholders in the room can identify structural and semantic connections, incongruities, and dependencies between items much more intuitively, reducing the potential for misunderstandings and inconsistencies that are otherwise easily overlooked in traditional modeling approaches.

A unique aspect of the IR method is that participants are encouraged to mark up the models with symbols ("annotations") that indicate value, effort and uncertainty drivers such as business value, complexity, security requirements, policy

Fig. 1 Canvases in an Interaction Room

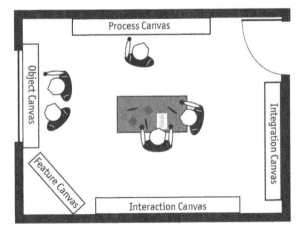

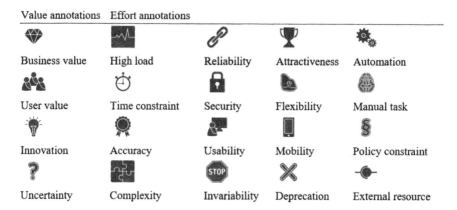

Value annotations   Effort annotations

Business value	High load	Reliability	Attractiveness	Automation
User value	Time constraint	Security	Flexibility	Manual task
Innovation	Accuracy	Usability	Mobility	Policy constraint
Uncertainty	Complexity	Invariability	Deprecation	External resource

Fig. 2 Value, effort and uncertainty annotations used in an Interaction Room

constraints, etc. (Fig. 2). These annotations serve as warning signs for issues that software engineers need to be aware of, and make valuable domain knowledge explicit that would otherwise remain implicit and cause costly defects in the software if not considered and resolved early on (Book et al. 2015).

Used this way, IR workshops can help to lay the foundation for a better mutual understanding and alignment of all stakeholders' needs, and for building software solutions that actually address those needs, thereby ensuring that complex IT projects provide high value to users and organizations.

The individual elements of the IR method—the canvases, annotations, workshop structure, and follow-up activities—were born out of many years of observations of stakeholders' struggles in dozens of large software projects in the insurance, healthcare, banking, telecommunications and public sector, and the realization that while the reasons for these struggles have been well-published since a long time (e.g. Curtis et al. 1988), established software process models and modeling tools provide little methodical support to avert them. Over the past years, we have used the Interaction Room method to provide consulting to over 20 industry clients from a broad range of domains, and refined it based on our experiences from those projects. In dozens of IR workshops, over 150 canvases have been filled with sketches, and over 1500 annotations have been applied to them. The clients' feedback and the project results have been nearly uniformly positive, with many customers finding it easier than usual to arrive at insights that provide actual value and are understood and supported by a heterogeneous group of stakeholders (Grapenthin et al. 2013, 2015; Book et al. 2014). A key to this high acceptance of the method certainly is its simplicity—several whiteboards, a stack of sticky notes for annotations, a notebook to record annotation details and trained coaches to moderate the session are all that is needed. However, from our project experience, we also found that working only with whiteboards and paper has certain drawbacks:

- While sketching on the whiteboards is pragmatic, editing the sketches can be cumbersome. Erasing and redrawing parts of sketches to make space for additional ideas, or cramming information onto the whiteboard's limited surface area, can make the sketches messy and hard to read, unless the IR coach invests continuous effort into refactoring the models on-the-go.
- Persisting the model sketches and annotations so that the workshop results can be accessed at any time by business and technical stakeholders even weeks after the workshop is cumbersome, as it requires either photographing the whiteboards or redrawing the contents in a digital modeling tool. Often, this means the results are static and end up not being used much beyond the workshop.
- Applying the traditional Interaction Room method in distributed teams is virtually impossible unless all team members travel to a joint workshop location. While this can be beneficial for a project kick-off, it is impractical for ongoing distributed team work.

Given these observations, we realized that the IR approach would benefit from careful digitization. Care was especially required to make sure that the "look & feel" of the method would not change despite the introduction of digital tools—namely, we did not want to sacrifice the method's ease of use that required no prior IT or modeling experience from any stakeholder, thereby letting everyone (business and technical stakeholders alike) act on a level playing field without one side dominating the tool and thus the discussion. Instead, our goal was to augment the existing method with digital features that would address exactly the shortcomings identified above.

2   The Augmented Interaction Room

To address the issues we observed with the original IR approach that relied solely on traditional whiteboards, we developed the Augmented Interaction Room (AugIR), a software that runs on several connected large interactive displays, mimicking the look & feel of traditional whiteboards, but offering additional features that provide higher usability and versatility of the model sketches (Fig. 3).

At its core, the AugIR enables the sketching of models on the large interactive screens using a pen whose movements are translated into digital ink strokes in real time. Going beyond the interaction that traditional whiteboards enable, the digital ink strokes can be grouped, rearranged and resized on the interactive display with simple touch gestures. Similarly, the whole drawing canvas can be zoomed and panned using simple gestures, giving users access to an essentially infinite digital whiteboard (Kleffmann et al. 2014).

The annotation of model elements that is performed using small sticky notes in the original IR is mirrored in the AugIR by dragging and dropping icons from an annotation palette onto model elements. Going beyond what is possible on the physical whiteboard, additional background information can be associated with

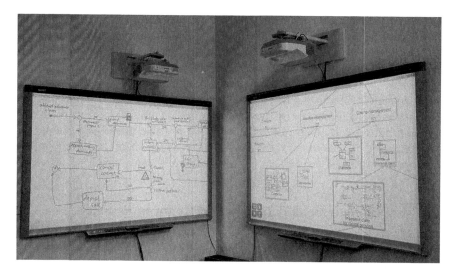

Fig. 3 Large interactive displays in an Augmented Interaction Room

each annotation icon in situ on the digital screen—either by handwriting or typing up a note, by recording an audio soundbite, or by linking to a file in a project repository, an intranet page or similar artifact.

The AugIR system itself is also continuously analyzing the model and identifying relationships between the model elements on different canvases (e.g. an object that is mentioned in an activity on the process canvas and defined in more detail on the object canvas). These relationships are noted by the system as so-called trace links. They serve two purposes: For one thing, they enable the efficient retrieval and navigation between related model sketches. For another, they enable the identification of correlations or conflicts between model annotations, e.g. when a warning annotation that has been applied to a data structure on the object canvas also impacts its use in an activity on the process canvas (Kleffmann et al. 2015).

Model sketches on the various canvases of an AugIR can be stored together when a meeting is adjourned, and retrieved at a later time when the meeting resumes or when individual team members would like to review parts of the model. A platform-independent remote viewing and sketching component enables team members to access the model sketches anytime, anywhere, on any device, and to edit them in parallel. This enables several forms of remote collaboration, such as asynchronous work with individual parts of a larger model, or collaboration on the same model with several teams working on large interactive displays in separate locations.

In combining these features, the digitization of the IR method makes the creation, manipulation and navigation of model sketches in the AugIR much easier and more efficient than the original whiteboard-based approach. In addition, the potential for distributed work enables wholly new forms of collaboration, extending the method's reach beyond collocated teams that become ever rarer in today's value chains.

The aim of the IR method has always been to facilitate the elicitation of knowledge and the mutual understanding in interdisciplinary teams, using pragmatic tools. The digitization of this approach does require a certain infrastructure investment in large interactive displays, which however pays back through the significantly increased usability and accessibility of the models, as well as the much higher volume of information that can be pragmatically associated with it. Last but not least, through the option of distributed work, the digital version of the IR method facilitates consulting modes that were not possible before, and enables the insights gained in the room to be disseminated much more effectively to the members of distributed teams.

3   Using the Augmented Interaction Room in Practice

In the following subsections, we will recount our experiences from using the AugIR in two consulting projects. We will focus on how the look & feel of the AugIR differed positively and negatively from the original, whiteboard-based version, and on how this digitization of the method affected the consulting style followed by the IR coaches. In evaluating the impact of the IR method's digitization, we look both at changes in the behavior and results observed on-site, as well as changes in the coaches' post-workshop responsibilities of interpreting the results and advising the customer on subsequent courses of action.

3.1   Case Study 1: Sprint Planning

The first case study was undertaken on-site at a small software development and consulting company in order to facilitate the sprint planning of an agile software project for developing an interactive, distributed software system.

From the beginning of the project, the IR method had been used on traditional whiteboards in order to define the project scope, to clarify the requirements and to analyze the business processes, business objects and system components. The whiteboards were photographed after each meeting to record the results.

Business stakeholders, product owners and developers were always involved in the sprint planning meetings. Unfortunately however, the business stakeholders were not always available on-site during the sprint. In these instances, questions and feedback had to be exchanged via telephone or e-mail during or after the meeting. None of these approaches were however perceived as satisfactory. This was mostly because the business stakeholders were not fully involved in the discussion and familiar with the model sketches on the IR canvases. Attempts at video-conferencing did not prove satisfactory either as the image quality was not sufficient to make out what was written on a whiteboard, much less perceive several boards simultaneously. Capturing the whiteboards photographically and e-mailing them to all team members after the meeting was tedious and had the disadvantage

Fig. 4 AugIR-supported collaboration scenarios in the first case study

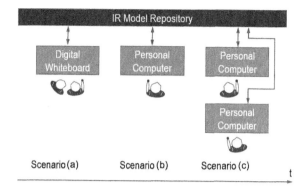

that these representations were not immediately editable. It was also difficult to remember all the decisions made during the discussion of the models, so information tended to get lost in the process.

Several sprints into the project, we introduced the AugIR to address these issues in the most common communication scenarios. As shown in Fig. 4 on the following page, we observed three main settings in which the stakeholders typically communicated over time. In scenario (a) a team consisting of both developer and business stakeholder discuss and model a requirement. The result is stored in the distributed model storage. Afterwards, in scenario (b) the developer refers to the created models when implementing the features in the current sprint. He does not change the model. If the developer has a question he invites the business stakeholder to the exact model where his question arises. He does not have to prepare something since both parties know the model. This is scenario (c) in which both stakeholders access the model simultaneously to clarify the requirement. Voice communication is done via telephone or other means, working out the consequences of decisions is done directly in the model itself. While these scenarios quite commonly occur in the sequence described here, they are independent and may occur in other constellations as well—usually e.g. in iterative fashion as the stakeholders refine and elaborate different aspects of a system over the course of several sprints.

The stakeholders found most beneficial in this setting that there was a single location where all models were stored and thus all decisions regarding the requirements were accessible. Stakeholders instantly knew how to reach each sketch again and used them as basis for subsequent discussions. It became easier for them to recreate the state of previous discussions in order to understand, explain or re-evaluate decisions after the fact. This resulted in saving considerable time that was usually expended at the beginnings of meetings in order to bring everyone up to speed. The visualization of the overall project structure helped stakeholders to remember the context of critical decisions. This translated to generally more productive meetings, which were building on previously achieved results rather than speculation and fragmentary memories of prior discussions. The canvases could also be easily shared with additional stakeholders to discuss matters requiring additional expertise.

3.2 Case Study 2: Distributed Project Scoping and Controlling

The second case study was undertaken in a team distributed across locations in Hamburg, Cologne and Essen, Germany, working on the scoping and controlling of a complex software platform developed jointly by five organizations from different domains (a software company, a telecommunication company, a university, a trade organization and a standardization body).

Each project partner was responsible for work packages related to their area of expertise. Monthly meetings of all partners were used to assess the status of the work packages and refine requirements stated in the project plan.

At the beginning of the project, the traditional IR method had been applied often and produced a large number of model sketches and requirements specifications on the whiteboards. These model sketches were usually photographed, redrawn in a modeling tool and uploaded to a central project repository available to all partners. Technical details related to these models were discussed bilaterally via teleconferences as needed.

We observed again that a lot of effort was spent on the appropriate dissemination of the IR results. Uploading and renaming photos or redrawing models took considerable effort. Moreover, the facts in the models soon diverged from the current understanding of the stakeholders; effort had to be spent each time a new detail was added to a model, in order to keep the models as up-to-date as possible. Updating a photo was perceived as unfeasible, and updating a model in a digital modeling tool was often neglected due to time constraints or missing experience with the modeling tool. We also observed that it was too difficult to bring previously created sketches into a meeting, as either they had to be printed out on large sheets of paper, which could not be edited easily, or they had to be redrawn on the IR whiteboards, which was not practical as the number of model sketches grew. Project partners therefore either printed out photographs of the whiteboards on smaller paper or used the redrawn models in their presentation. Both approaches had negative effects on maintaining focus during discussion. Either each stakeholder would scribble on his own printout which negated the shared workspace aspect of the IR, or the model was projected on a wall without a way to modify it, negating the immediacy of the IR method.

We introduced the AugIR to support the different communication scenarios in this project. Figure 5 shows the four most common scenarios. In scenario (a) we used a wall-sized display to perform an IR workshop like we would on a whiteboard. The models were saved in the model storage. After the meeting, each partner could access the models immediately in their own AugIR and use them as basis for their own refinements (scenario b). The models created during this refinement period were saved in the model storage as well. They could be accessed by the other partners at will (scenario c). During bilateral teleconferences, the AugIR provided the models from the model storage. In scenario (d), individual partners used their AugIRs simultaneously to discuss technical details and make decisions. While often

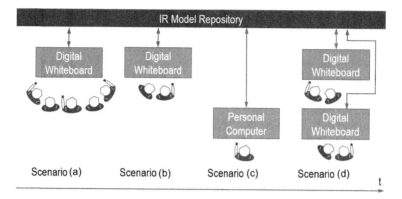

Fig. 5 AugIR-supported collaboration scenarios in the second case study

occurring in this sequence, the different usage scenarios were also employed individually as the partners' information and collaboration needs necessitated.

Introducing the AugIR in this setting had the immediate effect of reducing the time spent on meeting logistics. Existing material relevant to the discussion was brought into the AugIR from the model storage. Stakeholders were immediately familiar with the models since they looked the same as before. This helped with orientation in the models and with focusing the group during the workshop. Afterwards, the continuously accessible digital canvases served as the basis for creating detailed models and planning the subsequent implementation efforts. This proved to be useful during the bilateral teleconferences. Since all viewers could work on the same model simultaneously, a common understanding was reached faster than before.

4   Related Work

Several prior works advocate the use of large interactive screens in the domain of software development. For example, the NiCE Discussion Room (Haller et al. 2010) is a technically augmented meeting room that especially focuses on the integration of paper artifacts. The room is outfitted with a large display for collaborative work, onto which handwritten paper notes can be transferred via a special interface.

Chen, Grundy and Hosking (Chen et al. 2003, 2008) suggest a UML modeling tool that uses electronic whiteboards for free-hand diagram sketching in early project phases. The sketches can be transformed into computer-drawn diagrams and exported to other tools for further use.

Calico is a sketching tool that is especially suited for modeling during the early phases of a software development project (Mangano et al. 2010). It allows the designer to create free-hand sketches on electronic whiteboards or tablets.

By circumscribing an area on the board, the designer can create a so-called "scrap", which gives certain regions within the sketch an informal importance. The user can move the scraps and their content around, as well as combine and connect them to create relationships between them.

Tahuti (Hammond and Davis 2006) and Knight (Damm et al. 2000) allow users to draw diagrams on large multi-touch displays. The user can either choose to display all elements as they have been drawn in free-hand mode, or they can be interpreted as UML elements and replaced by the corresponding symbols. This replacement uses pattern recognition in multiple steps. The approach combines the simplicity of a paint tool with the editing support of a UML editor.

FlexiSketch (Wüest et al. 2013) is based on the assumption that most software engineers prefer paper and pencil when sketching ideas and performing modeling activities, especially when working in the field, e.g. gathering information from stakeholders. Therefore, FlexiSketch is a sketching tool for free-hand modeling, developed for the use on mobile devices. Users can draw informal sketches, enrich them with annotations, and later transform them into semi-formal models for further usage.

SourceVis addresses the fact that although most software projects are developed by teams of people, most visualization and modeling tools are primarily designed to support only a single user (Anslow et al. 2011). SourceVis therefore focuses on software visualization during collaboration by supporting the analysis of the structure, evolution and vocabulary of software systems.

However, all of these approaches merely provide interactive whiteboards as a drawing tool, rather than embedding them in a larger consulting methodology in which people can work with the models in a process that spans several locations, actors, and instances in time.

5   Discussion and Conclusion

In both case study projects, the introduction of the AugIR has proven beneficial. This can be ascribed to the improved access to the sketches created during the workshops, which are immediately visible and editable by all stakeholders regardless of their location. Since the mode of collaboration is essentially the same whether stakeholders work on the same or on distributed boards, the cooperative atmosphere fostered during the workshops (in which the IR coaches encourage business and technical stakeholders to communicate as equals, instead of letting one side dominate the discussion) is extended beyond the workshop environment and shapes the communication style throughout the project: interdisciplinary collaboration on models becomes easy and normal, even if the stakeholders are distributed, while any "entrenchment" of the business vs. technical departments, that communicate solely through documents and deadlines, is avoided. We believe that this shift in collaboration style and cooperative spirit has a more profound impact on the effectiveness of distributed teams than any particular methodical prescription for remote collaboration.

Another beneficial aspect is that the model storage provides a way for the sketches to evolve with a project. They do not have to be converted into another format—with straighter lines or rectangular boxes—to be useful. This way they provide the basis for an ongoing engagement with the contents of the project.

The stakeholders in the case study projects however also noted several critical aspects: Since all sketches are stored on a central server, stakeholders need to be online in order to work with a canvas. While this is not a problem for stakeholders using a large interactive display in a fixed location, it can be problematic for stakeholders who would like to contribute to the project from a remote location, e.g. while they are travelling.

Also, there is currently no integration between the AugIR and other tools in which the stakeholders might keep project-relevant information—whether it is model sketches created using other design tools, backlog items kept in other management tools, specifications, source code, bug reports, user feedback etc. Stakeholders currently need to keep track of these independently, and found it especially difficult to link these artefacts to the information on the IR canvas.

As we develop the AugIR approach further, we are therefore especially thriving to integrate the IR consulting method more tightly with established engineering methods and tools (e.g. project management approaches and bug tracking procedures) that can benefit from the added insight provided by the IR's annotated models.

In the future, we also plan to further support the ongoing engagement with the project by expanding the history capabilities of the AugIR. While the AugIR does support undoing actions, it is not yet possible to access arbitrary previous versions of a model, and recapitulate who made which changes at which time. We speculate that this will provide additional support for modeling activities that explore different alternatives before committing to one.

Furthermore, we plan to examine different moderation techniques for distributed modeling activities. The AugIR currently provides only a completely open editing mode, where every participant can draw, select, move, and annotate any element on the board. Discipline is needed in order to have productive modeling sessions. We plan to implement restrictions on concurrent editing to allow a certain kind of discipline while also retaining some of the collaborative and spontaneous feel of simultaneous work on a whiteboard.

Considering the "big picture" of the AugIR's applicability, we have found that the IR method is most suitable for supporting the early phases of IT projects: The identification of an organization's digitization potential and the formulation of digitization strategies, the scoping and requirements analysis of complex software projects, the evaluation of technologies and consideration of architectural decisions are activities that likely benefit most from the IR method's pragmatic approach, that prioritizes interdisciplinary understanding of value and effort drivers over the absolute correctness and completeness of specifications. After these initial strategic and scoping phases, which are often more consulting than engineering projects, traditional, stricter modeling techniques usually shift into focus as the projects turn into actual engineering projects and developers devise concrete software solutions.

In these phases, the AugIR still serves as a valuable tool as it enables a seamless refinement of informal into formal models, and continues to support remote collaboration among distributed teams. Its contribution in these phases however tends to be more technical than methodical.

Up to now, the IR method has been primarily designed for and applied in complex projects in the enterprise IT (or more generally, information systems) domain. Its potential in bringing stakeholders from diverse backgrounds together to facilitate cross-disciplinary understanding of domain requirements, technical capabilities, value, risk and effort drivers should however be transferrable to other software engineering sectors (and probably, other engineering disciplines in general) as well. In our ongoing work, we are therefore examining how the IR method can be applied to the design of cyber-physical systems, in which the close coupling to hardware components and physical constraints adds another dimension of challenges. We are also examining how an AugIR can be employed in the scientific and high-performance computing domain, where stakeholders from very different disciplines need to collaborate to design highly accurate models of real-world processes using highly specialized computing tools.

References

Anslow C, Marshall S, Noble J, Biddle R (2011) Interactive multi-touch surfaces for software visualization. In: Workshop on Data Exploration for Interactive Surfaces (DEXIS'11). ACM, New York, pp 20–23

Book M, Grapenthin S, Gruhn V (2012) Seeing the forest and the trees: Focusing team interaction on value and effort drivers. In: 20th International Symposium on the Foundations of Software Engineering (ACM SIGSOFT 2012 / FSE-20) New Ideas Track. ACM, New York, NY, art. no 30

Book M, Grapenthin S, Gruhn V (2014) Value-based migration of legacy data structures. In: Winkler D, Biffl S, Bergsmann J (eds) Software quality. Model-based approaches for advanced software and systems engineering. Proceedings of the 6th Software Quality Days (SWQD 2014), Lecture Notes in Business Information Processing. Springer, Berlin, pp 115–134

Book M, Grapenthin S, Gruhn V (2015) Highlighting value and effort drivers early in business and system models. In: Fujita H, Selamat A (eds) Intelligent Software Methodologies, Tools and Techniques. 13th International Conference (SoMeT 2014), Revised selected papers, Communications in Computer and Information Science. Springer, Berlin, pp 211–222

Chen Q, Grundy J, Hosking J (2003) An e-whiteboard application to support early design-stage sketching of UML diagrams. In: IEEE Symposium on Human Centric Computing Languages and Environments (HCC 2003). IEEE Computer Society, Washington, pp 219–226

Chen Q, Grundy J, Hosking J (2008) Sumlow: Early design-stage sketching of UML diagrams on an e-whiteboard. Software – Practice & Experience 38(9):961–994

Curtis B, Krasner H, Iscoe N (1988) A field study of the software design process for large systems. Commun ACM 31(11):1268–1287

Damm CH, Hansen KM, Thomsen M (2000) Tool support for cooperative object-oriented design: Gesture based modelling on an electronic whiteboard. In: Conference on Human Factors in Computing Systems (CHI 2000). ACM, New York, pp 518–525

Grapenthin S, Book M, Gruhn V, Schneider C, Völker K (2013) Reducing complexity using an Interaction Room – an experience report. In: ACM Special Interest Group on the Design of Communication Conference (SIGDOC 2013). ACM, New York, pp 71–76

Grapenthin S, Poggel S, Book M, Gruhn V (2015) Improving task breakdown comprehensiveness in agile projects with an Interaction Room. Information and Software Technology (INFSOF) 67:254–264

Haller M, Leitner J, Seifried T, Wallace JR, Scott SD, Richter C, Brandl P, Gokcezade A, Hunter S (2010) The NiCE discussion room: Integrating paper and digital media to support co-located group meetings. In: SIGCHI Conference on Human Factors in Computing Systems (CHI 2010). ACM, New York, pp 609–618

Hammond T, Davis R (2006) Tahuti: A geometrical sketch recognition system for UML class diagrams. ACM SIGGRAPH 2006 Courses. ACM, New York

Kleffmann M, Book M, Gruhn V (2014) Supporting collaboration of heterogeneous teams in an augmented team room. In: 6th International Workshop on Social Software Engineering (SSE'14) at 22nd ACM SIGSOFT International Symposium on the Foundations of Software Engineering (FSE 2014). ACM, New York, pp 9–16

Kleffmann M, Röhl S, Gruhn V, Book M (2015) Establishing and navigating trace links between elements of informal diagram sketches. In: 8th International Symposium on Software and Systems Traceability (SST 2015). IEEE Computer Society, Washington, DC, pp 1–7

Mangano N, Baker A, Dempsey M, Navarro E, van der Hoek A (2010) Software design sketching with Calico. In: IEEE/ACM International Conference on Automated Software Engineering (ASE 2010). ACM, New York, pp 23–32

Wüest D, Seyff N, Glinz M (2013) Flexisketch: A mobile sketching tool for software modeling. In: Uhler D, Mehta K, Wong JL (eds) Mobile Computing, Applications, and Services (MobiCase 2012). Lecture Notes of the Institute for Computer Sciences, Social Informatics and Telecommunications Engineering. Springer, Berlin, pp 225–244

Author Biographies

Erik Hebisch is Co-CEO of Interaction Room GmbH and doctoral candidate at paluno – The Ruhr Institute for Software Technology at the University of Duisburg-Essen. As an Interaction Room Coach, he has led over 15 Interaction Room workshops at organizations in the insurance and financial service domains and is responsible for the training of new coaches. His research focus is on the impact of quality and non-functional requirements on software architecture.

Simon Grapenthin is Co-CEO of Interaction Room GmbH and doctoral candidate at paluno – The Ruhr Institute for Software Technology at the University of Duisburg-Essen. As an Interaction Room Coach, he has led over 50 Interaction Room workshops at organizations in the financial service, trade and healthcare domains. His research areas are agile software development practices and pragmatic modeling techniques.

Matthias Book is Professor for Software Engineering at the University of Iceland. His research focus is on facilitating communication between distributed business and technical stakeholders in large software projects, and on pragmatic approaches to requirements engineering and modeling of complex software systems.

Markus Kleffmann is a doctoral candidate at paluno – The Ruhr Institute for Software Technology at the University of Duisburg-Essen and the lead developer of the Augmented Interaction Room software. His research focus is on human factors in software engineering, visualization and interaction techniques involving large interactive screens, and traceability between software model elements and artifacts.

Volker Gruhn holds the Chair for Software Engineering at the University of Duisburg-Essen. His research focus is on methods for industrial software engineering, as well as the effects of digital transformation on enterprises. He is Co-Founder and Chairman of the supervisory board of adesso AG, one of Germany's largest independent IT service providers with more than 2200 employees in 18 locations in Europe.

An Innovative Social Media Recruiting Framework for Human Resource Consulting

Ricardo Buettner and Ingo J. Timm

Abstract Recruiting of new employees is a key challenge for enterprises. Next to the skills and capability matching of applicants and job demands, the person-organizational environment fit is also crucial. As an increasing number of applicants provide personal information on social media, such as LinkedIn or XING, the question arises how can such information be used to achieve improved match-making. However, limited expertise in this area as well as legal and ethical issues prevent any straightforward application of sophisticated social media analysis in the process of recruiting. Thus, we propose an innovative consulting approach for human resource recruiting based on an automated assessment of the personality-organization environment fit. In our approach we show how an applicant's personality traits can be automatically derived from social media usage.

1 Introduction

Human resource (HR) consulting has seen a recent influx of electronic support tools and systems, in particular in e-recruiting (Buettner 2014). However, while existing e-recruiting consulting systems mainly focus on the problem of matching job demands and candidates' abilities, information about an applicant's personality that is needed to assess the person-organizational environment fit is not automatically taken into account. Such an assessment is necessary due to the fact that the fit between an employee's personality and the organizational environment (climate, culture, etc.) substantially influences job performance, job satisfaction, organizational commitment and employee turnover (Kristof 1996; Kristof-Brown et al. 2005;

R. Buettner (✉)
Faculty of Business Studies, Aalen University, Aalen, Germany
e-mail: ricardo.buettner@hs-aalen.de

I. J. Timm
Center for Informatics Research & Technologies (CIRT),
Trier University, Trier, Germany
e-mail: itimm@uni-trier.de

© Springer International Publishing AG 2018
V. Nissen (ed.), *Digital Transformation of the Consulting Industry*,
Progress in IS, https://doi.org/10.1007/978-3-319-70491-3_18

Verquer et al. 2003). Since social media are characterized by globally distributed users, dynamic interconnections and interactions, high accessibility, high speed of information distribution, and the opportunity to voluntarily provide personal information by users (Timm et al. 2016; Buettner and Buettner 2016; Buettner 2017), social media potentially contain fruitful information about a candidate's personality. That is why from an HR consulting perspective, social media not only provide the opportunity to communicate with potential employees, but applicants can also grant access to information relevant to assessment (i.e., personality related information).

Since human personality significantly influences how people think, feel and, in particular, behave (Barrick and Mount 1991; Judge et al. 1999), these traits remain quite stable over an entire lifetime and through varying situations (Costa and McCare 1992; Romero et al. 2009). It is therefore technically possible to predict a user's personality traits from their social media usage and digital footprints (Buettner 2014, 2016a, b, c, d). Despite the technical possibility of retrieving a user's personality from social media footprints, legal and ethical reasons impede the usage of Buettner's (2014) social media recruiting framework in HR consulting in Germany and the European Union. That is why we adapt Buettner's (2014) social media recruiting framework for an innovative HR consulting approach.

Next, we will sketch Buettner's (2014) social media recruiting framework and discuss related legal and ethical problems when using automated technology for recruiting decisions. After that, we propose the innovative social media recruiting framework for HR consulting before we offer indicative evaluations of the approach. Finally, we sketch the limitations of our framework and point to areas for further research.

2 Buettner's Social Media Recruiting Framework

Buettner (2014) developed a framework for social media recruiting covering the whole person-organization environment fit. This fit can be broken-down into sub-fits, with the most appropriate consisting of three all but disjoint sub-fits, which together almost cover the entire notion of the person-organization environment fit (Kristof-Brown et al. 2005). These sub-fits are

- Person-organization fit [between candidate personality and organizational culture, see Kristof (1996)],
- Person-group fit [matching of individual and group roles and interactions, see Werbel and Johnson (2001)], and
- Person-job fit [between a candidate's skills, knowledge, and abilities and job demands, see Edwards (1991)].

Since employees are most successful in organizations with a culture that is compatible with their personalities, an assessment of the person-organization fit

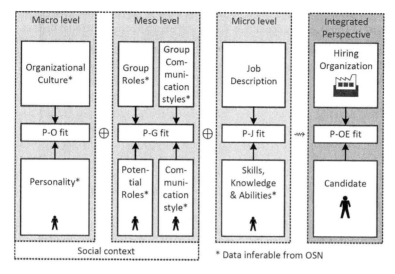

Fig. 1 Social media recruiting framework by Buettner (2014) (OSN—Online Social Network)

(macro level) is indicated and regularly carried out by HR consulting companies via questionnaires or by responding to the gut instinct of the representatives of the hiring organization. The person-group fit assessment (meso level) is related to social interactions (communication styles and group roles) within the workgroup between colleagues. In most companies, recruiters evaluate this fit through specific interview questions. Finally, on a micro level, recruiters evaluate the person-job fit based on the candidates' skills, knowledge, and abilities and the specific job demands. This is usually done by direct examinations of the candidates' CVs, testimonials and letters of reference together with the job description. An overview of investigations into these and further sub-fits can be found in Buettner (2014).

Buettner (2014) demonstrated in a conceptual way how information (e.g., personality traits) extracted from social media can be used to determine the person-organization environment fit. By calculating the person-organization environment fit and the corresponding sub-fits (person-organization, person-group, and person-job) instead of ignoring some of these sub-fits, the framework facilitates higher quality recommendations (see the following Fig. 1).

In addition, in a literature review comprising 275 articles Buettner (2016d) summarized stable and substantial relationships between online social networks indicators and the so-called big five personality traits of openness, conscientiousness, extraversion, agreeableness, and neuroticism (see Table 1).

While we also demonstrated that it is technically possible to predict a user's personality traits from an individual's social media usage (Buettner 2016a, b, c, d), we neglected some important legal and ethical problems of predicting personality for automated recruiting.

Table 1 Stable and substantial relationships between online social networks indicators and big five traits, (+)+ (very) positive correlation, (−)− (very) negative correlation (from Buettner 2016d)

Indicators/ features	Openness	Conscientiousness	Extraversion	Agreeableness	Neuroticism
Static profile (node) information					
No. of interests	+				
No. of groups/ categories					+
No. of profile pictures			++	+	−
Dynamic profile (node) information					
No. of profile picture changes	+		+		+
No. of general picture adds	+		+	+	
Usage intensity/frequency					
No. of logins			+	−	+
Time spent on OSN		−−	++		++
No. of other pages viewed		−	++	+	
Messages/communication					
No. of messages sent			++	+	−
No. of wall postings			++	+	+
No. of wall postings by others			+	+	
No. of faux pas (dirty words)		−−		−	
No. of blog entries	+				
Intensity of emotional content					+
Network properties					
No. of contacts			+	+	−
Network centrality	+			+	

3 Legal and Ethical Problems in Automated Recruiting Settings

Approaches like Buettner's social media recruiting framework are technically well suited to exploiting freely accessible information and utilizing them in decision making processes on many HR consulting related issues, e.g., applicant selection. However, according to German law (§6a BDSG), individual decisions (e.g., applicant rejections) that are only based on the automated processing of personal data are forbidden. Additionally, information in social media is provided according to the terms and conditions of the respective social network platform. Users often do not explicitly agree to having their data used within e-recruiting and application scenarios. Even if the user did sign an individual agreement with the potential employer, according to the planned introduction of the European basic regulations for data protection (EU-DSGVO), data use agreements between unequal partners are invalid.

Conventional approaches in big data analytics for overcoming data privacy regulations include de-personalizing information by aggregation, anonymization, or pseudonymization. However, in the context of HR consulting, in the subsequent application process it is important to know the identities of the specific applicants.

With respect to aspects of partner inequality and data privacy in the applicant-employer scenario, legal issues prevent an automated utilization of social media information. From an employer point of view, an HR representative could manually perform social media analyses. In contrast to an automated approach, manual analysis cannot reach a decision regarding cultural-personality-fit in a systematic and reproducible way. Furthermore, the HR representative not only derives relevant knowledge for the decision process but also "intimate" knowledge about the applicant—a potential colleague. Next to the legal perspective, this also raises ethical issues: is such an intimate analysis appropriate and does it potentially affect the working atmosphere in a company?

To solve these problems, we propose adding an impartial human agent to the applicant—employer scenario, who manually reflects on the fit between the applicant's personality and the company culture profile (an automatically generated decision proposal based on social media analysis, but a non-automated decision). Consequently, the approval between the applicant and the impartial human agent is valid from a legal perspective. As mentioned before, these impartial human agents could be employed by an HR consulting company.

4 Social Media Recruiting Framework for Human Resource Consulting

To avoid imbalances between applicants and employers we do not recommend providing direct access to Buettner's (2016d) personality prediction engine to employers or applicants. Instead, we suggest giving the engine to the HR consultants and so falling back on their original mediating function (Fig. 2).

HR consulting is mainly active in recruitment and selection activities as one of the eight HR core functions (Buettner 2015). Within this focus, classical HR consulting firms usually propose a set of suitable vacancy-specific candidates to the hiring organization. Searching for suitable candidates is very time-consuming and cost-intensive. Our approach thus gives HR consulting firms the opportunity to automatically receive recommendations from suitable candidates—based on social media analysis for personality-related information.

In the first step, the hiring organization requests that the HR consultants search for a specific employee and subsequently submits the organizational culture profile to the HR consulting firm (step 2). After that, the HR consulting firm actively searches for candidates or receives applications from interested people (step 3). Step 4 comprises the HR consulting firm's request for a personality assessment using the personality prediction web-service. After receiving approval for personal data mining and processing by the applicants, the personality prediction web-service

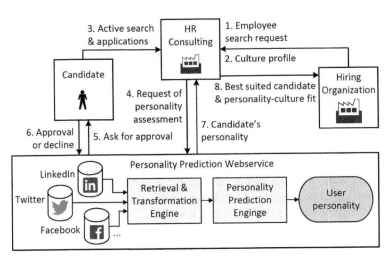

Fig. 2 A novel social media recruiting framework for HR consulting based on Buettner's (2016d) personality prediction engine

submits the candidates' personality traits to the HR consulting firm which selects the best suited applicant and submits this applicant including the personality-culture fit score to the hiring organization.

5 Demonstration

The personality prediction engine was evaluated using a dataset of the users' digital footprints on the social media platform www.XING.de. We electronically asked 760 working professionals who studied extra-occupationally at our university about their social media usage by applying the items shown in Table 2 on the following page. The call for participation was sent out with a link to the online questionnaire via our Germany-wide university. Please note that our university specializes in extra-occupational MBA and Bachelor students who all have working experience. 395 participants had a XING account (189 female, 206 male). Four were below 21 years, 259 between 21 and 30 years, 92 between 31 and 40 years, seven between 51 and 60 years and one person was over 60 years old.

Table 2 Items used for capturing the social media usage on XING (Buettner 2016d)

#	Item	Scale	Mean	SD
I_1	How often do you use XING?	[1-never…5-daily]	2.96	1.16
I_2	How often do you use the XING jobsearch function?	[1-never…5-daily]	1.70	0.87
I_3	How often do you use the XING blogging function?	[1-never…5-daily]	1.24	0.51
I_4	How often do you use the XING messaging function	[1-never…5-daily]	2.36	0.90
I_5	How often do you use the XING event organization function?	[1-never…5-daily]	1.14	0.41
I_6	How often do you use the XING event participation function?	[1-never…5-daily]	1.27	0.48
I_7	How often do you use XING's advantageous offers function?	[1-never…5-daily]	1.29	0.56
I_8	Have you filled out your educational background on XING?	[1-no/2-yes]	1.32	0.47
I_9	Have you filled out your work experience on XING?	[1-no/2-yes]	1.95	0.21
I_{10}	Have you filled out your organizations on XING?	[1-no/2-yes]	1.68	0.47
I_{11}	Have you filled out your interests on XING?	[1-no/2-yes]	1.73	0.44
I_{12}	Have you filled out your awards on XING?	[1-no/2-yes]	1.32	0.47
I_{13}	Have you filled out your language skills on XING?	[1-no/2-yes]	1.86	0.35
I_{14}	Have you filled out your haves on XING?	[1-no/2-yes]	1.73	0.44
I_{15}	Have you filled out your wants on XING?	[1-no/2-yes]	1.69	0.46
I_{16}	Have you filled out your about me information on XING?	[1-no/2-yes]	1.52	0.50
I_{17}	Do you have a XING premium membership?	[1-no/2-yes]	1.26	0.44
I_{18}	How many XING contacts do you have?	number	121	160

Table 3 Quality measures of the personality prediction engine (here C5.0 tree; from Buettner 2016c), ACC—accuracy, TPR—true positive rate (sensitivity), SPC—specificity, PPV—positive predictive value, NPV—negative predictive value (values above 0.5 are good values)

Personality traits	ACC	TPR	SPC	PPV	NPV
Openness	0.731	0.487	0.832	0.543	0.798
Conscientiousness	0.657	0.759	0.548	0.659	0.654
Extraversion	0.672	0.641	0.700	0.661	0.681
Agreeableness	0.664	0.609	0.714	0.661	0.667
Neuroticism	0.694	0.625	0.757	0.702	0.757
Ø	0.684	0.624	0.710	0.645	0.711

The big five personality traits were captured by referring to the *Ten Item Personality Inventory* by Gosling et al. (2003) using a five point Likert scale. This measurement constitutes a short but reliable personality questionnaire (see Gosling et al. 2003).

In a next step Buettner (2016c) applied machine learning algorithms (general regression models, support vector machine, C4.5, C5.0 and random forests as tree-based models) to predict the big five personality traits (openness, conscientiousness, extraversion, agreeableness, and neuroticism). In order to compare various machine learning algorithms the R $\times$ 64 3.2.2 environment (R Core Team 2015) combined with the caret package by Max Kuhn was used for all analyses. Based on the *Ten Item Personality Inventory* results, Buettner (2016c) had built two mean-balanced classes for each personality trait. For machine learning and evaluation purposes he split the n = 395 sample in a training partition ($n_T = 261$) and an evaluation partition ($n_E = 134$) and systematically compared the machine learning outputs in terms of accuracy, sensitivity, specificity, precision and negative predictive value. As a result he found that the C5.0 trees approach (cf. Kuhn and Johnson 2013) delivered the best output. Results are shown in the following Table 3.

Accuracy (ACC) is the proportion of correct classified subjects. Sensitivity (TPR) measures the proportion of true positives that are correctly identified as such (also called true positive rate). Specificity (SPC) measures the proportion of negatives that are correctly identified as such (also called the true negative rate). The positive and negative predictive values (PPV and NPV respectively) are the proportions of positive and negative results that are true positive and true negative results, respectively.

The C5.0 algorithm is the improved successor of C4.5 which is a decision tree algorithm originally proposed by Quinlan (1993) which is in turn an extension of Quinlan's ID3 algorithm and also uses the concept of information entropy (Loh 2008). The C5.0's predecessor C4.5 belongs to the most influential algorithms in the research community (Wu et al. 2008). With the C5.0 algorithm an impressive predictive gain was achieved of between 31.4 and 46.2%—which confirms that the social media platform XING.de contains very fruitful data for personality prediction. Compared to its predecessor C4.5, the C5.0 reached an overall accuracy gain of 26% (Table 4).

Table 4 Comparative table of quality measures for the C4.5 tree (from Buettner 2016a), ACC—accuracy, TPR—true positive rate (sensitivity), SPC—specificity, PPV—positive predictive value, NPV—negative predictive value (values above 0.5 are good values)

Personality traits	ACC	TPR	SPC	PPV	NPV
Openness	0.627	0.389	0.741	0.333	0.761
Conscientiousness	0.567	0.719	0.429	0.535	0.625
Extraversion	0.508	0.576	0.441	0.500	0.517
Agreeableness	0.470	0.485	0.454	0.478	0.462
Neuroticism	0.537	0.677	0.394	0.535	0.542
Ø	0.542	0.569	0.492	0.476	0.581

In summary, we found evaluative indications that the personality prediction engine works properly. Since personality traits are defined as "endogenous, stable, hierarchically structured basic dispositions governed by biological factors such as genes and brain structures" (Romero et al. 2009), not only behavioural observations but also digital social media footprints can be used to automatically predict a user's personality traits. This paves the way for the personality prediction web-service sketched in Fig. 2.

6 Conclusion, Limitations and Future Research

In the last decade, social media has become a valuable source of information for various applications. Until now, the major benefits have been felt by the social networks themselves, e.g., by profiling and selling personalized advertisement. In this paper, we introduced an approach for utilizing social media in a HR consulting scenario. We proposed an innovative consulting approach for HR recruiting based on the automated assessment of the personality-organization environment fit. In our approach we showed how an applicant's personality traits can be automatically derived from social media usage. On this basis, the personality-culture fit can be automatically computed and optimized which subsequently leads to higher job performance, job satisfaction, organizational commitment and lower employee turnover (Kristof 1996; Kristof-Brown et al. 2005; Verquer et al. 2003).

To overcome legal and ethical problems when analysing personality-related information directly, we proposed establishing a new field of business: HR consulting firms implementing the impartial human agent. On the one hand, such companies could provide the services to small and medium enterprises that are not capable of establishing a specified team on social media. On the other hand, the integration of a third-party overcomes the aforementioned legal and ethical issues. As a service provider, the impartial human agent would mine social media information on a detailed and potentially intimate scale.

References

Barrick MR, Mount MK (1991) The big five personality dimensions and job performance: a meta-analysis. Pers Psychol 44(1):1–26

Buettner R (2014) A framework for recommender systems in online social network recruiting. In: Proceedings of the 47th Hawaii international conference on system sciences (HICSS-47), Big Island, Hawaii, pp 1415–1424

Buettner R (2015) A systematic literature review of crowdsourcing research from a human resource management perspective. In: Proceedings of the 48th Hawaii international conference on system sciences (HICSS-48), Kauai, Hawaii, pp 4609–4618

Buettner R (2016a) Mining a user's personality from social media data: a comparison between the random forest and the C4.5 J48 based approach. In: Proceedings of the 78th Wissenschaftliche Jahrestagung des Verbandes der Hochschullehrer für Betriebswirtschaft, Munich

Buettner R (2016b) Personality as a predictor of business social media usage: An empirical investigation of XING usage patterns. In: Proceedings of the 20th Pacific Asia conference on information systems (PACIS), Chiayi, Taiwan, 27 June–1 July 2016

Buettner R (2016c) innovative personality-based digital services. In: Proceedings of the 20th Pacific Asia conference on information systems (PACIS), Chiayi, Taiwan, 27 June–1 July 2016

Buettner R (2016d) Predicting user behavior in electronic markets based on personality-mining in large online social networks: a personality-based product recommender framework. Electron Markets Int J Netw Bus, 1–19

Buettner R (2017) Getting a job via career-oriented social networking markets: The weakness of too many ties. Electron Markets Int Jd Netw Bus, 1–15

Buettner R, Buettner K (2016) A systematic literature review of twitter research from a socio-political revolution perspective. Proceeeding of 49th Hawaii international conference on system sciences (HICSS-49), Kauai, Hawaii, pp 2206–2215

Costa PT, McCrae RR (1992) Revised NEO personality inventory (NEO-PI-R) and the NEO five-factor inventory (NEO-FFI): professional manual. Psychological assessment resources, Odessa, FL, USA

Edwards JR (1991) Person-job fit: a conceptual integration, literature review, and methodological critique. In: Cooper CL, Robertson IT (eds) International review of industrial and organizational psychology. Wiley, Oxford, pp 283–357

Gosling SD, Rentfrow PJ, Swann WB Jr (2003) A very brief measure of the big-five personality domains. J Res Pers 37(6):504–528

Judge TA, Higgins CA, Thoresen CJ, Barrick MR (1999) The big five personality traits, general mental ability, and career success across the life span. Pers Psychol 52(3):621–652

Kristof AL (1996) Person-organization fit: An integrative review of its conceptualizations, measurement, and implications. Pers Psychol 49(1):1–49

Kristof-Brown AL, Zimmerman RD, Johnson EC (2005) Consequences of individuals' fit at work: a meta-analysis of person-job, person-organization, person-group, and person-supervisor fit. Pers Psychol 58(2):281–342

Kuhn M, Johnson K (2013) Applied predictive modeling. Springer, New York

Loh WY (2008) Classification and regression tree methods. In: Ruggeri F, Kenett RS and Faltin FW (eds) Encyclopedia of statistics in quality and reliability. Wiley, New York, pp 315–323

Quinlan JR (1993) C4.5: programs for machine learning. Morgan Kaufmann, San Mateo, CA

R Core Team (2015) R: a language and environment for statistical computing. R foundation for statistical computing. Vienna, Austria

Romero E, Villar P, Luengo MA, Gómez-Fraguela JA (2009) Traits, personal strivings and well-being. J Res Pers 43(4):535–546

Timm IJ, Berndt JO, Lorig F, Barth C, Bucher H-J (2016) Dynamic analysis of communication processes using twitter data. In: Proceedings of the second international conference on human and social analytics (HUSO), pp 14–22

Verquer ML, Beehr TA, Wagner SH (2003) A meta-analysis of relations between person-organization fit and work attitudes. J Vocat Behav 63(3):473–489

Werbel JD, Johnson DJ (2001) The use of person-group fit for employment selection: a missing link in person-environment fit. Hum Resour Manage 40(3):227–240

Wu X, Kumar V, Ross J, Quinlan J, Ghosh J, Yang Q, Motoda H, McLachlan GJ, Ng A, Liu B, Yu PS, Zhou ZH, Steinbach M, Hand DJ, Steinberg D (2008) Top 10 algorithms in data mining. Knowl Inf Syst 14(1):1–37

Author Biographies

Ricardo Buettner is a Professor of Data Science at Aalen University. He studied Computer Science (Dipl.-Inf.), Industrial Engineering and Management (Dipl.-Wirtsch.-Ing.), and Business Administration (Dipl.-Kfm.) and received his Ph.D. in Information Systems from Hohenheim University. After nine years working with the BMW Group, with experience in the fields of finance/controlling, marketing, strategy, R&D and HR, Ricardo joined the FOM University of Applied Sciences in 2009 before he moved to Aalen University in 2017.

Ingo J. Timm received a Diploma degree (1997), Ph.D. (2004), and Venia Legendi (2006) in Computer Science from University of Bremen. Ingo has been a PhD student, research assistant, visiting and senior researcher at University of Bremen, Technische Universität Ilmenau, and Indiana University Purdue University, Indianapolis (IUPUI). In 2006, he was appointed full Professor for Information Systems and Simulation at Goethe-University Frankfurt. Since the fall of 2010, he has held the Chair for Business Informatics at Trier University. In 2016, he founded and is now heading the Center for Informatics Research and Technology (CIRT) and its Research Lab on Simulation (TriLabS).

The Digitalization of Consulting and Auto-Assignment of Experts in the MedTech and Life Sciences Industries

Thorsten Knape, Moritz Fröhlich and Peter Hufnagl

Abstract The development of a technology product or process in the healthcare sector or the life science industry is generally characterized as being highly diversified and complex. Developing an electronic medical implant, for instance, requires an interdisciplinary team of engineers, computer and data scientists, chemists, biologists, and user experience (UX) designers. For consulting projects in the MedTech industry, this means that there is a high demand for specialized experts. The present work proposes an approach for digitalizing consulting to efficiently deal with the requirements of the high cost and low availability of experts in the medical technology sector. As a representative of a scientific consulting service for small and medium-sized enterprises (SMEs), we have designed an agile consulting digitalization process for the CBMI of the HTW Berlin. To this end, the first step is to realize a prototype system of an online consulting platform that finds and matches project partners having the same professional areas of interest. To illustrate and discuss our conceptual findings, this paper presents a scenario of the consulting process for product development in the medical sector.

1 Introduction

The Center of Biomedical Image and Information Processing (CBMI) is a scientific institute of the Hochschule für Technik und Wirtschaft—Berlin University of Applied Sciences (HTW Berlin), which has its main focus on digitalized health and

T. Knape (✉) · M. Fröhlich · P. Hufnagl
Center for Biomedical Image and Information Processing (CBMI),
Berlin University of Applied Sciences - Hochschule Für Technik
Und Wirtschaft (HTW), Berlin, Germany
e-mail: thorsten.knape@htw-berlin.de

M. Fröhlich
e-mail: moritz.froehlich@student.htw-berlin.de

P. Hufnagl
e-mail: hufnagl@htw-berlin.de

© Springer International Publishing AG 2018
V. Nissen (ed.), *Digital Transformation of the Consulting Industry*,
Progress in IS, https://doi.org/10.1007/978-3-319-70491-3_19

427

life sciences. It was established to combine this expertise with the areas of biomedical imaging and information processing and to provide a platform for joint research and development on the above topics. The CBMI scientific institute is planned as part of a larger organization, which includes a private research institute and a startup center. In this paper, the CBMI takes on the role of an innovation partner and technology consultant for SMEs in Germany in the MedTech industry. The term consulting is here understood as a professional service as defined by Nissen (2007).

The CBMI consulting firm work focuses on technology and management consulting as well as promoting cooperation between science and industry. The consultation has its purpose of supporting companies in successfully using the latest technology for creating their medical devices, medical software products (e.g. virtual microscopy for medical images with automated image processing based on machine learning algorithms) or improving their development process.

This could be the development of digital prototypes, e.g., mobile health apps or a prototype for using neural networks in the context of image processing. Also, a consulting process could result in recommendations for technology (tools, platforms, frameworks) required for the development of image processing software modules by machine learning.

The motivation for conceiving a digitally based consulting process is influenced by CBMI's customers, new data analytics possibilities, and its own organizational structure. CBMI customers have a growing need for specialized technical expertise in medical informatics and life sciences. The technical complexity and diversity of their questions are increasing. This requirement for specialization leads to a modularization of the CBMI consulting services, where a complex overall task is divided into smaller portions in a way that it can be addressed to individual experts. Afterward, the individual parts are reassembled to yield the total result. This approach is similar to crowdsourcing, where a crowd is used to "provide" a solution to a problem. This results in the need to find a suitable, digital-supported solution for distributing the tasks among several experts from the various disciplines at CBMI.

Furthermore, the transparency and financial accountability of the consulting projects should be improved, for example, as a time-boxed process. CBMI customers now demand a clearly defined scope for a solution within a short time; they want to influence the project process, and see intermediate results, e.g., as iteration steps in the app development and do not only demand theoretical concepts or general solutions. CBMI customers have an increasing need for solutions that are digitally integrated into their value chain. These are, for example, digital prototypes of a health app as a precursor for an iOS or Android app. A consulting process where iterative, digitized results are directly integrated into the customer product or process is of higher value to the CBMI customers than a traditional conceptual consulting strategy.

From the institutional point of view of the CBMI, the person of the consultant and his know-ledge is a particularly important success factor of the CBMI consulting. At the same time, this dependency on the availability of consultants is a risk factor, because the scientists are often only employed at the CBMI for two to three years. When an expert leaves the CBMI, it also loses his specific expertise. This all leads to the strategic requirement of operationalizing the consulting knowledge as a digital consulting offer, e.g. in the form of a software application. The prerequisite for this is a CBMI consulting process standardized within a definite scope so that the CBMI consultants can use these digital consulting applications repeatedly, achieving the same consulting quality. Also, the CBMI research areas with their digital focus (digital image processing, machine learning) support the realization of a digitalized consulting service. On the one hand, the requirements and results of the consulting work are already largely available in digital form. On the other hand, parts of the software research applications can be re-used in the development of consulting applications, e.g. data analysis modules. In addition, a digitalized consulting service allows CBMI employees to work as regular CBMI researchers as well as consultants because their personal on-site consulting work is minimized.

The following sections illustrate our concept of the CBMI consulting process and the first steps to realizing the development of a matching system. The intent of the CBMI system is to support professors, scientific staff, students, and companies in finding suitable project partners in a short time on an Internet platform. This will be enhanced in the future by various functionalities for joint consulting project work.

We explain the use of current and future technologies in the consulting process by using the development of a medical app as an example. Finally, we summarize the work and provide an outlook of the future development options.

2 Positioning the CBMI System as a Digitalized Consulting System

The long-term vision of the CBMI system is an application focusing on CBMI's entire technical consulting process. In a CBMI matching of project requirements and expert skills, the digitalization only influences the first part of the CBMI consulting value chain.

Johann et al. (2016) and Werth et al. (2016) show that digitalized consulting systems can be categorized into the extent to which they provide support for the consulting firm service and the extent to which the software tools are specialized for the consulting industry. According to these authors, the support for consulting firm services ranges from supporting functions and tasks by integrating tools into the value creation process of the customer up to replacing the consultant with a technical system. The degree of tool specialization starts with cross-sector tools, followed by tools specifically developed for consulting firm businesses and associated processes, up to automated self-service consulting. Figure 1 shows the corresponding positioning of the four archetypal IT-mediated categories of future consulting: Computer-Supported Consulting (CSC), Computer-Assisted Consulting (CAC), Computer-Controlled Consulting (CCC) and Computer-Executed Consulting (CEC).

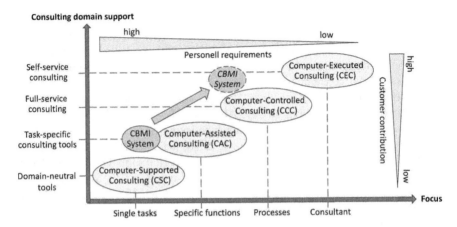

Fig. 1 Classification of digitalized consulting systems (based on Johann et al. (2016) and Werth et al. (2016))

The CBMI consulting process outlined in the next section will be a step-by-step digitized and automated one. Examples of software applications that are domain-neutral and are used for single tasks within the CBMI consulting work are spreadsheet and text processing applications for the general documentation and calculation tasks, presentation tools, virtual conference systems for reviews, and live webinar software for training. An advantage of this off-the-shelf software is that no significant development effort is required.

The first phase in the development of the CBMI system was the technical support for the CBMI task-specific functions. The starting point of development discussed in this contribution is matching the CBMI project requirements with the expert skills supported by a computer-assisted consulting system. The CBMI application is foreseen overall as a hybrid between an online self-service and a fully automated system.

3 CBMI—The Consulting Process

3.1 Process Overview

Figure 2 shows the consulting process of the CBMI, supported by digital tools. The process was developed in a startup mindset oriented on the methods of Agile Development, Lean Startup, and Design Thinking. The basis of the process design is an iterative agile approach in which the customer's complex problem (1.2 Problem Discovery) is subdivided into partial problems (2.1 Decomposing the Problem). Solutions for these subproblems are developed incrementally in cycles of fixed duration (3 CBMI Consulting Sprint) and delivered to the customer

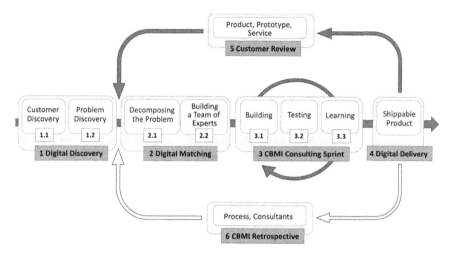

Fig. 2 CBMI—Agile consulting and innovation process

(4 Digital Delivery). Contrary to the traditional technology-oriented consulting method, there is no direct presentation of the technical solution. Instead, there is first developed an understanding of the customer's situation and background of the problem. In addition, the customer requirement for high-speed problem solving and its implementation by CBMI was considered to play a decisive role in the design of the process.

3.2 Technology-Supported Consulting Within the CBMI Process

3.2.1 Digital Discovery

In the *Digital Discovery* phase (Table 1), the emphasis is placed on empathy for the customer and his problem. It has to be clarified that if the consulting task can be solved with the resource pool available at CBMI, then the customer order can be accepted. This step is digitally supported by the CBMI matching system which quickly analyzes the number of available CBMI experts to solve the particular problem.

Data on the customer and the problem is collected by using mining algorithms and data analytics methods that evaluate data from company and product information available on the Internet (e.g., company website, social media data, interviews, publications) as well as the information from previous orders. For comprehending the task, the customer provides problem descriptions, e.g., scenarios, a list of requirements, photos, sketches.

Table 1 CBMI process step Digital Discovery

Step	Input	Processing	Result
1.1	Company website, Facebook, Twitter, publications, press, product information, interviews, photos, videos	Answers the question: Is the customer a suitable partner for CBMI?	Recommendation whether the company is a suitable partner, e.g., dashboard visualization, traffic light chart
1.2	Interviews, video, photo, sketches, 3D-CAD model, mockup	Answers the question: Is the problem solvable for CBMI?	Recommendation whether the problem is solvable for CBMI, traffic light chart
Technology	Data mining and data analytics using Apache Flink[a], e.g., speech to text, text/multimedia analytics, web crawler, social media analytics, CBMI project database		

[a]Apache Flink: https://flink.apache.org/

The result of the automated analysis of the CBMI system is visualized by a traffic light chart. If the result is not clear (yellow signal) the customer interview will be performed via a virtual conferencing tool to verify conscientiously the data analysis problem.

3.2.2 Digital Matching

The main area of application for the CBMI matching system is the step that selects the experts for the consulting sprint. For each sprint, for each new partial problem-solving task, the team of experts is newly formed, supported by the CBMI matching system to assure that the best-suited CBMI consultants are involved. Regular team events and training are designed to ensure a smooth collaboration between the various experts. The graph database Neo4J (see Sect. 4) is used for determining the best-matching consultants. The trend for modularization and specialization in the consulting sector is reflected in the matching steps (Table 2).

The complex problem is split up in a modular way to find the respective experts for executing the task. Moreover, the modular structure of the consulting service allows a step-by-step financial calculation and can be implemented transparently in a time-fixed sprint (e.g., days, weeks).

3.2.3 CBMI Consulting Sprint

The actual work of the CBMI team of experts takes place within the CBMI consulting sprint (Table 3). The target and scope are defined, starting from identifying the subproblem that is to be solved in the sprint. The strategy and concept are developed in close consultation with the customer. The CBMI sprint team then implements and evaluates the concept.

Table 2 CBMI process step Digital Matching

Step	Input	Processing	Result
2.1	Digitized problem description	Splitting up the problem into topic areas, formulating the partial tasks, identifying similar problems solved by CBMI in previous projects	Backlog with partial problems, concretized tasks by subject area, links to existing solutions of similar problems
2.2	Competence profiles of customers, experts	Digital matching to find suitable project partners	Recommendation of suitable project partners
Technology	Text analytics, digital matching with other customer problems in CBMI projects, CBMI matching system with shortest path algorithms in Neo4J, analytics, and matching of areas of interests (topics) of customers and experts, visual patterns. For further technical details, please see Sect. 4		

Table 3 CBMI process step CBMI Consulting Sprint

Step	Input	Processing	Result
3.1	Team of experts, backlog, digitization ideas, mockups, prototypes	Identifying the sprint problem, target, scope, measurements. building digital prototypes	Prototypes as solution of the sprint problem
3.2	Prototypes	Functional tests, usability tests, market acceptance tests with real user	Digital test results of prototypes
3.3	Test results	Comparing problem vs. solution	Lessons learned, recommendations for improvements
Technology	Prototyping tools, 3D and VR-models, simulations, video analytics, digital and web analytics, visual patterns		

For example, a prototype of a new medical device is to be built. Two sprint iteration cycles are performed for this purpose: sprint 1—the virtual prototype, and sprint 2—the hardware rapid prototype. After a digitally assisted problem and market analysis, CBMI engineers build a first virtual 3D model supported by a knowledge advisor module based on rules and best practices. The customers test this 3D model in a virtual reality test environment. At end of the sprint, the test results will be compared with the project target and requirements. The lessons learned are the input for the second sprint cycle of constructing a hardware rapid prototype.

3.2.4 Digital Delivery

At the end of the sprint, the achieved consulting result increment is integrated with the partial solutions realized so far and delivered to the customer, preferably digitally (Table 4).

3.2.5 Customer Review

In the review meeting, the consulting result is discussed critically with the client regarding the degree of achievement of the agreed sprint and project target (Table 5). For this purpose, the customer receives insight into the respective working phases, data, and access to prototypes. If the entire, complex problem of the customer has already been solved, then the consulting process ends. Else, the client updates his problem (backlog). A new sprint begins with the prioritization and selection of the next partial problem to be solved.

3.2.6 CBMI Retrospective

In the *CBMI retrospective* process step (Table 6), the CBMI team continuously analyzes and reflects its consulting expertise and process. The basis for this is the evaluation of the customer requirements, their thematic development and how well these were fulfilled from the customer's point of view.

The following architectural visual (Fig. 3) shows the different technologies of the CBMI system mentioned above, which process the transformation of knowledge and collect the required data. The analytics on data are processed based on information from OpenDB's, data collected by a web crawler, and project-specific

Table 4 CBMI process step Digital Delivery

Step	Input	Processing	Result
4	Applications, prototypes, test results, lessons learned	Automated provision of applications, prototypes	Iteration of product/ prototype is delivered to the customer
Technology	e.g. Virtualization tools, Docker, virtual machines, app distribution tools		

Table 5 CBMI process step Customer Review

Step	Input	Processing	Result
5	Iteration of product/ prototype, test results, lessons-learned, sprint and project targets	Analysis and evaluation of the sprint results from the point of view of the customer	Feedback from the customer, decision of project end or request of a new sprint with further specified problems
Technology	Presentation tools, virtual reality, virtual conferencing, feedback tools		

Table 6 CBMI process step CBMI Retrospective

Step	Input	Processing	Result
6	Lessons learned	CBMI internal analysis and evaluation of the consulting firm work and process quality	Recommendations for improvements for the CBMI consulting process, feedback for the consultants
Technology	Data analytics of customer requirements and feedback		

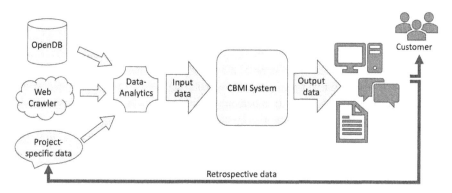

Fig. 3 Data flow of the CBMI system

data stored locally. Data analytics evaluate and choose the appropriate input data for a specific task. The data is then classified by CBMI's own ontology and is routed to the CBMI system to be a part of the interest matching and consulting digitalization process.

The following Sect. 4 explains the technical setup of the CBMI system. The output data of the CBMI system is then prepared for different targets as explained earlier. As shown in the agile consulting process in Fig. 2, the results are then split up into data for the customer (e.g. prototype or service) and data for the retrospective.

4 Technical Concept and Implementation of the CBMI System

Three structural layers were formed on database level for classifying the information of the CBMI system:

(a) Organizational groups,
(b) Persons,
(c) Areas of interests and competencies.

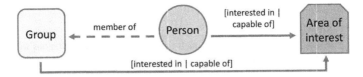

Fig. 4 Three structural layers of interest matching concept

Among these, the following relationships exist: people and groups are characterized by *areas of interests*, and persons are organized in groups. The memberships
in joint groups and common areas of interest or competencies allow the matching of
experts to the appropriate individual tasks. Moreover, a person may be a freelancer
who is not a member of a group. The person or group can either have an *interested
in* or *capable of* relationship to an area of interest, which means that the person has
an interest in solving a task or is capable of solving it. Therefore, a person on the
database level can be an expert or a person seeking advice. The areas of interest and
different competencies are categorized per CBMI's own ontology. This ontology
uses the algorithms of the data analytics digitally to ensure a matching of interests
and competencies. The three structural layers are shown in Fig. 4 on the following
page.

Figure 5 shows the view, application and the databases aspects of the layered
architecture of the CBMI system.

The two NoSQL databases employed by the application separate the search data
from the stored data. The CBMI system distinguishes between these two data types
for handling search requests and information lookup requests differently. The
reason for this is that the graph database Neo4J[1] is optimized for fast searching of
matching interests. On the one hand, the document database Apache CouchDB is
used for storing data such as user information and files (e.g. text or image files).
Graph databases, on the other hand, are used for storing data in a network that
resembles social networks. For the implementation, a graph database is used
because its data mapping structures resemble the patterns of persons with different
interests.

The two databases interconnect using Ektorp[2] on the Apache CouchDB[3] side
and the Neo4j Java driver[4] that is recommended by Neo4J. The web application is
built and operated with JavaServer Faces (JSF) and Primefaces[5] on Apache's
Tomcat Server.[6] JSF and Primefaces are used for the web-based development of a
user interface.

---

[1]Neo4J: https://neo4j.com/.

[2]Ektorp: http://ektorp.org/.

[3]Apache CouchDB: http://couchdb.apache.org/.

[4]Neo4j Java driver: https://neo4j.com/developer/java/.

[5]Primefaces: http://www.primefaces.org/.

[6]Tomcat Server: http://tomcat.apache.org/.

Fig. 5 CBMI system—layer architecture

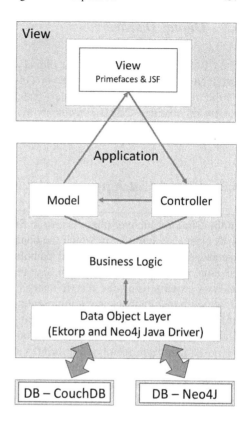

The application is written using the usual Model View Controller (MVC) pattern for web applications. The MVC pattern divides an application into three main components. In the view component, data are presented to the user, and the user interaction is accepted. The model component contains the data to be presented and the business logic. The controller component controls the flow of information to the View and thus specifies the program flow.

5 Scenario: Image Processing in Digital Pathology, App Prototype

The following scenario is intended to demonstrate the steps of the CBMI's consulting process: A small med-tech company, *Meyer GmbH*, is currently a provider of radiological image data analysis and wants to expand its service portfolio to analyzing pathological image information. Since the company lacks expertise in the field of pathological image data, Meyer asks for the consulting support of CBMI experts.

5.1 Digital Discovery

The CBMI process begins with the digital discovery phase (Table 7, Steps 1.1, 1.2) and then clarifies whether the Meyer GmbH is a suitable partner of the CBMI. Furthermore, an initial competency matching using the CBMI tool provides a variety of qualified CBMI consultants available, and so the order is accepted by CBMI.

5.2 Digital Matching

In the *Digital Matching* phase (Table 7, Steps 2.1, 2.2), Meyer GmbH is provided with plannable subtasks in which the consulting agreement is divided into partial, specialized problems, e.g., digital pathology, data analysis, and business model development. This modularization also represents the basis for the assembling a team of experts using the CBMI matching tool. Figure 6 shows a possible data structure in the graph database, representing persons with similar competencies in a group. In this example, Hufnagl is a suitable expert with competencies in digital pathology and business models. Based on these subject areas, he is automatically proposed as a team member for sprint A *Digital Pathology* and sprint C *Business Model*. After an automated check for the availability of experts, the customer receives the suggestion for the expert team members with their professional profiles (experience, skills).

Table 7 CBMI scenario: Digital Discovery, Digital Matching

Step	Input	Processing	Result
1.1	Small company, MedTech industry, analysis of radio-logical image data	Analysis: Is Meyer GmbH a suitable CBMI customer?	Yes
1.2	Problem formulation (not in detail): Technical and business concept for the analysis of pathological images?	Analysis: Does CBMI have suitable experts available in the area of pathological image processing?	Yes
2.1	Meyer's more specific task: A technical prototype of a software product and a business model for a digital analysis of pathological images	Splitting up the problem into technical, usability, and business tasks	Backlog with partial problems, specific questions, tasks
2.2	Digitalized profile of Meyer GmbH and the CBMI experts	Digital matching to find consulting experts in the domains relevant for Meyer GmbH	Recommendation of experts Hufnagl, Knape, and Fröhlich

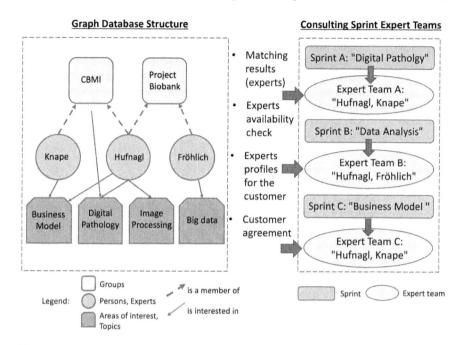

Fig. 6 Relations: Database section, Matching, Sprint expert team

If the customer does not accept the team members, then the next best suitable CBMI expert will be suggested, or external experts will be contacted through e.g. LinkedIn or Xing. If the customer accepts the experts, then the consulting sprint starts. For the other sprints, specialized team members are suggested accordingly. This provides for an effective and efficient planning for the consulting sprint.

5.3 CBMI Consulting Sprint, Digital Delivery, Review, and Retrospective

Three sprints, A, B, and C, are planned. The focus for the sprint A is the building and testing of an app prototype for pathological imaging. The second sprint B contains machine learning and artificial neural networks for image processing. The development of the business model happens in sprint C. All sprints consist of the steps three to six of Table 8, where Sprint A *Digital Pathology* (app prototyping) is described as a representative example.

Table 8 CBMI scenario: Consulting Sprint, Digital Delivery, Review, Retrospective

Step	Input	Processing	Result
3	Backlog	Building and usability testing of app prototype	App prototype tested for pathological images
4	App prototype	Distributing of app prototype to Meyer GmbH	App prototype can be tested by Meyer GmbH
5	App prototype, Sprint results	Review of the app prototype, sprint results	Feedback from Meyer GmbH, request for the next sprint
6	Feedback	Internal Review	Lessons learned

6 Conclusions

The need for increasing specialization among professionals for solving complex consulting challenges has led to a higher demand for experts in the MedTech industry. Moreover, the need has increased for customers to obtain digital consulting results. These can be integrated directly into their products or the value chain, e.g., in medical app development or in image processing applications. For fulfilling these requirements, the authors have demonstrated an approach using an IT-supported consulting process at CBMI of HTW Berlin as an example.

As the first implementation phase, this work made a presentation for the digitalization support for the automated formation of a team of experts. The appropriate consultants can be determined automatically based on the digital matching of the project requirements with the expert competencies. This has the potential of improving the staffing quality, speeding up the identification of suitable experts, and reducing the process cost. Our approach of selecting the experts is still based on the technical aspects. Here we plan to consider additional organizational and planning aspects, e.g., the handling of resource conflicts and more selection factors with regard to the personality of the experts for the customer. In addition, there are plans to expand the digitalization support to other consulting process steps. This could be an automated market and competition analysis and an automated analysis of the customer feedback in the retrospective phase as well as an improvement of the CBMI consulting digitalization process.

The implementation of a digital consulting process as suggested here carries some barriers and risks for consulting firms. First, it is necessary to make a substantial initial investment in the technology and its continuous support, considering also the ever-shortening technology lifecycles. Second, the availability of relevant expertise in data science can pose a problem. Third, there is the risk of customers not accepting the digital consulting services. However, it is reasonable to assume that the chances of acceptance of digital consultations increase with the trend of digital transformation in the industry sector. Customer problems will have more of a digital focus and customer experiences with digitalization in their organizations will increase. Therefore, consulting firms need to adopt corresponding procedures and tools to solve the customer problems with a digital focus while presenting themselves with a reputation of professional digitization experts.

In our opinion, other important success factors for customer acceptance of digitalized consulting involve a deep understanding of the customer's problem and the development of empathy for the customer. The emphasis here is not only placed on the immediate presentation of the technical solution to the customer but on the appreciation of the understanding of the customer and the operation of his environment. One important aspect of the future digital transformation in the consulting branch is the development of technical tools for an automated understanding of customer problems, business needs and technology capacities (such as human empathy).

Opportunities for implementing a consulting digitalization process exist, on the one hand, in the process organization: The prerequisite for a digital consulting service is the standardization of the consulting process. For this, we propose an agile, iterative approach. This offers transparency to the CBMI customers of the consulting service and the possibility to influence results already at an early stage. In addition, the development of digital consulting tools makes it possible to re-use these tools in other data science areas, e.g., in machine learning for digital image processing by the CBMI. It should be noted that the digital consulting services may reduce dependency on the individual consultants' expertise for the consulting firms. Specialized knowledge could potentially be digitized in software applications and be re-used by another consultant or by the customer himself in some form of self-service.

The next steps in the implementation of the CBMI system involve evaluating the customer feedback for the different supporting tools and technologies. Depending on this, the selected technology application is expanded or changed. An evaluation of the current face-to-face consulting services is also planned. Another avenue for future research is the optimization of the service portfolio for adjusting the content and results in a way to make them even more suitable for digital consulting services.

From our point of view, digitalized consulting will in the future be a key success factor in terms of the competitiveness, efficiency, and quality of consulting work. Digitalized consulting offers the opportunity for startups and small companies in the MedTech industry to offer consulting on a low financial budget. From a technical perspective, one of the relevant next steps for the consulting digitalization process is the integration and analysis of data science methods like machine learning or neural networks. Further research is needed to understand the potential and limits of digitalized consulting in different scenarios and industries. The added value of the digitally supported consulting process is to be presented to the customer, keeping up with the best practices and evidence of success. Thus, the digital transformation in the consulting industry will be the reference example for the professional services sector and become an essential, indispensable part of any future consultant's day.

References

Johann D, Greff T, Werth D (2016) On the effect of digital frontstores on transforming business
    models. In: Shishkov B (ed) Proceedings of the 6th international symposium on business
    modeling and software design. Rhodes, pp 64–72
Nissen V (ed) (2007) Consulting Research. Unternehmensberatung aus wissenschaftlicher
    Perspektive. DUV, Wiesbaden
Werth D, Greff T, Scheer AW (2016) Consulting 4.0 - Die Digitalisierung der Unternehmensberatung.
    HMD Praxis der Wirtschaftsinformatik 53(1):55–70

Author Biographies

Thorsten Knape is a researcher at the CBMI and has more than 15 years of experience as a senior
manager and consultant in the medical devices industries and research institutions. He holds a
Diploma in the field of Business Administration and Engineering, and a Master's degree in
Computer Sciences from the Beuth University of Applied Sciences Berlin. His current research
interests focus on the design and implementation of future digital consulting services, business
model innovations of medical apps and data-driven services.

Moritz Fröhlich is a Master student of Applied Computer Science at HTW Berlin. Additionally to
his studies, he is a software developer for Java and C#. He develops web applications in different
branches like healthcare, e-commerce and public sector. In agile projects, he executes the role of a
developer and the role of the Scrum Master and supports his team colleagues with qualified
knowledge. His expertise are the usage of graph databases like Neo4J and the hosting of web
applications in the cloud.

Peter Hufnagl studied Mathematics and Statistics at the Academy of Mining Freiberg. He focused
firstly on medical image analysis and developed frameworks for tumor characterization and drug
research. In the late nineties, he started do built telemedical solutions for doc-to-doc
communication and emergency care for ships and aircrafts. As head of Digital Pathology at the
Institute of Pathology at Charité Berlin, he is engaged in the application of virtual microscopy
systems and machine learning in histology. In 2016, he founded the Center for Biomedical Image
and Information Processing (CBMI) at the HTW University of Applied Sciences Berlin.

Printed by Books on Demand, Germany